Control Flow Semantics

Foundations of Computing
Michael Garey and Albert Meyer, editors

Control Flow Semantics

Jaco de Bakker and Erik de Vink

The MIT Press
Cambridge, Massachusetts
London, England

This book was set in LaTeX by the authors and was printed and bound in the United States of America.

Library of Congress Cataloging-in-Publication Data
Bakker, J. W. de (Jacobus Willem), 1939–
    Control flow semantics / Jaco de Bakker and Erik de Vink.
        p.   cm.–(Foundations of computing)
    Includes bibliographical references and index.
    ISBN 0-262-04154-5 (hc: alk. paper)
    1. Programming languages (Electronic computers)-Semantics. I. Vink, Erik de. II. Title.
III. Series.
QA76.7.B352   1996
005.13'1–dc20   95-47439
                                                                                            CIP

Contents

Series Foreword

Theoretical computer science has now undergone several decades of development. The "classical" topics of automata theory, formal languages, and computational complexity have become firmly established, and their importance to other theoretical work and to practice is widely recognized. Stimulated by technological advances, theoreticians have been rapidly expanding the areas under study, and the time delay between theoretical progress and its practical impact has been decreasing dramatically. Much publicity has been given recently to breakthroughs in cryptography and linear programming, and steady progress is being made on programming language semantics, computational geometry, and efficient data structures. Newer, more speculative, areas of study include relational databases, VLSI theory, and parallel and distributed computation. As this list of topics continues expanding, it is becoming more and more difficult to stay abreast of the progress that is being made and increasingly important that the most significant work be distilled and communicated in a manner that will facilitate further research and application of this work. By publishing comprehensive books and specialized monographs on the theoretical aspects of computer science, the series on Foundations of Computing provides a forum in which important research topics can be presented in their entirety and placed in perspective for researchers, students, and practitioners alike.

Michael R. Garey
Albert R. Meyer

Preface

Present-day programming languages exhibit an overwhelming variety of control flow notions. Our book is devoted to a comprehensive treatment of these, altogether developing operational and denotational semantic models for control flow in 27 languages. More specifically:

- We treat both traditional (e.g., assignment, iteration and recursion, locality) and modern concepts (such as process creation, action refinement, parallel objects, and the rendezvous construct).

- We deal with both *sequential* and *concurrent* languages, on the whole paying about equal attention to each of them.

- We investigate control flow concepts in imperative programming, but also—albeit to a lesser extent—in logic, object-oriented, and functional programming.

- Both schematic ("uniform," in our terminology) and state-based (interpreted or "nonuniform") languages are studied. In the former, the primitive actions are uninterpreted symbols, in the latter the primitives affect the state (e.g., through assignment statements).

- Both deterministic and (possibly unbounded) nondeterministic notions are considered. As to forms of parallelism, both uniform and nonuniform languages, and static and dynamic configurations will be treated. Not only interleaving but also noninterleaving models are presented, though in rather less detail.

- Throughout, finite and infinite behaviour will be specified in full detail.

For each of the 27 languages we develop its operational semantics based on the design of an appropriate labeled transition system specification (in the style of Plotkin's Structural Operational Semantics). In the denotational modeling, we apply the usual compositionality principle in mapping language constructs to elements of a mathematical domain, allowing the application of fixed point techniques to handle recursion. Sometimes, these domains have a linear structure, in that they consist of (functions to) (sets of) (finite or infinite) sequences. Other, more difficult ones are specified as solutions of *domain equations*. In all cases, we provide precise statements on how the operational ($\mathcal{O}$) and denotational ($\mathcal{D}$) models are related.

A large body of semantic definitional techniques will be used in designing these models. We list a few of them:

- We use both uniform (labeled) transition systems, with transitions of the form $s \xrightarrow{a} s'$, and systems with nonuniform transitions, written as $[s, \sigma] \to [s', \sigma']$. Here

s, s' are statements from the language at hand, a is an atomic action, and σ, σ' are semantic states (i.e., mappings from variables to values).

- We apply both finitely branching and image-finite transition systems, the latter to handle unbounded nondeterminacy.

- In the denotational semantics, we often use the powerful tool of *continuations.* In the design of the transition system specifications, we exploit their—not so standard—syntactic counterparts which we have baptized *resumptions.* The interplay between resumptions and continuations will be of the essence in most of the $\mathcal{O} = \mathcal{D}$ (or variations thereof) proofs.

All models to be described are based on mathematical entities (such as sequences, tree-like objects, or an occasional pomset) which provide a *full history* of the computation at hand. Our main motivation for this kind of modeling—to be contrasted in particular with approaches based on deriving the input/output function associated with a program—is

- the wish to deal with sequential and concurrent systems in one unified framework, together with

- the increased importance of *reactive,* in particular *embedded,* systems in contemporary programming practice, explaining

- the desire to treat finite and infinite behaviour as equally valid types of computation.

In accordance with the above, we have based our semantics on the use of topological, in particular *metric* structures. To be precise, we use *complete* metric spaces: all relevant limits have to be present to cater for infinite computations. We have several reasons for this choice:

- In a history-based model, there is a natural definition of a *distance* between two computations, viz. the following form of the classical Baire metric: two computations have a distance 2^{-n} when the first difference in their behaviour appears after n steps.

- The Baire metric is the starting point for the fruitful exploitation of a number of topological tools. In particular, we refer here to Banach's theorem, stating that each contractive function on a complete metric space has a unique fixed point.

- The use of Banach's theorem is pervasive throughout our work. It enables us to define—by uniqueness of the fixed point of an appropriate (higher-order) operator—both $\mathcal{O}$ and $\mathcal{D}$. Moreover, all semantic operators, ranging from, e.g., simple sequential composition through shared-variable parallelism to the rendezvous operator, are defined as fixed point of some higher-order mapping.

- Semantic domains $\mathbb{P}$ solving domain equations (isometries, to be precise) over complete metric spaces of the form $\mathbb{P} \simeq \mathcal{F}(\mathbb{P})$, for $\mathcal{F}$ a monotonic ("covariant") functor, may be solved as well by an appeal to Banach's theorem. The crucial step here is to set up a framework in which a distance between two complete metric spaces can be defined under certain conditions. Only for $\mathcal{F}$ nonmonotonic or "contravariant" will it be necessary to use tools from category theory. In an Appendix (written by J.J.M.M. Rutten), the solution method developed by America/Rutten (1989) will be described.

The above considerations should not be construed as claiming that metric spaces are the preferred mathematical structures in all semantic modeling. A crucial condition for their successful use is a natural intuition of *computational step* in the language paradigm at hand, such that performing the step contributes an observational element to the computational history. Once this condition is fulfilled, we have no need for the distinction between partial and total elements, a basic ingredient of all order-based semantics. For certain settings—the (untyped) lambda calculus being the prime example—our methodology is not suitable.[1]

We conclude this overview of the design principles of our work with one final remark: the number of languages treated may seem inordinately high and the question may arise whether, after dealing with a good part of them, treatment of further ones might not turn out to become a routine exercise. It has been our experience in studying the selection of 27 languages—still only a small sample of the richness and diversity in the world of programming languages—that this is not at all the case. Though the overall methodology in our semantic modeling stays the same throughout the book, in each individual case considerable variations turned out to be necessary, e.g., in the specification of the transition systems, in the definition of the underlying mathematical structures, or in the argument linking the operational and denotational semantics.

All references pertaining to the book are collected in the bibliographical notes at the end of each chapter. We have aimed at completeness in acknowledging the direct sources of our work, and at providing representative samples of related research. The field of semantics has become too vast to strive for completeness for the latter.

In the Appendices, we have put together some miscellaneous information. Appen-

---

[1]The domain equation $\mathbb{P} \simeq \mathbb{P} \xrightarrow{1} \mathbb{P}$ (the right-hand side denoting the function space of all nonexpansive mappings from $\mathbb{P}$ to $\mathbb{P}$) has only the one-point space as (ultra) metric solution. On the other hand, for nontrivial constants A, equations such as $\mathbb{P} \simeq A + (\mathbb{P} \xrightarrow{1} \mathbb{P})$ or $\mathbb{P} \simeq A \times (\mathbb{P} \xrightarrow{1} \mathbb{P})$ do have proper solutions.

dices A and B supply proofs of topological facts which we considered somewhat too advanced to incorporate them in the main text. Appendix C (by J.J.M.M. Rutten) describes a category-theory based method to solve domain equations $\mathbb{P} \simeq \mathcal{F}(\mathbb{P})$, where $\mathcal{F}$ is a functor which is possibly not covariant. (Chapter 18 illustrates the need for such an $\mathcal{F}$.) Appendix D provides some hints on further reading.

Our book has been written as an advanced text for senior undergraduate or graduate students and as a reference work for researchers interested in programming languages and their semantics, in concurrency theory, and in application of topology in computer science. To serve the latter audience, considerably more material has been included than can be covered in a one semester course on semantics. For such a course, the instructor might cover Chapters 1, 2, 4, a selection of (the first sections of) Chapters 5 to 8, and, possibly, Chapter 11. In the development of the metric framework (Section 1.1.2, Section 2.1), we have aimed at a complete—though elementary—treatment of the material, including full proofs of the results. In the subsequent semantic applications, it is usually sufficient to work solely with the theorems; familiarity with the techniques used in their proofs is not needed anymore. This holds as well for Chapter 11: Though it builds on the theory of domain equations of Chapter 10, it should be possible to provide only a quick introduction to the main results of this theory, and then to proceed with their application in the use of branching domains to model concurrency.

In order to enhance its use as a textbook, all (but one) of the chapters are provided with exercises, of a varying level of difficulty.

As a text for undergraduates, a substantial part of the material just indicated has been classroom tested for several years at the Vrije Universiteit Amsterdam. Graduate courses based on selected parts of our work have been given at various universities and institutes in Europe (Amsterdam, Rome, Warsaw, Turku, Turin). It seemed especially appropriate that the course in Warsaw was hosted by the Stefan Banach Centre.

Acknowledgments

We first learned about the use of metric spaces in semantics from Maurice Nivat through a memorable lecture series he gave in Amsterdam in 1978. Of seminal importance for our work was the collaboration with Jeff Zucker in the early eighties. We mention in particular his essential share in the development of the (ultra)metric perspective on solving domain equations, and their use in the modeling of imperative concurrency. In the early stages of the research reported here, John-Jules Meyer and Ernst-Rüdiger Olderog made a number of important contributions to it. Pierre America, Joost Kok and Jan Rutten have—in various combinations of joint papers, the majority of which were to become part of their Ph.D. theses—contributed decisively to the further development of the methodology set forth in our book. We are especially grateful to Jan Rutten who continued to play a leading role in the shaping of the more advanced parts of the theory. In addition, he read most of the drafts of our work—resulting in many amendments—and wrote Appendix C on the categorical approach to the solving of domain equations.

We owe our greatest debt to Franck van Breugel. He carefully scrutinized all successive drafts, providing detailed comments and suggestions for corrections and improvements on countless occasions. If the persons mentioned above were instrumental in the starting of the project, Franck was essential for its completion. Besides all this, a number of sections in the book are based on joint papers with Franck, and several significant ideas from his thesis have found their way into it.

We are furthermore grateful to many people for contributing to the sources on which our investigations are based, for critically reading (parts of) the many drafts of the material, and, more in general, for providing interest and encouragement during the demanding years of preparing the book. In the first category—restricting ourselves to sources from the Amsterdam group and its associates—we are indebted to Jan Bergstra, Frank de Boer, Arie de Bruin, Anton Eliëns, Eiichi Horita, Jan Willem Klop, Catuscia Palamidessi, Marcel de Rooy, Frank Stolker (for several exercises), and Jeroen Warmerdam. In the second group we owe much to the constructive comments by Marcello Bonsangue—who carefully went through the whole text and also prepared the indices—to Bart Jacobs, both for critical remarks and for incisive discussions on the principles of our enterprise, to Jean-Marie Jacquet (mostly pertaining to Chapter 15), and to Daniele Turi. For general support we are thankful to Ralph Back, Mariangiola Dezani, Tony Hoare, Furio Honsell, Marta Kwiatkowska, Mila Majster, Prakash Panangaden, Simona Ronchi della Rocca, and John Tucker.

Finally, we wish to express our thanks to Robert Prior at The MIT Press, as well as Albert Meyer and Michael Garey, for their willingness to publish the book in their Foundations of Computing series.

Jaco de Bakker   Erik de Vink
CWI and Vrije Universiteit   Vrije Universiteit
Amsterdam   Amsterdam

The 27 Languages

$\mathcal{L}_{rec}$ a uniform language with elementary actions,
          sequential composition and recursion

$\mathcal{L}_{wh}$ a nonuniform language with assignment statements,
          sequential composition, conditionals and the while statement

$\mathcal{L}_{cf}$ $\mathcal{L}_{rec}$ + nondeterminacy
          (the control flow of "context free" grammars)

$\mathcal{L}_{gc}$ the guarded commands language

$\mathcal{L}_{gt}$ $\mathcal{L}_{cf}$ with goto's replacing recursion

$\mathcal{L}_{par}$ $\mathcal{L}_{cf}$ + parallel composition

$\mathcal{L}_{pc}$ $\mathcal{L}_{cf}$ + process creation

$\mathcal{L}_{ra}$ $\mathcal{L}_{wh}$ + random assignment

$\mathcal{L}_{fm}$ $\mathcal{L}_{cf}$ + fair merge

$\mathcal{L}_{block}$ a nonuniform language with blocks and recursion

$\mathcal{L}_{fun}$ function procedures with parameters called-by-value

$\mathcal{L}_{svp}$ $\mathcal{L}_{wh}$ + shared variable parallelism

$\mathcal{L}_{cee}$ concurrent evaluation of expressions

$\mathcal{L}_{\mu}$ the μ-calculus

$\mathcal{L}_{bt}$ $\mathcal{L}_{rec}$ + backtracking

$\mathcal{L}_{fork}$ $\mathcal{L}_{wh}$ + the fork statement

$\mathcal{L}_{\delta}$ $\mathcal{L}_{cf}$ + deadlock

$\mathcal{L}_{syn}$ $\mathcal{L}_{par}$ + synchronization

$\mathcal{L}_{aw}$ $\mathcal{L}_{svp}$ + the await statement

$\mathcal{L}_{com}$ $\mathcal{L}_{svp}$ + value passing communication

$\mathcal{L}_{po}$ $\mathcal{L}_{svp}$ + parallel objects

$\mathcal{L}_{rv}$ $\mathcal{L}_{wh}$ + process creation and rendezvous

$\mathcal{L}_{atc}$ $\mathcal{L}_{par}$ + atomization and commit

$\mathcal{L}_{ref}$ $\mathcal{L}_{atc}$ + action refinement

$\mathcal{L}_{hcl}$ two versions (nonuniform/uniform) of Horn clause logic

$\mathcal{L}_{cc}$ a concurrent constraint language

$\mathcal{L}_{as,2}$ a language with second order assignment

Control Flow Semantics

Introduction

Semantics

In the study of the semantics of programming languages, one investigates ways of assigning *meanings* to programs. Expressed in mathematical terminology, one is interested in functions

$$\mathcal{M}\colon \mathcal{L} \to \mathbb{P},$$

where

- $\mathcal{L}$ is a programming language, i.e., a collection of programs. Usually, the *form* of the programs will be specified by some syntactic formalism: Languages such as Pascal or C have *grammars* to define their well-formed programs.

- $\mathbb{P}$ is a domain of meanings, i.e., a set of mathematical entities $p, q, \ldots$ which are chosen for the purpose of modeling (certain aspects of) the computation specified by the program. In general, in order to be able to express the meanings of the constructs from the language $\mathcal{L}$, the domain $\mathbb{P}$ will be equipped with some mathematical structure. For example, $\mathcal{L}$ may include operators such as addition ('+'), sequential composition (';') or iteration (e.g., in the form of the while...do construct), and the mathematical structure should enable us to define their effect in a rigorous manner.

- $\mathcal{M}$ is a mapping assigning to each program s in $\mathcal{L}$ its meaning $p = \mathcal{M}(s)$. Accordingly, the study of semantics centers around the development of methods to specify the functions $\mathcal{M}$ (and associated domains $\mathbb{P}$) for a range of languages $\mathcal{L}$.

Our work is devoted especially to *control flow* notions in programming. In the next section, we shall provide an introduction to this problem area. A large variety of control flow notions will be dealt with in the subsequent chapters, couched in terms of a wide spectrum of languages $\mathcal{L}$. In the present section, our aim is to provide the reader with an initial feeling for the process of designing, for a given $\mathcal{L}$, the semantic function $\mathcal{M}$ mapping it to some domain $\mathbb{P}$. We shall distinguish two ways of specifying such an $\mathcal{M}$, the first traditionally called the operational method, and the second the denotational one. That is, we shall be concerned with the two cases

$$\mathcal{O}\colon \mathcal{L} \to \mathbb{P}_O$$

and

$$\mathcal{D}\colon \mathcal{L} \to \mathbb{P}_D,$$

where the domain $\mathbb{P}_O$ and mapping $\mathcal{O}$ define the *operational semantics,* and $\mathbb{P}_D$ and $\mathcal{D}$ the *denotational semantics.* In this introduction, we shall not be fully precise in characterizing the two styles of definition. As to the operational one, it aims at capturing the operational intuition about program constructs by means of a so-called *transition system* $\mathcal{T}$, consisting of some axioms and rules, together with an associated mechanism of interpreting these in terms of what may be seen as the operations of an abstract machine. As to $\mathcal{D}$, its primary characteristic is that is is defined in a *compositional* manner, composing the meaning of a composite program piece from the meanings of its parts. (In Chapter 1, we shall come back to the terminology "denotational.")

As examples to illustrate the two ways of designing semantics, we shall introduce two simple languages with a clear operational intuition. We then develop both $\mathcal{O}$ and $\mathcal{D}$ for these two languages, and discuss for each of them the natural question as to how $\mathcal{O}$ and $\mathcal{D}$ are related.

Example 1 Let $(a, b, \ldots \in) A$ (see footnote[1]) be an alphabet, i.e., a finite nonempty set of symbols. Let us define the language $(w \in) W$, the collection of (structured) *words* over A, by the following syntax (which we assume to be self-explanatory):

$$w ::= a \mid (w \cdot w)$$

Thus, examples of elements from W are a, $(a \cdot b)$, $((a \cdot b) \cdot (c \cdot d))$ or $(a \cdot (b \cdot (c \cdot d)))$. For simplicity, we shall often omit the outermost parentheses around $(w_1 \cdot w_2)$. As meaning for an element $w \in W$ we take—for the purposes of this simple example— its *length*. Let $(n \in) \mathbb{N}$ be the set of nonnegative integers, and let $\mathbb{P}_O = \mathbb{P}_D = \mathbb{N}$. We shall define the two semantic mappings $\mathcal{O} \colon W \to \mathbb{P}_O$ and $\mathcal{D} \colon W \to \mathbb{P}_D$, where $\mathcal{O}$ is specified according to the operational model involving a transition system as announced above, and $\mathcal{D}$ is defined in a compositional manner. Next, we shall outline how it may be shown that $\mathcal{O} = \mathcal{D}$ on W. We begin with the definition of $\mathcal{O}$.

Let E be a special symbol standing for *termination*—it denotes that nothing is left to be done—and let v range over the set $V = W \cup \{E\}$. We shall specify $\mathcal{O}$ for W in terms of the transition system $\mathcal{T}_W$. Transitions—in the present setting— are entities of the form

$$(w, n) \to (v, n')$$

where $w \in W$, $v \in V$ and $n, n' \in \mathbb{N}$. The transition relation '$\to$'—specifying that the pair (w, n) can make a *step* resulting in the pair (v, n')—is determined as the

---

[1]The notation $(x, y, \ldots \in) X$ introduces a set X with variables $x, y, \ldots$ ranging over X.

(least[2]) relation satisfying the axioms and rules below:

- $$(a, n) \to (\mathrm{E}, n+1) \qquad\qquad\qquad\qquad\qquad\qquad (\mathrm{Ax})$$

- $$\frac{(w, n) \to (w', n')}{(w \cdot \bar{w}, n) \to (w' \cdot \bar{w}, n')} \qquad\qquad\qquad\qquad\qquad (\mathrm{R1})$$

- $$\frac{(w, n) \to (\mathrm{E}, n')}{(w \cdot \bar{w}, n) \to (\bar{w}, n')} \qquad\qquad\qquad\qquad\qquad (\mathrm{R2})$$

Examples　The following transitions can be derived from $\mathcal{T}_W$:

(1) $(a, 0) \to (\mathrm{E}, 1)$. This is immediate by (Ax).

(2) $((a \cdot b) \cdot c, 2) \to (b \cdot c, 3)$. This can be seen as follows: We have that $(a, 2) \to (\mathrm{E}, 3)$ by (Ax). Hence, by (R2), $(a \cdot b, 2) \to (b, 3)$. Then $((a \cdot b) \cdot c, 2) \to (b \cdot c, 3)$ follows by (R1).

(3) Also, for no $n \in \mathbb{N}$ do we have that $(a \cdot b, 0) \to (\mathrm{E}, n)$.

The next step is the definition of $\mathcal{O} : W \to \mathbb{P}_O$, based on the transitions of $\mathcal{T}_W$. Let us use the notation $(w_1, n_1) \to (w_2, n_2) \to (w_3, n_3) \to \dots$ as shorthand for the transitions

$$(w_1, n_1) \to (w_2, n_2)$$
$$(w_2, n_2) \to (w_3, n_3)$$
$$(w_3, n_3) \to \dots$$

We now define

$$\mathcal{O}(w) = n \quad \text{iff} \quad (w, 0) \to (w', 1) \to (w'', 2) \to \dots \to (\mathrm{E}, n).$$

For example, $\mathcal{O}((a \cdot b) \cdot (c \cdot d)) = \mathcal{O}(a \cdot (b \cdot (c \cdot d))) = 4$. Note that the definition of $\mathcal{O}$ is based (via (Ax)) on the repeated addition of 1 to some given length (initially 0), rather than on adding—for a composite w—the lengths of the two components. The latter approach will be the one adopted next:

We define $\mathcal{D} : W \to \mathbb{P}_D$ in a compositional manner. Let us make the natural assumption that we have available, on $\mathbb{N}$, the semantic operator '$+$' of addition.

---

[2]Formally, we define '$\to$' as the least (with respect to set inclusion) subset of $(W \times \mathbb{N}) \times (V \times \mathbb{N})$ which satisfies (Ax), (R1) and (R2). E.g., for all w, w', n, n', if $((w, n), (w', n')) \in \to$, then for any $\bar{w}$, $(((w \cdot \bar{w}), n), ((w' \cdot \bar{w}), n')) \in \to$, and similarly for the other cases.

Thus, for $n_1, n_2 \in \mathbb{N}$, we know how to determine $n_1 + n_2$. We then specify $\mathcal{D} \colon W \to \mathbb{P}_D$ by putting

$$
\begin{aligned}
\mathcal{D}(a) &= 1 \\
\mathcal{D}(w_1 \cdot w_2) &= \mathcal{D}(w_1) + \mathcal{D}(w_2)
\end{aligned}
$$

Examples

(1) $\mathcal{D}((a \cdot b) \cdot (c \cdot d)) = \mathcal{D}(a \cdot b) + \mathcal{D}(c \cdot d) = (\mathcal{D}(a) + \mathcal{D}(b)) + (\mathcal{D}(c) + \mathcal{D}(d)) = 2 + 2 = 4.$

(2) $\mathcal{D}(a \cdot (b \cdot (c \cdot d))) = \mathcal{D}(a) + (\mathcal{D}(b \cdot (c \cdot d))) = 1 + (\mathcal{D}(b) + \mathcal{D}(c \cdot d)) = 1 + (1 + (\mathcal{D}(c) + \mathcal{D}(d))) = 1 + (1 + (1 + 1)) = 4.$

We conclude Example 1 with a brief discussion on how to relate $\mathcal{O}$ and $\mathcal{D}$. In this simple example, it is easy to show that $\mathcal{O} = \mathcal{D}$ on W. We introduce the auxiliary mapping $\mathcal{E} \colon V \to \mathbb{N}$ by the clauses

$$
\begin{aligned}
\mathcal{E}(\mathrm{E}) &= 0 \\
\mathcal{E}(w) &= \mathcal{D}(w).
\end{aligned}
$$

We claim that, for each w, n, v, n' such that the transition

$$(w, n) \to (v, n') \tag{1}$$

can be derived from $\mathcal{T}_W$, we have that

$$\mathcal{E}(w) + n = \mathcal{E}(v) + n'. \tag{2}$$

We leave the simple proof of this—by induction on the structure of w and an analysis of the derivation of (1) from $\mathcal{T}_W$—to the reader. Now if $\mathcal{O}(w) = n$, we have, by the definition of $\mathcal{O}$,

$$(w, 0) \to (w', 1) \to \cdots \to (\mathrm{E}, n),$$

hence $\mathcal{E}(w) + 0 = \mathcal{E}(w') + 1 = \cdots = \mathcal{E}(\mathrm{E}) + n = n$. Since $\mathcal{D}(w) = \mathcal{E}(w) + 0 = n = \mathcal{O}(w)$, we have that $\mathcal{D}(w) = \mathcal{O}(w)$, for each $w \in W$, and $\mathcal{O} = \mathcal{D}$ on W follows.

Example 2 The second example treats the language $(r \in)$ *Reg* of *regular expressions*. The discussion of its semantics—assigning to each expression r the language associated with it—requires a small amount of basic notation from formal language theory, which we first recapitulate.

(1) Let $(a \in) A$ be an alphabet, let $(v, w \in) A^*$ be the set of all finite (possibly empty) words over A, and let vw denote the usual *concatenation* of the words v, w. (E.g., for $v = ab$, $w = cac$, $vw = abcac$.) The symbol ϵ denotes the empty word.

(2) Let $\mathbb{P} = \mathcal{P}(A^*)$ be the powerdomain over A^*, i.e., the collection of all subsets of A^*. For $L, L_1, L_2 \in \mathbb{P}$, we put $L_1.L_2 = \{ vw \mid v \in L_1, w \in L_2 \}$ and $L^* = \{\epsilon\} \cup L \cup L.L \cup \cdots = \bigcup_{n=0}^{\infty} L^n$.

We now discuss how to define the semantic mappings

$$\mathcal{O} \colon Reg \to \mathbb{P}_O$$
$$\mathcal{D} \colon Reg \to \mathbb{P}_D$$

where we put $\mathbb{P}_O = \mathbb{P}_D = \mathbb{P}$.

In the definition of $\mathcal{O}$, we employ once again a system, to be called $\mathcal{T}_{Reg}$, of axioms and rules. However, an essential new ingredient—not yet present in our treatment of W in Example 1—concerns the use of a succession of *labeled* transition steps $r_1 \xrightarrow{\alpha_1} r_2$, $r_2 \xrightarrow{\alpha_2} r_3$, $\cdots$, such that, for $r = r_1$, the outcome $\mathcal{O}(r)$ is composed from the successive labels $\alpha_1, \alpha_2, \cdots$—to be seen as the *observable* elements—distilled from these steps. This method of "executing" a language construct through a sequence of what may be seen as computational steps, and next collecting the successive observables in some form, is pervasive in all operational modeling described in our book.

We now turn to the precise definitions. First we give the syntax for $(r \in) Reg$. Let ϵ and $(a \in) A$ be as described above, and let $\emptyset$ be the symbol denoting the empty set. We define r by

$$r ::= a \mid \epsilon \mid \emptyset \mid (rr) \mid (r + r) \mid r^*.$$

Below, for notational convenience we shall often omit parentheses around composed regular expressions. The system $\mathcal{T}_{Reg}$ will be expressed in terms of transitions $r \xrightarrow{\alpha} r'$ or $r \xrightarrow{\alpha} \mathrm{E}$, where E is as in Example 1, and α either ranges over A or equals ϵ. We shall use the symbol t to denote either an element of Reg or E. We now define $\mathcal{T}_{Reg}$:

- $$a \xrightarrow{a} \mathrm{E} \qquad\qquad \epsilon \xrightarrow{\epsilon} \mathrm{E} \qquad\qquad\qquad\qquad\qquad \text{(Act 1,2)}$$

- $$\frac{r \xrightarrow{\alpha} r'}{r\bar{r} \xrightarrow{\alpha} r'\bar{r}} \qquad\qquad \frac{r \xrightarrow{\alpha} \mathrm{E}}{r\bar{r} \xrightarrow{\alpha} \bar{r}} \qquad\qquad\qquad\qquad \text{(Seq 1,2)}$$

- $$\frac{r \xrightarrow{\alpha} t}{r + \bar{r} \xrightarrow{\alpha} t} \qquad\qquad \frac{r \xrightarrow{\alpha} t}{\bar{r} + r \xrightarrow{\alpha} t} \qquad\qquad\qquad \text{(Choice 1,2)}$$

$$\cdot \qquad \frac{\epsilon + (rr^*) \overset{\alpha}{\to} t}{r^* \overset{\alpha}{\to} t} \qquad\qquad\qquad\qquad\qquad \text{(Star)}$$

The system $\mathcal{T}_{Reg}$ enables us to infer[3] transitions $r \overset{\alpha}{\to} t$. For example, we have that $ab \overset{a}{\to} b$ (by (Seq 2), since $a \overset{a}{\to} \mathrm{E}$), and $(a+b)^* \overset{a}{\to} (a+b)^*$, since $a+b \overset{a}{\to} \mathrm{E}$, whence, by (Seq 2), $(a+b)(a+b)^* \overset{a}{\to} (a+b)^*$, from which $(a+b)^* \overset{a}{\to} (a+b)^*$ follows by (Choice 2) and (Star).

Putting successive transition steps $r_1 \overset{\alpha_1}{\to} r_2$, $r_2 \overset{\alpha_2}{\to} r_3$, $\cdots$ together, we collect the outcome in the operational semantics $\mathcal{O} : Reg \to \mathbb{P}$ by defining

$$\mathcal{O}(r) = \{\, \alpha_1 \cdots \alpha_n \mid r = r_1 \overset{\alpha_1}{\to} r_2 \to \cdots \to r_n \overset{\alpha_n}{\to} \mathrm{E}, n \geq 1 \,\} \qquad\qquad (3)$$

Note that each of the α_i in (3) may equal ϵ and that, implicitly, we obtain as outcome $\mathcal{O}(r) = \emptyset$ in case we only have sequences of the form $r = r_1 \overset{\alpha_1}{\to} \cdots r_n \not\to$, $n \geq 1$. Here $r_n \not\to$ is short for $\neg\exists \alpha, r \, [\, r_n \overset{\alpha}{\to} r \,]$.

Example $\mathcal{O}(\epsilon + ab\emptyset) = \{\epsilon\}$, $\mathcal{O}((a+b)^*) = \{a,b\}^*$.

We next discuss how to define $\mathcal{D} : Reg \to \mathbb{P}$ in a compositional manner. Thanks to the simple syntactic structure of regular expressions, a particularly smooth definition by induction on the syntactic complexity of the argument r is possible. We put

$$\begin{aligned}
\mathcal{D}(\epsilon) &= \{\epsilon\} \\
\mathcal{D}(a) &= \{a\} \\
\mathcal{D}(\emptyset) &= \emptyset \\
\mathcal{D}(r_1 r_2) &= \mathcal{D}(r_1).\mathcal{D}(r_2) \\
\mathcal{D}(r_1 + r_2) &= \mathcal{D}(r_1) \cup \mathcal{D}(r_2) \\
\mathcal{D}(r^*) &= \mathcal{D}(r)^*.
\end{aligned}$$

Note how, on the right-hand sides of these equations, we employ semantic operators in the realm of $\mathbb{P}$, viz. concatenation ('.'), set-theoretic union ('$\cup$'), and the semantic '*'.

The relationship between $\mathcal{O}$ and $\mathcal{D}$ for Reg is simple. We have

$$\mathcal{O} \;=\; \mathcal{D}, \;\; \text{on } Reg.$$

---

[3]We here define as the relation generated by $\mathcal{T}_{Reg}$ the least set (with respect to set inclusion) of triples (r, α, t) satisfying the axioms and rules of $\mathcal{T}_{Reg}$. Again, this least set will be denoted by '$\to$', and we shall write $r \overset{\alpha}{\to} t$ instead of $(r, \alpha, t) \in \to$.

We shall not give a full proof of this result here. In essence, it is based on

- the fact that $\mathcal{O}$ can be shown to be compositional with respect to '.' and '+' (Note that this is not true by definition, but a special feature of $\mathcal{O}$ in this case.)
- the fact that $\mathcal{T}_{Reg}$ is interpreted as yielding the *least* set satisfying its axioms and rules
- the property that, for each $L \in \mathbb{P}$, we have that L^* is the least solution of the equation (for $X \in \mathbb{P}$)

$$X = \{\epsilon\} \cup L.X.$$

Combining these ingredients, an argument by induction on the complexity of r yields that $\mathcal{O}(r) = \mathcal{D}(r)$, for each r.

With these two examples, we have highlighted some key features of our semantic methodology:

- The operational semantics $\mathcal{O}$ is based on (a particular kind of formal system, viz.) a transition system[4], and, for a construct s, $\mathcal{O}(s)$ is obtained by collecting the labels from the successive steps as specified by this system, starting from s.
- The denotational semantics $\mathcal{D}$ is defined compositionally, using a correspondence between the syntactic operators from the language with appropriate operators on the semantic domain.
- For each $\mathcal{L}$, we wish to establish the relationship between $\mathcal{O}$ and $\mathcal{D}$.

For each of the examples, we discussed the design of the semantic models $\mathcal{O}$ and $\mathcal{D}$. Why are we interested in *two* semantics? Both $\mathcal{O}$ and $\mathcal{D}$ have a clear motivation. $\mathcal{O}(s)$ is defined in an algorithmic way, specifying which successive computation steps are to be taken while executing the program s. As we shall see, $\mathcal{O}$ *may* be—but often is not—compositional. That is, we shall encounter situations where, for some language operator—e.g., the binary operator 'op'—it is not possible to define a semantic $\hat{op}$ on the operational domain $\mathbb{P}_O$ such that $\mathcal{O}(s_1 \, op \, s_2) = \mathcal{O}(s_1) \, \hat{op} \, \mathcal{O}(s_2)$ holds. Still, there is always a strong reason to strive for a compositional semantics, viz. in view of the desirability of *modular* program design.

One would like to have at one's disposal a notion of program meaning $\mathcal{M}$ such that, in case $\mathcal{M}(s_1) = \mathcal{M}(s_2)$, then, for each "context" $C[\cdot]$—i.e., each larger

---

[4]Properly speaking, $\mathcal{T}$ is a transition system *specification*—much more about this in Chapter 1—but we ignore this distinction in the present introduction.

program in which s_1 or s_2 may be embedded—we have also that $\mathcal{M}(C[s_1]) = \mathcal{M}(C[s_2])$. The function $\mathcal{D}$ satisfies this property by definition, but an $\mathcal{O}$ which is not compositional does not. More in general, denotational semantics is a key tool in (the justification of) the design of program *logics*. Though not dealt with in the present treatise, the study of logics to derive program properties such as correctness, termination or equivalence provides compelling arguments for semantic modeling, especially in its denotational variety. On the other hand, operational semantics is motivated by the computational intuition it embodies. Frequently, a prototype implementation of a language can be based on the information contained in the transition system specifying its operational semantics.

After this preliminary outline of what semantic design is about, we devote the next section to a first overview of the area of control flow notions in programming.

Control Flow

Designers of contemporary programming languages have created an amazing variety of control flow notions and—maybe to a slightly lesser extent—of data types. In our book, we concentrate on the control flow aspects of programming, largely ignoring the issues having to do with (the specification of) static information such as data structures, types, etc. Even so, we face a demanding task in surveying the mass of control flow structures which have been put forward in language design over the years. In this section, we shall provide a preliminary classification of the notions to be treated later in much more detail. Altogether, our work is organized around 27 languages[5], and no more than a first overview is possible at this stage.

"Control flow" refers to the body of concepts having to do with the way in which a program specifies the successive steps to be taken during its execution. This formulation leads in a natural way to a distinction between the program primitives specifying the atomic or indivisible steps in this execution, and the operators used to compose more complex programs from simpler ones. We discuss both of these somewhat further.

Primitives The choice of the elementary actions constituting the basis for a language has a decisive impact on its design and, consequently, on its semantics. Classical imperative languages have assignment statements $v := e$ (for e an expression the value of which is to be assigned to the variable v) as basic building blocks[6].

---

[5]In fact, "languages" may be too ambitious a term; it is used primarily to simplify the terminology. Properly speaking, we should use instead something like "cluster of language notions."

[6]We abstract here from the possibility that the execution of $v := e$ has to be subdivided in smaller steps, e.g., when the evaluation of e is a complex process.

On the other hand, so-called process description languages—which play a prominent role in the study of parallel or concurrent processing—are built from atomic actions which are no more than symbols from some alphabet. At a different level of articulation, the primitive processes $a, b, \ldots$ may be equipped with some detailed description, but at the level of the, mostly parallel, system, the $a, b, \ldots$ are taken as atomic. Clearly, this has important consequences for the choice of the semantic domain $\mathbb{P}$. In modeling the former case—with assignments as atoms—one works with states and state-transforming functions. Here a state is to be taken as a function linking variables to their values. For the latter, the entities in $\mathbb{P}$ are no more than (sets of) sequences of symbols or (generalizations of) labeled tree structures. At the present stage, we will not discuss this any further. Suffice it to say that the difference between state-based and symbol-based primitives is a key distinction in all later developments. Elsewhere, one may encounter the distinction as "interpreted" versus "schematic." In logic, one calls it "first-order" versus "propositional." To avoid biasing the reader with too much connotation from earlier terminology, we shall consistently use the pair of terms "nonuniform" versus "uniform" for the two approaches.

Besides primitives of the form $v := e$ or simple atoms $a, b, \ldots$, we shall encounter further cases which may be seen as intermediate between these two. Rather than leaving the $a, b, \ldots$ completely schematic or uninterpreted, one may view them as equipped with some—maybe varying—interpretation, where the states they manipulate are not necessarily the mappings (from variables to values) as mentioned above, but may be chosen instead to accommodate a range of other programming paradigms. A modest number of examples of this will be treated in due course[7].

Composition rules We next list some organizing principles for program composition operators.

- The first group of program constructors are the, mostly binary, operators such as sequential composition (';') or choice ('+' in the uniform setting, selection based on a *test* in the nonuniform one). Operations such as these are of paramount importance in imperative languages, present in some form in all their instances. In case the choices just mentioned allow more than one outcome, the phenomenon of *nondeterminacy* enters the scene, with far-reaching consequences for the semantic modeling. In addition to these main operations, there are several somewhat more special ones. An example is the "backtracking" version of choice. A representative

---

[7]For the reader familiar with logic programming, we mention two examples. In the first, states are instantiated to substitutions and the interpretation of actions is expressed in terms of *unification*. In the second, states are collections of facts, and the atomic actions have to do with adding information to, or inferring information from, such collections.

sample of such operations will also be studied.

- The second group of control flow operators consists of the notions of *recursion* and *iteration*. Both of these serve to prescribe repeated execution of parts of a program, and, as such, are essential elements of the expressive power of a programming language. The ability to specify nonterminating behaviour is an indispensable element for what is called—in computability theory—the "universal" power of a language. Accordingly, maybe the most important underlying principle for our semantic methodology is the insistence on considering terminating and nonterminating behaviour as equally important or desirable. Many computing systems have as aim to provide continuously available services, without a predetermined time by which a service is to terminate. Our semantic domains are, in all cases, organized in order that they can accommodate such *reactive systems*, essentially by keeping a full record of the computation—which may well be infinite. As an additional benefit of such a history-based model, we have a natural basis to model the execution of parallel programs (more about this in a moment). For sequential languages, the input/output model is also attractive: the semantic design is then aimed at determining the function linking the output of the computation to its input. For the general goal we have set ourselves—modeling both finite and infinite behaviour, and both sequential and parallel programming by means of one unified methodology—the I/O model is not suited.

- A further group of control flow notions has to do with parallel program execution as specified, e.g., by the parallel composition operator '$\|$'. Based on the way we (mostly) model this notion—to be called the "interleaving" approach—it has a natural interpretation as a symmetric variant of sequential composition. Important further notions which usually appear together with '$\|$' are *deadlock, synchronization* and *communication*. The way in which two parallel components may interact can be controlled by an atomization operator (and associated version, called "commit," of sequential composition), turning certain parts of the program into atoms which are not amenable to interrupts from parallel processes.

- Closely connected with the just mentioned concepts from parallel programming are those of *static* versus *dynamic* configurations of processes. We shall investigate two forms of expanding a given configuration by the creation of new processes. We also discuss means to encapsulate the activities of a given process by providing it with its own local state—effectively protecting it towards interference from other processes—and explicitly prescribing the way processes may communicate. By doing this, we shall be able to render some of the flavour of concurrent object-oriented programming.

• Largely orthogonal to the above group of concepts, there is the issue of *locality* and *scope* of variables. We shall provide a modest treatment of this by introducing the classical semantic notion of an *environment* for variables. This refines the earlier mapping from variables to values by introducing addresses as an intermediate layer. Exploiting this notion, we next study one parameter mechanism for procedures, viz. "call-by-value." Further parameter mechanisms have been dealt with in considerable detail in many earlier semantic investigations of (primarily) sequential languages. We here approach the borderline between the world of control flow notions and that of functional languages—with vast expanses of research dealing with type theory, polymorphism, higher-order notions and (models for) the lambda calculus. Apart from a few skirmishes in the borderland of imperative and functional territory (Sections 6.2 and 7.2, Chapter 18), we refrain from attacking the problems in the functional world, if only since we expect that the history-oriented methodology will be less effective in dealing with them.

With this listing of control flow primitives and main notions which may be encountered in contemporary programming languages, we close this introductory chapter. All issues alluded to here will return extensively in the chapters to come. The reader should now be ready to study Part I of our book, which is devoted primarily to an exposition of the general principles of our methodology.

I FUNDAMENTALS

Part I presents the fundamental principles of our methodology. For both uniform (schematic) and nonuniform (state-based) language families, we introduce basic examples, and use them to illustrate the central concepts of the method at work, such as complete metric spaces, transition system specifications, higher-order operators and fixed point techniques, and resumptions versus continuations. Especially Chapters 1 and 2 are essential for all subsequent developments. Chapter 3 is devoted to some variations on earlier themes and could be kept for a second round of study.

1 Recursion and Iteration

In Chapter 1, we present the first part of the fundamentals of our methodology for the design of control flow semantics. Two simple languages will be used as vehicles to introduce the basic semantic techniques and mathematical structures which underly all subsequent definitions. In Section 1.1, we shall discuss a very simple language, to be called $\mathcal{L}_{rec}$, with programs built from elementary actions (i.e., symbols from some alphabet) through sequential composition and, possibly recursive, procedures. Recursion is the key concept here. It induces the possibility of *infinite* behaviour, and thus necessitates the introduction of mathematical structures with some form of *limit* for its rigorous treatment. In our methodology, *metric spaces* will serve as the underlying universe, allowing us to borrow several—mostly elementary—results from metric topology. In Section 1.2, we shall be concerned with a second language ($\mathcal{L}_{wh}$) which looks quite different from the first one. It includes a small sample of real-life programming constructs such as assignment statements, sequential composition, conditionals and the while statement. Though $\mathcal{L}_{wh}$ is syntactically rather different from $\mathcal{L}_{rec}$, its semantic analysis will exhibit a surprisingly large similarity to the method used for the investigation of $\mathcal{L}_{rec}$.

In Chapter 1, we shall develop a substantial part of our semantic methodology, and it is essential that the reader obtains a good understanding of the techniques to be described. Though these may seem overly demanding for the study of such simple languages, the reader will be amply rewarded when, in later chapters, he will see how they can be fruitfully applied to a wide variety of, sometimes advanced, control flow notions. One last introductory remark: Chapter 1 is concerned solely with *deterministic* programs. Nondeterminacy will be dealt with in Chapter 2. Some new mathematical material will be required, but the key tools as described in Chapter 1 will retain their central role, both in Chapter 2 and in all later chapters.

1.1 Recursion—transition systems and higher-order definitions

Section 1.1 uses $\mathcal{L}_{rec}$ as a means to introduce and study a first group of fundamental concepts in semantics. As we saw in the introduction, two types of semantic modelling will be distinguished, viz.

- *operational* semantics
- *denotational* semantics.

The first kind of semantics will be based on the design of a *transition system*, or, more precisely, a transition system *specification*, for $\mathcal{L}_{rec}$. By this we refer to a certain mathematical object, comparable to an automaton as studied in formal language theory. Roughly, a transition system for $\mathcal{L}_{rec}$ has the programs for $\mathcal{L}_{rec}$ as its configurations (to be compared with the states of an automaton), and the transitions between successive configurations model the evolving of the computation as prescribed by the initial program. The transitions between successive configurations are specified by a formal system with axioms and rules which together capture the meaning of the $\mathcal{L}_{rec}$-constructs. Each transition results in an "observable" action, and the collection of all successive such actions constitutes the operational semantics of the program. The fact that this model has much of the flavour of an abstract machine explains the qualification "operational."

The second type of semantics is, traditionally, called "denotational." This terminology stems from the principle that "programming constructs denote values." Denotational semantics is not based on transition systems. Rather, it adheres to the "compositionality principle," stating that the meaning of a program is composed from the meanings of its constituent parts. Though appealingly simple, this principle raises several subsidiary questions. Here we only mention the way to handle recursion, for which additional techniques in terms of so-called fixed point definitions are necessary. Fortunately, our basing the semantic models on metric topology pays off nicely, since we can exploit a powerful classical result (Banach's fixed point theorem).

For all semantic definitions in Chapter 1—and virtually everywhere later—we use a technique in terms of so-called higher-order operators. E.g., for $\mathcal{L}_{rec}$ both the operational semantics ($\mathcal{O}$) and the denotational semantics ($\mathcal{D}$), and the (semantic) sequential composition operator ('$;$'), will be defined using some higher-order mapping. We refrain from trying to explain this idea further at the present stage—it would require some minimum of notation to describe—but warn the reader that it will probably appear somewhat daunting at first sight. However, the technique is used all through our book, so a large collection of examples will become available to familiarize him with this method.

A natural question raised by the above concerns the relationship between the operational and denotational semantics for $\mathcal{L}_{rec}$. As main theorem of Section 1.1 we shall obtain the equivalence of $\mathcal{O}$ and $\mathcal{D}$ for $\mathcal{L}_{rec}$. This will, in fact, be the first instalment of a long list of results. In all languages studied in our work we shall present precise statements about the relationship between $\mathcal{O}$ and $\mathcal{D}$ for the language under consideration. In the simpler cases, we shall be able to obtain an equivalence result. For the harder languages studied later in our book, the situation will be less simple, and the formulation and proof of the relationship between $\mathcal{O}$ and $\mathcal{D}$ will throughout be a main goal of our semantic investigations.

Section 1.1 is organized in four subsections. After presenting the syntax and operational semantics for $\mathcal{L}_{rec}$ (of the so-called "direct" kind), we devote a separate subsection to some basic metric topology. In a first round, the reader may wish to study here only the definitions and statements of the theorems, without aiming at a full grasp of (the details of) the proofs. This remark also applies to subsequent occasions where we present some mathematical background. Usually, it is not necessary to have a full command over the mathematical details in order to appreciate the metric machinery at work in the semantic definitions. Sections 1.1.3 and 1.1.4 then bring the (higher-order) definitions of $\mathcal{D}$ and $\mathcal{O}$, culminating in the theorem that $\mathcal{O} = \mathcal{D}$ on $\mathcal{L}_{rec}$.

1.1.1 Syntax and operational semantics

The programs of the language $\mathcal{L}_{rec}$ are composed of *statements* and *declarations*. Statements ($s \in$) *Stat*—this notation should be taken as introducing a set *Stat* with s a variable ranging over it—are put together from basic components using (just) one composition rule. The basic components are

(1) The set ($a \in$) *Act* of *actions*. The elements of *Act* may be seen as *abstract* operations which we leave without further interpretation. (In later chapters we often specialize the actions in *Act* to commands which are indeed associated with some meaning, such as assignment statements.) For the moment, we do not care whether *Act* is a finite or infinite set.

(2) The set ($x \in$) *PVar* of *procedure variables*. Procedure variables will obtain a meaning through a declaration, to be supplied as part of a program. An occurrence of some x in a statement—a *call* of x—will invoke execution of the statement associated with x in the declaration, this statement being called the procedure body for x. Again, it is immaterial whether *PVar* is finite or infinite.

The composition rule of $\mathcal{L}_{rec}$ is that of sequential composition, yielding the composed statement ($s_1;s_2$) from the constituents s_1 and s_2. It is read as: s_1 followed by s_2.

Besides the set ($s \in$) *Stat* we shall also introduce the set ($g \in$) *GStat*—a subset of *Stat*—of so-called *guarded* statements. These play a role in the format for declarations; a guarded statement starts with an action, thus "guarding" the procedure variables which may occur in it. The reason for introducing this restriction will become amply clear in the sequel. In the specification of the syntax of $\mathcal{L}_{rec}$, we shall use a—we hope mostly self-explanatory—syntactic formalism, with '::=' to be read as "is defined as" and with '|' as "or." The entities occurring on the right-hand side

of the syntactic definitions are either given a priori (such as the symbols '(', ')' or
';', and the $a \in Act$ or $x \in PVar$), or they are recursive occurrences of the entities
being defined. (The reader who has not seen this type of syntactic definition before
may want to consult Exercise 1.16).[1]

Definition 1.1 Let $(a \in) Act$ and $(x \in) PVar$ be given sets.

(a) The set $(s \in) Stat$ is given by

$$s ::= a \mid x \mid (s;s).$$

(b) The set $(g \in) GStat$ is given by

$$g ::= a \mid (g;s).$$

(where s is as defined in part (a)).

(c) The set $(D \in) Decl$ of *declarations* is given by[2]

$$Decl = PVar \rightarrow GStat.$$

(d) The set $(\pi \in) \mathcal{L}_{rec}$ of *programs* is given by

$$\mathcal{L}_{rec} = Decl \times Stat.$$

Examples

(1) The expressions $(a_1;(a_2;a_3))$, $((a_1;a_2);a_3)$, $((a;x);y)$ and $(x;y)$ are statements.

(2) We write $(x \Leftarrow g \mid s)$ and $(x_1 \Leftarrow g_1, \ldots, x_n \Leftarrow g_n \mid s')$ for programs $(D|s)$ and
$(D'|s')$ where the declarations D and D' are such that $D(x) = g$ and $D'(x_i) = g_i$,
for $i = 1, \ldots, n$, respectively.

(3) Examples of $\mathcal{L}_{rec}$-programs are $(D|(a;b))$, $(x \Leftarrow (a;x) \mid (x;b))$,
$(x \Leftarrow (a;y), y \Leftarrow (b;x) \mid x)$.

---

[1]The exercises are collected at the end of each chapter (and numbered $i.j$, for the j-th exercise
of Chapter i).

[2]For sets M, N, we write $M \rightarrow N$ for the set of all functions from M to N.

The general format adopted in Definition 1.1 will be used all through our book. Syntactic subdefinitions are not subscripted, in order not to overload the notation. However, the main definitions—e.g., of the language at hand, here $\mathcal{L}_{rec}$—are subscripted with an abbreviation for the language (or main language construct) to be studied. Implicitly, all further syntactic (and other) notions occurring in a given section are to be taken as subscripted in a similar manner.

An $\mathcal{L}_{rec}$-program thus is a pair $(D|s)$—with '|' used as a separator for easier readability—with $D \in Decl$ and $s \in Stat$. A declaration D is a function assigning a body $D(x)$ in $GStat$ to each procedure variable x. A statement $s \in Stat$ is either a single action $a \in Act$, a procedure variable $x \in PVar$—to be taken as a call of x—or a sequential composition $(s_1;s_2)$. We shall mostly drop the outermost parentheses when dealing with sequential composition. Inner parentheses will be omitted once we have settled associativity of ';'. That is, we shall write $s_1;s_2$ rather than $(s_1;s_2)$. Also, after having proved associativity of ';', we shall write $s_1;s_2;s_3$ for either $(s_1;s_2);s_3$ or $s_1;(s_2;s_3)$.

By allowing only guarded statements to act as procedure bodies, we exclude, e.g., bindings of the form

$$D(x) = x;a \text{ or } D(x) = y, D(y) = x ,$$

and also $D(x) = y, D(y) = a$. Guardedness may be formulated also in the following way: Let us call an action a *exposed* in a, a procedure variable x exposed in x, and an action or procedure variable exposed in $s_1;s_2$ whenever it is exposed in s_1. We then have that only an action may occur exposed in a guarded statement g.

We now turn to a discussion of the first main type of semantics, viz. the *operational* semantics for $\mathcal{L}_{rec}$. The qualification "operational" indicates that we want to base this style of semantics on some form of operational intuition. The formalism to make this precise relies on two important notions, viz. that of

- a *transition system*

and of

- a *transition system specification*.

We begin with the introduction of the first notion.

Definition 1.2 A transition system $\mathcal{T}$ is a triple $(Conf, Obs, \rightarrow)$, where

- $(c \in) Conf$ is a set of *configurations*

- $(a \in)$ *Obs* is a set of *observations*
- '$\rightarrow$' is a subset of *Conf* $\times$ *Obs* $\times$ *Conf*, i.e., we have

$$\rightarrow \; \subseteq \; Conf \times Obs \times Conf.$$

In this definition, we take *Conf* and *Obs* as abstract sets, both of which may be infinite. We shall always write $c \xrightarrow{a} c'$ instead of $(c, a, c') \in \; \rightarrow$. Abstracting from the observations a, we see that '$\rightarrow$' determines a *relation* on *Conf*; accordingly, '$\rightarrow$' is called "the relation of T." A transition system T may be seen as an abstract machine, determining computations in a natural way: Each $c \in Conf$ can be viewed as a configuration of the machine, and a transition $c \xrightarrow{a} c'$ specifies a transition from configuration c to configuration c', with a as observable result. Also, successive steps $c \xrightarrow{a_1} c_1$, $c_1 \xrightarrow{a_2} c_2$, ..., when put together in

$$c \xrightarrow{a_1} c_1 \xrightarrow{a_2} c_2 \rightarrow \ldots \xrightarrow{a_n} c_n \rightarrow \ldots \tag{1.1}$$

determine a *computation sequence*, with the sequence $a_1 \cdot a_2 \cdot \ldots \cdot a_n \cdot \ldots$ as observable behavior. This view leads to a few further points:

(1) The wish to concatenate the $a_1, a_2, \ldots$ implies that we should take *Obs* as an *alphabet*, with associated concatenation operator '$\cdot$'.

(2) A sequence (1.1) may either go on indefinitely—producing an infinite sequence $a_1 \cdot a_2 \cdots$—or it may end in a configuration c_n such that, for *no* a and $\bar{c}$, we have $c_n \xrightarrow{a} \bar{c}$. In that case, the sequence (1.1) terminates with c_n.

We introduce two notations associated with a transition system T.

Notation 1.3 Let $T = (Conf, Obs, \rightarrow)$ be given.

(a) For each $c \in Conf$, the *successor set* $\mathcal{S}(c)$ is given by

$$\mathcal{S}(c) = \{\, \langle a, c' \rangle \mid c \xrightarrow{a} c' \,\}$$

(b) We write $c \nrightarrow$ in case $\neg\exists a, c' \colon c \xrightarrow{a} c'$, or, equivalently, in case $\mathcal{S}(c) = \emptyset$.

Rather than continuing at this stage with the presentation of examples of transition systems, we turn to the discussion of the second important notion, viz. of a *transition system specification*. Indeed, the wish to *specify* transition systems, in particular to find means to *define* the transition relation '$\rightarrow$' by additional techniques, has led to the introduction of the fruitful notion of transition system specification. Throughout our book, all definitions of operational semantics will be based on instances of this notion.

Definition 1.4   A transition system specification is a four-tuple $\mathcal{T} = (Conf, Obs, \rightarrow, Spec)$. The sets $Conf$, Obs, and '$\rightarrow$' (a subset of $Conf \times Obs \times Conf$) are as before. The specification $Spec$ consists of a set of n (≥ 1) *axioms* and m (≥ 0) *rules*. The axioms and rules of $Spec$ determine the transition relation '$\rightarrow$' in the following way:

(1) Each axiom is a construct of the form $c \xrightarrow{a} c'$. It specifies that all tuples of the form (c, a, c') belong to '$\rightarrow$'.

(2) A rule is a construct of the form

$$\frac{c_1 \xrightarrow{a_1} c'_1, \ldots, c_k \xrightarrow{a_k} c'_k}{c \xrightarrow{a} c'}. \qquad (1.2)$$

The intended meaning of a rule (1.2) is given by the following implication.

If, for all $i = 1, \ldots, k$, $(c_i, a_i, c'_i) \in \rightarrow$, then $(c, a, c') \in \rightarrow$. $\qquad (1.3)$

Here (1.3) should be taken in the sense that it is universally quantified over all configurations and observations occurring in it.

(3) '$\rightarrow$' is the *least* set—with respect to the subset ordering—which satisfies specifications (1) and (2).

The condition that '$\rightarrow$' be the least set as specified should become clear once it is noted that the full set $U \stackrel{df}{=} Conf \times Obs \times Conf$ trivially satisfies conditions (1) and (2). In general, this may hold as well for many subsets of U, and we are interested in the least of them, containing no more (and also no less) triples than determined by the specification. (In Exercise 1.3 it is shown that such a least set can always be found.)

Remark In later chapters, we shall sometimes use systems with countably many axioms, rules or premises in a rule. "Rules" will often be used as shorthand for "axioms and rules."

Some examples are in order to illustrate the important notion of a transition system specification.

Example 1 Let $(\mathbb{N}, 0, s)$ be the set of natural numbers with zero 0 and successor function s. Let $\mathcal{T} = (\mathbb{N}, \{<\}, \rightarrow, Spec)$ where the set Obs is, simply, the singleton set $\{<\}$, and $Spec$ consists of one axiom and two rules

- $$0 \xrightarrow{<} s(n) \tag{Ax}$$

- $$\frac{n \xrightarrow{<} m}{s(n) \xrightarrow{<} s(m)} \tag{R1}$$

- $$\frac{n \xrightarrow{<} m, \ m \xrightarrow{<} p}{n \xrightarrow{<} p} \tag{R2}$$

It will not be difficult for the reader to convince himself that, by this $Spec$, we have that $(n, <, m) \in \ \rightarrow$ iff $n < m$, where the second '$<$' is the usual order relation on $\mathbb{N}$. Note in particular how the implicit quantification in rules (R1), (R2) is to be taken as $\forall n, m [n \xrightarrow{<} m \Rightarrow s(n) \xrightarrow{<} s(m)]$ and $\forall n, m, p [n \xrightarrow{<} m \wedge m \xrightarrow{<} p \Rightarrow n \xrightarrow{<} p]$, respectively.

Example 2 (this example has more interesting observations)
Let $M = (Q, \Sigma, \delta, q_0, F)$ be a finite automaton, with $(q \in) Q$ the set of states, $(a \in) \Sigma$ the alphabet, and $\delta \colon Q \times \Sigma \rightarrow \mathcal{P}(Q)$ the transition function. Here $\mathcal{P}(Q)$ denotes the powerset of Q, i.e., the collection of all subsets of Q. (The initial state q_0 and the final states F will play no role in our example.) Let $(w \in) \Sigma^*$ be—as usual— the set of all (finite) words over Σ, and let ϵ denote the empty word. With M we may associate the following transition system specification $\mathcal{T}_M = (Q, \Sigma^*, \rightarrow, Spec)$, where $Spec$ consists of two axioms and one rule:

- $$q \xrightarrow{\epsilon} q \tag{Ax1}$$
- $$q \xrightarrow{a} q' \qquad \text{if } q' \in \delta(q, a) \tag{Ax2}$$

- $$\frac{q \xrightarrow{a} q' \qquad q' \xrightarrow{w} q''}{q \xrightarrow{aw} q''} \tag{R}$$

We leave it to the reader to verify that *Spec* determines ' → ' such that $q \xrightarrow{w} q'$ iff $q' \in \delta(q, w)$ (with $\delta \colon Q \times \Sigma^* \to \mathcal{P}(Q)$ as usual in automata theory).

The key idea of using a transition system specification as a means to specify an abstract machine on which the operational semantics may be based is the following: We take the programs of the language—or, sometimes, constructs which are slight variations on the programs—as configurations of the system. Next, we view the transitions as specified by *Spec* as *computation steps,* in each case yielding the corresponding observation $a \in Obs$ as visible result of the step. Altogether, our strategy will be to specify transitions $c \xrightarrow{a} c'$, with c (almost) a program, by means of a suitable system of axioms and rules, varying according to the language considered at each given moment. Furthermore, the specification will be *structured* in the sense that the axioms and rules are *syntax-directed*: each syntactic (sub)construct of the language corresponds to some axiom or rule which determines how to execute the construct concerned.

We shall now present the transition system specification $\mathcal{T}_{rec}$, to be used for the semantics of $\mathcal{L}_{rec}$. The configurations of $\mathcal{T}_{rec}$ are almost the programs of $\mathcal{L}_{rec}$. More precisely, we take $Conf = Decl \times Res$, where $(r \in) Res$ is a new syntactic class of so-called *resumptions,* to be introduced now. Let E be a special symbol standing for *termination.* (E abbreviates the *empty* remaining statement.)

Definition 1.5 The set $(r \in) Res$ is given by

$r ::= \mathrm{E} \mid s$.

In other words, $Res = Stat \cup \{\mathrm{E}\}$, i.e., a resumption is either a statement, or the special symbol E. (In later chapters, we shall often work with resumptions embodying additional structure. Throughout our book, resumptions will serve as the main ingredient of the configurations of any transition system.)

We shall adopt the convention that a configuration E;s—terminate and then continue with s—will be syntactically identified with s. (This convention will allow a somewhat more concise formulation of the specification.) Here—and everywhere later—we shall use '$\equiv$' to denote syntactic identity.

Notation 1.6 For each $s \in Stat$, we have E;$s \equiv s$.

We proceed with the definition of $\mathcal{T}_{rec}$.

Definition 1.7 $\mathcal{T}_{rec} = (Decl \times Res, Act, \rightarrow, Spec)$. The transitions of $\mathcal{T}_{rec}$ are tuples of the form

$$((D_1|r_1), a, (D_2|r_2)) . \tag{1.4}$$

We shall always be concerned with (1.4) only in cases where $D_1 = D_2$. For brevity, we shall use the notation

$$r_1 \xrightarrow{a}_D r_2 \tag{1.5}$$

rather than (1.4) with $D = D_1 = D_2$. The axioms and rules of $Spec$ are the following

- $$a \xrightarrow{a}_D \mathrm{E} \tag{Act}$$

- $$\frac{g \xrightarrow{a}_D r}{x \xrightarrow{a}_D r} \qquad \text{if } D(x) = g \tag{Rec}$$

- $$\frac{s_1 \xrightarrow{a}_D r_1}{s_1;s_2 \xrightarrow{a}_D r_1;s_2} \tag{Seq}$$

The specification $Spec$ employs one axiom and two rules. Throughout, these refer to one given, fixed declaration D. The operational intuition of the axiom (Act) is, simply that an action a can make a transition towards E—and thus terminate—while producing a as observable. The rule (Rec) states that, in order to see which transition can be made by a procedure variable x, one should look for the transitions possible for $g = D(x)$—the body associated with x in the declaration D. The rule (Seq) covers two subcases, depending on whether $r \equiv \mathrm{E}$ or $r \equiv s_1' \in Stat$, viz.

$$\frac{s_1 \xrightarrow{a}_D \mathrm{E}}{s_1;s_2 \xrightarrow{a}_D \mathrm{E};s_2} \quad \text{and} \quad \frac{s_1 \xrightarrow{a}_D s_1'}{s_1;s_2 \xrightarrow{a}_D s_1';s_2} .$$

By the convention stated earlier, $\mathrm{E};s_2 \equiv s_2$, and the first subcase can be read as: If we know that s_1 terminates after performing an a-step, then, for any s_2, the statement $s_1;s_2$ can make an a-step to s_2. The second subcase states that, if s_1 can make an a-step to some s_1', then, for any s_2, $s_1;s_2$ can make an a-step to $s_1';s_2$. Together, the rule (Seq) specifies that the first step of $s_1;s_2$ always equals the first step of s_1.

Examples

(1) With respect to a fixed declaration D,

$$(a_1;a_2);a_3 \xrightarrow{a_1}_D a_2;a_3,$$

since $a_1 \xrightarrow{a_1}_D E$ by (Act), hence $a_1;a_2 \xrightarrow{a_1}_D a_2$ by (Seq), hence $(a_1;a_2);a_3 \xrightarrow{a_1}_D a_2;a_3$ again by (Seq). Also

$$a_1;(a_2;a_3) \xrightarrow{a_1}_D a_2;a_3,$$

since $a_1 \xrightarrow{a_1}_D E$ by (Act), from which $a_1;(a_2;a_3) \xrightarrow{a_1}_D a_2;a_3$ follows directly by (Seq).

(2) If $x \Leftarrow a;x$, we have

$$x;b \xrightarrow{a}_D x;b,$$

for $a \xrightarrow{a}_D E$ by (Act), so $a;x \xrightarrow{a}_D x$ by (Seq), hence $x \xrightarrow{a}_D x$ by (Rec) since $D(x) = a;x$. From this $x;b \xrightarrow{a}_D x;b$ follows by (Seq).

Some simple properties of $\mathcal{T}_{rec}$ can already be stated.

Lemma 1.8

(a) For all a, r, $x \xrightarrow{a}_D r$ iff $D(x) \xrightarrow{a}_D r$.

(b) For all a, r,

$$s_1;s_2 \xrightarrow{a}_D r \Longleftrightarrow \exists r_1[(s_1 \xrightarrow{a}_D r_1) \wedge (r \equiv r_1;s_2)] .$$

(c) For all a,

$$\exists r_1[(s_1;s_2);s_3 \xrightarrow{a}_D r_1] \Longleftrightarrow \exists r_2[s_1;(s_2;s_3) \xrightarrow{a}_D r_2]$$

Proof We leave parts (a) and (b) as exercises, and prove only part (c). We have

$$\exists r_1[(s_1;s_2);s_3 \xrightarrow{a}_D r_1]$$
$$\Leftrightarrow [\text{part (b)}] \; \exists r_{12}, r_1[((s_1;s_2) \xrightarrow{a}_D r_{12}) \wedge (r_1 \equiv r_{12};s_3)]$$
$$\Leftrightarrow \exists \bar{r}, r_{12}, r_1[(s_1 \xrightarrow{a}_D \bar{r}) \wedge (r_{12} \equiv \bar{r};s_2) \wedge (r_1 \equiv r_{12};s_3)]$$

$\Leftrightarrow \exists \bar{r}[(s_1 \xrightarrow{a}_D \bar{r}) \wedge \exists r_{12}, r_1[(r_{12} \equiv \bar{r}; s_2) \wedge (r_1 \equiv r_{12}; s_3)]]$

$\Leftrightarrow$ [such r_{12}, r_1 can always be found] $\exists \bar{r}[s_1 \xrightarrow{a}_D \bar{r}]$.

Similarly, we can show that

$\exists r_2[s_1; (s_2; s_3) \xrightarrow{a}_D r_2] \iff \exists \bar{r}[s_1 \xrightarrow{a}_D \bar{r}]$

and the desired result follows.   □

It is of some importance to note here that it is not true that, for all a, r,

$(s_1; s_2); s_3 \xrightarrow{a}_D r \iff s_1; (s_2; s_3) \xrightarrow{a}_D r$.

E.g., we have, putting $s_1 \equiv (a;b)$, $s_2 \equiv c$, $s_3 \equiv d$, that $((a;b);c);d \xrightarrow{a}_D (b;c);d$, but $(a;b);(c;d) \xrightarrow{a}_D b;(c;d)$. Though, as we shall prove later, $(b;c);d$ and $b;(c;d)$ have the same *meaning*—their operational semantics coincide—we do not have that they are *syntactically* the same.

We next state a general property of the transition sytem $\mathcal{T}_{rec}$, viz. that it is *deterministic*. More precisely, we have that, for each (D and) s, there is a unique pair $\langle a, r \rangle$ such that $s \xrightarrow{a}_D r$. Moreover, for $r \equiv \mathrm{E}$ we have *no* transition $\mathrm{E} \xrightarrow{a}_D r'$. Besides as a fact with some interest of its own, the property will serve as an occasion to introduce an important proof technique. Let us recall our earlier definition of successor set (Notation 1.3a): $\mathcal{S}(D|r) = \{ \langle a, (D|r') \rangle \mid r \xrightarrow{a}_D r' \}$. We shall show

Lemma 1.9

(a) $|\mathcal{S}(D|E)| = 0$.

(b) $|\mathcal{S}(D|s)| = 1$, *for each* $s \in Stat$.

We here use the notation that, for any set A, $|A|$ is the cardinality (number of elements) of A—in our book either a natural number, or '∞' indicating that A is an infinite set.

In the proof of the lemma, we shall use the so-called *weight function* of a configuration $(D|r)$, say $wgt(D|r)$, as defined in

Definition 1.10 The function $wgt: Decl \times Res \to \mathbb{N}$ is defined by

$$
\begin{aligned}
wgt(D|\text{E}) &= 0 \\
wgt(D|a) &= 1 \\
wgt(D|x) &= wgt(D|D(x)) + 1 \\
wgt(D|s_1;s_2) &= wgt(D|s_1) + 1\,.
\end{aligned}
$$

Note carefully that, for $r \in Stat$, $wgt(D|r)$ is not defined by induction on the syntactic complexity of r—since $D(x)$ is not syntactically simpler than x. Thus, the question arises as to whether $wgt(D|r)$ is well-defined. It is here that our restriction to *guarded* statements in declarations plays an essential role. We have

Lemma 1.11 $wgt(D|r)$ *is well-defined for each* $(D|r)$.

Proof Clear for $r \equiv \text{E}$. We next discuss the case $r \in Stat$ and first treat the subcase $r \in GStat$. We prove that, for each $g \in GStat$, $wgt(D|g)$ is well-defined. We have, by definition of wgt,

$$
\begin{aligned}
wgt(D|a) &= 1 \\
wgt(D|g;s) &= wgt(D|g) + 1\,,
\end{aligned}
$$

and we see that $wgt(D|g)$ is well-defined by induction on the syntactic complexity of g. We now tackle the general case, again arguing by syntactic induction. The cases $s \equiv a$ and $s \equiv s_1;s_2$ are clear. The case $s \equiv x$ follows by the subcase just shown, since $wgt(D|x) = wgt(D|D(x)) + 1$, with $D(x) \in GStat$. $\square$

We are now ready for the

Proof of Lemma 1.9.   Induction on $wgt(D|r)$. Clearly $|\mathcal{S}(D|\text{E})| = 0$. Next, we consider $r \in Stat$. Three subcases.

[a]   Clear, since $\mathcal{S}(D|a) = \{(a, (D|\text{E})\}$.

[x]   Since $\mathcal{S}(D|x) = \mathcal{S}(D|D(x))$ (Lemma 1.8a), the result follows by the induction hypothesis (and the fact that $wgt(D|D(x)) < wgt(D|x)$).

[$s_1;s_2$]   Since $|\mathcal{S}(D|s_1;s_2)| = |\mathcal{S}(D|s_1)|$ (a consequence of Lemma 1.8b), the result is again clear by induction. $\square$

Exercise 1.2 emphasizes the essential role of the guardedness requirement in Lemma 1.9 and 1.11.

The main purpose of $\mathcal{T}_{rec}$ is to use it as a basis for the definition of the operational semantics for $\mathcal{L}_{rec}$. In this, the notion of a computation sequence determined by

$\mathcal{T}_{rec}$—cf. formula (1.1)—will be important. First, we state the domain and codomain for $\mathcal{O}_d$, where $\mathcal{O}$ stands—here and everywhere later—for *operational* semantics and the subscript d indicates its *direct* version (to be contrasted with later forms of $\mathcal{O}$, cf. Section 1.1.4).

The domain of $\mathcal{O}_d$ is *Decl* × *Res*, and its codomain $\mathbb{P}_O$ is given in

Definition 1.12 $\mathbb{P}_O = Act^\infty$, where $Act^\infty = Act^* \cup Act^\omega$.

As we saw earlier, we want to view *Act* as an alphabet; Act^∞ is then given as the union of Act^* (the set of all *finite* words over *Act*) and Act^ω (the set of all *infinite* words over *Act*). For the moment, we assume that the reader has an intuitive understanding of Act^∞. In Section 1.1.2, we shall present the elementary mathematical properties of A^∞, for A any alphabet.

At last, we are ready for the main definition of this subsection.

Definition 1.13 $\mathcal{O}_d$:*Decl* × *Res* → $\mathbb{P}_O$ is given by

$$\mathcal{O}_d(D|r) = \begin{cases} a_1 a_2 \cdots a_n & \text{if } r \xrightarrow{a_1}_D r_1 \xrightarrow{a_2}_D \ldots \xrightarrow{a_n}_D r_n \equiv \mathrm{E} \\ a_1 a_2 \cdots & \text{if } r \xrightarrow{a_1}_D r_1 \xrightarrow{a_2}_D \ldots \, . \end{cases}$$

Examples $\mathcal{O}_d(D|(a_1;a_2);a_3) = \mathcal{O}_d(D|a_1;(a_2;a_3)) = a_1 a_2 a_3$,
$\mathcal{O}_d(x \Leftarrow a;x \mid x;b) = aaa \cdots = a^\omega$, $\mathcal{O}_d(x \Leftarrow a;y, y \Leftarrow b;x \mid x) = ababab \cdots = (ab)^\omega$.

Definition 1.13 states that the operational meaning of $(D|r)$ equals the sequence of all observations (all actions) produced successively by the transitions starting from $(D|r)$. Note that, by Lemma 1.9, there is always at most one way to continue a computation sequence. We note

- for each (D and) r, the induced computation sequences may be finite (terminating with $r_n \equiv \mathrm{E}$) or infinite

- in case $r \equiv \mathrm{E}$, the definition specializes to $\mathcal{O}_d(D|\mathrm{E}) = \epsilon$ (with ϵ the empty word in Act^∞).

We draw attention to an essential difference between our interpretation of the syntactic versus the semantic definitions for $\mathcal{L}_{rec}$. A program *text* is, by definition, finite: the number of applications of a recursive step in specifying the syntax of a program according to Definition 1.1 is always finite. On the other hand, the *meaning* of a program may involve both finite and infinite entities (here sequences of actions from Act). This phenomenon is of paramount importance for the theory to be developed subsequently, since the possible presence of infinite objects puts much heavier demands on the underlying mathematical structures.

Though the definition of $\mathcal{O}_d$ captures, in a natural way, our operational understanding of programs in $\mathcal{L}_{rec}$, several further tools have to be developed in order that we may prove some basic properties of $\mathcal{O}_d$. For example, we have

Lemma 1.14

(a) $\mathcal{O}_d(D|x) = \mathcal{O}_d(D|D(x))$.

(b) $\mathcal{O}_d(D|(s_1;s_2);s_3) = \mathcal{O}_d(D|s_1;(s_2;s_3))$.

The proof of part (a) is an easy exercise (based on Lemma 1.8a). However, we are not able to prove part (b) at the present stage, the reason being that the possible presence of infinite sequences in the outcomes prohibits the use of any argument based on induction (e.g., on the number of steps in the computation sequence on which the $\mathcal{O}_d(\cdot)$ are based). The problem signalled here will be attacked by the development of a mathematical framework allowing proofs about infinite objects, viz. that of *metric spaces*. In the next subsection, we shall present the first principles of this framework; later, various extensions will be developed (in particular in Section 2.1, Chapter 10, and the Appendices). In Section 1.1.3 we shall introduce a second type of semantics in the definition of which metric spaces play a fundamental role. We shall return to $\mathcal{O}$ for $\mathcal{L}_{rec}$ in Section 1.1.4, proving Lemma 1.14b as a side result.

1.1.2   Metric spaces

As we saw in the preceding subsection, a program from $\mathcal{L}_{rec}$—as well as from all further languages studied in our book—may prescribe an infinite computation. In order to argue about such computations and establish their properties in a mathematically rigorous manner, we must have available a notion of a *limit*. A natural way to proceed is to base ourselves on the same foundations as in mathematical analysis, viz. on the theory of *metric spaces*. Whereas in analysis a substantial part of the theory is developed for the sets $\mathbb{R}, \mathbb{R}^2, \ldots, \mathbb{R}^n, \ldots$ (the real line, real plane, ... , real n-space, ... , all instances of metric spaces), in control flow semantics the metric space of *words* over some alphabet—and a host of generalizations thereof—will play a central role.

So let us begin with defining the notion of a metric space.

Definition 1.15

(a) A metric space is a pair (M, d), with $(x, y, z \in) M$ a nonempty set and $d: M \times M \to \mathbb{R}_{\geq 0}$, i.e., d is a function—called the *distance*—from $M \times M$ to the set $\mathbb{R}_{\geq 0}$ of nonnegative reals. Moreover, d is required to satisfy the three postulates

(M1)	$d(x, y) = 0 \Leftrightarrow x = y$
(M2)	$d(x, y) = d(y, x)$
(M3)	$d(x, y) \leq d(x, z) + d(z, y)$.

(b) An *ultrametric* space is a pair (M, d) with M as before and $d: M \times M \to \mathbb{R}_{\geq 0}$ satisfying (M1), (M2) and (M4):

(M4)	$d(x, y) \leq max\{ d(x, z), d(z, y) \}$.

A distance function satisfying (M1), (M2) and (M3) will be called a *metric*. If d satisfies (M1), (M2) and (M4) it is called an *ultrametric*.

Postulate (M1) expresses that the distance between two points x and y is 0 precisely when $x = y$. (M2) is the symmetry law, and (M3) is the so-called triangle inequality (cf. Example (1) below). Note how (M4) strengthens (M3): whenever d satisfies (M4), it certainly satisfies (M3). Thus, each ultrametric space is a metric space. Ultrametric spaces are not so much important in the general theory of metric spaces; however, for the theory underpinning the various semantic models investigated in the sequel, (M4) is frequently of the essence.

Some simple examples of metric spaces are the following:

Examples

(1) ($\mathbb{R}$ and $\mathbb{R}^2$ with the Euclidean metric) For two real numbers $x, y \in \mathbb{R}$ we put

$$d_1(x, y) = |x - y|.$$

For two pairs $x = (x_1, x_2)$, $y = (y_1, y_2)$ in the plane $\mathbb{R}^2$ we put

$$d_2(x, y) = \sqrt{(y_1 - x_1)^2 + (y_2 - x_2)^2}.$$

$(\mathbb{R}, d_1)$ and $(\mathbb{R}^2, d_2)$ are metric spaces. E.g., the triangle inequality in $\mathbb{R}^2$ states the well-known fact that, for any triangle ABC, the length of AB is at most the sum of the lengths of AC and CB. Neither d_1 nor d_2 are ultrametrics.

(2) ($\mathbb{R}^2$ with the so-called Manhattan metric) As alternative for the metric d_2 from example (1) we may take

$$d_3(x, y) = |y_1 - x_1| + |y_2 - x_2|.$$

(3) Let M be any nonempty set. The *discrete* metric d on M is given by

$$d(x, y) \;\; = \;\; \begin{cases} 0 & \text{if } x = y \\ 1 & \text{if } x \neq y \end{cases}.$$

(4) Each discrete metric is an ultrametric. Another example is the following: Let $\mathbb{N}$ be the set of natural numbers. Let $d: \mathbb{N} \times \mathbb{N} \to \mathbb{R}_{\geq 0}$ be given by

$$d(n, m) \;\; = \;\; \begin{cases} 0 & \text{if } n = m \\ 2^{-min(n,m)} & \text{if } n \neq m. \end{cases}$$

Then d is an ultrametric.

For each space (M, d) and each nonempty $X \subseteq M$, we have that $(X, d{\upharpoonright}(X \times X))$—where $d{\upharpoonright}(X \times X)$ denotes the function d restricted to the domain $X \times X$—is also a metric space.

A space (M, d) is called *A-bounded*, for some real number $A \geq 0$, in case $d(x, y) \leq A$, for all x, y. In fact, almost all spaces considered in our book will be 1-bounded.

A major role in our theory will be played by the space of words over some alphabet. Accordingly, we shall use it as a running example in this subsection, and pay special attention to its properties.

An alphabet A is a nonempty (finite or infinite) set, the elements of which are called *symbols*. We denote by A^* the set of all *finite* strings (sequences of symbols) over A, and by A^ω the set of all *infinite* strings. Moreover, we put (as in Definition 1.12), $A^\infty = A^* \cup A^\omega$, i.e., the elements of A^∞ are either finite or infinite strings. Elements of A are also called *letters*, elements of A^∞ are mostly called *words*. The empty word (sequence of zero letters) will be denoted by ϵ. For $a \in A$, a^n denotes the string consisting of n letters a $(n \geq 0)$, and a^ω the infinite string of a's. We use a^* as shorthand for the set $\{a\}^* = \{a^n \mid n \in \mathbb{N}\}$ (with the convention that $0 \in \mathbb{N}$), i.e., the set of all finite sequences of a's. On A^∞ we assume the pre-fixing operation '$\cdot$', yielding $a \cdot w$ for $a \in A$ and $w \in A^\infty$. Here $a \cdot w$ denotes the string with a as its first letter and the n-th letter of w as its $n+1$-st letter (and no

$n + 1$-st letter if w has no n-th letter). Note that each nonempty word w in A^∞ can be written as $w = a \cdot v$, for suitable $a \in A$ and $v \in A^\infty$. (In the next subsection, we shall define the *concatenation* for two arbitrary words $v, w \in A^\infty$.)

Each finite word in A^* has a *length,* as defined in

Definition 1.16 $lgt: A^* \to \mathbb{N}$ is defined by

$$
\begin{aligned}
lgt(\epsilon) &= 0 \\
lgt(a \cdot w) &= 1 + lgt(w) \,.
\end{aligned}
$$

It will be convenient to put $lgt(w) = \infty$ when $w \in A^\omega$ and to assume some natural rules to calculate with ∞, such as

- $n + \infty = \infty + n = \infty$

- $n < \infty$, $min\{\, n, \infty \,\} = n$, $max\{\, n, \infty \,\} = \infty$,

etc.

For later use we mention an alternative—and more precise—way of viewing sequences, viz. as *functions.*

Definition 1.17 A finite word in A^∞ is a function $w: \{\, 1, \ldots, n \,\} \to A$, for some $n \geq 0$. In case $n = 0$, i.e., for the function from $\emptyset$ to A, we shall always use the name ϵ. If $w(i) = a$, we say that a is the i-th element of w, for $1 \leq i \leq n$. An infinite word is a function $w: \mathbb{N}_> \to A$ (where $\mathbb{N}_> = \mathbb{N} \setminus \{0\}$). If $w(i) = a$, we say that a is the i-th element of w, for $i \geq 1$.

On the way to the definition of a metric on A^∞, we introduce the *truncation* $w[n]$, for $w \in A^\infty$ and $n \in \mathbb{N}$.

Definition 1.18

(a)
$$
\begin{aligned}
w[0] &= \epsilon \\
\epsilon[n + 1] &= \epsilon \\
(a \cdot v)[n + 1] &= a \cdot (v[n]) \,.
\end{aligned}
$$

(b) For $X \subseteq A^\infty$, we put $X[n] = \{\, w[n] \mid w \in X \,\}$.

Examples

(1) $abc[0] = \epsilon$, $abc[1] = a$, $abc[2] = ab$, $abc[3] = abc$, $abc[n] = abc$, for $n \geq 4$.

(2) $a^{\omega}[n] = a^n$ (with $a^0 = \epsilon$).

As elementary properties of truncation we have

Lemma 1.19 *For each* $v, w \in A^{\infty}$, $n, m \in \mathbb{N}$,

(a) $v[n] = w[n] \Rightarrow \forall m \leq n(v[m] = w[m])$.

(b) $w[n][m] = w[min\{n, m\}]$.

(c) *If* $v \neq w$ *then* $v[n] \neq w[n]$, *for some* $n > 0$.

Proof Parts (a) and (b) are left as exercises, part (c) follows by a case analysis (based on Definition 1.17). E.g., if $v, w \in A^{\omega}$ and $v \neq w$ then $v(i) \neq w(i)$, for some $i \geq 1$, and $v[i] \neq w[i]$ follows. The other cases are left to the reader. $\square$

We are now ready for

Definition 1.20 (Baire-distance) Let A be some alphabet. The so-called Baire-distance $d_B : A^{\infty} \times A^{\infty} \to \mathbb{R}_{\geq 0}$ is given by

$$d_B(v, w) = \begin{cases} 0 & \text{if } v = w \\ 2^{-n} & \text{where } n = max\{k \mid v[k] = w[k]\}, \text{ if } v \neq w. \end{cases} \qquad (1.6)$$

In words, $d_B(v, w) = 0$ in case $v = w$, and, for $v \neq w$, $d_B(v, w) = 2^{-n}$, for n the length of the longest common prefix of v and w. Note that, by Lemma 1.19c, if $v \neq w$ then, for some k, $v[k] \neq w[k]$, thus (1.6) is well-defined (the *max* as indicated exists).

Examples

(1) $d(abc, abe) = 2^{-2} = \frac{1}{4}$, since $abc[2] = ab = abe[2]$, but $abc[3] = abc \neq abe = abe[3]$.

(2) $d(ab, abce) = 2^{-2} = \frac{1}{4}$, since $ab[2] = ab = abce[2]$, but $ab[3] = ab \neq abc = abce[3]$.

(3) $d(\epsilon, w) = 1$, for $w \neq \epsilon$.

(4) $d(cab, ab) = 1$ since $cab[0] = \epsilon = ab[0]$ but $cab[1] = c \neq a = ab[1]$.

(5) $d(a^n, a^{\omega}) = 2^{-n}$.

Some first properties of the Baire-distance are listed in

Lemma 1.21

(a) $d_B(v, w) \leq 2^{-n} \iff v[n] = w[n]$

(b) $d_B(v, v[n]) \leq 2^{-n}$

(c) $d_B(a \cdot v, a \cdot w) = \frac{1}{2} d_B(v, w)$.

Proof Exercise.   □

The Baire-distance d_B turns A^∞ into an ultrametric space:

Theorem 1.22 (A^∞, d_B) *is an ultrametric space.*

Proof We verify that d_B satisfies (M1), (M2) and (M4). (M1) and (M2) are immediate by (1.6). (M4) requires more work. We have to show that, for each $w, v, u \in A^\infty$,

$$d_B(v, w) \leq max\{\, d_B(v, u), d_B(u, w)\,\}. \tag{1.7}$$

In case $max\{\, d_B(v, u), d_B(u, w)\,\} = 0$, we have $d_B(v, u) = 0$ and $d_B(u, w) = 0$, hence $v = u$ and $u = w$, implying that $v = w$ and $d_B(v, w) = 0$. Now assume $max\{\, d_B(v, u), d_B(u, w)\,\} = 2^{-n}$, for some $n \geq 0$. Since $d_B(v, u) \leq 2^{-n}$ and $d_B(u, w) \leq 2^{-n}$, by Lemma 1.21a we have $v[n] = u[n]$ and $u[n] = w[n]$, hence $v[n] = w[n]$. Again by Lemma 1.21a, we obtain $d_B(v, w) \leq 2^{-n}$, from which (1.7) follows.   □

We next present the first round of elementary properties of metric spaces. In Chapter 2.1 and Chapter 10, we shall develop some further theory; the harder proofs will be relegated to Appendix A. Altogether, we aim at the development of some powerful tools to work with in our semantic modeling. In particular, we shall present a number of classical theorems which will turn out to be fundamental for our methodology—with Banach's fixed point theorem (Theorem 1.34) as first main example.

The first subtopic concerns the way in which metric spaces may be composed from given spaces.

Definition 1.23

(a) Let (M_1, d_1) and (M_2, d_2) be given (ultra) metric spaces. We define the *product* space $(M_1 \times M_2, d_P)$ and the *disjoint union* space $(M_1 + M_2, d_U)$ by putting

- $M_1 \times M_2 = \{ (x,y) \mid x \in M_1, y \in M_2 \}$
- $d_P((x,y),(x',y')) = max\{ d_1(x,x'), d_2(y,y') \}$
- $M_1 + M_2 = (\{1\} \times M_1) \cup (\{2\} \times M_2)$
- $d_U(x,y) = \begin{cases} d_i(x',y') & \text{if } x = (i,x'), y = (i,y'), i = 1,2 \\ 1 & \text{otherwise.} \end{cases}$

(b) Let (M,d) be a 1-bounded metric space, and let X be any set. We define the *function* space $(X \to M, d_F)$ by putting

- $X \to M$ is the set of all functions from X to M
- $d_F(f,g) = sup\{ d(f(x),g(x)) \mid x \in X \}$.

Remarks

(1) The disjoint union construction ensures that in the outcome $M_1 + M_2$, we can always determine whether an element $x \in M_1 + M_2$ "stems from" M_1 or M_2. E.g., for $M_1 = \{a,b\}$, $M_2 = \{b,c\}$, we have that $M_1 + M_2 = \{ \langle 1,a \rangle, \langle 1,b \rangle, \langle 2,b \rangle, \langle 2,c \rangle \}$, whereas $M_1 \cup M_2 = \{ a,b,c \}$ (with '$\cup$' the ordinary set-union).

(2) The proviso that M be 1-bounded in clause (b) ensures that the *sup* as given in the definition indeed exists. (Note that A-bounded, for any $A \in \mathbb{R}_{\geq 0}$, would work as well). Without the condition, we might have that $sup\{ d(f(x),g(x)) \mid x \in X \} = \infty$, violating the condition that the codomain of d equals $\mathbb{R}_{\geq 0}$.

Of course, we have to verify that the constructions just given indeed yield (1-bounded) (ultra) metric spaces when applied to given (1-bounded) (ultra) metric spaces. This is the contents of

Lemma 1.24

(a) If (M_1, d_1), (M_2, d_2) are *1-bounded metric spaces, then so are* $(M_1 \times M_2, d_P)$ *and* $(M_1 + M_2, d_U)$.

(b) If (M,d) *is a (1-bounded) metric space, then so is* $(X \to M, d_F)$.

(c,d) *As (a),(b) with "ultrametric" replacing "metric."*

Proof

(a) We only discuss the product space, and leave the disjoint union case as an exercise. We have to check (M1), (M2) and (M3).

(M1) $d_P((x,y),(x',y')) = 0$
     $\Leftrightarrow$ [def. d_P] $max\{\, d_1(x,x'), d_2(y,y')\,\}= 0$
     $\Leftrightarrow$ [property max] $d_1(x,x') = 0 \wedge d_2(y,y') = 0$
     $\Leftrightarrow$ [d_1, d_2 satisfy (M1)] $x = x' \wedge y = y'$
     $\Leftrightarrow$ $(x,y) = (x',y')$.

(M2)   Obvious.

(M3) $d_P((x,x'),(z,z')) + d_P(z,z'),(y,y'))$
   $=$ [def. d_P] $max\{\, d_1(x,z), d_2(x',z')\,\}+max\{\, d_1(z,y), d_2(z',y')\,\}$
   $\geq$ [property max] $max\{\, d_1(x,z) + d_1(z,y), d_2(x',z') + d_2(z',y')\,\}$
   $\geq$ [d_1, d_2 satisfy (M3)] $max\{\, d_1(x,y), d_2(x',y')\,\}$
   $=$ [def. d_P] $d_P((x,x'),(y,y'))$.

Preservation of 1-boundedness is trivial.

(b) We only discuss (M3). Let $f, g, h \in X \rightarrow M$.

    $d(f,h) + d(h,g)$
   $=$ [def. d_F] $sup\{\, d(f(x), h(x)) \mid x \in X\,\}+sup\{\, d(h(x), g(x)) \mid x \in X\,\}$
   $\geq$ [property sup] $sup\{\, d(f(x), h(x)) + d(h(x), g(x)) \mid x \in X\,\}$
   $\geq$ [d satisfies (M3)] $sup\{\, d(f(x), g(x)) \mid x \in X\,\}$
   $=$ [def. d_F] $d(f,g)$.

(c,d) Exercise. $\square$

In the sequel, we shall mostly drop subscripts from the various metrics, and simply write d rather than d_P, d_U, or d_F (or d_B). Only when confusion may arise, shall we be explicit about the metrics concerned. Also, we shall often simply write "the metric spaces M, M_1, …," when we should, more fully, specify them as (M, d), (M_1, d_1), …, or even as (M, d_M), (M_1, d_{M_1}), …. .

We proceed with the introduction of some central notions in the theory of metric spaces, viz. those of *convergent sequence* and *limit*, and of *Cauchy sequence*. An infinite sequence $x_0, x_1, \ldots$ from a space M will be denoted by $(x_n)_{n=0}^{\infty}$, or, mostly, by $(x_n)_n$. A subsequence of $(x_n)_n$ is an infinite sequence $(x_{n_k})_k$, with $n_k < n_{k'}$ if $k < k'$. Occasionally, we shall also employ the notation $(x_{f(n)})_n$ for a subsequence of $(x_n)_n$, where we assume that $f: \mathbb{N} \rightarrow \mathbb{N}$ is a function such that $f(n) < f(n')$ for $n < n'$.

Definition 1.25

(a) $(x_n)_n$ is a convergent sequence with limit x whenever

$$\forall \varepsilon > 0 \exists i \forall j \geq i \left[d(x_j, x) \leq \varepsilon \right].$$ (1.8)

(b) $(x_n)_n$ is a Cauchy sequence whenever

$$\forall \varepsilon > 0 \exists i \forall j, k \geq i \left[d(x_j, x_k) \leq \varepsilon \right].$$ (1.9)

In case (1.8) holds we also say that $(x_n)_n$ *converges to* x, and we write $lim_n x_n = x$. Sometimes, we shall also use the notation "$x_n \rightarrow x$ for $n \rightarrow \infty$."

Examples (Each example specifies the relevant metric space.)

(1) $(\mathbb{R}, d_{\mathbb{R}})$ $lim_n 2^{-n} = 0$, $lim_n \frac{n}{n+1} = 1$. If $a_n \leq b_n$, all n, then $lim_n a_n \leq lim_n b_n$.

(2) (M, d) If $lim_n x_n = x$ and $lim_n x_n = y$, then $x = y$.

(3) (A^∞, d) $lim_n w[n] = w$. If $A = \{a_0, a_1, \dots\}$ then $lim_n a_0^n a_n = a_0^\omega$ and $lim_n a_0 a_1 \cdots a_n = a_0 a_1 \cdots$. (A^*, d) The Cauchy sequence $(a^n)_n$ does not have a limit in A^* (since $a^\omega \notin A^*$).

(4) $lim_n x_n = x$ (in (M, d)) $\Leftrightarrow$ $lim_n d(x_n, x) = 0$ (in $(\mathbb{R}, d_{\mathbb{R}})$).

(5) If $(x_n)_n$ converges to x, then so does each subsequence $(x_{n_k})_k$. If $(x_n)_n$ is a Cauchy sequence, then so is each of its subsequences.

We leave to the reader the easy proof of

Lemma 1.26 *Each convergent sequence is a Cauchy sequence.* $\square$

As example (3) above shows, the converse of this lemma does not hold: It is not true, in general, that each Cauchy sequence is convergent. Spaces in which this property does hold are called *complete*.

Definition 1.27 A metric space (M, d) in which each Cauchy sequence converges to an element of M is called complete.

Examples

(1) Let d be short for the Euclidean metric $d_{\mathbb{R}}$ on $\mathbb{R}$. Let $[0, 1] = \{ x \in \mathbb{R} \mid 0 \leq x \leq 1 \}$ and $[0, 1) = \{ x \in \mathbb{R} \mid 0 \leq x < 1 \}$. Then $([0, 1], d)$ is complete, but $([0, 1), d)$ is not. E.g., the Cauchy sequence $(\frac{n}{n+1})_n$ has no limit in $[0, 1)$.

(2) Every space with the discrete metric is complete.

The property of completeness of a metric space, and some of its consequences, in particular Theorem 1.34, are crucial for our semantic domains. Briefly, completeness guarantees that limits are available, whenever necessary. Theorem 1.34 (Banach's fixed point theorem) ensures that a powerful definitional (and proof-) technique may be invoked on numerous occasions.

A natural question regarding the notion of completeness is whether it is preserved by the constructions of Definition 1.23. The answer is affirmative:

Lemma 1.28 *If (M_1, d_1), (M_2, d_2) and (M, d) are complete, then so are $(M_1 \times M_2, d)$, $(M_1 + M_2, d)$ and $(X \to M, d)$.*

Proof

(a) $(M_1 \times M_2, d)$ Let[3] $(x_n, y_n)_n$ be a Cauchy sequence in $M_1 \times M_2$. This implies that $(x_n)_n$ is a Cauchy sequence in M_1 and $(y_n)_n$ a Cauchy sequence in M_2. By the completeness of M_1 and M_2, we have that $(x_n)_n$ has a limit, say x ($x \in M_1$), and $(y_n)_n$ has a limit, say y ($y \in M_2$). It follows that $(x_n, y_n)_n$ has a limit (x, y) in $M_1 \times M_2$.

(b) $(M_1 + M_2, d)$ Let $(x_n)_n$ be a Cauchy sequence in $(M_1 + M_2, d)$. Then, clearly, for almost all n (i.e., all but a finite number of exceptions) we have that $x_n = (1, x'_n)$ or $x_n = (2, x'_n)$, with $(x'_n)_n$ a Cauchy sequence in M_1 or M_2, respectively. The desired result is then immediate by the completeness of M_1 and M_2.

(c) $(X \to M, d)$ Let $(f_n)_n$ be a Cauchy sequence in $(X \to M, d)$. We must find f such that $lim_n f_n = f$. Firstly, we observe that, since $(f_n)_n$ is a Cauchy sequence in $X \to M$, $((f_n(x))_n$ is a Cauchy sequence in M, for each x. This holds since from

$$\forall \varepsilon > 0 \exists i \forall j, k \geq i [d(f_j, f_k) \leq \varepsilon]$$

one may infer that, for each x,

$$\forall \varepsilon > 0 \exists i \forall j, k \geq i [d(f_j(x), f_k(x)) \leq \varepsilon] . \tag{1.10}$$

Next, we put[4] $F = \lambda x . lim_n f_n(x)$, and show that $lim_n f_n = f$. Choose x and $\varepsilon > 0$. By (1.10), we have that we can find some $i \in \mathbb{N}$ such that, for all $j, k \geq i$,

$$d(f_j(x), f_k(x)) \leq \varepsilon/2 .$$

---

[3] Recall the convention of dropping outer parentheses, i.e., to write $(x_n, y_n)_n$ rather than $((x_n, y_n))_n$.

[4] The notation $\lambda x. \ldots$ is used for the function mapping argument x to result $\ldots$.

Since $(f_k(x))_k$ converges to $f(x)$, we have that $d(f_k(x), f(x)) \le \varepsilon/2$, for k sufficiently large. Using (M3) we obtain that $d(f_j(x), f(x)) \le \varepsilon/2 + \varepsilon/2 = \varepsilon$, for $j \ge i$. Therefore, for $j \ge i$,

$$sup\{\, d(f_j(x), f(x)) \mid x \in X \,\} \le \varepsilon \,.$$

Altogether, we have established that

$$\forall \varepsilon > 0 \exists i \forall j \ge i [d(f_j, f) \le \varepsilon] \,,$$

i.e., that $lim_n f_n = f$. □

As indicated already, complete spaces are essential in our methodology, since they guarantee the existence of limits. As we saw above, (A^*, d) is not complete. We now establish the important

Theorem 1.29 (A^∞, d) *is complete.*

Proof Let $(w_n)_n$ be a Cauchy sequence in A^∞. Without loss of generality (cf. Exercise 1.4c) we may assume

$$\forall i, j \ge k \, [d(w_i, w_j) \le 2^{-k}] \,. \tag{1.11}$$

We distinguish two cases: (1) $\exists N \forall i [lgt(w_i) \le N]$; (2) $\forall N \exists i [lgt(w_i) > N]$. Case (1): By the definition of lgt, we have that $w_i[N] = w_i$, for all i. Furthermore, we have $d(w_i, w_N) \le 2^{-N}$, for all $i \ge N$. Hence (Lemma 1.21a) $w_i = w_i[N] = w_N[N] = w_N$, for all $i \ge N$. Conclusion: $lim_i w_i = w_N$.

Case (2): Choose a subsequence $(w'_n)_n$ such that $\forall n [lgt(w'_n) \ge n]$. We put $a_1^{(n)} \ldots a_n^{(n)}$ such that $w'_n = a_1^{(n)} \ldots a_n^{(n)} w''_n$, for some $w''_n \in A^\infty$. *Claim:* if $i \le n, m$ then $a_i^{(n)} = a_i^{(m)}$. *Proof of the claim:* Suppose that, for some n, m, $i \le n, m$ and $a_i^{(n)} \ne a_i^{(m)}$. Then $a_1^{(n)} \ldots a_i^{(n)} \ne a_1^{(m)} \ldots a_i^{(m)}$. Hence, $w'_n[i] \ne w'_m[i]$, so $d(w'_n, w'_m) > 2^{-i}$, contradicting (1.11). Now put $w = a_1^{(1)} a_2^{(2)} \cdots \in A^\omega$. For $n \in \mathbb{N}$ we have

$$w[n] = a_1^{(1)} \ldots a_n^{(n)} = a_1^{(n)} \ldots a_n^{(n)} = w'_n[n] \,.$$

Hence $d(w, w'_n) \le 2^{-n}$, for each $n \in \mathbb{N}$. Conclusion: $w = lim_n w'_n = lim_n w_n$. □

The metric space (A^*, d) is a subspace of the complete metric space (A^∞, d). This is an instance of a general result, stating that *each* metric space can be enlarged to a complete space—with the given space as a subspace—by the addition of suitable limit points. A rigorous proof of this proposition is rather involved, and postponed till Appendix A. (The proposition will, in fact, not be needed till Chapter 10.)

The last important topic of our first introduction to metric space theory concerns some fundamental properties of functions between spaces, viz. of a function being *continuous, nonexpansive, $(\alpha-)$contractive,* and *α-Lipschitz.*

Definition 1.30 Let (M_1, d_1), (M_2, d_2) be metric spaces and $f: M_1 \rightarrow M_2$.

(a) f is called continuous whenever, for each convergent sequence $(x_n)_n$, with $lim_n x_n = x$, we have that

$$\lim_n f(x_n) = f(x).$$

(b) Let α be a real number with $0 \le \alpha \le 1$. The function f is called α-Lipschitz if, for each $x, y \in M_1$,

$$d_2(f(x), f(y)) \le \alpha \cdot d_1(x, y).$$

(c) A function f which is 1-Lipschitz is usally called *nonexpansive.* If f is α-Lipschitz for some α, $0 \le \alpha < 1$, then f is called *α-contractive.* The function is called contractive if it is α-contractive for some α $(0 \le \alpha < 1)$.

(d) The collection of all α-Lipschitz functions from M_1 to M_2 is denoted by $M_1 \xrightarrow{\alpha} M_2$.

Examples

(1) The identity function $\lambda x.x$ is nonexpansive. Each constant function is 0-contractive.

(2) Let $f: (\mathbb{R}, d_\mathbb{R}) \rightarrow (\mathbb{R}, d_\mathbb{R})$ be given by $f(x) = \frac{1}{3}x$. Then: f is $\frac{1}{3}$-contractive.

(3) Let $f: (A^\infty, d) \rightarrow (A^\infty, d)$ be given by $f(x) = a \cdot x$. Then: f is $\frac{1}{2}$-contractive.

As first simple lemma connecting the various properties of functions we have

Lemma 1.31

(a) Each contractive function is nonexpansive.

(b) Each α-Lipschitz function is continuous.

Proof

(a) Clear from the definitions.

(b) Let $f: M_1 \to M_2$ be α-Lipschitz. We leave the case $\alpha = 0$ to the reader. Assume $0 < \alpha \leq 1$. Let $(x_n)_n$ be a converging sequence with limit x. Choose $\varepsilon > 0$. Then, by the definition of convergent sequence,

$$\exists i \forall j \geq i \, [d_1(x_j, x) \leq \varepsilon/\alpha] \, .$$

Since f is α-Lipschitz, we obtain from this

$$\exists i \forall j \geq i \, [d_2(f(x_j), f(x)) \leq \varepsilon],$$

implying that $lim_n f(x_n) = f(x)$. $\qquad\qquad\qquad\qquad\qquad\qquad\qquad\qquad$ $\square$

Thus, e.g., nonexpansiveness is a stronger property than continuity (cf. Exercise 1.6c). Since almost all functions encountered below will turn out to be nonexpansive, continuity as such will play a minor role in our considerations. Only a few properties will be expressed in terms of continuity in general. A first example is

Lemma 1.32 *The mapping $d: M \times M \to \mathbb{R}_{\geq 0}$ is continuous.*

Proof Let $(x_n, y_n)_n$ be a convergent sequence in $M \times M$ with limit (x, y). We have to verify that $lim_n d(x_n, y_n) = d(x, y)$. Since $lim_n (x_n, y_n) = (x, y)$, we have that $lim_n x_n = x$, $lim_n y_n = y$. Using the fourth example after Definition 1.25, we obtain

$$d(x, y) - lim_n d(x_n, y_n)$$
$$= lim_n (d(x, y) - d(x_n, y_n))$$
$$\leq lim_n (d(x_n, x) + d(y_n, y))$$
$$= 0 \, .$$

Symmetrically, $d(x, y) - lim_n d(x_n, y_n) \geq 0$, and $d(x, y) = lim_n d(x_n, y_n)$ follows.
$\square$

The function spaces $M_1 \overset{1}{\to} M_2$ and $M_1 \overset{\alpha}{\to} M_2$ $(0 \leq \alpha < 1)$ are complete in case M_2 is complete. This is the contents of

Lemma 1.33 *Let (M_2, d_2) be complete. Then, for each (M_1, d_1) and each α with $0 \le \alpha \le 1$, the space $M_1 \overset{\alpha}{\to} M_2$ is complete.*

Proof Assume $0 \le \alpha \le 1$. We already saw (Lemma 1.28) that each Cauchy sequence of functions $(f_n)_n$ in $M_1 \to M_2$—and, hence, also in $M_1 \overset{1}{\to} M_2$—has a limit. We now show that, in case all f_n, $n = 0, 1, \ldots$ are α-Lipschitz, then so is $f = lim_n f_n$. We have, for any $x, y \in M_1$,

$d_2(f(x), f(y))$

$= d_2((lim_n f_n)(x), (lim_n f_n)(y))$

$= d_2(lim_n f_n(x), lim_n f_n(y))$

$= [\text{Lemma 1.32}] \; lim_n d_2(f_n(x), f_n(y))$

$\le [\text{all } f_n \text{ are } \alpha\text{-Lipschitz}] \; \alpha \cdot d_1(x, y) .$ □

We have now arrived at the main theorem of this subsection, viz. Banach's fixed point theorem. This theorem will turn out to be a cornerstone for all subsequent developments.

Theorem 1.34 *(Banach) Let (M, d) be a complete metric space, and let $f : M \to M$ be a contractive function. Then*

(a) *There exists $x \in M$ such that $f(x) = x$.*

(b) *The fixed point is unique: If $f(x) = x$, $f(y) = y$, then $x = y$. We shall write $\mathrm{fix}(f)$ for the unique fixed point of f.*

(c) *$\mathrm{fix}(f) = lim_n f^n(x_0)$, where $x_0 \in M$ is arbitrary, $f^0(x_0) = x_0$, $f^{n+1}(x_0) = f(f^n(x_0))$. (Thus, $\mathrm{fix}(f)$ may be obtained by iterating f starting from an arbitrary point x_0 in M.)*

Proof Let f be α-contractive, for some α, $0 \le \alpha < 1$. Let x_0 be arbitrary in M and consider the sequence

$$x_0, f(x_0), f^2(x_0), \ldots \tag{1.12}$$

The main technical step is to prove that (1.12) is a Cauchy sequence. This is shown below. Once this has been established, the rest is easy: Since M is complete, the Cauchy sequence $(f^n(x_0))_n$ has a limit, say $x = lim_n f^n(x_0)$. Since f is α-contractive, it is certainly continuous. Therefore,

$$f(x) = f(\lim_n f^n(x_0)) = \lim_n f(f^n(x_0)) = \lim_n f^n(x_0) = x .$$

Moreover, in case $f(y) = y$, then, since f is α-contractive,

$$d(x, y) = d(f(x), f(y)) \le \alpha \cdot d(x, y).$$

Since $\alpha < 1$, this is only possible if $d(x, y) = 0$, i.e., if $x = y$.

There remains to prove that the sequence (1.12) is a Cauchy sequence. Let $d(x_0, f(x_0)) = \beta$. Then, for any $j, k \in \mathbb{N}$ with $j < k$ we have

$$d(f^j(x_0), f^k(x_0))$$
$$\le d(f^j(x_0), f^{j+1}(x_0)) + \ldots + d(f^{k-1}(x_0), f^k(x_0))$$
$$\le \alpha^j \cdot \beta + \ldots + \alpha^{k-1} \cdot \beta$$
$$\le \alpha^j \cdot \beta \cdot (1 + \alpha + \ldots)$$
$$= \alpha^j \cdot \beta \cdot \frac{1}{1-\alpha}.$$

Since $\alpha < 1$, α^j and, therefore, $\alpha^j \cdot \frac{\beta}{1-\alpha}$ can be made arbitrarily small by taking j sufficiently large, thus establishing that $(f^n(x_0))_n$ is a Cauchy sequence. $\square$

Examples

(1) Let $f: (\mathbb{R}, d_{\mathbb{R}}) \to (\mathbb{R}, d_{\mathbb{R}})$ be given by $f(x) = \frac{x+1}{2}$. Put $x_0 = 0$, $x_{n+1} = \frac{x_n+1}{2}$. Then $\text{fix}(f) = \lim_n \frac{n}{n+1} = 1$.

(2) Let $f: (A^\infty, d) \to (A^\infty, d)$ be given by $f(x) = a \cdot x$. Put $x_0 = b$, $x_{n+1} = a \cdot x_n$. Then $\text{fix}(f) = \lim_n a^n b = a^\omega$.

(3) Let $\rho: (\mathbb{R}^2, d_{\mathbb{R}^2}) \to (\mathbb{R}^2, d_{\mathbb{R}^2})$ be given by $\rho(x, y) = (\frac{y}{2}, -\frac{x}{2})$, i.e., ρ is a combined rotation over $\frac{\pi}{2}$ and multiplication with $\frac{1}{2}$ with respect to the origin $(0, 0)$. Then $\text{fix}(\rho) = (0, 0)$.

Many more applications of Theorem 1.34 will follow in the remainder of the book.

1.1.3 Denotational semantics

Operational semantics for programming languages are based on transition systems. In this subsection, we introduce *denotational* semantics ($\mathcal{D}$) as the second main branch of semantics, with $\mathcal{L}_{rec}$ as the first example language for which $\mathcal{D}$ will be developed.

The first underlying principle of denotational semantics:

Program constructs denote values.

Note the term "denote" explaining the qualification "denotational." Thus, in designing $\mathcal{D}$ we firstly shall have to specify which domain of values is to be used as codomain for $\mathcal{D}$. Calling this domain $(p \in) \mathbb{P}_D$—D for denotational—we have to define, for each $(\pi \in) \mathcal{L}$,

$$\mathcal{D}: \mathcal{L} \to \mathbb{P}_D .$$

Thus, $\mathcal{D}(\pi) = p$ expresses that program π denotes p as its value.

Now the key question is, of course, how $\mathcal{D}$ is to be designed. Rather than using a transition system—as we did for $\mathcal{O}_d$ in Section 1.1.1—we base the definition of $\mathcal{D}$ on the second principle of denotational semantics, viz. the *compositionality principle*:

> *The meaning of a whole is composed from the meaning of its constituent parts.*

The compositionality principle induces a definition driven by the syntactic structure of the constructs (mostly statements) concerned. Moreover, for each syntactic operator (part of the syntax of the language), say $\mathsf{op}_{\mathrm{syn}}$, a corresponding semantic operator (defined on $\mathbb{P}_D$), say $\mathsf{op}_{\mathrm{sem}}$, should be defined. Next, equations such as the following are used in defining $\mathcal{D}$:

$$
\begin{aligned}
\mathcal{D}(s_1 \, \mathsf{op}_{\mathrm{syn}} \, s_2) &= \mathcal{D}(s_1) \, \mathsf{op}_{\mathrm{sem}} \, \mathcal{D}(s_2) \\
\mathcal{D}(\mathsf{op}_{\mathrm{syn}} \, s) &= \mathsf{op}_{\mathrm{sem}} \, \mathcal{D}(s) ,
\end{aligned}
$$

in the case that $\mathsf{op}_{\mathrm{syn}}$ is a binary or unary operator, respectively. In the special case that $\mathcal{D}$ is to be applied to a language constant, say α, we want that $\mathcal{D}(\alpha) = \bar{\alpha}$, where $\bar{\alpha}$ is the denotation or value (in $\mathbb{P}_D$) of the language element α. (In many cases, it will be possible to simply take $\bar{\alpha} = \alpha$.)

In order to focus on the compositionality pattern, we dropped the declaration D from the equations. Reinstalling the D, and specializing to the ';' from $\mathcal{L}_{rec}$, we want to have that

$$\mathcal{D}(D|s_1;s_2) = \mathcal{D}(D|s_1);\mathcal{D}(D|s_2) ,$$

where the ';' on the left-hand side is the syntactic sequential composition, and the ';' on the right-hand side is the semantic sequential composition, i.e., a—still to be defined—mapping from $\mathbb{P}_D \times \mathbb{P}_D$ to $\mathbb{P}_D$.

While applying the compositionality principle, we face a special problem when dealing with recursion. Let us take $\mathcal{L}_{rec}$ as an example. Since the meaning of a procedure variable x equals the meaning of its associated body $D(x)$ (cf. Lemma 1.14a), we want to have that

$$\mathcal{D}(D|x) = \mathcal{D}(D|D(x)).$$ (1.13)

It should be noted that (1.13) is not an instance of the compositionality principle, since it is not the case that $D(x)$ is a syntactic constituent of x (which, as a single symbol from $PVar$, has no proper constituents at all). Rather, (1.13) is a further property which we require from the denotational definitions when (some form of) recursion is present. Ultimately, we shall have to make sure that a certain fixed point result holds, reflecting that x and $D(x)$ have the same meaning. A good part of the present subsection will be devoted to this. The tools of complete metric spaces, in particular Banach's theorem, will play a central role here.

Before we confront the problem of recursion, let us first settle the other issues having to do with the definition of $\mathcal{D}$ for $\mathcal{L}_{rec}$. We begin with the introduction of the corresponding $\mathbb{P}_D$.

Definition 1.35 $\mathbb{P}_D \stackrel{df}{=} Act^\infty \setminus \{\epsilon\}$.

Thus, $\mathbb{P}_D$ is as $\mathbb{P}_O$ for $\mathcal{L}_{rec}$, apart from the deletion of ϵ. As we shall see soon (cf. Exercise 1.13), it will be convenient to have no ϵ in $\mathbb{P}_D$. By the previous subsection, we know that $\mathbb{P}_D$, equipped with the Baire-metric, is a complete ultrametric space (Theorems 1.22 and 1.29). We note that each element p in $\mathbb{P}_D$ is (nonempty, hence) of the form $a \in Act$ or $a \cdot p'$, with $a \in Act$ and $p' \in \mathbb{P}_D$.

After having chosen $\mathbb{P}_D$, we firstly stipulate that, as denotation of an action $a \in Act$, we simply take a itself. That is, we put

$$\mathcal{D}(D|a) \;=\; a.$$

Next, we define the semantic operator ';' from $\mathbb{P}_D \times \mathbb{P}_D$ to $\mathbb{P}_D$. Intuitively, we want ';' to satisfy

$$\begin{aligned} a;p &= a \cdot p \\ (a \cdot p');p &= a \cdot (p';p). \end{aligned}$$ (1.14)

It should be observed, however, that these two clauses do not constitute a definition without further justification. Since we also have infinite words in $\mathbb{P}_D$—necessary to model the possibly infinite behaviour of recursive procedures—the definition cannot be justified by induction on the length of the first argument. Instead, we will justify the definition based on (1.14) by an appeal to Banach's theorem (Theorem 1.34). In fact, the type of argument to be used here will be pervasive in all of our book.

Definition 1.36 The semantic operator $;: \mathbb{P}_D \times \mathbb{P}_D \xrightarrow{1} \mathbb{P}_D$ is the unique nonexpansive function satisfying

$$
\begin{aligned}
;(a, p) &= a \cdot p \\
;(a \cdot p', p) &= a \cdot ;(p', p) .
\end{aligned}
\tag{1.15}
$$

In giving the definition of ';', we have anticipated—by our use of '$\xrightarrow{1}$'—the fact that ';' will be a nonexpansive mapping. Also, we have rewritten (1.14) into (1.15)—replacing the infix notation for ';' by a more functional notation—in order to prepare the way for the subsequent arguments. Note that (1.15) presupposes the existence of the prefix-operator $a \cdot (\cdot)$. For this, cf. Section 1.1.2.

We shall now establish that there exists a unique mapping in $\mathbb{P}_D \times \mathbb{P}_D \xrightarrow{1} \mathbb{P}_D$, satisfying (1.15). In order to set the stage for an application of Banach's theorem, we first remark that the class of operators $Op = \mathbb{P}_D \times \mathbb{P}_D \xrightarrow{1} \mathbb{P}_D$, the (nonexpansive) function space containing the sought-for ';', is a complete metric space (by the completeness of $\mathbb{P}_D$ and Lemma 1.33). Secondly, we define a transformation

$$
\Omega_; : Op \to Op
$$

derived from (1.15) in a way to be made precise in a moment. Since $\Omega_;$ maps each operator (element of Op) to another operator (again an element of Op), we baptize $\Omega_;$ a *higher-order* (sometimes also called higher-type) operator. We shall, moreover, ensure that $\Omega_;$ is defined such that it is a contractive mapping from Op to Op. By Banach's theorem, $\Omega_;$ then has a unique fixed point, and it is our aim to define $\Omega_;$ such that we can take $; = fix(\Omega_;)$, i.e., we *define* ';' as the unique fixed point of $\Omega_;$—which exists by the contractiveness of $\Omega_;$.

Having explained the general pattern, there remains the crucial step: how to base the definition of $\Omega_;$ on (1.15). It should be noted that it is our task to define $\Omega_;$ on *any* operator in Op, say on any $\phi \in Op$. In specifying $\Omega_;(\phi)$, we have to describe the outcome of $\Omega_;(\phi)(p_1, p_2)$, for all p_1, p_2. Since, as saw above, p_1 is either of the form $a (\in Act)$ or of the form $a \cdot p'$, we must give rules for both $\Omega_;(\phi)(a, p_2)$ and $\Omega_;(\phi)(a \cdot p', p_2)$. At this point, we can follow the pattern of (1.15). We put

$$
\begin{aligned}
\Omega_;(\phi)(a, p_2) &= a \cdot p_2 \\
\Omega_;(\phi)(a \cdot p', p_2) &= a \cdot \phi(p', p_2) .
\end{aligned}
\tag{1.16}
$$

Note how (1.16) is very close to (1.14). Recalling our aim that we want to be able to put $; = fix(\Omega_;)$, whence $\Omega_;(;) = ;$, and filling in ';' for ϕ in (1.16), we obtain

$$;(a, p_2) \;=\; a \cdot p_2$$
$$;(a \cdot p', p_2) \;=\; a \cdot ;(p', p_2)$$

which coincides with (1.15). Summarizing, there remains the proof of

Lemma 1.37 *Let* $(\phi \in)\, Op = \mathbb{P}_D \times \mathbb{P}_D \xrightarrow{1} \mathbb{P}_D$, *and let the mapping* $\Omega_; : Op \to Op$ *be given by (1.16). Then* $\Omega_;$ *is* $\frac{1}{2}$-*contractive (in* ϕ).

Proof Take $\phi_1, \phi_2 \in Op$. It suffices to show

$$d(\Omega_;(\phi_1)(p_1, p_2), \Omega_;(\phi_2)(p_1, p_2)) \le \tfrac{1}{2} d(\phi_1, \phi_2)\,.$$

We consider two cases.

$$\begin{aligned}
[a] \quad & d(\Omega_;(\phi_1)(a, p_2), \Omega_;(\phi_2)(a, p_2)) \\
= \;& d(a \cdot p_2, a \cdot p_2) \\
= \;& 0 \;\le\; \tfrac{1}{2} d(\phi_1, \phi_2).
\end{aligned}$$

$$\begin{aligned}
[a \cdot p'] \quad & d(\Omega_;(\phi_1)(a \cdot p', p_2), \Omega_;(\phi_2)(a \cdot p', p_2)) \\
= \;& [\text{def. } \Omega_;]\; d(a \cdot \phi_1(p', p_2), a \cdot \phi_2(p', p_2)) \\
= \;& [\text{def. } d \text{ on } \mathbb{P}_D]\; \tfrac{1}{2} d(\phi_1(p', p_2), \phi_2(p', p_2)) \\
\le \;& [\text{def. } d(\phi_1, \phi_2)]\; \tfrac{1}{2} d(\phi_1, \phi_2). \qquad\qquad \square
\end{aligned}$$

Example We have

$$ab;cde = (a \cdot b);cde = a \cdot (b;cde) = a \cdot (b \cdot cde) = abcde.$$

We also have $a^\omega;cde = a^\omega$. This can be seen as follows: $a^\omega = a \cdot a^\omega$, so $a^\omega;cde = (a \cdot a^\omega);cde = a \cdot (a^\omega;cde)$. Therefore

$$d_B(a^\omega;cde, a^\omega) = d_B(a \cdot (a^\omega;cde), a \cdot a^\omega) = \tfrac{1}{2} d_B(a^\omega;cde, a^\omega)$$

by Lemma 1.21c. From this we derive

$$d_B(a^\omega;cde, a^\omega) = 0$$

and $a^\omega;cde = a^\omega$ follows by condition (M1) for d_B.

Before we continue with the design of $\mathcal{D}$ for $\mathcal{L}_{rec}$, we first state a simple property of ';' in the next lemma, viz. its associativity. The proof technique used in this lemma constitutes a second important tool in proving properties in a metric setting—the first one being the use of Banach's theorem.

Lemma 1.38 *For each $p_1, p_2, p_3 \in \mathbb{P}_D$, $(p_1;p_2);p_3 = p_1;(p_2;p_3)$.*

Proof The idea of the proof is to introduce ε as the largest possible distance between $(p_1;p_2);p_3$ and $p_1;(p_2;p_3)$—taken over all p_1, p_2, p_3 in $\mathbb{P}_D$—and to show that $\varepsilon \leq \varepsilon/2$, which implies $\varepsilon = 0$, whence the distance referred to must be 0, implying the desired result. Thus we put

$$\varepsilon = sup\{\, d((p_1;p_2);p_3, p_1;(p_2;p_3)) \mid p_1, p_2, p_3 \in \mathbb{P}_D \,\}$$

and we derive that $\varepsilon \leq \varepsilon/2$. Choose any p_1, p_2, p_3. We distinguish two cases.

$[p_1 = a] \qquad d((a;p_2);p_3, a;(p_2;p_3))$

$\qquad = \quad$ [def. of ';'] $d(a \cdot (p_2;p_3), a \cdot (p_2;p_3)))$

$\qquad = \quad 0\,.$

$[p_1 = a \cdot p'] \qquad d(((a \cdot p');p_2);p_3, (a \cdot p');(p_2;p_3))$

$\qquad = \quad$ [def. of ';'] $d((a \cdot ((p';p_2);p_3), a \cdot (p';(p_2;p_3)))$

$\qquad = \quad \frac{1}{2}d((p';p_2);p_3, p';(p_2;p_3))$

$\qquad \leq \quad \frac{1}{2}sup\{\, d((p';p_2);p_3, p';(p_2;p_3)) \mid p', p_2, p_3 \in \mathbb{P}_D \,\}$

$\qquad = \quad \varepsilon/2\,.$ $\qquad\qquad\qquad\qquad\qquad\qquad\qquad\qquad\qquad\qquad\qquad\qquad$ $\square$

We proceed with the definition of $\mathcal{D}$ for $\mathcal{L}_{rec}$. Putting the earlier definitions together, we want $\mathcal{D}$ to satisfy

Definition 1.39 $\mathcal{D}: \mathcal{L}_{rec} \to \mathbb{P}_D$ is given by

$$
\begin{aligned}
\mathcal{D}(D|a) &= a \\
\mathcal{D}(D|x) &= \mathcal{D}(D|D(x)) \\
\mathcal{D}(D|s_1;s_2) &= \mathcal{D}(D|s_1);\mathcal{D}(D|s_2)\,.
\end{aligned}
\qquad (1.17)
$$

Examples

(1) $\quad \mathcal{D}(D|(a_1;a_2);a_3)$

$\quad = \mathcal{D}(D|a_1;a_2);\mathcal{D}(D|a_3)$

$\quad = (\mathcal{D}(D|a_1);\mathcal{D}(D|a_2));\mathcal{D}(D|a_3)$

$\quad = (a_1;a_2);a_3$

$\quad = (a_1 \cdot a_2);a_3$

$\quad = a_1 \cdot a_2 \cdot a_3$

$= a_1 a_2 a_3$

$\mathcal{D}(D|a_1;(a_2;a_3))$

$= \mathcal{D}(D|a_1);\mathcal{D}(D|a_2;a_3)$

$= \mathcal{D}(D|a_1);(\mathcal{D}(D|a_2);\mathcal{D}(D|a_3))$

$= a_1;(a_2;a_3)$

$= a_1 \cdot (a_2 \cdot a_3)$

$= a_1 a_2 a_3$

(2) Suppose $D(x) = a;x$, then we have

$D(D|x;b)$

$= \mathcal{D}(D|x);\mathcal{D}(D|b)$

$= \mathcal{D}(D|a;x);\mathcal{D}(D|b)$

$= (\mathcal{D}(D|a);D(D|x));\mathcal{D}(D|b)$

$= (a \cdot \mathcal{D}(D|x));\mathcal{D}(D|b)$

$= a \cdot (\mathcal{D}(D|x);\mathcal{D}(D|b))$

$= a \cdot \mathcal{D}(D|x;b)$

by definition. So

$d_B(\mathcal{D}(D|x;b), a^\omega) = d_B(a \cdot \mathcal{D}(D|x;b), a \cdot a^\omega) = \frac{1}{2} d_B(\mathcal{D}(D|x;b), a^\omega).$

Therefore $d_B((\mathcal{D}(D|x;b), a^\omega) = 0$ and $\mathcal{D}(D|x;b) = a^\omega$ follows.

As we already saw, it requires additional justification that these three clauses together uniquely determine a value $\mathcal{D}(D|s)$, for each $s \in Stat$. Simple structural induction—i.e., induction on the syntactic complexity of s—does not work, since $D(x)$ is not, syntactically, simpler than x. As possible alternative one might try to base the induction on $wgt(D|s)$—with wgt as given in Definition 1.10. However, then the case $s_1;s_2$ does not work, since we do not have, in general, that $wgt(D|s_2) < wgt(D|s_1;s_2)$. Note how the latter fact prohibits an argument that $\mathcal{D}(D|s_1;s_2)$ is well-defined from the well-definedness of both $\mathcal{D}(D|s_1)$ and $\mathcal{D}(D|s_2)$.

It will not come as a surprise that we justify Definition 1.39 by another appeal to Banach's theorem. Similar to what we did for ';', we define the set of all semantic mappings $(S \in) Sem_D = \mathcal{L}_{rec} \to \mathbb{P}_D$, and next characterize $\mathcal{D}$ as unique fixed point of a suitable—contractive higher-order—mapping $\Psi: Sem_D \to Sem_D$. Since $\mathbb{P}_D$ and, hence, Sem_D is a complete metric space, we then have the appropriate setting for Banach's theorem. The way we define $\Psi(S)$ will be inferred from the clauses (1.17) in Definition 1.39—similar to the way $\Omega_;$ followed the clauses (1.15). In the left-hand side, we replace $\mathcal{D}$ by $\Psi(S)$, and in the right-hand side we replace $\mathcal{D}$ by either $\Psi(S)$ or by S alone. More specifically, we repeat $\Psi(S)$ only for programs of weight less than that of the program on the left-hand side. For example, we define

$$\Psi(S)(D|s_1;s_2) \;\; = \;\; \Psi(S)(D|s_1);S(D|s_2)$$

since, in general, $wgt(D|s_i) < wgt(D|s_1;s_2)$ for $i = 1$, but not for $i = 2$.

The full definition of Ψ is contained in

Definition 1.40 Let $(S \in) Sem_D = \mathcal{L}_{rec} \to \mathbb{P}_D$. The mapping $\Psi{:}Sem_D \to Sem_D$ is given by

$$\begin{array}{rcl}
\Psi(S)(D|a) & = & a \\
\Psi(S)(D|x) & = & \Psi(S)(D|D(x)) \\
\Psi(S)(D|s_1;s_2) & = & \Psi(S)(D|s_1);S(D|s_2) \,.
\end{array}$$

Note how this definition is organized such that well-definedness of $\Psi(S)$, for each argument $(D|s)$, is easily obtained by induction on $wgt(D|s)$.

The next step is to establish that Ψ is $\frac{1}{2}$-contractive in S. As auxiliary result in the proof of this fact we shall use a lemma on ';', stating an important property of ';' (which will also be used frequently in later chapters).

Lemma 1.41 For each $p_1, p_2, \bar{p}_1, \bar{p}_2 \in \mathbb{P}_D$ we have

$$d(p_1;p_2, \bar{p}_1;\bar{p}_2) \leq max\{\, d(p_1, \bar{p}_1), \tfrac{1}{2}d(p_2, \bar{p}_2) \,\}\,. \tag{1.18}$$

We shall base the proof on the definition of ; $= fix(\Omega_;)$. By Banach's theorem, we know that we may take ; $= lim_i\, \Omega_;^i(\phi_0)$, for some arbitrary $\phi_0 \in Op$. We now argue as follows. We first state the generalized version of (1.18), with ϕ replacing ';'.

$$d(\phi(p_1, p_2), \phi(\bar{p}_1, \bar{p}_2)) \leq max\{\, d(p_1, \bar{p}_1), \tfrac{1}{2}d(p_2, \bar{p}_2) \,\}\,. \tag{1.19}$$

As next step, we exhibit some special ϕ_0 for which it is immediate that it satisfies (1.19). E.g., it suffices to take $\phi_0 \in Op$ defined by $\phi_0(p_1, p_2) = p_1$ for all p_1, p_2.

Next we show the following *Claim*: For all ϕ, if ϕ satisfies (1.19) then $\Omega_;(\phi)$ satisfies (1.19). This will constitute the main technical part of the proof, and is elaborated below. Taking this for granted for the moment, we complete the proof as follows. Let $\phi_i = \Omega_;^i(\phi_0)$, $i = 0, 1, \cdots$. By induction on i, one obtains that (1.19) holds for each ϕ_i, $i = 0, 1, \cdots$. By an elementary property of limits (on $[0,1]$) we consequently have that

$$\lim_i d(\phi_i(p_1, p_2), \phi_i(\bar{p}_1, \bar{p}_2)) \leq max\{\, d(p_1, \bar{p}_1), \tfrac{1}{2}d(p_2, \bar{p}_2) \,\}.$$

Next, by the continuity of d we obtain

$$d(\lim_i \phi_i(p_1, p_2), \lim_i \phi_i(\bar{p}_1, \bar{p}_2)) \leq max\{\, d(p_1, \bar{p}_1), \tfrac{1}{2}d(p_2, \bar{p}_2) \,\}.$$

Since $lim_i \phi_i(p_1, p_2) = (lim_i \phi_i)(p_1, p_2)$ and $; = lim_i \phi_i$, the desired result follows.

There remains the proof of the claim. We distinguish eight cases, depending on the form of p_1 and $\bar{p}_1$, viz. $p_1 = a$, $\bar{p}_1 = \bar{a}$; $p_1 = a$, $\bar{p}_1 = \bar{a} \cdot \bar{p}_1'$; $p_1 = a \cdot p_1'$, $\bar{p}_1 = \bar{a}$; $p_1 = a \cdot p_1'$, $\bar{p}_1 = \bar{a} \cdot \bar{p}_1'$ with $a = \bar{a}$ or $a \neq \bar{a}$. Of the four subcases with $a = \bar{a}$, we discuss the hardest one: $p_1 = a \cdot p_1'$, $\bar{p}_1 = a \cdot \bar{p}_1'$, leaving the others as an exercise. We have

$$d(\Omega_;(\phi)(a \cdot p_1', p_2), \Omega_;(\phi)(a \cdot \bar{p}_1', \bar{p}_2))$$
$$= d(a \cdot \phi(p_1', p_2), a \cdot \phi(\bar{p}_1', \bar{p}_2))$$
$$= \tfrac{1}{2}d(\phi(p_1', p_2), \phi(\bar{p}_1', \bar{p}_2))$$
$$\leq [\text{assumption on } \phi]\ \tfrac{1}{2}max\{\, d(p_1', \bar{p}_1'), \tfrac{1}{2}d(p_2, \bar{p}_2) \,\}$$
$$\leq max\{\, d(a \cdot p_1', a \cdot \bar{p}_1'), \tfrac{1}{2}d(p_2, \bar{p}_2) \,\}. \qquad \square$$

We have now all ingredients for the proof of

Lemma 1.42 *Let* $\Psi \colon Sem_D \to Sem_D$ *be as in Definition 1.40. Then*

(a) Ψ *is* $\tfrac{1}{2}$*-contractive (in S).*

(b) *Putting* $\mathcal{D} = \text{fix}(\Psi)$, $\mathcal{D}$ *is the unique function satisfying (1.17).*

Proof

(a) Clearly, $\Psi(S)(D|s) \neq \epsilon$, for all S, D, s. Now let S_1, S_2 be arbitrary elements of Sem_D. We verify that

$$d(\Psi(S_1)(D|s), \Psi(S_2)(D|s)) \leq \tfrac{1}{2}d(S_1, S_2),$$

by induction on $wgt(D|s)$. One subcase.

$[s_1;s_2]$ $d(\Psi(S_1)(D|s_1;s_2), \Psi(S_2)(D|s_1;s_2))$
$\quad = \quad$ [def. Ψ] $d(\Psi(S_1)(D|s_1);S_1(D|s_2), \Psi(S_2)(D|s_1);S_2(D|s_2))$
$\quad \leq \quad$ [Lemma 1.41]
$\qquad max\{\, d(\Psi(S_1)(D|s_1), \Psi(S_2)(D|s_1)), \frac{1}{2}d(S_1(D|s_2), S_2(D|s_2))\,\}$
$\quad \leq \quad$ [ind. hyp. for $(D|s_1)$, def. of $d(S_1, S_2)$] $\frac{1}{2}d(S_1, S_2)$.

(b) Clear. $\square$

Now that $\mathcal{D}$ has been put on a solid basis, we can show various simple properties such as

Lemma 1.43

(a) $\mathcal{D}(D|(s_1;s_2);s_3) = \mathcal{D}(D|s_1;(s_2;s_3))$.

(b) Let $D(x) = a;x$. Then $\mathcal{D}(D|x) = a^\omega$.

Proof

(a) Easy by the definition of $\mathcal{D}$ and the associativity of the semantic ';' (Lemma 1.38).

(b) Since $\mathcal{D}(D|x) = \mathcal{D}(D|a;x) = a \cdot \mathcal{D}(D|x)$, we have that $\mathcal{D}(D|x)$ is the fixed point of the $\frac{1}{2}$-contractive mapping $\lambda p.(a \cdot p)\colon \mathbb{P}_D \to \mathbb{P}_D$, and the result follows by Banach's theorem.

An alternative proof of Lemma 1.43b is given in Exercise 1.14 (cf. also the Example following Definition 1.39).

1.1.4   Equivalence of $\mathcal{O}$ and $\mathcal{D}$

After having defined both the operational ($\mathcal{O}_d$) and the denotational ($\mathcal{D}$) semantics for $\mathcal{L}_{rec}$, the question arises as to how $\mathcal{O}_d$ and $\mathcal{D}$ are related. We recall that $\mathcal{O}_d(D|s)$, for $(D|s) \in \mathcal{L}_{rec}$, was defined (Definition 1.13), on the basis of the transition system specification $\mathcal{T}_{rec}$, as the (finite or infinite) sequence of actions labeling the successive transitions produced starting from $(D|s)$. On the other hand, $\mathcal{D}$ was defined in a compositional manner, and its justification was given in terms of a contractive higher-order mapping Ψ such that $\mathcal{D} = fix(\Psi)$. The fundamental idea in relating operational and denotational semantics for $\mathcal{L}_{rec}$ consists in defining the operational semantics ($\mathcal{O}$) for $\mathcal{L}_{rec}$ as well in terms of a contractive mapping, say Φ, where this Φ is based on the transition system $\mathcal{T}_{rec}$ in a manner to be specified soon. Putting

$$\mathcal{O} = fix(\Phi), \qquad\qquad\qquad\qquad\qquad\qquad\qquad\qquad (1.20)$$

the first question to be addressed is how this $\mathcal{O}$ relates to the earlier $\mathcal{O}_d$, and it will be easy to check that $\mathcal{O} = \mathcal{O}_d$. The main benefit of introducing $\mathcal{O}$ through (1.20) is that it allows another application of Banach's theorem (the third in Section 1.1!): we shall show that

$$\Phi(\mathcal{D}) = \mathcal{D} . \tag{1.21}$$

This claim should carefully be distinguished from the earlier fact that $\mathcal{D} = \mathit{fix}(\Psi)$, whence $\Psi(\mathcal{D}) = \mathcal{D}$. The formula involving Ψ was used to justify the definition of $\mathcal{D}$, whereas (1.21) is a further property of $\mathcal{D}$, ultimately relying on properties of $\mathcal{T}_{rec}$ (through the dependence of Φ on $\mathcal{T}_{rec}$). Thus, a separate proof of (1.21) will have to be provided. Once this has been achieved, we have that $\mathcal{O} = \mathcal{D}$, by the uniqueness of the fixed point of Φ (and formula (1.20)). Actually, since $\mathcal{O}$ will be defined on $Decl \times Res$ rather than on $\mathcal{L}_{rec}$ (note that $\mathcal{L}_{rec} = Decl \times Stat \subsetneq Decl \times Res$), we shall use a slight extension of (1.21), involving a denotational meaning function $\mathcal{E}$ defined on all of $Decl \times Res$. As first step, we introduce the contractive higher-order mapping Φ and the associated $\mathcal{O}$. For $\mathbb{P}_O$, recall Definition 1.12.

Definition 1.44 Let $(S \in) Sem_O = Decl \times Res \to \mathbb{P}_O$.

(a) The mapping $\Phi: Sem_O \to Sem_O$ is given by

$$
\begin{aligned}
\Phi(S)(D|\mathrm{E}) &= \epsilon \\
\Phi(S)(D|s) &= a \cdot S(D|r), \quad \text{where } s \xrightarrow{a}_D r.
\end{aligned}
$$

(b) $\mathcal{O} = \mathit{fix}(\Phi)$.

Remark Recall that, by (the proof of) Lemma 1.9, for each s there is precisely one pair $\langle a, r \rangle$ such that $s \xrightarrow{a}_D r$, implying well-definedness of $\Phi(S)(D|s)$.

We now check that Φ is $\frac{1}{2}$-contractive:

Lemma 1.45 $\Phi: Sem_O \to Sem_O$ is $\frac{1}{2}$-contractive (in S).
Proof We show that, for all S_1, S_2 and all $(D|r)$,

$$d(\Phi(S_1)(D|r), \Phi(S_2)(D|r)) \le \tfrac{1}{2} d(S_1, S_2) .$$

The case $r \equiv \mathrm{E}$ is immediate. Now take $r \equiv s$, and assume $s \xrightarrow{a}_D \bar{r}$. We then have

$$d(\Phi(S_1)(D|s), \Phi(S_2)(D|s))$$

$$= d(a \cdot S_1(D|\bar{r}), a \cdot S_2(D|\bar{r}))$$
$$= \tfrac{1}{2}d(S_1(D|\bar{r}), S_2(D|\bar{r}))$$
$$\leq \tfrac{1}{2}d(S_1, S_2) \ . \qquad\qquad\qquad\qquad\qquad\qquad\qquad\qquad \square$$

Example Note $\mathcal{O} = \Phi(\mathcal{O})$. We have

$$\mathcal{O}(D|(a_1;a_2);a_3)$$
$$= a_1 \cdot \mathcal{O}(D|a_2;a_3)$$
$$= a_1 \cdot a_2 \cdot \mathcal{O}(D|a_3)$$
$$= a_1 \cdot a_2 \cdot a_3 \cdot \mathcal{O}(D|\mathrm{E})$$
$$= a_1 \cdot a_2 \cdot a_3 \cdot \epsilon$$
$$= a_1 a_2 a_3$$

From $\mathcal{O}(x \Leftarrow a;x|x;b) = a \cdot \mathcal{O}(x \Leftarrow a;x|x;b)$ it follows that $\mathcal{O}(x \Leftarrow a;x|x;b) = a^\omega$.
Likewise, since $\mathcal{O}(x \Leftarrow a;y, y \Leftarrow b;x \mid x) = a \cdot \mathcal{O}(x \Leftarrow a;y, y \Leftarrow b;x \mid y) = a \cdot b \cdot \mathcal{O}(x \Leftarrow a;y, y \Leftarrow b;x \mid x)$ we have that $\mathcal{O}(x \Leftarrow a;y, y \Leftarrow b;x \mid x) = (ab)^\omega$.

Using, as always below, the notation $\mathcal{O}[\![\cdot]\!]$ for $\mathcal{O}$ when restricted to the language at hand—here $\mathcal{L}_{rec}$—we have the

Definition 1.46 $\mathcal{O}[\![D|s]\!] = \mathcal{O}(D|s)$.

For consistency in notation, we shall also use $\mathcal{D}[\![D|s]\!] = \mathcal{D}(D|s)$. (Though not very informative at the present stage, the notations $\mathcal{O}[\![D|s]\!]$ and $\mathcal{D}[\![D|s]\!]$ will serve some purpose on later occasions.)

The next step is to show $\mathcal{O} = \mathcal{O}_d$ (on $Decl \times Res$). By Banach, it suffices to show that $\Phi(O_d) = \mathcal{O}_d$.

Lemma 1.47 *For each $(D|r)$, $\Phi(\mathcal{O}_d)(D|r) = \mathcal{O}_d(D|r)$.*

Proof Clear for $r \equiv \mathrm{E}$. Now take $r \equiv s$, and assume $s \xrightarrow{a}_D \bar{r}$. We then have, by the definition of Φ,

$$\Phi(\mathcal{O}_d)(D|s) = a \cdot \mathcal{O}_d(D|\bar{r}) \ .$$

Also, by the definition of $\mathcal{O}_d$, one immediately sees that

$$\mathcal{O}_d(D|s) = a \cdot \mathcal{O}_d(D|\bar{r})$$

and the desired result follows. $\square$

We finally turn to the comparison of $\mathcal{O}$ and $\mathcal{D}$. As indicated already, we introduce $\mathcal{E}$ as extension of $\mathcal{D}$ to the domain $Decl \times Res$.

Definition 1.48 $\mathcal{E}: Decl \times Res \rightarrow \mathbb{P}_O$ is given by $\mathcal{E}(D|\mathrm{E}) = \epsilon$, $\mathcal{E}(D|s) = \mathcal{D}(D|s)$.

We are now ready for the proof of

Lemma 1.49 $\Phi(\mathcal{E}) = \mathcal{E}$, on $Decl \times Res$.

Proof We show that $\Phi(\mathcal{E})(D|r) = \mathcal{E}(D|r)$, by induction on $wgt(D|r)$. We omit the case that $r \equiv \mathrm{E}$, and discuss three subcases for $r \equiv s$.

$[a]$ $\Phi(\mathcal{E})(D|a)$

$= $ [def. Φ, $a \xrightarrow{a}_D \mathrm{E}$] $a \cdot \mathcal{E}(D|\mathrm{E})$

$= $ [def. $\mathcal{E}$] $a \cdot \epsilon$

$= $ a

$= $ [def. $\mathcal{E}, \mathcal{D}$] $\mathcal{E}(D|a)$

$[x]$ Let $D(x) = g$. Note that $x \xrightarrow{a}_D r \Leftrightarrow g \xrightarrow{a}_D r$ (by Lemma 1.8a), hence $\Phi(\mathcal{E})(D|x) = \Phi(\mathcal{E})(D|g)$, by the definition of Φ. Now

$\Phi(\mathcal{E})(D|x)$

$= $ $\Phi(\mathcal{E})(D|D(x))$

$= $ [ind. hyp.] $\mathcal{E}(D|D(x))$

$= $ [def. $\mathcal{E}, \mathcal{D}$] $\mathcal{D}(D|x)$.

$[s_1;s_2]$ Extending our earlier definitions, we put $\epsilon;p = p$. Assume $s_1;s_2 \xrightarrow{a}_D r$. Then we have $(s_1 \xrightarrow{a}_D r_1) \wedge (r \equiv r_1;s_2)$, for some suitable r_1 (Lemma 1.8b). Moreover, $\mathcal{E}(D|r) = \mathcal{E}(D|r_1;s_2) = \mathcal{E}(D|r_1);\mathcal{E}(D|s_2)$, by the definition of $\mathcal{E}$ and the compositionality of $\mathcal{D}$. Therefore,

$\Phi(\mathcal{E})(D|s_1;s_2)$

$= $ $a \cdot \mathcal{E}(D|r)$

$= $ $a \cdot (\mathcal{E}(D|r_1);\mathcal{E}(D|s_2))$

$= $ [def. ';'] $(a \cdot \mathcal{E}(D|r_1));\mathcal{E}(D|s_2)$

$= $ [def. Φ, $s_1 \xrightarrow{a}_D r_1$] $\Phi(\mathcal{E})(D|s_1);\mathcal{E}(D|s_2)$

$= $ [ind. hyp.] $\mathcal{E}(D|s_1);\mathcal{E}(D|s_2)$

$= $ [def. $\mathcal{E}, \mathcal{D}$] $\mathcal{E}(D|s_1;s_2)$. $\square$

We draw attention to the fact that this style of argument—which we shall invoke many times on later occasions—is based purely on (induction on) $wgt(D|r)$, irrespective of the question whether any of the intermediate outcomes $\mathcal{E}(D|r')$ encountered in the calculations is finite or infinite.

We finally have arrived at the main result of Section 1.1.

Theorem 1.50 $\mathcal{O}[\![\pi]\!] = \mathcal{D}[\![\pi]\!]$, *for each* $\pi \in \mathcal{L}_{rec}$.

Proof By Lemma 1.49 and Banach's theorem, we have that $\mathcal{O} = \mathcal{E}$ on $Decl \times Res$. Restricting this to $\mathcal{L}_{rec} = Decl \times Stat$, we obtain the result as stated.   □

The reader may recall that we still owe him a proof of Lemma 1.14b, viz. that $\mathcal{O}(D|(s_1;s_2);s_3) = \mathcal{O}(D|s_1;(s_2;s_3))$. This result is now immediate by Lemma 1.43 and the equivalence of $\mathcal{O}$ and $\mathcal{D}$, as just obtained.

1.2 Iteration
—a nonuniform language with continuation semantics

In Section 1.1, we have laid the foundations for the semantic definitions of all languages to be studied in our book. Though $\mathcal{L}_{rec}$ is extremely simple, it is used as a vehicle to introduce already a sizable proportion of the techniques to be applied later. Summarizing, we shall go on using complete metric spaces, transition system specifications and higher-order mappings for defining (and proving properties of) operational and denotational semantics, and semantic operators. In Section 1.2, we discuss a seemingly very different—and somewhat more realistic—language including at least a few "real-life" notions such as assignments, conditionals and while statements. The basic difference between this language—to be called $\mathcal{L}_{wh}$, with "wh" abbreviating *while* —and $\mathcal{L}_{rec}$ is that the atomic constituents of $\mathcal{L}_{wh}$ have their own interpretation, viz. as transformations of so-called *states*, whereas the atoms of $\mathcal{L}_{rec}$ are just symbols from the alphabet Act. Assignments are built from simple variables and expressions, thus requiring the introduction of some further syntactic classes. The (dynamically changing) bindings between the variables and their values will be recorded in the states, another fundamental notion in semantics. We furthermore use this section to introduce a new semantic technique, viz. that of *continuations*. These serve a variety of purposes in semantic design. Their first—and maybe most typical—use is in the handling of sequential composition, as will be described in Section 1.2.2. Many further instances of applying continuations will be encountered in later chapters.

1.2.1   Syntax and operational semantics

The language $\mathcal{L}_{wh}$ looks quite different from $\mathcal{L}_{rec}$—details will follow in a moment. Still, for its semantic treatment we shall be able to use all the main tools as developed for $\mathcal{L}_{rec}$, to which we add two fundamental new techniques, viz. the use of

- *states*

and of

- *continuations.*

Contrary to $\mathcal{L}_{rec}$, the language $\mathcal{L}_{wh}$ is what we like to call *nonuniform*, i.e., its atomic constituents are actions which do have their own meaning (rather than the simple $a \in Act$), viz. *assignment statements*. Assignment statements *depend* on the (current) state, which may explain the terminology of "nonuniform" (to be contrasted with the "uniform" actions from *Act*, the effect of which does not depend on the state). The introduction of these constructs presupposes the availability of two basic syntactic classes, viz.

- the class $(v \in) IVar$ of *individual variables*
- the class $(e \in) Exp$ of *expressions.*

Though different from *PVar*, the class *IVar* is comparable in that it is, simply, an abstract set, the elements of which have no further structure. The syntactic class $(e \in) Exp$ will be treated in some detail in Section 1.2.3. For the moment the reader may think of simple expressions as in PASCAL such as $v + 1$, $v_1 + v_2$, or $v_1 > v_2$. More specifically, we assume that all expressions are such that their evaluation always terminates (in a unique value) and that no side-effects are invoked in this evaluation. (In Section 1.2.3 we shall make precise what we mean by a side-effect.) Included in the class of expressions are the so-called *logical expressions*, evaluation of which yields a truth-value, say an element of the set $\{tt, ff\}$.

The language $\mathcal{L}_{wh}$ exhibits a second important difference with $\mathcal{L}_{rec}$ in that its programs have no declaration component. Instead, we here encounter a special form of recursion, viz. the so-called *iteration* in the form of the while statement while e do s od. We assume that the reader is familiar with the basic equivalence characterizing the while statement:

while e do s od = if e then (s;while e do s od) else skip fi .   (1.22)

In (1.22) we have used two further ingredients of $\mathcal{L}_{wh}$, the conditional construct if e then s_1 else s_2 fi and the skip-statement skip. Altogether, we have as syntax for $\mathcal{L}_{wh}$

Definition 1.51

(a) $s\,(\in Stat) ::= v := e \mid$ skip $\mid (s;s) \mid$ if e then s else s fi $\mid$ while e do s od.

(b) $(\pi \in)\,\mathcal{L}_{wh} = Stat.$

Examples

(1) $(v_1 := 1; v_2 := 2); v_3 := 3,\ v_1 := 1; (v_2 := 2; v_3 := 3)$

(2) $v := v_1;$ if $v_1 < v_2$ then $v := v_2$ else skip fi

(3) while $v < 5$ do $v := v + 1$ od

(4) while true do skip od.

Remarks

(1) Here—and in all subsequent comparable settings—we shall assume that the constructs of our language are *well-typed*. In the present case this means that the expressions e occurring in if e then s_1 else s_2 fi and in while e do s od are logical (also called "boolean"), i.e., that their evaluation—see Section 1.2.3 for details—delivers one of the two truth-values tt or ff.

(2) In $\mathcal{L}_{wh}$, there is no explicit role for guarded statements. However, implicitly $\mathcal{L}_{wh}$ does satisfy a guardedness requirement, in that the while statement while e do s od may be seen as a syntactic alternative for the $\mathcal{L}_{rec}$-construct as specified by $D(x) =$ if e then $(s;x)$ else skip fi (cf. Exercise 1.20). This $D(x)$ deserves to be called guarded (at least in x).

Now that individual variables have appeared on the scene, it is natural to introduce the first main new notion of this section, viz. that of a *state*. Programs in $\mathcal{L}_{wh}$—and, in general, in nonuniform languages—transform states, where a state is a mapping assigning *values* to individual variables. The nature of the collection of values is of no importance for our considerations. For definiteness, the reader may assume that the set of values consists of the set $\mathbb{Z}$ of integers and the truth-values $\{\,tt, ff\,\}$. Here, $\mathbb{Z}$ may be replaced by any other structure, but we shall always require that $\{\,tt, ff\,\}$ is a subset of the set of values. Altogether we have

Definition 1.52

(a) ($\alpha \in$) *Val* is the set of values. We require that *Val* includes the truth-values *tt* and *ff* as elements.

(b) ($\sigma \in$) $\Sigma = IVar \to Val$ is the set of *states*, i.e., of functions with domain *IVar* and range *Val*.

The definitions of both $\mathcal{O}$ and $\mathcal{D}$ for $\mathcal{L}_{wh}$ will employ the states σ in an essential manner. As part of their definition, we shall need the definition of the value of an expression e in a state σ. The evaluation function, say $\mathcal{V}$, is to be given as a mapping

$$\mathcal{V}: Exp \to \Sigma \to Val, \tag{1.23}$$

i.e., we want rules to evaluate, for each e and σ, the value $\alpha = \mathcal{V}(e)(\sigma)$. We shall return to this in Section 1.2.3, where we shall specify $\mathcal{V}$ both according to the operational and the denotational semantics style. Right now, we assume that $\mathcal{V}$ from (1.23) is already available, and concentrate on the design of $\mathcal{O}$ and $\mathcal{D}$ for the control flow features of $\mathcal{L}_{wh}$. One notation—with some associated properties—is necessary before we can start with the design of the transition system specification $\mathcal{T}_{wh}$ for $\mathcal{L}_{wh}$. The definition introduces the so-called *update* of a state:

Definition 1.53 For $\sigma \in \Sigma$, $\alpha \in Val$, $v \in IVar$ we use the notation $\sigma\{\alpha/v\}$ for the state which is like σ, except for its value in v which equals α. That is, $\sigma\{\alpha/v\}$ is the function

$$\sigma\{\alpha/v\}(v') = \begin{cases} \alpha & \text{if } v \equiv v' \\ \sigma(v') & \text{if } v \not\equiv v' . \end{cases}$$

Some elementary properties of this notation, tacitly used in the sequel, are given in

Lemma 1.54 *For each* $\sigma \in \Sigma$, $\alpha_1, \alpha_2 \in Val$, $v, v_1, v_2 \in IVar$, *we have*

(a) $\sigma\{\sigma(v)/v\} = \sigma$.

(b) $\sigma\{\alpha_1/v_1\}\{\alpha_2/v_2\} = \begin{cases} \sigma\{\alpha_2/v_2\} & \text{if } v_1 \equiv v_2 \\ \sigma\{\alpha_2/v_2\}\{\alpha_1/v_1\} & \text{if } v_1 \not\equiv v_2. \end{cases}$

Proof Exercise.   □

We proceed with the definition of the transition system $\mathcal{T}_{wh}$. The configurations of $\mathcal{T}_{wh}$ consist of *pairs* $[r, \sigma]$, with r a resumption and σ a state. States σ are as just introduced. Resumptions are given in

Definition 1.55 $r \, (\in Res) ::= \text{E} \mid (s\text{:}r)$.

The net effect of this definition is that a resumption r is a construct of the form $(s_1\text{:}(s_2\text{:} \ldots (s_n\text{:E}) \ldots))$, $n \geq 0$, i.e., a sequence of $n \geq 0$ statements ending in E (again with the connotation "termination"). Resumptions of this form live up to their name: a pair $s\text{:}r$ will obtain meaning such that—for given σ—s is executed, yielding some intermediate result, and execution is then to be *resumed* with that of r. The idea that configurations consist of $[r, \sigma]$-pairs is natural, in that the abstract machine performing the transitions, at each moment has to have available both the current program (in the form of the r) and the state σ, incorporating the current values of the program variables. The transitions of $\mathcal{T}_{wh}$ are triples of the form $([r_1, \sigma_1], \sigma, [r_2, \sigma_2])$, or, in terms of the ' $\rightarrow$ ' notation,

$$[r_1, \sigma_1] \xrightarrow{\sigma} [r_2, \sigma_2] \, . \tag{1.24}$$

We see that as *Obs* we have taken the set of states Σ. Now it will turn out that (almost) all transition systems used in our book employing states (we will warn the reader when an exception appears) satisfy that $\sigma = \sigma_2$: the observable element coincides with the state *after* the transition has been performed. This fact will allow us to use as notation for nonuniform transitions

$$[r_1, \sigma_1] \rightarrow [r_2, \sigma_2],$$

dropping the observation σ from $\xrightarrow{\sigma}$, since the σ always equals σ_2.

Before presenting $\mathcal{T}_{wh}$, we need one further notational convention. We shall often—here and later—use rules of the form

$$\frac{[r_2, \sigma_2] \rightarrow [r, \sigma]}{[r_1, \sigma_1] \rightarrow [r, \sigma]} \tag{1.25}$$

prescribing that, in order to evaluate $[r_1, \sigma_1]$, it is necessary to evaluate $[r_2, \sigma_2]$. If the latter configuration makes a transition to $[r, \sigma]$, then so does the former. As a convenient abbreviation for (1.25) we shall use $[r_1, \sigma_1] \rightarrow_0 [r_2, \sigma_2]$, where ' $\rightarrow_0$ ' is to be read as a *zero-step*, i.e., a step without observable effect. This notation will be useful in

Definition 1.56 $\mathcal{T}_{wh} = (Res \times \Sigma, \Sigma, \rightarrow, Spec)$, where $Spec$ consists of

- $[(v := e):r, \sigma] \rightarrow [r, \sigma\{\alpha/v\}]$ where $\alpha = \mathcal{V}(e)(\sigma)$ (Ass)

- $[\text{skip}:r, \sigma] \rightarrow [r, \sigma]$ (Skip)

- $[(s_1;s_2):r, \sigma] \rightarrow_0 [s_1:(s_2:r), \sigma]$ (Seq)

- $[\text{if } e \text{ then } s_1 \text{ else } s_2 \text{ fi}:r, \sigma] \rightarrow_0 [s_1:r, \sigma]$ if $\mathcal{V}(e)(\sigma) = tt$ (If 1)
  $[\text{if } e \text{ then } s_1 \text{ else } s_2 \text{ fi}:r, \sigma] \rightarrow_0 [s_2:r, \sigma]$ if $\mathcal{V}(e)(\sigma) = ff$ (If 2)

- $[\text{while } e \text{ do } s \text{ od}:r, \sigma] \rightarrow_0$ (While)
  $[\text{if } e \text{ then } (s;\text{while } e \text{ do } s \text{ od}) \text{ else skip fi}, \sigma]$

A precise definition of $\mathcal{V}(e)(\sigma)$ follows in Section 1.2.3. $Spec$ consists of two axioms ((Ass) and (Skip)) and four rules ((Seq), (If 1), (If 2) and (While)). Clearly, the rules in $Spec$ are organized in the syntax directed style as announced in our earlier discussion preceding Definition 1.5.

Examples

(1) Since $[v := v_2:\text{E}, \sigma\{1/v, 1/v_1, 2/v_2\}] \rightarrow [\text{E}, \sigma\{2/v, 1/v_1, 2/v_2\}]$ we have

$[\text{if } v_1 < v_2 \text{ then } v := v_2 \text{ else skip fi}:\text{E}, \sigma\{1/v, 1/v_1, 2/v_2\}] \rightarrow$
$\quad [\text{E}, \sigma\{2/v, 1/v_1, 2/v_2\}].$

Similarly, since $[\text{skip};\text{E}, \sigma\{2/v, 2/v_1, 1/v_2\}] \rightarrow [\text{E}, \sigma\{2/v, 2/v_1, 1/v_2\}]$ we have

$[\text{if } v_1 < v_2 \text{ then } v := v_2 \text{ else skip fi}:\text{E}, \sigma\{2/v, 2/v_1, 1/v_2\}] \rightarrow$
$\quad [\text{E}, \sigma\{2/v, 2/v_1, 1/v_2\}].$

(2) Put, for the moment $s_{\text{wh}} \equiv \text{while } v < 5 \text{ do } v := v + 1 \text{ od}$. We have

$[v := v + 1:(s_{\text{wh}}:r), \sigma\{4/v\}] \rightarrow [s_{\text{wh}}:r, \sigma\{5/v\}]$ by (Ass),

$[(v := v + 1;s_{\text{wh}}):r, \sigma\{4/v\}] \rightarrow [s_{\text{wh}}:r, \sigma\{5/v\}]$ by (Seq) from (1),

$[\text{if } v < 5 \text{ then } (v := v + 1;s_{\text{wh}}) \text{ else skip fi}:r, \sigma\{4/v\}] \rightarrow$
$\quad [s_{\text{wh}}:r, \sigma\{5/v\}]$ by (If) from (3), and therefore

$[\text{while } v < 5 \text{ do } v := v + 1 \text{ od}:r, \sigma\{4/v\}] \rightarrow$
$\quad [\text{while } v < 5 \text{ do } v := v + 1 \text{ od}:r, \sigma\{5/v\}]$ by (While) from (3).

Now that $\mathcal{T}_{wh}$ is available, we may define $\mathcal{O}$ for $\mathcal{L}_{wh}$ in a way which closely follows that of $\mathcal{O}$ for $\mathcal{L}_{rec}$. We begin with the introduction of the operational codomain.

Definition 1.57 $\mathbb{P}_O = \Sigma \to \Sigma^\infty$.

Just as we did for Act^∞ we view Σ^∞ (and $\Sigma \to \Sigma^\infty$) as a complete (ultra) metric space, by using the Baire-metric on Σ^∞. This allows us to base the definition of

$$\mathcal{O}[\![\cdot]\!]: \mathcal{L}_{wh} \to \mathbb{P}_O$$

on a higher-order contractive mapping, just as done for $\mathcal{L}_{rec}$. Of course, we might also begin by introducing a directly defined $\mathcal{O}_d$ (mimicking Definition 1.13). However, here and almost everywhere below, we shall skip the step introducing $\mathcal{O}_d$, and immediately define $\mathcal{O}$ as fixed point. Usually, it is easy to prove that $\mathcal{O}_d = \mathcal{O}$, following the argument as applied earlier for $\mathcal{L}_{rec}$. (Note, however, that this does depend on the fact that the codomains of $\mathcal{O}_d$ and $\mathcal{O}$ coincide. Here, this is trivial by definition. In later instances, it may require extra effort to establish this fact.)

Definition 1.58

(a) Let $(S \in) \mathit{Sem}_O = \mathit{Res} \times \Sigma \to \Sigma^\infty$. We define $\Phi: \mathit{Sem}_O \to \mathit{Sem}_O$ by putting

$$\begin{aligned} \Phi(S)(\mathrm{E}, \sigma) &= \epsilon \\ \Phi(S)(s{:}r, \sigma) &= \sigma' \cdot S(r', \sigma'), \quad \text{if } [s{:}r, \sigma] \to [r', \sigma']. \end{aligned}$$

(b) The mapping $\mathcal{O}: \mathit{Res} \times \Sigma \to \Sigma^\infty$ is given as $\mathcal{O} = \mathit{fix}(\Phi)$.

(c) $\mathcal{O}[\![\cdot]\!]: \mathcal{L}_{wh} \to \mathbb{P}_O$ is given by $\mathcal{O}[\![s]\!] = \lambda\sigma.\mathcal{O}(s{:}\mathrm{E}, \sigma)$.

Note how the observable σ' is delivered as first step in the result $\sigma' \cdot S(r', \sigma')$ in the same way as the action a was produced as first step in $a \cdot S(r)$ for $\mathcal{L}_{rec}$. Also note how $\mathcal{O}$ is defined on $\mathit{Res} \times \Sigma$, yielding elements in Σ^∞, and how $\mathcal{O}[\![\cdot]\!]$ is defined on $\mathcal{L}_{wh}$ yielding results in $\Sigma \to \Sigma^\infty$. Moreover, the argument s of $\mathcal{O}[\![\cdot]\!]$ is turned into an element of Res by postfixing it with E. (All this is necessary since the transition system approach requires configurations in $\mathit{Res} \times \Sigma$, whereas the "ultimate" $\mathcal{O}[\![\cdot]\!]$ expects elements of $\mathcal{L}_{wh}$ as arguments.)

Examples

(1) $\quad \mathcal{O}[\![(v_1 := 1; v_2 := 2); v_3 := 3]\!](\sigma)$

$\quad = \mathcal{O}(((v_1 := 1; v_2 := 2); v_3 := 3){:}\mathrm{E}, \sigma)$

$\quad = \sigma\{1/v_1\} \cdot \mathcal{O}(v_2 := 2{:}(v_3 := 3{:}\mathrm{E}), \sigma\{1/v_1\})$

$\quad = \sigma\{1/v_1\} \cdot \sigma\{1/v_1, 2/v_2\} \cdot \mathcal{O}(v_3 := 3{:}\mathrm{E}, \sigma\{1/v_1, 2/v_2\})$

$$\begin{aligned}
&= \sigma\{1/v_1\} \cdot \sigma\{1/v_1, 2/v_2\} \cdot \sigma\{1/v_1, 2/v_2, 3/v_3\} \cdot \\
&\quad \mathcal{O}(\text{E}, \sigma\{1/v_1, 2/v_2, 3/v_3\}) \\
&= \sigma\{1/v_1\} \cdot \sigma\{1/v_1, 2/v_2\} \cdot \sigma\{1/v_1, 2/v_2, 3/v_3\} \cdot \epsilon \\
&= \sigma\{1/v_1\} \sigma\{1/v_1, 2/v_2\} \sigma\{1/v_1, 2/v_2, 3/v_3\}.
\end{aligned}$$

(2) $\quad \mathcal{O}[\![\text{while } v < 5 \text{ do } v := v + 1 \text{ od}]\!](\sigma\{1/v\})$

$$\begin{aligned}
&= \mathcal{O}(\text{while } v < 5 \text{ do } v := v + 1 \text{ od:E}, \sigma\{1/v\}) \\
&= \sigma\{2/v\} \cdot \mathcal{O}(\text{while } v < 5 \text{ do } v := v + 1 \text{ od:E}, \sigma\{2/v\}) \\
&= \sigma\{2/v\} \cdot \sigma\{3/v\} \cdot \mathcal{O}(\text{while } v < 5 \text{ do } v := v + 1 \text{ od:E}, \sigma\{3/v\}) \\
&= \sigma\{2/v\} \cdot \sigma\{3/v\} \cdot \sigma\{4/v\} \cdot \mathcal{O}(\text{while } v < 5 \text{ do } v := v + 1 \text{ od:E}, \sigma\{4/v\}) \\
&= \sigma\{2/v\} \cdot \sigma\{3/v\} \cdot \sigma\{4/v\} \cdot \sigma\{5/v\} \cdot \\
&\quad \mathcal{O}(\text{while } v < 5 \text{ do } v := v + 1 \text{ od:E}, \sigma\{5/v\}) \\
&= \sigma\{2/v\} \cdot \sigma\{3/v\} \cdot \sigma\{4/v\} \cdot \sigma\{5/v\} \cdot \mathcal{O}(\text{skip:E}, \sigma\{5/v\}) \\
&= \sigma\{2/v\} \cdot \sigma\{3/v\} \cdot \sigma\{4/v\} \cdot \sigma\{5/v\} \cdot \sigma\{5/v\} \cdot \mathcal{O}(\text{E}, \sigma\{5/v\}) \\
&= \sigma\{2/v\} \cdot \sigma\{3/v\} \cdot \sigma\{4/v\} \cdot \sigma\{5/v\} \cdot \sigma\{5/v\} \cdot \epsilon \\
&= \sigma\{2/v\} \sigma\{3/v\} \sigma\{4/v\} \sigma\{5/v\} \sigma\{5/v\}.
\end{aligned}$$

A number of facts have to be verified in order to justify Definition 1.58. The first one is

Lemma 1.59 *For each s, r, σ.*

(a) $\mid \mathcal{S}(\text{E}, \sigma) \mid = 0$

(b) $\mid \mathcal{S}(s{:}r, \sigma) \mid = 1.$

Thus, $\mathcal{T}_{wh}$ is deterministic, just as $\mathcal{T}_{rec}$. In the proof we use a weight function which is very similar to the one used in Section 1.1.1:

Definition 1.60 *wgt: $Res \cup Stat \to \mathbb{N}$ is given by*

$$\begin{aligned}
wgt(\text{E}) &= 0 \\
wgt(s{:}r) &= wgt(s) \\
wgt(v := e) &= wgt(\text{skip}) = 1 \\
wgt(s_1;s_2) &= wgt(s_1) + 1 \\
wgt(\text{if } e \text{ then } s_1 \text{ else } s_2 \text{ fi}) &= max\{\, wgt(s_1), wgt(s_2)\,\} + 1 \\
wgt(\text{while } e \text{ do } s \text{ od}) &= \\
wgt(\text{if } e \text{ then } (s;&\text{while } e \text{ do } s \text{ od}) \text{ else skip fi}) + 1\,.
\end{aligned}$$

As a consequence of this definition we obtain that

$$wgt(\text{while } e \text{ do } s \text{ od}) = wgt(s) + 3,$$

a fact which is the key step in the proof (left as Exercise 1.18a) that $wgt(r)$ and $wgt(s)$ are well-defined. We leave as another exercise (Exercise 1.18b) the easy proof of Lemma 1.59, based on induction on $wgt(r)$. As a corollary to this lemma, we have that the clause for $\Phi(S)(s{:}r, \sigma)$ in Definition 1.58 is well-defined, since there is always precisely one step $[s{:}r, \sigma] \rightarrow [r', \sigma']$ possible.

One important step remains in the justification of the definition of $\mathcal{O} = fix(\Phi)$:

Lemma 1.61 *The mapping Φ is $\frac{1}{2}$-contractive in S.*

Proof Let $S_1, S_2 \in Sem_O$. We show that, for all σ, $d(\Phi(S_1)(r, \sigma), \Phi(S_2)(r, \sigma)) \leq \frac{1}{2}d(S_1, S_2)$. The case $r \equiv \mathrm{E}$ is clear. If $r \equiv s{:}\bar{r}$, we have

$$d(\Phi(S_1)(s{:}\bar{r}, \sigma), \Phi(S_2)(s{:}\bar{r}, \sigma))$$
$$= [\text{by the definition of } \Phi, \text{ assuming } [s{:}\bar{r}, \sigma] \rightarrow [r', \sigma']]$$
$$\quad d(\sigma' \cdot S_1(r', \sigma'), \sigma' \cdot S_2(r', \sigma'))$$
$$= \tfrac{1}{2}d(S_1(r', \sigma'), S_2(r', \sigma'))$$
$$\leq \tfrac{1}{2}d(S_1, S_2). \qquad \qquad \qquad \qquad \qquad \qquad \square$$

Altogether, we have completed the first task of this section, viz. to define the operational semantics for $\mathcal{L}_{wh}$. We now turn to its denotational semantics.

1.2.2 Denotational semantics, equivalence of $\mathcal{O}$ and $\mathcal{D}$

The most striking feature of the denotational semantics for $\mathcal{L}_{wh}$ is the use of so-called *continuations*. Continuations are the denotational counterpart of resumptions. Whereas the latter specify the remainder of the program which is still to be executed (the r in $s{:}r$), the former embody the *meaning* of this remainder. Thus, resumptions are syntactic entities, whereas continuations are semantic ones. Occasionally, we shall want to refer to both types of notions in one phrase. We then use the phrase *prolongation*, thus referring to either a resumption or a continuation.

Let $(\gamma \in) \, Cont$ be the set of continuations. Since the meaning of the remainder of a program is an entity of the same kind as the meaning of a program itself, it is not surprising that we simply take $Cont = \mathbb{P}_D$, where $\mathbb{P}_D$ is, in turn, equal to $\Sigma \rightarrow \Sigma^{\infty}$ (i.e., $\mathbb{P}_D = \mathbb{P}_O$, with $\mathbb{P}_O$ as in Subsection 1.2.1). Below, the *empty* continuation $\lambda\sigma.\epsilon$ will play a special role (to be compared with that of the resumption E). Therefore, we give a special name to it, viz. γ_{ϵ}.

The denotational semantics $\mathcal{D}$ has two arguments, viz. a statement s and a continuation γ, i.e., $\mathcal{D}$ is of type

$$\mathcal{D}\colon Stat \to Cont \to \mathbb{P}_D$$

and, for $s \in Stat$, $\gamma \in Cont$, $\mathcal{D}(s)(\gamma)$ determines the meaning of s in a context where we already know that the meaning of the remaining program (the part after s) has the value γ. At first sight, this approach may seem rather paradoxical: while executing s, how can we already know the meaning γ of that part of the program that is to come after s? In other words, this approach seems counter to our intuition that a program is evaluated from left to right. However, by considering a few special cases the reader may appreciate that the use of continuations does make sense:

(1) Evaluating a complete program s may be achieved by determining $\mathcal{D}(s)(\gamma_\epsilon)$: s is evaluated in a context where nothing remains to be done. (We here find the denotational counterpart of the operational step going from s to $s{:}E$ in Definition 1.58c.)

(2) The meaning of $s_1;s_2$ for a continuation γ, i.e., $\mathcal{D}(s_1;s_2)(\gamma)$, is specified as the meaning of s_1 for continuation $\mathcal{D}(s_2)(\gamma)$, i.e., we shall require

$$\mathcal{D}(s_1;s_2)(\gamma) = \mathcal{D}(s_1)(\mathcal{D}(s_2)(\gamma)). \tag{1.26}$$

(1.26) is, in fact, the key rule for the use of continuations. In words, executing $s_1;s_2$ for continuation γ amounts to the execution of s_1 for a continuation consisting of the execution of s_2 for continuation γ. (Here the operational counterpart is the (Seq)-rule $[(s_1;s_2){:}r, \sigma] \to_0 [s_1{:}(s_2{:}r), \sigma]$.)

(3) As last subcase we look at the assignment statement. We shall use

$$\mathcal{D}(v := e)(\gamma) = \lambda\sigma.\sigma\{\alpha/v\} \cdot \gamma(\sigma\{\alpha/v\}). \tag{1.27}$$

This clause is to be understood as follows: The meaning of the assignment statement $v := e$ for continuation γ (recall that γ is an element of the set $\Sigma \to \Sigma^\infty$) and the state σ is a sequence consisting of the concatenation of

- the updated state $\sigma_1 = \sigma\{\alpha/v\}$, for $\alpha = \mathcal{V}(e)(\sigma)$

- the sequence (say ρ) resulting from supplying the result σ_1 as input to the continuation function γ. Since γ has been determined—by the very mechanism we are now describing—as the meaning of the part of the program following $v := e$, we know that $\rho = \gamma(\sigma\{\alpha/v\})$ (with $\rho \in \Sigma^\infty$) is the to be expected outcome when that part of the program is executed for input state $\sigma_1 = \sigma\{\alpha/v\}$.

Altogether, the result $\sigma\{\alpha/v\}\cdot\gamma(\sigma\{\alpha/v\})$ is the outcome of executing an assignment statement.

After this outline of the definition of $\mathcal{D}$, the reader should not have too much difficulty in understanding the next definition. Similar to the situation for $\mathcal{L}_{rec}$, we first give a number of defining equations for $\mathcal{D}$, and then invoke an additional argument to show that these equations taken together uniquely specify a function.

Definition 1.62 Let $\mathbb{P}_D = \Sigma \to \Sigma^\infty$.

(a) Let $(\gamma \in)\,Cont = \mathbb{P}_D$, and let $\gamma_\epsilon = \lambda\sigma.\epsilon$.

(b) Let $\mathcal{D}\colon \mathcal{L}_{wh} \to Cont \to \mathbb{P}_D$ be the function satisfying

$$
\begin{aligned}
\mathcal{D}(v := e)(\gamma)(\sigma) &= \sigma\{\alpha/v\} \cdot \gamma(\sigma\{\alpha/v\}), \quad \text{where } \alpha = \mathcal{V}(e)(\sigma) \\
\mathcal{D}(\text{skip})(\gamma)(\sigma) &= \sigma \cdot \gamma(\sigma) \\
\mathcal{D}(s_1;s_2)(\gamma)(\sigma) &= \mathcal{D}(s_1)(\mathcal{D}(s_2)(\gamma))(\sigma)
\end{aligned}
$$

$$
\mathcal{D}(\text{if } e \text{ then } s_1 \text{ else } s_2 \text{ fi})(\gamma)(\sigma) = \left\{ \begin{array}{ll} \mathcal{D}(s_1)(\gamma)(\sigma) & \text{if } \mathcal{V}(e)(\sigma) = tt \\ \mathcal{D}(s_2)(\gamma)(\sigma) & \text{if } \mathcal{V}(e)(\sigma) = f\!f \end{array} \right.
$$

$$
\begin{aligned}
\mathcal{D}(\text{while } e \text{ do } s \text{ od})(\gamma)(\sigma) \\
= \mathcal{D}(\text{if } e \text{ then } (s;\text{while } e \text{ do } s \text{ od}) \text{ else skip fi})(\gamma)(\sigma).
\end{aligned}
$$

(c) $\mathcal{D}[\![\cdot]\!]\colon \mathcal{L}_{wh} \to \mathbb{P}_D$ is given by $\mathcal{D}[\![s]\!] = \mathcal{D}(s)(\gamma_\epsilon)$.

Examples

(1)
$$
\begin{aligned}
&\mathcal{D}((v_1 := 1;v_2 := 2);v_3 := 3)(\gamma_\epsilon)(\sigma) \\
&= \mathcal{D}(v_1 := 1;v_2 := 2)\big(\mathcal{D}(v_3 := 3)(\gamma_\epsilon)\big)(\sigma) \\
&= \mathcal{D}(v_1 := 1)\Big(\mathcal{D}(v_2 := 2)\big(\mathcal{D}(v_3 := 3)(\gamma_\epsilon)\big)\Big)(\sigma) \\
&= \sigma\{1/v_1\} \cdot \mathcal{D}(v_2 := 2)\big(\mathcal{D}(v_3 := 3)(\gamma_\epsilon)\big)(\sigma\{1/v_1\}) \\
&= \sigma\{1/v_1\} \cdot \sigma\{1/v_1, 2/v_2\} \cdot \mathcal{D}(v_3 := 3)(\gamma_\epsilon)(\sigma\{1/v_1, 2/v_2\}) \\
&= \sigma\{1/v_1\} \cdot \sigma\{1/v_1, 2/v_2\} \cdot \sigma\{1/v_1, 2/v_2, 3/v_3\} \cdot \gamma_\epsilon(\sigma\{1/v_1, 2/v_2, 3/v_3\}) \\
&= \sigma\{1/v_1\} \cdot \sigma\{1/v_1, 2/v_2\} \cdot \sigma\{1/v_1, 2/v_2, 3/v_3\} \cdot \epsilon \\
&= \sigma\{1/v_1\}\sigma\{1/v_1, 2/v_2\}\sigma\{1/v_1, 2/v_2, 3/v_3\}.
\end{aligned}
$$

(2) Abbreviating while $v < 5$ do $v := v + 1$ od by s_{wh} we have

$$
\begin{aligned}
&\mathcal{D}(\text{while } v < 5 \text{ do } v := v + 1 \text{ od})(\gamma_\epsilon)(\sigma\{1/v\}) \\
&= \mathcal{D}(\text{if } v < 5 \text{ then } (v := v + 1;s_{\text{wh}}) \text{ else skip fi})(\gamma_\epsilon)(\sigma\{1/v\})
\end{aligned}
$$

$$= \mathcal{D}(v := v + 1; s_{\mathrm{wh}})(\gamma_\epsilon)(\sigma\{1/v\})$$
$$= \mathcal{D}(v := v + 1)(\mathcal{D}(s_{\mathrm{wh}})(\gamma_\epsilon))(\sigma\{1/v\})$$
$$= \sigma\{2/v\} \cdot \mathcal{D}(s_{\mathrm{wh}})(\gamma_\epsilon)(\sigma\{2/v\})$$
$$= \ldots$$
$$= \sigma\{2/v\} \cdot \sigma\{3/v\} \cdot \sigma\{4/v\} \cdot \sigma\{5/v\} \cdot \mathcal{D}(s_{\mathrm{wh}})(\gamma_\epsilon)(\sigma\{5/v\})$$
$$= \sigma\{2/v\} \cdot \sigma\{3/v\} \cdot \sigma\{4/v\} \cdot \sigma\{5/v\} \cdot$$
$$\quad \mathcal{D}(\text{if } v < 5 \text{ then } (v := v + 1; s_{\mathrm{wh}}) \text{ else skip fi})(\gamma_\epsilon)(\sigma\{5/v\})$$
$$= \sigma\{2/v\} \cdot \sigma\{3/v\} \cdot \sigma\{4/v\} \cdot \sigma\{5/v\} \cdot \mathcal{D}(\text{skip})(\gamma_\epsilon)(\sigma\{5/v\})$$
$$= \sigma\{2/v\} \cdot \sigma\{3/v\} \cdot \sigma\{4/v\} \cdot \sigma\{5/v\} \cdot \sigma\{5/v\} \cdot \gamma_\epsilon(\sigma\{5/v\})$$
$$= \sigma\{2/v\} \cdot \sigma\{3/v\} \cdot \sigma\{4/v\} \cdot \sigma\{5/v\} \cdot \sigma\{5/v\} \cdot \epsilon$$
$$= \sigma\{2/v\}\sigma\{3/v\}\sigma\{4/v\}\sigma\{5/v\}\sigma\{5/v\}.$$

Our task in justifying this definition is somewhat harder than what we had to do for $\mathcal{L}_{rec}$, due to the complications caused by the presence of the continuations. In fact, we shall have to rely on a property of $\mathcal{D}(s)$ which we have not encountered for ($\mathcal{D}$ for) $\mathcal{L}_{rec}$, viz. that $\mathcal{D}(s)$—note that this is a function of argument γ—is $\frac{1}{2}$-contractive in γ. Since $\mathcal{D}$ is—as before—obtained as fixed point of a contractive higher-order mapping $\Psi: Sem_D \to Sem_D$, we shall have to build this property of being $\frac{1}{2}$-contractive in γ into the domain of meanings Sem_D. That is, we take

$$(S \in) Sem_D = Stat \to Cont \xrightarrow{\frac{1}{2}} \mathbb{P}_D . \tag{1.28}$$

Note the appearance of the '$\xrightarrow{\frac{1}{2}}$', replacing the earlier '$\to$'. Altogether, we shall show

Lemma 1.63 *Let Sem_D be as in (1.28), and let $\Psi: Sem_D \to Sem_D$ be given as*

$$\Psi(S)(v := e)(\gamma)(\sigma) \;=\; \sigma\{\alpha/v\} \cdot \gamma(\sigma\{\alpha/v\}), \;\; \text{where } \alpha = \mathcal{V}(e)(\sigma)$$
$$\Psi(S)(\text{skip})(\gamma)(\sigma) \;=\; \sigma \cdot \gamma(\sigma)$$
$$\Psi(S)(s_1; s_2)(\gamma)(\sigma) \;=\; \Psi(S)(s_1)(S(s_2)(\gamma))(\sigma)$$
$$\Psi(S)(\text{if } e \text{ then } s_1 \text{ else } s_2 \text{ fi})(\gamma)(\sigma) \;=\; \begin{cases} \Psi(S)(s_1)(\gamma)(\sigma) & \text{if } \mathcal{V}(e)(\sigma) = tt \\ \Psi(S)(s_2)(\gamma)(\sigma) & \text{if } \mathcal{V}(e)(\sigma) = ff \end{cases}$$
$$\Psi(S)(\text{while } e \text{ do } s \text{ od})(\gamma)(\sigma)$$
$$\qquad = \Psi(S)(\text{if } e \text{ then } (s; \text{while } e \text{ do } s \text{ od}) \text{ else skip fi})(\gamma)(\sigma).$$

Then

(a) $\Psi(S)(s)$ is $\frac{1}{2}$-contractive in γ.

(b) Ψ *is* $\frac{1}{2}$*-contractive in* S.

Proof

(a) Choose S, s, γ_1, γ_2 and σ. We show that

$$d(\Psi(S)(s)(\gamma_1)(\sigma), \Psi(S)(s)(\gamma_2)(\sigma)) \leq \tfrac{1}{2}d(\gamma_1, \gamma_2),$$

by induction on $wgt(s)$. Three subcases.

$[v := e]$ Then

$$\begin{aligned}
&d(\sigma\{\alpha/v\} \cdot \gamma_1(\sigma\{\alpha/v\}), \sigma\{\alpha/v\} \cdot \gamma_2(\sigma\{\alpha/v\})) \\
&= \quad \tfrac{1}{2}d(\gamma_1(\sigma\{\alpha/v\}), \gamma_2(\sigma\{\alpha/v\})) \\
&\leq \quad \tfrac{1}{2}d(\gamma_1, \gamma_2).
\end{aligned}$$

$[s_1;s_2]$ Then

$$\begin{aligned}
&d(\Psi(S)(s_1;s_2)(\gamma_1)(\sigma), \Psi(S)(s_1;s_2)(\gamma_2)(\sigma)) \\
&= \quad d(\Psi(S)(s_1)(S(s_2)(\gamma_1))(\sigma), \Psi(S)(s_1)(S(s_2)(\gamma_2))(\sigma)) \\
&\leq \quad [\text{ind. hyp for } s_1] \; \tfrac{1}{2}d(S(s_2)(\gamma_1), S(s_2)(\gamma_2)) \\
&\leq \quad [S \in Sem_D] \; \tfrac{1}{2} \cdot \tfrac{1}{2}d(\gamma_1, \gamma_2) \\
&\leq \quad \tfrac{1}{2}d(\gamma_1, \gamma_2).
\end{aligned}$$

[while e do s od]   Immediate by induction, since $wgt($while e do s od$)$
   $> wgt($if e then $(s;$while e do s od$)$ else skip fi$)$.

(b) Choose $S_1, S_2, s, \gamma, \sigma$. We show that

$$d(\Psi(S_1)(s)(\gamma)(\sigma), \Psi(S_2)(s)(\gamma)(\sigma)) \leq \tfrac{1}{2}d(S_1, S_2),$$

by induction on $wgt(s)$. One subcase.

$[s_1;s_2]$ We have

$$\begin{aligned}
&d(\Psi(S_1)(s_1;s_2)(\gamma)(\sigma), \Psi(S_2)(s_1;s_2)(\gamma)(\sigma)) \\
&= \quad d(\Psi(S_1)(s_1)(S_1(s_2)(\gamma))(\sigma), \Psi(S_2)(s_1)(S_2(s_2)(\gamma))(\sigma)) \\
&\leq \quad [d \text{ is an ultrametric}] \\
&\quad max\{ \; d(\Psi(S_1)(s_1)(S_1(s_2)(\gamma))(\sigma), \Psi(S_1)(s_1)(S_2(s_2)(\gamma))(\sigma)), \\
&\qquad\qquad d(\Psi(S_1)(s_1)(S_2(s_2)(\gamma))(\sigma), \Psi(S_2)(s_1)(S_2(s_2)(\gamma))(\sigma)) \; \} \\
&\leq \quad [\text{part (a), ind. hyp. for } s_1] \\
&\quad max\{ \tfrac{1}{2}d(S_1(s_2)(\gamma), S_2(s_2)(\gamma)), \tfrac{1}{2}d(S_1, S_2) \} \\
&\leq \quad \tfrac{1}{2}d(S_1, S_2).
\end{aligned}$$

$\square$

Remarks

(1) Note how the step based on the ultrametricity of d is of the form $d(a, b) \leq max\{\, d(a, c), d(c, b)\,\}$ where the c is chosen such that the remaining argument goes through.

(2) One might argue that there are reasons to cast doubt on the well-formedness of Definition 1.62 as a *denotational* definition: For $s \equiv$ while e do s_1 od, $\mathcal{D}(s)$ is defined in terms of a larger construct (viz. if e then $(s_1;s)$ else skip fi) involving s itself as a constituent. There are ways to remedy this problem. A first example (for a language with a construct very similar to the while statement) will be discussed in Section 3.1, and a more general analysis (for $\mathcal{L}_{rec}$) follows in Chapter 8.

Having completed the (justification of the) definition of $\mathcal{D}$, we establish the equivalence of $\mathcal{O}[\![\cdot]\!] = \mathcal{D}[\![\cdot]\!]$ on $\mathcal{L}_{wh}$. As we did for $\mathcal{L}_{rec}$, we shall want to apply Banach's theorem to the mapping Φ characterizing $\mathcal{O}$, and obtain something like $\Phi(\mathcal{D}) = \mathcal{D}$. Since $\mathcal{O}$ and $\Phi(\mathcal{O})$ act on pairs $[r, \sigma]$, whereas $\mathcal{D}$ acts on statements (and $\mathcal{D}(s)(\gamma)$ on states), there is a slight mismatch here, which we remedy by the introduction of two auxiliary (denotational-like) mappings, viz. $\mathcal{E}$ and $\mathcal{E}^*$.

Definition 1.64

(a) $\mathcal{E} \colon Res \to \mathbb{P}_O$ is given by

$$\begin{aligned}
\mathcal{E}(\mathrm{E}) &= \gamma_\epsilon \\
\mathcal{E}(s{:}r) &= \mathcal{D}(s)(\mathcal{E}(r))\,.
\end{aligned}$$

(b) $\mathcal{E}^* \colon Res \times \Sigma \to \Sigma^\infty$ is given by

$$\mathcal{E}^*(r, \sigma) = \mathcal{E}(r)(\sigma)\,.$$

The crucial fixed point property can now be demonstrated for $\mathcal{E}^*$:

Lemma 1.65

$$\Phi(\mathcal{E}^*) = \mathcal{E}^*\,. \tag{1.29}$$

In proving (1.29), we follow an argument based on a property linking the system $\mathcal{T}_{wh}$ and $\mathcal{E}^*$:

Lemma 1.66

(a) $\mathcal{E}^*((s_1;s_2){:}r,\sigma) = \mathcal{E}^*(s_1{:}(s_2{:}r),\sigma)$

(b) $\mathcal{E}^*(\text{if } e \text{ then } s_1 \text{ else } s_2 \text{ fi}{:}r,\sigma)$
$\quad = \text{ if } \mathcal{V}(e)(\sigma) \text{ then } \mathcal{E}^*(s_1{:}r,\sigma) \text{ else } \mathcal{E}^*(s_2{:}r,\sigma) \text{ fi}$

(c) $\mathcal{E}^*(\text{while } e \text{ do } s \text{ od}{:}r,\sigma)$
$\quad = \mathcal{E}^*(\text{if } e \text{ then } (s;\text{while } e \text{ do } s \text{ od}) \text{ else skip fi}{:}r,\sigma).$

Proof We only discuss cases 1.66a and 1.66c. The desired results are immediate by the following calculations involving $\mathcal{E}$:

$[(s_1{:}s_2){:}r,\sigma]$ We have

$$\mathcal{E}((s_1;s_2){:}r) = \mathcal{D}(s_1;s_2)(\mathcal{E}(r)) = \mathcal{D}(s_1)(\mathcal{D}(s_2)(\mathcal{E}(r)))$$
$$= \mathcal{D}(s_1)(\mathcal{E}(s_2{:}r)) = \mathcal{E}(s_1{:}(s_2{:}r)).$$

$[\text{while } e \text{ do } s \text{ od}{:}r,\sigma]$ Putting $s_w \equiv \text{while } e \text{ do } s \text{ od}$ we have

$$\mathcal{E}(s_w{:}r) = \mathcal{D}(s_w)(\mathcal{E}(r)) = \mathcal{D}(\text{if } e \text{ then } (s;s_w) \text{ else skip fi})(\mathcal{E}(r))$$
$$= \mathcal{E}(\text{if } e \text{ then } (s;s_w) \text{ else skip fi}{:}r). \qquad \square$$

We now give the

Proof of Lemma 1.65 We show that, for each r,σ

$$\Phi(\mathcal{E}^*)(r,\sigma) = \mathcal{E}^*(r,\sigma)\,,$$

by induction on $wgt(r)$. Two cases:

$[(v := e){:}r']\qquad \Phi(\mathcal{E}^*)((v := e){:}r',\sigma)$
$\quad = \quad [\alpha = \mathcal{V}(e)(\sigma)]\ \sigma\{\alpha/v\} \cdot \mathcal{E}^*(r',\sigma\{\alpha/v\})$
$\quad = \quad \sigma\{\alpha/v\} \cdot \mathcal{E}(r')(\sigma\{\alpha/v\})$
$\quad = \quad \mathcal{D}(v := e)(\mathcal{E}(r'))(\sigma)$
$\quad = \quad \mathcal{E}((v := e){:}r')(\sigma)$
$\quad = \quad \mathcal{E}^*((v := e){:}r',\sigma)\,.$

$[(s_1;s_2){:}r']\qquad \Phi(\mathcal{E}^*)((s_1;s_2){:}r',\sigma)$
$\quad = \quad [\text{def. } \mathcal{T}_{wh}]\ \Phi(\mathcal{E}^*)(s_1{:}(s_2{:}r'),\sigma)$
$\quad = \quad [\text{ind. hyp.}]\ \mathcal{E}^*(s_1{:}(s_2{:}r'),\sigma)$
$\quad = \quad [\text{Lemma 1.66}]\ \mathcal{E}^*((s_1;s_2){:}r',\sigma)\,. \qquad\qquad \square$

This brings us to the final equivalence result.

Theorem 1.67 $\mathcal{O}[\![\pi]\!] = \mathcal{D}[\![\pi]\!]$, *for each* $\pi \in \mathcal{L}_{wh}$.

Proof Let $s \in \mathcal{L}_{wh}$ and $\sigma \in \Sigma$. Then

$$\mathcal{O}[\![s]\!](\sigma) = \mathcal{O}(s{:}\mathrm{E}, \sigma) = \mathcal{E}^*(s{:}\mathrm{E}, \sigma) = \mathcal{D}(s)(\gamma_\epsilon)(\sigma) = \mathcal{D}[\![s]\!](\sigma). \qquad \square$$

We close this section with a remark on the use of continuations for the denotational semantics for $\mathcal{L}_{wh}$. Though a quite convenient tool, they are by no means essential. A direct semantics, involving an explicit definition of sequential composition on the domain $\Sigma \to \Sigma^\infty$, is feasible as well, though somewhat awkward in its technical details (Exercise 1.19). In most of the sequential languages to be discussed later—especially the nonuniform ones—we shall indeed employ continuations. In a setting with parallelism—many examples will appear in Parts II and III—continuations will be used only in an exceptional case.

1.2.3 Semantics for expressions

So far, we have paid little attention to expressions. We assumed no more than the existence of

- a class of individual variables $(v \in)$ *IVar*
- a class of expressions $(e \in)$ *Exp*.

Moreover, we assumed given a function $\mathcal{V}{:}\, Exp \to \Sigma \to Val$, such that, for $\alpha = \mathcal{V}(e)(\sigma)$, α could be taken as the value of the expression e in state σ. We shall now provide the details omitted up till now, starting with the syntax for *Exp*. In this, we take three sets as starting points:

- $(v \in)$ *IVar*, as introduced already
- $(\alpha \in)$ *Const* $=$ *Val*. We do not bother to distinguish between some α taken as a syntactic constant and as a semantic value.
- $(u \in)$ *Constr*, the set of *constructors*. Constructors will act as function symbols given at the outset (to be contrasted with program-declared functions to be introduced in Chapter 6.2). With each $u \in$ *Constr*, we assume given an arity function $ar{:}\, Constr \to \mathbb{N}$, with $ar(u) = k \geq 1$. Moreover, we assume, for each u, an interpretation $\hat{u}{:}\, Val^k \to Val$ where $k = ar(u)$.

We now give

Definition 1.68 $e ::= \alpha \mid v \mid u(e_1, \ldots, e_k)$, for $k = \text{ar}(u)$.

Examples $<(v, 5), +(v, 1), +(+(v, 2), +(3, 4)), +(+(v_1, v_2), +(3, 4))$.

We next develop the operational semantics for *Exp*. Once again, this is based on a transition system specification, as described in

Definition 1.69 $\mathcal{T}_{exp} = (Exp, \Sigma, \rightarrow, Spec)$. Transitions are here written as $[e_1, \sigma] \rightarrow e_2$ (rather than $e_1 \overset{\sigma}{\rightarrow} e_2$). *Spec* consists of

- $$[\alpha, \sigma] \rightarrow \alpha \qquad\qquad\qquad\qquad\text{(Val)}$$

- $$[v, \sigma] \rightarrow \sigma(v) \qquad\qquad\qquad\qquad\text{(IVar)}$$

- $$\frac{[e_1, \sigma] \rightarrow \alpha_1, \ldots, [e_k, \sigma] \rightarrow \alpha_k}{[u(e_1, \ldots, e_k), \sigma] \rightarrow \hat{u}(\alpha_1, \ldots, \alpha_k)} \qquad\qquad\text{(Constr)}$$

Note how, in the rule (Constr), the right-hand side $\hat{u}(\alpha_1, \ldots, \alpha_k)$ appearing in the conclusion, determines a value in *Val* by the definition of $\hat{u}$.

Example Suppose $\sigma(v_1) = 1$, $\sigma(v_2) = 2$ and that '+' has the usual interpretation.

(1) $[v_1, \sigma] \rightarrow 1$, $[v_2, \sigma] \rightarrow 2$, so $[+(v_1, v_2), \sigma] \rightarrow 3$.

(2) $[3, \sigma] \rightarrow 3$, $[4, \sigma] \rightarrow 4$, so $[+(3, 4), \sigma] \rightarrow 7$.

(3) From (1) and (2) it follows by (Constr) that

$[+(+(v_1, v_2), +(3, 4)), \sigma] \rightarrow 10$.

The definition of $\mathcal{O}: Exp \rightarrow \Sigma \rightarrow Val$ based on $\mathcal{T}_{exp}$ is much simpler than the definitions encountered so far, since there is no need to cope with possibly infinite behaviour. (Even stronger, we even do not need *sequences* of transitions.) We have

Definition 1.70 $\mathcal{O}(e)(\sigma) = \alpha$ iff $[e, \sigma] \rightarrow \alpha$.

Examples Again assume $\sigma(v_1) = 1$, $\sigma(v_2) = 2$. $\mathcal{O}(v_1)(\sigma) = 1$, $\mathcal{O}(+(v_1, v_2)) = 3$, $\mathcal{O}(+(+(v_1, v_2), +(3,4))) = 10$.

In the denotational definition for *Exp*, we can be equally quick. No more is needed than a simple definition by structural induction on e.

Definition 1.71 $\mathcal{V}$:*Exp* $\to \Sigma \to$ *Val* is given by

$$
\begin{aligned}
\mathcal{V}(\alpha)(\sigma) &= \alpha \\
\mathcal{V}(v)(\sigma) &= \sigma(v) \\
\mathcal{V}(u(e_1, \ldots, e_k))(\sigma) &= \hat{u}(\mathcal{V}(e_1)(\sigma), \ldots, \mathcal{V}(e_k)(\sigma)) \; .
\end{aligned}
$$

Examples

(1) Let the infix written '$<$' be the interpretation for $< \, \in$ *Constr*.

$$
\begin{aligned}
&\mathcal{V}(<(v, 5))(\sigma\{4/v\}) \\
&= \mathcal{V}(v)(\sigma\{4/v\}) < \mathcal{V}(5)(\sigma\{4/v\}) \\
&= \sigma\{4/v\}(v) < 5 \\
&= 4 < 5 \\
&= tt.
\end{aligned}
$$

(2) Let the infix written '$+$' be the interpretation of $+ \in$ *Constr* and assume $\sigma(v_1) = 1$, $\sigma(v_2) = 2$. We then have

$$
\begin{aligned}
&\mathcal{V}(+(+(v_1, v_2), +(3, 4)))(\sigma) \\
&= \mathcal{V}(+(v_1, v_2))(\sigma) + \mathcal{V}(+(3, 4))(\sigma) \\
&= (\mathcal{V}(v_1)(\sigma) + \mathcal{V}(v_2)(\sigma)) + (\mathcal{V}(3)(\sigma) + \mathcal{V}(4)(\sigma)) \\
&= (1 + 2) + (3 + 4) \\
&= 3 + 7 \\
&= 10.
\end{aligned}
$$

Well-definedness of $\mathcal{V}$ on *Exp* is immediate.
Of course, we have

Lemma 1.72 $\mathcal{O} = \mathcal{V}$ *on Exp.*

Proof We show that, for all e and σ, $\mathcal{O}(e)(\sigma) = \mathcal{V}(e)(\sigma)$, by structural induction on e. One subcase.

$[u(e_1, \ldots, e_k)]$ We have

$$\mathcal{O}(u(e_1, \ldots, e_k))(\sigma) = \alpha$$
$$\Leftrightarrow \quad [\text{def. } \mathcal{O}] \; [u(e_1, \ldots, e_k), \sigma] \to \alpha$$
$$\Leftrightarrow \quad [\text{rule (Constr)}] \; [e_1, \sigma] \to \alpha_1, \ldots, [e_k, \sigma] \to \alpha_k, \; \alpha = \hat{u}(\alpha_1, \ldots, \alpha_k)$$
$$\Leftrightarrow \quad [\text{def. } \mathcal{O}] \; \mathcal{O}(e_1)(\sigma) = \alpha_1, \ldots, \mathcal{O}(e_k)(\sigma) = \alpha_k, \; \alpha = \hat{u}(\alpha_1, \ldots, \alpha_k)$$
$$\Leftrightarrow \quad [\text{ind. hyp.}] \; \mathcal{V}(e_1)(\sigma) = \alpha_1, \ldots, \mathcal{V}(e_k)(\sigma) = \alpha_k, \; \alpha = \hat{u}(\alpha_1, \ldots, \alpha_k)$$
$$\Leftrightarrow \quad [\text{def. } \mathcal{V}] \; \mathcal{V}(u(e_1, \ldots, e_k))(\sigma) = \alpha \; . \qquad \qquad \qquad \square$$

Compared to the complications we faced when dealing with $\mathcal{L}_{rec}$ or (the control flow of) $\mathcal{L}_{wh}$, all the above is remarkably simple. (The reader will appreciate here how the guarantee of finite behaviour greatly simplifies the analysis.) In later chapters, we shall deal with situations where there is a more interesting interplay between statements and expressions. More specifically, we shall investigate *function procedures*—a means for the programmer to introduce functions—in Chapter 6.2, and concurrent evaluation of expressions in Chapter 7.2. In both settings, we shall develop definitions in which there is a non-trivial interference between the evaluation of the expressions and statements concerned. One remark anticipating this (fulfilling an earlier promise): We say that the evaluation of an expression exhibits a *side-effect* (on the state), when, instead of $\mathcal{V}(e)(\sigma) = \alpha$, it is meaningful to write $\mathcal{V}(e)(\sigma) = \langle \alpha, \sigma' \rangle$. The latter equation expresses that the evaluation of e in σ both delivers a value α and an, in general changed, state σ'. Many details will appear in the announced chapters.

1.3   Exercises

Exercise 1.1 Assume the definitions of Section 1.1.1. Let D be such that $D(x) = a;y$, $D(y) = b;x$. Determine $wgt(D|x)$ and $\mathcal{O}_d(D|x)$.

Exercise 1.2 Suppose that we do not require D to be guarded for each argument, say by replacing $(D \in) \, Decl = PVar \to GStat$ by $(D \in) \, Decl = PVar \to Stat$. Use the example $\pi = (x \Leftarrow x;a|x)$ to show that $\mathcal{O}_d(\pi)$ and $wgt(\pi)$ are then undefined, and that Lemma 1.9b no longer holds.

Exercise 1.3 Let $T = (Conf, Obs, \rightarrow, Spec)$ be a transition system specification, and put $\mathcal{U} = Conf \times Obs \times Conf$. Prove that

(a) $\mathcal{U}$ satisfies $Spec$ (irrespective of the form of $Spec$).

(b) Let $X_1, X_2 \subseteq \mathcal{U}$. If X_1, X_2 satisfy $Spec$, then so does $X_1 \cap X_2$.

(c) There exists a *least* set (viz. '$\rightarrow$') satisfying $Spec$. (Hint: Take $\rightarrow\ =\ \bigcap\{X \subseteq \mathcal{U} \mid X$ satisfies $Spec\}$.)

Exercise 1.4

(a) If a Cauchy sequence has a convergent subsequence, then it is convergent.

(b) Let $(a, b \in) A$ be some alphabet. Prove that $(a^n b^n)_n$ is a Cauchy sequence in (A^*, d_B) and that $(a^n b^n)_n$ converges to a^ω in (A^∞, d_B).

(c) Let $(w_n)_n$ be a Cauchy sequence in (A^∞, d_B). Prove that $(w_n)_n$ has a subsequence $(w_{f(n)})_n$ such that

$$\forall k \forall i, j \geq k\ [d_B(w_{f(i)}, w_{f(j)}) \leq 2^{-k}].$$

Exercise 1.5 Let $a \in A$, $w \in A^\infty$. Define $a \cdot w$ based on Definition 1.17.

Exercise 1.6

(a) Let $(\mathbb{R}, d_\mathbb{R})$ be the space of real numbers. Let $\beta \in [0, 1]$. Show that $f : \mathbb{R} \rightarrow \mathbb{R}$ given by $f(x) = \beta \cdot x$ is α-Lipschitz for each α, $\beta \leq \alpha \leq 1$.

(b) Let M, M_1, M_2 be metric spaces, and let $f_i : M \rightarrow M_i$, $i = 1, 2$. Let $f = \langle f_1, f_2 \rangle : M \rightarrow M_1 \times M_2$ be given by $f(x) = \langle f_1(x), f_2(x) \rangle$.

   (i) Show that, if f_1, f_2 are continuous then so is f.

   (ii) Let f_i be α_i-Lipschitz, $i = 1, 2$. Determine (the least) α such that $\langle f_1, f_2 \rangle$ is α-Lipschitz.

(c) Give an example of a function which is continuous but not nonexpansive.

Exercise 1.7 Let $(x \in) M$, $(y \in) N$ be complete metric spaces. Assume that $f: M \to (N \to N)$ is α-Lipschitz in x and contractive in y. Show that

$$d(\text{fix}(f(x)), \text{fix}(f(x'))) \leq \alpha \cdot d(x, x'),$$

for all $x, x' \in M$.

Exercise 1.8 Let (M, d) be a metric space and let $x \in M$, $f: M \to M$ be such that $x = \text{fix}(f \circ f)$ (i.e., x is the unique fixed point of the function $f \circ f = \lambda y.f(f(y))$). Prove that $x = \text{fix}(f)$.

Exercise 1.9 Prove Lemma 1.19a,b and Lemma 1.21.

Exercise 1.10 Let *Fun* be a collection of function symbols with $\text{ar}(f) \in \mathbb{N}$ the *arity* of f (required number of arguments). Assume that *Fun* contains at least one 0-ary function symbol (i.e., a constant), and define *Term* as the least set satisfying

$$Term \;=\; \{\, f(t_1, ..., t_n) \mid f \in Fun, \text{ar}(f) = n, t_1, ..., t_n \in Term \,\}.$$

For $s, t \in Term$ with $s = f(t_1, ..., t_n)$, $t = g(t'_1, ..., t'_m)$, we define

$$d(s, t) \;=\; \begin{cases} 1 & \text{if } f \neq g \\ \frac{1}{2} max\{\, d(t_i, t'_i) \mid 1 \leq i \leq n = \text{ar}(f) \,\} & \text{if } f = g \text{ and } \text{ar}(f) > 0. \\ 0 & \text{if } f = g \text{ and } \text{ar}(f) = 0. \end{cases}$$

Prove that *Term* is an ultrametric space. Is *Term* complete?

Exercise 1.11 Define, for any $a \in A$, a relation $\xrightarrow{a} \; \subseteq A^\infty \times A^\infty$ by putting $w \xrightarrow{a} w'$ iff $w = a \cdot w'$. Define, inductively,

$$\begin{aligned} \sim_0 \;&=\; A^\infty \times A^\infty \\ \sim_{n+1} \;&=\; \{\, (w_1, w_2) \in A^\infty \times A^\infty \mid \\ & \qquad (w_1 \xrightarrow{a} w'_1 \Rightarrow \exists w'_2 \, [w_2 \xrightarrow{a} w'_2 \wedge w'_1 \sim_n w'_2]) \wedge \\ & \qquad (w_2 \xrightarrow{a} w'_2 \Rightarrow \exists w'_1 \, [w_1 \xrightarrow{a} w'_1 \wedge w'_1 \sim_n w'_2]) \,\}. \end{aligned}$$

Prove that, for all $v, w \in A^\infty$,

$$d_B(v, w) \;=\; inf\{\, 2^{-n} \mid v \sim_n w \,\}.$$

Infer that, putting $\sim \, = \bigcap_n \sim_n$, we have that $v \sim w$ iff $d_B(v, w) = 0$ (iff $v = w$).

Exercise 1.12 Let $(p_1, p_2 \in) Act^\infty$ and $;: Act^\infty \times Act^\infty \to Act^\infty$ be as in Section 1.1.3.

(a) Prove $a^\omega; b = a^\omega$, $a^n; a^\omega = a^\omega$, $n \geq 0$.

(b) Let $\hat{;}: Act^\infty \times Act^\infty \to Act^\infty$ be given by $p_1 \hat{;} p_2 = p_1$, for $p_1 \in Act^\omega$, $\epsilon \hat{;} p = p$, $(a \cdot p') \hat{;} p = a \cdot (p' \hat{;} p)$, for $p' \in Act^*$. Prove that '$;$' is well-defined and that $\hat{;} = ;$.

Exercise 1.13 Show by an example that Lemma 1.41 does not hold on Act^∞ $(= \mathbb{P}_D \cup \{\epsilon\})$.

Exercise 1.14 Let Ψ be as in Definition 1.40, let $S_0 = \lambda \pi.a$ and $S_{n+1} = \Psi(S_n)$, $n = 0, 1, \ldots$.

(a) Show that $\mathcal{D} = lim_n S_n$.

(b) Let $\pi = (x \Leftarrow a; x \mid x)$. Determine $S_0(\pi)$ and $S_{n+1}(\pi)$, $n = 0, 1, \ldots$.

(c) Prove Lemma 1.43b using that $\mathcal{D}(\pi) = lim_n S_n(\pi)$.

Exercise 1.15 Let Ψ be as in Definition 1.40 and $\mathcal{O}$ as in Definition 1.44a.

(a) Prove that $\Psi(\mathcal{O}) = \mathcal{O}$ (without using Theorem 1.50), and use this to obtain an alternative proof of Theorem 1.50.

(b) Prove Theorem 1.50 using the '$\varepsilon \leq \frac{1}{2}\varepsilon$' principle.

Exercise 1.16 Put $A = Act \cup PVar \cup \{(,),;\}$, and let $(v, w \in) A^*$ be as usual. Let $(V, W \in) \mathcal{P}(A^*)$ be the collection of all subsets of A^*. On A^* and $\mathcal{P}(A^*)$ we assume the standard concatenation operators, e.g., $VW = \{vw \mid v \in V, w \in W\}$.

(a) Let $Stat_0 = \emptyset$, $Stat_{n+1} = Act \cup PVar \cup \{(\}Stat_n\{;\}Stat_n\{)\}$. Prove that $Stat$ (as in Definition 1.1) $= \bigcup_{n=0}^{\infty} Stat_n$.

(b) Let $\Omega: \mathcal{P}(A^*) \to \mathcal{P}(A^*)$ be given by $\Omega(V) = Act \cup PVar \cup \{(\}V\{;\}V\{)\}$. Show that $Stat$ is the *least* fixed point of Ω, i.e., that $\Omega(Stat) = Stat$, and that, for each W such that $\Omega(W) = W$, we have that $Stat \subseteq W$.

(c) Formulate the counterpart of parts (a) and (b) for the set $GStat$.

Exercise 1.17 Prove Lemma 1.54.

Exercise 1.18 Let *wgt* be as in Definition 1.60.

(a) Prove that *wgt* is well-defined.

(b) Prove Lemma 1.59.

Exercise 1.19 Design operational and denotational semantics for $\mathcal{L}_{wh}$ in terms of simple resumptions ($r ::= \mathrm{E} \mid s$) and without continuations. (Hint: the key part is the definition, for $p_1, p_2 \in \Sigma \to \Sigma^\omega \cup \Sigma^+$, of the concatenation $p_1 \hat{;} p_2$. Let $last\colon \Sigma^+ \to \Sigma$ be the function yielding the last element of a (finite nonempty) sequence. We put

$$p_1 \hat{;} p_2(\sigma) \;=\; \left\{ \begin{array}{ll} p_1(\sigma) & \text{if } p_1(\sigma) \in \Sigma^\omega \\ p_1(\sigma); p_2(last(p_1(\sigma))) & \text{otherwise} \end{array} \right.$$

where ';' is the usual concatenation on Σ^∞.)

Exercise 1.20 Design syntax and semantics of a nonuniform language with recursion (and without while statements), say $\mathcal{L}_{rec,n}$, and show that, for each $s \in \mathcal{L}_{wh}$ there exists $\pi \in \mathcal{L}_{rec,n}$ such that $\mathcal{D}[\![s]\!] = \mathcal{D}[\![\pi]\!]$. (Hint: use declarations $x \Leftarrow$ if e then $s;x$ else skip fi.)

Exercise 1.21 Consider the repeat statement

$s_r =$ repeat s until e end,

with as characterizing equivalence

$s_r \;=\; s;$if $\neg e$ then $s;s_r$ else skip fi.

Design $\mathcal{O}$ and $\mathcal{D}$ for a language incorporating this construct, and prove $\mathcal{O}[\![\cdot]\!] = \mathcal{D}[\![\cdot]\!]$.

Exercise 1.22 (The '$\varepsilon \le \frac{1}{2}\varepsilon$' principle and the unique fixed point principle based on Banach's theorem are equivalent.)

Principle 1 Let M be a metric space, and let $x, y \in M$. If $d(x, y) \le \frac{1}{2}d(x, y)$, then $x = y$. (We usually apply the principle to the case $f, g \colon M_1 \to M_2$, with $\varepsilon = d(f, g) = sup\{\, d(f(x), g(x)) \mid x \in M_1 \,\}$.)

Principle 2 Let M be a metric space, and let $x, y \in M$. If there exists an $\frac{1}{2}$-contractive function $f \colon M \to M$ such that $f(x) = x$, $f(y) = y$, then $x = y$.

Show that Principle 1 $\leftrightarrow$ Principle 2. (Hint: To show '$\Leftarrow$', take $M = \{x, y\}$, and take for f the identity function which is $\frac{1}{2}$-contractive on M by assumption. To show '$\Rightarrow$', assume that f satisfies the given conditions. Then $d(x, y) = d(f(x), f(y)) \le \frac{1}{2}d(x, y)$.)

1.4   Bibliographical notes

Ever since the advent of machine independent general purpose programming languages such as LISP ([McC62]) or Algol 60 ([Nau63]), a variety of methods has been proposed to model their semantics. The operational style of semantics goes back to the early sixties, in which period a number of definitional approaches based on abstract machines were developed, e.g., Landin's SECD machine ([Lan64]) or the Vienna Definition Language ([LW71]). The use of labeled transition systems in designing semantics seems to originate with Keller ([Kel76]). Shortly afterwards Plotkin (partly in joint work with Hennessy) successfully advocated the use of transition system specifications in operational semantics ([HP79, Plo81], see also [Plo77]). At present, this definitional approach—also known as the SOS (for Structural Operational Semantics) method—has become the predominant one in operational semantics.

The principles of denotational semantics were developed by Scott and Strachey from 1969 onwards, see, e.g., [Sco70, SS71]. In order to deal with recursive constructs, one has to use domains which allow the definition of fixed points. Various mathematical structures have been used for this purpose. During the first decade, ordered sets were used primarily (see the textbooks [Sto77, Gor79] and the monograph [MS76]). Often, these sets are defined as solutions of recursive equations (cf. [Sco76, SP82]). In the late seventies, the use of *metric spaces* in semantics was proposed by Arnold and Nivat ([Niv79, AN80a, AN80b, ANN85]). The solving of domain equations over metric spaces was first studied by De Bakker and Zucker ([BZ82]). In a series of subsequent papers, De Bakker and his coworkers (the so-called Amsterdam Concurrency Group or ACG) have designed metric semantic models for a large number of programming notions. An introductory paper is [BM88]; in several theses, the methodology has been applied to a variety of language paradigms and associated foundational problems (America and Rutten [AR89a], Kok [Kok89], Eliëns [Eli92], Horita [Hor93b], and Van Breugel [Bre94b]). The book [BR92] contains a selection of the papers from a decade work of ACG. [Bre94b] provides a comprehensive account of the use of topological (in particular metric) models in semantics, including several more advanced investigations not dealt with in the present book.

Metric denotational semantics has also been studied, e.g., by the Programming Research Group of Oxford University ([RR88, Ree89]) and by Majster-Cederbaum et al. ([MZ91, MZ94]). Metric techniques in designing operational semantics (for recursion) are investigated in [Bru84]; [Kui81] uses metric tools to prove an operational and a denotational semantics equivalent for a simple language. (More references and applications of metric semantics by ACG and other groups will follow in subsequent bibliographical sections.)

Metric spaces are a specialization of topological spaces. A standard text on topology is [Eng89]; see also [Smy92]. Our notion of Baire metric is a variation on the definition in [Bai09]. Banach's theorem is from [Ban22]. Besides its use in the *definition* of various entities as unique fixed points of some contractive endofunction (on a complete space), it also induces the unique fixed point principle as a tool to prove elements of a metric space equal. In semantics, this proof principle has been introduced by Kok and Rutten in the important paper [KR90]. The use of higher-order operators in the definition of both $\mathcal{O}$ and $\mathcal{D}$ is also from [KR90]. Prior, Hennessy and Plotkin ([HP79]) presented an order-theoretic variant of the proof principle based on the Knaster-Tarski theorem ([Kna28, Tar55]). (The latter is the order-theoretic analogue of Banach's theorem, stating that each monotonic endofunction on a complete lattice has a *least* fixed point.) The proof technique which we have baptized the '$\varepsilon \leq \varepsilon/2$' principle is probably standard in general metric studies; in semantics, it was first applied in [ABKR89]. Exercise 1.22 is due to Van Breugel.

The programming constructs of recursion and iteration are fundamental in all (higher) programming languages. Recursion dates back to the notion of recursive function in mathematical logic (e.g., [Kle52]). In programming, its first appearance was in languages such as LISP ([McC62]) or ALGOL 60 ([Nau63]). The rudimentary language $\mathcal{L}_{rec}$ in which we have embedded recursion is in fact a simplified version of the notion of a context free language as standard in formal language theory (cf. also the bibliographical notes in Section 2.3). The fixed point approach to recursion is pervasive in all of (denotational) semantics; for further references cf. Section 8.6. The terminology of uniform versus nonuniform was introduced in [BKMOZ85, BMOZ88]. The guardedness condition (which plays a key role as well in many subsequent chapters) corresponds to the Greibach condition in formal language theory (cf. [Niv79]). The use of the empty resumption E originates with [Apt83]. Zero-step transitions have been introduced in [Bak91].

States (in the form $\Sigma = IVar \rightarrow Val$) are a standard notion in all semantic modeling, used in some form in each of the semantic methodologies. Continuations constitute a classical tool in denotational semantics. They originate with Wadsworth ([SW74]) and Mazurkiewicz ([Maz71]). (A historical overview can be found in [Rey93].) The systematic use of resumptions in operational semantics as a counterpart of continuations is due to the present authors (e.g., [BV91]). Our use of the *wgt*-function (in Chapter 1 and *passim* in later chapters) systematizes earlier complexity arguments as used, e.g., in [BM88] or [KR90].

2 Nondeterminacy

In this chapter we study the programming notion of nondeterminacy. Computations may be nondeterminate in the sense that their outcome is not uniquely defined. Rather, the possible results are specified as belonging to a *set*, say X, of outcomes. Recalling that $|X|$ stands for the number of elements in X, we may, in general, have both $|X| > 1$ or $|X| = 0$ (in addition to the case $|X| = 1$, as we had so far). We shall also encounter the case that $|X| = \infty$, i.e., X has an infinite number of elements.

Clearly, the possibility of sets of outcomes requires an extension of the metric framework as introduced in Chapter 1. Both in the general setting (for a metric space (M, d)) and in the specialized (semantic) situation with spaces such as (Act^∞, d_B), we always worked with (distances on) single elements. More specifically, both for $(s \in) \mathcal{L}_{rec}$ and $(s \in) \mathcal{L}_{wh}$, we have that $\mathcal{O}[\![s]\!]$ (and $\mathcal{D}[\![s]\!]$) deliver *points* in a space $((Act^\infty, d)$ and $(\Sigma \to \Sigma^\infty, d)$, respectively). We are now setting the stage for the semantic modeling of programming constructs where sets of results may be delivered. Mathematically, this induces the need to study, besides spaces (M, d) as already considered, also spaces $(\mathcal{P}(M), d')$, where $\mathcal{P}(M)$ denotes the *power set* (all subsets) of M, and d' is a distance still to be defined (in terms of the given d). It will turn out that the metric framework cannot be developed for $\mathcal{P}(M)$ in general, but for certain special kinds of subsets of M, viz. the *closed* subsets and the *compact* subsets. Both these notions are central in general topology, and we have an extensive collection of topological properties at our disposal to exploit in our semantic investigations. Fortunately, only a modest number of classical results will be needed for our purposes. In general, we shall be concerned primarily with the powerdomain of compact sets, to be denoted by $\mathcal{P}_{co}(M)$; the powerdomain $\mathcal{P}_{cl}(M)$ of closed subsets will play a secondary role. (It will appear especially in Chapters 5 to 7.) As we shall see, compactness is a generalization of finiteness. Since most of the forms of nondeterminacy as studied in our book can be seen, operationally, as having a *finitary* nature (the technical term is "finitely branching," a key property of transition systems), it is to be expected that the compactness property is fundamental in our studies.

In Section 2.1 we present the metric tools necessary to deal with spaces of sets, also called *hyperspaces*. Section 2.2 is devoted to a simple extension of $\mathcal{L}_{rec}$ with nondeterminacy. We add the language construct $s_1 + s_2$ to the syntax for $\mathcal{L}_{rec}$, with the intended interpretation that either s_1 or s_2 is to be executed. In this way, we introduce a basic form of nondeterminacy into the language. Let us call the extended language $\mathcal{L}_{cf}$ (the reasons for the abbreviation "*cf*" will be disclosed soon). Once the metric means to deal with hyperspaces have been developed, we shall be able to design the semantics for $\mathcal{L}_{cf}$ in a way which closely follows the general approach as described earlier for $\mathcal{L}_{rec}$. In fact, with the combined results for metric spaces (Section 1.1.2) and metric hyperspaces (Section 2.1), we have available a powerful set of tools, sufficient for all semantic modeling in Parts I and II of our treatise (altogether dealing with 17 languages). Only in Part III will the need arise for another chapter devoted to the mathematical foundations, this time dealing with so-called *domain equations*.

2.1   Metric hyperspaces

For (M, d) a metric space, we shall introduce the notions of a closed and a compact subset of M, and the associated powerdomains $(\mathcal{P}_{cl}(M), d')$ and $(\mathcal{P}_{co}(M), d')$, for d' a distance on (closed or compact) sets still to be defined. As fundamental results of this section we already mention

- the definition of d' as the so-called *Hausdorff distance* d_H
- the theorems (by *Hahn* and *Kuratowski*) stating that, for (M, d) complete, $(\mathcal{P}_{cl}(M), d')$ and $(\mathcal{P}_{co}(M), d')$ are also complete
- various closure properties involving compactness, stating its preservation under, e.g., continuous mappings, product, or union (over a finite or, even, a compact (explanations follow) index set)
- the characterization of compactness as a limit case of finiteness.

  Unless explicitly stated otherwise, from now on all metrics considered are assumed to be 1-bounded, i.e., distances range from 0 up to 1.

2.1.1   Closed sets

Definition 2.1   Let (M, d) be a metric space.

(a) A subset X of M is called *closed* if each convergent sequence $(x_n)_n$, with $x_n \in X$, $n = 0, 1, \ldots$, has its limit x in X.

(b) For $X \subseteq M$, $\bar{X}$ denotes the smallest closed set containing X, i.e., we put $\bar{X} = \bigcap \{ Y \mid X \subseteq Y, Y \text{ closed} \}$. We call $\bar{X}$ the *closure* of X.

Examples   Let (M, d) be a metric space.

(1) $\emptyset$ and M are closed.

(2) If X_i, $i = 1, \ldots, n$, is closed, then $\bigcup_{i=1}^{n} X_i$ is closed.

(3) If I is an arbitrary index set, and all X_i, $i \in I$, are closed, then $\bigcap_{i \in I} X_i$ is closed.

(4) If X_i is closed in (M_i, d_i), $i = 1, 2$, then $X_1 \times X_2$ is closed in $(M_1 \times M_2, d_P)$.

(5) X is closed iff $X = \bar{X}$. Also $\bar{\bar{X}} = \bar{X}$; $X \subseteq Y \Rightarrow \bar{X} \subseteq \bar{Y}$.

We write $\mathcal{P}_{cl}(M)$ for the collection of all closed subsets of M, and $\mathcal{P}_{ncl}(M)$ for the collection of all *nonempty* and closed subsets of M.

Our first task is to define a *metric* on $\mathcal{P}_{cl}(M)$ in terms of the given metric d. For this purpose, we use a classical definition, viz. the so-called Hausdorff distance on sets. In words, we put $d_H(X, Y) = \alpha$, if α is the least among (or, more precisely, the infimum over) all numbers such that, for all $x \in X$ there exists $y \in Y$ with $d(x, y) < \alpha$, and symmetrically. This is stated formally in

Definition 2.2 Let (M, d) be a metric space, and let $X, Y \subseteq M$. We define the *Hausdorff distance* d_H on $\mathcal{P}(M) \times \mathcal{P}(M)$ by putting

$$d_H(X, Y) \;=\; inf\{\, \alpha > 0 \mid \forall x \in X \exists y \in Y [d(x, y) < \alpha] \qquad (2.1)$$
$$\wedge\, \forall y \in Y \exists x \in X [d(x, y) < \alpha]\,\},$$

with the convention that $inf(\emptyset) = 1$.

Remark Note that in this definition we do not (yet) require that X and Y be closed. As we shall see in a moment, the result that d_H is a metric does rely on X, Y being closed.

Examples

(1) $d_H(\{x\}, \{y\}) = d(x, y)$

(2) $d_H(\{\, \epsilon, a, \ldots, a^n \,\}, a^*) = 2^{-n}$

(3) $d_H(a^*, a^* \cup \{a^\omega\}) = 0$.

The key theorem on d_H is

Theorem 2.3

(a) If (M,d) is a metric space, then $(\mathcal{P}_{cl}(M), d_H)$ is a metric space.

(b) As part (a), with "ultrametric" replacing "metric."

Proof

(a) We verify conditions (M1), (M2) and (M3) from Definition 1.15.

(M1) First assume $X = Y$. Since, for each $\alpha > 0$, we have that $\forall x \in X \exists y \in Y[d(x,y) < \alpha]$ (simply take $y = x$), we have $d_H(X,Y) = inf\{\alpha \mid \alpha > 0\} = 0$. Conversely, assume $d_H(X,Y) = 0$. Let $x \in X$ and choose, for each $n \in \mathbb{N}$, $y_n \in Y$ such that $d(x, y_n) < 2^{-n}$. Then $lim_n y_n = x$. Since $(y_n)_n$ is a convergent sequence in the closed set Y, we have $x \in Y$, hence $X \subseteq Y$. Symmetrically, we obtain $Y \subseteq X$, and $X = Y$ follows.

(M2) Clear from the symmetry in the definition of d_H.

(M3) Choose $X, Y, Z \in \mathcal{P}_{cl}(M)$. Put

$$A_1 = \{\alpha > 0 \mid \forall x \in X \exists z \in Z[d(x,z) < \alpha] \text{ and symmetrically }\}$$
$$A_2 = \{\alpha > 0 \mid \forall z \in Z \exists y \in Y[d(z,y) < \alpha] \text{ and symmetrically }\}.$$

Choose some $\alpha_1 \in A_1$, $\alpha_2 \in A_2$. Let $x \in X$. Choose $z \in Z$ such that $d(x,z) < \alpha_1$. Choose $y \in Y$ such that $d(z,y) < \alpha_2$. Then $d(x,y) < \alpha_1 + \alpha_2$, by (M3) for (M,d). Hence $\forall x \in X \exists y \in Y[d(x,y) < \alpha_1 + \alpha_2]$. Similarly, $\forall y \in Y \exists x \in X[d(y,x) < \alpha_1 + \alpha_2]$. Thus $d_H(X,Y) \leq \alpha_1 + \alpha_2$. Taking infima over A_1 and A_2, we obtain $d_H(X,Y) \leq d_H(X,Z) + d_H(Z,Y)$, as desired.

(b) The proof of $(M4)$ is very similar to that of (M3), and left as an exercise. □

The next example is important in semantics.

Example For $a \in A$, $X \subseteq A^\infty$, we put $a \cdot X = \{a \cdot x \mid x \in X\}$. In $(\mathcal{P}_{ncl}(A^\infty), d_H)$ we have that $d_H(a \cdot X, a \cdot Y) = \frac{1}{2} d_H(X,Y)$. The example $d_H(a \cdot \emptyset, a \cdot \{b\}) = 1 \neq \frac{1}{2} d(\emptyset, \{b\}) = \frac{1}{2}$ shows that the restriction to *nonempty* sets is essential here.

We draw special attention to this example. As will become clear in due course, e.g., in Lemma 2.33, it motivates the restriction to the powerdomain of *nonempty* (closed or compact) sets in all semantic applications studied in Parts I and II.

A useful property of d_H which we shall often use in later arguments is

Lemma 2.4 *Let $n \geq 1$, $X_i, Y_i \in \mathcal{P}_{cl}(M)$, $i = 1, \ldots, n$, and let $X = \bigcup_{i=1}^{n} X_i$, $Y = \bigcup_{i=1}^{n} Y_i$. Then*

$$d_H(X, Y) \leq max\{\, d_H(X_i, Y_i) \mid 1 \leq i \leq n\,\}.$$

Proof We apply a simple property of the (order on) real numbers, viz. that, in order to prove $\alpha_1 \leq \alpha_2$ for $\alpha_1, \alpha_2 \geq 0$, it is sufficient to show that $\forall \epsilon > 0\,[\alpha_2 < \epsilon \Rightarrow \alpha_1 \leq \epsilon]$. Choose $\epsilon > 0$ such that $max\{\, d_H(X_i, Y_i) \mid 1 \leq i \leq n\,\} < \epsilon$. Choose $x \in X$, say $x \in X_i$, for some i, $1 \leq i \leq n$. We can choose $y \in Y_i$ such that $d(x, y) < \epsilon$ (Exercise 2.7). So $\forall x \in X \exists y \in Y[d(x, y) < \epsilon]$. Similarly, $\forall y \in Y \exists x \in X[d(x, y) < \epsilon]$. Hence, $d_H(X, Y) \leq \epsilon$. Conclusion: $d_H(X, Y) \leq max\{\, d_H(X_i, Y_i) \mid 1 \leq i \leq n\,\}$.

In the statement of this lemma, we used that $\bigcup_{i=1}^{n} X_i$ is closed for X_i closed, $1 \leq i \leq n$. In general, $\bigcup_{i \in I} X_i$ is not closed for an arbitrary index set I (cf. Exercise 2.1). In case we do know, by some additional argument, that the X_i, $i \in I$, are such that $\bigcup_{i \in I} X_i$ *is* closed, then the above lemma applies as well, since the argument in its proof does not rely on the finiteness of I. In its general form, the lemma reads as follows:

Lemma 2.5 *Let X_i, Y_i, $i \in I$ be closed sets, and assume that we have that $X = \bigcup_{i \in I} X_i$, $Y = \bigcup_{i \in I} Y_i$ are closed. Then we have*

$$d_H(X, Y) \leq sup\{\, d_H(X_i, Y_i) \mid i \in I\,\}.$$

Example Let $A = \{\, a_i \mid i \in I\,\}$ be an infinite alphabet, and let $X, X_i, Y_i \subseteq A^{\infty}$. Let $a \cdot X$ be as before. Assume the discrete metric on A. We have

(a) If X_i is closed for all $i \in I$, then $\bigcup_{i \in I}(a_i \cdot X_i)$ is closed.

(b) If X_i, Y_i are nonempty and closed for all $i \in I$, then

$$d_H(\bigcup_{i \in I}(a_i \cdot X_i), \bigcup_{i \in I}(a_i \cdot Y_i)) \leq \tfrac{1}{2} \cdot sup\{\, d_H(X_i, Y_i) \mid i \in I\,\}.$$

The Hausdorff distance, as given in Definition 2.2, expresses the distance between sets directly in terms of the distance between points. An alternative definition which is, in fact, somewhat more customary, uses the definition of the distance between a point and a set as an intermediate step:

Definition 2.6 Let (M, d) be a metric space, and let $X, Y \subseteq M$.

(a) $d'(x, Y) = inf\{ d(x, y) \mid y \in Y \}$, with the convention that $inf(\emptyset) = 1$.

(b) $d'_H(X, Y) = max\{ sup_{x \in X} d'(x, Y), sup_{y \in Y} d'(y, X) \}$, with the convention $sup(\emptyset) = 0$.

Examples

(1) $d'_H(\{x\}, \{y\}) = max\{ d'(x, \{y\}), d'(y, \{x\}) \} = d(x, y)$.

(2) We have $d'(a^i, a^*) = 0$, $d'(a^i, \{ \epsilon, a, \ldots, a^n \}) = 0$ for $0 \leq i \leq n$ and $d'(a^i, \{ \epsilon, a, \ldots, a^n \}) = 2^{-n}$ for $i > n$. Hence

$$d'_H(\{ \epsilon, a, \ldots, a^n \}, a^*)$$
$$= max\{ sup\{ d'(a^i, a^*) \mid 0 \leq i \leq n \},$$
$$sup\{ d'(a^i, \{ \epsilon, a, \ldots, a^n \}) \mid i \geq 0 \} \}$$
$$= max\{ 0, 2^{-n} \}$$
$$= 2^{-n}.$$

(3) Since

$$d'(a^\omega, a^*) = inf\{ d(a^\omega, a^i) \mid i \geq 0 \} = inf\{ 2^{-i} \mid i \geq 0 \} = 0,$$

we have $d'_H(a^*, a^* \cup \{a^\omega\}) = 0$.

It is not too difficult to show that d_H and d'_H coincide.

Lemma 2.7 $d_H = d'_H$.

Proof Let $X, Y \subseteq M$. Suppose $d'_H(X, Y) < d_H(X, Y)$. Choose $\alpha > 0$ such that $d'_H(X, Y) < \alpha < d_H(X, Y)$. Then we have $\exists x \in X \forall y \in Y[d(x, y) \geq \alpha]$ or $\exists y \in Y \forall x \in X[d(x, y) \geq \alpha]$. So $\exists x \in X[d'(x, Y) \geq \alpha]$ or $\exists y \in Y[d'(y, X) \geq \alpha]$. Thus, $sup_{x \in X} d'(x, Y) \geq \alpha$ or $sup_{y \in Y} d'(y, X) \geq \alpha$. Hence $d'_H(X, Y) \geq \alpha$, contradicting our choice for α. Now suppose $d_H(X, Y) < d'_H(X, Y)$. Choose $\alpha > 0$ such that $d_H(X, Y) < \alpha < d'_H(X, Y)$. We then have that $\forall x \in X \exists y \in Y[d(x, y) < \alpha]$ and $\forall y \in Y \exists x \in X[d(y, x) < \alpha]$. So $\forall x \in X[d'(x, Y) < \alpha]$ and $\forall y \in Y[d'(y, X) < \alpha]$, and we infer that $sup_{x \in X} d(x, Y) \leq \alpha$ and $sup_{y \in Y} d'(y, X) \leq \alpha$. Therefore, $d'_H(X, Y) \leq \alpha$, contradicting our choice for α. $\square$

In choosing between the equivalent definitions of d_H and d'_H, we have preferred to work with d_H, since it is somewhat more convenient technically. When we specialize (M, d) to (A^∞, d_B), it is possible to show that the Hausdorff metric d_H as determined by the Baire metric d_B according to the general scheme of Definition 2.2 (formula (2.1)), satisfies a property which clearly brings out its structural relationship with d_B. Recall that we put, for each $X \subseteq A^\infty$, $X[n] = \{ x[n] \mid x \in X \}$. Now instead of applying (2.1), we may also adopt the pattern from the definition of d_B, as described in

Definition 2.8 Let (A^∞, d_B) be as before, and let $X, Y \subseteq A^\infty$. We put

$$d_B^+(X, Y) \quad = \quad \begin{cases} 0 & \text{if } X = Y \\ 2^{-n} & \text{where } n = max\{ k \mid X[k] = Y[k] \}, \text{ if } X \neq Y. \end{cases}$$

Examples

(1) We have $\{w\}[k] = \{v\}[k]$ iff $w[k] = v[k]$. So $d_B^+(\{w\}, \{v\}) = d_B(w, v)$.

(2) $\{ \epsilon, a, \ldots, a^n \}[n] = a^*[n] = \{ \epsilon, a, \ldots, a^n \}$,
$\{ \epsilon, a, \ldots, a^n \}[n+1] = \{ \epsilon, a, \ldots, a^n \} \neq \{ \epsilon, a, \ldots, a^n, a^{n+1} \} = a^*[n+1]$. Therefore, $d_B^+(\{ \epsilon, a, \ldots, a^n \}, a^*) = 2^{-n}$.

(3) For all n, $a^*[n] = \{ \epsilon, a, \ldots, a^n \} = (a^* \cup \{a^\omega\})[n]$. Hence $d_B^+(a^*, a^* \cup \{a^\omega\}) = 0$.

Our confidence in the usefulness of the general definition of d_H for our aims is clearly supported by the following

Lemma 2.9 For each $X, Y \in \mathcal{P}_{cl}(A^\infty)$ we have that

$$d_H(X, Y) = d_B^+(X, Y).$$

Proof We first prove an auxiliary
Claim: $\forall n \in \mathbb{N}[\forall x \in X \exists y \in Y[d(x, y) \leq 2^{-n}] \Leftrightarrow (X[n] \subseteq Y[n])]$.
Proof of the claim: Choose $n \in \mathbb{N}$ and assume $\forall x \in \exists y \in Y[d(x, y) \leq 2^{-n}]$. Choose $x \in X$. Then $d(x, y) \leq 2^{-n}$, for some $y \in Y$. By Lemma 1.21a, we have $x[n] = y[n]$. So $x[n] \in Y[n]$, hence $X[n] \subseteq Y[n]$. Conversely, suppose $x \in X$. Since $x[n] \in X[n]$, we can choose $y \in Y$ such that $x[n] = y[n]$. Again by Lemma 1.21a, we have $d(x, y) \leq 2^{-n}$. Hence $\forall x \in X \exists y \in Y[d(x, y) \leq 2^{-n}]$. This proves the claim.
In order to prove that $d_H(X, Y) = d_B^+(X, Y)$, we argue as follows: If $X = Y$, the result is clear. Now assume $X \neq Y$. We have

$d_H(X, Y)$

$= inf\{\, \alpha > 0 \mid \forall x \in X \exists y \in Y [d(x, y) < \alpha] \text{ and symmetrically}\,\}$

$= [\text{Exercise 2.6}]$
$\quad inf\{\, 2^{-n} \mid \forall x \in X \exists y \in Y [d(x, y) \le 2^{-n}] \text{ and symmetrically}\,\}$

$= [\text{by the claim}] \; inf\{\, 2^{-n} \mid (X[n] \subseteq Y[n]) \wedge (Y[n] \subseteq X[n])\,\}$

$= inf\{\, 2^{-n} \mid X[n] = Y[n]\,\}$

$= [X \ne Y] min\{\, 2^{-n} \mid X[n] = Y[n]\,\}$

$= d_B^+(X, Y).$ $\qquad\qquad\qquad\qquad\qquad\qquad\qquad\qquad\qquad\qquad\qquad\qquad$ □

Thus, the Hausdorff distance based on d_B (according to (2.1)), and the direct definition of d_B^+ adopting the scheme of the definition of d_B, coincide.

With Lemma 2.9, we have completed the introduction of d_H, and the discussion of the variations in its definition. We now turn to the presentation of its first fundamental property. In Section 1.1.2, we followed a scheme where, after introducing various ways of constructing composed metric spaces from given ones, we next established that all given constructions preserve completeness. We shall now present the same kind of result for the closed powerdomain operator, as stated in the important

Theorem 2.10 *(Hahn) Let (M, d) be a complete metric space.*

(a) If $(X_n)_n$ is a Cauchy sequence in $(\mathcal{P}_{ncl}(M), d_H)$, then

$$\lim_n X_n = \{\, \lim_n x_n \mid x_n \in X_n, n = 0, 1, \ldots, \qquad\qquad (2.2)$$
$$(x_n)_n \text{ Chaucy sequence in } M \,\}.$$

(b) If $(X_n)_n$ is a Cauchy sequence in $(\mathcal{P}_{cl}(M), d_H)$ then either, for almost all n, $X_n = \emptyset$, and $\lim_n X_n = \emptyset$, or for almost all n, $X_n \ne \emptyset$ (say for $n \ge N$), and

$$\lim_n X_n = \{\, \lim_{n \ge N} x_n \mid x_n \in X_n, n \ge N, \qquad\qquad (2.3)$$
$$(x_n)_{n=N}^{\infty} \text{ Cauchy sequence in } M \,\}.$$

(c) $(\mathcal{P}_{cl}(M), d_H)$ and $(\mathcal{P}_{ncl}(M), d_H)$ are complete metric spaces.

Proof Since the details of the proof are somewhat complicated and not used in later arguments, we postpone it to Appendix A, Theorem A.1. $\qquad\qquad$ □

This theorem finishes the groundwork for the semantic treatment of nondeterminacy. All computations in languages with some element of nondeterminacy will deliver *closed* sets of outcomes. However, it will turn out that in the majority of cases an even stronger property will be satisfied, viz. that of compactness—for our purposes a generalization of finiteness. Compactness has better closure properties than closedness, thus enabling us to prove several additional results for most of our semantic models.

2.1.2 Compact sets

The first acquaintance with the notion of a compact set—in the framework of a mathematical study of programming semantics—is probably best expressed in terms of the following characterization: Let (M, d) be a complete metric space.

> $X \subseteq M$ is called compact whenever we have that $X = \lim_n X_n$, where each X_n, $n = 0, 1, \ldots$, is a *finite* subset of M (and the limit is with respect to d_H).

This definition provides a direct intuition for the (semantic) role of compactness. This will become especially manifest in Section 2.2, when we discuss the property of a transition system being *finitely branching,* and the associated result that a finitely branching transition system induces a compact semantics. However, from the point of view of a smooth mathematical development, we find it preferable to take a different starting point, as expressed in the next definition. Later (Theorem 2.20) we shall show that the just given characterization coincides with that of the next definition.

Definition 2.11

(a) Let (M, d) be a metric space. A set $X \subseteq M$ is called compact whenever each infinite sequence $(x_n)_n$ in X has a convergent subsequence with limit in X.

(b) The metric space (M, d) is called compact whenever M is a compact subset (according to part (a)) of M.

Examples

- a^* is not closed nor compact (with respect to A^∞ and d_B).
- $a^* \cup \{a^\omega\}$ is compact.

- A^∞ is compact for A finite, and closed but not compact for A infinite. In the latter case the sequence $(a_i)_i$ with $a_i \in A$ pairwise distinct constitutes a sequence without a convergent subsequence.

As immediate consequence of the definition we have

Lemma 2.12

(a) Each finite set is compact.

(b) Each compact set is closed.

(c) Each compact space is complete.

Proof

(a) Exercise.

(b) Let $(x_n)_n$ be a convergent sequence in the compact set X, and let $(x_{n_k})_k$ be the convergent subsequence for which we have—by the compactness definition—that $lim_k\, x_{n_k} = x\,(\in X)$. Since, a fortiori, $lim_n\, x_n = x$, we have shown that X is closed.

(c) Immediate by part (b).   □

The question may arise whether there is a property P such that we have

X is compact $\Longleftrightarrow$ X is closed and X satisfies P

In the setting of a complete metric space (M, d), the answer is affirmative—with P being the property of being "totally bounded" (cf. Exercise 2.12)—but this notion will not be applied in our semantic studies.

Compactness is preserved by finite unions and products, and by the application of a continuous function. The first two properties also hold for closed sets (cf. Examples (2) and (4) following Definition 2.1), but the last one does not (Exercise 2.8). In fact, preservation of compactness under continuous mappings—in our setting in the form of nonexpansive mappings—is crucial for a good part of our investigations.

Lemma 2.13 *Let (M, d), (M_1, d_1), (M_2, d_2) be metric spaces.*

(a) If X_1, X_2 are compact subsets of (M, d), then so is $X_1 \cup X_2$.

(b) If X_i is compact in (M_i, d_i), $i = 1, 2$, then $X_1 \times X_2$ is compact in $(M_1 \times M_2, d_P)$.

(c) If $f: M_1 \to M_2$ is continuous and X is compact in M_1, then $f(X) \overset{df}{=} \{\, f(x) \mid x \in X \,\}$ is compact in M_2.

Proof

(a) Exercise.

(b) Let $(x_n, y_n)_n$ be an infinite sequence in $M_1 \times M_2$. Then $(x_n)_n$ is an infinite sequence in M_1, which has a convergent subsequence $(x_{n_k})_k$. For easier notation, we rather write $(x_{f(k)})_k$, with $f \colon \mathbb{N} \to \mathbb{N}$ such that $f(k) < f(k')$ for $k < k'$. The corresponding sequence $(y_{f(k)})_k$ in M_2 has, in turn, a convergent subsequence $(y_{f(g(\ell))})_\ell$. Since each infinite subsequence of a convergent sequence is itself convergent, we have that $(x_{f(g(\ell))}, y_{f(g(\ell))})_\ell$ is the desired convergent subsequence of $(x_n, y_n)_n$.

(c) Let $(y_n)_n$ be an infinite sequence in $f(X)$. Then, for some $(x_n)_n$ in X we have $f(x_n) = y_n$, $n = 0, 1, \ldots$. By the compactness of X, $(x_n)_n$ has a convergent subsequence $(x_{n_k})_k$, with limit x. By the continuity of f, we have that $lim_k f(x_{n_k}) = f(x)$. Now putting $y_{n_k} = f(x_{n_k})$ we have that $lim_k y_{n_k} = f(x)$, and we have identified a convergent subsequence of $(y_n)_n$. □

Similarly to what we saw for $\mathcal{P}_{cl}(M)$ and $\mathcal{P}_{ncl}(M)$, we have that the (nonempty) compact powerdomain operators $\mathcal{P}_{co}(M)$ and $\mathcal{P}_{nco}(M)$ preserve completeness. This is the content of the next theorem, due to Kuratowski (and, once again, stated without proof).

Theorem 2.14 *(Kuratowski) Let (M, d) be a complete metric space.*

(a) As in Theorem 2.10, with $\mathcal{P}_{co}(\cdot)$ and $\mathcal{P}_{nco}(\cdot)$ replacing $\mathcal{P}_{cl}(\cdot)$ and $\mathcal{P}_{ncl}(\cdot)$.

(b) $(\mathcal{P}_{co}(M), d_H)$ and $(\mathcal{P}_{nco}(M), d_H)$ are complete.

Proof See Appendix A, Theorem A.2. □

With Kuratowski's theorem, we have reached a point in the hyperspace theory of compact sets comparable to that of Hahn's theorem in the theory for closed sets. We shall now discuss a number of further properties of compactness which extend those valid for closedness in an essential way. (Recall that Lemma 2.13c already provided a first example of this.) In Lemma 2.13a, we stated that the finite union of compact sets is compact. We shall now describe a setting where this result is strengthened to a theorem concerning *compact* unions of compact sets. The notion of compact union requires some explanation. Let (M, d) be as usual, and let $(\bar{M}, \bar{d}) = (\mathcal{P}_{co}(M), d_H)$ be the hyperspace of compact subsets of M. In $\bar{M}$, we can also single out subsets: a subset $\bar{X}$ of $\bar{M}$ is a set, the elements of which are themselves subsets of M. Figure 2.1 illustrates the situation.

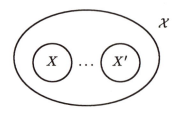

Figure 2.1

That is, the set $\mathcal{X}$ has as elements the "points" $X, \ldots, X', \ldots$, each a subset of M. Now one might be interested in $Y \overset{df}{=} \bigcup \{ X \mid X \in \mathcal{X} \}$, i.e., the union (over the "index set" $\mathcal{X}$) of all X belonging to $\mathcal{X}$. Clearly, this will result in another subset of M. Now the question to which all this leads is: Is Y itself a compact set? The (affirmative) answer is provided in

Theorem 2.15 *(Michael) Let (M, d) be complete, and let $(\mathcal{P}_{co}(M), d_H)$ be as before. If $\mathcal{X}$ is a compact subset of $(\mathcal{P}_{co}(M), d_H)$, then $\bigcup \mathcal{X} = \bigcup \{ X \mid X \in \mathcal{X} \}$ is a compact subset of (M, d).*

Proof Let $(x_n)_n$ be an infinite sequence in $\bigcup \mathcal{X}$. Choose, for all n, some X_n in $\mathcal{X}$ such that $x_n \in X_n$. Since $(X_n)_n$ is an infinite sequence in the compact set $\mathcal{X}$, there exists a strictly increasing mapping $f \colon \mathbb{N} \to \mathbb{N}$ such that $(X_{f(n)})_n$ is a convergent subsequence with limit, say X, in $\mathcal{X}$. Clearly, $X \subseteq \bigcup \mathcal{X}$. By Kuratowski's theorem, X is itself compact. Choose, for all n, some $y_n \in X$ such that $d(x_{f(n)}, y_n) \leq 2 \cdot d_H(X_n, X)$ (cf. Exercise 2.7). Since $(y_n)_n$ is an infinite sequence in the compact set X there exists a strictly increasing mapping $g \colon \mathbb{N} \to \mathbb{N}$ such that $(y_{g(n)})_n$ is a convergent sequence with limit, say y, in X. We have $lim_n\, x_{f(g(n))} = y$, since

$$d(x_{f(g(n))}, y)$$
$$\leq\ d(x_{f(g(n))}, y_{g(n)}) + d(y_{g(n)}, y)$$
$$\leq\ 2 \cdot d_H(X_{f(g(n))}, X) + d(y_{g(n)}, y)$$
$$\to 0\ \text{[if } n \to \infty.\text{]}$$

So $(x_n)_n$ has a converging subsequence, namely $(x_{f(g(n))})_n$. Moreover, $lim_n\, x_{f(g(n))} = y \in X \subseteq \bigcup \mathcal{X}$. $\qquad\square$

Remark Michael's theorem is also valid in the form: The compact union of a family of closed sets is closed (cf. Exercise 2.11a). However, this form of the theorem will not be used.

We next discuss an important application of Theorem 2.15. Recall that, in Lemma 2.13c, we stated that a continuous function maps compact sets to compact sets: If $f: (M_1, d_1) \to (M_2, d_2)$ is continuous, and $f(X)$ is defined as $\{ f(x) \mid x \in X \}$, then, for $X \in \mathcal{P}_{co}(M_1)$, $f(X) \in \mathcal{P}_{co}(M_2)$. In our semantic investigations, we will often encounter the situation that M_2 is itself a powerdomain, say of compact subsets of some space M. Let X be a compact subset of M_1. Frequently, we are not only interested in $f(X) = \{ f(x) \mid x \in X \}$, but rather in $\hat{f}(X)$ as defined in

$$\hat{f}(X) = \bigcup \{ f(x) \mid x \in X \}. \tag{2.4}$$

Since the situation may appear somewhat confused, let us spell out what happens here. Firstly, since each $f(x)$ belongs to M_2, $f(X)$ is a set of points in M_2. Since M_2 is itself a hyperspace (of subsets of M), $f(X)$ is in fact a set of subsets of M. Thus, it is meaningful to take the union of all these subsets, and this is precisely what is expressed by formula (2.4). Now what happens with the various outcomes for X compact and f continuous? This is stated in

Lemma 2.16 *Let (M, d) and (M_1, d_1) be complete metric spaces, and let $(M_2, d_2) = (\mathcal{P}_{co}(M), d_H)$. Let $f: (M_1, d_1) \to (M_2, d_2)$ be continuous, Then, for X compact in M_1, $\hat{f}(X)$ is compact in M.*

Proof By Lemma 2.13c, for X compact in M_1, $f(X) = \{ f(x) \mid x \in X \}$ is a compact subset of M_2 ($= \mathcal{P}_{co}(M)$). By Michael's theorem, $\hat{f}(X) = \bigcup \{ f(x) \mid x \in X \}$ is a compact subset of M. $\qquad \square$

We shall often appeal to Lemma 2.16 in later applications in a setting where f is contractive or nonexpansive. As we shall prove in the next lemma, $\hat{f}$ inherits the property of being contractive or nonexpansive (in addition to the property of delivering compact results). Therefore, we call the next lemma the "Lifting Lemma": it lifts a property of a function on points to a property of functions on sets.

Lemma 2.17 *(Lifting Lemma) Let $f: (M_1, d_1) \to (\mathcal{P}_{co}(M), d_H)$ be nonexpansive or α-contractive (and all spaces concerned complete). Then $\hat{f}$, as defined above, is a nonexpansive or α-contractive function of type $(\mathcal{P}_{co}(M_1), (d_1)_H) \to (\mathcal{P}_{co}(M), d_H)$.*

Proof We only discuss the case that f is α-contractive for some α, $0 \leq \alpha < 1$. Clearly, f is continuous. By Lemma 2.16, the codomain of $\hat{f}$ equals $\mathcal{P}_{co}(M)$. There remains the proof that $\hat{f}$ is α-contractive. We know that, for each $x, x' \in M_1$, $d_H(f(x), f(x')) \leq \alpha \cdot d_1(x, x')$. We have to show that $d_H(\hat{f}(X), \hat{f}(X')) \leq \alpha \cdot (d_1)_H(X, X')$ for $X, X' \in \mathcal{P}_{co}(M_1)$. Suppose $(d_1)_H(X, X') < \beta$, for some $\beta > 0$. Let $y \in \hat{f}(X)$, say $y = f(x)$, for some $x \in X$. Choose $x' \in X'$ such that $d_1(x, x') < \beta$. Then $d_H(f(x), f(x')) \leq \alpha \cdot \beta$. A similar symmetric result holds. Hence $d_H(\hat{f}(X), \hat{f}(X')) \leq \alpha \cdot \beta$. Taking the infimum over β, we obtain $d_H(\hat{f}(X), \hat{f}(X')) \leq \alpha \cdot (d_1)_H(X, X')$.   □

In a number of instances below, we shall encounter the Lifting Lemma in a form where f is a function of $n > 1$ variables. Also, mixed versions where f is nonexpansive in one variable and α-contractive in another variable will be used. We leave to the reader the details of the statement and proof of the Lifting Lemma in its (slightly) generalized form.

The theorems of Kuratowski and Michael, and the Lifting Lemma, will constitute the main tools to be exploited in later chapters (when dealing with compact sets, as we mostly will be). For completeness sake—now using this word with its usual English language connotation—and to fulfill our promise concerning the characterization of compactness in terms of limits of finite sets, we close this subsection with the discussion of a few further properties of compact sets. Some new notions and techniques will be employed which will not be applied again before Chapter 10. Accordingly, the remainder of this section may be skipped at first reading.

We begin by stating another definition of compactness (which is, in fact, the form in which it occurs mostly in general topology). In order to distinguish the present notion from the one in Definition 2.11, we shall refer to the newly to be defined one as that of topological compactness. A few preliminary definitions are in order. Let (M, d) be a metric space. A subset X of M is called *open* in case $M \setminus X$ is closed. A *cover* of X is a family of sets $\mathcal{A} = \{ A_i \mid A_i \subseteq M, i \in I \}$, such that $X \subseteq \bigcup \mathcal{A}$. The cover $\mathcal{A}$ is called open if all its elements A_i, $i \in I$, are open. A subcover of $\mathcal{A}$ is a cover $\mathcal{A}' = \{ A_i \mid A_i \subseteq M, i \in I' \}$, with $I' \subseteq I$. A cover is called finite in case $|I| < \infty$. We now give

Definition 2.18 A subset X of a metric space (M, d) is called topologically compact in case each open cover of X has a finite subcover (of X). The space (M, d) is called topologically compact in case each open cover of M has a finite subcover (of M).

The two characterizations of compactness (the one of Definition 2.11, also called *sequential* compactness, and the one of Definition 2.18, also simply called compactness) coincide.

Theorem 2.19 *Let (M, d) be a metric space. A subset X of M is compact (according to Definition 2.11) iff it is topologically compact (according to Definition 2.18).*

Proof See Appendix, Theorem A.4. □

The topologically compactness definition will turn out to be advantageous at a few occasions in our work. To begin with, it is used in the already announced

Theorem 2.20 X *is compact in* (M, d) *whenever* $X = lim_n X_n$, *with* X_n *finite,* $n = 0, 1, \ldots$ *(and the limit is taken with respect to* d_H*).*

Proof Clearly, each finite set is compact. Since the limit of a converging sequence of compact sets is compact (by Kuratowski's theorem), we have that $lim_n X_n$ is compact for X_n, $n = 0, 1, \ldots$, finite. We now prove the reverse implication. Let, for each $x \in M$, $B_\varepsilon(x)$ denote the "open ε-ball around x," i.e., the set

$\{ y \mid d(x, y) < \varepsilon \}$.

Clearly, for each n, the family $\{ B_{2^{-n}}(x) \mid x \in X \}$ is an open cover of X. Since X is compact, there exists a finite subset of X, say X_n, such that $\{ B_{2^{-n}}(x) \mid x \in X_n \}$ covers X. Consequently,

$$\forall x \in X \exists x' \in X_n [d(x, x') < 2^{-n}]. \tag{2.5}$$

Since $X_n \subseteq X$, we certainly have

$$\forall x \in X_n \exists x' \in X [d(x, x') < 2^{-n}]. \tag{2.6}$$

Putting (2.5) and (2.6) together, and taking the infimum we may conclude that $d_H(X, X_n) \leq 2^{-n}$, for each n, and $lim_n X_n = X$ follows. □

We close this subsection with the discussion of an important property characterizing compactness in the setting of (A^∞, d_B). Once again, finiteness is the crucial notion here:

Lemma 2.21 *Let (A^∞, d_B) be as before. A closed set $X \subseteq A^\infty$ is compact whenever $X[n]$ is finite, for each $n \geq 0$.*

Proof We first show that, for X compact, $X[n]$ is finite for each n. Assume that $X[n]$ is infinite, for some n. We then may choose a sequence $(x_k)_k$ in X such that $x_i[n] \neq x_j[n]$, for $i \neq j$. By Lemma 1.21a, we have that $d(x_i, x_j) > 2^{-n}$, for $i \neq j$. Thus, $(x_k)_k$ has no convergent subsequence, contradicting the compactness of X. Conversely, if $X[n]$ is finite for each n, then $X = \lim_n X[n]$ is compact by Theorem 2.20.   □

2.2 Nondeterministic choice—the compact powerdomain

Section 2.2 brings the first example of a language with a form of nondeterminacy: the computations prescribed by the programs in this language involve moments of *choice*—with the induced effect of *sets* of outcomes—and the machinery of metric hyperspaces, in particular the use of compact powerdomains, is required for the semantic definitions.

In Sections 2.2.1 and 2.2.2, we closely follow the definitional format as introduced earlier in Sections 1.1.1, 1.1.3 and 1.1.4. In Section 2.2.3, we describe as well a continuation style (denotational) definition for our language. In this way, we are in a position to compare two styles—direct and continuation-based—of denotational semantics, and make precise statements about their relationships.

2.2.1 Syntax and operational semantics

The (uniform) language studied in this section is an extension of $\mathcal{L}_{rec}$ of Section 1.1. To the basic constructs of $\mathcal{L}_{rec}$, viz. actions, procedure variables—with the possibility of recursion—and sequential composition, we add as second composition operator that of *nondeterministic choice*, syntactically expressed as $s_1 + s_2$. The execution of $s_1 + s_2$ proceeds by choosing arbitrarily between the two operands s_1 and s_2, and executing the chosen one. For example, the execution of $(a;b) + c$ leads to the execution of either $(a;b)$ (with ab as outcome), or of c (with c as outcome). Combining the two results in a *set* of outcomes yields $\{ab, c\}$ as semantics for $(a;b) + c$. The wish to handle sets of outcomes explains the need for the development, in the previous section, of a metric framework to handle spaces of sets. For our present purposes—and the great majority of the subsequent ones—we shall be able to make fruitful use of *compact* sets (here with sequences over Act as elements).

The language to be investigated is called $\mathcal{L}_{cf}$—with cf abbreviating "context free." The reason for this terminology is the close structural similarity between the programs of $\mathcal{L}_{cf}$ and context free grammars. Both are built on the same notions, viz.

- actions or terminal symbols
- sequential composition and nondeterministic choice
- recursion in terms of declarations or production rules.

(Of course, we are here comparing the $\mathcal{L}_{cf}$-programs with context free grammars producing finite *and infinite* words.)

We now give the syntactic definitions for $\mathcal{L}_{cf}$. This follows the format as used for $\mathcal{L}_{rec}$; in particular, we observe a return of the notion of *guarded* statement. The sets $(a \in) Act$ and $(x \in) PVar$ are as in Section 1.1.

Definition 2.22

(a) $s\,(\in Stat) ::= a \mid x \mid (s;s) \mid (s+s)$.

(b) $g\,(\in GStat) ::= a \mid (g;s) \mid (g+g)$.

(c) $(D \in) Decl = PVar \to GStat$.

(d) $(\pi \in) \mathcal{L}_{cf} = Decl \times Stat$.

Examples $(D|a;(b+c))$, $(D|(a;b)+(a;c))$, $(x \Leftarrow (a;x)+b \mid x;c)$.

Remark The definition of $(g \in) GStat$ may be understood in terms of the notion of "exposed" (as discussed in Section 1.1.1) by adding the clauses that an action a is exposed in $s_1 + s_2$ whenever it is exposed in s_1 or s_2, and similarly for a procedure variable x. The definition of $GStat$ implies that, as before, only actions occur exposed in any $g \in GStat$.

In later definitions and examples we often drop parentheses, adopting the convention that ';' binds tighter than '+'. For example, $a;b+c$ is to be read as $((a;b)+c)$ rather than as $(a;(b+c))$.

The operational semantics for $\mathcal{L}_{cf}$ is—as always—given in terms of a transition system specification. Resumptions are as in Section 1.1, but now with respect to $\mathcal{L}_{cf}$. That is, each $r\,(\in Res)$ is either equal to the empty resumption E or to some s (from $Stat$ as in Definition 2.1a). The identification of E;r and r is imposed as before. We now define $\mathcal{T}_{cf}$.

Definition 2.23 $\mathcal{T}_{cf} = (Decl \times Res, Act, \rightarrow, Spec)$. *Spec consists of the following axiom and three rules. (Again, the notation $r \xrightarrow{a}_D r'$ for $((D|r), a, (D|r')) \in \rightarrow$ is adopted.)*

- $$a \xrightarrow{a}_D E \qquad\qquad\qquad\qquad\qquad\qquad\qquad\qquad\qquad\qquad \text{(Act)}$$

- $$\frac{g \xrightarrow{a}_D r}{x \xrightarrow{a}_D r} \qquad \text{if } D(x) = g \qquad\qquad\qquad\qquad\qquad\qquad \text{(Rec)}$$

- $$\frac{s_1 \xrightarrow{a}_D r_1}{s_1;s_2 \xrightarrow{a}_D r_1;s_2} \qquad\qquad\qquad\qquad\qquad\qquad\qquad\qquad \text{(Seq)}$$

- $$\frac{s \xrightarrow{a}_D r}{s + s' \xrightarrow{a}_D r} \qquad\qquad\qquad\qquad\qquad\qquad\qquad\qquad \text{(Choice)}$$
$$s' + s \xrightarrow{a}_D r$$

The rule (Choice) has (one premise and) two conclusions; it expresses that from the premise *both* conclusions may be inferred. That is, it is an abbreviation for the two rules

$$\frac{s \xrightarrow{a}_D r}{s + s' \xrightarrow{a}_D r} \quad , \quad \frac{s \xrightarrow{a}_D r}{s' + s \xrightarrow{a}_D r} \quad .$$

Due to the presence of nondeterminacy in $\mathcal{L}_{cf}$, we cannot expect that Lemma 1.9 (stating $|\mathcal{S}(D|r)| = 0$ or 1) holds as well in the present setting. Instead, we establish a more general property, stating that, for each $D \in Decl$ and $r \in Res$, the set of successors $\mathcal{S}(D|r)$, as determined by $\mathcal{T}_{cf}$, is *finite* (and nonempty for $r \not\equiv E$).

Lemma 2.24 *For each $(D|r)$, $\mathcal{S}(D|r)$ is finite and $r \not\equiv E \Leftrightarrow \mathcal{S}(D|r) \neq \emptyset$.*

In order to prove the lemma, we extend the weight function as given in Definition 1.10:

Definition 2.25 $wgt: Decl \times Res \rightarrow \mathbb{N}$ *is given by*

$$
\begin{aligned}
wgt(D|\mathrm{E}) &= 0 \\
wgt(D|a) &= 1 \\
wgt(D|x) &= wgt(D|D(x)) + 1 \\
wgt(D|s_1;s_2) &= wgt(D|s_1) + 1 \\
wgt(D|s_1 + s_2) &= max\{\, wgt(D|s_1), wgt(D|s_2)\,\} + 1.
\end{aligned}
$$

Well-definedness of wgt is shown, as before, first for all $g \in GStat$ and, next, for all $s \in Stat$.

We are ready for the

Proof of Lemma 2.24. Induction on $wgt(D|r)$. All cases are as for Lemma 1.9, but for the final one:

$[s_1 + s_2]$ Clearly $s_1 + s_2 \xrightarrow{a}_D r$ iff $s_1 \xrightarrow{a}_D r$ or $s_2 \xrightarrow{a}_D r$. Thus, $\mathcal{S}(D|s_1 + s_2) = \mathcal{S}(D|s_1) \cup \mathcal{S}(D|s_2)$, and the result follows by the definition of $wgt(D|s_1 + s_2)$ and the induction hypothesis.   □

It is important to note that Lemma 2.24 depends crucially on the requirement that $D(x)$ is guarded. Consider, for example, a "declaration" such as

$$D(x) = (x;a) + b. \tag{2.7}$$

Note that this $D(x)$ is unguarded, since x is exposed in $(x;a)$, hence also in $(x;a) + b$. We have, since $b \xrightarrow{b}_D \mathrm{E}$, that $(x;a) + b \xrightarrow{b}_D \mathrm{E}$, whence, by (Rec),

$$x \xrightarrow{b}_D \mathrm{E}.$$

From this, by (Seq), $x;a \xrightarrow{b}_D a$, whence, by (Choice), $(x;a) + b \xrightarrow{b}_D a$, and

$$x \xrightarrow{b}_D a$$

follows. Similarly, we derive

$$x \xrightarrow{b}_D a;a.$$

Continuing in this way, we obtain $x \xrightarrow{b}_D a;a;\cdots;a$, for any sequence of actions a, and we have shown that $\mathcal{S}(D|x)$ is infinite for $D(x)$ as in (2.7).

The property expressed by Lemma 2.24 is a fundamental one for transition systems in general. For this, reason, they have obtained a special name.

Definition 2.26 A transition system $\mathcal{T} = (Conf, Obs, \rightarrow)$, such that $\mathcal{S}(c)$ is finite for each $c \in Conf$, is called *finitely branching*.

The property of being finitely branching of a transition system induces a topological property of the operational semantics associated with the system. We first adapt the definition of *direct* operational semantics, as given in Definition 1.13 for $\mathcal{L}_{rec}$, to the present situation where *sets* of sequences (rather than just sequences) of actions are delivered. That is, we define $\mathcal{O}_d: Decl \times Res \to \mathcal{P}(Act^\infty)$ in

Definition 2.27

$$\mathcal{O}_d(D|r) \quad = \quad \{\, a_1 a_2 \cdots a_n \mid r \xrightarrow{a_1}_D r_1 \xrightarrow{a_2}_D \cdots \xrightarrow{a_n}_D r_n \equiv \mathrm{E} \,\} \cup$$
$$\{\, a_1 a_2 \cdots a_n \cdots \mid r \xrightarrow{a_1}_D r_1 \xrightarrow{a_2}_D \cdots \xrightarrow{a_n}_D r_n \cdots \,\}.$$

This definition expresses that $\mathcal{O}_d(D|r)$ is obtained by collecting all finite and infinite transition sequences starting from r, and concatenating the actions labeling the successive transitions. Here a sequence terminates precisely when the last resumption equals E. Note how the presence of nondeterminacy in $\mathcal{L}_{cf}$ induces the possibility of more than one sequence $r \xrightarrow{a_1}_D r_1 \xrightarrow{a_2}_D \cdots$ starting with any given r.

A first simple property of $\mathcal{O}_d(D|r)$ for $\mathcal{L}_{cf}$ is

Lemma 2.28 $\mathcal{O}_d(D|r) \neq \emptyset$ for each $(D|r) \in Decl \times Res$.

Proof Immediate by Definition 2.27, since $\mathcal{O}_d(D|\mathrm{E}) = \{\epsilon\}$. $\qquad\qquad\qquad\square$

We now turn to the statement of the topological property of transition systems in general referred to above. Since we know, from Lemma 2.20, that compactness is the limit-case of finiteness, we are already prepared for the proposition that the operational semantics associated with a finitely branching transition system is *compact*. For completeness sake, we restate Definition 2.27 for arbitrary transition systems.

Definition 2.29 Let $\mathcal{T} = (Conf, Obs, \to)$ be a transition system. We define $\mathcal{O}_d: Conf \to \mathcal{P}(Obs^\infty)$ as follows:

$$\mathcal{O}_d(c) \quad = \quad \{\, a_1 a_2 \cdots a_n \mid c \xrightarrow{a_1} c_1 \xrightarrow{a_2} c_2 \cdots \xrightarrow{a_n} c_n \not\to \,\} \cup$$
$$\{\, a_1 a_2 \cdots a_n \cdots \mid c \xrightarrow{a_1} c_1 \xrightarrow{a_2} c_2 \cdots \xrightarrow{a_n} c_n \cdots \,\}.$$

We then have the fundamental

Theorem 2.30 Let $\mathcal{T} = (Conf, Obs, \to)$ be a finitely branching transition system. Then $\mathcal{O}_d(c)$ is compact subset of Obs^∞, for each $c \in Conf$.

Since the proof of this theorem is somewhat involved, we shall not present it here. It will be given in Appendix B, Theorem B.2.

Combining Lemma 2.28 and Theorem 2.30, we have

Lemma 2.31 *As range for the mapping* $\mathcal{O}_d\colon Decl \times Res \to \mathcal{P}(Act^\infty)$ *we may take*

$$\mathbb{P}_O = \mathcal{P}_{nco}(Act^\infty)$$

where $\mathcal{P}_{nco}(Act^\infty)$ *stands for the powerdomain of all nonempty and compact subsets of* Act^∞.

By Theorem 2.14 we know that $\mathbb{P}_O$ is a *complete* metric space. This allows us to follow Section 1.1.4 in supplying an alternative definition for the operational semantics for $\mathcal{L}_{cf}$ in terms of a (contractive) higher-order operator. As before, this definition will in particular prove useful when we compare $\mathcal{O}$ and $\mathcal{D}$ for $\mathcal{L}_{cf}$.

The higher-order definition of $\mathcal{O}$ follows:

Definition 2.32

(a) Let $(S \in)\, Sem_O = Decl \times Res \to \mathbb{P}_O$ and let $\Phi\colon Sem_O \to Sem_O$ be given by

$$\begin{aligned}
\Phi(S)(D|\mathrm{E}) &= \{\epsilon\} \\
\Phi(S)(D|s) &= \bigcup\{\, a \cdot S(D|r) \mid s \xrightarrow{a}_D r \,\}.
\end{aligned}$$

(b) $\mathcal{O} = \text{fix}(\Phi)$, $\mathcal{O}[\![\cdot]\!]\colon Decl \times Stat \to \mathbb{P}_O$ is given by $\mathcal{O}[\![D|s]\!] = \mathcal{O}(D|s)$.

Various comments are in order to understand and justify this definition. We first look at the clause for $\Phi(S)(D|s)$. Let S be any given meaning function (from $Sem_O = Decl \times Res \to \mathbb{P}_O$), and let $(D|s) \in Decl \times Res$. In order to determine $\Phi(S)(D|s)$, we consult $\mathcal{T}_{cf}$, and see for which (a, r) we may infer that $s \xrightarrow{a}_D r$. Note that, by nondeterminacy, there may be more than one such (a, r). For each (a, r), we firstly obtain $S(D|r)$—the S-meaning of the configuration $(D|r)$ to be executed next—and prefix it by the observation a, the first step resulting from executing $(D|s)$. Note that, by the definition of Sem_O, $S(D|r)$ delivers a set of sequences, and it is meaningful to prefix this set by a. (For each $p \in \mathbb{P}_O$, $a \cdot p$ equals the set of all $a \cdot q$, for $q \in p$.) Since there are, in general, several (a, r) and associated $a \cdot S(D|r)$, we take their union $\bigcup\{\, a \cdot S(D|r) \mid s \xrightarrow{a}_D r \,\}$ as specified.

Examples

(1) $\mathcal{O}(D|a;(b+c))$

  $= a \cdot \mathcal{O}(D|b+c)$

  $= a \cdot (b \cdot \mathcal{O}(D|\mathrm{E}) \cup c \cdot \mathcal{O}(D|\mathrm{E}))$

  $= a \cdot (b \cdot \{\epsilon\} \cup c \cdot \{\epsilon\})$

  $= a \cdot (\{b\} \cup \{c\})$

  $= a \cdot \{b, c\}$

  $= \{ab, ac\}$

(2) $\mathcal{O}(D|a;b + a;c)$

  $= a \cdot \mathcal{O}(D|b) \cup a \cdot \mathcal{O}(D|c)$

  $= a \cdot b \cdot \mathcal{O}(D|\mathrm{E}) \cup a \cdot c \cdot \mathcal{O}(D|\mathrm{E})$

  $= a \cdot b \cdot \{\epsilon\} \cup a \cdot c \cdot \{\epsilon\}$

  $= \{ab\} \cup \{ac\}$

  $= \{ab, ac\}$

(3) Assume $D(x) = a;x + b$. Then we have $x \xrightarrow{a}_D x$ and $x \xrightarrow{b}_D \mathrm{E}$. Hence

  $\mathcal{O}(D|x)$

  $= a \cdot \mathcal{O}(D|x) \cup b \cdot \mathcal{O}(D|\mathrm{E})$

  $= a \cdot \mathcal{O}(D|x) \cup \{b\}.$

We claim $\mathcal{O}(D|x) = a^* \cdot \{b\} \cup \{a^\omega\}$. This can be seen as follows:

  $d(\mathcal{O}(D|x), a^* \cdot \{b\} \cup \{a^\omega\})$

  $= d(a \cdot \mathcal{O}(D|x) \cup \{b\}, a \cdot (a^* \cdot \{b\} \cup \{a^\omega\}) \cup \{b\})$

  $= [\text{Lemma } 2.4]$

    $max\{ d(a \cdot \mathcal{O}(D|x), a \cdot (a^* \cdot \{b\} \cup \{a^\omega\})), d(\{b\}, \{b\}) \}$

  $= \tfrac{1}{2} d(\mathcal{O}(D|x), a^* \cdot \{b\} \cup \{a^\omega\}).$

Thus $d(\mathcal{O}(D|x), a^* \cdot \{b\} \cup \{a^\omega\}) = 0$ and $\mathcal{O}(D|x) = a^* \cdot \{b\} \cup \{a^\omega\}$.

We next discuss well-definedness of $\Phi(S)$, i.e., we investigate whether $\Phi(S)(D|r)$ is nonempty and compact for each $(D|r)$. Clearly, $\Phi(S)(D|\mathrm{E})$ is well-defined. As to $\Phi(S)(D|s)$, we have to check whether the set $\bigcup\{ a \cdot S(D|r) \mid s \xrightarrow{a}_D r \}$ is nonempty and compact. Since $S(D|s) \neq \emptyset$, nonemptiness is clear. Also, $S(D|r)$ and, hence, $a \cdot S(D|r)$ is compact for each a and $(D|r)$. Moreover, since there are only finitely many (a, r) such that $s \xrightarrow{a}_D r$ (Lemma 2.24), the union on the right-hand side of the equation for $\Phi(S)(D|s)$ is taken over a finite index set, and the outcome is compact (by Lemma 2.13).

Finally, we verify that Φ is $\tfrac{1}{2}$-contractive in S.

Lemma 2.33 $\Phi \in Sem_O \xrightarrow{\frac{1}{2}} Sem_O$.

Proof Take $S_1, S_2 \in Sem_O$. We show that

$$d(\Phi(S_1)(D|r), \Phi(S_2)(D|r)) \leq \tfrac{1}{2}d(S_1, S_2),$$

for each $(D|r)$. The case $r \equiv \mathrm{E}$ is clear. Otherwise, we have

$d(\Phi(S_1)(D|s), \Phi(S_2)(D|s))$
$= d(\bigcup\{a \cdot S_1(D|r) \mid s \xrightarrow{a}_D r\}, \bigcup\{a \cdot S_2(D|r) \mid s \xrightarrow{a}_D r\})$
$\leq$ [Lemma 2.4] $max\{d(a \cdot S_1(D|r), a \cdot S_2(D|r)) \mid s \xrightarrow{a}_D r\}$
$= [S_1(D|r), S_2(D|r) \neq \emptyset]\ \tfrac{1}{2} max\{d(S_1(D|r), S_2(D|r)) \mid s \xrightarrow{a}_D r\}$
$\leq \tfrac{1}{2}d(S_1, S_2).$ $\square$

We draw attention to the step depending on $S_1(D|r), S_2(D|r) \neq \emptyset$. Cf. the discussion following Theorem 2.3, emphasizing the importance of working with nonempty sets.

Altogether, we have obtained that Φ is a $\tfrac{1}{2}$-contractive mapping on the complete metric space Sem_O (since $\mathbb{P}_O$ is a complete metric space, so is $Decl \times Res \to \mathbb{P}_O$); hence, its unique fixed point $\mathcal{O}$ exists. Just as we did for $\mathcal{O}_d$ in Section 1.1, it is easy to show that $\Phi(\mathcal{O}_d) = \mathcal{O}_d$, and $\mathcal{O} = \mathcal{O}_d$ on $Decl \times Res$ follows.

We conclude this subsection with the analogue of Lemma 1.14.

Lemma 2.34

(a) $\mathcal{O}(D|x) = \mathcal{O}(D|D(x))$.

(b) $\mathcal{O}(D|s_1;(s_2;s_3)) = \mathcal{O}(D|(s_1;s_2);s_3)$.

Proof

(a) Direct by the (Rec)-rule from $\mathcal{T}_{cf}$.

(b) Put

$$\varepsilon = sup\{d(\mathcal{O}(D|s_1;(s_2;s_3)), \mathcal{O}(D|(s_1;s_2);s_3)) \mid s_1, s_2, s_3 \in Stat\}.$$

We shall show $\varepsilon \leq \varepsilon/2$, implying the desired result. We have

$\mathcal{O}(D|(s_1;s_2);s_3)$
$= \bigcup\{a \cdot \mathcal{O}(D|s_2;s_3) \mid s_1 \xrightarrow{a}_D \mathrm{E}\} \cup \bigcup\{a \cdot \mathcal{O}(D|(s';s_2);s_3) \mid s_1 \xrightarrow{a}_D s'\}$

and similarly for $\mathcal{O}(D|s_1;(s_2;s_3))$. Now

$$d(\mathcal{O}(D|s_1;(s_2;s_3)), \mathcal{O}(D|(s_1;s_2);s_3))$$
$$\leq d(\bigcup\{a \cdot \mathcal{O}(D|s';(s_2;s_3)) \mid s_1 \xrightarrow{a} s'\}, \bigcup\{a \cdot \mathcal{O}(D|(s';s_2);s_3) \mid s_1 \xrightarrow{a} s'\})$$
$$\leq [\text{Lemma 2.4}]$$
$$\quad max\{\tfrac{1}{2}d(\mathcal{O}(D|s';(s_2;s_3)), \mathcal{O}(D|(s';s_2);s_3)) \mid s_1 \xrightarrow{a}_D s'\}$$
$$\leq \tfrac{1}{2}max\{d(\mathcal{O}(D|s';(s_2;s_3)), \mathcal{O}(D|(s';s_2);s_3)) \mid s', s_2, s_3 \in Stat\}$$
$$\leq \varepsilon/2. \hspace{8cm} \square$$

We have completed the development of $\mathcal{O}$ for $\mathcal{L}_{cf}$. We saw that, apart from the introduction of sets—and associated topological machinery for hyperspaces—the definitions strongly resemble those for $\mathcal{L}_{rec}$. A similar comment will hold for the denotational semantics for $\mathcal{L}_{cf}$ which we shall present in the next subsection.

2.2.2 Denotational semantics, equivalence of $\mathcal{O}$ and $\mathcal{D}$

The denotational semantics $\mathcal{D}$ for $\mathcal{L}_{cf}$ will first be given in the style which follows closely what we did for $\mathcal{L}_{rec}$. Later (Section 2.2.3) we shall discuss how a definition with *continuations* may be given which resembles what we did for $\mathcal{L}_{wh}$.

We begin with the introduction of the denotational codomain $\mathbb{P}_D$, and the various operators on $\mathbb{P}_D$ which are the counterparts of the syntactic composition rules. We recall that $\mathbb{P}_D$ for $\mathcal{L}_{rec}$ was taken as $Act^\infty \setminus \{\epsilon\}$. Since we here work with sets of results, we take as codomain for $\mathcal{D}$ the set $\mathcal{P}(Act^\infty \setminus \{\epsilon\})$. By the results of the previous subsection, we expect that we may specialize this to $\mathcal{P}_{nco}(Act^\infty \setminus \{\epsilon\})$, i.e., the collection of all nonempty and compact subsets of $Act^\infty \setminus \{\epsilon\}$. Indeed, we shall take

$$(p \in)\mathbb{P}_D = \mathcal{P}_{nco}(\mathbb{Q}_D)$$
$$(q \in)\mathbb{Q}_D = Act^\infty \setminus \{\epsilon\}.$$

(Introducing the separate name $\mathbb{Q}_D$ for $Act^\infty \setminus \{\epsilon\}$ will turn out useful in the sequel.) Our task is now firstly to define the semantic operators on this $\mathbb{P}_D$ and to show that these operators preserve nonemptiness and compactness. We do this in

Definition 2.35

(a) $; : \mathbb{P}_D \times \mathbb{P}_D \to \mathbb{P}_D$ is given as

$$p_1;p_2 = \{q_1;q_2 \mid q_1 \in p_1, q_2 \in p_2\}. \hspace{3cm} (2.8)$$

(b) $+ : \mathbb{P}_D \times \mathbb{P}_D \to \mathbb{P}_D$ is given as

$$p_1 + p_2 = p_1 \cup p_2. \hspace{4.5cm} (2.9)$$

In this definition, the ';' on the right-hand side of (2.8) is the sequential composition as defined in Definition 1.36. The '∪' on the right-hand side of (2.9) is, simply, the set-theoretic union.

We have

Lemma 2.36

(a) If $p_1, p_2 \in \mathbb{P}_D$ then $p_1;p_2 \in \mathbb{P}_D$ and $p_1 + p_2 \in \mathbb{P}_D$.

(b) The operators ';' and '+' are nonexpansive on $\mathbb{P}_D \times \mathbb{P}_D$.

(c) (strengthening of (b)) For each $p_1, p_2, \bar{p}_1, \bar{p}_2$ we have

$$d(p_1;p_2, \bar{p}_1;\bar{p}_2) \leq max\{\, d(p_1, \bar{p}_1), \tfrac{1}{2}d(p_2, \bar{p}_2) \,\}.$$

(d) For each $p_1, p_2, p_3 \in \mathbb{P}_D$,

$$
\begin{aligned}
(p_1;p_2);p_3 &= p_1;(p_2;p_3) \\
(p_1 + p_2);p_3 &= (p_1;p_3) + (p_2;p_3) \\
p_1;(p_2 + p_3) &= (p_1;p_2) + (p_1;p_3).
\end{aligned}
$$

Proof

(a) For ';' this follows from the Lifting Lemma (Lemma 2.17), and for '+' from Lemma 2.13.

(b) For ';' this follows from the Lifting Lemma and for '+' from Lemma 2.4.

(c) By the (generalized) Lifting Lemma.

(d) Clear from Definition 2.35 and earlier results.   □

Remarks

(1) Note that, similar to what we had in Section 1.1.3, part (c) does not hold if we allow $\epsilon \in p_1$ or $\epsilon \in p_2$.

(2) The identities mentioned in Lemma 2.36d are just a few examples of a much larger collection. A systematic study of the axiomatics and model theory of equational systems of this kind—especially in a setting where parallel composition is also included as operator—is made in Process Algebra, cf. the references for Chapter 4.

After having ascertained that we have the appropriate semantic operators available, it is not difficult to generalize the method used to define $\mathcal{D}$ in Section 1.1.3 to the present situation. We first supply the defining equations for $\mathcal{D}$, and then prove that these equations can be satisfied uniquely by another argument in terms of a contractive higher-order mapping.

Definition 2.37

(a) $\mathcal{D}: \mathcal{L}_{cf} \to \mathbb{P}_D$ is given as the (unique) function satisfying

$$
\begin{aligned}
\mathcal{D}(D|a) &= \{a\} \\
\mathcal{D}(D|x) &= \mathcal{D}(D|D(x)) \\
\mathcal{D}(D|s_1;s_2) &= \mathcal{D}(D|s_1);\mathcal{D}(D|s_2) \\
\mathcal{D}(D|s_1 + s_2) &= \mathcal{D}(D|s_1) + \mathcal{D}(D|s_2).
\end{aligned}
$$

Here the operators ';', '+' on the right-hand side of the equations are as in Definition 2.35.

(b) $\mathcal{D}[\![D|s]\!] = \mathcal{D}(D|s)$.

Once again, the somewhat vacuous clause (b) is included for consistency with the definitions of $\mathcal{D}[\![\cdot]\!]$ elsewhere in our book.

Examples

(1) $\mathcal{D}(D|a;(b+c))$
$= \mathcal{D}(D|a);\mathcal{D}(D|b+c)$
$= \{a\};(\mathcal{D}(D|b) + \mathcal{D}(D|c))$
$= \{a\};(\{b\} + \{c\})$
$= \{a\};\{b,c\}$
$= \{a;b, a;c\}$
$= \{ab, ac\}$

(2) $\mathcal{D}(D|a;b + a;c)$
$= \mathcal{D}(D|a;b) + \mathcal{D}(D|a;c)$
$= (\mathcal{D}(D|a);\mathcal{D}(D|b)) + (\mathcal{D}(D|a);\mathcal{D}(D|c))$
$= (\{a\};\{b\}) + (\{a\};\{c\})$
$= \{ab\} \cup \{ac\}$
$= \{ab, ac\}$

(3) Suppose $D(x) = a;x + b$. Since

$$\mathcal{D}(D|x)$$
$$= \mathcal{D}(D|a;x + b)$$
$$= \mathcal{D}(D|a;x) + \mathcal{D}(D|b)$$
$$= (\mathcal{D}(D|a);\mathcal{D}(D|x)) + \{b\}$$
$$= (\{a\};\mathcal{D}(D|x)) + \{b\}$$
$$= (a \cdot \mathcal{D}(D|x)) + \{b\},$$

it follows that $d(\mathcal{D}(D|x), a^* \cdot \{b\} \cup \{a^\omega\}) = 0$ and $\mathcal{D}(D|x) = a^* \cdot \{b\} \cup \{a^\omega\}$.

The justification of Definition 2.37 follows in

Lemma 2.38 *Let* $(S \in) Sem_D = \mathcal{L}_{cf} \to \mathbb{P}_D$, *and let* $\Psi \colon Sem_D \to Sem_D$ *be given as*

$$\begin{aligned}
\Psi(S)(D|a) &= \{a\} \\
\Psi(S)(D|x) &= \Psi(S)(D|D(x)) \\
\Psi(S)(D|s_1;s_2) &= \Psi(S)(D|s_1);S(D|s_2) \\
\Psi(S)(D|s_1 + s_2) &= \Psi(S)(D|s_1) + \Psi(S)(D|s_2).
\end{aligned}$$

Then

(a) $\Psi(S)(D|s)$ *is well-defined (i.e., nonempty and compact) for each* $(D|s)$.

(b) Ψ *is* $\frac{1}{2}$*-contractive in* S.

Proof

(a) Induction on $wgt(D|s)$ using lemma 2.36, part (a).

(b) Take some S_1, S_2. Two subcases.

$[s_1;s_2]$ $d(\Psi(S_1)(D|s_1;s_2), \Psi(S_2)(D|s_1;s_2))$
$= \ d(\Psi(S_1)(D|s_1);S_1(D|s_2), \Psi(S_2)(D|s_1);S_1(D|s_2))$
$\leq \ $ [Lemma 2.36c]
$\quad max\{\, d(\Psi(S_1)(D|s_1), \Psi(S_2)(D|s_1)), \frac{1}{2}d(S_1(D|s_2), S_2(D|s_2))\,\}$
$\leq \ $ [ind. hyp. for $(D|s_1)$, def. $d(S_1, S_2)$] $\frac{1}{2}d(S_1, S_2)$.

$[s_1 + s_2]$ $d(\Psi(S_1)(D|s_1 + s_2), \Psi(S_2)(D|s_1 + s_2))$
$= \ d(\Psi(S_1)(D|s_1) + \Psi(S_1)(D|s_2), \Psi(S_2)(D|s_1) + \Psi(S_2)(D|s_2))$
$\leq \ $ ['+' is nonexpansive]
$\quad max\{\, d(\Psi(S_1)(D|s_1), \Psi(S_2)(D|s_1)),$
$\qquad\quad d(\Psi(S_1)(D|s_2), \Psi(S_2)(D|s_2))\,\}$
$\leq \ $ [ind. hyp. for $(D|s_1), (D|s_2)$] $\frac{1}{2}d(S_1, S_2)$. $\square$

We see that, though all facts stated here concern sets rather than just sequences, the pattern in the semantic definitions and justifications has hardly changed. In fact, the proof of the first subcase just displayed is identical to what we gave in Lemma 1.42. A very similar observation holds for the final part of this subsection, in which we shall establish that $\mathcal{O} = \mathcal{D}$ on $\mathcal{L}_{cf}$.

We first introduce $\mathcal{E}$ as extension of $\mathcal{D}$ to $Decl \times Res \to \mathbb{P}_O$.

Definition 2.39 $\mathcal{E}(D|\mathrm{E}) = \{\epsilon\}$, $\mathcal{E}(D|s) = \mathcal{D}(D|s)$.

Next, we show, for Φ as in Definition 2.32,

Lemma 2.40 $\Phi(\mathcal{E}) = \mathcal{E}$, on $Decl \times Res$.

Proof We show that, for each $(D|r)$, $\Phi(\mathcal{E})(D|r) = \mathcal{E}(D|r)$, using induction on $wgt(D|r)$. One subcase.

$[s_1 + s_2]$ Recall that

$$s_1 + s_2 \xrightarrow{a}_D r \text{ iff } s_1 \xrightarrow{a}_D r \text{ or } s_2 \xrightarrow{a}_D r. \tag{2.10}$$

We also have

$$\mathcal{E}(D|s_1 + s_2) = \mathcal{E}(D|s_1) + \mathcal{E}(D|s_2). \tag{2.11}$$

Now

$$
\begin{aligned}
&\Phi(\mathcal{E})(D|s_1 + s_2) \\
&= \bigcup \{ a \cdot \mathcal{E}(D|r) \mid s_1 + s_2 \xrightarrow{a}_D r \} \\
&= [\text{by } (2.10)] \bigcup \{ a \cdot \mathcal{E}(D|r) \mid s_1 \xrightarrow{a}_D r \} \cup \bigcup \{ a \cdot \mathcal{E}(D|r) \mid s_2 \xrightarrow{a}_D r \} \\
&= [\text{def. } \Phi] \; \Phi(\mathcal{E})(D|s_1) \cup \Phi(\mathcal{E})(D|s_2) \\
&= [\text{ind. hyp.}] \; \mathcal{E}(D|s_1) \cup \mathcal{E}(D|s_2) \\
&= [\text{by } (2.11)] \; \mathcal{E}(D|s_1 + s_2). \qquad \qquad \square
\end{aligned}
$$

Lemma 2.40 constitutes the main step in the proof of

Theorem 2.41 $\mathcal{O}[\![\pi]\!] = \mathcal{D}[\![\pi]\!]$, for each $\pi \in \mathcal{L}_{cf}$.

Proof We have, for each $(D|s) \in \mathcal{L}_{cf}$, $\mathcal{O}[\![D|s]\!] = \mathcal{O}(D|s) = \mathcal{E}(D|s) = \mathcal{D}[\![D|s]\!]$, where the second equality follows from Lemma 2.40 and the definition of $\mathcal{O}$. $\square$

2.2.3 A continuation semantics for $\mathcal{L}_{cf}$

So far, we have dealt with two uniform languages ($\mathcal{L}_{rec}$ and $\mathcal{L}_{cf}$) and one nonuniform language ($\mathcal{L}_{wh}$). Whereas the former two were treated in terms of simple resumptions ($r ::= \mathrm{E} \mid s$) and without continuations, for the latter we used more structured resumptions ($r ::= \mathrm{E} \mid (s{:}r)$), and continuations in the definition of $\mathcal{D}$. In order to complete the picture, we now supply as well a continuation based semantics for $\mathcal{L}_{cf}$. In order to facilitate comparison of $\mathcal{O}$ and the new $\mathcal{D}$, we also update the operational semantics for $\mathcal{L}_{cf}$ in terms of a treatment based on structured resumptions. This is what we do first.

Definition 2.42 $r\,(\in Res') ::= \mathrm{E} \mid (s{:}r)$.

We shall not need the identification rule $\mathrm{E};r \equiv r$ for the r as defined here.

The adapted transition system specification for $\mathcal{L}_{cf}$ has the following form:

Definition 2.43 $\mathcal{T}_{cf}' = (Decl \times Res', Act, \rightarrow, Spec')$, where $Spec'$ consists of one axiom and three rules. (In the rules, we use the notation $r_1 \rightarrow_{0,D} r_2$ as shorthand for

$$\frac{r_2 \xrightarrow{a}_D r}{r_1 \xrightarrow{a}_D r},$$

cf. the definition of $\mathcal{T}_{wh}$.)

- $\quad a{:}r \xrightarrow{a}_D r$ \hfill (Act)

- $\quad x{:}r \rightarrow_{0,D} D(x){:}r$ \hfill (Rec)

- $\quad (s_1;s_2){:}r \rightarrow_{0,D} s_1{:}(s_2{:}r)$ \hfill (Seq)

- $\quad (s_1 + s_2){:}r \rightarrow_{0,D} s_1{:}r$ \hfill (Choice)

  $\quad (s_1 + s_2){:}r \rightarrow_{0,D} s_2{:}r$

In the notation for $Spec'$, we have taken the usual liberties in suppressing some parentheses.

The operational semantics obtained from $\mathcal{T}_{cf}'$ is given in

Definition 2.44

(a) $\mathcal{O}': Decl \times Res' \to \mathbb{P}_O$ is the unique mapping satisfying

$$\mathcal{O}'(D|\mathrm{E}) = \{\epsilon\}$$
$$\mathcal{O}'(D|s\text{:}r) = \bigcup\{\, a \cdot \mathcal{O}'(D|\bar{r}) \mid s\text{:}r \xrightarrow{a}_D \bar{r}\,\},$$

with ' $\to$ ' determined by $Spec'$.

(b) $\mathcal{O}'[\![D|s]\!] = \mathcal{O}'(D|s\text{:}\mathrm{E})$.

We omit justification of the well-definedness of $\mathcal{O}'$. The modified ($\mathcal{T}'_{cf}$ and) $\mathcal{O}'$ yields the same result as the earlier $\mathcal{O}$ (from definition 2.32). The proof requires some effort:

Lemma 2.45 $\mathcal{O}'[\![\pi]\!] = \mathcal{O}[\![\pi]\!]$, *for $\pi \in \mathcal{L}_{cf}$.*

Proof We extend our earlier defintion of ';' by putting $\{\epsilon\}; p = p; \{\epsilon\} = p$. We shall show that

$$\mathcal{O}'(D|s\text{:}r) = \mathcal{O}(D|s); \mathcal{O}'(D|r). \tag{2.12}$$

Taking $r \equiv \mathrm{E}$, the desired result then follows. The proof of (2.12) requires an application of the $\varepsilon \leq \varepsilon/2$ argument. Let us put

$$\varepsilon = sup\{\, d(\mathcal{O}'(D|s\text{:}r), \mathcal{O}(D|s); \mathcal{O}'(D|r)) \mid D \in Decl, r \in Res', s \in Stat\,\}.$$

We show that $\varepsilon \leq \varepsilon/2$ by induction on $wgt(D|s\text{:}r)$, where the function $wgt: Decl \times Res' \to \mathbb{N}$ is given as follows: $wgt(D|\mathrm{E}) = 0$, $wgt(D|s\text{:}r) = wgt(D|s)$, with $wgt(D|s)$ as in Definition 2.25. We treat two subcases.

$[x\text{:}r]$ Then

$$\mathcal{O}'(D|x\text{:}r)$$
$$= \;\; \mathcal{O}'(D|D(x)\text{:}r)$$
$$= \;\; [\text{ind. hyp.}] \;\; \mathcal{O}(D|D(x)); \mathcal{O}'(D|r)$$
$$= \;\; [\text{Lemma 2.34a}] \;\; \mathcal{O}(D|x); \mathcal{O}'(D|r).$$

$[(s_1;s_2)\text{:}r]$ This case is more involved. We use the fact that, for any $p, p_1, p_2 \in \mathbb{P}_O$ such that $\epsilon \notin p$, we have that $d(p;p_1, p;p_2) \leq \frac{1}{2}d(p_1, p_2)$ (an easy corollary of Lemma 2.36c).

$$d(\mathcal{O}'(D|(s_1;s_2)\text{:}r), \mathcal{O}(D|s_1;s_2); \mathcal{O}'(D|r))$$

$$
\begin{aligned}
&= \quad \text{[by } \mathcal{T}'_{cf}, \text{ Theorem 2.41, and associativity of `;']} \\
&\quad\ d(\mathcal{O}'(D|s_1{:}(s_2{:}r)), \mathcal{O}(D|s_1);(\mathcal{O}(D|s_2);\mathcal{O}'(D|r))) \\
&= \quad \text{[ind. hyp.] } d(\mathcal{O}(D|s_1);\mathcal{O}'(D|s_2{:}r), \mathcal{O}(D|s_1);(\mathcal{O}(D|s_2);\mathcal{O}'(D|r))) \\
&\leq \quad \tfrac{1}{2}d(\mathcal{O}'(D|s_2{:}r), \mathcal{O}(D|s_2);\mathcal{O}'(D|r)) \\
&\leq \quad \text{[def. } \varepsilon] \ \varepsilon/2,
\end{aligned}
$$

where we have used the easily proven fact that $\epsilon \notin \mathcal{O}(D|s)$, for each $(D|s) \in \mathcal{L}_{cf}$.

That $\mathcal{O}'[\![\pi]\!] = \mathcal{O}[\![\pi]\!]$ is now immediate from (2.12). $\square$

We continue with the introduction of the continuation-style denotational semantics $\mathcal{D}'$ for $\mathcal{L}_{cf}$. Now we put $(p \in) \mathbb{P}_D = \mathcal{P}_{nco}(Act^\infty)$ and we take $(\gamma \in) Cont = \mathbb{P}_D$, with $\gamma_\epsilon = \{\epsilon\}$. The first, easy, step consists in defining prefixing on $Cont$:

Definition 2.46 For $a \in Act$, $\gamma \in Cont$, we put

$$
a \cdot \gamma = \{\, a \cdot q \mid q \in \gamma \,\}.
$$

Next, we take, for $p_1, p_2 \in \mathbb{P}_D$, $p_1 + p_2$ with the same meaning as before. The semantic `;' has no role here, since the use of continuations renders this operator superfluous.

The definition of $\mathcal{D}'$ follows.

Definition 2.47

(a) $\mathcal{D}' : \mathcal{L}_{cf} \to Cont \overset{\frac{1}{2}}{\to} \mathbb{P}_D$ is the unique function satisfying

$$
\begin{aligned}
\mathcal{D}'(D|a)(\gamma) &= a \cdot \gamma \\
\mathcal{D}'(D|x)(\gamma) &= \mathcal{D}'(D|D(x))(\gamma) \\
\mathcal{D}'(D|s_1;s_2)(\gamma) &= \mathcal{D}'(D|s_1)(\mathcal{D}'(D|s_2)(\gamma)) \\
\mathcal{D}'(D|s_1 + s_2)(\gamma) &= \mathcal{D}'(D|s_1)(\gamma) + \mathcal{D}'(D|s_2)(\gamma).
\end{aligned}
$$

(b) $\mathcal{D}'[\![D|s]\!] = \mathcal{D}'(D|s)(\gamma_\epsilon)$.

The argument showing well-definedness of $\mathcal{D}'$ is almost identical to the one used for the same claim for $\mathcal{D}$ on $\mathcal{L}_{wh}$. More specifically, we may show the following

Lemma 2.48 *Let* $(S \in)Sem'_D = \mathcal{L}_{cf} \to Cont \xrightarrow{\frac{1}{2}} \mathbb{P}_D$, *and let* $\Psi': Sem'_D \to Sem'_D$
be given by

$$
\begin{aligned}
\Psi'(S)(D|a)(\gamma) &= a \cdot \gamma \\
\Psi'(S)(D|x)(\gamma) &= \Psi'(S)(D|D(x))(\gamma) \\
\Psi'(S)(D|s_1;s_2)(\gamma) &= \Psi'(S)(D|s_1)(S(D|s_2)(\gamma)) \\
\Psi'(S)(D|s_1 + s_2)(\gamma) &= \Psi'(S)(D|s_1)(\gamma) + \Psi'(S)(D|s_2)(\gamma).
\end{aligned}
$$

Then

(a) Ψ' *is well-defined, i.e.,* $\Psi'(S)(D|s)(\gamma) \in \mathbb{P}_D$, *for each* $S \in Sem'_D$, $(D|s) \in \mathcal{L}_{cf}$,
$\gamma \in Cont$, *and* $\Psi'(S)(D|s)$ *is* $\frac{1}{2}$-*contractive in* γ.

(b) Ψ' *is* $\frac{1}{2}$-*contractive in* S.

Proof The details of the proof are virtually the same as those of the proof of Lemma 1.63, and left as an exercise. □

It is not difficult to relate $\mathcal{O}'$ and $\mathcal{D}'$. Following the technique as first described for $\mathcal{L}_{wh}$, we introduce

Definition 2.49 $\mathcal{E}': Decl \times Res' \to \mathbb{P}_O$ *is given by*

$$
\begin{aligned}
\mathcal{E}'(D|\mathrm{E}) &= \{\epsilon\} \\
\mathcal{E}'(D|s{:}r) &= \mathcal{D}'(D|s)(\mathcal{E}'(D|r)).
\end{aligned}
$$

Next, we show, for Φ' the higher-order mapping (implicitly) used to define $\mathcal{O}'$,

Lemma 2.50 $\Phi'(\mathcal{E}') = \mathcal{E}'$.

The next lemma is the counterpart of Lemma 1.66.

Lemma 2.51

(a) *If* $r \to_{0,D} r'$, *and* r *is not of the form* $(s_1 + s_2){:}\bar{r}$, *then* $\mathcal{E}'(D|r) = \mathcal{E}'(D|r')$.

(b) $\mathcal{E}'(D|(s_1 + s_2){:}\bar{r}) = \mathcal{E}'(D|s_1{:}\bar{r}) \cup \mathcal{E}'(D|s_2{:}\bar{r})$.

Proof Exercise. □

We now give the

Proof of Lemma 2.50 We show that, for each $(D|r)$, $\Phi'(\mathcal{E}')(D|r) = \mathcal{E}'(D|r)$, by induction on $wgt(D|r)$. Two subcases.

$[x{:}r]$ $\quad \Phi'(\mathcal{E}')(D|x{:}r)$

$\quad = \quad$ [def. $\mathcal{T}'_{cf}$] $\Phi'(\mathcal{E}')(D|D(x){:}r)$

$\quad = \quad$ [ind. hyp.] $\mathcal{E}'(D|D(x){:}r)$

$\quad = \quad$ [Lemma 2.51] $\mathcal{E}'(D|x{:}r)$.

$[(s_1 + s_2){:}r]$ $\quad \Phi'(\mathcal{E}')(D|(s_1 + s_2){:}r)$

$\quad = \quad$ [def. $\mathcal{T}'_{cf}$] $\Phi'(\mathcal{E}')(D|s_1{:}r) \cup \Phi'(\mathcal{E}')(D|s_2{:}r)$

$\quad = \quad$ [ind. hyp] $\mathcal{E}'(D|s_1{:}r) \cup \mathcal{E}'(D|s_2{:}r)$

$\quad = \quad$ [Lemma 2.51] $\mathcal{E}'(D|(s_1 + s_2){:}r)$. $\qquad\qquad\qquad\square$

The equivalence of $\mathcal{O}'$ and $\mathcal{D}'$ on $\mathcal{L}_{cf}$ now immediately follows.

Theorem 2.52 $\mathcal{O}'[\![\pi]\!] = \mathcal{D}'[\![\pi]\!]$, for $\pi \in \mathcal{L}_{cf}$.

Proof Immediate from the definitions and Lemma 2.50. $\qquad\qquad\qquad\square$

One final task remains, viz. to establish the relationship between $\mathcal{D}$ and $\mathcal{D}'$. Mimicking what we showed for $\mathcal{O}$ and $\mathcal{O}'$, we here have

Lemma 2.53

(a) For each $(D|s) \in \mathcal{L}_{cf}$, $p \in \mathbb{P}_D (= Cont)$,

$$\mathcal{D}(D|s);p = \mathcal{D}'(D|s)(p)$$

(b) $\mathcal{D}[\![D|s]\!] = \mathcal{D}'[\![D|s]\!]$.

Proof We only treat part (a). Let $\varepsilon = sup\{\, d(\mathcal{D}(D|s);p, \mathcal{D}'(D|s)(p)) \mid D \in Decl, s \in Stat \,\}$. We show $\varepsilon \leq \varepsilon/2$ by induction on $wgt(D|s)$. Two subcases.

$[x]$ $\quad \mathcal{D}(D|x);p = \mathcal{D}(D|D(x));p =$ [ind. hyp.] $\mathcal{D}'(D|D(x))(p) = \mathcal{D}'(D|x)(p)$.

$[s_1{;}s_2]$ $\quad$ Take any D, s_1, s_2, p. Then

$\quad d(\mathcal{D}(D|s_1{;}s_2);p, \mathcal{D}'(D|s_1{;}s_2)(p))$

$\quad = \quad$ [def. $\mathcal{D}, \mathcal{D}'$] $d(\mathcal{D}(D|s_1);(\mathcal{D}(D|s_2);p), \mathcal{D}'(D|s_1)(\mathcal{D}'(D|s_2)(p)))$

$\quad = \quad$ [ind. hyp. for s_1] $d(\mathcal{D}'(D|s_1)(\mathcal{D}(D|s_2);p), \mathcal{D}'(D|s_1)(\mathcal{D}'(D|s_2)(p)))$

$\quad \leq \quad$ [$\mathcal{D}'(D|s)$ is $\frac{1}{2}$-contractive in γ] $\frac{1}{2}d(\mathcal{D}(D|s_2);p, \mathcal{D}'(D|s_2)(p))$

$\quad \leq \quad \varepsilon/2$. $\qquad\qquad\qquad\qquad\qquad\qquad\qquad\qquad\qquad\qquad\square$

This concludes our treatment of the continuation semantics for $\mathcal{L}_{cf}$, thus bringing our comparative semantic analysis of $\mathcal{L}_{cf}$ to an end. Now that Chapter 2 has been completed, we have laid the foundations for the development of the semantics for a large variety of further control flow notions to be treated in Part II. Most of this will not demand further metric tools (a modest exception appearing in Chapter 5). Only in Part III will we need essential extensions of the basic metric theory as used so far.

Before embarking upon all this—applications in Part II, further theory in Part III—we first devote a separate chapter to some mild variations on the themes elaborated up till now.

2.3   Exercises

Exercise 2.1 Give an example of a metric space (M, d) and of closed sets X_i, $X_i \subseteq M$, $i \in I$ (I an arbitrary index set) such that $\bigcup_{i \in I} X_i$ is not closed.

Exercise 2.2 Let d'_H be as in Definition 2.6. Prove $\bar{X} = \{ x \mid d'_H(x, X) = 0 \}$.

Exercise 2.3 Prove that $d_H(\{x\}, \{y\}) = d(x, y)$.

Exercise 2.4 Prove that the operation of set-intersection ('$\cap$') is not nonexpansive (on $(\mathcal{P}_{ncl}(M), d_H) \times (\mathcal{P}_{ncl}(M), d_H) \to (\mathcal{P}_{cl}(M), d_H)$).

Exercise 2.5 Let (M, d) be a (1-bounded) metric space. Let X be any set, and let $Y \subseteq X$. Let $f, g \colon X \to M$ be functions. Prove $d_H(f(Y), g(Y)) \leq d_F(f, g)$.

Exercise 2.6 Let $p \colon [0, 1] \to \{tt, ff\}$ be such that, if $\alpha \leq \beta$ then $p(\alpha) \Rightarrow p(\beta)$. Show that $inf\{ \alpha \in [0, 1] \mid p(\alpha) \} = inf\{ 2^{-n} \mid p(2^{-n}) \}$.

Exercise 2.7

(a) Let $X, Y \in (\mathcal{P}_{ncl}(M), d_H)$. Prove that, for all $\varepsilon > 0$,

$$d_H(X,Y) \leq \varepsilon \iff \forall \delta > 0 \, [\forall x \in X \exists y \in Y \, (d(x,y) \leq \varepsilon + \delta) \wedge$$
$$\forall y \in Y \exists x \in X \, (d(x,y) \leq \varepsilon + \delta) \quad].$$

(b) Let $X, Y \in (\mathcal{P}_{nco}(M), d_H)$. Prove

$$\forall x \in X \exists y \in Y \, [d(x,y) = d_H(X,Y)] \wedge \forall y \in Y \exists x \in X \, [d(x,y) = d_H(X,Y)].$$

Exercise 2.8 Let $\mathbb{R}_{\geq} = [0, \infty)$ be equipped with the usual metric, and let $f \colon \mathbb{R}_{\geq} \to \mathbb{R}_{\geq}$ be given by $f(x) = 2^{-x}$. Show that f is a continuous function which maps the closed set $[0, \infty)$ to the nonclosed set $(0, 1]$.

Exercise 2.9 Explain why Lemma 2.21 requires the set X to be closed.

Exercise 2.10 Explain that it is not possible to prove Lemma 2.53 directly from (2.12), using Theorem 2.41 and Theorem 2.52.

Exercise 2.11

(a) Prove that, for $\mathcal{X} \in \mathcal{P}_{co}(\mathcal{P}_{cl}(M))$, $\bigcup \mathcal{X} \in \mathcal{P}_{cl}(M)$.

(b) Prove that the mappings

$$\bigcup \colon \mathcal{P}_{co}(\mathcal{P}_{co}(M)) \to \mathcal{P}_{co}(M)$$
$$\bigcup \colon \mathcal{P}_{co}(\mathcal{P}_{cl}(M)) \to \mathcal{P}_{cl}(M)$$

are nonexpansive.

Exercise 2.12 Let (M, d) be a metric space, and let $X \subseteq M$. We call X *totally bounded* whenever, for each $\varepsilon > 0$, we have that X can be covered by a *finite* collection of open ε-balls. (That is, putting $B_\varepsilon(x) = \{ y \mid d(x,y) < \varepsilon \}$, we have that, for all $\varepsilon > 0$, $X \subseteq \bigcup \{ B_\varepsilon(x) \mid x \in F \}$, F a finite subset of M.) Prove that, for (M, d) complete, we have

X is compact $\iff$ X is closed and totally bounded.

(Hint: A proof may be based on Theorem A.4 of Appendix A.)

Exercise 2.13 Consider the setting of Lemma 2.45. Define $\mathcal{P} \colon Decl \times Res \to \mathbb{P}_O$ by putting $\mathcal{P}(D|E) = \{\epsilon\}$, $\mathcal{P}(D|s{:}r) = \mathcal{O}(D|s); \mathcal{O}'(D|r)$. Prove that $\Phi'(\mathcal{P}) = \mathcal{P}$, and use this to obtain a proof of the lemma replacing the '$\varepsilon \leq \varepsilon/2$' proof principle by the (usual) unique fixed point principle.

Exercise 2.14 (This exercise continues Exercise 1.11.) Let $(p \in) \mathbb{P} = \mathcal{P}_{ncl}(Act^\infty \setminus \{\epsilon\}) \cup \{\{\epsilon\}\}$, let $p_a = \{ q \mid a \cdot q \in p, q \neq \epsilon \}$, and let '$\xrightarrow{a}$' be the following relation on $\mathbb{P}$:

$$\begin{cases} p \xrightarrow{a} p_a & \text{if } p_a \neq \emptyset \\ p \xrightarrow{a} \{\epsilon\} & \text{if } a \in p. \end{cases}$$

Define, inductively, $\sim_0 = \mathbb{P} \times \mathbb{P}$, and

$$\sim_{n+1} = \{ (p_1, p_2) \mid \exists p_1' \, [p_1 \xrightarrow{a} p_1' \Rightarrow \exists p_2' \, [p_2 \xrightarrow{a} p_2' \wedge p_1' \sim_n p_2']] $$
$$\text{and vice-versa} \} \,.$$

Prove that, for all $p_1, p_2 \in \mathbb{P}$,

$$d_H(p_1, p_2) \;=\; inf\{\, 2^{-n} \mid p_1 \sim_n p_2 \,\}\,.$$

Infer that, putting $\sim \,=\, \bigcap_n \sim_n$, we have that $p_1 \sim p_2$ iff $d_H(p_1, p_2) = 0$ (iff $p_1 = p_2$).

2.4   Bibliographical notes

The definition of the Hausdorff metric and Theorem 2.3 are due to [Hau14]. The theorems of Hahn and Kuratowski are from [Hah32] and [Kur56], respectively. Michael's theorem is from [Mic51]. The equivalence—for metric spaces—of our definition of compactness (Definition 2.11) and the usual topological one (Definition 2.18) is a classical result due to Hausdorff and Gross ([Hau14, Gro14]); preservation of compactness by continuous maps is from [Ale27]. The theorem stating the compactness of the (operational) semantics associated with a finitely branching transition system seems to be folklore; for a rigorous proof see, e.g., [Bre94b] (and our Appendix B). Our lifting lemma is a variation on a similar result in a cpo-setting (cpo for complete partial order) in [MV88].

The language $\mathcal{L}_{cf}$ generalizes the well-known notion of a context free language as studied in formal language theory (e.g., [HU79]), in that we allow the production of finite *and infinite* words. In that respect, our treatment continues earlier work of Nivat ([Niv77, Niv78]), where fixed point properties of infinitary languages are studied. The equivalence of $\mathcal{O}$ and $\mathcal{D}$ for $\mathcal{L}_{cf}$ extends a classical result for the finitary case by Schutzenberger ([Sch63]). The theory of infinitary languages has strong connections with automata theory over infinite words, cf. [HR85, Tho90a].

Nondeterminacy is a central notion in programming. Its origins can be traced back both to automata theory, to phenomena in the physical world in which the computers executing our programs operate, and to notions in programming languages themselves. In its simplest form, these are exemplified by the operator '+' for $\mathcal{L}_{cf}$. Other constructs embodying forms of nondeterminacy are Dijkstra's guarded commands (cf. Chapter 3) and the wide spectrum of notions of (interleaving) parallelism studied in several of the later chapters (Chapters 4, 7, 11–16).

3 Variations

This chapter is devoted to a study of several variations on the themes as developed in Chapters 1 and 2. Two seemingly disparate language concepts are treated, viz. that of guarded commands and that of goto statements. Though neither of them requires the introduction of new metric tools, they both demand for their semantic definitions some techniques which are not quite as smooth as the ones applied so far.

Guarded commands constitute a variation on (the language with) while statements. Two new topics are addressed, one on the language level, and one on the semantic description level. The new language notion is that of *deadlock* (here synonymous with "abort")—a notion which is to play a key role in Part III, where various forms of parallelism are studied. For the moment, the consequences of the presence of deadlock are not as drastic as in Part III, where an essential extension of the linear domains used till now will turn out to be necessary. Still, some not so transparent semantic calculations are in order for its full analysis. The second topic involves a different denotational treatment of recursion (here in the form of iteration): rather than using the "global" technique where $\mathcal{D}$ is defined, for the program as a whole, as fixed point of one higher order operator, we adopt the approach which is properly compositional: For each $s, \mathcal{D}(s)$ is expressed in terms of the meanings of its constituents. In contrast with the global technique, we now follow a "local" method, in that we determine a fixed point for each iteration statement occurring in the program.

The section on goto statements—here introduced in terms of a simple variation on $\mathcal{L}_{cf}$—has as main feature the specification of continuations by means of a *system* of equations. This section is included not so much because the technique to be described is of special mathematical interest. Rather, the motivation for it is primarily historical, since continuations were conceived originally to handle goto statements.

3.1 Guarded commands—$\mathcal{D}$ without higher order

The language $\mathcal{L}_{gc}$ studied in this section brings some modest variations on $\mathcal{L}_{wh}$. Firstly, it includes a form of nondeterminism, necessitating an extension of the semantic framework as developed for $\mathcal{L}_{wh}$ with the use of (compact) powerdomains. No more than a small change with respect to the powerdomains as used for $\mathcal{L}_{cf}$ will be needed here. Secondly, $\mathcal{L}_{gc}$ has a form of *deadlock*—a programming phenomenon in which no further action is possible. In the design of $\mathcal{T}_{gc}$, this will become visible in

the presence of resumptions $r \not\equiv E$ for which no transition is possible. Semantically, a special symbol δ will be used to model deadlock, and some new rules to handle δ will be introduced. As further feature of our semantic model for $\mathcal{L}_{gc}$ we mention the way we define $\mathcal{D}$ for $\mathcal{L}_{gc}$. Contrary to what we did everywhere before, we shall *not* introduce a higher-order mapping Ψ, and put

$$\mathcal{D} = \text{fix}(\Psi). \tag{3.1}$$

Rather, we give a properly compositional definition of $\mathcal{D}(s)$ for all $s \in \mathcal{L}_{gc}$, including the case that s involves a form of iteration. Thus, for each s, $\mathcal{D}(s)$ will be composed, by means of suitable semantic operators, in terms of $\mathcal{D}(s')$, with s' a proper (syntactic) constituent of s. Briefly, instead of following a *global* fixed point definition of $\mathcal{D}$, as in (3.1), we now adopt a *local* approach, in that we invoke a fixed point definition specifically to deal with the iterative construct—a variation on the while statement—of $\mathcal{L}_{gc}$.

3.1.1 Syntax and operational semantics

$\mathcal{L}_{gc}$ is a nonuniform language with individual variables $(v \in) IVar$ and expressions $(e \in) Exp$ as before. The sequential composition $(s;s)$ is the standard one. New constructs appear as variations on the conditional and while statement from $\mathcal{L}_{wh}$ in a way which exhibits a form of nondeterminism.

Definition 3.1

(a) $s (\in Stat) ::= v := e \mid \text{skip} \mid (s;s) \mid \text{if } g \text{ fi} \mid \text{do } g \text{ od}.$

(b) $g (\in Guard) ::= (e \rightarrow s) \mid g \square g.$

(c) $(\pi \in) \mathcal{L}_{gc} = Stat.$

Remark In clause (b), the (intended) type of e is logical.

Examples if $(v < 0 \rightarrow u := -1) \square (v > 0 \rightarrow u := 1)$ fi,
do $(v < 5 \rightarrow v := v + 1)$ od, if $(\text{true} \rightarrow v := 1) \square (\text{true} \rightarrow v := 2)$ fi.

Notation 3.2 Throughout this section, we shall use the notation s_{if} for a typical if-statement if g fi $\equiv$ if $(e_1 \rightarrow s_1) \square \ldots \square (e_n \rightarrow s_n)$ fi $(n \geq 1)$, and the notation s_{do} for a typical do-statement do g od $\equiv$ do $(e_1 \rightarrow s_1) \square \ldots \square (e_n \rightarrow s_n)$ od $(n \geq 1)$.

Though resembling them in their name, the guards $g\,(\in Guard)$ are completely different (both syntactically and as to their intended meaning) from the guarded statements from $\mathcal{L}_{rec}$ or $\mathcal{L}_{cf}$.

Informally, the meaning of if g fi and do g od can be explained as follows: Let $g \equiv (e_1 \rightarrow s_1)\square \ldots \square (e_n \rightarrow s_n),\ n \geq 1$.

- $s_{\mathrm{if}} \equiv$ if g fi is executed in state σ by nondeterministically selecting some i such that e_i is true in σ, and then executing s_i. In case none of the e_i is true in σ, the statement s_{if} deadlocks, i.e., no further execution is possible (neither of s_{if} nor of any statement embracing s_{if}).

- $s_{\mathrm{do}} \equiv$ do g od is executed in state σ by nondeterministically selecting some i such that e_i is true in σ, and then executing $(s_i;s_{\mathrm{do}})$. In case none of the e_i is true in σ, the statement s_{do} is equivalent to skip.

The transition system specification $\mathcal{T}_{gc}$ is given as a variation on $\mathcal{T}_{wh}$ incorporating the operational intuition as just described.

Definition 3.3

(a) $r\,(\in Res) ::= \mathrm{E}|(s{:}r)$.

(b) $\mathcal{T}_{gc} = (Res \times \Sigma, \Sigma, \rightarrow, Spec)$, where $Spec$ consists of—the notation is as for $\mathcal{T}_{wh}$—

- $\quad [(v := e){:}r, \sigma] \rightarrow [r, \sigma\{\alpha/v\}] \qquad$ where $\alpha = \mathcal{V}(e)(\sigma)$ $\hfill$ (Ass)

- $\quad [\mathsf{skip}{:}r, \sigma] \rightarrow [r, \sigma]$ $\hfill$ (Skip)

- $\quad [(s_1;s_2){:}r, \sigma] \rightarrow_0 [s_1{:}(s_2{:}r), \sigma]$ $\hfill$ (Seq)

- $\quad [\mathsf{if}\ (e_1 \rightarrow s_1)\square \ldots \square (e_n \rightarrow s_n)\ \mathsf{fi}{:}r, \sigma] \rightarrow_0 [s_i{:}r, \sigma]$ $\hfill$ (If)

  $$\text{if } \mathcal{V}(e_i)(\sigma) = tt \text{ for some } i,\ 1 \leq i \leq n$$

- $\quad [\mathsf{do}\ (e_1 \rightarrow s_1)\square \ldots \square (e_n \rightarrow s_n)\ \mathsf{od}{:}r, \sigma] \rightarrow_0$ $\hfill$ (Do 1)

  $$[(s_i;\mathsf{do}\ (e_1 \rightarrow s_1)\square \ldots \square (e_n \rightarrow s_n)\ \mathsf{od}){:}r, \sigma]$$

  $$\text{if } \mathcal{V}(e_i)(\sigma) = tt \text{ for some } i,\ 1 \leq i \leq n$$

- $\quad [\mathsf{do}\ (e_1 \rightarrow s_1)\square \ldots \square (e_n \rightarrow s_n)\ \mathsf{od}{:}r, \sigma] \rightarrow_0 [\mathsf{skip}{:}r, \sigma]$ $\hfill$ (Do 2)

  $$\text{if } \mathcal{V}(e)(\sigma) = f\!f, \text{ for all } i,\ 1 \leq i \leq n$$

As important—albeit somewhat hidden—feature of $\mathcal{T}_{gc}$ we observe that *no* transitions are defined for an if-statement for which none of the e_i is true in the present state. In general, we shall say that $[r, \sigma]$ *blocks* if no transition is possible (according to $\mathcal{T}_{gc}$) for $[r, \sigma]$, i.e., if $\mathcal{S}(r, \sigma) = \emptyset$. We use $[r, \sigma] \not\rightarrow$ as short-hand for '$[r, \sigma]$ blocks'. As first lemma concerning this notion—which also takes into account the way in which a configuration $[r, \sigma]$ may block due to constituents of r—we have

Lemma 3.4 *Let* $g \equiv (e_1 \rightarrow s_1) \square \ldots \square (e_n \rightarrow s_n)$.

(a) $[\text{if } g \text{ fi}:r, \sigma] \not\rightarrow$ *iff* $\forall i[\mathcal{V}(e_i)(\sigma) = \mathit{ff} \vee [s_i:r, \sigma] \not\rightarrow]$.

(b) $[\text{do } g \text{ od}:r, \sigma] \not\rightarrow$ *iff*
$\exists i[\mathcal{V}(e_i)(\sigma) = \mathit{tt}] \wedge \forall i[\mathcal{V}(e_i)(\sigma) = \mathit{tt} \Rightarrow [(s_i;\text{do } g \text{ od}):r, \sigma] \not\rightarrow]$.

Proof By the definition of the (If) and (Do)-rules in $\mathcal{T}_{gc}$. $\qquad\qquad\square$

The possibility of blocking explains a new type of clause in the definition of $\mathcal{O}$ based on $\mathcal{T}_{gc}$ which we shall soon present. By way of preparation, we introduce the special symbol δ to reflect the situation where a configuration $[r, \sigma]$, with $r \not\equiv \mathrm{E}$, cannot make a transition. This in turn induces the need for an extension of the domain of possible outcomes. Whereas for $\mathcal{L}_{wh}$ we used $\mathbb{P}_O = \Sigma \rightarrow \Sigma^\infty$, we now use

$$\mathbb{P}_O = \Sigma \rightarrow \mathcal{P}_{nco}(\Sigma_\delta^\infty) \qquad\qquad (3.2)$$

where

Definition 3.5 $\Sigma_\delta^\infty = \Sigma^* \cup \Sigma^* \cdot \{\delta\} \cup \Sigma^\omega$.

Thus, Σ_δ^∞ consists of all finite or infinite sequences of states (i.e., Σ^∞ as used before), together with the set of finite sequences of states with δ concatenated at the end.

We are now ready for

Definition 3.6

(a) Let $(S \in) \mathit{Sem}_O = \mathit{Res} \times \Sigma \rightarrow \mathcal{P}_{nco}(\Sigma_\delta^\infty)$. We define $\Phi: \mathit{Sem}_O \rightarrow \mathit{Sem}_O$ by putting

$$\Phi(S)(\mathrm{E}, \sigma) = \{\epsilon\}$$

$$\Phi(S)(s:r, \sigma) = \begin{cases} \{\delta\} & \text{if } [s:r, \sigma] \not\rightarrow \\ \bigcup \{\sigma' \cdot S(r', \sigma') \mid [s:r, \sigma] \rightarrow [r', \sigma']\} & \text{otherwise.} \end{cases}$$

(b) $\mathcal{O}: Res \times \Sigma \rightarrow \mathcal{P}_{nco}(\Sigma_\delta^\infty)$ is given as $\mathcal{O} = fix(\Phi)$.

(c) $\mathcal{O}[\![\cdot]\!]: \mathcal{L}_{gc} \rightarrow \mathbb{P}_O$ is given as $\mathcal{O}[\![s]\!] = \lambda\sigma.\mathcal{O}(s{:}E, \sigma)$.

Examples

(1) $\mathcal{O}[\![\text{if } (v < 0 \rightarrow u := -1)\square(v > 0 \rightarrow u := 1) \text{ fi}]\!](\sigma\{10/v\})$
$= \mathcal{O}(\text{if } (v < 0 \rightarrow u := -1)\square(v > 0 \rightarrow u := 1) \text{ fi}{:}E, \sigma\{10/v\})$
$= \sigma\{10/v, 1/u\} \cdot \mathcal{O}(E, \sigma\{10/v, 1/u\})$
$= \sigma\{10/v, 1/u\} \cdot \{\epsilon\}$
$= \{\sigma\{10/v, 1/u\}\}$

(2) $\mathcal{O}[\![\text{if } (v < 0 \rightarrow u := -1)\square(v > 0 \rightarrow u := 1) \text{ fi}]\!](\sigma\{0/v\})$
$= \mathcal{O}(\text{if } (v < 0 \rightarrow u := -1)\square(v > 0 \rightarrow u := 1) \text{ fi}, \sigma\{0/v\})$
$= \{\delta\}$

(3) $\mathcal{O}[\![\text{do } (v < 5 \rightarrow v := v + 1) \text{ od}]\!](\sigma\{4/v\})$
$= \mathcal{O}(\text{do } (v < 5 \rightarrow v := v + 1) \text{ od}, \sigma\{4/v\})$
$= \sigma\{5/v\} \cdot \mathcal{O}(\text{do } (v < 5 \rightarrow v := v + 1) \text{ od}, \sigma\{5/v\})$
$= \sigma\{5/v\} \cdot \sigma\{5/v\} \cdot \mathcal{O}(E, \sigma\{5/v\})$
$= \{\sigma\{5/v\}\sigma\{5/v\}\}$

(4) $\mathcal{O}[\![\text{if } (\text{true} \rightarrow v := 1)\square(\text{true} \rightarrow v := 2) \text{ fi}]\!](\sigma)$
$= \mathcal{O}(\text{if } (\text{true} \rightarrow v := 1)\square(\text{true} \rightarrow v := 2) \text{ fi}{:}E, \sigma)$
$= \sigma\{1/v\} \cdot \mathcal{O}(E, \sigma\{1/v\}) \cup \sigma\{2/v\} \cdot \mathcal{O}(E, \sigma\{2/v\})$
$= \{\sigma\{1/v\}, \sigma\{2/v\}\}$

$\cdot$

Just as we had to do in Section 1.2, various facts have to be verified. The main tool is, again, the weight function, as given in

Definition 3.7 $wgt: Res \cup Stat \rightarrow \mathbb{N}$ is given by

$$
\begin{aligned}
wgt(E) &= 0 \\
wgt(s{:}r) &= wgt(s) \\
wgt(v := e) &= wgt(\text{skip}) = 1 \\
wgt(s_1{;}s_2) &= wgt(s_1) + 1 \\
wgt(\text{if } g \text{ fi}) &= max\{\, wgt(s_i) \mid 1 \leq i \leq n \,\} + 1 \\
wgt(\text{do } g \text{ od}) &= max\{\, wgt(s_i) + 1 \mid 1 \leq i \leq n \,\} + 1.
\end{aligned}
$$

Well-definedness of *wgt* is immediate by induction on the syntactic complexity of its argument.

We now state

Lemma 3.8

(a) T_{gc} is finitely branching.

(b) $\Phi(S)(r,\sigma) \in \mathcal{P}_{nco}(\Sigma_\delta^\infty)$, for each S, r, σ.

(c) Φ is $\frac{1}{2}$-contractive in S.

Proof

(a) Using induction on $wgt(r)$, we may show that $0 \leq |\mathcal{S}(r,\sigma)| < \infty$, for each r and σ. For the s_{if} and s_{do} cases the results follow immediately by the identities

$$
\begin{aligned}
\mathcal{S}(s_{if}{:}r,\sigma) &= \bigcup\{\mathcal{S}(s_i{:}r,\sigma) \mid \mathcal{V}(e_i)(\sigma) = tt\} \\
\mathcal{S}(s_{do}{:}r,\sigma) &= \bigcup\{\mathcal{S}((s_i;s_{do}){:}r,\sigma) \mid \mathcal{V}(e_i)(\sigma) = tt\} \cup \\
&\quad \{\mathcal{S}(\mathsf{skip}{:}r,\sigma) \mid \forall i[\mathcal{V}(e_i)(\sigma) = ff\,]\}.
\end{aligned}
$$

(b) Clear if $r \equiv \mathrm{E}$ or $[r,\sigma] \not\to$. In case $[s{:}r,\sigma] \to [r',\sigma']$ we know, by part (a), that only finitely many such $[r',\sigma']$ are possible. Hence, the union on the right-hand side of the clause for $\Phi(S)(s{:}r)(\sigma)$ is taken over a finite index set. Since each of the sets $\sigma' \cdot S(r',\sigma')$ is (nonempty and) compact (by the assumption on S), so is the result of uniting them.

(c) Standard. $\square$

Remark In order to complete the above argument, we also have to verify that $\mathcal{O}_d(r,\sigma)$ is compact, for each r,σ. Note that we cannot simply invoke Theorem 2.30 in the form as stated, since in T_{gc} we have *two* cases where $[r,\sigma]$ cannot make a step, viz. $r \equiv \mathrm{E}$, or $r \not\equiv E$ and $[r,\sigma] \not\to$. In Exercise 3.4, we show how to handle this.

One final point concerning the operational semantics for $\mathcal{L}_{gc}$ is worth mentioning. Viewing δ as indicating deadlock—no further action is possible—it is natural to expect that δ is not delivered as a possible outcome *together* with (i.e., as element of the same set as) some alternatives: in case an alternative is present, there is no reason to signal deadlock as a result of the computation. In formal terms, this is expressed by the claim that either $\mathcal{O}(r)(\sigma) = \{\delta\}$, or $\mathcal{O}(r)(\sigma)$ is a (nonempty and compact) subset of $\Sigma^* \cup \Sigma^+ \cdot \{\delta\} \cup \Sigma^\omega$. (Here Σ^+ is the set of all nonempty sequences of states; note that $\delta \notin \Sigma^+ \cdot \{\delta\}$.) This is the content of the next lemma.

Lemma 3.9 *For each r, σ, either*

- $\mathcal{O}(r)(\sigma) = \{\delta\}$

or

- $\mathcal{O}(r)(\sigma) \in \mathcal{P}_{nco}(\Sigma^* \cup \Sigma^+ \cdot \{\delta\} \cup \Sigma^\omega)$.

Proof Immediate by the way $\{\delta\}$ is delivered as outcome in the clause for $\Phi(S)(s{:}r)(\sigma)$.   □

In the next subsection, where we design the denotational semantics for $\mathcal{L}_{gc}$, we will have to make sure that the denotational counterpart of the lemma holds as well (anticipating the desired $\mathcal{O}[\![\cdot]\!] = \mathcal{D}[\![\cdot]\!]$ result).

3.1.2   Denotational semantics, equivalence of $\mathcal{O}$ and $\mathcal{D}$

The denotational semantics $\mathcal{D}$ for $\mathcal{L}_{gc}$ uses continuations in the same way as was the case with $\mathcal{D}$ for $\mathcal{L}_{wh}$. The main new element in the definition of $\mathcal{D}$ concerns the way fixed points are used to handle the do ... od construct. We first state the definitions of $\mathbb{P}_D$ and *Cont*.

Definition 3.10

(a) $\mathbb{P}_D = \Sigma \to \mathcal{P}_{nco}(\Sigma_\delta^\infty)$.

(b) $(\gamma \in)\, Cont = \mathbb{P}_D,\ \gamma_\epsilon = \lambda\sigma.\{\epsilon\}$.

Thus, $\mathbb{P}_D$ coincides with $\mathbb{P}_O$ from Section 3.1.1, and *Cont* equals $\mathbb{P}_D$.

Next, we state the definition of $\mathcal{D}$. Various explanations will follow the definition, having to do with the handling of δ and, especially, with the fixed point treatment of do g od.

Definition 3.11 Below, we assume g to be of the form $(e_1 \to s_1)\square \ldots \square(e_n \to s_n)$.

(a) $\mathcal{D}{:}\, \mathcal{L}_{gc} \to Cont \xrightarrow{\frac{1}{2}} \mathbb{P}_D$ is given by

$$\begin{aligned}
\mathcal{D}(v := e)(\gamma)(\sigma) &= \sigma\{\alpha/v\} \cdot \gamma(\sigma\{\alpha/v\}), \quad \text{where } \alpha = \mathcal{V}(e)(\sigma) \\
\mathcal{D}(\mathsf{skip})(\gamma)(\sigma) &= \sigma \cdot \gamma(\sigma) \\
\mathcal{D}(s_1;s_2)(\gamma)(\sigma) &= \mathcal{D}(s_1)(\mathcal{D}(s_2)(\gamma))(\sigma) \\
\mathcal{D}(\mathsf{if}\ g\ \mathsf{fi})(\gamma)(\sigma) &= \\
&\quad \bigcup\{\mathcal{D}(s_i)(\gamma)(\sigma) \mid (\mathcal{V}(e_i)(\sigma) = t\!t) \wedge (\mathcal{D}(s_i)(\gamma)(\sigma) \neq \{\delta\})\} \cup \\
&\quad\ \ \{\delta \mid \forall i[(\mathcal{V}(e_i)(\sigma) = f\!f) \vee (\mathcal{D}(s_i)(\gamma)(\sigma) = \{\delta\})]\}
\end{aligned}$$

$$\mathcal{D}(\mathsf{do}\ g\ \mathsf{od})(\gamma)(\sigma) = \mathit{fix}(\Omega_{\mathsf{do}\,g\,\mathsf{od}}(\gamma))(\sigma),$$

where the mapping $\Omega_{\mathsf{do}\,g\,\mathsf{od}} \colon \mathit{Cont} \xrightarrow{\frac{1}{2}} (\mathbb{P}_D \xrightarrow{\frac{1}{2}} \mathbb{P}_D)$ is given by

$$\begin{aligned}
\Omega_{\mathsf{do}\,g\,\mathsf{od}}(\gamma)(p)(\sigma) &= \\
&\bigcup\{\mathcal{D}(s_i)(p)(\sigma) \mid (\mathcal{V}(e_i)(\sigma) = t\!t) \wedge (\mathcal{D}(s_i)(p)(\sigma) \neq \{\delta\})\} \cup \\
&\bigcup\{\sigma \cdot \gamma(\sigma) \mid \forall i[\mathcal{V}(e_i)(\sigma) = f\!f]\} \cup \\
&\ \ \{\delta \mid \exists i[\mathcal{V}(e_i)(\sigma) = t\!t] \wedge \forall i[\mathcal{V}(e_i)(\sigma) = t\!t \Rightarrow \mathcal{D}(s_i)(p)(\sigma) = \{\delta\}]\}.
\end{aligned}$$

(b) $\mathcal{D}[\![\pi]\!] = \mathcal{D}(\pi)(\gamma_\epsilon).$

Examples

(1) Let $s_{\mathrm{if}} \equiv \mathsf{if}\ (v < 0 \to u := -1) \,\square\, (v > 0 \to u := 1)\ \mathsf{fi}.$

$\quad \mathcal{D}[\![s_{\mathrm{if}}]\!](\sigma\{10/v\})$

$\quad = \mathcal{D}(s_{\mathrm{if}})(\gamma_\epsilon)(\sigma\{10/v\})$

$\quad = \mathcal{D}(u := 1)(\gamma_\epsilon)(\sigma\{10/v, 1/u\})$

$\quad = \sigma\{10/v, 1/u\} \cdot \gamma_\epsilon(\sigma\{10/v, 1/u\})$

$\quad = \sigma\{10/v, 1/u\} \cdot \{\epsilon\}$

$\quad = \{\sigma\{10/v, 1/u\}\}$

(2) $\quad \mathcal{D}[\![s_{\mathrm{if}}]\!](\sigma\{0/v\})$

$\quad = \mathcal{D}(s_{\mathrm{if}})(\gamma_\epsilon)(\sigma\{0/v\})$

$\quad = \{\delta\}$

(3) Let $g \equiv (v < 5 \to v := v + 1).$

$\quad \mathcal{D}[\![\mathsf{do}\ g\ \mathsf{od}]\!](\sigma\{4/v\})$

$\quad = \mathcal{D}(\mathsf{do}\ g\ \mathsf{od})(\gamma_\epsilon)(\sigma\{4/v\})$

$\quad = \Omega_{\mathsf{do}\,g\,\mathsf{od}}(\gamma_\epsilon)\big(\mathcal{D}(\mathsf{do}\ g\ \mathsf{od})(\gamma_\epsilon)\big)(\sigma\{4/v\})$

$$
\begin{aligned}
&= \mathcal{D}(v := v + 1)\big(\mathcal{D}(\text{do } g \text{ od})(\gamma_\epsilon)\big)(\sigma\{4/v\}) \\
&= \sigma\{5/v\} \cdot \mathcal{D}(\text{do } g \text{ od})(\gamma_\epsilon)(\sigma\{5/v\}) \\
&= \sigma\{5/v\} \cdot \Omega_{\text{do } g \text{ od}}(\gamma_\epsilon)(\mathcal{D}(\text{do } g \text{ od})(\gamma_\epsilon))(\sigma\{5/v\}) \\
&= \sigma\{5/v\} \cdot \sigma\{5/v\} \cdot \gamma_\epsilon(\sigma\{5/v\}) \\
&= \sigma\{5/v\} \cdot \sigma\{5/v\} \cdot \{\epsilon\} \\
&= \{\sigma\{5/v\}\sigma\{5/v\}\}
\end{aligned}
$$

(4) Let $s_{\text{if}} \equiv \text{if } (\text{true} \rightarrow v := 1)\square(\text{true} \rightarrow v := 2) \text{ fi}$.

$$
\begin{aligned}
&\mathcal{D}[\![s_{\text{if}}]\!](\sigma) \\
&= \mathcal{D}(s_{\text{if}})(\gamma_\epsilon)(\sigma) \\
&= \mathcal{D}(v := 1)(\gamma_\epsilon)(\sigma) \cup \mathcal{D}(v := 2)(\gamma_\epsilon)(\sigma) \\
&= \sigma\{1/v\} \cdot \gamma_\epsilon(\sigma\{1/v\}) \cup \sigma\{2/v\} \cdot \gamma_\epsilon(\sigma\{2/v\}) \\
&= \sigma\{1/v\} \cdot \{\epsilon\} \cup \sigma\{2/v\} \cdot \{\epsilon\} \\
&= \{\, \sigma\{1/v\}, \sigma\{2/v\} \,\}.
\end{aligned}
$$

The first three clauses of this definition (for $v := e$, skip and $(s_1;s_2)$) should be clear—they are identical to the corresponding clauses for $\mathcal{L}_{wh}$. The clauses for $\mathcal{D}(\text{if } g \text{ fi})$ and $\mathcal{D}(\text{do } g \text{ od})$ need several further comments. Firstly, we note that they are expressed in terms of $\mathcal{D}(s_i)$ (and of $\mathcal{V}(e_i)$), thus substantiating our earlier claim that $\mathcal{D}$ for $\mathcal{L}_{gc}$ is defined in a properly compositional way: the s_i (and e_i) are syntactic constituents of the g concerned.

Secondly, let us consider the definition of $\mathcal{D}(\text{if } g \text{ fi})(\gamma)(\sigma)$. In case one or more e_i are found for which both $\mathcal{V}(e_i)(\sigma) = tt$ and $\mathcal{D}(s_i)(\gamma)(\sigma) \neq \{\delta\}$, we take the union, over all such i, of the outcomes $\mathcal{D}(s_i)(\gamma)(\sigma)$. If no such i exists, we deliver $\{\delta\}$ as outcome. Note carefully that in the first summand of the result (the $\bigcup\{\dots\}$ part), terms equal to $\{\delta\}$ are excluded. In this way, we ensure that, if $\delta \in \mathcal{D}(s_{\text{if}})(\gamma)(\sigma)$, then $\mathcal{D}(s_{\text{if}})(\gamma)(\sigma) = \{\delta\}$. (In words, $\mathcal{D}(s_{\text{if}})(\gamma)(\sigma)$ may deadlock only if no alternatives are present.) For example, take $s' \equiv \text{if } (\text{false} \rightarrow v := 0) \text{ fi}$ and $s'' \equiv \text{if } (\text{true} \rightarrow s')\square(\text{true} \rightarrow v := 1) \text{ fi}$. We have $\mathcal{D}(s')(\gamma_\epsilon)(\sigma) = \{\delta\}$ and $\mathcal{D}(s'')(\gamma_\epsilon)(\sigma) = \{\sigma\{1/v\}\}$. Without the proviso as just described (i.e., without the condition $\mathcal{D}(s_i)(\gamma)(\sigma) \neq \{\delta\}$), we would deliver $\mathcal{D}(s'')(\gamma_\epsilon)(\sigma) = \{\delta, \sigma\{1/v\}\}$. The need to design $\mathcal{D}$ as just described arises from the operational understanding of $\mathcal{L}_{gc}$ (cf. the definition of $\mathcal{O}$ for $\mathcal{L}_{gc}$ and especially Lemma 3.9), and the desire to ensure that $\mathcal{O} = \mathcal{D}$ on $\mathcal{L}_{gc}$.

The hardest clause is the one for $\mathcal{D}(\text{do } g \text{ od})(\gamma)$. The way $\mathcal{D}(\text{do } g \text{ od})(\gamma)$ deals with the possible presence of deadlock is close to what we saw for $\mathcal{D}(\text{if } g \text{ fi})(\gamma)$. Three possibilities arise (see below for details on p):

(1) There exists at least one i $(1 \leq i \leq n)$ such that $\mathcal{V}(e_i)(\sigma) = tt$ and $\mathcal{D}(s_i)(p)(\sigma) \neq \{\delta\}$. Then the union, over all such i, of the $\mathcal{D}(s_i)(p)(\sigma)$ is delivered.

(2) For all i, $\mathcal{V}(e_i)(\sigma) = ff$. Then $\sigma \cdot \gamma(\sigma)$ is delivered, i.e., the result equals the denotational counterpart of the skip-statement.

(3) Neither (1) or (2) applies, i.e., for some i, $\mathcal{V}(e_i)(\sigma) = tt$, and for all true e_i, the corresponding s_i deadlocks. Then the do g od statement deadlocks as well.

There remains the need of an explanation of the fixed point aspects of the clause for $\mathcal{D}(\text{do } g \text{ od})$. We first present some informal comments, and then formally justify the definition, in so far as the existence of the (unique) fixed point of $\Omega_{\text{do } g \text{ od}}(\gamma)$ is concerned. Let us, for the moment, use p_{do} as an abbreviation for $\mathcal{D}(\text{do } g \text{ od})(\gamma) = fix(\Omega_{\text{do } g \text{ od}}(\gamma))$. By the definition of $\Omega_{\text{do } g \text{ od}}(\gamma)$ and the fact that $\Omega_{\text{do } g \text{ od}}(\gamma)(p_{\text{do}}) = p_{\text{do}}$, we obtain the equality

$$p_{\text{do}} = \lambda\sigma.(\ \bigcup\{\mathcal{D}(s_i)(p_{\text{do}})(\sigma) \mid (\mathcal{V}(e_i)(\sigma) = tt) \wedge (\mathcal{D}(s_i)(p_{\text{do}})(\sigma) \neq \{\delta\})\ \}$$
$$\cup \bigcup\{\sigma \cdot \gamma(\sigma) \mid \ldots\ \} \cup \{\delta \mid \ldots\ \}).$$

In words, the meaning of do g od (for continuation γ and state σ) equals the union of

- all $\mathcal{D}(s_i)(p_{\text{do}})(\sigma)$ such that $\mathcal{V}(e_i)(\sigma) = tt$ and $\mathcal{D}(s_i)(p_{\text{do}})(\sigma) \neq \{\delta\}$
- $\sigma \cdot \gamma(\sigma)$ in case, for all i, $\mathcal{V}(e_i)(\sigma) = ff$
- δ, in case neither of the first two conditions applies.

We see that this definition of $p_{\text{do}} = \mathcal{D}(\text{do } g \text{ od})(\gamma)$ amounts to the semantic equality of the two statements

do g od $\equiv$ do $(e_1 \rightarrow s_1)\square \ldots \square(e_n \rightarrow s_n)$ od

and

$$\text{if } (e_1 \rightarrow (s_1;\text{do } g \text{ od}))\square \ldots \square(e_n \rightarrow (s_n;\text{do } g \text{ od}))\square \tag{3.3}$$
$$(\neg e_1 \wedge \ldots \wedge \neg e_n \rightarrow \text{skip}) \text{ fi}$$

(Note that the if $\ldots$ fi statement in (3.3) will execute skip in case none of the e_i, $1 \leq i \leq n$, is true.) Altogether, the do g od construct executes, in a nondeterministic fashion, some s_i for which e_i is true, and then iterates do g od (*unless* all such s_i deadlock, in which case do g od deadlocks as well). The latter iteration is taken care of by the fixed point p_{do} of $\Omega_{\text{do } g \text{ od}}(\gamma) = \lambda p.\Omega_{\text{do } g \text{ od}}(\gamma)(p)$. This brings us to the final step: the proof that $\Omega_{\text{do } g \text{ od}}(\gamma)$ is $\frac{1}{2}$-contractive in p. The proof uses that $\mathcal{D}(s)$ is $\frac{1}{2}$-contractive in γ.

Lemma 3.12

(a) $\Omega_{\mathrm{do}\, g\, \mathrm{od}}(\gamma)$ is $\frac{1}{2}$-contractive in p, for each γ.

(b) $\Omega_{\mathrm{do}\, g\, \mathrm{od}}$ is $\frac{1}{2}$-contractive in γ.

(c) $\mathcal{D}(s)$ is $\frac{1}{2}$-contractive in γ.

(d) For all γ, γ', $\mathcal{D}(s)(\gamma)(\sigma) = \{\delta\}$ iff $\mathcal{D}(s)(\gamma')(\sigma) = \{\delta\}$.

Proof We show the assertions simultaneously by induction on the syntactic complexity $c(s)$ (and $c(\mathrm{do}\, g\, \mathrm{od})$), defined as follows

$$
\begin{aligned}
c(v := e) &= c(\mathsf{skip}) = 1 \\
c(s_1; s_2) &= c(s_1) + c(s_2) + 1 \\
c(\mathsf{if}\ g\ \mathsf{fi}) &= max\{\, c(s_i) \mid 1 \le i \le n \,\} + 1 \\
c(\mathsf{do}\ g\ \mathsf{od}) &= max\{\, c(s_i) \mid 1 \le i \le n \,\} + 1
\end{aligned}
$$

(Note carefully how $c(s)$ differs form $wgt(s)$.) We omit the basis step of the induction.

(a) Take γ, p_1, p_2 and σ arbitrarily. Put $C_j(i) \equiv \mathcal{V}(e_i)(\sigma) = tt \wedge \mathcal{D}(s_i)(p_j)(\sigma) = \{\delta\}$, $D \equiv \forall i\,[\, \mathcal{V}(e_i)(\sigma = ff\,]$, $E_j \equiv \neg D \wedge \forall i\,[\, \neg C_j(i)\,]$, $(j = 1, 2)$. By the induction hypothesis for part (c) we have

$$
\forall i\,[\, C_1(i) \Leftrightarrow C_2(i)\,] \ \text{ and } \ E_1 \Leftrightarrow E_2. \tag{3.4}
$$

Therefore

$$
\begin{aligned}
&d(\Omega_{\mathrm{do}\, g\, \mathrm{od}}(\gamma)(p_1)(\sigma), \Omega_{\mathrm{do}\, g\, \mathrm{od}}(\gamma)(p_2)(\sigma)) \\
&= d(\ \textstyle\bigcup\{\mathcal{D}(s_i)(p_1)(\sigma) \mid C_1(i)\} \cup \bigcup\{\sigma \cdot \gamma(\sigma) \mid D\} \cup \{\delta \mid E_1\}, \\
&\qquad \textstyle\bigcup\{\mathcal{D}(s_i)(p_2)(\sigma) \mid C_2(i)\} \cup \bigcup\{\sigma \cdot \gamma(\sigma) \mid D\} \cup \{\delta \mid E_2\}\ ) \\
&\le [\text{Lemma 2.4, eq. (3.4)}]\ max\{\, d(\mathcal{D}(s_i)(p_1)(\sigma), \mathcal{D}(s_i)(p_2)(\sigma)) \\
&\le [\text{ind. hyp. part (c)}]\ \tfrac{1}{2}d(p_1, p_2),
\end{aligned}
$$

(where the maximum equals 0 if for no i, $C_1(i)$ holds).

(b) Similar to part (a).

(c) Three cases are to be verified. Take γ_1, γ_2 and σ arbitrarily.

$$
\begin{aligned}
[s_1; s_2]\quad &d(\mathcal{D}(s_1)(\mathcal{D}(s_2)(\gamma_1))(\sigma), \mathcal{D}(s_1)(\mathcal{D}(s_2)(\gamma_2))(\sigma)) \\
&\le\ [\text{ind. hyp. for } s_1]\ \tfrac{1}{2}d(\mathcal{D}(s_2)(\gamma_1), \mathcal{D}(s_2)(\gamma_2)) \\
&\le\ [\text{ind. hyp. for } s_2]\ \tfrac{1}{2} \cdot \tfrac{1}{2}d(\gamma_1, \gamma_2) \\
&\le\ \tfrac{1}{2}d(\gamma_1, \gamma_2).
\end{aligned}
$$

[if g fi] Put $C_j(i) \equiv (\mathcal{V}(e_i)(\sigma) = tt) \wedge (\mathcal{D}(s_i)(\gamma)(\sigma) \neq \{\delta\})$, $(j = 1, 2)$. By the induction hypothesis for part (a), we now have

$$d(\mathcal{D}(\text{if } g \text{ fi})(\gamma_1)(\sigma), \mathcal{D}(\text{if } g \text{ fi})(\gamma_2)(\sigma))$$
$$= \quad d(\; \bigcup\{\,\mathcal{D}(s_i)(\gamma_1)(\sigma) \mid C_1(i)\,\} \cup \{\,\delta \mid \forall i\,[\,\neg C_1(i)\,]\,\},$$
$$\qquad\quad \bigcup\{\,\mathcal{D}(s_i)(\gamma_2)(\sigma) \mid C_2(i)\,\} \cup \{\,\delta \mid \forall i\,[\,\neg C_1(i)\,]\,\}\;)$$
$$\leq \quad [\text{Lemma 2.4}]\; max\{\, d(\mathcal{D}(s_i)(\gamma_1)(\sigma), \mathcal{D}(s_i)(\gamma_2)(\sigma)) \mid C_1(i)\,\}$$
$$\leq \quad [\text{ind. hyp part (c)}]\; \tfrac{1}{2} d(\gamma_1, \gamma_2).$$

[do g od] By the induction step verified already for parts (a) and (b) we have $\Omega_{\text{do } g \text{ od}} \in Conf \xrightarrow{\frac{1}{2}} (\mathbb{P}_D \xrightarrow{\frac{1}{2}} \mathbb{P}_D)$. Therefore, by Exercise 1.7,

$$d(\text{fix}(\Omega_{\text{do } g \text{ od}}(\gamma_1)), \text{fix}(\Omega_{\text{do } g \text{ od}}(\gamma_2))) \leq \tfrac{1}{2} d(\gamma_1, \gamma_2). \qquad (3.5)$$

From this we directly obtain

$$d(\mathcal{D}(\text{do } g \text{ od})(\gamma_1), \mathcal{D}(\text{do } g \text{ od})(\gamma_2)) \leq \tfrac{1}{2} d(\gamma_1, \gamma_2)$$

from the definition.

(d) Exercise. $\square$

Altogether, we have justified the denotational (here, properly compositional) definition of $\mathcal{D}$ for $\mathcal{L}_{gc}$. Lest the reader gets the impression that the "local" fixed point approach to iteration—with a fixed point clause to be invoked for each single do g od-construct—is essential for the present case, we point out that a *global* approach—with $\mathcal{D} = \text{fix}(\Psi)$, Ψ close to the mapping used for $\mathcal{L}_{wh}$—is equally possible. Our main aim with the present way of defining $\mathcal{D}$ was to introduce an interesting variation on the—so far—standard method. (In Chapter 8, we shall discuss some further variations on the fixed point techniques used in dealing with recursion.)

As usual, the last topic to be addressed concerns the equivalence of $\mathcal{O}$ and $\mathcal{D}$. We follow the familiar route: The mappings $\mathcal{E} \colon Res \to \mathbb{P}_D$ and $\mathcal{E}^* \colon Res \times \Sigma \to \mathcal{P}_{nc}(\Sigma_\delta^\infty)$ are given by

$$\mathcal{E}(\text{E}) \quad = \quad \lambda\sigma.\{\epsilon\}$$
$$\mathcal{E}(s\colon r) \quad = \quad \mathcal{D}(s)(\mathcal{E}(r))$$
$$\mathcal{E}^*(r, \sigma) \quad = \quad \mathcal{E}(r)(\sigma).$$

Before establishing that $\mathcal{E}^*$ is a fixed point of Φ (from Definition 3.6), we prove an auxiliary lemma relating operational and denotational deadlock:

Lemma 3.13 *For all s, r, σ*

$[s{:}r,\sigma] \not\rightarrow \;$ *iff* $\mathcal{D}(s)(\mathcal{E}(r))(\sigma) = \{\delta\}$.

Proof Induction on $c(s)$. One subcase:

`[if g fi]   [if g fi:$r,\sigma] \not\rightarrow$

$\quad\Leftrightarrow\quad$ [Lemma 3.4a] $\forall i[(\mathcal{V}(e_i)(\sigma) = \mathit{ff}) \vee [s_i{:}r,\sigma] \not\rightarrow\,]$

$\quad\Leftrightarrow\quad$ [ind. hyp.] $\forall i[(\mathcal{V}(e_i)(\sigma) = \mathit{ff}) \vee (\mathcal{D}(s_i)(\mathcal{E}(r))(\sigma) = \{\delta\})]$

$\quad\Leftrightarrow\quad$ [def. $\mathcal{D}$] $\mathcal{D}(\text{if } g \text{ fi})(\mathcal{E}(r))(\sigma) = \{\delta\}$. $\square$

We next show

Lemma 3.14 $\Phi(\mathcal{E}^*) = \mathcal{E}^*$, *on Res* $\times \Sigma$.

Proof We prove that, for each r,σ, $\Phi(\mathcal{E}^*)(r,\sigma) = \mathcal{E}^*(r,\sigma)$, using induction on $wgt(r)$. One subcase.

[do g od:r']   Choose some σ. We first discuss the case that [do g od:$r',\sigma] \not\rightarrow$. Then

$\qquad \Phi(\mathcal{E}^*)(\text{do } g \text{ od:}r',\sigma)$

$\quad = \quad$ [def. Φ] $\{\delta\}$

$\quad = \quad$ [Lemma 3.13] $\mathcal{D}(\text{do } g \text{ od})(\mathcal{E}(r'))(\sigma)$

$\quad = \quad$ [def. $\mathcal{E}^*$] $\mathcal{E}^*(\text{do } g \text{ od:}r',\sigma)$.

Otherwise ($C(i)$ and D are as in the proof of Lemma 3.12)

$\qquad \Phi(\mathcal{E}^*)(\text{do } g \text{ od:}r',\sigma)$

$\quad = \quad$ [def. $\mathcal{T}_{gc}$, Lemma 3.4b, Lemma 3.13]
$\qquad \bigcup\{\, \Phi(\mathcal{E}^*)((s_i;\text{do } g \text{ od}){:}r',\sigma) \mid C(i)\,\}\cup\{\, \Phi(\mathcal{E}^*)(\text{skip:}r'\sigma) \mid D\,\}$

$\quad = \quad$ [ind. hyp.] $\bigcup \mathcal{E}^*((s_i;\text{do } g \text{ od}){:}r',\sigma) \mid C(i)\,\}\cup\{\, \mathcal{E}^*(\text{skip:}r',\sigma) \mid D\,\}$

$\quad = \quad$ [def. $\mathcal{E}, \mathcal{E}^*$]
$\qquad \bigcup\{\, \mathcal{D}(s_i;\text{do } g \text{ od})(\mathcal{E}(r'))(\sigma) \mid C(i)\,\}\cup\{\, \mathcal{D}(\text{skip})(\mathcal{E}(r))(\sigma) \mid D\,\}$

$\quad = \quad$ [def. $\mathcal{D}$] $\mathcal{D}(\text{do } g \text{ od})(\mathcal{E}(r'))(\sigma)$

$\quad = \quad \mathcal{E}^*(\text{do } g \text{ od:}r',\sigma)$. $\square$

This brings us to the final

Theorem 3.15 $\mathcal{O}[\![\pi]\!] = \mathcal{D}[\![\pi]\!]$, *for* $\pi \in \mathcal{L}_{gc}$.

Proof Standard from Lemma 3.14 and the definitions of $\mathcal{O}[\![\cdot]\!]$ and $\mathcal{D}[\![\cdot]\!]$. $\square$

3.2   Goto statements—systems of continuations

Historically, continuations as a tool in (denotational) semantics were first introduced in order to deal with goto statements. Now that the reader has acquired
already ample experience with the use of continuations, he will have little difficulty
in appreciating their use in the present section which deals with a simple (uniform)
sequential language with goto's. Maybe the most unusual element here is the way
we have organized the syntax such that the treatment of $\mathcal{L}_{gt}$ may be seen as a
modest variation on that of $\mathcal{L}_{cf}$.

3.2.1   Syntax and operational semantics

We introduce a finite set of labels $(L \in) Lab = \{L_1, \ldots L_n\}$. Goto statements
are constructs of the form goto L, and labeled statements appear (implicitly, see
the discussion at the end of Section 3.2.2 for more explanation) as $L{:}g$. The set
$(a \in)Act$ is as always.

Definition 3.16

(a) $s(\in Stat) ::= a \mid \text{goto } L \mid (s;s) \mid (s+s)$

(b) $g(\in GStat) ::= a \mid (g;s) \mid (g+g)$

(c) $(d \in) Decl = Lab \rightarrow GStat$

(d) $(\pi \in) \mathcal{L}_{gt} = Decl \times Stat.$

Examples

(1) $(D|\text{goto } L_2)$ with $Lab = \{L_1, L_2, L_3\}$, $D(L_i) = a_i$, $i = 1, 2, 3$

(2) $(D|\text{goto } L_1)$ with $Lab = \{L_1\}$, $D(L_1) = (a;\text{goto } L_1) + b$

(3) $(D|\text{goto } L_1;d)$ with $Lab = \{L_1, L_2, L_3\}$, $D(L_1) = a;\text{goto } L_1$, $D(L_2) = b$ and
     $D(L_3) = c.$

At the end of this section we shall discuss how a program written in a more
familiar syntax of a language with goto statements, say of the form

$L_1{:}g_1;L_2{:}g_2;\ldots;L_n{:}g_n$

may be expressed by an equivalent program in $\mathcal{L}_{gt}$. By way of informal explanation
we note that $\mathcal{L}_{gt}$ will be treated as $\mathcal{L}_{cf}$, but with one essential difference: whereas

for a procedure call x, after execution of $D(x)$ the program execution resumes with that of the statement immediately following x, for a goto statement goto L_i, execution consists in that of $D(L_i)$, after which the program execution (ignores the statement following goto L_i and) resumes with the execution of goto L_{i+1}.

We proceed with the definition of the operational semantics for $\mathcal{L}_{gt}$. The resumptions $(r \in)Res$ are the usual ones for a simple sequential language.

Definition 3.17 $r(\in Res) ::= \mathrm{E} \mid (s{:}r)$.

The transition system $\mathcal{T}_{gt}$ is given in

Definition 3.18 $\mathcal{T}_{gt} = (Decl \times Res, Act, \rightarrow, Spec)$, where $Spec$ consists of

- $$a{:}r \xrightarrow{a}_D r \tag{Act}$$

- $$\mathrm{goto}\ L_i{:}r \rightarrow_{0,D} (D(L_i);\mathrm{goto}\ L_{i+1}){:}\mathrm{E}, \quad 1 \le i \le n{-}1 \tag{Goto}$$

  $$\mathrm{goto}\ L_n{:}r \rightarrow_{0,D} D(L_n){:}\mathrm{E}$$

- $$(s_1;s_2){:}r \rightarrow_{0,D} s_1{:}(s_2{:}r) \tag{Seq}$$

- $$(s_1 + s_2){:}r \rightarrow_{0,D} s_1{:}r \tag{Choice}$$

  $$(s_1 + s_2){:}r \rightarrow_{0,D} s_2{:}r$$

We draw particular attention to the (Goto) rule. Three points are of importance:

(1) the "body" $D(L_i)$ associated with L_i in the declaration is executed first; next

(2) execution continues with that of goto L_{i+1} (to which the (Goto)-rule applies again);

(3) the resumption r is thrown away, and E replaces it.

The weight function $wgt{:} Decl \times (Res \cup Stat) \rightarrow \mathbb{N}$ is given in

Definition 3.19

$$(\mathrm{a}) \quad \begin{aligned} wgt(D|\mathrm{E}) &= 0 \\ wgt(D|s{:}r) &= wgt(D|s) + wgt(D|r) \end{aligned}$$

(b)
$$
\begin{aligned}
wgt(D|a) &= 1 \\
wgt(D|\text{goto } L) &= wgt(D|D(L)) + 2 \\
wgt(D|s_1;s_2) &= wgt(D|s_1) + 1 \\
wgt(D|s_1 + s_2) &= max\{\, wgt(D|s_1), wgt(D|s_2)\,\} + 1
\end{aligned}
$$

The proof of the next lemma will explain the reason for the '$+2$' in the clause for $wgt(D|\text{goto } L)$. We have

Lemma 3.20

(a) wgt is well-defined.

(b) If $r_1 \to_{0,D} r_2$, then $wgt(D|r_1) > wgt(D|r_2)$.

Proof

(a) Well-definedness of $wgt(D|s)$ follows by structural induction on, first, each $g \in$ $GStat$ and, next, each $s \in Stat$. Well-definedness of $wgt(D|r)$ is then immediate by structural induction on r.

(b) One subcase.

$[(D|\text{goto } L_i{:}r)]$

$$
\begin{aligned}
&\quad wgt(D|\text{goto } L_i{:}r) \\
&= wgt(D|\text{goto } L_i) + wgt(D|r) \\
&= wgt(D|D(L_i)) + 2 + wgt(D|r) \\
&> wgt(D|D(L_i)) + 1 + wgt(D|\text{E}) \\
&= wgt(D|D(L_i);\text{goto } L_{i+1}) + wgt(D|\text{E}) \\
&= wgt(D|(D(L_i);\text{goto } L_{i+1}){:}\text{E}). \qquad\qquad \square
\end{aligned}
$$

Using the wgt function, it is not difficult to show

Lemma 3.21 $\mathcal{T}_{gt}$ *is finitely branching.*
Proof Exercise. $\square$

We can now define $\mathcal{O}$ for $\mathcal{L}_{gt}$ based on $\mathcal{T}_{gt}$. We use $(p \in) \mathbb{P}_O = \mathcal{P}_{nco}(Act^\infty)$ and prefixing on $\mathbb{P}_O$ as before.

Definition 3.22

(a) $\mathcal{O}: Decl \times Res \to \mathbb{P}_O$ is the unique function satisfying

$$\begin{aligned}
\mathcal{O}(D|\text{E}) &= \{\epsilon\} \\
\mathcal{O}(D|s{:}r) &= \bigcup\{\, a \cdot \mathcal{O}(D|r') \mid s{:}r \xrightarrow{a}_D r' \,\}\,.
\end{aligned}$$

(b) $\mathcal{O}[\![D|s]\!] = \mathcal{O}(D|s{:}\text{E})$.

Examples

(1) Assume $Lab = \{\, L_1, L_2, L_3 \,\}$ and $D(L_i) = a_i$, $(i = 1, 2, 3)$.

$\mathcal{O}[\![D|\text{goto } L_2]\!]$
$= \mathcal{O}(D|\text{goto } L_2{:}\text{E})$
$= a_2 \cdot \mathcal{O}(D|\text{goto } L_3{:}\text{E})$
$= a_2 \cdot a_3 \cdot \mathcal{O}(D|\text{E})$
$= a_2 \cdot a_3 \cdot \{\epsilon\}$
$= \{a_2 a_3\}$

(2) Assume $Lab = \{L_1\}$ and $D(L_1) = (a;\text{goto } L_1) + b$.

$\mathcal{O}[\![D|\text{goto } L_1]\!]$
$= \mathcal{O}(D|\text{goto } L_1{:}\text{E})$
$= a \cdot \mathcal{O}(D|\text{goto } L_1{:}\text{E}) \cup b \cdot \mathcal{O}(D|\text{E})$
$= a \cdot \mathcal{O}[\![D|\text{goto } L_1]\!] \cup \{b\}$.

From this it folllows that $\mathcal{O}[\![D|\text{goto } L_1]\!] = a^* \cdot \{b\} \cup \{a^\omega\}$.

(3) Assume $Lab = \{\, L_1, L_2, L_3 \,\}$, $D(L_1) = a;\text{goto } L_1$, $D(L_2) = b$, $D(L_3) = c$.

$\mathcal{O}[\![D|\text{goto } L_1;d]\!]$
$= a \cdot \mathcal{O}(D|(\text{goto } L_1;\text{goto } L_2){:}\text{E})$
$= a \cdot a \cdot \mathcal{O}(D|(\text{goto } L_1;\text{goto } L_2){:}(\text{goto } L_1{:}\text{E})$
$= \ldots$

We obtain $\mathcal{O}[\![D|\text{goto } L_1;d]\!] = \{a^\omega\}$.

3.2.2   Denotational semantics, equivalence of $\mathcal{O}$ and $\mathcal{D}$

The denotational semantics for $\mathcal{L}_{gt}$ relies on the use of continuations. More specifically, for a program with n label declarations $D(L_i) = g_i$, $1 \leq i \leq n$, the continuations will be specified as the solution of a system of n *equations*.

Let $(p \in)\mathbb{P}_D$ and $+: \mathbb{P}_D \times \mathbb{P}_D \to \mathbb{P}_D$ be as before, and let $(\gamma \in)Cont = \mathbb{P}_D$, with $\gamma_\epsilon = \{\epsilon\}$. The definition of $\mathcal{D}$ is given in

Definition 3.23

(a) Let $(S \in)Sem_D = Decl \times Stat \to Cont \xrightarrow{1} \mathbb{P}_D$. The operator $\Psi: Sem_D \to Sem_D$ is defined by putting

$$
\begin{aligned}
\Psi(S)(D|a)(\gamma) &= a \cdot \gamma \\
\Psi(S)(D|s_1;s_2)(\gamma) &= \Psi(S)(D|s_1)(S(D|s_2)(\gamma)) \\
\Psi(S)(D|s_1 + s_2)(\gamma) &= \Psi(S)(D|s_1)(\gamma) + \Psi(S)(D|s_2)(\gamma) \\
\Psi(S)(D|\text{goto } L_i)(\gamma) &= \gamma_i, \;\; 1 \leq i \leq n, \text{ where} \\
&\qquad \gamma_i = \Psi(S)(D|D(L_i))(\gamma_{i+1}), \;\; 1 \leq i \leq n-1 \\
&\qquad \gamma_n = \Psi(S)(D|D(L_n))(\gamma_\epsilon)
\end{aligned}
$$

(b) $\mathcal{D} = \text{fix}(\Psi)$, $\mathcal{D}[\![D|s]\!] = \mathcal{D}(D|s)(\gamma_\epsilon)$.

Examples

(1) Assume $Lab = \{\,L_1, L_2, L_3\,\}$ and $D(L_i) = a_i$, $(i = 1, 2, 3)$.

$\mathcal{D}[\![D|\text{goto } L_2]\!]$

$= \mathcal{D}(D|\text{goto } L_2)(\gamma_\epsilon)$

$= \mathcal{D}(D|a_2)(\gamma_3)$

$= a_2 \cdot \gamma_3$

$= a_2 \cdot \mathcal{D}(D|a_3)(\gamma_\epsilon)$

$= a_2 \cdot a_3 \cdot \gamma_\epsilon$

$= \{a_2 a_3\}$

(2) Assume $Lab = \{L_1\}$ and $D(L_1) = (a;\text{goto } L_1) + b$.

$\mathcal{D}[\![D|\text{goto } L_1]\!]$

$= \mathcal{D}(D|\text{goto } L_1)(\gamma_\epsilon)$

$= \mathcal{D}(D|a;\text{goto } L_1 + b)(\gamma_\epsilon)$

$$= \mathcal{D}(D|a;\text{goto } L_1)(\gamma_\epsilon) + \mathcal{D}(D|b)(\gamma_\epsilon)$$

$$= \mathcal{D}(D|a)\big(\mathcal{D}(D|\text{goto } L_1)(\gamma_\epsilon)\big) + b \cdot \gamma_\epsilon$$

$$= a \cdot \mathcal{D}(D|\text{goto } L_1)(\gamma_\epsilon) + \{b\}$$

from which we obtain $\mathcal{D}[\![D|\text{goto } L_1]\!] = \mathcal{D}(D|\text{goto } L_1)(\gamma_\epsilon) = a^* \cdot \{b\} \cup \{a^\omega\}$.

(3) Assume $Lab = \{\, L_1, L_2, L_3 \,\}$, $D(L_1) = a;\text{goto } L_1$, $D(L_2) = b$, $D(L_3) = c$.

$\mathcal{D}[\![D|\text{goto } L_1;d]\!]$

$$= \mathcal{D}(D|\text{goto } L_1;d)(\gamma_\epsilon)$$

$$= \mathcal{D}(D|\text{goto } L_1)\big(\mathcal{D}(D|d)(\gamma_\epsilon)\big)$$

$$= \mathcal{D}(D|a;\text{goto } L_1)(\gamma_2)$$

$$= a \cdot \mathcal{D}(D|\text{goto } L_1)(\gamma_2)$$

$$= a \cdot \mathcal{D}(D|a;\text{goto } L_1)(\gamma_2).$$

Therefore $\mathcal{D}[\![D|\text{goto } L_1;d]\!] = \mathcal{D}(D|a;\text{goto } L_1)(\gamma_2) = a \cdot \mathcal{D}(D|a;\text{goto } L_1)(\gamma_2) = \{a^\omega\}$.

Definition 3.23 is justified in

Lemma 3.24 *For each S, D, s, γ*

(a) $\epsilon \notin \Psi(S)(D|s)(\gamma)$.

(b) $\Psi(S)$ is well-defined.

(c) $\Psi(S)(D|s)$ is $\frac{1}{2}$-contractive (in γ).

(d) Ψ is $\frac{1}{2}$-contractive (in S).

Proof

(a) Exercise.

(b) We first show that $\Psi(S)(D|g)$ is well-defined by structural induction on g. Next, we show that $\Psi(S)(D|s)$ is well-defined for each s, using the definitions of the γ_i, $1 \le i \le n$, and the just mentioned result for the g to deal with the case $s \equiv \text{goto } L_i$, $1 \le i \le n$.

(c) Structural induction on s. Two subcases.

[a] $d(\Psi(S)(D|a)(\gamma'), \Psi(S)(D|a)(\gamma'')) = d(a \cdot \gamma', a \cdot \gamma'') = \frac{1}{2}d(\gamma', \gamma'')$.

[goto L_i] $d(\Psi(S)(D|\text{goto } L_i)(\gamma'), \Psi(S)(D|\text{goto } L_i)(\gamma''))$
$$= d(\gamma_{i+1}, \gamma_{i+1})$$
$$= 0 \le \tfrac{1}{2}d(\gamma', \gamma'').$$

(d) Choose some γ. We use structural induction first on g, then on s. Two subcases.

[$g;s$] $\quad d(\Psi(S_1)(D|g;s)(\gamma), \Psi(S_2)(D|g;s)(\gamma))$
$\qquad = \quad d(\Psi(S_1)(D|g)(S_1(D|s)(\gamma)), \Psi(S_2)(D|g)(S_2(D|s)(\gamma)))$
$\qquad \leq \quad$ [ultrametricity]
$\qquad\qquad max\{\ d(\Psi(S_1)(D|g)(S_1(D|s)(\gamma)), \Psi(S_1)(D|g)(S_2(D|s)(\gamma))),$
$\qquad\qquad\qquad d(\Psi(S_1)(D|g)(S_2(D|s)(\gamma)), \Psi(S_2)(D|g)(S_2(D|s)(\gamma)))\ \}$
$\qquad \leq \quad$ [part (c), ind. hyp. for g]
$\qquad\qquad max\{\ \frac{1}{2}d(S_1(D|s)(\gamma), S_2(D|s)(\gamma)), \frac{1}{2}d(S_1, S_2)\ \}$
$\qquad \leq \quad \frac{1}{2}d(S_1, S_2)\ .$

[goto L_i] Let

$$\gamma_i' \ = \ \Psi(S_1)(D|D(L_i))(\gamma_{i+1}'), \quad 1 \leq i \leq n-1$$
$$\gamma_i'' \ = \ \Psi(S_2)(D|D(L_i))(\gamma_{i+1}''), \quad 1 \leq i \leq n-1$$
$$\gamma_n' \ = \ \Psi(S_1)(D|D(L_n))(\gamma_\epsilon)$$
$$\gamma_n'' \ = \ \Psi(S_2)(D|D(L_n))(\gamma_\epsilon).$$

It is sufficient to show that $d(\gamma_i', \gamma_i'') \leq \frac{1}{2}d(S_1, S_2)$, $i = 1, \ldots, n$. Clearly, we have, by the result already obtained for each $(D|g)$, that $d(\gamma_n', \gamma_n'') \leq \frac{1}{2}d(S_1, S_2)$. We now prove the desired result for any i, $1 \leq i \leq n-1$, under the assumption that we have obtained it already for $i + 1$:

$\quad d(\gamma_i', \gamma_i'')$
$\quad = \quad d(\Psi(S_1)(D|D(L_i))(\gamma_{i+1}'), \Psi(S_2)(D|D(L_i))(\gamma_{i+1}''))$
$\quad \leq \quad$ [ultrametricity]
$\qquad max\{\ d(\Psi(S_1)(D|D(L_i))(\gamma_{i+1}'), \Psi(S_1)(D|D(L_i))(\gamma_{i+1}'')),$
$\qquad\qquad d(\Psi(S_1)(D|D(L_i))(\gamma_{i+1}''), \Psi(S_2)(D|D(L_i))(\gamma_{i+1}''))\ \}$
$\quad \leq \quad$ [part (c), and the result for $(D|g)$]
$\qquad max\{\ \frac{1}{2}d(\gamma_{i+1}', \gamma_{i+1}''), \frac{1}{2}d(S_1, S_2)\ \}$
$\quad \leq \quad$ [assumption for $i + 1$] $\frac{1}{2}d(S_1, S_2)$. $\square$

Below, we shall need the

Lemma 3.25

$$\mathcal{D}(D|\text{goto } L_i)(\gamma) \ = \ \mathcal{D}(D|D(L_i);\text{goto } L_{i+1})(\gamma_\epsilon), \quad i = 1, \ldots, n-1$$
$$\mathcal{D}(D|\text{goto } L_n)(\gamma) \ = \ \mathcal{D}(D|D(L_n))(\gamma_\epsilon).$$

Proof The case $i = n$ is immediate by the definition of $\mathcal{D}$. If $i < n$ we have

$\mathcal{D}(D|\text{goto } L_i)(\gamma)$

$$= \text{[def. } \mathcal{D}\text{] } \mathcal{D}(D|D(L_i))(\gamma_{i+1})$$

$$= \text{[def. } \mathcal{D}(D|\text{goto } L_{i+1})(\gamma)\text{] } \mathcal{D}(D|D(L_i))(\mathcal{D}(D|\text{goto } L_{i+1})(\gamma_\epsilon))$$

$$= \mathcal{D}(D|D(L_i);\text{goto } L_{i+1})(\gamma_\epsilon). \qquad \square$$

As next step to show $\mathcal{O} = \mathcal{D}$, we introduce the intermediate semantics $\mathcal{E}$.

Definition 3.26 $\mathcal{E}: Decl \times Res \to \mathbb{P}_O$ is given by

$$\mathcal{E}(D|\text{E}) = \gamma_\epsilon$$
$$\mathcal{E}(D|s{:}r) = \mathcal{D}(D|s)(\mathcal{E}(D|r)).$$

In the familiar way, we have

Lemma 3.27 If $r_1 \to_{0,D} r_2$ by (Goto) or (Seq), then $\mathcal{E}(D|r_1) = \mathcal{E}(D|r_2)$. If $r \to_{0,D} r'$ and $r \to_{0,D} r''$ (by (Choice)), then $\mathcal{E}(D|r) = \mathcal{E}(D|r') + \mathcal{E}(D|r'')$.

Proof One subcase.

$$\text{[goto } L_i\text{]} \quad \mathcal{E}(D|\text{goto } L_i{:}r)$$

$$= \text{[def. } \mathcal{E}\text{] } \mathcal{D}(D|\text{goto } L_i)(\mathcal{E}(D|r))$$

$$= \text{[Lemma 3.25] } \mathcal{D}(D|D(L_i);\text{goto } L_{i+1})(\gamma_\epsilon)$$

$$= \text{[def. } \mathcal{E}\text{] } \mathcal{E}(D|(D(L_i);\text{goto } L_{i+1}){:}\text{E}). \qquad \square$$

It is now routine to show

Theorem 3.28

(a) $\Phi(\mathcal{E}) = \mathcal{E}$, where Φ is the operator used (implicitly) in the definition of $\mathcal{O}$.

(b) $\mathcal{O} = \mathcal{E}$.

(c) $\mathcal{O}[\![\pi]\!] = \mathcal{D}[\![\pi]\!]$, for each $\pi \in \mathcal{L}_{gt}$.

Proof

(a) We prove by induction on $wgt(D|r)$ that $\Phi(\mathcal{E})(D|r) = \mathcal{E}(D|r)$, for each $(D|r)$. The proof uses the definition of $\mathcal{T}_{gt}$ and Lemma 3.27.

(b) Standard.

(c) $\mathcal{O}[\![(D|s)]\!] = \mathcal{O}(D|s{:}\text{E}) = \mathcal{E}(D|s{:}\text{E}) = \mathcal{D}(D|s)(\gamma_\epsilon) = \mathcal{D}[\![(D|s)]\!]. \qquad \square$

We conclude our treatment of $\mathcal{L}_{gt}$ with the promised explanation how to map a traditional program with goto statements to an element from $\mathcal{L}_{gt}$. Let

$$\pi \equiv L_1{:}g_1; \ldots; L_n{:}g_n$$

be the given program (with the g_i as in Definition 3.16; see also the final comment below). According to the standard interpretation of this program, execution starts at L_1, i.e., with that of g_1, and each g_i has g_{i+1} as its successor, $1 \leq i \leq n-1$. The program terminates if and when execution of g_n terminates. Moreover, each goto L_i (occurring in some g_j) transfers control to the statement g_i (labeled by L_i). In an equivalent notation employing declarations, the information contained in π may be represented by the (intermediate) program

$$\pi_1 \equiv (\tilde{D}|\text{goto } L_1),$$

where $\tilde{D}(L_i) = g_i;\text{goto } L_{i+1}$, $1 \leq i \leq n-1$, and $\tilde{D}(L_n) = g_n$.

According to the definitions of $\mathcal{O}$ and $\mathcal{D}$ for $\mathcal{L}_{gt}$, the linking statements goto L_{i+1}, $1 \leq i \leq n-1$, are supplied automatically, and the final result of the transformation will have the form

$$\pi_2 \equiv (D|\text{goto } L_1)$$

with $D(L_i) = g_i$, $1 \leq i \leq n$. The reader will have no difficulty in convincing himself that the execution of π_2—according to the $\mathcal{O}$ or $\mathcal{D}$ as given in Definition 3.22 or 3.23—has the same effect as the standard execution of π. Of course, this only holds since we have defined the semantics for π_2 in a way which essentially differs from the treatment of recursive procedures. Recapitulating our earlier discussions, we contrast the treatment of $\ldots$ goto $L_i; s' \ldots$ (in $\mathcal{L}_{gt}$) with that of $\ldots x; s' \ldots$ (in $\mathcal{L}_{cf}$). Whereas the former resumes, after performing $D(L_i)$, with the execution of goto L_{i+1}, the latter resumes, after performing $D(x)$, with the execution of s'. It is precisely at this point that the prolongation machinery plays an essential role.

One final comment on the restriction to guarded statements. Clearly, the metric space approach does not allow treatment of essentially unguarded programs such as $(D|\text{goto } L)$ with $D(L) = \text{goto } L$. (In the same vein, a "program" $(x \Leftarrow x|x)$ is syntactically disallowed in all languages (to be) considered.) For $\mathcal{L}_{gt}$—and as well for the languages $\mathcal{L}_{rec}, \ldots$—one also has forms of "inessential" unguardedness, as suggested by the simple example where $Lab = \{L_1, L_2\}$, $D(L_1) = \text{goto } L_2$, $D(L_2) = g$. The reader will have no problem in replacing this incorrect D by an amended D'.

3.3   Exercises

Exercise 3.1 Let $\mathcal{O}$ be as in Definition 3.6. Determine

$$\mathcal{O}[\![\text{if } z \neq 0 \to x := y + z \text{ fi};y := y - z]\!]$$

for

(a) $\sigma\{5/y\}\{2/z\}$

(b) $\sigma\{5/y\}\{0/z\}$.

Exercise 3.2

(a) Assuming a language which contains both while statements and guarded commands, prove the semantic equivalence of

do $e \to s$ od and while e do s od.

(b) Assume that $\mathcal{L}_{wh}$ is extended with the nondeterministic construct $s + s$. Discuss the (non)equivalence of the statements

do $e_1 \to s_1 \square e_2 \to s_2$ od

and

while $e_1 \vee e_2$ do
    if $e_1 \wedge e_2$ then $s_1 + s_2$ else
        if e_1 then s_1 else if e_2 then s_2 else skip fi fi
    fi od.

Exercise 3.3 Discuss how $\mathcal{D}$ may be defined for $\mathcal{L}_{gc}$ using the '$\mathcal{D} = fix(\Psi)$' style of definition.

Exercise 3.4 Let $\Sigma_\delta = \Sigma \cup \{\delta\}$, and let $\mathcal{T}'_{gc} = (Res \times \Sigma, \Sigma_\delta, \to')$ be defined as follows: '$\to$'' contains all triples $([r, \sigma], \sigma', [r', \sigma'])$ from '$\to$' (as specified by $\mathcal{T}_{gc}$), together with the transitions

$[r, \sigma] \xrightarrow{\delta}{}' [\mathrm{E}, \sigma],$

whenever $r \not\equiv \mathrm{E}$ and $[r, \sigma] \not\rightarrow$. Let $\mathcal{O}'$ be derived from $\mathcal{T}'_{gc}$ in the usual way. Show that

- $\mathcal{T}'_{gc}$ is finitely branching
- Theorem 2.30 holds for $\mathcal{T}'_{gc}$
- $\mathcal{O}' = \mathcal{O}$, on $Res \times \Sigma$.

Exercise 3.5 Let $\mathcal{O}$ be as in Definition 3.22. Determine $\mathcal{O}[\![D|a;(\text{goto } L_1;c)]\!]$, where $D(L_1) = b;\text{goto } L_2$, $D(L_2) = a + c$.

Exercise 3.6 Let $\mathcal{D}$ be as in Definition 3.23. Let $Lab = \{ L_1, \ldots, L_n \}$, and let D be such that $D(L_i) = g_i$, $i = 1, \ldots, n$. Prove

$$\mathcal{D}[\![D|\text{goto } L_1]\!]$$
$$=$$
$$\mathcal{D}(D|g_1)(\mathcal{D}(D|g_2))(\ldots(\mathcal{D}[\![D|g_n]\!])\ldots).$$

Exercise 3.7 Let $\mathcal{L}_{gt,n}$ be a nonuniform version of $\mathcal{L}_{gt}$, with $(s \in) Stat$ defined by

$s ::= v := e \mid \text{skip} \mid (s;s) \mid \text{if } e \text{ then } s \text{ else } s \text{ fi} \mid \text{goto } L,$

where $(L \in) Lab$, $Decl$ etc. are similar to Definition 3.16. Design operational and denotational semantics for $\mathcal{L}_{gt,n}$, prove their equivalence, and show that, for each $s \in \mathcal{L}_{wh}$, there exists $\pi \in \mathcal{L}_{gt,n}$ such that $\mathcal{D}[\![s]\!] = \mathcal{D}[\![\pi]\!]$.

3.4 Bibliographical notes

Guarded commands were introduced in [Dij75]. (There are minor discrepancies between our semantics for $\mathcal{L}_{gc}$ and Dijkstra's intended one, e.g., with respect to his identifying deadlock with divergence.) The "local" fixed point approach introduced in Section 3.1 is, in fact, the traditional one as described in standard texts such as [Sto77, Bak80] (for languages in the spirit of $\mathcal{L}_{wh}$). The metric semantics for $\mathcal{L}_{gc}$ given in Section 3.1 has not been published before.

Goto statements were of some importance in the history of denotational semantics in that they gave rise to the first use of continuations ([SW74]). The way we massage a program with goto's into a form which is close to an element of $\mathcal{L}_{cf}$ goes back to a classical paper by Van Wijngaarden ([Wij66]).

II LINEAR MODELS

Part II, entitled *Linear Models,* builds on the foundations laid in Part I, in that no new metric machinery is developed. All domains used here are ultimately based on *sequences*—to be contrasted with Part III, where *branching* domains are applied throughout. The control flow notions studied in Part II are both of the more classical/sequential kind—such as locality, or the μ-calculus as syntactic format for recursive procedures—and of the modern/concurrent type, e.g., process creation, fair merge, or the fork statement. Most of the chapters of Part II consist of two sections, the first one presenting the basic version of the notion to be studied, and the second one devoted to a semantically more demanding variation or extension.

4 Uniform Parallelism

Chapter 4 is devoted to a study of *uniform parallelism*. We shall discuss two (different) ways to add parallelism to $\mathcal{L}_{cf}$:

- The first extension is expressed in terms of the (binary) operator of *parallel composition*, written as $s_1 \| s_2$. The resulting language is called $\mathcal{L}_{par}$.

- The second extension involves the (unary) operator of process creation, written as $\mathsf{new}(s)$. The resulting language is called $\mathcal{L}_{pc}$.

Parallel composition will be taken in the "interleaving" sense, i.e., the parallel execution of s_1 and s_2 consists in the arbitrary merge of the constituent actions of s_1 and s_2, provided the *order* in which these actions occur in s_1 and s_2, respectively, is preserved. The process creation construct $\mathsf{new}(s)$ is executed as follows: Assume that already n (≥ 0) processes are active, and are being executed in parallel. Then an $n+1$-st process is created, with body s, and its execution is initiated in parallel to the existing n processes. This brief description requires some further elaboration, and it is precisely that which will be provided in the semantics discussed in Section 4.2.

Section 4.1 on $\mathcal{L}_{par}$ is a fairly straightforward extension of Section 2.2, in that parallel composition requires—both for the operational and the denotational models—two-sided versions of the definitions provided earlier for ';'. Process creation is rather different; its semantics relies heavily on the use of resumptions and continuations.

Nonuniform versions of parallelism will be investigated in Chapter 7, and various extensions of both the uniform and the nonuniform variety in Part III.

4.1 Parallel composition—introduction of '$\|$'

This section brings the first instalment of our semantic analysis of the programming construct of *parallel composition*. In later chapters, we shall encounter several variations and extensions of this important concept. In the present one, we focus on one of the more basic forms of parallelism, syntactically (and semantically) expressed by the operator '$\|$'. That is, we shall study the parallel composition $s_1 \| s_2$ of the two statements s_1 and s_2 (and the corresponding semantic composition $p_1 \| p_2$ working on two elements p_1, p_2 from $\mathbb{P}_D$). As first approximation of the intended effect of $s_1 \| s_2$ one may say that it consists of the *arbitrary interleaving* of the actions resulting from the execution of s_1 and s_2, respectively.

What do we mean by 'arbitrary interleaving'? This is best explained by providing an informal description of the arbitrary interleavings of two action sequences, i.e., two words q_1, q_2 in Act^*. (In this informal introduction, we omit the case that q_1 or q_2 is infinite; cf. Exercise 4.2.) We say that a word q is a possible interleaving of q_1 and q_2 in case we can find words $x_i, y_i \in Act^*$, $i = 1, \ldots, n$ $(n \geq 0)$, such that

$$
\begin{aligned}
q_1 &= x_1 x_2 \cdots x_n \\
q_2 &= y_1 y_2 \cdots y_n \\
q &= x_1 y_1 x_2 y_2 \cdots x_n y_n.
\end{aligned} \tag{4.1}
$$

Note carefully that each of the x_i, y_i is a *word*—not just a single action—and may equal ϵ. Some examples may help. Let $q_1 = ab$, $q_2 = cde$. The *set* of interleavings $q_1 \| q_2$ includes the elements

$q = acbde$ and $q = cdaeb$

(and many more). The first is obtained from (4.1) by taking, for example, $x_1 = a$, $y_1 = c$, $x_2 = b$, $y_2 = de$, and the second by taking $x_1 = \epsilon$, $y_1 = cd$, $x_2 = a$, $y_2 = e$, $x_3 = b$, $y_3 = \epsilon$.

As second example, consider the case $q_1 = a^n$ $(n \geq 0)$, $q_2 = b$. Then $q_1 \| q_2 = \{ a^k b a^\ell \mid k, \ell \geq 0, k + \ell = n \}$.

Briefly, $q_1 \| q_2$ equals the set of all sequences which are formed by an arbitrary merge of the successive actions in q_1 and q_2, *provided* that it is *order-preserving*, i.e., that the (precedence) order in which the constituent actions of q_i appear in this merge equals their order in the q_i, $i = 1, 2$. For example, the sequence bca is *not* an element of $(ab) \| c$, since the order of a before b in q_1 is not preserved in bca.

As announced already, the parallel composition $s_1 \| s_2$ will be taken in the sense of this arbitrary interleaving. Operationally, one may understand this by specifying the execution of $s_1 \| s_2$ as the interleaving of the actions making up the execution of s_1 and s_2, respectively, in such a way that the scheduling in which s_1 and s_2 get their turn in the execution is arbitrary, but for its obeying the following two conditions

- the order in which the actions occur in each of s_1 and s_2, respectively, is preserved in the execution of $s_1 \| s_2$

- the execution of $s_1 \| s_2$ terminates precisely when both s_1 and s_2 terminate.

(Below, we shall discuss a possibly unexpected consequence of the second condition in case we also take infinite behaviour into account, having to do with the notion of *fair* versus *unfair* execution.)

The above description of parallel execution is geared to a model with one processor which allocates its resources alternatingly to the two programs. In a multiprocessor model, one may want to avoid the interleaving view, and look for a definition which embodies *simultaneity*: in executing $s_1 \| s_2$, s_1 is executed (on machine M_1) simultaneously with s_2 (as executed on M_2). This demands another type of (operational and denotational) semantics, and will be dealt with in Part IV, Chapter 16.

After this informal introduction, we proceed with the formal definitions for $\mathcal{L}_{par}$.

4.1.1   Syntax and operational semantics

The syntax of $\mathcal{L}_{par}$ is obtained from that of $\mathcal{L}_{cf}$ by adding the construct $s_1 \| s_2$ as possibility for s (and $g_1 \| g_2$ as possibility for g).

Definition 4.1

(a) $s \, (\in Stat) ::= a \mid x \mid (s;s) \mid (s + s) \mid (s \| s)$.

(b) $g \, (\in GStat) ::= a \mid (g;s) \mid (g + g) \mid (g \| g)$.

(c) $(D \in) Decl = PVar \rightarrow GStat$.

(d) $(\pi \in) \mathcal{L}_{par} = Decl \times Stat$.

Examples $(D \mid a \| (b;c))$, $(x \Leftarrow (a \| b); x \mid x)$, $(x \Leftarrow a; x \mid x \| b)$, $(x \Leftarrow a; x, y \Leftarrow b; y \mid x \| y) \in \mathcal{L}_{par}$.

Remarks

(1) From now on we shall, apart from a few (rare) exceptions, omit explicit mentioning of the declaration D. *This applies to the present and to all subsequent chapters!* Always, we assume some fixed D as given, and all considerations in any given argument refer to this fixed D.

(2) The definition of g embodies the idea that an action or a procedure variable occurs guarded in $g_1 \| g_2$ in case it occurs guarded in both g_1 and g_2. Accordingly, we have that, e.g., $a \| x \notin GStat$. Operationally, one may understand this by the fact that $a \| x$ may *start* with the execution of x (cf. the definition of $\mathcal{T}_{par}$ below).

(3) $\mathcal{L}_{par}$ is nondeterministic, not only because of the presence of $s_1 + s_2$ (as in $\mathcal{L}_{cf}$), but also since the interleaving interpretation of '$\|$' implies the making of (many) choices.

For the class of resumptions for $\mathcal{L}_{par}$ we return to the simplest format:

Definition 4.2 $r\ (\in Res) ::= \mathrm{E} \mid s$.

We identify $\mathrm{E};s$ with s (as before). Moreover, $\mathrm{E}\|s$ and $s\|\mathrm{E}$ are also identified with s.

Contrary to what we saw for $\mathcal{L}_{cf}$, it is not a feasible alternative to work with resumptions defined by $r ::= \mathrm{E} \mid (s{:}r)$. We shall return to this point after the definition of $\mathcal{T}_{par}$, which we now give.

Definition 4.3 $\mathcal{T}_{par} = (Res, Act, \rightarrow, Spec)$. $Spec$ is obtained by adding to $Spec$ from $\mathcal{T}_{cf}$ a rule (actually a pair of rules) to handle '$\|$':

- $$a \xrightarrow{a} \mathrm{E} \tag{Act}$$

- $$\frac{D(x) \xrightarrow{a} r}{x \xrightarrow{a} r} \tag{Rec}$$

- $$\frac{s \xrightarrow{a} r}{s;\bar{s} \xrightarrow{a} r;\bar{s}} \tag{Seq}$$

- $$\frac{s \xrightarrow{a} r}{s + \bar{s} \xrightarrow{a} r} \tag{Choice}$$
  $$\bar{s} + s \xrightarrow{a} r$$

- $$\frac{s \xrightarrow{a} r}{s \| \bar{s} \xrightarrow{a} r \| \bar{s}} \tag{Par}$$
  $$\bar{s} \| s \xrightarrow{a} \bar{s} \| r$$

Compared to the transition system specification $\mathcal{T}_{cf}$ (Definition 2.23), the rule (Par) is new. From $s \xrightarrow{a} r$, we may infer $s \| \bar{s} \xrightarrow{a} r \| \bar{s}$ and $\bar{s} \| s \xrightarrow{a} \bar{s} \| r$. Accordingly, for the first step to be taken by $s_1 \| s_2$, one (i.e., the executing abstract machine specified by $\mathcal{T}_{par}$) may take either the first step of s_1 or the first step of s_2. By the convention on the use of the resumption r, we obtain as special cases that from $s \xrightarrow{a} \mathrm{E}$ we may infer $s \| \bar{s} \xrightarrow{a} \bar{s}$ and $\bar{s} \| s \xrightarrow{a} \bar{s}$.

The way in which $\mathcal{O}$ is based on $\mathcal{T}_{par}$ is just as for $\mathcal{T}_{cf}$. We give

Definition 4.4

(a) $\mathbb{P}_O = \mathcal{P}_{nco}(Act^\infty)$.

(b) $\mathcal{O}: Res \to \mathbb{P}_O$ is the unique function satisfying $\mathcal{O}(E) = \{\epsilon\}$ and

$$\mathcal{O}(s) \;=\; \bigcup\{\, a \cdot \mathcal{O}(r) \mid s \xrightarrow{a} r \,\}.$$

(c) $\mathcal{O}[\![\pi]\!] = \mathcal{O}(\pi)$, for $\pi \in \mathcal{L}_{par}$.

Examples $\mathcal{O}[\![a \,\|\, (b;c)]\!] = \{\, abc, bac, bca \,\}$,
$\mathcal{O}[\![x \Leftarrow x;a \mid x \,\|\, b]\!] = \{\, a^n ba^\omega \mid n \geq 0 \,\} \cup \{a^\omega\}$,
$\mathcal{O}[\![x \Leftarrow a;x, y \Leftarrow b;y \mid x \,\|\, y]\!] = \{\, a, b \,\}^\omega$.

Justification of Definition 4.4 uses the customary argument. The weight-function is extended with the clause

$$wgt(s_1 \,\|\, s_2) = max\{\, wgt(s_1), wgt(s_2) \,\} + 1$$

(the other clauses being as in Definition 2.25). It is then easy to show

Lemma 4.5 *With respect to $\mathcal{T}_{par}$, we have $|\mathcal{S}(E)| = 0$ and, for each $r \not\equiv E$,*

$$0 < |\mathcal{S}(r)| < \infty.$$

Proof Induction on $wgt(r)$. The only new case is when r is of the form $s_1 \,\|\, s_2$. We then use $s_1 \,\|\, s_2 \xrightarrow{a} r$ iff $(s_1 \xrightarrow{a} r' \wedge r \equiv r' \,\|\, s_2) \vee (s_2 \xrightarrow{a} r'' \wedge r \equiv s_1 \,\|\, r'')$, from which we infer $|\mathcal{S}(s_1)| \leq |\mathcal{S}(s_1 \,\|\, s_2)| \leq |\mathcal{S}(s_1)| + |\mathcal{S}(s_2)|$, and the desired result follows by induction. $\qquad\square$

We leave it as an exercise to supply—for later use—a suitable Φ characterizing $\mathcal{O}$, and the proof of its $\frac{1}{2}$-contractiveness.

Remark We owe the reader a comment on the definition of *Res*. Imagine that we want to extend the scheme from Definition 2.42 to cater for parallel composition. A plausible route would be to introduce as definition

$$r ::= E \mid (s{:}r) \mid (r_1, r_2), \tag{4.2}$$

where $(s{:}r)$ deals with sequential composition as before, and where (r_1, r_2) is intended to cover the case of parallel execution of r_1 and r_2—for which suitable rules in, say $\mathcal{T}'_{par}$ would then have to be included. Furthermore, $\mathcal{T}'_{par}$ would include all the rules of $\mathcal{T}'_{cf}$, to which a rule to handle $(s_1 \| s_2){:}r$ would have to be added. Now the problem is that no suitable rule of the form $(s_1 \| s_2){:}r \to_0 \ldots$ is known. The reader should contrast this with the situation for the language of the next section (with *process creation*) where resumptions defined by (4.2) are, in fact, precisely what we want. In Exercise 4.3 we shall mention an adaptation of (4.2) which does work for $\mathcal{L}_{par}$, albeit at the price of complicating both (4.2) and some of the corresponding denotational definitions.

4.1.2   Denotational semantics, equivalence of $\mathcal{O}$ and $\mathcal{D}$

The design of $\mathcal{D}$ for $\mathcal{L}_{par}$ follows quite closely that of $\mathcal{D}$ for $\mathcal{L}_{cf}$. Only one new definition is needed, viz. that of the semantic '$\|$'. In fact, most of the present subsection will be concerned with defining '$\|$', with investigating its properties, and with the induced extensions in the proof that $\mathcal{O} = \mathcal{D}$ on $\mathcal{L}_{par}$.

We first recall

Definition 4.6

(a) $(q \in) \mathbb{Q}_D = Act^\infty \setminus \{\epsilon\}$.

(b) $(p \in) \mathbb{P}_D = \mathcal{P}_{nco}(\mathbb{Q}_D)$.

We now turn to the definition of $\| : \mathbb{P}_D \times \mathbb{P}_D \to \mathbb{P}_D$. We proceed in two stages, just as we did for '$;$' from $\mathcal{L}_{cf}$ (recall that the first stage for '$;$' was part of the definitions for $\mathcal{L}_{rec}$). That is, we shall first define '$\|$' on *words* (delivering sets of words), and next apply the Lifting Lemma, obtaining '$\|$' acting on *sets* of words (and delivering sets of words again). In the definition of $\| : \mathbb{Q}_D \times \mathbb{Q}_D \to \mathbb{P}_D$, we use as an auxiliary operator the so-called *left merge* $\mathbb{Q}_D \times \mathbb{Q}_D \to \mathbb{P}_D$. The (intended) relationship between the two operators is expressed in

$$q_1 \| q_2 \quad = \quad (q_1 \mathbin{\underline{\|}} q_2) \cup (q_2 \mathbin{\underline{\|}} q_1). \tag{4.3}$$

The meaning of $q_1 \mathbin{\underline{\|}} q_2$ is almost that of $q_1 \| q_2$, but for the additional requirement that the first step of $q_1 \mathbin{\underline{\|}} q_2$ has to be taken by q_1. Symmetrically, of course, the first step of $q_2 \mathbin{\underline{\|}} q_1$ has to be taken by q_2, and (4.3) expresses no more than the simple fact that the first step of $q_1 \| q_2$ is to be taken either by q_1 or by q_2. (For the corresponding operational intuition, the reader may recall our comment explaining the rule (Par) from $\mathcal{T}_{par}$.)

We next present the formal details in

Definition 4.7

(a) Let $(\phi \in) \, Op = \mathbb{Q}_D \times \mathbb{Q}_D \xrightarrow{1} \mathbb{P}_D$. The operators $\Omega_{\|}: Op \to Op$ and $\Omega_;: Op \to Op$ are given by

$$
\begin{array}{rcl}
\Omega_{\|}(\phi)(q_1, q_2) & = & \Omega_;(\phi)(q_1, q_2) \cup \Omega_;(\phi)(q_2, q_1) \\
\Omega_;(\phi)(a, q) & = & \{a \cdot q\} \\
\Omega_;(\phi)(a \cdot q', q) & = & a \cdot \phi(q', q)
\end{array}
$$

(b) The operators $\|, \underline{\|} \in Op$ are given as $\| = \mathit{fix}(\Omega_{\|})$, $\underline{\|} = \Omega_;(\|)$.

We leave as an exercise the following two facts about $\Omega_;$ and $\Omega_{\|}$:

(a) $\Omega_;$ and $\Omega_{\|}$ are $\frac{1}{2}$-contractive (in ϕ).

(b) If ϕ is nonexpansive, then so are $\Omega_;(\phi)$ and $\Omega_{\|}(\phi)$.

Note how the requirement that sets be delivered explains the singleton set $\{a \cdot q\}$ on the right-hand side of $\Omega_;(\phi)(a, q)$. Also note how (4.3) follows as a consequence of this definition, by specializing ϕ to $\|$, and using $\| = \mathit{fix}(\Omega_{\|})$ and $\underline{\|} = \Omega_;(\|)$.

Examples $a \| bc = \{\, abc, bac, bca \,\}$,
$a^\omega \| b = \{\, a^n b a^\omega \mid n \geq 0 \,\} \cup \{\, a^\omega \,\}$,
$a^\omega \| b^\omega = \{\, a, b \,\}^\omega$.

As first property of '$\|$' and '$\underline{\|}$' we have the usual

Lemma 4.8 '$\|$' and '$\underline{\|}$' are nonexpansive in both their arguments.

Proof We only discuss '$\|$'. Since $\Omega_{\|}: Op \xrightarrow{\frac{1}{2}} Op$ and Op is a complete metric space, we have that $\| = \mathit{fix}(\Omega_{\|})$ is an element of Op, and the nonexpansiveness of '$\|$' follows. $\square$

We now extend $\|, \underline{\|}: \mathbb{Q}_D \times \mathbb{Q}_D \to \mathbb{P}_D$ to mappings (with the same name) of type $\mathbb{P}_D \times \mathbb{P}_D \to \mathbb{P}_D$.

Definition 4.9

(a) $p_1 \| p_2 = \bigcup \{ q_1 \| q_2 \mid q_1 \in p_1, q_2 \in p_2 \}$.

(b) $p_1 \mathbin{\underline{\|}} p_2 = \bigcup \{ q_1 \mathbin{\underline{\|}} q_2 \mid q_1 \in p_1, q_2 \in p_2 \}$.

By the Lifting Lemma, we immediately obtain

Lemma 4.10 *The mappings* $\|, \underline{\|} : \mathbb{P}_D \times \mathbb{P}_D \to \mathbb{P}_D$ *are well-defined and nonexpansive.*

Our next result expresses various basic properties of the operators '$\|$' and '$\underline{\|}$'.

Lemma 4.11

(a) $p_1 \| p_2 = (p_1 \mathbin{\underline{\|}} p_2) \cup (p_2 \mathbin{\underline{\|}} p_1)$.

(b) $p_1 \| p_2 = p_2 \| p_1$.

(c) $p \| (p_1 \cup p_2) = (p \| p_1) \cup (p \| p_2)$, $(p_1 \cup p_2) \| p = (p_1 \| p) \cup (p_2 \| p)$.

(d) As (c), with '$\underline{\|}$' replacing '$\|$'.

(e) $(p_1 \| p_2) \| p_3 = p_1 \| (p_2 \| p_3)$.

Proof

(a) By (4.3) and Definition 4.9.

(b) By part (a) and the commutativity of '$\cup$'.

(c) We only discuss right-distributivity. We have

$(p_1 \cup p_2) \| p$

$= \bigcup \{ q' \| q \mid q' \in p_1 \cup p_2, q \in p \}$

$= \bigcup \{ q' \| q \mid q' \in p_1, q \in p \} \cup \bigcup \{ q' \| q \mid q' \in p_2, q \in p \}$

$= (p_1 \| p) \cup (p_2 \| p)$

(d) Similar to (c).

(e) By the definition of '$\|$' (Definition 4.9) and part (c), it is sufficient to show that $(q_1 \| q_2) \| \{ q_3 \} = \{ q_1 \} \| (q_2 \| q_3)$ for all $q_1, q_2, q_3 \in \mathbb{Q}_D$. We use another instance of the $\varepsilon \leq \varepsilon / 2$ argument. Let

$\varepsilon \quad = \quad sup \{ d((q_1 \| q_2) \| \{ q_3 \}, \{ q_1 \} \| (q_2 \| q_3)) \mid q_1, q_2, q_3 \in \mathbb{Q}_D \}$.

We shall show that $\varepsilon \le \varepsilon/2$, from which the desired result follows in the familiar way. We only discuss the case that $q_1 = a \cdot q'$, $q_2 = b \cdot q''$, $q_3 = c \cdot q'''$, leaving the (simpler) cases that $q_i \in Act$, $i = 1, 2$ or 3, to the reader. We have

$(q_1 \| q_2) \| \{q_3\}$

$= ((a \cdot q') \| (b \cdot q'')) \| \{q_3\}$

$= [\text{def. } \|] \ (a \cdot (q' \| q_2) \cup b \cdot (q_1 \| q'')) \| \{q_3\}$

$= [\text{part (c)}] \ (a \cdot (q' \| q_2)) \| \{q_3\} \cup (b \cdot (q_1 \| q'')) \| \{c \cdot q'''\}$

$= [\text{def. } \|] \ a \cdot ((q' \| q_2) \| \{q_3\}) \cup c \cdot (a \cdot (q' \| q_2) \| \{q'''\}) \cup$
$\qquad\qquad b \cdot ((q_1 \| q'') \| \{q_3\}) \cup c \cdot (b \cdot (q_1 \| q'') \| \{q'''\})$

$= [\text{def. } \|] \ a \cdot ((q' \| q_2) \| \{q_3\}) \cup b \cdot ((q_1 \| q'') \| \{q_3\}) \cup c \cdot ((q_1 \| q_2) \| \{q'''\}),$

and similarly

$\{q_1\} \| (q_2 \| q_3)$

$= a \cdot (\{q'\} \| (q_2 \| q_3)) \cup b \cdot (\{q_1\} \| (q'' \| q_3)) \cup c \cdot (\{q_1\} \| (q_2 \| q''')).$

Hence, using Lemma 2.4,

$d((q_1 \| q_2) \| \{q_3\}, \{q_1\} \| (q_2 \| q_3))$

$= d(\ a \cdot ((q' \| q_2) \| \{q_3\}) \cup b \cdot ((q_1 \| q'') \| \{q_3\}) \cup c \cdot ((q_1 \| q_2) \| \{q'''\}),$
$\qquad a \cdot (\{q'\} \| (q_2 \| q_3)) \cup b \cdot (\{q_1\} \| (q'' \| q_3)) \cup c \cdot (\{q_1\} \| (q_2 \| q''')))$

$\le \frac{1}{2} max\{ \ d((q' \| q_2) \| \{q_3\}, \{q'\} \| (q_2 \| q_3)),$
$\qquad\qquad d((q_1 \| q'') \| \{q_3\}, \{q_1\} \| (q'' \| q_3)),$
$\qquad\qquad d((q_1 \| q_2) \| \{q'''\}, \{q_1\} \| (q_2 \| q''')) \ \}$

$\le \varepsilon/2.$ $\square$

We add two remarks concerning the definition of '$\|$'.

Remarks

(1) It should be noted that the definition of '$\|$' allows so-called *unfair* results in case (at least) one of the two operands is infinite (i.e., in case $p_i \cap Act^\omega \ne \emptyset$, $i = 1$ or 2). E.g., we have $\{a^\omega\} \| \{b\} = \{a^n b a^\omega \mid n \ge 0\} \cup \{a^\omega\}$ and we see that an outcome in which all steps consist of a-actions only is allowed by the definition. In fact, $\{a^\omega\} \| \{b\}$ is the (unique) solution of the equation

$$p = a \cdot p \cup b \cdot \{a^\omega\} \tag{4.4}$$

and the solution set p contains a^ω. Thus, there exists an execution of $a^\omega \| b$ where b never gets its turn, and one may want to call this an *unfair* execution. (In

Exercise 4.4, we shall present a few more examples.) In Section 5.3, we shall discuss how the definition of '$\parallel$' may be refined to include only *fair* merges—where each operand which has not yet finished its execution eventually gets its turn in the (scheduling of the) interleavings.

(2) An alternative definition of the semantic '$\parallel$' may be given which avoids the use of the Lifting Lemma, and instead directly uses Michael's theorem (Theorem 2.15) for its justification. This runs as follows: Let $(\phi \in)\, Op = \mathbb{P}_D \times \mathbb{P}_D \xrightarrow{1} \mathbb{P}_D$, and $Op' = \mathbb{Q}_D \times \mathbb{Q}_D \xrightarrow{1} \mathbb{P}_D$. $\Omega_\parallel, \Omega_;: Op \to Op$ and $\Omega_{;\prime}: Op \to Op'$ are given by

$$
\begin{aligned}
\Omega_\parallel(\phi)(p_1, p_2) &= \Omega_;(\phi)(p_1, p_2) \cup \Omega_;(\phi)(p_2, p_1) \\
\Omega_;(\phi)(p_1, p_2) &= \bigcup \{\, \Omega_{;\prime}(\phi)(q_1, q_2) \mid q_1 \in p_1, q_2 \in p_2 \,\} \\
\Omega_{;\prime}(\phi)(a, q) &= \{a \cdot q\} \\
\Omega_{;\prime}(\phi)(a \cdot q', q) &= a \cdot \phi(\{q'\}, \{q\}).
\end{aligned}
$$

Now put, just as before, $\parallel = \mathit{fix}(\Omega_\parallel)$, $\underline{\parallel} = \Omega_;(\parallel)$. We can justify this definition, concentrating on the question whether the right-hand side of the clause for $\Omega_;(p_1, p_2)$ is compact, as follows: Let us put $F = \lambda(q_1, q_2).\Omega_{;\prime}(\phi)(q_1, q_2)$. Clearly, for each q_1, q_2, $F(q_1, q_2)$ is a compact set (by the definition of the codomain for $\Omega_{;\prime}(\phi)$). By the definition of $\Omega_{;\prime}$ (and the assumption on ϕ), we have that F is (nonexpansive, hence) continuous. Therefore, by Lemma 2.13c, $F(p_1, p_2) = \{\, F(q_1, q_2) \mid q_1 \in p_1, q_2 \in p_2 \,\}$ is a compact set (the elements of which are in turn compact sets), i.e., an element of $\mathcal{P}_{co}(\mathbb{P}_D)$. By Michael's theorem (Theorem 2.15), we then infer that $\bigcup F(p_1, p_2)$ is compact (i.e., an element of $\mathbb{P}_D$).

We have discussed this alternative to the definition of '$\parallel$' since we shall encounter a similar style of defining '$\parallel$' on several occasions in later chapters.

We are now ready for the definition of $\mathcal{D}: \mathcal{L}_{par} \to \mathbb{P}_D$. The operators ';' and '+' on $\mathbb{P}_D$ are as in Section 2.2.2.

Definition 4.12

(a) $\mathcal{D}: \mathcal{L}_{par} \to \mathbb{P}_D$ is the unique function satisfying

$$
\begin{aligned}
\mathcal{D}(a) &= \{a\} \\
\mathcal{D}(x) &= \mathcal{D}(D(x)) \\
\mathcal{D}(s_1 \,\mathrm{op}\, s_2) &= \mathcal{D}(s_1) \,\mathrm{op}\, \mathcal{D}(s_2), \quad \mathrm{op} \in \{;, +, \parallel\}.
\end{aligned}
$$

(b) $\mathcal{D}[\![\pi]\!] = \mathcal{D}(\pi)$, for $\pi \in \mathcal{L}_{par}$.

Existence and uniqueness of $\mathcal{D}$ are straightforward by introducing a suitable Ψ—extending the definition used in the proof of Lemma 2.38—and putting $\mathcal{D} = fix(\Psi)$.

Examples

(1) For the example programs introduced above we have
$\mathcal{D}[\![a \,\|\,(b;c)]\!] = \{\, abc, bac, bca \,\}$,
$\mathcal{D}[\![x \Leftarrow x;a \mid x \,\|\, b]\!] = \{\, a^n ba^\omega \mid n \geq 0 \,\} \cup \{a^\omega\}$,
$\mathcal{D}[\![x \Leftarrow a;x, y \Leftarrow b;y \mid x \,\|\, y]\!] = \{\, a, b \,\}^\omega$.

(2) Assume $D(x) = (a \,\|\, b);x$. Then we have

$\mathcal{D}[\![x]\!]$
$= \mathcal{D}((a \,\|\, b);x)$
$= \mathcal{D}(a \,\|\, b);\mathcal{D}(x)$
$= (\mathcal{D}(a) \,\|\, \mathcal{D}(b));\mathcal{D}(x)$
$= (\{a\} \,\|\, \{b\});\mathcal{D}(x)$
$= \{\, ab, ba \,\};\mathcal{D}(x)$.

From this we derive $\mathcal{D}(x) = \{\, ab, ba \,\}^\omega$.

The reader may wonder whether a definition of $\mathcal{D}$ for $\mathcal{L}_{par}$ based on continuations is also feasible. Similar to what we saw earlier for $\mathcal{O}$, the answer to this question is negative. It is an open problem how to extend the machinery of Section 2.2.3 with a clause covering the case $\mathcal{D}(s_1 \,\|\, s_2)(\gamma)$, the reason being that a definition of $\mathcal{D}(s_1 \,\|\, s_2)(\gamma)$ in terms of $\mathcal{D}(s_1)(\gamma_1)$ and $\mathcal{D}(s_2)(\gamma_2)$—for suitable γ_1, γ_2—is not available (cf. however, Exercise 4.5).

There remains the proof that $\mathcal{O} = \mathcal{D}$ on $\mathcal{L}_{par}$. The first step is, again, simple.

Definition 4.13 $\mathcal{E}: Res \rightarrow \mathbb{P}_O$ is defined by putting $\mathcal{E}(\mathrm{E}) = \{\epsilon\}$, $\mathcal{E}(s) = \mathcal{D}(s)$.

We next verify that $\mathcal{E}$ is a fixed point of the operator Φ (implicitly) defining the operational semantics $\mathcal{O}$.

Lemma 4.14 $\Phi(\mathcal{E}) = \mathcal{E}$.

Proof First, put, for $q \in Act^\infty$, $\epsilon \,\|\!\_\, q = q \,\_\!\| \, \epsilon = \epsilon \,\|\, q = q \,\_\!\|\!\_\, \epsilon$, and let '$\|\!\_$' and '$\|$' on $\mathbb{P}_O$ be the respective liftings. Next, we show that, for all r, $\Phi(\mathcal{E})(r) = \mathcal{E}(r)$, by induction on $wgt(r)$. All cases are as in the proof of Lemma 2.40, but for the new case

$[s_1 \| s_2]$ We have

$\Phi(\mathcal{E})(s_1 \| s_2)$

$=$ [def. Φ] $\bigcup \{ a \cdot \mathcal{E}(r) \mid s_1 \| s_2 \overset{a}{\to} r \}$

$=$ [rule (Par) from $\mathcal{T}_{par}$]

$\quad \bigcup \{ a \cdot \mathcal{E}(r_1 \| s_2) \mid s_1 \overset{a}{\to} r_1 \} \cup \bigcup \{ a \cdot \mathcal{E}(s_1 \| r_2) \mid s_2 \overset{a}{\to} r_2 \}$

$=$ [def. $\mathcal{D}, \mathcal{E}$]

$\quad \bigcup \{ a \cdot (\mathcal{E}(r_1) \| \mathcal{E}(s_2)) \mid s_1 \overset{a}{\to} r_1 \} \cup \bigcup \{ a \cdot (\mathcal{E}(s_1) \| \mathcal{E}(r_2)) \mid s_2 \overset{a}{\to} r_2 \}$

$=$ [def. $\parallel$]

$\quad \bigcup \{ (a \cdot \mathcal{E}(r_1)) \parallel \mathcal{E}(s_2) \mid s_1 \overset{a}{\to} r_1 \} \cup \bigcup \{ (a \cdot \mathcal{E}(r_2)) \parallel \mathcal{E}(s_1) \mid s_2 \overset{a}{\to} r_2 \}$

$=$ [Lemma 4.5, 4.11]

$\quad (\bigcup \{ a \cdot \mathcal{E}(r_1) \mid s_1 \overset{a}{\to} r_1 \}) \parallel \mathcal{E}(s_2) \cup (\bigcup \{ a \cdot \mathcal{E}(r_2) \mid s_2 \overset{a}{\to} r_2 \}) \parallel \mathcal{E}(s_1)$

$=$ [def. Φ] $\Phi(\mathcal{E})(s_1) \parallel \mathcal{E}(s_2) \cup \Phi(\mathcal{E})(s_2) \parallel \mathcal{E}(s_1)$

$=$ [ind. hyp.] $\mathcal{E}(s_1) \parallel \mathcal{E}(s_2) \cup \mathcal{E}(s_2) \parallel \mathcal{E}(s_1)$

$=$ [def. $\|$] $\mathcal{E}(s_1) \| \mathcal{E}(s_2)$

$=$ [def. $\mathcal{D}, \mathcal{E}$] $\mathcal{E}(s_1 \| s_2)$.

$\qquad\qquad\qquad\qquad\qquad\qquad\qquad\qquad\qquad\qquad\qquad\qquad\qquad\qquad$ $\square$

In the usual way, we now obtain

Theorem 4.15 $\mathcal{O}[\![\pi]\!] = \mathcal{D}[\![\pi]\!]$, for $\pi \in \mathcal{L}_{par}$.

This result concludes our comparative analysis of $\mathcal{L}_{par}$. As one of the benefits of the general semantic methodology, we were able to develop this analysis as a fairly minor extension to that of $\mathcal{L}_{cf}$. Though languages with parallelism are, conceptually, rather more demanding than sequential ones, this has not (yet) become very manifest in the definitions so far. In later chapters, we shall discuss several extensions to $\mathcal{L}_{par}$. E.g., a nonuniform version—with '$\|$' added to $\mathcal{L}_{wh}$—will be treated in Chapter 7. Essentially new phenomena appear when we add the notion of *deadlock* (cf. the discussion of $\mathcal{L}_{gc}$ in Chapter 3), requiring a substantial extension of the metric framework (to be dealt with in Part III). Before coming to all this, we first discuss, in the next section, a fairly modest variation on (the '$\|$'-version of) uniform parallelism, viz. the notion of *process creation*.

4.2   Process creation—parallel resumptions

In this section we discuss a new way of introducing parallel execution in a programming language, viz. through the notion of *process creation*. Syntactically, process creation will be expressed by the construct new(s). This concept may be understood as follows: at each moment during execution of a program, $n \geq 1$ "processes" are active. Initially, $n = 1$. When, during execution of one of these processes, the construct new(s) is encountered, a new process with body s starts executing in parallel to the n processes already active (and n is increased by 1). Execution of the complete program terminates when all constituent processes running in parallel have finished. As we shall see in a moment, the language $\mathcal{L}_{pc}$—which includes process creation as main characteristic concept—has only implicit parallelism (through the new-construct), and no explicit parallelism (in the form of '$\|$' in the syntax). Contrary to the situation for $\mathcal{L}_{par}$, the semantics for process creation can be handled smoothly by the use of (an extended version of) resumptions.

4.2.1 Syntax and operational semantics

The syntax for $\mathcal{L}_{pc}$ has a uniform basis (comparable to that of $\mathcal{L}_{rec}$ or $\mathcal{L}_{cf}$), employing the usual sets $(a \in)\, Act$ and $(x \in)\, PVar$. In the definition of the class of guarded statements $GStat$, a complication is encountered which will be explained after the definition.

Definition 4.16

(a) $s(\in Stat) ::= a \mid x \mid (s;s) \mid (s+s) \mid$ new(s).

(b) The sets of *guarded* statements $(g \in)\, GStat$ and *strictly guarded* statements $(h \in)\, HStat$ are defined by

$$g ::= h \mid (g;g) \mid (g+g) \mid \text{new}(g)$$
$$h ::= a \mid (h;s) \mid (h+h).$$

(c) $(D \in)\, Decl = PVar \to GStat$, $(\pi \in)\, \mathcal{L}_{pc} = Decl \times Stat$.

Examples

(1) new($a;b$);$c \in Stat$. This statement will obtain the same meaning as the $\mathcal{L}_{par}$-statement $(a;b)\|c$.

(2) $a;$new($b_1;$new($b_2;c_1$);c_2);$c_3 \in Stat$. This statement will obtain the same meaning as the $\mathcal{L}_{par}$-statement $a;(b_1;((b_2;c_1)\|c_2))\|c_3$.

(3) $(x \Leftarrow a_1;$new(b_1);$y, y \Leftarrow a_2;x \mid y;b_2) \in \mathcal{L}_{pc}$, but $(x \Leftarrow (\text{new}(a);x) + b \mid x) \notin \mathcal{L}_{pc}$, since new($a$);$x \notin GStat$.

Remark The distinction between guarded and strictly guarded statements is necessary since, as we shall see, process creation does not necessarily result in the guarding of procedure variables. E.g., in the construct new$(a);x$, the variable x occurs unguarded. The semantic definitions to be given later will result in the same meaning for this statement as that for the $\mathcal{L}_{par}$-statement $a\|x$. Clearly, the latter construct may *begin* with the execution of x, thus violating the guardedness condition. Through the extra clause involving $(h \in) HStat$, it is ensured that occurrences of x in some $g \in GStat$ are preceded by an elementary action which is not in the scope of some new$(\cdot)$-construct.

We continue with the preparations for the definition of $\mathcal{T}_{pc}$. The absence of '$\|$' in the syntax for $\mathcal{L}_{pc}$ is compensated for by the introduction of an explicit parallel construct in the set of resumptions $(r \in) Res$.

Definition 4.17 Let E be as always.

(a) $r\,(\in Res) ::= \mathrm{E} \mid (s{:}r) \mid (r,r)$.

(b) By convention, we identify (E, r) and (r, E) with r.

The resumption (r_1, r_2) should be read as: execute r_1 and r_2 in parallel. As we shall see in a moment, the transition rules for (r_1, r_2) in $\mathcal{T}_{pc}$ mimic those for $(s_1\|s_2)$ in $\mathcal{T}_{par}$.

Definition 4.18 $\mathcal{T}_{pc} = (Res, Act, \rightarrow, Spec)$. *Spec consists of the following axiom and rules:*

- $$a{:}r \xrightarrow{a} r \qquad\qquad\qquad\qquad\qquad\qquad\qquad\qquad \text{(Act)}$$

- $$x{:}r \rightarrow_0 D(x){:}r \qquad\qquad\qquad\qquad\qquad\qquad\quad \text{(Rec)}$$

- $$(s_1;s_2){:}r \rightarrow_0 s_1{:}(s_2{:}r) \qquad\qquad\qquad\qquad\quad \text{(Seq)}$$

- $$(s_1 + s_2){:}r \rightarrow_0 s_1{:}r \qquad\qquad\qquad\qquad\qquad \text{(Choice)}$$
  $$(s_1 + s_2){:}r \rightarrow_0 s_2{:}r$$

- $$\text{new}(s){:}r \rightarrow_0 (s{:}\mathrm{E}, r) \qquad\qquad\qquad\qquad\qquad \text{(New)}$$

- $$\dfrac{r_1 \xrightarrow{a} r_2}{(r, r_1) \xrightarrow{a} (r, r_2)} \qquad\qquad\qquad\qquad\qquad\qquad \text{(Par)}$$
  $$(r_1, r) \xrightarrow{a} (r_2, r)$$

$\mathcal{T}_{pc}$ has the familiar rules for (Act), (Rec), (Seq) and (Choice). The rule (New) expresses that, in order to execute $\mathsf{new}(s)$ with resumption r, we start a new process with body s and resumption E, and put this in parallel to r. Finally, the rule (Par) has the same form as the rule (Par) from Section 4.1.

Examples

(1) Since

- $(\mathsf{new}(a;b);c){:}\mathrm{E} \to_0 \mathsf{new}(a;b){:}(c{:}\mathrm{E})$
- $\mathsf{new}(a;b){:}(c{:}\mathrm{E}) \to_0 ((a;b){:}\mathrm{E}, c{:}\mathrm{E})$
- $(a;b){:}\mathrm{E} \to_0 a{:}(b{:}\mathrm{E})$
- $a{:}(b{:}\mathrm{E}) \xrightarrow{a} b{:}\mathrm{E}$
- $c{:}\mathrm{E} \xrightarrow{c} \mathrm{E}$

we obtain by (Par)—also applying the $(\mathrm{E}, r) \equiv r$ identification—that
$$(\mathsf{new}(a;b);c){:}\mathrm{E} \xrightarrow{a} (b{:}\mathrm{E}, c{:}\mathrm{E})$$
and also
$$(\mathsf{new}(a;b);c){:}\mathrm{E} \xrightarrow{c} (a;b){:}\mathrm{E}.$$

(2) Suppose $x \Leftarrow \mathsf{new}(a;x);b$. Then we have

- $x{:}\mathrm{E} \to_0 (\mathsf{new}(a;x);b){:}\mathrm{E}$
- $(\mathsf{new}(a;x);b){:}\mathrm{E} \to_0 \mathsf{new}(a;x){:}(b{:}\mathrm{E})$
- $\mathsf{new}(a;x){:}(b{:}\mathrm{E}) \to_0 ((a;x){:}\mathrm{E}, b{:}\mathrm{E}).$

Hence, by (Par) and (Seq),
$$x{:}\mathrm{E} \xrightarrow{a} (x{:}\mathrm{E}, b{:}\mathrm{E})$$
and
$$x{:}\mathrm{E} \xrightarrow{b} (a;x){:}\mathrm{E}.$$

The definition of $\mathcal{O}$ for $\mathcal{L}_{pc}$ follows the usual pattern. As always so far, we have that $\mathcal{T}_{pc}$ is finitely branching. For the proof we use a *weight*-function $wgt\colon Res \to \mathbb{N}$ which satisfies the following properties:

- $wgt(r_1) > wgt(r_2)$, for each rule $r_1 \to_0 r_2$ in $\mathcal{T}_{pc}$
- $wgt((r_1, r_2)) > max\{\, wgt(r_1), wgt(r_2)\,\}$, for $r_1, r_2 \not\equiv \mathrm{E}$.

It will be more convenient to postpone introduction of this function till the next subsection (Definition 4.25): It is rather involved, and may be better appreciated when the reader has developed some more familiarity with the notion of process creation.

Lemma 4.19 $\mathcal{T}_{pc}$ *is finitely branching.*

Proof (Assuming the function wgt to be defined.) Show by induction on $wgt(r)$, that the set $\{\langle a, r'\rangle \mid r \xrightarrow{a} r'\}$ is (nonempty and) finite for each r with $r \not\equiv$ E.

The definition of $\mathcal{O}$ now follows.

Definition 4.20 Let $(p \in)\,\mathbb{P}_O = \mathcal{P}_{nco}(Act^\infty)$.

(a) $\mathcal{O}: Res \to \mathbb{P}_O$ is the unique function satisfying $\mathcal{O}(\mathrm{E}) = \{\epsilon\}$ and, for $r \not\equiv$ E,

$$\mathcal{O}(r) \;=\; \bigcup\{a \cdot \mathcal{O}(r') \mid r \xrightarrow{a} r'\}.$$

(b) $\mathcal{O}[\![s]\!] = \mathcal{O}(s{:}\mathrm{E})$.

Justification of this definition may be given in the usual way.

Examples

(1) $\mathcal{O}[\![\mathsf{new}(a;b);c]\!]$
   $= \mathcal{O}(\mathsf{new}(a;b);c{:}\mathrm{E})$
   $= a \cdot \mathcal{O}(b{:}\mathrm{E}, c{:}\mathrm{E}) \;\cup\; c \cdot \mathcal{O}(a;b{:}\mathrm{E})$
   $= a \cdot (b \cdot \mathcal{O}(c{:}\mathrm{E}) \cup c \cdot \mathcal{O}(b{:}\mathrm{E})) \cup c \cdot a \cdot \mathcal{O}(b{:}\mathrm{E})$
   $= \ldots$
   $= \{abc, acb, cab\}$

(2) Suppose $x \Leftarrow \mathsf{new}(a;x)$. We then have $\mathcal{O}(x{:}\mathrm{E}) = \mathcal{O}(a;x{:}\mathrm{E}) = \mathcal{O}(a{:}(x{:}\mathrm{E})) = a \cdot \mathcal{O}(x{:}\mathrm{E})$, hence $\mathcal{O}(x{:}\mathrm{E}) = \{a^\omega\}$. Therefore
   $\mathcal{O}(x{:}\mathrm{E}, b{:}\mathrm{E})$
   $= a \cdot \mathcal{O}(x{:}\mathrm{E}, b{:}\mathrm{E}) \;\cup\; b \cdot \mathcal{O}(x{:}\mathrm{E})$
   $= a \cdot \mathcal{O}(x{:}\mathrm{E}, b{:}\mathrm{E}) \;\cup\; \{ba^\omega\}$
   from which $\mathcal{O}(x{:}\mathrm{E}, b{:}\mathrm{E}) = \{a^\omega\} \cup \{a^n ba^\omega \mid n \geq 0\}$ follows. So
   $\mathcal{O}[\![x;b]\!]$

$$\begin{aligned}
&= \mathcal{O}(x;b{:}\mathrm{E}) \\
&= \mathcal{O}(a;x{:}\mathrm{E}, b{:}\mathrm{E}) \\
&= a \cdot \mathcal{O}(x{:}\mathrm{E}, b{:}\mathrm{E}) \;\cup\; b \cdot \mathcal{O}(a;x{:}\mathrm{E}) \\
&= a \cdot (\{a^\omega\} \cup \{\, a^n b a^\omega \mid n \geq 0 \,\}) \;\cup\; b \cdot \{a^\omega\} \\
&= \{a^\omega\} \cup \{\, a^n b a^\omega \mid n \geq 0 \,\}.
\end{aligned}$$

4.2.2   Denotational semantics, equivalence of $\mathcal{O}$ and $\mathcal{D}$

In the denotational semantics for $\mathcal{L}_{pc}$, continuations play an important role. Let $\mathbb{P}_D = \mathcal{P}_{nco}(Act^\infty)$ [1], let $(\gamma \in) Cont = \mathbb{P}_D$, and let $\gamma_\epsilon = \{\epsilon\}$. We shall use the *semantic* operator '$\|$' as defined in the previous section. Note that this use of '$\|$' does not contradict the absence from $\mathcal{L}_{pc}$ of '$\|$' as *syntactic* construct. The operator '$+$' will be as in Chapter 2, i.e., it denotes set-theoretic union. In addition to some clauses for $\mathcal{D}$ which are familiar from previous chapters, a new clause will appear dealing with the new-construct. As a result of this clause we shall obtain that, for a statement new(s) and continuation γ,

$$\mathcal{D}(\mathsf{new}(s))(\gamma) = \mathcal{D}(s)(\gamma_\epsilon)\|\gamma. \tag{4.5}$$

The reader who compares this with the operational rule for (New), viz.

$$\mathsf{new}(s){:}r \rightarrow_0 (s{:}\mathrm{E}, r),$$

will have no difficulty in understanding (4.5): The continuations γ and γ_ϵ correspond to the resumptions r and E, respectively, and the semantic '$\|$' operator, putting two elements from $\mathbb{P}_D$ in parallel, corresponds to the syntactic $(\cdot, \cdot)$-construct putting two resumptions in parallel.

Before presenting the definition of $\mathcal{D}$ as fixed point of some higher-order Ψ, we need a definition of $wgt(s)$ which is somewhat more subtle than the definitions encountered earlier, the reason being the different role of the h, g and s statements already mentioned above. (The definition of $wgt(s)$ is not yet the definition of $wgt(r)$ as announced before the proof of Lemma 4.19.)

Definition 4.21 $wgt{:}\mathcal{L}_{pc} \rightarrow \mathbb{N}$ is defined by

---

[1] Contrary to the situation in Section 4.1, the presence of ϵ is necessary here.

$$
\begin{aligned}
wgt(a) &= 1 \\
wgt(x) &= wgt(D(x)) + 1 \\
wgt(h;s) &= wgt(h) + 1 \\
wgt(s_1;s_2) &= wgt(s_1) + wgt(s_2) + 1, \quad \text{for } s_1 \notin HStat \\
wgt(s_1 + s_2) &= max\{\, wgt(s_1), wgt(s_2) \,\} + 1 \\
wgt(\mathsf{new}(s)) &= wgt(s) + 1.
\end{aligned}
$$

It is easy to show

Lemma 4.22 *wgt is well-defined on $\mathcal{L}_{pc}$.*

Proof By structural induction on first h, next g and then s.   □

We can now give

Definition 4.23

(a) Let $(S \in) Sem_D = \mathcal{L}_{pc} \to Cont \xrightarrow{1} \mathbb{P}_D$, and let $\Psi\colon Sem_D \to Sem_D$ be defined as follows

$$
\begin{aligned}
\Psi(S)(a)(\gamma) &= a \cdot \gamma \\
\Psi(S)(x)(\gamma) &= \Psi(S)(D(x))(\gamma) \\
\Psi(S)(h;s)(\gamma) &= \Psi(S)(h)(S(s)(\gamma)) \\
\Psi(S)(s_1;s_2)(\gamma) &= \Psi(S)(s_1)(\Psi(S)(s_2)(\gamma)), \quad s_1 \notin HStat \\
\Psi(S)(s_1 + s_2)(\gamma) &= \Psi(S)(s_1)(\gamma) + \Psi(S)(s_2)(\gamma) \\
\Psi(S)(\mathsf{new}(s))(\gamma) &= \Psi(S)(s)(\gamma_\epsilon) \| \gamma.
\end{aligned}
$$

(b) $\mathcal{D} = fix(\Psi)$, $\mathcal{D}[\![s]\!] = \mathcal{D}(s)(\gamma_\epsilon)$.

Examples

(1) $\mathcal{D}[\![\mathsf{new}(a;b);c]\!] = \mathcal{D}(\mathsf{new}(a;b);c)(\gamma_\epsilon) = \{ab\} \| \{c\}$.

(2) Suppose $x \Leftarrow \mathsf{new}(a;x);b$. Then we have

$\mathcal{D}(x)(\gamma_\epsilon)$

$= \mathcal{D}(\mathsf{new}(a;x))(\mathcal{D}(b)(\gamma_\epsilon))$

$= \mathcal{D}(a;x)(\gamma_\epsilon) \| \mathcal{D}(b)(\gamma_\epsilon)$

$= \mathcal{D}(a)\big(\mathcal{D}(x)(\gamma_\epsilon)\big) \| b \cdot \{\epsilon\}$

$$= (a \cdot \mathcal{D}(x)(\gamma_\epsilon)) \| \{b\}$$
$$= [\text{Eq. (4.3)}] \; a \cdot (\mathcal{D}(x)(\gamma_\epsilon) \| \{b\}) \; \cup \; b \cdot a \cdot \mathcal{D}(x)(\gamma_\epsilon)$$

from which it follows that

$$\mathcal{D}[\![x]\!] = \{ \, w \in \{a,b\}^\omega \mid \natural_b(v) \leq \natural_a(v) + 1 \text{ for each prefix } v \text{ of } w \, \}.$$

(Here $\natural_a(v)$ denotes the number of a's in v, and likewise for $\natural_b(v)$. A proof of the equality, though, is not easy to obtain.)

The next lemma supports the definition of $\mathcal{D}$.

Lemma 4.24 *For each $S \in Sem_D$*

(a) For each $s \in \mathcal{L}_{pc}$, $\gamma \in Cont$, we have

(i) $\Psi(S)(s)(\gamma)$ is nonempty and compact

(ii) $\Psi(S)(s)$ is nonexpansive (in γ)

(b) For each $h \in HStat$ it holds that $\Psi(S)(h)$ is $\frac{1}{2}$-contractive (in γ).

(c) Ψ is $\frac{1}{2}$-contractive (in S).

Proof

(a) Claim (i) follows by induction on $wgt(s)$. Consider, for example, the case $s_1 ; s_2$, for $s_1 \notin HStat$. Then, by induction, $\Psi(S)(s_2)(\gamma)$ is well-defined and, for each γ, $\Psi(S)(s_1)(\gamma)$ is nonempty and compact. Hence, in particular $\Psi(S)(s_1)(\Psi(S)(s_2)(\gamma))$ is nonempty and compact. The other cases are either direct, or follow since the operators '$+$', '$\|$' preserve nonemptiness and compactness. Clause (ii) is left as an exercise.

(b) Easy by induction on $wgt(h)$, starting from the basic case

$$d(\Psi(S)(a)(\gamma_1), \Psi(S)(a)(\gamma_2)) = d(a \cdot \gamma_1, a \cdot \gamma_2) = \tfrac{1}{2} d(\gamma_1, \gamma_2) \, .$$

(c) Choose some γ. Three subcases.

$[h;s]$ $d(\Psi(S_1)(h;s)(\gamma), \Psi(S_2)(h;s)(\gamma))$
$= \quad d(\Psi(S_1)(h)(S_1(s)(\gamma)), \Psi(S_2)(h)(S_2(s)(\gamma)))$
$\leq \quad [d \text{ an ultrametric}]$
$\qquad max\{ \; d(\Psi(S_1)(h)(S_1(s)(\gamma)), \Psi(S_1)(h)(S_2(s)(\gamma))),$
$\qquad\qquad d(\Psi(S_1)(h)(S_2(s)(\gamma)), \Psi(S_2)(h)(S_2(s)(\gamma))) \; \}$
$\leq \quad [\text{part (b), ind. hyp.}] \; max\{ \; \tfrac{1}{2} d(S_1(s)(\gamma), S_2(s)(\gamma)), \tfrac{1}{2} d(S_1, S_2) \; \}$

$\leq \quad \frac{1}{2}d(S_1, S_2).$

$[s_1;s_2]$ where $s_1 \notin HStat.$

$\quad d(\Psi(S_1)(s_1;s_2)(\gamma), \Psi(S_2)(s_1;s_2)(\gamma))$

$\quad = \quad d(\Psi(S_1)(s_1)(\Psi(S_1)(s_2)(\gamma)), \Psi(S_2)(s_1)(\Psi(S_2)(s_2)(\gamma)))$

$\quad \leq \quad [\text{ultrametricity}]$

$\qquad max\{ \ d(\Psi(S_1)(s_1)(\Psi(S_1)(s_2)(\gamma)), \Psi(S_1)(s_1)(\Psi(S_2)(s_2)(\gamma))),$

$\qquad\qquad d(\Psi(S_1)(s_1)(\Psi(S_2)(s_2)(\gamma)), \Psi(S_2)(s_1)(\Psi(S_2)(s_2)(\gamma))) \ \}$

$\quad \leq \quad [\text{part (a)ii, ind. hyp. for } s_1]$

$\qquad max\{ \ d(\Psi(S_1)(s_2)(\gamma), \Psi(S_2)(s_2)(\gamma)), \frac{1}{2}d(S_1, S_2) \ \} .$

$\quad \leq \quad [\text{ind. hyp. for } s_2] \ \frac{1}{2}d(S_1, S_2).$

$[\text{new}(s)]$ $d(\Psi(S_1)(\text{new}(s))(\gamma), \Psi(S_2)(\text{new}(s))(\gamma))$

$\quad = \quad d(\Psi(S_1)(s)(\gamma_\epsilon)\|\gamma, \Psi(S_2)(s)(\gamma_\epsilon)\|\gamma)$

$\quad \leq \quad [\| \text{ nonexpansive}] \ d(\Psi(S_1)(s)(\gamma_\epsilon), \Psi(S_2)(s)(\gamma_\epsilon))$

$\quad \leq \quad [\text{ind. hyp.}] \ \frac{1}{2}d(S_1, S_2).$ □

Remark The mapping $\Psi(S)(s)$ is, in general, not $\frac{1}{2}$-contractive in γ. This is due to the new-construct. We have, e.g.,

$$d(\Psi(S)(\text{new}(s))(\gamma_1), \Psi(S)(\text{new}(s))(\gamma_2))$$
$$= d(\Psi(S)(s)(\gamma_\epsilon)\|\gamma_1, \Psi(S)(s)(\gamma_\epsilon)\|\gamma_2)$$
$$\leq d(\gamma_1, \gamma_2),$$

where the last inequality holds since '$\|$' is nonexpansive (rather than $\frac{1}{2}$-contractive) in its second argument. For a program h, with $h \in HStat$, we do have that $\Psi(S)(h)$ is $\frac{1}{2}$-contractive (in γ), cf. part (b) of the lemma. This is explained by the fact that no h-statement begins with a statement of the form $\text{new}(h')$. The reason for the difference in treatment of $h;s$ versus $s_1;s_2$, with $s_1 \notin HStat$ should now also be clear.

Having defined both $\mathcal{O}$ and $\mathcal{D}$ for $\mathcal{L}_{pc}$, we next treat the issue of their equivalence. We shall show that, indeed, $\mathcal{O}[\![\pi]\!] = \mathcal{D}[\![\pi]\!]$, for each $\pi \in \mathcal{L}_{pc}$. The proof of this fact is more complicated than that of the same claim for $\mathcal{L}_{par}$. Due to the presence of the new-construct, we need a more involved weight function on $Decl \times Res$. (The earlier given definition of wgt on $Stat$, cf. Definition 4.21, will play no role in what follows.) As announced already, the main purpose of the definition of $wgt(r)$ is to ensure that, for $r_1 \to_0 r_2$, we have that $wgt(r_1) > wgt(r_2)$, cf. the proof of Lemma 4.19.

We shall compose the definition of $wgt(r)$ from two parts—both of which happen to be independent of the declaration D—viz. $k(r)$ and $c(r)$. The former counts the number of unguarded occurrences of procedure variables in r, the latter is a version of the syntactic complexity of r.

Definition 4.25

(a) The functions $k \colon Res \to \mathbb{N}$ and $c \colon Res \cup Stat \to \mathbb{N}$ are given by

$$k(\mathrm{E}) = 0, \ k(r_1, r_2) = k(r_1) + k(r_2)$$
$$k(a{:}r) = 0, \ k(x{:}r) = 1 + k(r)$$
$$k((s_1;s_2){:}r) = k(s_1{:}(s_2{:}r)), \ k((s_1 + s_2){:}r) = max\{\, k(s_1{:}r), k(s_2{:}r)\,\}$$
$$k(\mathrm{new}(s){:}r) = k(s{:}\mathrm{E}) + k(r),$$

$$c(\mathrm{E}) = 0, \ c(s{:}r) = c(s) + c(r), \ c(r_1, r_2) = c(r_1) + c(r_2)$$
$$c(a) = c(x) = 1, \ c(s_1;s_2) = c(s_1 + s_2) = c(s_1) + c(s_2) + 1$$
$$c(\mathrm{new}(s)) = c(s) + 1.$$

(b) Let '$>$' be the standard ordering on $\mathbb{N}$. The so-called lexicographic ordering '$\geq_\ell$' on $\mathbb{N}^2$ is given by $\langle n_1, n_2 \rangle <_\ell \langle n_1', n_2' \rangle$ iff either $n_1 < n_1'$, or $n_1 = n_1'$ and $n_2 < n_2'$. The mapping $wgt \colon Decl \times Res \to (\mathbb{N}^2, \geq_\ell)$ is given by $wgt(r) = \langle k(r), c(r) \rangle$.

Note that, by clause (b), $wgt(r)$ is ordered lexicographically. The key lemma for this weight function will now be given. The definitions have been organized such that if $r_1 \to_0 r_2$, then either the number of unguarded occurrences of a procedure variable decreases from r_1 to r_2 (i.e., k decreases in value), or, if not, then the syntactic complexity decreases from r_1 to r_2 (i.e., c decreases in value).

Lemma 4.26

(a) c is well-defined for each r, s, and $c(r) > 0$ for $r \not\equiv \mathrm{E}$.

(b) k is well-defined for each r, and $k(r) \geq 0$.

(c) $k(h{:}r) = 0$.

(d) $k(g{:}r) \leq k(r)$.

(e) If $r_1 \to_0 r_2$, then $wgt(r_1) > wgt(r_2)$. Also,

$$wgt(r_1, r_2) > max\{\, wgt(r_1), wgt(r_2)\,\}.$$

Proof

(a) Structural induction on s and r.

(b) Induction on $c(r)$.

(c) Structural induction on h. One subcase.

$[h;s]$ $k((h;s){:}r) = k(h{:}(s{:}r)) = 0$, by the induction hypothesis, since h is syntactically smaller than $(h;s)$.

(d) Structural induction on g. Two subcases.

$[(g_1;g_2){:}r]$ We have
$$k((g_1;g_2){:}r) = k(g_1{:}(g_2{:}r))$$
$$\leq [\text{ind. hyp. for } g_1]\ k(g_2{:}r)$$
$$\leq [\text{ ind. hyp. for } g_2]\ k(r).$$

$[\text{new}(g){:}r]$ We have $k(\text{new}(g){:}r) = k(g{:}\mathrm{E}) + k(r) \leq k(\mathrm{E}) + k(r) = k(r)$.

(e) Two subcases.

$[x{:}r]$ $k(x{:}r) = 1 + k(r) > k(r) \geq k(D(x){:}r)$, by part (d), since $D(x) \in GStat$.

$[\text{new}(s){:}r]$ $k(\text{new}(s){:}r) = k(s{:}\mathrm{E}) + k(r) = k(s{:}\mathrm{E}, r)$ and $c(\text{new}(s){:}r) = c(\text{new}(s)) + c(r) = c(s) + 1 + c(r) > c(s{:}\mathrm{E}) + c(r) = c(s{:}\mathrm{E}, r)$. Hence $wgt(\text{new}(s){:}r) > wgt(s{:}\mathrm{E}, r)$. $\square$

$\mathcal{O}$ and $\mathcal{D}$ will be connected using an intermediate semantics $\mathcal{E}{:}Decl \times Res \to \mathbb{P}_O$. The purpose of $\mathcal{E}$ is to extend $\mathcal{D}$ from $Decl \times Stat$ to $Decl \times Res$.

Definition 4.27

$$\mathcal{E}(\mathrm{E})\ \ =\ \ \gamma_\epsilon$$
$$\mathcal{E}(s{:}r)\ \ =\ \ \mathcal{D}(s)(\mathcal{E}(r))$$
$$\mathcal{E}(r_1, r_2)\ \ =\ \ \mathcal{E}(r_1)\|\mathcal{E}(r_2).$$

$\mathcal{E}$ is the denotational counterpart of $\mathcal{O}$. In fact, we shall show that $\Phi(\mathcal{E}) = \mathcal{E}$, from which $\mathcal{O} = \mathcal{E}$ is immediate by Banach's theorem. We extend the semantic operators to all of $\mathbb{P}_O$ in the usual way. Next, we show

Lemma 4.28

(a) $\mathcal{E}(a{:}r) = a \cdot \mathcal{E}(r)$.

(b) *If $r_1 \to_0 r_2$ by one of the rules (Rec), (Seq) or (New), then $\mathcal{E}(r_1) = \mathcal{E}(r_2)$.
If $r \to_0 r'$ and $r \to_0 r''$ (both by (Choice)), then $\mathcal{E}(r) = \mathcal{E}(r') + \mathcal{E}(r'')$.*

Proof One subcase.

$[(\text{new}(s){:}r)] \quad \mathcal{E}(\text{new}(s){:}r)$

$\quad = \quad [\text{def. } \mathcal{E}] \ \mathcal{D}(\text{new}(s))(\mathcal{E}(r))$

$\quad = \quad [\text{def. } \mathcal{D}] \ \mathcal{D}(s)(\gamma_\epsilon) \| \mathcal{E}(r)$

$\quad = \quad [\text{def. } \mathcal{E}] \ \mathcal{E}(s{:}\text{E}) \| \mathcal{E}(r)$

$\quad = \quad [\text{def. } \mathcal{E}] \ \mathcal{E}(s{:}\text{E}, r).$ $\qquad\qquad\qquad\qquad\qquad\qquad\qquad$ $\square$

After these preparations, it is no more difficult to show

Lemma 4.29 *For all r,*

$$\Phi(\mathcal{E})(r) = \mathcal{E}(r).$$

Proof Induction on $wgt(r)$. Two subcases

$[\text{new}(s){:}r] \quad \Phi(\mathcal{E})(\text{new}(s){:}r)$

$\quad = \quad [\text{def. } \mathcal{T}_{pc}] \ \Phi(\mathcal{E})(s{:}\text{E}, r)$

$\quad = \quad [\text{ind. hyp.}] \ \mathcal{E}(s{:}\text{E}, r)$

$\quad = \quad [\text{Lemma 4.28}] \ \mathcal{E}(\text{new}(s){:}r).$

$[(r_1, r_2)] \quad \text{Let } r_1, r_2 \not\equiv \text{E}.$
$\qquad \Phi(\mathcal{E})(r_1, r_2)$

$\quad = \quad [\text{def. } \mathcal{T}_{pc}] \ \bigcup\{ a \cdot \mathcal{E}(r_1', r_2) \mid r_1 \xrightarrow{a} r_1' \} \cup (\text{symm.})$

$\quad = \quad [\text{def. } \mathcal{E}, \|] \ \bigcup\{ a \cdot \mathcal{E}(r_1') \mid r_1 \xrightarrow{a} r_1' \} \| \mathcal{E}(r_2) \cup (\text{symm.})$

$\quad = \quad [\text{def. } \Phi] \ \Phi(\mathcal{E})(r_1) \| \mathcal{E}(r_2) \cup (\text{symm.})$

$\quad = \quad [\text{ind. hyp., def. } \|] \ \mathcal{E}(r_1) \| \mathcal{E}(r_2)$

$\quad = \quad [\text{def. } \mathcal{E}] \ \mathcal{E}(r_1, r_2).$ $\qquad\qquad\qquad\qquad\qquad\qquad$ $\square$

Finally we conclude with

Theorem 4.30

(a) $\mathcal{O} = \mathcal{E}$.

(b) $\mathcal{O}[\![\pi]\!] = \mathcal{D}[\![\pi]\!]$, *for* $\pi \in \mathcal{L}_{pc}$.

Proof

(a) Direct.

(b) Let $\pi = s \in \textit{Stat}$. Then $\mathcal{O}[\![\pi]\!] = \mathcal{O}(s{:}E) = \mathcal{E}(s{:}E) = \mathcal{D}(s)(\gamma_\epsilon) = \mathcal{D}[\![\pi]\!]$. $\square$

Having arrived at the end of the section on process creation, we add a comment on the relationship between $\mathcal{L}_{par}$ and $\mathcal{L}_{pc}$. Since the syntactic new-construct is modeled in terms of the semantic '$\|$' operator, it may be tempting to conjecture that $\mathcal{L}_{pc}$ and $\mathcal{L}_{par}$ have the same expressive power. The following proposition shows that this is not true.

Proposition 4.31 $\mathcal{L}_{pc}$ *and* $\mathcal{L}_{par}$ *are incomparable, i.e.*

(a) There exists a program $\pi_1 \in \mathcal{L}_{par}$ *such that for no* $\pi_2 \in \mathcal{L}_{pc}$ *we have*

$$\mathcal{O}[\![\pi_1]\!] = \mathcal{O}[\![\pi_2]\!].$$

(b) There exists a program $\pi_2 \in \mathcal{L}_{pc}$ *such that for no* $\pi_1 \in \mathcal{L}_{par}$ *we have*

$$\mathcal{O}[\![\pi_2]\!] = \mathcal{O}[\![\pi_1]\!].$$

The proof of part (a) is easy: Take, for example, the program $(a\|b);c$. No program in $\mathcal{L}_{pc}$ is able to reflect the effect of this program, since, in $\mathcal{L}_{pc}$, constituent parallel processes may terminate only upon termination of the complete program. The proof of part (b) is more involved (it needs a counter example involving recursion), and is omitted here.

4.3   Exercises

Exercise 4.1 Let s_1, s_2, $\mathcal{O}$ and '$\|$' be as in Section 4.1. Prove that $\mathcal{O}(s_1\|s_2) = \mathcal{O}(s_1)\|\mathcal{O}(s_2)$, without appealing to Theorem 4.15.

Exercise 4.2 (Direct definition of '$\|$' for finite and infinite words.) Let A, B be two, possibly infinite, alphabets, and let $h: A \to B^*$ be a given mapping. Let, for $u \in B^*$, $v \in B^\infty$, $u.v$ be defined by putting $\epsilon.v = v$, $(a \cdot u').v = a \cdot (u'.v)$. We say that h is homomorphically extended to a mapping $h: A^\infty \to B^\infty$ if it satisfies $h(\epsilon) = \epsilon$, $h(a \cdot w) = h(a).h(w)$, for each $w \in A^\infty$. Let $h^{-1}(w) = \{\, u \mid h(u) = w \,\}$. Let '$\leq$' on $A^\infty \times A^\infty$ be defined as: $w_1 \leq w_2$ iff $\exists u\,[\, w_1.u = w_2 \,]$, where $w_1.u$ is as above for $w_1 \in A^*$, and $w_1.u = w_1$, for $w_1 \in A^\omega$.

For any A, let $\bar{A} = \{\, \bar{a} \mid a \in A \,\}$, and similarly for $\bar{\bar{A}}$. We define $\| : A^\infty \times A^\infty \to \mathcal{P}(A^\infty)$ as follows: Let $h, h_1, h_2: \bar{A} \cup \bar{\bar{A}} \to A^*$ be given by

$$
\begin{array}{ccccc}
h(\bar{a}) & = & h(\bar{\bar{a}}) & = & a \\
h_1(\bar{a}) & = & h_2(\bar{\bar{a}}) & = & a \\
h_2(\bar{a}) & = & h_1(\bar{\bar{a}}) & = & \epsilon,
\end{array}
$$

and their homomorphic extensions. We now put, for $w_1, w_2 \in A^*$,

$$
w_1 \| w_2 \;=\; \{\, w \in A^* \mid \exists w' \in h^{-1}(w)\,[\, h_1(w') = w_1, h_2(w') = w_2 \,] \,\},
$$

and, for $w_1 \in A^\omega$ or $w_2 \in A^\omega$,

$$
w_1 \| w_2 \;=\; \{\, w \in A^\omega \mid \exists w' \in h^{-1}(w)\,[\, h_1(w') \leq w_1, h_2(w') \leq w_2 \,] \,\}.
$$

Prove that the operator '$\|$' as defined here coincides with the operator '$\|$' from Definition 4.7 (when the latter is adapted to the domain $A^\infty \times A^\infty \to \mathcal{P}(A^\infty)$).

Exercise 4.3 (A variation on *Res* for $\mathcal{L}_{par}$.) Define $(r \in)$ *Res'* by

$$
r ::= \mathrm{E} \mid (s{:}r) \mid (r, r){:}r
$$

with the identification $(\mathrm{E}, \mathrm{E}){:}r \equiv r$. Let $\mathcal{T}'_{par}$ be defined to consist of the rules (Act), (Rec), (Seq) and (Choice) as in $\mathcal{T}'_{cf}$ (Definition 2.43) and, in addition, of the rules

$$
\frac{(s_1{:}\mathrm{E}, s_2{:}\mathrm{E}){:}r \xrightarrow{a} \bar{r}}{(s_1 \| s_2){:}r \xrightarrow{a} \bar{r}}
$$

$$
\frac{r_1 \xrightarrow{a} r_1'}{\begin{array}{l} (r_1, r_2){:}r \xrightarrow{a} (r_1', r_2){:}r \\ (r_2, r_1){:}r \xrightarrow{a} (r_2, r_1'){:}r \end{array}}
$$

Discuss T'_{par} and the associated $\mathcal{O}': Res' \to \mathbb{P}_O$. E.g., define the appropriate *wgt*-function, prove that T'_{par} is finitely branching, and formulate and prove the relationship between $\mathcal{O}$ and $\mathcal{O}'$.

Exercise 4.4

(a) Let $\pi = (x \Leftarrow a; x \mid x \| s)$. Then $a^\omega \in \mathcal{O}(\pi)$.

(b) Let $\pi = (x \Leftarrow a; x \ y \Leftarrow b; y \mid x \| y)$. Then $\{a, b\}^*; \{a^\omega, b^\omega\} \subseteq \mathcal{O}(\pi)$.

Exercise 4.5 ($\mathcal{D}$ with continuations for $\mathcal{L}_{par}$.) We define a ternary operator (with three arguments) $\|: Act^\infty \times Act^\infty \times Act^\infty \to \mathcal{P}_{nco}(Act^\infty)$ as the unique function satisfying

$$
\begin{aligned}
\|(\epsilon, \epsilon, q) &= \{q\} \\
\|(a \cdot q, \epsilon, q'') &= a \cdot \|(q, \epsilon, q'') \\
\|(\epsilon, a' \cdot q', q'') &= a' \cdot \|(\epsilon, q', q'') \\
\|(a \cdot q, a' \cdot q', q'') &= a \cdot \|(q, a' \cdot q', q'') \cup a' \cdot \|(a \cdot q, q', q'').
\end{aligned}
$$

We put $\|(p_1, p_2, p) = \bigcup\{ \|(q_1, q_2, q) \mid q_1 \in p_1, q_2 \in p_2, q \in p\}$ and we write $(p_1 \| p_2)(p)$ for $\|(p_1, p_2, p)$. Let $\mathbb{P}_D = (\gamma \in) Cont = \mathcal{P}_{nco}(Act^\infty)$, and let $\gamma_\epsilon = \{\epsilon\}$. We define $\mathcal{D}': \mathcal{L}_{par} \to Cont \xrightarrow{1} \mathbb{P}_D$ as the unique mapping satisfying the clauses of Definition 2.45 and, in addition,

$$
\mathcal{D}'(s_1 \| s_2)(\gamma) = (\mathcal{D}'(s_1)(\gamma_\epsilon) \| \mathcal{D}'(s_2)(\gamma_\epsilon))(\gamma).
$$

Formulate and prove the various lemmas justifying these definitions, and investigate the relationship between $\mathcal{D}'$ and $\mathcal{O}'$ as in Exercise 4.3.

Exercise 4.6 Let $\mathcal{L}$ be a language including both the '$\|$' and the new($\cdot$)-constructs. Prove the semantic equivalence of the two programs π_1, π_2 from $\mathcal{L}$:

$$
\begin{aligned}
\pi_1 &= (x \Leftarrow a; \text{new}(x) \mid x) \\
\pi_2 &= (y \Leftarrow a; (a \| y) \mid y).
\end{aligned}
$$

Exercise 4.7 Prove the semantic equivalence of the following two $\mathcal{L}_{pc}$-programs:

$(D \mid \text{new}(\text{new}(a); b); c)$ and $(D \mid \text{new}(a); (\text{new}(b); c))$.

(Hint: use the associativity of the semantic '$\|$'.)

Exercise 4.8 Let Ψ, S, g, γ be as in Section 4.2 (in particular Definition 4.23). Give an example to show that $\Psi(S)(g)$ is not, in general, $\frac{1}{2}$-contractive in γ.

Exercise 4.9 (The "step semantics" for $\mathcal{L}_{par}$.) Let Act be as usual, and let $(\alpha \in) Act^{ext} = \mathcal{P}_{fn}(Act)$, the collection of all finite nonempty subsets of Act. We write $(\alpha =) [a_1, \ldots, a_n]$, $n \geq 1$, for a typical element of Act^{ext}. We design $\mathcal{O}$ and $\mathcal{D}$ for $\mathcal{L}_{par}$ with respect to the extended alphabet Act^{ext}. The key extension to $\mathcal{T}_{par}$ (as in Definition 4.3) is the replacement of (Par) by the rule

$$
\bullet \quad \frac{s_1 \xrightarrow{\alpha_1} r_1 \qquad s_2 \xrightarrow{\alpha_2} r_2}{s_1 \| s_2 \xrightarrow{\alpha_1 \cup \alpha_2} r_1 \| r_2} \quad \cdot
$$

E.g., $(a;b) \| c \xrightarrow{[a,c]} b \xrightarrow{[b]} E$, and for $D(x) = a;x$, $D(y) = b;y$, we have $\mathcal{O}(D \mid x \| y) = [a, b]^\omega$. The denotational '$\|$'-operator is the unique mapping satisfying $\epsilon \| q = q \| \epsilon = \{q\}$ and $(\alpha_1 \cdot q_1) \| (\alpha_2 \cdot q_2) = (\alpha_1 \cup \alpha_2) \cdot (q_1 \| q_2)$ (with the usual extension based on the Lifting Lemma). Complete the definitions as outlined above, formulate and prove the mathematical properties supporting them, and discuss the relationship between $\mathcal{O}$ and $\mathcal{D}$ for the step semantics. Also consider the effect of replacing Act^{ext} by the collection of all (finite nonempty) *multisets* over Act.

4.4   Bibliographical notes

Process description languages of the uniform variety—of which $\mathcal{L}_{par}$ is a particularly simple example—have been studied extensively since the early eighties. The classical source for this is Milner's CCS ([Mil80]). (The second parallel language playing a seminal role in concurrency research, viz. Hoare's CSP ([Hoa78, Hoa85]) is, in fact, a nonuniform language to be studied in Chapter 12.) Both CCS and CSP contain important further concepts—especially synchronization and communication—which are not present in $\mathcal{L}_{par}$ but will be investigated in later chapters (Chapters 11 to 13).

Our treatment of parallel composition in the simple form as in $\mathcal{L}_{par}$ goes back to [BZ82, BBKM84] and, in particular, [BM88]. The latter paper contains already most of the key ideas described in Chapter 4. The transition system for $\mathcal{L}_{par}$ was strongly influenced by the SOS-style semantics of [HP79].

The construct of process creation is a considerably simplified version of a notion from the language POOL (for Parallel Object-Oriented Language) as described in [AR89a]. (More about this will follow in Chapter 13.) In the paper [AB88], process creation is investigated in depth for a hierarchy of languages. In [BV92], a treatment of process creation in the framework of process algebra (cf. [BW91a]) is given, partly building on properties of this operation. Another presentation of the continuation style treatment of process creation is given in [BV91]. The result stating that $\mathcal{L}_{par}$ and $\mathcal{L}_{pc}$ are incomparable is due to [AA88].

The benefits of the higher-order method in comparing $\mathcal{O}$ and $\mathcal{D}$ are especially manifest when looking at earlier work of ACG on languages of the $\mathcal{L}_{par}$-family, where we did not yet use higher-order techniques: The complexity of papers such as [BMOZ88] by far exceeds that of the present approach.

Some further ACG sources dealing with simple (uniform) parallelism are

- [BM87], where some technical results relating metric techniques with cpo-based tools are developed (results which are refined and extended in [Hor93b])

- [MV89b], where several variations on $\mathcal{L}_{par}$, e.g., dealing with so-called "step semantics," are treated

- [Bak89], where a concise overview is given of much of the material referred to above.

Concurrency constitutes a vast area of research, and we can only provide here a few pointers to the available literature: Standard texts are

- [Hoa85]—an influential textbook on CSP—

- [BW91a]—providing an introduction to "process algebra," where a wide spectrum of notions in concurrency is treated in an axiomatic (mostly equational) style—

- [Hen88, Mil89, Old91]—more advanced texts, with a wealth of further material.

The volumes [Bes93, JP94] contain two recent proceedings of the annual conference on concurrency theory.

5 Unbounded Nondeterminism

The nondeterminacy studied in Section 2.2 has a finitary nature. The construct $s_1 + s_2$ determines a finite choice, and the associated transition system is of the finitely branching variety. Moreover, the semantic domains could be expressed in terms of the *compact* powerdomain—recall that the property of compactness can be seen as a limit case of finiteness (Theorem 2.20). For a number of programming constructs, this form of "bounded" nondeterminism does not suffice, since they exhibit what may be called *unbounded* nondeterministic behaviour in an intrinsic way. Two examples of such notions will be discussed in the present chapter, viz. the *random assignment* and the *fair merge*. The first of these—though arguably of a noncomputable nature—clearly serves our purposes of illustrating the theme of this chapter in a convincing way. The second construct is important since it both brings out a possible defect in our earlier treatment of the '$\|$'-operator, and it provides a nice application of the tools to be introduced. This machinery consists in a generalization of the basic ingredients in our semantic modelling. Firstly, we shall present an extension of the notion of finitely branching transition system to the so-called *image-finite* systems. Secondly, we shall replace our use of the powerdomain of (nonempty) compact sets by that of (nonempty) *closed* sets. The key property of (preservation of) completeness still applies (by Hahn's theorem), but a few other issues, especially the definition of the semantic operators, require some new techniques.

The programming concepts studied in the present chapter may be deemed to be of somewhat secondary importance in the world of programming languages. This certainly does not hold for the notion of *locality*, which we shall study in depth in the next chapter, and which also requires the tools of image-finite transition systems and closed powerdomains.

Since the material in the section on the fair merge is of a rather technical flavour—and the proofs are somewhat more demanding mathematically—the reader may wish to skip this at first reading. Later chapters will not depend on it in an essential manner.

5.1 Image-finite transition systems—closed replaces compact

So far, all transition systems used for semantic specification were of the finitely branching variety (Lemmas 1.9, 1.59, 2.24, 3.8, 3.21, 4.5 and 4.19). The languages studied in this chapter require a more general notion, viz. that of an *image-finite* transition system. We devote the present section to a general introduction of this notion and its key properties. In Sections 5.2 and 5.3, we then present two simple examples of the new concept. In Chapter 6, a more elaborate example will be treated.

Let $T = (Conf, Obs, \rightarrow)$ be a transition system. We recall the following definitions and theorem.

(1) T is called finitely branching whenever, for each $c \in Conf$, the successor set

$$S(c) \;=\; \{\, \langle a, c' \rangle \mid c \overset{a}{\rightarrow} c' \,\}$$

is finite.

(2) $\mathcal{O}_d \colon Conf \rightarrow \mathcal{P}(Obs^\infty)$ is defined as

$$\mathcal{O}_d(c) \;=\; \{\, a_1 a_2 \cdots a_n \mid c \overset{a_1}{\rightarrow} c_1 \overset{a_2}{\rightarrow} \ldots \overset{a_n}{\rightarrow} c_n \nrightarrow \,\} \cup \tag{5.1}$$
$$\{\, a_1 a_2 \cdots a_n \cdots \mid c \overset{a_1}{\rightarrow} c_1 \overset{a_2}{\rightarrow} \ldots \overset{a_n}{\rightarrow} c_n \ldots \,\} \,.$$

(3) For T finitely branching, $\mathcal{O}_d(c)$ is a (nonempty and) compact set, for each $c \in Conf$.

We moreover showed that, for finitely branching T, the direct definition of the operational semantics in terms of the $\mathcal{O}_d$ as just given coincides with the $\mathcal{O}$ defined in the familiar fashion in terms of a contractive higher-order Φ:

Theorem 5.1 *Let $(S \in) Sem = Conf \rightarrow \mathcal{P}_{nco}(Obs^\infty)$, and let $\Phi \colon Sem \rightarrow Sem$ be given by*

$$\Phi(S)(c) \;=\; \begin{cases} \{\epsilon\} & \text{if } c \nrightarrow \\ \bigcup \{\, a \cdot S(c') \mid c \overset{a}{\rightarrow} c' \,\} & \text{otherwise.} \end{cases}$$

Let $\mathcal{O} = \mathrm{fix}(\Phi)$. Then $\mathcal{O}$ is well-defined and $\mathcal{O}_d = \mathcal{O}$.

We now generalize the above to the so-called image-finite transition systems.

Definition 5.2 A transition system T is called *image-finite* whenever, for all $c \in Conf$ and $a \in Obs$, the set

$$\{\, c' \mid c \overset{a}{\rightarrow} c' \,\}$$

is finite.

Note the essential difference with the notion of finitely branching transition system. Whereas in the latter, for each c there are finitely many (a, c') such that $c \xrightarrow{a} c'$, here we require that for each c and a, there are finitely many c' such that $c \xrightarrow{a} c'$. In a situation where Obs itself is an infinite set, a transition system may well be image-finite without being finitely branching. As somewhat contrived example consider $Conf = \mathbb{N} = \{0, 1, \dots\}$, $Obs = \mathbb{N}$, and '$\rightarrow$' specified by $n \xrightarrow{k} k$, for all $n, k \in \mathbb{N}$. Examples with some semantic content follow in Sections 5.2 and 5.3.

For any $\mathcal{T}$—and thus, a fortiori, for image-finite $\mathcal{T}$—we may define $\mathcal{O}_d(c)$ as specified above. An important property of $\mathcal{O}_d(c)$ for the image-finite case is

Theorem 5.3 *For each image-finite $\mathcal{T}$ we have that $\mathcal{O}_d(c)$ is a (nonempty and) closed subset of Obs^∞, for each $c \in Conf$.*

Proof See Appendix B, Theorem B.2. $\qquad\qquad\qquad\qquad\qquad\qquad\qquad\qquad\square$

As we discussed in some detail in Section 2.1 on metric hyperspaces, closed sets enjoy fewer properties than compact sets (e.g., they lack preservation under continuous mappings). Still, there is one important property which remains valid, viz. preservation of completeness (Hahn's theorem, Appendix A, Theorem A.1): If (M, d) is complete, then $(\mathcal{P}_{ncl}(M), d_H)$ is also complete. Thanks to this theorem, we may apply the familiar apparatus defining operational semantics in terms of contractive higher-order mappings as well in a situation where the range of $\mathcal{O}$ consists of closed (rather than compact) sets. We now discuss Theorem 5.1 in the version where closed replaces compact:

Theorem 5.4 *Let $\mathcal{T}$ be an image-finite transition system, and let $\mathcal{O}_d$ be defined as in (5.1). Let us assume the discrete metric on Obs, the Baire metric on Obs^∞, and the Hausdorff metric on $\mathcal{P}_{ncl}(Obs^\infty)$. Let $(S \in) Sem = Conf \rightarrow \mathcal{P}_{ncl}(Obs^\infty)$, and let $\Phi: Sem \rightarrow Sem$ be defined by*

$$\Phi(S)(c) = \begin{cases} \{\epsilon\} & \text{if } c \not\rightarrow \\ \bigcup\{a \cdot S(c') \mid c \xrightarrow{a} c'\} & \text{otherwise.} \end{cases}$$

Let $\mathcal{O} = \text{fix}(\Phi)$. Then $\mathcal{O}$ is well-defined, and $\mathcal{O} = \mathcal{O}_d$.

Proof The only new element in the proof is that, for each c, the set $\Phi(S)(c) = \bigcup\{a \cdot S(c') \mid c \xrightarrow{a} c'\}$ is a closed set. By assumption, each $S(c')$ is a closed set. Also, by the image-finiteness of $\mathcal{T}$, for each given c and a, only finitely many c', say $c'_1, \dots c'_n$, are possible such that $c \xrightarrow{a} c'$. Since each Cauchy sequence in $\Phi(S)(c)$ is, eventually, in some $a \cdot (S(c'_1) \cup \dots \cup S(c'_n))$—recall that we assumed the discrete

metric on *Obs* and that the union of finitely many closed sets is closed—the desired
result follows.   □

Theorem 5.4 tells us that the property that $\mathcal{O} = \mathcal{O}_d$ holds for any image-finite
transition system—and not only for finitely branching systems. Of course, the
finitely branching property does deliver additional structure, in that the outcome
of $\mathcal{O}$ (or $\mathcal{O}_d$) for any c is a compact (rather than just a closed) set.

After thus having set the stage for the general use of image-finite transition
systems, we now proceed with the discussion of two example languages.

5.2   Random assignment—the closed powerdomain

The first application of the tools developed in Section 5.1 concerns a language with
random assignment ($\mathcal{L}_{ra}$). This notion will be studied in the setting of an enlarged
$\mathcal{L}_{wh}$ (the language with while statements). We shall develop the semantic models
for $\mathcal{L}_{ra}$ as a direct extension of our earlier results for $\mathcal{L}_{wh}$. Note, however, that the
validity of this extension depends crucially on Theorems 5.3 and 5.4.

5.2.1   Syntax and operational semantics

The basic new ingredient for $\mathcal{L}_{ra}$ is the "random assignment," syntactically written
as $v := ?$, and to be interpreted as: choose, randomly, an element α of the domain
of values *Val*, and set v to α. As soon as *Val* is infinite, this introduces an element
of "unbounded" nondeterminacy in the language: the number of possibilities for
α is unbounded in that any of the—arbitrarily many—elements of *Val* may be
chosen. Assuming the discrete metric on *Val*, it is clear that *Val* is not compact.
Take, for example, $Val = \mathbb{N} = \{0, 1, \dots\}$ as a set in which we do not have that
each infinite sequence has a converging subsequence. We thus see that unbounded
nondeterminacy introduces an element of noncompactness in our metric framework,
whence the need for resorting to image-finiteness.

We proceed with the precise definitions.

Definition 5.5 Let $(v \in)\,IVar$, $(e \in)Exp$ be as usual.

(a) $s\,(\in Stat) ::= \quad v := e \mid \mathsf{skip} \mid (s;s) \mid \mathsf{if}\ e\ \mathsf{then}\ s\ \mathsf{else}\ s\ \mathsf{fi} \mid$
$\qquad\qquad\qquad\quad \mathsf{while}\ e\ \mathsf{do}\ s\ \mathsf{od} \mid v := ?$

(b) $(\pi \in)\,\mathcal{L}_{ra} = Stat$

(c) $r\,(\in Res) ::= \mathrm{E} \mid (s{:}r).$

Statements and resumptions for $\mathcal{L}_{ra}$ are as to be expected, with $v := ?$ as the only new feature. $\mathcal{T}_{ra}$ is given in

Definition 5.6 $\mathcal{T}_{ra} = (Res \times \Sigma, \Sigma, \rightarrow, Spec)$, where $Spec$ consists of the rules from $\mathcal{T}_{wh}$, together with the rule

- $[(v := ?){:}r, \sigma] \rightarrow [r, \sigma\{\alpha/v\}]$ for (any) $\alpha \in Val$ (Rand)

In our subsequent discussion of $\mathcal{T}_{ra}$, we assume that Val is an infinite set. The rules in $\mathcal{T}_{ra}$ look deceptively simple, in that they consist of the rules of $\mathcal{T}_{wh}$, together with the seemingly innocent rule (Rand). Note, however, that (Rand) specifies, for a fixed pair $[(v := ?){:}r, \sigma]$ a choice between as many alternatives as there are elements in Val. Thus, it is here that we find the announced appearance of unbounded nondeterminacy. Taking $Conf = Res \times \Sigma$ and $Obs = \Sigma$, it is also clear that we have

Lemma 5.7 $\mathcal{T}_{ra}$ is image-finite.

Proof Recalling our convention that the observable element in a transition $[r, \sigma] \rightarrow [r', \sigma']$ is σ' we must show that, for each $[r, \sigma]$ and σ', the set

$$\{ [r', \sigma'] \mid [r, \sigma] \rightarrow [r', \sigma'] \} \tag{5.2}$$

is a finite set. Now this is easily proved by structural induction on r. In fact, we have that the set (5.2) is a singleton set for each $[r, \sigma]$ and σ'. $\square$

Theorem 5.4 provides a safe basis for the definition of $\mathcal{O}$ for $\mathcal{L}_{ra}$. That is, we may adopt the usual higher-order definition for $\mathcal{O}$ and obtain its well-definedness—and equivalence with $\mathcal{O}_d$—as a direct consequence of the results of Section 5.1. This is done in

Definition 5.8

(a) $\mathbb{P}_O = \Sigma \rightarrow \mathcal{P}_{ncl}(\Sigma^\infty)$.

(b) $\mathcal{O}: Res \times \Sigma \rightarrow \mathcal{P}_{ncl}(\Sigma^\infty)$ is the unique function satisfying $\mathcal{O}(\mathrm{E}, \sigma) = \{\epsilon\}$ and

$$\mathcal{O}(s{:}r, \sigma) = \bigcup \{ \sigma' \cdot \mathcal{O}(r', \sigma') \mid [s{:}r, \sigma] \rightarrow [r', \sigma'] \}.$$

(c) $\mathcal{O}[\![\cdot]\!]: \mathcal{L}_{ra} \rightarrow \mathbb{P}_O$ is given by $\mathcal{O}[\![s]\!] = \lambda\sigma.\mathcal{O}(s{:}\mathrm{E}, \sigma)$.

We have

Lemma 5.9 $\mathcal{O}$ *is well-defined.*

Proof By the discreteness of *Val*, Σ is discrete as well. The desired result now follows as a corollary of Theorem 5.4. $\square$

5.2.2   Denotational semantics, equivalence of $\mathcal{O}$ and $\mathcal{D}$

We can be extremely brief in this subsection. The whole machinery developed so far applies, with $\mathcal{P}_{ncl}(\cdot)$ replacing $\mathcal{P}_{nco}(\cdot)$. The only new element is the definition of $\mathcal{D}$ for $v := ?$.

Definition 5.10

(a) Let $(\gamma \in) \, Cont = \mathbb{P}_D = \Sigma \to \mathcal{P}_{ncl}(\Sigma^\infty)$, and let $\gamma_\epsilon = \lambda\sigma.\{\epsilon\}$. Let $(S \in) \, Sem = Stat \to Cont \xrightarrow{1} \mathbb{P}_D$, and let $\Psi: Sem \to Sem$ be given by

$$\Psi(S)(v := e)(\gamma) \;=\; \lambda\sigma.\bigcup\{\,\sigma\{\alpha/v\} \cdot \gamma(\sigma\{\alpha/v\}) \mid \alpha = \mathcal{V}(e)(\sigma)\,\}$$
$$\Psi(S)(v := ?)(\gamma) \;=\; \lambda\sigma.\bigcup\{\,\sigma\{\alpha/v\} \cdot \gamma(\sigma\{\alpha/v\}) \mid \alpha \in Val\,\},$$

together with clauses which exactly copy those as given for $\mathcal{L}_{wh}$—but now, of course, with respect to the $\mathbb{P}_D$ specified above.

(b) $\mathcal{D} = fix(\Psi)$, $\mathcal{D}[\![s]\!] = \mathcal{D}(s)(\gamma_\epsilon)$.

The only point which may not be immediately obvious is whether the second clause above has as right-hand side a set (say $\gamma_?(\sigma)$) which is indeed closed for each σ. Since we assumed the discrete metric on *Val*, each Cauchy sequence in $\gamma_?(\sigma)$ is eventually in one of the $\sigma\{\alpha/v\} \cdot \gamma(\sigma\{\alpha/v\})$, where α is some element of *Val*. By the assumption on γ, each of these sets is closed, and the desired well-definedness of $\Psi(S)$ follows.

The proof that $\mathcal{O}[\![\cdot]\!] = \mathcal{D}[\![\cdot]\!]$ for $\mathcal{L}_{ra}$ is standard and omitted.

5.3   Fair merge—enforcing image-finiteness

In our treatment of $\mathcal{L}_{par}$ in Section 4.1, we observed that the parallel composition as introduced there may lead to *unfair* computations. The composition $p_1 \| p_2$ may include outcomes in which not all of the actions of one of the two operands occur. E.g., we have that $a^\omega \in a^\omega \| b$ (thus ignoring b), or $a^k b^\ell a^\omega \in a^\omega \| b^\omega$, for each $k, \ell \geq 0$ (thus ignoring all but a finite number of the b's). The *fair* merge (say '$\|_f$') avoids this phenomenon. By definition, $p_1 \|_f p_2$ consists of precisely those elements of $p_1 \| p_2$ where *all* actions of p_1 and p_2 are included. For example, for the case $a^\omega \|_f b^\omega$ we have (putting $a^+ = a \cdot a^*$, $b^+ = b \cdot b^*$), that

$$a^\omega \|_f b^\omega \qquad\qquad (5.3)$$
$$= (a^+ b^+)^\omega \cup (b^+ a^+)^\omega$$
$$= \{ a^{n_1} b^{n_2} a^{n_3} \cdots \mid n_k > 0, k = 1, 2, \ldots \} \cup$$
$$\{ b^{m_1} a^{m_2} b^{m_3} \cdots \mid m_k > 0, k = 1, 2, \ldots \}.$$

One problem in handling the fair merge should already be manifest from this discussion. Consider once more the example $a^\omega \|_f b$. This set equals

$$\{ a^k b a^\omega \mid k \geq 0 \}, \qquad\qquad (5.4)$$

but this is a non-closed set. It contains the Cauchy sequence $(a^k b a^\omega)_k$, but not its limit a^ω. This example makes it clear that a simple application of the metric machinery as developed so far will not work, since the requirement that all sets considered be closed is an essential feature of the theory. Rather, we shall have to resort to some new techniques in order to provide satisfactory semantic definitions for the fair merge. The key idea in defining $p_1 \|_f p_2$ is inspired by formula (5.3) for $a^\omega \|_f b^\omega$: We shall ensure that, for arbitrary p_1, p_2, $p_1 \|_f p_2$ alternatingly allows an arbitrary (but positive) number of steps from each of the operands—of course only as long as there are steps to be performed at all by any one of these. This scheme avoids the situation that, from a certain moment on, all steps are made solely by one of the two operands, ignoring the other one.

Though not difficult in outline, the details of this scheme require some care. We shall attack the problem of defining the operational semantics for $\mathcal{L}_{fm}$ as a second application of the use of image-finite transition systems. Once the way to handle $\|_f$ in $\mathcal{T}_{fm}$ is understood, it will not be too hard to appreciate the denotational definition of '$\|_f$' in terms of another higher-order definitional scheme. Note the occurrence of "arbitrary number" in the explanation of $p_1 \|_f p_2$ just given. In fact, the successive choices of these arbitrary numbers—cf. the $n_1, n_2, \ldots, m_1, m_2, \ldots$ of example (5.3)—closely resemble the random choice feature in Section 5.2: The way in which we shall model fair merge below incorporates an element of random choice in an essential way. As additional feature we shall now be dealing with a systematic *iteration* of such choices.

One final introductory remark. As we shall see, the use of an image-finite transition system relies on a definitional scheme where the choices (the $n_1, n_2, \ldots$) are in some way "encoded" in the actions of the language. This scheme is on the one hand essential for the mathematical justification of the definitions. On the other hand, one might argue that it introduces an artificial element in the semantics for $\mathcal{L}_{fm}$ which is absent from the language models as presented so far. However, a more natural approach which both fits into the simple metric framework we use throughout our work, and also avoids all coding tricks, is not known to date.

5.3.1   Syntax and operational semantics

The language $\mathcal{L}_{fm}$ with *fair merge* is, syntactically, a simple variation on $\mathcal{L}_{par}$, in that '$\|_f$' replaces '$\|$'. The sets $(a \in) Act$ and $(x \in) PVar$ are as usual for a uniform language.

Definition 5.11

(a) $s\,(\in Stat) ::= a \mid x \mid (s;s) \mid (s+s) \mid (s \|_f s)$

(b) $g\,(\in GStat) ::= a \mid (g;s) \mid (g+g) \mid (g \|_f g)$

(c) $(D \in) Decl$ is as usual, $\mathcal{L}_{fm} = Decl \times Stat$.

In the definition of $\mathcal{T}_{fm}$, we shall use resumptions r which include the simple cases as before (E, $s \in Stat$), and also constructs of the form $s_1 \mathbin{\|\!\|}^n s_2$ with $s_1, s_2 \in \mathcal{L}_{fm}$ and $n\ (\geq 0)$ a natural number. The intended interpretation of the construct $s_1 \mathbin{\|\!\|}^n s_2$ is that those computations of $s_1 \|_f s_2$ are singled out where the first $n\ (\geq 0)$ steps are made by s_1. As a consequence of this interpretation we have that $s_1 \mathbin{\|\!\|}^0 s_2$ starts with a step from s_2, and $s_1 \mathbin{\|\!\|}^{n+1} s_2$ starts with a step from s_1 (leading to r_1, say), after which the statement $r_1 \mathbin{\|\!\|}^n s_2$ is executed. Since the '$\mathbin{\|\!\|}^n$' construct may occur nested, we shall in fact use $r \mathbin{\|\!\|}^n r$ rather than $s \mathbin{\|\!\|}^n s$ in the syntax for $(r \in) Res$. (Further explanation of the '$\mathbin{\|\!\|}^n$'-technique will follow after we have presented $\mathcal{T}_{fm}$.)

Definition 5.12 $r\,(\in Res) ::= \mathrm{E} \mid s \mid (r \mathbin{\|\!\|}^n r)\ (n \geq 0)$.

We shall identify E;r and E $\mathbin{\|\!\|}^n r$ $(n \geq 0)$ with r.

In the definition of $\mathcal{T}_{fm}$, we shall use an enlarged version of Act, say $Act^{ext} = Act \times \mathbb{N}^*$, where $\mathbb{N}^*$ is the set of all finite (possibly empty) sequences of natural numbers. The purpose of Act^{ext} is to leave a trace of the successive (random) choices made in executing $s_1 \|_f s_2$, in that the number of execution slots $(n_k, m_k, k \geq 1)$ allotted in turn to s_1 and s_2 (or s_2 and s_1) is stored. More precisely, for $a \in Act$, $\nu \in \mathbb{N}^*$, $\alpha = (a, \nu) \in Act^{ext}$, we shall use $\alpha n \overset{df}{=} (a, \nu n)$ to record n as the most recent such choice. (Some study of the rules in $\mathcal{T}_{fm}$ for $r_1 \mathbin{\|\!\|}^n r_2$ will probably be needed to fully understand this.)

Definition 5.13

(a) $(\alpha \in) \, Act^{ext} = Act \times \mathbb{N}^*$.

(b) $\mathcal{T}_{fm} = (Res, Act^{ext}, \rightarrow, Spec)$, where $Spec$ is defined as follows.

- $$a \xrightarrow{(a,\epsilon)} E \tag{Act}$$

- $$\frac{D(x) \xrightarrow{\alpha} r}{x \xrightarrow{\alpha} r} \tag{Rec}$$

(Seq) and (Choice) are as usual (with $\alpha \in Act^{ext}$ replacing $a \in Act$)

- $$\frac{s_1 \, \|^{0} \, s_2 \xrightarrow{\alpha} r}{s_1 \, \|_f \, s_2 \xrightarrow{\alpha} r} \tag{Fair, init}$$

$$s_2 \, \|_f \, s_1 \xrightarrow{\alpha} r$$

- $$\frac{s_2 \xrightarrow{\alpha} r_2}{s_1 \, \|^{0} \, s_2 \xrightarrow{\alpha n} r_2 \, \|^{n} \, s_1} \quad (n \geq 0) \tag{Fair, 0}$$

- $$\frac{s_1 \xrightarrow{\alpha} r_1}{s_1 \, \|^{n+1} \, s_2 \xrightarrow{\alpha} r_1 \, \|^{n} \, s_2} \quad (n \geq 0) \tag{Fair, $n+1$}$$

The rules (Act), (Rec), (Seq) and (Choice) are the standard ones. The new part in $\mathcal{T}_{fm}$ consists in the three (Fair, $\cdot$) rules:

(1) The rule (Fair, init) has as intended effect that $s_1 \, \|_f \, s_2$ satisfies the semantic equation

$$s_1 \, \|_f \, s_2 \;=\; (s_1 \, \|^{0} \, s_2) + (s_2 \, \|^{0} \, s_1) \, .$$

Thus, the fair merge $s_1 \, \|_f \, s_2$ is initialized by stating that its first step is either taken by s_2 ($s_1 \, \|^{0} \, s_2$ allows no first step from s_1), or by s_1 (similarly). So far, little news. The interesting part comes next:

(2) The rule (Fair, 0) expresses that $r_1 \, \|^{0} \, r_2$ is executed by first executing a step (say α) by r_2 leading to r_2', and next choosing n ($n \geq 0$) for the number of steps to be taken by r_2' in the further execution (of $r_2' \, \|^{n} \, r_1$). Note carefully that the n as

chosen here is postfixed to the α, yielding the step αn as the resulting transition. Without this update from α to αn, the system T_{fm} would not be image-finite (more about this in a moment).

(3) The rule (Fair, $n+1$) expresses that $r_1 \, \|\!\!\!\sqsubset^{n+1} r_2$ is executed by first executing a step (say α) by r_1 leading to r_1', and then continuing with $r_1' \, \|\!\!\!\sqsubset^n r_2$.

Examples

(1) By (Fair,0) we have

$$a \, \|\!\!\!\sqsubset^0 b \xrightarrow{(b,n)} a,$$

since $b \xrightarrow{(b,\epsilon)} \mathrm{E}$, $(b,\epsilon)n = (b,n)$ and $\mathrm{E} \, \|\!\!\!\sqsubset^n a \equiv a$. Also $a \, \|\!\!\!\sqsubset^{n+1} b \xrightarrow{(a,\epsilon)} b$ by (Fair,$n+1$) since $a \xrightarrow{(a,\epsilon)} \mathrm{E}$ and $\mathrm{E} \, \|\!\!\!\sqsubset^n b \equiv b$.

(2) We have

$$a \, \|_f \, (b;c) \xrightarrow{(b,n)} c \, \|\!\!\!\sqsubset^n a$$

for $n \geq 0$, since $b;c \xrightarrow{(b,\epsilon)} c$, so $a \, \|\!\!\!\sqsubset^0 (b;c) \xrightarrow{(b,n)} c \, \|\!\!\!\sqsubset^n a$ by (Fair,0) from which $a \, \|_f \, (b;c) \xrightarrow{(b,n)} c \, \|\!\!\!\sqsubset^n a$ follows by (Fair,init). Also

$$a \, \|_f \, (b;c) \xrightarrow{(a,n)} b;c$$

for $n \geq 0$, since $a \xrightarrow{(a,\epsilon)} \mathrm{E}$, so $b;c\|\!\!\!\sqsubset^0 a \xrightarrow{(a,n)} b;c$ by (Fair,0) from which $a\|_f(b;c) \xrightarrow{(a,n)} b;c$ follows by (Fair,init).

(3) Suppose $D(x) = a;x$. Then we have

$$x \, \|\!\!\!\sqsubset^0 b \xrightarrow{(b,n)} x$$

for $n \geq 0$, and

$$x \, \|\!\!\!\sqsubset^{n+1} b \xrightarrow{(a,\epsilon)} x \, \|\!\!\!\sqsubset^n b$$

by (Act), (Seq), (Rec) and (Fair,$n+1$), respectively.

(4) It holds that

$(a \parallel_f b) \parallel_f c \xrightarrow{(a,nm)} b \parallel^m c.$

This can be seen as follows: $a \xrightarrow{(a,\epsilon)} \mathrm{E}$ by (Act), so $b \parallel^0 a \xrightarrow{(a,n)} b$ (with $n \geq 0$), so $a \parallel_f b \xrightarrow{(a,n)} b$ by (Fair,init), hence $c \parallel^0 (a \parallel_f b) \xrightarrow{(a,nm)} b \parallel^m c$ (with $m \geq 0$) and therefore $(a \parallel_f b) \parallel_f c \xrightarrow{(a,nm)} b \parallel^n c$ (with $m \geq 0$) again by (Fair,init).

As announced, $\mathcal{T}_{fm}$ satisfies

Lemma 5.14 $\mathcal{T}_{fm}$ *is image-finite.*

Proof Let $wgt(r)$ be defined in the usual way (where $wgt(r_1 \parallel^n r_2) = wgt(r_1) + wgt(r_2)+1$). We use induction on $wgt(r)$; the interesting case is that $r \equiv r_1 \parallel^0 r_2$: By the induction hypothesis we have that , for each r_2 and α, $|\{\, r_2' \mid r_2 \xrightarrow{\alpha} r_2' \,\}| < \infty$. As a consequence, for each r_1, r_2, α and n, $|\{\, (r_2' \parallel^n r_1) \mid r_1 \parallel^0 r_2 \xrightarrow{\alpha n} r_2' \parallel^n r_1 \,\}| < \infty$ as well, thus settling the central case of the proof. □

The way in which $\mathcal{O}$ for $\mathcal{L}_{fm}$ is obtained from $\mathcal{T}_{fm}$ is standard.

Definition 5.15 We assume the discrete metric on Act^{ext}.

(a) $\mathbb{P}_O = \mathcal{P}_{ncl}((Act^{ext})^\infty)$.

(b) $\mathcal{O}: Res \to \mathbb{P}_O$ is the unique function satisfying $\mathcal{O}(\mathrm{E}) = \{\epsilon\}$, and, for $r \not\equiv \mathrm{E}$,

$$\mathcal{O}(r) \;=\; \bigcup\{\, \alpha \cdot \mathcal{O}(r') \mid r \xrightarrow{\alpha} r' \,\}.$$

(c) $\mathcal{O}[\![\pi]\!] = \mathcal{O}(\pi)$, for $\pi \in \mathcal{L}_{fm}$.

Examples

(1) $\mathcal{O}(a \parallel_f (b;c))$
    $= \{\, (a,n)(b,\epsilon)(c,\epsilon), (b,0)(a,n)(c,\epsilon), (b,n+1)(c,\epsilon)(a,\epsilon) \mid n \geq 0 \,\}$

(2) $\mathcal{O}((a \parallel_f b) \parallel_f c)$
    $= \{\, (a,n0)(c,m)(b,\epsilon), (a,n(m+1))(b,\epsilon)(c,\epsilon),$
        $(b,n0)(c,m)(a,\epsilon), (b,n(m+1))(a,\epsilon)(c,\epsilon),$
        $(c,n)(a,m)(b,\epsilon), (c,n)(b,m)(a,\epsilon) \mid n,m \geq 0 \,\}.$
    Note $\mathcal{O}((a \parallel_f b) \parallel_f c) \neq \mathcal{O}(a \parallel_f (b \parallel_f c))$.

Remark It may be instructive to see what happens when we do not invoke the technique of "remembering" the choice n in αn: Imagine that this feature is deleted from $\mathcal{T}_{fm}$, resulting in a system $\mathcal{T}'_{fm}$ where all actions are simply labelled by some $a \in Act$. A *direct* definition of $\mathcal{O}_d \colon Res \to \mathcal{P}(Act^\infty)$ is still possible (as it is for any $\mathcal{T}$). However, for, e.g., the program $\pi \equiv (x \Leftarrow a;x \mid x \parallel_f b)$, we would obtain as outcome for $\mathcal{O}_d[\![\pi]\!]$ the nonclosed set $\{\, a^k ba^\omega \mid k \geq 0 \,\}$.

5.3.2 Denotational semantics, equivalence of $\mathcal{O}$ and $\mathcal{D}$

The denotational semantics for $\mathcal{L}_{fm}$ is obtained in a fairly straightforward manner from its operational one. We shall use $\mathbb{P}_D$, $\mathbb{Q}_D$ as given in

Definition 5.16

(a) $\mathbb{Q}_D = (Act^{ext})^\infty \setminus \{\epsilon\}$, $\mathbb{P}_D = \mathcal{P}_{ncl}(\mathbb{Q}_D)$.

(b) The operators ';', '+' on $\mathbb{P}_D$ are as in Section 4.1.

One main job is to define $p_1 \parallel_f p_2$. Following what we did for the operational construct $s_1 \parallel^n s_2$, we shall introduce its denotational counterpart $p_1 \parallel^n p_2$. In explaining its intended meaning, it is convenient to first consider the special case that $p_1 = a \cdot p'$, $p_2 = b \cdot p''$, say. Now we want to define the operations such that we have

$$
\begin{aligned}
\bullet \qquad p_1 \parallel_f p_2 &= (p_1 \parallel^0 p_2) \cup (p_2 \parallel^0 p_1) \\
\bullet \qquad p_1 \parallel^0 (b \cdot p'') &= \textstyle\bigcup_{n \in \mathbb{N}} b \cdot (p'' \parallel^n p_1) \\
\bullet \qquad (a \cdot p') \parallel^{n+1} p_2 &= a \cdot (p' \parallel^n p_2) \,.
\end{aligned}
\tag{5.5}
$$

Note how these formulae follow the pattern in (Fail,init), (Fail,0) and (Fail,$n+1$) from $\mathcal{T}_{fm}$. E.g., the second rule prescribes that $p_1 \parallel^0 (b \cdot p'')$ takes (zero steps from p_1 and) its first step (viz. b) from $p_2 = b \cdot p''$, and then continues with $p'' \parallel^n p_1$ (prescribing n steps from p''), for arbitrary $n \geq 0$. For a full definition, we must firstly include here as well the mechanism of storing the random choices in the elementary actions, and secondly we must cater for the situation that p_1, p_2 have more than one possible initial step (rather than just the a and b, as in the special case just described). For this purpose, we introduce a new

Notation 5.17 For $p \in \mathbb{P}_D$, $q \in \mathbb{Q}_D$, and $\alpha \in Act^{ext}$, we put

$$
p_\alpha = \{\, q \mid \alpha \cdot q \in p, q \neq \epsilon \,\} \,.
$$

Thus, p_α is obtained by deleting the initial α from all words from p which have α as proper prefix (i.e., $\exists q \neq \epsilon \, [\, \alpha q \in p \,]$). Note that p_α may well equal $\emptyset$ (and thus not belong to $\mathbb{P}_D$). We now turn (5.5) into a general (higher-order) definition, using the notation just introduced to control the possible initial steps from p_1 or p_2. As further new element, compared to the $\Omega_\parallel$ as introduced in Section 4.1, we have that $\Omega_\parallel$ here has the natural number n as an additional argument.

Definition 5.18

(a) Let $(\phi \in) Op = \mathbb{N} \to (\mathbb{P}_D \times \mathbb{P}_D) \xrightarrow{1} \mathbb{P}_D$, and let $\Omega_\parallel \colon Op \to Op$ be given by

$$\Omega_\parallel(\phi)(0)(p_1, p_2)$$
$$= \bigcup \{\, \alpha n \cdot \phi(n)((p_2)_\alpha, p_1) \mid (p_2)_\alpha \neq \emptyset \,\} \cup \bigcup \{\, \alpha n \cdot p_1 \mid \alpha \in p_2 \,\}$$
$$\Omega_\parallel(\phi)(n+1)(p_1, p_2)$$
$$= \bigcup \{\, \alpha \cdot \phi(n)((p_1)_\alpha, p_2) \mid (p_1)_\alpha \neq \emptyset \,\} \cup \bigcup \{\, \alpha \cdot p_2 \mid \alpha \in p_1 \,\}.$$

(b) $\parallel^n = (\mathrm{fix}(\Omega_\parallel))(n)$, $n = 0, 1, \ldots$.

(c) $p_1 \parallel_f p_2 = (p_1 \parallel^0 p_2) \cup (p_2 \parallel^0 p_1)$.

Example Let $\alpha, \beta \in Act^{ext}$. From

$$\{\alpha^\omega\} \parallel^0 \{\beta\} = (\beta m) \cdot \{\alpha^\omega\}, \quad m \geq 0$$
$$\{\alpha^\omega\} \parallel^{n+1} \{\beta\} = \alpha \cdot (\{\alpha^\omega\} \parallel^n \{\beta\})$$

one obtains by induction

$$\{\alpha^\omega\} \parallel^n \{\beta\} = \{\alpha^n(\beta m)\alpha^\omega\}.$$

Hence,

$$\{\alpha^\omega\} \parallel_f \{\beta\}$$
$$= \{\alpha^\omega\} \parallel^0 \{\beta\} \cup \{\beta\} \parallel^0 \{\alpha^\omega\}$$
$$= \{\, (\beta n)\alpha^\omega, (\alpha n)\alpha^n(\beta m)\alpha^\omega \mid n, m \geq 0 \,\}.$$

We have

Lemma 5.19 $\|^n$ *(and $\|_f$) is well-defined.*

Proof It is not difficult to see that $\Omega_\|$ is $\frac{1}{2}$-contractive in ϕ. Also, for each $p \in \mathbb{P}_D$ we have that, since $p \neq \emptyset, \{\epsilon\}$, for at least one α we have that $p_\alpha \neq \emptyset$ or $\alpha \in p$ (or both), establishing that the right-hand side of the clauses for $\Omega_\|(\phi)(n)(p_1, p_2)$ is nonempty in all cases considered. There remains the issue of closedness of these right-hand sides. We only discuss the case $\Omega_\|(\phi)(0)(p_1, p_2)$. Let us abbreviate the first term on its right-hand side by $X = \bigcup\{\alpha n \cdot X_n \mid n \geq 0\}$. By assumption, for each n, the set $X_n = \phi(n)((p_2)_\alpha, p_1)$ is closed and, hence, so is $\alpha n \cdot X_n$. By the discreteness of Act^{ext}, each Cauchy sequence in X is eventually in some $\alpha n \cdot X_n$, thus establishing that X is closed. The closedness of $\bigcup\{\alpha \cdot p_1 \mid \alpha \in p_2\}$ is immediate from the closedness of p_1 (and the discreteness of Act^{ext}). $\qquad\square$

As direct variation on earlier results, one may now prove

Lemma 5.20

(a) '$\|_f$' is nonexpansive in both arguments, and both left- and right-distributive with respect to '$\cup$'.

(b) As part (a), with '$\|^n$' replacing '$\|_f$', for each $n \geq 0$.

(c) '$\|_f$' is associative.

Proof An extension of earlier results, and left to the reader. $\qquad\square$

Now that we have completed the definition of '$\|_f$', it is straightforward to define $\mathcal{D}$ for $\mathcal{L}_{fm}$:

Definition 5.21

(a) $\mathcal{D}: \mathcal{L}_{fm} \to \mathbb{P}_D$ is the unique function satisfying

$$\begin{aligned}
\mathcal{D}(a) &= \{(a, \epsilon)\} \\
\mathcal{D}(x) &= \mathcal{D}(D(x)) \\
\mathcal{D}(s_1 \text{ op } s_2) &= \mathcal{D}(s_1) \text{ op } \mathcal{D}(s_2), \quad \text{op} \in \{\,;, +, \|_f\,\}.
\end{aligned}$$

(b) $\mathcal{D}[\![s]\!] = \mathcal{D}(s)$.

Examples

(1) $\mathcal{D}[\![a \parallel_f (b;c)]\!]$

$= \{(a,\epsilon)\} \parallel_f \{(b,\epsilon)(c,\epsilon)\}$

$= \{\, (b,0)(a,n)(c,\epsilon), (b,n+1)(c,\epsilon)(a,\epsilon), (a,n)(b,\epsilon)(c,\epsilon) \mid n \geq 0 \,\}.$

(2) Suppose $D(x) = a;x$. Then we have

$\mathcal{D}[\![x \parallel_f b]\!]$

$= \{(a,\epsilon)^\omega\} \parallel_f \{(b,\epsilon)\}$

$= \{\, (\beta n)\alpha^\omega, (\alpha n)\alpha^n(\beta m)\alpha^\omega \mid n, m \geq 0 \,\}.$

We conclude with the proof of the equivalence of $\mathcal{O}$ and $\mathcal{D}$ on $\mathcal{L}_{fm}$. Let us assume the natural extension of the semantic operators to $\mathbb{P}_O$, let Φ be the operator used to define $\mathcal{O}$ on Res, and let $\mathcal{E}\colon Res \to \mathbb{P}_D$ be given by $\mathcal{E}(\mathrm{E}) = \{\epsilon\}$, $\mathcal{E}(s) = \mathcal{D}(s)$, and $\mathcal{E}(r_1 \parallel^n r_2) = \mathcal{E}(r_1) \parallel^n \mathcal{E}(r_2)$. We have

Theorem 5.22 $\Phi(\mathcal{E})(r) = \mathcal{E}(r)$, *for each* $r \in Res$.

Proof Induction on $wgt(r)$. One subcase.

$[r_1 \parallel^0 r_2]$ Assume $r_2 \not\equiv \mathrm{E}$.

$\mathcal{E}(r_1 \parallel^0 r_2)$

$= \;\; \mathcal{E}(r_1) \parallel^0 \mathcal{E}(r_2)$

$= \;\; \text{[ind. hyp.]}\; \mathcal{E}(r_1) \parallel^0 \Phi(\mathcal{E})(r_2)$

$= \;\; \mathcal{E}(r_1) \parallel^0 (\bigcup\{\, \alpha \cdot \mathcal{E}(s_2) \mid r_2 \overset{\alpha}{\to} s_2 \,\} \cup \{\, \alpha \mid r_2 \overset{\alpha}{\to} \mathrm{E} \,\})$

$= \;\; \bigcup\{\, \alpha n \cdot (\bigcup\{\, \mathcal{E}(s_2) \mid r_2 \overset{\alpha}{\to} s_2 \,\} \parallel^n \mathcal{E}(r_1) \mid r_2 \overset{\alpha}{\to} s_2 \,\} \cup$
$\quad\;\; \bigcup\{\, \alpha n \cdot \mathcal{E}(r_1) \mid r_2 \overset{\alpha}{\to} \mathrm{E} \,\}$

$= \;\; \bigcup\{\, \alpha n \cdot \bigcup\{\, \mathcal{E}(s_2) \parallel^n \mathcal{E}(r_1) \mid r_2 \overset{\alpha}{\to} s_2 \,\} \mid r_2 \overset{\alpha}{\to} s_2 \,\} \cup$
$\quad\;\; \bigcup\{\, \alpha n \cdot \mathcal{E}(r_1) \mid r_2 \overset{\alpha}{\to} \mathrm{E} \,\}$

$= \;\; \bigcup\{\, \alpha n \cdot (\mathcal{E}(s_2) \parallel^n \mathcal{E}(r_1)) \mid r_2 \overset{\alpha}{\to} s_2 \,\} \cup \bigcup\{\, \alpha n \cdot \mathcal{E}(r_1) \mid r_2 \overset{\alpha}{\to} \mathrm{E} \,\}$

$= \;\; \bigcup\{\, \alpha n \cdot \mathcal{E}(s_2 \parallel^n r_1) \mid r_2 \overset{\alpha}{\to} s_2 \,\} \cup \bigcup\{\, \alpha n \cdot \mathcal{E}(r_1) \mid r_2 \overset{\alpha}{\to} \mathrm{E} \,\}$

$= \;\; \bigcup\{\, \alpha \cdot \mathcal{E}(r) \mid r_1 \parallel^0 r_2 \overset{\alpha}{\to} r \,\}$

$= \;\; \Phi(\mathcal{E})(r_1 \parallel^0 r_2).$ $\square$

Finally, we have the usual

Corollary 5.23 $\mathcal{O}[\![\pi]\!] = \mathcal{D}[\![\pi]\!]$, for $\pi \in \mathcal{L}_{fm}$.

5.4   Exercises

Exercise 5.1 Consider the "program" $(x \Leftarrow (x;a) + b \mid x)$. Show that, when such a program is allowed, $\mathcal{T}_{cf}$ (as in Section 2.2) is not even image-finite.

Exercise 5.2 Let, in the setting of $\mathcal{L}_{ra}$, $D(x) = s_1;x$, $D(y) = s_2;y$. Let the set *Val* as used in the interpretation of $v := ?$ be given as $Val = \mathbb{N}_{>0}$ (the set of positive integers). Consider the scheme for executing $x \parallel_f y$ as expressed by the following program (executed over the domain of nonnegative integers):

$v_1 := ?; v_2 := ?;$
while true do
    if $v_1 \leq v_2$
    then $(s_1; v_1 := ?; v_2 := v_2 - 1)$
    else $(s_2; v_2 := ?; v_1 := v_1 - 1)$
    fi
od.

Discuss how this scheme corresponds to the operational semantics for $x \parallel_f y$ as embodied in $\mathcal{T}_{fm}$.

Exercise 5.3 Explain why we assume the discrete metric on Act^{ext}, e.g., in Definition 5.15 (instead of using an alternative such as d_B from Definition 1.20 for the alphabet $A = Act \cup \mathbb{N}$).

Exercise 5.4

(a) Prove that $\mathcal{O}[\![x \Leftarrow a;x \mid x \parallel_f b]\!] = $
    $\{ (b,k) \cdot (a, \epsilon)^\omega \mid k \geq 0 \} \cup \{ (a, \ell) \cdot (a, \epsilon)^\ell \cdot (b,k) \cdot (a, \epsilon)^\omega \mid k, \ell \geq 0 \}$.

(b) Determine $\mathcal{O}[\![x \Leftarrow a;x, y \Leftarrow b;y \mid x \parallel_f y]\!]$.

Exercise 5.5 Prove that T'_{fm} (introduced after Definition 5.15) is not image-finite.

Exercise 5.6 Let $abs: Act^{ext} \to Act$ and its extension

$$abs: \mathcal{P}_{ncl}((Act^{ext})^{\infty}) \to \mathcal{P}(Act^{\infty})$$

be defined as suggested by the formulae

$$
\begin{aligned}
abs(a, n_1 n_2 \cdots n_k) &= a \\
abs(\alpha_1 \alpha_2 \cdots) &= abs(\alpha_1) \cdot abs(\alpha_2) \cdot \cdots \\
abs(p) &= \{\, abs(q) \mid q \in p \,\}.
\end{aligned}
$$

Let $\mathcal{O}_d: \mathcal{L}_{fm} \to \mathcal{P}(Act^{\infty})$ be as given in (5.1), on the basis of '$\to$' from T'_{fm}. Let $\mathcal{O}: \mathcal{L}_{fm} \to \mathbb{P}_O$ be as in Definition 5.15. Show that $abs \circ \mathcal{O} = \mathcal{O}_d$. (Note that this result has no denotational counterpart.)

5.5 Bibliographical notes

In Section 2.3 we noted that the precise origins of the theorem stating that finitely branching transition systems determine compact sets is unknown (to us). The same comment applies to the result that image-finite transition systems specify *closed* operational semantics: we do not know of a reference containing precisely this fact. Both results are reminiscent of König's lemma ([Kön26]). Related results have been presented by Landweber (Corollary 3.2 of [Lan69]), Arnold (Proposition 3.2 of [Arn83]) and in [BMOZ88] (Theorem 2.4.10) or [BK90] (Lemma 3.7). [Bre94b] contains a precise proof of Theorem 5.3 (as does our Appendix B). The result stated in Theorem 5.4 is also contained in [BM88] or [BK90].

The problematic role of *unbounded* nondeterminacy in semantics has been well-known for some time. In a cpo-setting, continuity of various operators is at stake, and a variety of techniques to deal with this problem have been proposed. Cf. [Bak80] for a statement of the problem (and [Bak76] for an erroneous claim stemming from ignoring this issue). Apt and Plotkin ([AP86]) investigate what happens when the unboundedness is restricted to a countable version. Other treatments based on ordered structures are [Bac83] and [Hes92].

The observation that the use of closed sets allows a smooth treatment of, e.g., random assignment was first made in [BZ82].

Fairness is a notoriously difficult notion in programming theory. We refer to the book by Francez ([Fra86]) for a comprehensive treatment (though focusing primarily on proof-theoretic rather than on semantic topics). The method we describe in

Section 5.3 goes back to [BZ83a, BZ83b], where the metric machinery—albeit of the branching variety as described in Part III—is used to formulate a *scheduling* approach to the fair merge, in turn basing itself on ideas of Plotkin ([Plo82]). The current form of the transition system $\mathcal{T}_{fm}$ is due to Van Breugel (personal communication). In [RZ92], several ideas from [BZ83a, BZ83b] are further elaborated.

An essentially different way of linking metric techniques to fairness has been proposed by Degano and Montanari ([DM84], cf. also [Cos85]). Rather than using one and the same definition of the metric concerned—as we do throughout—they use a metric which is, as it were, dependent on the language construct considered. The latter idea is also crucial in the work of [DNPY92] (see also [PN92]) where some fundamental theorems are obtained relating (a wide class of) fairness notions, corresponding notions of ultrametrics, and certain complexity classes in the arithmetic recursion hierarchy.

6 Locality

Variables may be "local" to a piece of program: their life time begins at the start of the execution of that program piece, and ends upon its completion. A customary term to denote the program part involved is "block," and the first section of this chapter is devoted to the semantic analysis of this notion. A block is characterized by the presence—normally at its start—of a *declaration,* followed by one or more statements, the whole embraced by opening and closing parentheses (traditionally written as begin and end). The declaration, say 'var v', introduces the individual variable v, with as "scope" (synonymous for "life time") the program part between the begin and end of the block concerned. A declaration var v introduces v with an as yet unknown value. In other words, v is uninitialized at its declaration. In a case where the value of v is retrieved before proper initialization of v has taken place, some *arbitrary* value is then delivered. (In some implementations, an error message might result instead, but this is not the interpretation we have chosen to model.) Accordingly, the block begin var v; $w := v$ end (assuming w to be known from an earlier declaration) has the same effect upon w as the random assignment $w := ?$. Therefore, we shall have to invoke the machinery of image-finite transition systems for the modelling of blocks, in a way which closely resembles what we did for $\mathcal{L}_{ra}$ in Section 5.2.

Some further issues induced by the presence of blocks in a programming language will be described below, when we provide more details on their semantic features. Briefly, we shall discuss

- the possibility of "holes" in the scope of a variable
- the distinction between "static" and "dynamic" scope for procedures.

A second (cluster of) notion(s) where locality plays a central role is that of procedures *with parameters.* In Section 6.2, we shall focus on the study of the mechanism of "call-by-value," since it is probably the most important variety of parameter passing. Moreover, the way we model it provides a clear application of the techniques developed in Section 6.1. As we shall see, call-by-value may be modelled by a form of blocks with *initialized* declarations. As a consequence, in Section 6.2 we shall return to a fully deterministic setting.

Section 6.2 will, in fact, be dealing with call-by-value for *function* procedures, i.e., for procedures which, after possibly effecting one or more state changes, result in a value (from *Val*) as final outcome. (A classical case of a recursive function procedure is the factorial function.) We have chosen this concept as a means to illustrate the use of a further semantic tool, viz. the distinction between *statement*

and *expression* prolongations (resumptions and continuations), and the definition
of the denotational semantic mappings $\langle \mathcal{D}, \mathcal{V} \rangle$ as a simultaneous fixed point of a
pair of mappings.

6.1   Blocks—environments for individual variables

The language $\mathcal{L}_{block}$ is a variation of $\mathcal{L}_{wh}$, in that

- the block construct begin var v; s end is added
- while statements are replaced by (recursive) procedures.

In the construct begin var v; s end, we distinguish the *defining* occurrence of v
immediately following the var symbol, and all remaining occurrences (in s), which
we shall call *applied* occurrences.

A consequence of the presence of the block concept is that it is now meaningful
to require that all individual variables in a program be declared, i.e., that for each
occurrence of some v in some statement of the program, it is possible to determine
a declaration var v such that the occurrence at hand is an applied occurrence
of v (with respect to the indicated declaration). Consider, e.g., the situation of
Figure 6.1.

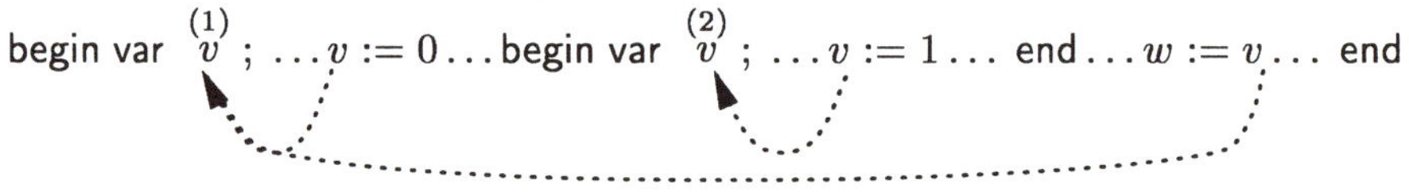

begin var $\overset{(1)}{v}$; $\ldots v := 0 \ldots$ begin var $\overset{(2)}{v}$; $\ldots v := 1 \ldots$ end $\ldots w := v \ldots$ end

Figure 6.1

In this program, we observe two declarations of the (same) variable v. The
occurrence of v in $v := 0$ identifies the outermost declaration (for convenience
marked by [(1)]), and the occurrence of v in $v := 1$ identifies the innermost declaration
(marked by [(2)]). Moreover, the v in $w := v$ identifies the defining v marked by [(1)]
rather than the v marked by [(2)]. Thus, Figure 6.1 also illustrates the phenomenon
of a *hole* in the scope of a variable: In the scope of the v of the outermost block,
the inner block induces a hole, in that the v's occurring in the latter block have
their own identity (which is different from that of the outer v).

The variable w from Figure 6.1 is not declared in the program as displayed. If
w has not been declared in some embracing block—not visible in Figure 6.1—two
possibilities remain:

- the declaration of w has erroneously been omitted. This situation will be signalled by the delivery of an error message in the form of the "undefined" state (details follow).

- the variable w is *global*. This term applies to a situation where the variable is not programmer declared, but still known to the (operating) system in which the program concerned is executed. A typical example is the use of some library or system variables which are assumed as already given at the outset for each program (execution).

Altogether, we are faced with the task of designing a model which incorporates (at least) the following three phenomena

- the distinction between undeclared and uninitialized variables, the former leading to an error message and the latter to a form of random assignment

- the correspondence between applied and defining occurrences of variables, and the possibility of holes in the scope of a variable

- global variables which are (not programmer declared but still) known to the system, as exemplified by library names.

To this list, we should add one further topic (static versus dynamic scope for procedures) which we shall explain in a moment. In fact, it will turn out that the machinery to be developed to cope with the above three problems also allows us to handle this point.

The key to the solution of the problems as just outlined consists in the introduction of an additional layer in the mechanism as used so far to control storage and retrieval of values for individual variables. Till now, the simple picture was as in Figure 6.2a,

Figure 6.2a

depicting the role of states $\sigma\ (\in \Sigma)$ as mappings from $(v \in)\ IVar$ to $(\alpha \in)\ Val$. We now add a layer of *addresses* $(a \in)\ Addr$, together with mappings $(\rho \in)\ Env$ of so-called *environments*. See Figure 6.2b.

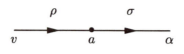

Figure 6.2b

That is, we introduce the collection of environments $(\rho \in)$ *Env* as a set of mappings from $(v \in)$ *IVar* to $(a \in)$ *Addr*, and amend the notion of state, in that a state is now a mapping from *Addr* to *Val*. For each v, $a = \rho(v)$ determines the address associated with v in the (current) environment ρ, and $\alpha = \sigma(a) = \sigma(\rho(v))$ determines its current value. States are, as before, affected by assignment statements, whereas environments are controlled by declarations. Environments are, in fact, *partial* mappings. Their domain of definedness grows (with v) with the processing of a declaration var v (unless v was declared before, in which case a *fresh* address is associated with v), and shrinks (with v) at the moment of the corresponding block exit. This view also allows us to provide a satisfactory model for the global variables: we simply assume an initial environment ρ_0, with domain $dom(\rho_0)$, say, and process the programmer-supplied declarations as extensions/deletions starting from this given domain.

Finally, we can now explain the announced static/dynamic scope distinction for procedures. Consider the following program (in a syntax which is the natural nonuniform counterpart of that of the uniform $\mathcal{L}_{rec}$):

$$(x \Leftarrow \ldots v := 0 \ldots \mid \ldots \mathsf{begin}\ \mathsf{var}\ \overset{(1)}{v}\ ;\ v := 1 \ldots x \ldots w := v \ldots \mathsf{end} \ldots)$$

Here, the procedure x is called inside the scope of the locally declared v, whereas the body of x has an occurrence of (the same) v (in $v := 0$). The question now arises how this occurrence is handled during the call of x. The "dynamic scope" rule takes the replacement of x by its body literally in that, after this replacement, the v from the body identifies the v from the declaration (marked by [(1)]) as its defining occurrence. Accordingly, the effect of $w := v$ is to set w to 0. In the "static scope" approach, the v of the body is identified at the moment of declaration, here as determined by the initial environment. As a consequence, the call of x does not affect the value of the local v (which remains 1), and the assignment $w := v$ sets w to 1.

In many languages, the static scope rule is the preferred one, and we have chosen to model this below. The technique to be used for this purpose consists in carrying the initial environment, say ρ_0, along in all semantic definitions, in the same way as we do this (albeit implicitly in the notation) with the declaration D. At the moment of a procedure call, the current environment is stored somewhere, and the initial environment is installed as current environment. Upon exit from the procedure body the stored environment is reinstalled as the current environment.

Though adding a nontrivial level of complexity to the semantic modelling, in defense of the environment machinery one may point out that firstly it is sufficiently powerful to deal in one go with a number of not so simple aspects of locality, and secondly that it is in fact a natural counterpart of the dominant implementation model for block-structured languages, where program variables are mapped in some way to (a stack of) machine addresses, i.e., locations in memory where values may be stored.

6.1.1 Syntax and operational semantics

Let $(v \in) \mathit{IVar}$, $(e \in) \mathit{Exp}$ and $(x \in) \mathit{PVar}$ be as usual. We introduce $\mathcal{L}_{block}$ as a variation on $\mathcal{L}_{wh}$. Firstly, we add the block-construct begin var v; s end. Secondly, we replace the while statement by recursion; this is motivated by our wish to address the problems having to do with static scope.

Definition 6.1

(a) $s\,(\in \mathit{Stat}) ::= v := e \mid (s;s) \mid x \mid$ if e then s else s fi $\mid$ begin var v; s end

(b) $(D \in) \mathit{Decl} = \mathit{PVar} \rightarrow \mathit{Stat}$

(c) $(\pi \in) \mathcal{L}_{block} = \mathit{Decl} \times \mathit{Stat}$.

Remark No special class of guarded statements is introduced for $\mathcal{L}_{block}$. We shall avoid the issues relating to guardedness by postulating a skip step in the handling of (recursive) procedures, both in the operational and the denotational model. As we shall see, this induces contractivity of the relevant operators in a straightforward way. In the present circumstances, this approach slightly simplifies our semantic design.

We need various preparations for the definition of $\mathcal{O}$ for $\mathcal{L}_{block}$. The first step introduces the notion of *address,* and associated definitions.

Definition 6.2

(a) Let *Addr* be an infinite set of addresses, the structure of which is left unspecified (but see requirement (b) below). Let $\perp_A$ be a new symbol (not in *Addr*) denoting the "undefined" address, and let, similarly, $\perp_\Sigma$ denote the "undefined" state. The following sets are defined

$$
\begin{aligned}
\Sigma &= Addr \rightarrow Val \\
(a \in) Addr_\perp &= Addr \cup \{\perp_A\} \\
(\sigma \in) \Sigma_\perp &= \Sigma \cup \{\perp_\Sigma\} \\
(\rho \in) Env &= IVar \rightarrow Addr_\perp .
\end{aligned}
$$

We moreover put

$$
\begin{aligned}
dom(\rho) &= \{\, v \mid \rho(v) \neq \perp_A \,\} \\
cod(\rho) &= \{\, a \mid v \in dom(\rho), a = \rho(v) \,\} .
\end{aligned}
$$

The update notation $\rho\{a/v\}$ is defined by putting

$$
\begin{aligned}
\rho\{a/v\}(w) &= \rho(w), \text{ for } v \not\equiv w \\
\rho\{a/v\}(v) &= a .
\end{aligned}
$$

(b) We postulate, for each $\rho \in Env$,

(i) $Addr \setminus cod(\rho) \neq \emptyset$

(ii) ρ is a 1–1 function on its domain $dom(\rho)$.

The above definitions and conditions may be understood as follows. For each v, $a = \rho(v)$ yields the address associated with v, and $\sigma(a) = \sigma(\rho(v))$ yields the (current) value of v. The equality

$$\rho(v) = \perp_A \tag{6.1}$$

may be taken as stating that the address associated with v by ρ is undefined. During the execution of a program, encountering some v for which (6.1) holds may be seen as an error situation: We shall design our semantics such that (6.1) only occurs for variables which are neither declared locally nor globally (i.e., which are not in the domain of the initial environment). The state $\perp_\Sigma$ will be yielded as a result—possibly preceded by a sequence of proper ($\neq \perp_\Sigma$) states—when a situation where (6.1) holds occurs. The domain $dom(\rho)$ of ρ, i.e., the set of all variables v for which $\rho(v) \neq \perp_A$, is in particular of importance when we process a local declaration. Let var v be the declaration concerned, and let ρ be the current environment. We distinguish two possibilities:

- $v \in dom(\rho)$, i.e., v was already declared in an embracing block. We then update ρ to $\rho\{a/v\}$, where a is some fresh address ($\neq \perp_A$), i.e., $a \in Addr \setminus cod(\rho)$.
- $v \notin dom(\rho)$, i.e., $\rho(v) = \perp_A$, implying that v was not declared in an embracing block. We now extend $dom(\rho)$ with v; the same notation $\rho\{a/v\}$ now denotes an extension of ρ which has $a (\neq \perp_A)$ as value in v.

Remark Traditionally, in semantics the symbol '$\perp$' (pronounced as "bottom") is used to denote the undefined object (often indexed by the structure for which it represents "undefined," such as in '$\perp_A$' or '$\perp_\Sigma$'). There is no *essential* reason, however, why we could not use the δ-symbol, as used previously in Chapter 3 (and to be used *passim* in Part III) with the connotation of ("abort" or) deadlock.

The intended effect of the environment machinery may be somewhat difficult to digest at the present stage. We therefore recommend that the reader also takes into account the subsequent definition of $\mathcal{T}_{block}$ before aiming at a full understanding of the notions involved. One final remark on clause b(i) of the definition. This clause amounts to the requirement that always an unused address may be found. It allows us to consistently use environments which are 1–1 on their domain. (Of course, since $\rho(w)$ is constant—viz. equal to $\perp_A$—on all $w \notin dom(\rho)$, ρ is injective *only* on $dom(\rho)$.)

In the sequel, we shall have occasion to use the following simple lemma (cf. Lemma 1.54):

Lemma 6.3

(a) *For each ρ, v_1, v_2, a_1, a_2,*

$$\rho\{a_1/v_1\}\{a_2/v_2\} = \begin{cases} \rho\{a_2/v_2\} & \text{if } v_1 \equiv v_2 \\ \rho\{a_2/v_2\}\{a_1/v_1\} & \text{if } v_1 \not\equiv v_2. \end{cases}$$

(b) *For each ρ, v, we have $\rho\{\rho(v)/v\} = \rho$.*

Proof Exercise.   □

We now proceed with the specification of $\mathcal{T}_{block}$. We shall define it as a triple of a somewhat more complex structure than used so far, viz. consisting of

$Conf = Decl \times Env \times Res \times Env \times \Sigma$
$Obs = \Sigma$
Spec to be given below.

The set *Res* consists of the usual resumptions, together with two extensions which we need for technical reasons (cf. Definition 6.6). Transitions for $\mathcal{T}_{block}$ will be written as

$$[r, \rho, \sigma] \rightarrow_{\rho_0} [r', \rho', \sigma'] \, .$$

The $[r, \sigma]$ and $[r', \sigma']$ components of this transition are familiar; the fixed declaration D is, once more, suppressed. The ρ_0-subscript of '$\rightarrow$' is the so-called initial environment. Just as D, ρ_0 remains fixed throughout the execution. Its role is to act as a means to "declare" the individual variables of the program which are not declared in some local declaration (such as the library variables mentioned earlier). The ρ, ρ' are the *current* environments. Due to the effect of executing a block, the current environment ρ will be changed to some ρ'. Other programming constructs affecting ρ will be discussed later. $\mathcal{T}_{block}$ will be designed such that, for transitions stemming from the execution of a program, we always have that $dom(\rho_0) \subseteq dom(\rho)$ and $dom(\rho_0) \subseteq dom(\rho')$.

Three further preparations are in order before we can give $\mathcal{T}_{block}$. Firstly, we define a function *ivar*, which collects the individual variables occurring in an expression or assignment statement. This function will have a role in checking whether variables are declared.

Definition 6.4

(a) $ivar(\alpha) = \emptyset$, $ivar(v) = \{v\}$, $ivar(u(e_1, \ldots, e_\ell)) = \bigcup_{k=1}^{\ell} ivar(e_k)$.

(b) $ivar(v := e) = \{v\} \cup ivar(e)$.

Secondly, we amend the definition of the semantics for $e \in Exp$ to the presence of environments. For simplicity, we only present the modified $\mathcal{V}$, omitting the (obvious) consequences for $\mathcal{O}$. We shall invoke the definition of $\mathcal{V}(e)(\rho)(\sigma)$ only in the case that $ivar(e) \subseteq dom(\rho)$, hence the following

Definition 6.5 The function $\mathcal{V}: Exp \rightarrow Env \rightarrow \Sigma \rightarrow Val$ is defined by putting

- if $ivar(e) \subseteq dom(\rho)$

$$
\begin{aligned}
\mathcal{V}(\alpha)(\rho)(\sigma) &= \alpha \\
\mathcal{V}(v)(\rho)(\sigma) &= \sigma(\rho(v)) \\
\mathcal{V}(u(e_1, \ldots, e_\ell))(\rho)(\sigma) &= \hat{u}(\mathcal{V}(e_1)(\rho)(\sigma), \ldots, \mathcal{V}(e_\ell)(\rho)(\sigma)) \, .
\end{aligned}
$$

- if $ivar(e) \nsubseteq dom(\rho)$, $\mathcal{V}(e)(\rho)(\sigma)$ is not defined.

Thirdly, we introduce *Res* as a syntactic class which is like our usual set of resumptions (for simple sequential languages), but with two extra statements. These extra statements are introduced especially for the purpose of defining $\mathcal{T}_{block}$. Accordingly, the language $\mathcal{L}_{block}$ is not affected by their introduction. The rules (Reset 1,2) will handle these extra statements; recall that $a \in Addr_\perp$.

Definition 6.6 $r(\in Res)$ ::= E $\mid$ $(s{:}r)$ $\mid$ $(v := a){:}r$ $\mid$ $reset(\rho){:}r$.

At last, we are ready for the definition of $\mathcal{T}_{block}$.

Definition 6.7 $\mathcal{T}_{block} = (Decl \times Env \times Res \times Env \times \Sigma, \Sigma, \rightarrow, Spec)$, where $Spec$ consists of the axioms and rules listed below. In all of them, we assume that ρ_0 is the initial environment and that $\sigma \neq \perp_\Sigma$. The meaning of the notation $\rightarrow_{0,\rho_0}$ should be clear.

- $$[(v := e){:}r, \rho, \sigma] \rightarrow_{\rho_0} [r, \rho, \sigma\{\alpha/a\}] \qquad \text{if } ivar(v := e) \subseteq dom(\rho) \qquad \text{(Ass)}$$
  where $a = \rho(v)$, $\alpha = \mathcal{V}(e)(\rho)(\sigma)$

- $$[(s_1;s_2){:}r, \rho, \sigma] \rightarrow_{0,\rho_0} [s_1{:}(s_2{:}r), \rho, \sigma] \qquad \text{(Seq)}$$

- $$[x{:}r, \rho, \sigma] \rightarrow_{\rho_0} [D(x){:}(reset(\rho){:}r), \rho_0, \sigma] \qquad \text{(Rec)}$$

- $$[\text{if } e \text{ then } s_1 \text{ else } s_2 \text{ fi}{:}r, \rho, \sigma] \rightarrow_{0,\rho_0} [s_1{:}r, \rho, \sigma] \qquad \text{(If 1)}$$
  $$\text{if } ivar(e) \subseteq dom(\rho), \mathcal{V}(e)(\rho)(\sigma) = tt$$

- a symmetric rule in case $\mathcal{V}(e)(\rho)(\sigma) = f\!f$ \qquad (If 2)

- $$[\text{begin var } v; s \text{ end}{:}r, \rho, \sigma] \rightarrow_{\rho_0} \qquad \text{(Block)}$$
  $$[s{:}((v := \rho(v)){:}r), \rho\{a/v\}, \sigma\{\alpha/a\}]$$

  where both the following conditions hold

  - a is an arbitrary element in $Addr \setminus cod(\rho)$

  - α is an arbitrary element in Val

- $$[(v := a){:}r, \rho, \sigma] \rightarrow_{0,\rho_0} [r, \rho\{a/v\}, \sigma] \qquad \text{(Reset 1)}$$

- $$[reset(\rho){:}r, \rho_1, \sigma] \rightarrow_{0,\rho_0} [r, \rho, \sigma] \qquad \text{(Reset 2)}$$

Much of the above should already be clear on the basis of our earlier discussions. We draw attention to a few specific points.

(1) As usual, no transitions are defined for $[E, \rho, \sigma]$.

(2) Furthermore, no transitions are defined for $[r, \rho, \perp_\Sigma]$ or for any of the cases where the stated conditions are not satisfied, in particular for (Ass), (If 1) and (If 2).

(3) The rule (Ass) combines two features. Firstly, it requires that all relevant variables be declared, i.e., contained in the domain of the current ρ. Secondly, it refines the update of (the value of) v as encountered in earlier treatments to an update of the value stored in the address $a = \rho(v)$ associated with v by ρ.

(4) The recursion rule is, partly, familiar in that the execution of x is replaced by the execution of $D(x)$, partly new in the handling of the environments. The initial environment ρ_0 is installed as current environment, and the current environment ρ is temporarily dumped, to be reinstalled upon completion of the execution of $D(x)$ as a result of the $reset(\rho)$ statement, cf. also the (Reset 2) rule. The explicit step ('$\rightarrow_{\rho_0}$' rather than '$\rightarrow_{0,\rho_0}$') avoids the imposing of guardedness restrictions.

(5) The (If 1), (If 2) rules should be clear.

(6) The (Block) rule either overwrites the current ρ with a fresh a for v—in case $v \in dom(\rho)$—or extends the domain of ρ to $dom(\rho) \cup \{v\}$—in case $v \notin dom(\rho)$. By the postulate on $Addr$, it is always possible to find a fresh a as specified. Moreover, an arbitrary initial value α is assigned to the address a associated with v. Furthermore, the auxiliary assignment $v := \rho(v)$ is included in the resumption on the right-hand side of the rule, with the purpose of resetting ρ in v to its old value (valid before performing the transition at hand) after completion of the execution of s. In this way, upon exit of the block concerned, ρ is reset to this old value (possibly '$\perp_A$').

(7) The effect of the first reset-rule is like an assignment, but affecting ρ rather than σ. The second reset-rule overwrites the current environment ρ_1 by the to be reinstalled environment ρ. Both rules are of the $\rightarrow_0$-variety; this simplifies the comparison with $\mathcal{D}$ below.

The arbitrary choice of a and α in the (Block)-rule has as a consequence that $\mathcal{T}_{block}$ is (not finitely branching but) image-finite. This may be shown in essentially the same way as we did for $\mathcal{L}_{ra}$ in Section 5.2. We omit details of this proof; all we do here is to provide a definition for $wgt(r)$, which is then to be used in the proof in the standard way.

Definition 6.8 $wgt\colon Res \cup Stat \to \mathbb{N}$ is given by

(a) $wgt(\mathrm{E}) = 0$
$wgt(s{:}r) = wgt(s) + wgt(r)$
$wgt((v := a){:}r) = wgt(reset(\rho){:}r) = 1 + wgt(r).$

(b) $wgt(v := e) = wgt(x) = wgt(\mathsf{begin\ var\ } v;\ s\ \mathsf{end}) = 1$
$wgt(s_1;s_2) = wgt(s_1) + wgt(s_2) + 1$
$wgt(\mathsf{if\ } e \mathsf{\ then\ } s_1 \mathsf{\ else\ } s_2 \mathsf{\ fi}) = max\{\, wgt(s_1), wgt(s_2)\,\} + 1.$

The function wgt has been designed such that the following (variation on the) familiar lemma holds:

Lemma 6.9 *If* $[r_1, \rho, \sigma] \to_{0,\rho_0} [r_2, \rho, \sigma]$, *then* $wgt(r_1) > wgt(r_2)$.

Remark Thanks to the fact that recursion specifies an explicit step, we can define $wgt(x)$ in an especially simple way.

Now that $\mathcal{T}_{block}$ has been specified, the definition of $\mathcal{O}$ for $\mathcal{L}_{block}$ requires only little more work.

Definition 6.10

(a) Let $\Sigma_\perp^\infty = \Sigma^* \cup \Sigma^* \cdot \{\perp_\Sigma\} \cup \Sigma^\omega$, and let $\mathbb{P}_O = Env \to \Sigma_\perp \to \mathcal{P}_{ncl}(\Sigma_\perp^\infty)$.

(b) $\mathcal{O}\colon Decl \times Env \times Res \times Env \times \Sigma_\perp \to \mathcal{P}_{ncl}(\Sigma_\perp^\infty)$ is the unique function satisfying $\mathcal{O}(\rho_0|r, \rho, \perp_\Sigma) = \{\perp_\Sigma\}$, and, for $\sigma \neq \perp_\Sigma$,

$$\mathcal{O}(\rho_0|\mathrm{E}, \rho, \sigma) \;=\; \{\epsilon\}\,,$$

and, for $r \not\equiv \mathrm{E}$,

$$\mathcal{O}(\rho_0|r, \rho, \sigma)$$
$$= \begin{cases} \{\perp_\Sigma\} & \text{if } [r, \rho, \sigma] \not\to_{\rho_0} \\ \bigcup\{\sigma' \cdot \mathcal{O}(\rho_0|r', \rho', \sigma') \mid [r, \rho, \sigma] \to_{\rho_0} [r', \rho', \sigma']\} & \text{otherwise} \end{cases}$$

(c) $\mathcal{O}[\![\cdot]\!]\colon \mathcal{L}_{block} \to \mathbb{P}_O$ is given by

$$\mathcal{O}[\![s]\!] \;=\; \lambda\rho.\lambda\sigma.\mathcal{O}(\rho|s{:}\mathrm{E}, \rho, \sigma)\,.$$

Remark In the above definition—and everywhere below in Chapter 6—we do not bother to distinguish between $\perp_\Sigma$ (from $\Sigma_\perp$) and the one-element sequence $\langle \perp_\Sigma \rangle$ (from $\Sigma_\perp^\infty$).

Note how, in clause (c), both the initial and the current environment are initialized to ρ. Well-definedness of $\mathcal{O}$ for $\mathcal{L}_{block}$ is an immediate corollary of the image-finiteness of $\mathcal{T}_{block}$. Details are omitted since they are immediate on the basis of our earlier discussion in (Section 5.1 and) Section 5.2 on $\mathcal{L}_{ra}$.

Examples

(1) Suppose u is not declared by ρ, i.e., $\rho(u) = \perp_A$.

$\mathcal{O}[\![\text{begin var } v; v := u \text{ end}]\!](\rho)(\sigma)$

$= \mathcal{O}(\rho|\text{begin var } v; v := u \text{ end}:E, \rho, \sigma)$

$= \sigma \cdot \bigcup \{ \mathcal{O}(\rho|v := u{:}v := \rho(v){:}E, \rho\{a/v\}, \sigma\{\alpha/v\}) \mid a \text{ fresh}, \alpha \text{ arb.} \}$

$= [ivar(v := u) = \{v, u\} \not\subseteq dom(\rho\{a/v\})] \; \sigma \cdot \{\perp_\Sigma\}$

$= \{\sigma \perp_\Sigma\}.$

(2) Suppose $\rho(u) = a$, $\rho(v) = a_0$, $\sigma(a_0) = \alpha_0$.

$\mathcal{O}[\![\text{begin var } v; v := 2 \text{ end};u := v]\!](\rho)(\sigma)$

$= \mathcal{O}(\rho|\text{begin var } v; v := 2 \text{ end};u := v{:}E, \rho, \sigma)$

$= \bigcup \{ \sigma\{\alpha_1/a_1\} \cdot$
$\qquad \mathcal{O}(\rho|v := 2{:}v := a_0{:}u := v{:}E, \rho\{a_1/v\}, \sigma\{\alpha_1/a_1\}) \mid$
$\qquad\qquad a_1 \text{ fresh}, \alpha_1 \text{ arb.} \}$

$= [\rho\{a_1/v\}(v) = a_1]$
$\quad \bigcup \{ \sigma\{\alpha_1/a_1\} \cdot \sigma\{2/a_1\} \cdot$
$\qquad \mathcal{O}(\rho|v := a_0{:}u := v{:}E, \rho\{a_1/v\}, \sigma\{2/a_1\}) \mid a_1 \text{ fresh}, \alpha_1 \text{ arb.} \}$

$= [\rho\{a_1/v\}\{a_0/v\} = \rho]$
$\quad \bigcup \{ \sigma\{\alpha_1/a_1\} \cdot \sigma\{2/a_1\} \cdot$
$\qquad \mathcal{O}(\rho|u := v{:}E, \rho, \sigma\{2/a_1\}) \mid a_1 \text{ fresh}, \alpha_1 \text{ arb.} \}$

$= \bigcup \{ \sigma\{\alpha_1/a_1\} \cdot \sigma\{2/a_1\} \cdot \sigma\{2/a_1, \alpha_0/a\} \cdot$
$\qquad \mathcal{O}(\rho|E, \rho, \sigma\{2/a_1, \alpha_0/a\}) \mid a_1 \text{ fresh}, \alpha_1 \text{ arb.} \}$

$= \{ \sigma\{\alpha_1/a_1\}\sigma\{2/a_1\}\sigma\{2/a_1, \alpha_0/a\} \mid a_1 \text{ fresh}, \alpha_1 \text{ arb.} \}.$

(3) Suppose $\rho(v) = a_0$, $\sigma(a_0) = \alpha_0$ and $D(x) = v := 0$.

$\mathcal{O}[\![\text{begin var } v; x;u := v \text{ end};u := v]\!](\rho)(\sigma)$

$= \mathcal{O}(\rho|\text{begin var } v; x;u := v \text{ end};u := v{:}E, \rho, \sigma)$

$$= \bigcup \{\, \sigma\{\alpha_1/a_1\} \cdot$$
$$\mathcal{O}(\rho|x;u := v:v := a_0:u := v:\mathrm{E}, \rho\{a_1/v\}, \sigma\{\alpha_1/a_1\}) \mid$$
$$a_1 \text{ fresh, } \alpha_1 \text{ arb.} \}$$
$$= \bigcup \{\, \sigma\{\alpha_1/a_1\} \cdot \sigma\{\alpha_1/a_1\} \cdot$$
$$\mathcal{O}(\rho|v := 0\text{:}reset(\rho\{a_1/v\})\text{:}u := v:v := a_0;u := v:\mathrm{E},$$
$$\rho, \sigma\{\alpha_1/a_1\}) \mid a_1 \text{ fresh, } \alpha_1 \text{ arb.} \}$$
$$= \bigcup \{\, \sigma\{\alpha_1/a_1\}^2 \cdot \sigma\{\alpha_1/a_1, 0/a_0\} \cdot$$
$$\mathcal{O}(\rho|reset(\rho\{a_1/v\})\text{:}u := v:v := a_0;u := v:\mathrm{E},$$
$$\rho, \sigma\{\alpha_1/a_1, 0/a_0\}) \mid a_1 \text{ fresh, } \alpha_1 \text{ arb.} \}$$
$$= \bigcup \{\, \sigma\{\alpha_1/a_1\}^2 \cdot \sigma\{\alpha_1/a_1, 0/a_0\} \cdot$$
$$\mathcal{O}(\rho|u := v:v := a_0;u := v:\mathrm{E},$$
$$\rho\{a_1/v\}, \sigma\{\alpha_1/a_1, 0/a_0\}) \mid a_1 \text{ fresh, } \alpha_1 \text{ arb.} \}$$
$$= [\rho\{a_1/v\}(u) = \rho(u) = a, \mathcal{V}(v)(\rho\{a_1/v\})(\sigma\{\alpha_1/a_1\}) = \alpha_1]$$
$$\bigcup \{\, \sigma\{\alpha_1/a_1\}^2 \cdot \sigma\{\alpha_1/a_1, 0/a_0\} \cdot \sigma\{\alpha_1/a_1, 0/a_0, \alpha_1/a\} \cdot$$
$$\mathcal{O}(\rho|v := a_0\text{:}u := v:\mathrm{E}, \rho\{a_1/v\}, \sigma\{\alpha_1/a_1, 0/a_0, \alpha_1/a\}) \mid$$
$$a_1 \text{ fresh, } \alpha_1 \text{ arb.} \}$$
$$= [\rho\{a_1/v\}\{a_0/v\} = \rho]$$
$$\bigcup \{\, \sigma\{\alpha_1/a_1\}^2 \cdot \sigma\{\alpha_1/a_1, 0/a_0\} \cdot \sigma\{\alpha_1/a_1, 0/a_0, \alpha_1/a\} \cdot$$
$$\mathcal{O}(\rho|u := v:\mathrm{E}, \rho, \sigma\{\alpha_1/a_1, 0/a_0, \alpha_1/a\}) \mid a_1 \text{ fresh, } \alpha_1 \text{ arb.} \}$$
$$= \bigcup \{\, \sigma\{\alpha_1/a_1\}^2 \cdot \sigma\{\alpha_1/a_1, 0/a_0\} \cdot$$
$$\sigma\{\alpha_1/a_1, 0/a_0, \alpha_1/a\} \cdot \sigma\{\alpha_1/a_1, 0/a_0, 0/a\} \cdot$$
$$\mathcal{O}(\mathrm{E}, \rho, \sigma\{\alpha_1/a_1, 0/a_0, 0/a\}) \mid a_1 \text{ fresh, } \alpha_1 \text{ arb.} \}$$
$$= \{\, \sigma\{\alpha_1/a_1\}^2 \sigma\{\alpha_1/a_1, 0/a_0\} \sigma\{\alpha_1/a_1, 0/a_0, \alpha_1/a\} \cdot$$
$$\sigma\{\alpha_1/a_1, 0/a_0, 0/a\}) \mid a_1 \text{ fresh, } \alpha_1 \text{ arb.} \}.$$

6.1.2   Denotational semantics, equivalence of $\mathcal{O}$ and $\mathcal{D}$

The framework for the definition of $\mathcal{D}$ has the usual ingredients—continuations, $\mathcal{D}$ as fixed point of a higher-order Ψ—and, in addition, uses environments in a manner which closely follows the approach already described for the operational semantics.

Definition 6.11

(a) $\mathbb{P}_D = Env \rightarrow \Sigma_\perp \rightarrow \mathcal{P}_{ncl}(\Sigma_\perp^\infty)$.

(b) $(\gamma \in)\, Cont = \mathbb{P}_D,\ \gamma_\epsilon = \lambda\rho.\lambda\sigma.\text{if } \sigma =\perp_\Sigma \text{ then } \{\perp_\Sigma\} \text{ else } \{\epsilon\} \text{ fi}.$

(c) $\mathcal{D}\text{:} Env \times Stat \rightarrow Cont \xrightarrow{1} \mathbb{P}_D$ is the unique function satisfying

$$\mathcal{D}(\rho_0|s)(\gamma)(\rho)(\perp_\Sigma) = \{\perp_\Sigma\}$$

and, for $\sigma \neq \perp_\Sigma$,

- $\mathcal{D}(\rho_0|v := e)(\gamma)(\rho)(\sigma) =$
  - $\sigma\{\alpha/a\} \cdot \gamma(\rho)(\sigma\{\alpha/a\})$, if $ivar(v := e) \subseteq dom(\rho)$,
    where $a = \rho(v)$, $\alpha = \mathcal{V}(e)(\rho)(\sigma)$
  - $\{\perp_\Sigma\}$, otherwise
- $\mathcal{D}(\rho_0|s_1;s_2)(\gamma)(\rho)(\sigma) = \mathcal{D}(\rho_0|s_1)(\mathcal{D}(\rho_0|s_2)(\gamma))(\rho)(\sigma)$
- $\mathcal{D}(\rho_0|x)(\gamma)(\rho)(\sigma) = \sigma \cdot \mathcal{D}(\rho_0|D(x))(\lambda\bar{\rho}.\gamma(\rho))(\rho_0)(\sigma)$
- $\mathcal{D}(\rho_0|\text{if } e \text{ then } s_1 \text{ else } s_2 \text{ fi})(\gamma)(\rho)(\sigma) =$
  - $\mathcal{D}(\rho_0|s_1)(\gamma)(\rho)(\sigma)$, if $ivar(e) \subseteq dom(\rho)$, $\mathcal{V}(e)(\rho)(\sigma) = tt$
  - $\mathcal{D}(\rho_0|s_2)(\gamma)(\rho)(\sigma)$, if $ivar(e) \subseteq dom(\rho)$, $\mathcal{V}(e)(\rho)(\sigma) = ff$
  - $\{\perp_\Sigma\}$, if $ivar(e) \not\subseteq dom(\rho)$
- $\mathcal{D}(\rho_0|\text{begin var } v; s \text{ end})(\gamma)(\rho)(\sigma)$
  $$= \bigcup\{\sigma\{\alpha/a\} \cdot \mathcal{D}(\rho_0|s)(\lambda\bar{\rho}.\gamma(\rho))(\rho\{a/v\})(\sigma\{\alpha/a\}) \mid$$
  $$a \in Addr \setminus cod(\rho), \alpha \in Val\}.$$

(d) $\mathcal{D}[\![s]\!] = \lambda\rho.\mathcal{D}(\rho|s)(\gamma_\epsilon)(\rho).$

The following explanations may help.

(1) The clauses for $v := e$ and if e then s_1 else s_2 fi are easily understood on the basis of the corresponding transition rules.

(2) The case $s \equiv x$ has three aspects—all mimicking the operational meaning embodied in the (Rec)-rule—

  (a) x is replaced by $D(x)$.

  (b) The current environment ρ is replaced by the initial environment ρ_0 (valid at the moment of the declaration of x).

  (c) The continuation γ is modified such that its first action will be to reinstall ρ.

(3) The clause for the block begin var v; s end combines the following

  (a) Some new address a is associated with v, and a is initialized to the arbitrary value α.

  (b) The meaning of s is determined for the new $\rho' = \rho\{a/v\}$ and $\sigma' = \sigma\{\alpha/a\}$.

  (c) Upon exit of the block, the current environment is reset to ρ. Note the difference here with the operational treatment, where ρ is explicitly reset only in the argument v (viz. to $\rho(v)$). Though we might have copied this in the denotational clause, we prefer not to do so, since we feel that a global resetting of the environment is more denotational in spirit. It will be one of the proof obligations in establishing $\mathcal{O} = \mathcal{D}$ for $\mathcal{L}_{block}$ to show that both approaches yield the same effect.

(d) In defining $\mathcal{D}[\![s]\!]$, we supply the initial environment ρ and, moreover, initialize the current environment to the initial environment. The nil continuation $\gamma_\epsilon = \lambda\rho.\lambda\sigma.\text{if } \sigma = \perp_\Sigma \text{ then } \{\perp_\Sigma\} \text{ else } \{\epsilon\} \text{ fi}$ has the usual role.

Examples

(1) Let $\rho(u) = \perp_A$.

$\mathcal{D}[\![\text{begin var } v; v := u \text{ end}]\!](\rho)(\sigma)$

$= \mathcal{D}(\rho|\text{begin var } v; v := u \text{ end})(\gamma_\epsilon)(\rho)(\sigma)$

$= \bigcup\{\, \sigma\{\alpha/a\} \cdot \mathcal{D}(\rho|v := u)(\lambda\bar{\rho}.\gamma_\epsilon(\rho))(\rho\{a/v\})(\sigma\{\alpha/a\}) \mid$
$\qquad a \text{ fresh}, \alpha \text{ arb.}\,\}$

$= [ivar(v := u) = \{v, u\} \not\subseteq dom(\rho\{\alpha/v\})]$
$\quad \bigcup\{\, \sigma\{\alpha/a\} \cdot \{\perp_\Sigma\} \mid a \text{ fresh}, \alpha \text{ arb.}\,\}$

$= \{\, \sigma\{\alpha/a\}\, \perp_\Sigma \mid a \text{ fresh}, \alpha \text{ arb.}\,\}.$

(2) Let $\rho(u) = a$, $\rho(v) = a_0$, $\sigma(a_0) = \alpha_0$.

$\mathcal{D}[\![\text{begin var } v; v := 2 \text{ end}; u := v]\!](\rho)(\sigma)$

$= \mathcal{D}(\rho|\text{begin var } v; v := 2 \text{ end}; u := v)(\gamma_\epsilon)(\rho)(\sigma)$

$= \mathcal{D}(\rho|\text{begin var } v; v := 2 \text{ end})(\mathcal{D}(\rho|u := v)(\gamma_\epsilon))(\rho)(\sigma)$

$= \bigcup\{\, \sigma\{\alpha_1/a_1\} \cdot$
$\qquad \mathcal{D}(\rho|v := 2)(\lambda\bar{\rho}.\mathcal{D}(\rho|u := v)(\gamma_\epsilon)(\rho))(\rho\{a_1/v\})(\sigma\{\alpha_1/a_1\}) \mid$
$\qquad\qquad a_1 \text{ fresh}, \alpha_1 \text{ arb.}\,\}$

$= [\rho\{a_1/v\}(v) = a_1]$
$\quad \bigcup\{\, \sigma\{\alpha_1/a_1\} \cdot \sigma\{2/a_1\} \cdot$
$\qquad (\lambda\bar{\rho}.\mathcal{D}(\rho|u := v)(\gamma_\epsilon)(\rho))(\rho\{a_1/v\})(\sigma\{2/a_1\}) \mid$
$\qquad\qquad a_1 \text{ fresh}, \alpha_1 \text{ arb.}\,\}$

$= \bigcup\{\, \sigma\{\alpha_1/a_1\} \cdot \sigma\{2/a_1\} \cdot \mathcal{D}(\rho|u := v)(\gamma_\epsilon)(\rho)(\sigma\{2/a_1\}) \mid$
$\qquad\qquad a_1 \text{ fresh}, \alpha_1 \text{ arb.}\,\}$

$= [\rho(u) = a, \mathcal{V}(v)(\rho)(\sigma\{2/a_1\}) = \sigma(a_0) = \alpha_0]$
$\quad \bigcup\{\, \sigma\{\alpha_1/a_1\} \cdot \sigma\{2/a_1\} \cdot \sigma\{2/a_1, \alpha_0/a\} \cdot \gamma_\epsilon(\rho)(\sigma\{2/a_1, \alpha_0/a\}) \mid$
$\qquad\qquad a_1 \text{ fresh}, \alpha_1 \text{ arb.}\,\}$

$$= \{\, \sigma\{\alpha_1/a_1\}\sigma\{2/a_1\}\sigma\{2/a_1,\alpha_0/a\} \mid a_1 \text{ fresh}, \alpha_1 \text{ arb.}\,\}$$

(3) Let $\rho(u) = a, \rho(v) = a_0$, $\sigma(a_0) = \alpha_0$, $D(x) = v := 0$.

$$\mathcal{D}[\![\text{begin var } v; x; u := v \text{ end}; u := v]\!](\rho)(\sigma)$$

$$= \mathcal{D}(\rho|\text{begin var } v; x; u := v \text{ end}; u := v)(\gamma_\epsilon)(\rho)(\sigma)$$

$$= \mathcal{D}(\rho|\text{begin var } v; x; u := v \text{ end})\big(\mathcal{D}(\rho|u := v)(\gamma_\epsilon)\big)(\rho)(\sigma)$$

$$= \bigcup\{\, \sigma\{\alpha_1/a_1\} \cdot$$
$$\mathcal{D}(x; u := v)\big(\lambda\bar{\rho}.\mathcal{D}(\rho|u := v)(\gamma_\epsilon)(\rho)\big)(\rho\{a_1/v\})(\sigma\{\alpha_1/a_1\}) \mid$$
$$a_1 \text{ fresh}, \alpha_1 \text{ arb}\,\}$$

$$= \bigcup\{\, \sigma\{\alpha_1/a_1\} \cdot \mathcal{D}(\rho|x)\big(\mathcal{D}(\rho|u := v)(\lambda\bar{\rho}.\mathcal{D}(\rho|u := v)(\gamma_\epsilon)(\rho))\big)$$
$$(\rho\{a_1/v\})(\sigma\{\alpha_1/a_1\}) \mid a_1 \text{ fresh}, \alpha_1 \text{ arb}\,\}$$

$$= \bigcup\{\, \sigma\{\alpha_1/a_1\} \cdot \sigma\{\alpha_1/a_1\} \cdot \mathcal{D}(\rho|v := 0)$$
$$\Big(\lambda\bar{\bar{\rho}}.\mathcal{D}(\rho|u := v)(\lambda\bar{\rho}.\mathcal{D}(\rho|u := v)(\gamma_\epsilon)(\rho))(\rho\{a_1/v\})\Big)$$
$$(\rho)(\sigma\{\alpha_1/a_1\}) \mid a_1 \text{ fresh}, \alpha_1 \text{ arb}\,\}$$

$$= \bigcup\{\, \sigma\{\alpha_1/a_1\} \cdot \sigma\{\alpha_1/a_1\} \cdot \sigma\{\alpha_1/a_1, 0/a_0\} \cdot$$
$$\Big(\lambda\bar{\bar{\rho}}.\mathcal{D}(\rho|u := v)(\lambda\bar{\rho}.\mathcal{D}(\rho|u := v)(\gamma_\epsilon)(\rho))(\rho\{a_1/v\})\Big)$$
$$(\rho)(\sigma\{\alpha_1/a_1, 0/a_0\}) \mid a_1 \text{ fresh}, \alpha_1 \text{ arb}\,\}$$

$$= \bigcup\{\, \sigma\{\alpha_1/a_1\} \cdot \sigma\{\alpha_1/a_1\} \cdot \sigma\{\alpha_1/a_1, 0/a_0\} \cdot$$
$$\mathcal{D}(\rho|u := v)(\lambda\bar{\rho}.\mathcal{D}(\rho|u := v)(\gamma_\epsilon)(\rho))$$
$$(\rho\{a_1/v\})(\sigma\{\alpha_1/a_1, 0/a_0\}) \mid a_1 \text{ fresh}, \alpha_1 \text{ arb}\,\}$$

$$= \bigcup\{\, \sigma\{\alpha_1/a_1\}^2 \cdot \sigma\{\alpha_1/a_1, 0/a_0\} \cdot \sigma\{\alpha_1/a_1, 0/a_0, \alpha_1/a\} \cdot$$
$$\mathcal{D}(\rho|u := v)(\gamma_\epsilon)(\rho)(\sigma\{\alpha_1/a_1, 0/a_0, \alpha_1/a\})$$
$$\mid a_1 \text{ fresh}, \alpha_1 \text{ arb}\,\}$$

$$= \bigcup\{\, \sigma\{\alpha_1/a_1\}^2 \cdot \sigma\{\alpha_1/a_1, 0/a_0\} \cdot \sigma\{\alpha_1/a_1, 0/a_0, \alpha_1/a\} \cdot$$
$$\sigma\{\alpha_1/a_1, 0/a_0, 0/a\} \cdot \gamma_\epsilon(\rho)(\sigma\{\alpha_1/a_1, 0/a_0, 0/a\}) \mid$$
$$a_1 \text{ fresh}, \alpha_1 \text{ arb}\,\}$$

$$= \{\, \sigma\{\alpha_1/a_1\}^2\sigma\{\alpha_1/a_1, 0/a_0\}\sigma\{\alpha_1/a_1, 0/a_0, \alpha_1/a\}$$
$$\sigma\{\alpha_1/a_1, 0/a_0, 0/a\} \mid a_1 \text{ fresh}, \alpha_1 \text{ arb}\,\}$$

We follow the usual route to establish that $\mathcal{O}$ and $\mathcal{D}$ coincide. We first define an intermediate $\mathcal{E}$:

Definition 6.12 $\mathcal{E}: Env \times Res \to Cont$ is defined by putting

$$\begin{aligned}
\mathcal{E}(\rho_0|\mathrm{E}) &= \gamma_\epsilon \\
\mathcal{E}(\rho_0|s{:}r) &= \mathcal{D}(\rho_0|s)(\mathcal{E}(\rho_0|r)) \\
\mathcal{E}((\rho_0|v := a){:}r) &= \lambda\rho.\mathcal{E}(\rho_0|r)(\rho\{a/v\}) \\
\mathcal{E}(\rho_0|reset(\bar{\rho}){:}r) &= \lambda\rho.\mathcal{E}(\rho_0|r)(\bar{\rho}).
\end{aligned}$$

Similarly to what we saw before, below we also need the mapping $\mathcal{E}^*$: $Env \times Res \times Env \times \Sigma_\perp \to \mathbb{P}_O$, defined by

$$\mathcal{E}^*(\rho_0|r, \rho, \sigma) \;=\; \mathcal{E}(\rho_0|r)(\rho)(\sigma) \,.$$

A useful technical lemma—with as main role to aid in showing that the operational and denotational way of resetting ρ upon block exit coincide—is now presented.

Lemma 6.13 *For all ρ, if $\gamma_1(\rho) = \gamma_2(\rho)$, then $\mathcal{D}(\rho_0|s)(\gamma_1)(\rho) = \mathcal{D}(\rho_0|s)(\gamma_2)(\rho)$.*

Remark Note the way in which we quantify over ρ: equivalence of γ_1 and γ_2 is only required for some given ρ, in order that the stated conclusion (for that γ_1, γ_2 and ρ) holds.

Proof Assume $\gamma_1(\rho) = \gamma_2(\rho)$. We use structural induction on s in proving that $\mathcal{D}(\rho_0|s)(\gamma_1)(\rho)(\sigma) = \mathcal{D}(\rho_0|s)(\gamma_2)(\rho)(\sigma)$. Without lack of generality we assume that all individual variables have been declared, and that $\sigma \neq \perp_\Sigma$. Four subcases:

$[v := e]$ $\quad \mathcal{D}(\rho_0|v := e)(\gamma_1)(\rho)(\sigma)$

$\qquad = \quad \sigma\{\alpha/a\} \cdot \gamma_1(\rho)(\sigma\{\alpha/a\})$

$\qquad = \quad \sigma\{\alpha/a\} \cdot \gamma_2(\rho)(\sigma\{\alpha/a\})$

$\qquad = \quad \mathcal{D}(\rho_0|v := e)(\gamma_2)(\rho)(\sigma)$

$\qquad$ where $a = \rho(v)$, $\alpha = \mathcal{V}(e)(\rho)(\sigma)$.

$[s_1; s_2]$ $\quad$ Two applications of the induction hypothesis.

$[x]$ $\quad \mathcal{D}(\rho_0|x)(\gamma_1)(\rho)(\sigma)$

$\qquad = \quad \sigma \cdot \mathcal{D}(\rho_0|D(x))(\lambda\bar{\rho}.\gamma_1(\rho))(\rho_0)(\sigma)$

$\qquad = \quad \sigma \cdot \mathcal{D}(\rho_0|D(x))(\lambda\bar{\rho}.\gamma_2(\rho))(\rho_0)(\sigma)$

$\qquad = \quad \mathcal{D}(\rho_0|x)(\gamma_2)(\rho)(\sigma) \,.$

$[\text{begin var } v; s \text{ end}]$ $\quad \mathcal{D}(\rho_0|\text{begin var } v; s \text{ end})(\gamma_1)(\rho)(\sigma)$

$\qquad = \quad \bigcup\{\sigma\{\alpha/a\} \cdot \mathcal{D}(\rho_0|s)(\lambda\bar{\rho}.\gamma_1(\rho))(\rho\{a/v\})(\sigma\{\alpha/a\}) \mid$
$\qquad\qquad\qquad\qquad\qquad\qquad\qquad\qquad a \in Addr \setminus cod(\rho), \alpha \in Val \,\}$

$\qquad = \quad \bigcup\{\sigma\{\alpha/a\} \cdot \mathcal{D}(\rho_0|s)(\lambda\bar{\rho}.\gamma_2(\rho))(\rho\{a/v\})(\sigma\{\alpha/a\}) \mid$
$\qquad\qquad\qquad\qquad\qquad\qquad\qquad\qquad a \in Addr \setminus cod(\rho), \alpha \in Val \,\}$

$\qquad = \quad \mathcal{D}(\rho_0|\text{begin var } v; s \text{ end})(\gamma_2)(\rho)(\sigma) \,.$ $\qquad\qquad\qquad\qquad$ $\square$

Let Φ be the higher-order operator defining $\mathcal{O}$. We have

Lemma 6.14 $\Phi(\mathcal{E}^*) = \mathcal{E}^*$.

Proof We show that, for each r, ρ, σ, $\Phi(\mathcal{E}^*)(r, \rho, \sigma) = \mathcal{E}^*(r, \rho, \sigma)$. Without lack of generality, take $\sigma \neq \perp_\Sigma$ and assume that all relevant variables have been declared. We use induction on $wgt(r)$. Three subcases.

$[x{:}r]$ $\Phi(\mathcal{E}^*)(\rho_0|x{:}r, \rho, \sigma)$

$\quad = \quad$ [def. Φ] $\sigma \cdot \mathcal{E}^*(\rho_0|D(x){:}(reset(\rho){:}r), \rho_0, \sigma)$

$\quad = \quad$ [def. $\mathcal{E}^*$] $\sigma \cdot \mathcal{E}(\rho_0|D(x){:}(reset(\rho){:}r))(\rho_0)(\sigma)$

$\quad = \quad$ [def. $\mathcal{E}$] $\sigma \cdot \mathcal{D}(\rho_0|D(x))(\mathcal{E}(\rho_0|reset(\rho){:}r))(\rho_0)(\sigma)$

$\quad = \quad$ [def. $\mathcal{E}$] $\sigma \cdot \mathcal{D}(\rho_0|D(x))(\lambda\bar\rho.\mathcal{E}(\rho_0|r)(\rho))(\rho_0)(\sigma)$

$\quad = \quad$ [def. $\mathcal{D}$] $\mathcal{D}(\rho_0|x)(\mathcal{E}(\rho_0|r))(\rho)(\sigma)$

$\quad = \quad$ [def. $\mathcal{E}$] $\mathcal{E}(\rho_0|x{:}r)(\rho)(\sigma)$

$\quad = \quad$ [def. $\mathcal{E}^*$] $\mathcal{E}^*(\rho_0|x{:}r, \rho, \sigma)$.

$[\text{begin var } v; \; s \text{ end}{:}r]$ We have

$$\mathcal{E}(\rho_0|(v := \rho(v)){:}r)(\rho\{a/v\}) \tag{6.2}$$

$\quad = \quad \mathcal{E}(\rho_0|r)(\rho\{a/v\}\{\rho(v)/v\})$

$\quad = \quad \mathcal{E}(\rho_0|r)(\rho)$

$\quad = \quad (\lambda\bar\rho.\mathcal{E}(\rho_0|r)(\rho))(\rho\{a/v\})$.

Therefore,

$\quad \Phi(\mathcal{E}^*)(\rho_0|\text{begin var } v; \; s \text{ end}, \rho, \sigma)$

$\quad = \quad$ [def. Φ] $\bigcup\{ \sigma\{\alpha/a\} \cdot \mathcal{E}^*(\rho_0|s{:}((v := \rho(v)){:}r), \rho\{a/v\}, \sigma\{\alpha/a\}) \mid$
$\qquad\qquad\qquad\qquad a \in Addr \setminus cod(\rho), \alpha \in Val \}$

$\quad = \quad \bigcup\{ \sigma\{\alpha/a\} \cdot \mathcal{D}(\rho_0|s)(\mathcal{E}(\rho_0|(v := \rho(v)){:}r))(\rho\{a/v\})(\sigma\{\alpha/a\}) \mid$
$\qquad\qquad\qquad\qquad a \in Addr \setminus cod(\rho), \alpha \in Val \}$

$\quad = \quad$ [by Lemma 6.13, eq. (6.2)]
$\qquad \bigcup\{ \sigma\{\alpha/a\} \cdot \mathcal{D}(\rho_0|s)(\lambda\bar\rho.\mathcal{E}(\rho_0|r)(\rho))(\rho\{a/v\})(\sigma\{\alpha/a\}) \mid$
$\qquad\qquad\qquad\qquad a \in Addr \setminus cod(\rho), \alpha \in Val \}$

$\quad = \quad \mathcal{D}(\rho_0|\text{begin var } v; \; s \text{ end})(\mathcal{E}(\rho_0|r))(\rho)(\sigma)$

$\quad = \quad \mathcal{E}^*(\rho_0|\text{begin var } v; \; s \text{ end}{:}r, \rho, \sigma)$.

$[(v := a){:}r]$ $\Phi(\mathcal{E}^*)(\rho_0|(v := a){:}r, \rho, \sigma)$

$$
\begin{aligned}
&= \quad \Phi(\mathcal{E}^*)(\rho_0|r, \rho\{a/v\}, \sigma) \\
&= \quad [\text{ind. hyp.}] \ \mathcal{E}^*(\rho_0|r, \rho\{a/v\}, \sigma) \\
&= \quad \mathcal{E}^*(\rho_0|(v := a){:}r, \rho, \sigma) \, .
\end{aligned}
$$

$\square$

The desired result now follows in the customary manner:

Theorem 6.15

(a) $\mathcal{O} = \mathcal{E}^*$.

(b) $\mathcal{O}[\![s]\!] = \mathcal{D}[\![s]\!]$.

Proof Part (a) is clear by Lemma 6.14 and Banach's theorem. Part (b) is immediate by the definitions and part (a). $\square$

6.2 Function procedures with parameters called-by-value —statement and expression prolongations

As a second example of a construct in which locality plays a key role, we treat procedures *with parameters*. More specifically, we shall be concerned with the parameter mechanism of "call-by-value." We have singled out this mechanism—preferring it to several other systems not treated in our work—since it is both in wide-spread use and it provides a nice application of the techniques developed in Section 6.1. Let us consider a procedure x declared—in a provisional syntax—as $x \Leftarrow (\text{formal } v;\ s)$, indicating that x has v as formal parameter (tacitly assumed to be of the "call-by-value" kind), and s as body. A call $x(e)$—with e as actual parameter—is, in essence, equivalent to the execution of the block begin var $v; v :=$ $e; s$ end, i.e., of a block with the local v *initialized* to e, and with s as its statement part.

Rather than illustrating call-by-value for procedures of the "statement-variety," we shall in fact be concerned with procedures of the "expression-variety," i.e., of so-called *function procedures*. This will enable us to achieve a second aim with the present section, viz. the treatment of non-trivial expressions. Recall that, so far, all languages considered were either uniform or, when nonuniform, contained only simple expressions without side effects or the possibility of nontermination. We now introduce the language $\mathcal{L}_{fun}$ which (is nonuniform and) allows us to focus on more realistic expressions. Firstly, they may involve, besides the constructors u, also function procedures declared in the program. Secondly, these expressions may incur side-effects, i.e., changes of the state.

As often before, the semantic models developed in this section will rely heavily on the use of prolongations (resumptions and continuations). As new phenomenon we distinguish, for both classes, two kinds of prolongations, viz., *statement* resumptions versus *expression* resumptions, and similarly *statement* continuations versus *expression* continuations.

Contrary to the (unbounded) nondeterminism present in the block construct of Section 6.1, in the present section we shall deal with deterministic programs only. This stems from the fact that the local variables (i.e., the formals) in a call-by-value setting are all *initialized*, thus avoiding the "arbitrary initial value" issues which played an important role above.

6.2.1 Syntax and operational semantics

Let $(v \in) IVar$ and $(\alpha \in) Val$ be as before. Let $(f \in) FSym$ be a class of *function symbols*. These serve as extension of the constructors $(u \in) Constr$ as introduced earlier: Whereas the latter are given at the outset, together with an *interpretation* yielding $\hat{u}: Val^k \to Val$ as meaning for each u, the functions f are to be *declared* by the programmer, and will obtain a meaning by the semantic definitional mechanism we are about to describe.

To avoid notational overhead by allowing an arbitrary number of arguments for the u- and f-constructs, we shall, in the present section, agree that both u and f have precisely two arguments.

In view of balancing the total syntactic complexity, whereas the expressions in $\mathcal{L}_{fun}$ are rather more involved than the earlier ones, the statements will be extremely simple.

Definition 6.16

(a) $e \, (\in Exp) ::= \alpha \mid v \mid u(e, e) \mid f(e, e) \mid \text{if } e \text{ then } e \text{ else } e \text{ fi} \mid (s;e)$

(b) $s \, (\in Stat) ::= v := e \mid (s;s)$

(c) $(D \in) Decl = FSym \to IVar \times IVar \times Exp$

(d) $(\pi \in) \mathcal{L}_{fun} = Decl \times Stat.$

We shall always write $D(f) \equiv \lambda(v_1, v_2).e$—rather than just $D(f) = \langle v_1, v_2, e \rangle$—in order to emphasize the role of the v_1, v_2 as parameters of the function f.

In the design of the operational semantics for $\mathcal{L}_{fun}$, we shall use the sets $(\sigma \in) \Sigma_\perp$, $(a \in) Addr_\perp$ and $(\rho \in) Env$ as in Section 6.1. We shall use two kinds of resumptions, viz., statement resumptions $(r \in)$ *SRes* and expression resumptions $(g \in)$ *ERes*. We shall also make use of a few auxiliary mappings $\phi\colon Env \times \Sigma_\perp \to Env \times \Sigma_\perp$, which will be applied in certain transformations motivated by locality concerns.

Definition 6.17

(a) $r (\in SRes) ::= \text{E} \mid (s{:}r) \mid \text{if } \alpha \text{ then } r \text{ else } r \text{ fi} \mid (e{:}g) \mid r\langle a \leftarrow \alpha \rangle \mid (\phi{:}r)$

(b) $g (\in ERes) ::= \lambda \alpha.r.$

The statement resumptions E and $(s{:}r)$ are familiar, and the conditional resumption should be clear. The construct $(e{:}g)$ expresses that the expression e has to be evaluated (this will take $n \geq 0$ steps) and, eventually, its result, say $\bar{\alpha}$, should be passed on to the expression resumption g. By clause (b), such a g is always of the form $\lambda \alpha.r$. Thus, it is a function which, when supplied with an argument $\bar{\alpha}$, delivers as a result the statement resumption r with $\bar{\alpha}$ syntactically substituted for α (to be denoted by $r[\bar{\alpha}/\alpha]$). Altogether, execution of $(e{:}\lambda\alpha.r)$ amounts to the evaluation of e and, next, continuation with the new $r[\bar{\alpha}/\alpha]$. The construct $r\langle a \leftarrow \alpha \rangle$ plays a role in the handling of the assignment statement. Its effect will be that α is assigned to the address a, after which execution continues with r. The construct $\phi{:}r$, finally, will play an auxiliary role in certain transformations having to do with the (re)setting of ρ, σ, as prescribed by locality considerations. More specifically, we shall employ a function ϕ of a particular form, viz. $\phi = set(\rho, \psi)$. Here $\psi\colon \Sigma \to \Sigma$ is a mapping to be defined later. The intended meaning of $set(\rho, \psi)$ is given by

$$set(\rho, \psi) \quad = \quad \lambda(\bar{\rho}, \bar{\sigma}).(\rho, \psi(\bar{\sigma})).$$

Thus, for given $\bar{\rho}, \bar{\sigma}$, applying $set(\rho, \psi)$ delivers a pair with ρ as current environment and $\psi(\bar{\sigma})$ as current state (cf. the rule (Set) in $\mathcal{T}_{fun}$). For brevity, we shall use $set(\rho)$ as abbreviation for $set(\rho, \lambda\bar{\sigma}.\bar{\sigma})$.

The transition system $\mathcal{T}_{fun}$ resembles $\mathcal{T}_{block}$ in its use of both environments $\rho \ (\in Env)$ and states $\sigma \ (\in \Sigma_\perp)$. The role of the initial environment ρ_0, and the way static scope is treated in $\mathcal{L}_{fun}$ are exactly as for $\mathcal{T}_{block}$.

Definition 6.18 $\mathcal{T}_{fun} = (Env \times SRes \times Env \times \Sigma_\perp, \Sigma_\perp, \to, Spec)$. We adopt the conventions that (D is suppressed throughout and)

- The initial environment ρ_0 is written as a subscript on the '$\to$' (resulting in '$\to_{\rho_0}$'); this brings out that ρ_0 remains constant through all transitions.

- The $\to_0$-notation is as usual (and here takes the form of '$\to_{0,\rho_0}$'). In case both ρ and σ are not affected by the transition, they will not be written.

- All transitions specified below assume that $\sigma \neq \perp_\Sigma$.

- All bound variables α, α_1, α_2, β, (in $\lambda\alpha.\cdots$, etc.) are chosen *fresh* (i.e., occurring in the constructs concerned only where explicitly indicated).

Spec consists of the following axioms and rules:

- $[(v := e):r, \rho, \sigma] \rightarrow_{0,\rho_0} [e:\lambda\alpha.r\langle\rho(v)\leftarrow\alpha\rangle, \rho, \sigma]$ if $v \in dom(\rho)$ (Ass 1)

- $(s_1;s_2):r \rightarrow_{0,\rho_0} s_1:(s_2:r)$ (Seq 1)

- $\bar{\alpha}:\lambda\alpha.r \rightarrow_{0,\rho_0} r[\bar{\alpha}/\alpha]$ (Val)

- $[v:g, \rho, \sigma] \rightarrow_{\rho_0} [\sigma(\rho(v)):g, \rho, \sigma]$ if $v \in dom(\rho)$ (IVar)

- $u(e_1, e_2):g \rightarrow_{0,\rho_0} e_1:\lambda\alpha_1.(e_2:\lambda\alpha_2.\hat{u}(\alpha_1, \alpha_2):g)$ (Constr)

- $[f(e_1, e_2):\lambda\beta.r, \rho, \sigma] \rightarrow_{\rho_0}$ (Fun)
    $[e_1:\lambda\alpha_1.(e_2:\lambda\alpha_2.(set(\rho_0\{a_1/v_1, a_2/v_2\},$
          $\lambda\bar{\sigma}.\bar{\sigma}\{\alpha_1/a_1, \alpha_2/a_2\}):(e:\lambda\beta.(set(\rho):r)))), \rho, \sigma]$
    where $D(f) = \lambda(v_1, v_2).e$, and $a_1, a_2 \in Addr \setminus cod(\rho_0)$

- if e then e_1 else e_2 fi$:g \rightarrow_{0,\rho_0} e:\lambda\alpha.$if α then $e_1:g$ else $e_2:g$ fi   (If 1)

- $(s;e):g \rightarrow_{0,\rho_0} s:(e:g)$ (Seq 2)

- if tt then r_1 else r_2 fi $\rightarrow_{0,\rho_0} r_1$ (If 2)

- if ff then r_1 else r_2 fi $\rightarrow_{0,\rho_0} r_2$ (If 3)

- $[r\langle a\leftarrow\alpha\rangle, \rho, \sigma] \rightarrow_{\rho_0} [r, \rho, \sigma\{\alpha/a\}]$ (Ass 2)

- $[set(\rho', \psi):r, \rho, \sigma] \rightarrow_{0,\rho_0} [r, \rho', \psi(\sigma)]$ (Set)

Some explanations of $\mathcal{T}_{fun}$ follow.

(1) To elaborate an assignment $v := e$, for given r, ρ, σ, the expression e is evaluated (requiring $n \geq 0$ steps), and the result, say $\bar{\alpha}$, is passed on to the expression resumption $g = \lambda\alpha.r\langle a\leftarrow\alpha\rangle$, with $a = \rho(v)$ (assuming $v \in dom(\rho)$). By an application of (Val), $\bar{\alpha}$ will be substituted for α in g. Next, the rule (Ass 2) will accomplish the desired state transformation, resulting in the updated state $\sigma\{\alpha/a\}$ and the statement resumption r. Note how (Ass 2) requires an explicit step.

(2) The *only* rules which specify explicit steps are (Ass 2), (IVar) and (Fun). That is, in these rules we use ' $\to_{\rho_0}$ '; in all other rules, we use transitions of the ' $\to_{0,\rho_0}$ ' kind.

(3) The rules (Seq 1), (Seq 2) and (If 2), (If 3) should be clear. The rule (If 1) prepares the way for the evaluation of e; depending on its outcome, eventually either the resumption $e_1{:}g$ or $e_2{:}g$ will be chosen.

(4) The rule for $v{:}g$, for given ρ, σ, applies σ to $a = \rho(v)$ (assuming $v \in dom(\rho)$), thus yielding $\alpha = \sigma(a)$ as value to be passed on (by (Val)) to g.

(5) The rule for $u(e_1, e_2)$ evaluates the expressions e_1 and e_2—in that order—storing the values as arguments of the respective mappings $\lambda\alpha_1.\cdots$ and $\lambda\alpha_2.\cdots$. The function $\hat{u}$—the interpretation of the constructor u—is next applied to (the values stored in) the α_1, α_2, and the result $\hat{u}(\alpha_1, \alpha_2)$ is determined and passed on to g. Note: a treatment of the expression $u(e_1, e_2)$ which evaluates e_1 and e_2 *in parallel* is also possible. However, this requires a rather more complex strategy which will be described in Section 7.2.

(6) The rule for $f(e_1, e_2)$ is the most complex one of $\mathcal{T}_{fun}$. Let us assume some $g = \lambda\beta.r$, ρ and σ, and let $D(f) = \lambda(v_1, v_2).e$. The following takes place

- e_1 and e_2 are evaluated, resulting in values (to be stored in) α_1, α_2

- a new block is opened, with the initial environment ρ_0 as the current environment (updated in arguments v_1, v_2 to fresh addresses a_1, a_2—to avoid nondeterminacy here one should take the *first* such addresses), and with the state (current upon completion of the evaluation of e_1 and e_2) to be updated in a_1, a_2 to α_1, α_2

- the expression e—the "body" of f—is evaluated, resulting in a value (to be stored in) β

- the environment is (re)set upon completion of e (to the former value ρ)

- the computation resumes with that of r.

(7) The rule (Set) has the effect as described after Definition 6.17.

Remarks

(1) The scheme as employed in $\mathcal{T}_{fun}$ is organized solely in terms of transitions of the type $[r, \rho, \sigma] \to [r', \rho', \sigma']$ (forgetting for the moment about the ρ_0). The dual task of specifying rules for statements *and* expressions is handled by the two types of resumptions. An alternative would be to employ a "many-sorted" transition system, where transitions of, essentially, both the types $s_1 \to s_2$ and $e_1 \to e_2$ (not

writing the various additional components) are used. In Section 7.2, we shall discuss a transition system (for the parallel or *concurrent* evaluation of expressions) which indeed uses transitions of both types.

(2) Contrary to what we did in $\mathcal{T}_{block}$, we have here employed (re)set-operators affecting the environment as a whole (rather than only in the arguments v_1 and v_2). This approach facilitates comparison with the denotational semantics for $\mathcal{L}_{fun}$, allowing us to avoid duplicating the argument of Lemma 6.13.

We now come to the definition of $\mathcal{O}$ for $\mathcal{L}_{fun}$. It will be convenient to slightly extend $\mathcal{T}_{fun}$, in order to be able to treat the "abnormal termination" cases—where $\bot_\Sigma$ is to be delivered—in a unified manner. We do this in

Definition 6.19 Let $\mathcal{T}'_{fun}$ be as $\mathcal{T}_{fun}$, with following two rules added

- $[(v := e){:}r, \rho, \sigma] \to {}_{\rho_0}[\mathrm{E}, \rho, \bot_\Sigma]$, if $v \notin dom(\rho)$
- $[v{:}g, \rho, \sigma] \to {}_{\rho_0}[\mathrm{E}, \rho, \bot_\Sigma]$, if $v \notin dom(\rho)$.

We next define $\mathbb{P}_O$ and $\mathcal{O}$ for $\mathcal{L}_{fun}$. In this definition, the transition relation $\to'_{\rho_0}$ is that of $\mathcal{T}'_{fun}$.

Definition 6.20

(a) $\Sigma_\bot^\infty = \Sigma^* \cup \Sigma^\omega \cup \Sigma^* \cdot \{\bot_\Sigma\}$

(b) $\mathbb{P}_O = Env \to \Sigma_\bot \to \Sigma_\bot^\infty$

(c) $\mathcal{O}{:}\, Env \times SRes \times Env \times \Sigma_\bot \to \Sigma_\bot^\infty$ is the unique function satisfying

$\mathcal{O}(\rho_0 | r, \rho, \sigma) =$

- $\sigma' \cdot \mathcal{O}(\rho_0 | r', \rho', \sigma')$, if $[r, \rho, \sigma] \to'_{\rho_0}[r', \rho', \sigma']$

- ϵ, if $[r, \rho, \sigma] \not\to'_{\rho_0}$, $\sigma \neq \bot_\Sigma$

- $\bot_\Sigma$, if $[r, \rho, \sigma] \not\to'_{\rho_0}$, $\sigma = \bot_\Sigma$.

(d) $\mathcal{O}[\![\cdot]\!]{:}\, \mathcal{L}_{fun} \to \mathbb{P}_O$ is given by

$$\mathcal{O}[\![s]\!] = \lambda\rho.\lambda\sigma.\mathcal{O}(\rho | s{:}\mathrm{E}, \rho, \sigma)\,.$$

Example Suppose $D(f) = \lambda(v_1, v_2).v_1 * v_2$, $\rho(v) = a$, $\rho(w) = a'$, $\sigma(a) = 1$ and '$\hat{+}$', '$\hat{*}$' the interpretations of $+, * \in Constr$.

$\mathcal{O}[\![v := f(v, (w := 1; w + w))]\!](\rho)(\sigma)$

$= \mathcal{O}(\rho \mid v := f(v, (w := 1; w + w)){:}\mathrm{E}, \rho, \sigma)$

$= \mathcal{O}(\rho \mid f(v, (w := 1; w + w)){:}\lambda\alpha.\mathrm{E}\langle a \leftarrow \alpha\rangle, \rho, \sigma)$

$= \sigma \cdot \mathcal{O}\Big(\rho \mid v{:}\lambda\alpha_1.\big((w := 1; w + w){:}\lambda\alpha_2.$
$\qquad\quad \big(set(\rho\{a_1/v_1, a_2/v_2\}, \lambda\bar{\sigma}.\bar{\sigma}\{\alpha_1/a_1, \alpha_2/a_2\}){:}$
$\qquad\qquad (v_1 * v_2{:}\lambda\beta.(set(\rho){:}\mathrm{E}\langle a \leftarrow \beta\rangle))))\big), \rho, \sigma\Big)$

$= [\sigma(\rho(v)) = 1]$
$\quad \sigma \cdot \sigma \cdot \mathcal{O}\Big(\rho \mid 1{:}\lambda\alpha_1.\big((w := 1; w + w){:}\lambda\alpha_2.$
$\qquad\quad \big(set(\rho\{a_1/v_1, a_2/v_2\}, \lambda\bar{\sigma}.\bar{\sigma}\{\alpha_1/a_1, \alpha_2/a_2\}){:}$
$\qquad\qquad (v_1 * v_2{:}\lambda\beta.(set(\rho){:}\mathrm{E}\langle a \leftarrow \beta\rangle))))\big), \rho, \sigma\Big)$

$= \sigma^2 \cdot \mathcal{O}(\rho \mid (w := 1; w + w){:}\lambda\alpha_2.$
$\qquad \big(set(\rho\{a_1/v_1, a_2/v_2\}, \lambda\bar{\sigma}.\bar{\sigma}\{1/a_1, \alpha_2/a_2\}){:}$
$\qquad\quad (v_1 * v_2{:}\lambda\beta.(set(\rho){:}\mathrm{E}\langle a \leftarrow \beta\rangle))), \rho, \sigma)$

$= \sigma^2 \cdot \mathcal{O}\Big(\rho \mid w := 1{:}\big((w + w){:}\lambda\alpha_2.$
$\qquad \big(set(\rho\{a_1/v_1, a_2/v_2\}, \lambda\bar{\sigma}.\bar{\sigma}\{1/a_1, \alpha_2/a_2\}){:}$
$\qquad\quad (v_1 * v_2{:}\lambda\beta.(set(\rho){:}\mathrm{E}\langle a \leftarrow \beta\rangle)))\big), \rho, \sigma\Big)$

$= [\rho(w) = a']$
$\quad \sigma^2 \cdot \mathcal{O}\Big(\rho \mid 1{:}\lambda a'.\big((w + w){:}\lambda\alpha_2.$
$\qquad \big(set(\rho\{a_1/v_1, a_2/v_2\}, \lambda\bar{\sigma}.\bar{\sigma}\{1/a_1, \alpha_2/a_2\}){:}$
$\qquad\quad (v_1 * v_2{:}\lambda\beta.(set(\rho){:}\mathrm{E}\langle a \leftarrow \beta\rangle)))\big)\langle a' \leftarrow \alpha'\rangle, \rho, \sigma\Big)$

$= \sigma^2 \cdot \mathcal{O}\Big(\rho \mid \big((w + w){:}\lambda\alpha_2.$
$\qquad \big(set(\rho\{a_1/v_1, a_2/v_2\}, \lambda\bar{\sigma}.\bar{\sigma}\{1/a_1, \alpha_2/a_2\}){:}$
$\qquad\quad (v_1 * v_2{:}\lambda\beta.(set(\rho){:}\mathrm{E}\langle a \leftarrow \beta\rangle)))\big)\langle a' \leftarrow 1\rangle, \rho, \sigma\Big)$

$= \sigma^2 \cdot \sigma\{1/a'\} \cdot \mathcal{O}(\rho \mid (w + w){:}\lambda\alpha_2.$
$\qquad \big(set(\rho\{a_1/v_1, a_2/v_2\}, \lambda\bar{\sigma}.\bar{\sigma}\{1/a_1, \alpha_2/a_2\}){:}$
$\qquad\quad (v_1 * v_2{:}\lambda\beta.(set(\rho){:}\mathrm{E}\langle a \leftarrow \beta\rangle))), \rho, \sigma\{1/a'\})$

$$= \ldots$$

$$= \sigma^2 \cdot \sigma\{1/a'\}^3 \cdot \mathcal{O}(\rho \mid 2{:}\lambda\alpha_2.$$
$$\big(set(\rho\{a_1/v_1, a_2/v_2\}, \lambda\bar{\sigma}.\bar{\sigma}\{1/a_1, \alpha_2/a_2\}){:}$$
$$(v_1 * v_2{:}\lambda\beta.(set(\rho){:}\mathrm{E}\langle a \leftarrow \beta\rangle)))\big), \rho, \sigma\{1/a'\})$$

$$= \sigma^2 \cdot \sigma\{1/a'\}^3 \cdot \mathcal{O}(\rho \mid$$
$$\big(set(\rho\{a_1/v_1, a_2/v_2\}, \lambda\bar{\sigma}.\bar{\sigma}\{1/a_1, 2/a_2\}){:}$$
$$(v_1 * v_2{:}\lambda\beta.(set(\rho){:}\mathrm{E}\langle a \leftarrow \beta\rangle)))\big), \rho, \sigma\{1/a'\})$$

$$= \sigma^2 \cdot \sigma\{1/a'\}^3 \cdot \mathcal{O}(\rho \mid$$
$$(v_1 * v_2{:}\lambda\beta.(set(\rho){:}\mathrm{E}\langle a \leftarrow \beta\rangle)),$$
$$\rho\{a_1/v_1, a_2/v_2\}, \sigma\{1/a', 1/a_1, 2/a_2\})$$

$$= \ldots$$

$$= \sigma^2 \cdot \sigma\{1/a'\}^3 \cdot \sigma\{1/a', 1/a_1, 2/a_2\}^2 \cdot \mathcal{O}(\rho \mid$$
$$(set(\rho){:}\mathrm{E}\langle a \leftarrow 2\rangle)), \rho\{a_1/v_1, a_2/v_2\}, \sigma\{1/a', 1/a_1, 2/a_2\})$$

$$= \sigma^2 \cdot \sigma\{1/a'\}^3 \cdot \sigma\{1/a', 1/a_1, 2/a_2\}^2 \cdot \mathcal{O}(\rho \mid$$
$$\mathrm{E}\langle a \leftarrow 2\rangle, \rho, \sigma\{1/a', 1/a_1, 2/a_2\})$$

$$= \sigma^2 \cdot \sigma\{1/a'\}^3 \cdot \sigma\{1/a', 1/a_1, 2/a_2\}^2 \cdot \sigma\{1/a', 1/a_1, 2/a_2, 2/a\}.$$

6.2.2 Denotational semantics, equivalence of $\mathcal{O}$ and $\mathcal{D}$

The definition of the denotational semantics $\mathcal{D}$ for *Stat* will use the denotational semantics $\mathcal{V}$ for *Exp* and vice versa. For this reason, $\mathcal{D}$ and $\mathcal{V}$ will be defined as the *simultaneous* fixed point of a higher-order mapping in two arguments.

Let $\mathbb{P}_D = \mathbb{P}_O$. In the definition of $\mathcal{D}, \mathcal{V}$, continuations play, once again, a crucial role. For statements, we shall use statement continuations $(\gamma \in) SCont = \mathbb{P}_D$, and for expressions we use expression continuations $(\kappa \in) ECont = Val \rightarrow \mathbb{P}_D$. The former will correspond to the $r \in SRes$, the latter to the $g \in ERes$. Let $\gamma_\epsilon = \lambda\rho.\lambda\sigma.$if $\sigma = \bot_\Sigma$ then $\bot_\Sigma$ else ϵ fi, and $\kappa_\epsilon = \lambda\alpha.\gamma_\epsilon$ be the respective nil-continuations.

Definition 6.21

(a) Let

$$
\begin{aligned}
(S \in) SSem_D &= Env \times Stat \rightarrow SCont \xrightarrow{1} \mathbb{P}_D \\
(T \in) ESem_D &= Env \times Exp \rightarrow ECont \xrightarrow{1} \mathbb{P}_D .
\end{aligned}
$$

We shall define the mapping $\Psi\colon SSem_D \times ESem_D \to SSem_D \times ESem_D$ by supplying the various argument cases for $\Psi(S,T)$. Let us put, for brevity, $\Psi(S,T) = (\hat{S}, \hat{T})$. Thus, $\hat{S} \in SSem_D$, $\hat{T} \in ESem_D$. In the various clauses for $\hat{S}, \hat{T}$, we shall not only suppress the declarations D, but also the (initial) environment ρ_0. Moreover, we shall use $\gamma\langle a \leftarrow \alpha\rangle$ as abbreviation for the statement continuation which handles the assignment of α to a, i.e., as short-hand for $\lambda\rho.\lambda\sigma.\sigma\{\alpha/a\} \cdot \gamma(\rho)(\sigma\{\alpha/a\})$. We now list the various cases for $\hat{S}, \hat{T}$:

$$
\begin{aligned}
\hat{S}(v := e)(\gamma)(\rho) &= \lambda\sigma.\text{if } (\sigma = \perp_\Sigma) \vee v \notin dom(\rho) \text{ then } \perp_\Sigma \text{ else}\\
&\qquad \hat{T}(e)(\lambda\alpha.\gamma\langle\rho(v) \leftarrow \alpha\rangle)(\rho)(\sigma) \text{ fi}\\
\hat{S}(s_1;s_2)(\gamma)(\rho) &= \hat{S}(s_1)(\hat{S}(s_2)(\gamma))(\rho)
\end{aligned}
$$

and

$$
\begin{aligned}
\hat{T}(\alpha)(\kappa)(\rho) &= \kappa(\alpha)(\rho)\\
\hat{T}(v)(\kappa)(\rho) &= \lambda\sigma.\text{if } (\sigma = \perp_\Sigma) \vee (v \notin dom(\rho)) \text{ then } \perp_\Sigma \text{ else}\\
&\qquad \sigma \cdot \kappa(\sigma(\rho(v)))(\rho)(\sigma) \text{ fi}\\
\hat{T}(u(e_1,e_2))(\kappa)(\rho) &= \hat{T}(e_1)(\lambda\alpha_1.\hat{T}(e_2)(\lambda\alpha_2.\kappa(\hat{u}(\alpha_1,\alpha_2))))(\rho)\\
\hat{T}(f(e_1,e_2))(\kappa)(\rho) &=
\end{aligned}
$$

$$
\begin{aligned}
&\lambda\sigma.\text{if } \sigma = \perp_\Sigma \text{ then } \perp_\Sigma \text{ else } \sigma \cdot \hat{T}(e_1)\big(\lambda\alpha_1.\hat{T}(e_2)\big(\lambda\alpha_2.\lambda\bar{\rho}.\lambda\bar{\sigma}.\\
&\quad T(e)(\lambda\beta.\lambda\bar{\bar{\rho}}.\kappa(\beta)(\rho))(\rho_0\{a_1/v_1, a_2/v_2\})\\
&\quad (\bar{\sigma}\{\alpha_1/a_1, \alpha_2/a_2\})\big)\big)(\rho)(\sigma) \text{ fi}
\end{aligned}
$$

where ρ_0 is the initial environment, $D(f) = \lambda(v_1, v_2).e$,
a_1, a_2 are (the first) fresh addresses from $Addr \setminus cod(\rho_0)$

$$
\begin{aligned}
\hat{T}(\text{if } e \text{ then } e_1 \text{ else } e_2 \text{ fi})(\kappa)(\rho) &\\
&= \hat{T}(e)(\lambda\beta.\text{if } \beta \text{ then } \hat{T}(e_1)(\kappa) \text{ else } \hat{T}(e_2)(\kappa) \text{ fi})(\rho)\\
\hat{T}(s;e)(\kappa)(\rho) &= \hat{S}(s)(\hat{T}(e)(\kappa))(\rho).
\end{aligned}
$$

(b) $(\mathcal{D}, \mathcal{V}) = fix(\Psi)$, $\mathcal{D}[\![s]\!] = \lambda\rho.\lambda\sigma.\mathcal{D}(\rho, s)(\gamma_\epsilon)(\rho)(\sigma)$.

We draw attention to a few points of explanation concerning this definition.

(1) All but one of the clauses express $\hat{S}(s)$ and $\hat{T}(e)$ in terms of either given entities, or of $\hat{S}(s')$ and $\hat{T}(e')$ for s', e' which are syntactically simpler than s, e. The only exception is the clause for $f(e_1, e_2)$ where the meaning of the body e (associated with f through D) is invoked. Note carefully that we use here $T(e)$ rather than $\hat{T}(e)$. (Cf. our earlier use, e.g., in Definition 1.40, of $\Psi(S)(s_1);S(s_2)$ rather than of $\Psi(S)(s_1);\Psi(S)(s_2)$.)

(2) In two clauses, we check whether a variable (say v) has been declared, viz. whether $v \in dom(\rho)$. If not, we deliver '$\perp_\Sigma$' as outcome.

(3) The clauses follow closely the operational rules from $\mathcal{T}_{fun}$. This is especially facilitated by the correspondence between the syntactic resumptions and the semantic continuations.

(4) The rule for $v := e$—for given γ, ρ—may be understood as follows: Assuming $v \in dom(\rho)$, $a = \rho(v)$, we evaluate e and the result α is assigned to a, as expressed by the updated continuation $\gamma\langle a \leftarrow \alpha\rangle$.

(5) The clauses for $(s_1;s_2)$ and $(s;e)$ are standard applications of the continuation mechanism.

(6) The clause for the conditional expression specifies that e is evaluated first and, depending upon the outcome, the execution continues with that of e_1 or e_2.

(7) The value of α for expression continuation κ is simply $\kappa(\alpha)$. The value of v for given κ, ρ and $\sigma(\neq \perp_\Sigma)$ is determined as follows: If $v \in dom(\rho)$, $a = \rho(v)$ then a skip step is performed, delivering σ. Next, the evaluation is continued with $\kappa(\sigma(a))(\rho)(\sigma)$. If $v \notin dom(\rho)$ or $\sigma = \perp_\Sigma$ then '$\perp_\Sigma$' is delivered.

(8) The clause for $u(e_1, e_2)$ follows the transition rule from $\mathcal{T}_{fun}$ for this case. The reader should keep in mind here the correspondence between the $\alpha{:}g$ construct in the operational, and the $\kappa(\alpha)$ entity in the denotational model.

(9) The construct $f(e_1, e_2)$ is treated as follows (for given κ, ρ, $\sigma \neq \perp_\Sigma$):

  • A skip step, resulting in σ, is delivered, after which

  • The arguments e_1, e_2 are evaluated in the order as given (in the environment ρ and state σ), resulting in the values α_1, α_2

  • The body e of f is evaluated in the initial environment ρ_0, with v_1, v_2 set to the fresh addresses a_1, a_2, and the then current state $\bar{\sigma}$ with a_1, a_2 set to α_1, α_2, respectively

  • The first step of the continuation for e is to reset the environment to the (current) ρ.

After this informal explanation, we present the formal justification of the definition of $(\mathcal{D}, \mathcal{V})$ in

Lemma 6.22 Let $(\hat{S}, \hat{T}) = \Psi(S, T)$ be as in Definition 6.21. Then

(a) $\hat{S}(s)$ is $\frac{1}{2}$-contractive (in γ).

(b) $\hat{T}(e)$ *is nonexpansive (in κ).*

(c) Ψ *is $\frac{1}{2}$-contractive (in (S,T)).*

Proof

(a,b) The proofs are standard—for $\hat{S}(s)$ ultimately relying on the $\lambda\sigma.\sigma\{\}\cdot\gamma(\cdot)$ step in the clause for the assignment statement—and omitted.

(c) We use simultaneous induction on the complexity of (s,e), and we only discuss the subcase $f(e_1, e_2)$. For easier notation, we simplify this case to $f(e_1)$, leaving the full case as an exercise. Choose some κ, ρ, $\sigma \neq \perp_\Sigma$. We use ultrametricity in the usual way and obtain

$$d(\hat{T}_1(f(e_1))(\kappa)(\rho)(\sigma), \hat{T}_2(f(e_1))(\kappa)(\rho)(\sigma))$$

$= $ [writing $(-)$ for arguments not depending on T_1, T_2]
$$d(\sigma\cdot\hat{T}_1(e_1)(\lambda\alpha_1.T_1(e)(-))(\rho)(\sigma), \sigma\cdot\hat{T}_2(e_1)(\lambda\alpha_1.T_2(e)(-))(\rho)(\sigma))$$

$\leq$ [prop. d, ultrametricity] $\frac{1}{2} max\{$
$$d(\hat{T}_1(e_1)(\lambda\alpha_1.T_1(e)(-))(\rho)(\sigma), \hat{T}_1(e_1)(\lambda\alpha_1.T_2(e)(-))(\rho)(\sigma)),$$
$$d(\hat{T}_1(e_1)(\lambda\alpha_1.T_2(e)(-))(\rho)(\sigma), \hat{T}_2(e_1)(\lambda\alpha_1.T_2(e)(-))(\rho)(\sigma))\,\}$$

$\leq$ [part (b), ind. hyp. for e_1]
$$\tfrac{1}{2} max\{\, d(\lambda\alpha_1.T_1(e)(-), \lambda\alpha_1.T_2(e)(-)), \tfrac{1}{2}\cdot d(T_1, T_2)\,\}$$

$\leq \frac{1}{2}d(T_1, T_2)\,.$ $\qquad\qquad\square$

Example

$$\mathcal{D}[\![v := f(v, (w := 1; w + w))]\!](\rho)(\sigma)$$

$$= \mathcal{D}(v := f(v, (w := 1; w + w)))(\gamma_\epsilon)(\rho)(\sigma)$$

$$= \mathcal{V}(f(v, (w := 1; w + w)))(\lambda\alpha.\gamma_\epsilon\langle a \leftarrow \alpha\rangle)(\rho)(\sigma)$$

$$= \sigma\cdot\mathcal{V}(v)\big(\lambda\alpha_1.\mathcal{V}(w := 1; w + w)$$
$$\big(\lambda\alpha_2.\lambda\bar{\rho}.\lambda\bar{\sigma}.\mathcal{V}(v_1 * v_2)(\lambda\beta.\lambda\bar{\bar{\rho}}.\gamma_\epsilon\langle a \leftarrow \beta\rangle(\rho))$$
$$(\rho\{a_1/v_1, a_2/v_2\})(\bar{\sigma}\{\alpha_1/a_1, \alpha_2/a_2\})))\big)(\rho)(\sigma)$$

$$= \sigma\cdot\sigma\cdot\mathcal{V}(w := 1; w + w)$$
$$\big(\lambda\alpha_2.\lambda\bar{\rho}.\lambda\bar{\sigma}.\mathcal{V}(v_1 * v_2)(\lambda\beta.\lambda\bar{\bar{\rho}}.\gamma_\epsilon\langle a \leftarrow \beta\rangle(\rho))$$
$$(\rho\{a_1/v_1, a_2/v_2\})(\bar{\sigma}\{1/a_1, \alpha_2/a_2\}))(\rho)(\sigma)$$

$$= \sigma^2\cdot\mathcal{D}(w := 1)$$

$$\big(\mathcal{V}(w+w)\big(\lambda\alpha_2.\lambda\bar{\rho}.\lambda\bar{\sigma}.\mathcal{V}(v_1 * v_2)(\lambda\beta.\lambda\bar{\bar{\rho}}.\gamma_\epsilon\langle a \leftarrow \beta\rangle(\rho))$$
$$(\rho\{a_1/v_1, a_2/v_2\})(\bar{\sigma}\{1/a_1, \alpha_2/a_2\})))\big)(\rho)(\sigma)$$

$$= \sigma^2 \cdot \sigma\{1/a'\} \cdot \mathcal{V}(w+w)$$
$$\big(\lambda\alpha_2.\lambda\bar{\rho}.\lambda\bar{\sigma}.\mathcal{V}(v_1 * v_2)(\lambda\beta.\lambda\bar{\bar{\rho}}.\gamma_\epsilon\langle a \leftarrow \beta\rangle(\rho))$$
$$(\rho\{a_1/v_1, a_2/v_2\})(\bar{\sigma}\{1/a_1, \alpha_2/a_2\}))\big)(\rho)(\sigma\{1/a'\})$$

$$= \ldots$$

$$= \sigma^2 \cdot \sigma\{1/a'\}^3 \cdot \mathcal{V}(2)$$
$$\big(\lambda\alpha_2.\lambda\bar{\rho}.\lambda\bar{\sigma}.\mathcal{V}(v_1 * v_2)(\lambda\beta.\lambda\bar{\bar{\rho}}.\gamma_\epsilon\langle a \leftarrow \beta\rangle(\rho))$$
$$(\rho\{a_1/v_1, a_2/v_2\})(\bar{\sigma}\{1/a_1, \alpha_2/a_2\}))\big)(\rho)(\sigma\{1/a'\})$$

$$= \sigma^2 \cdot \sigma\{1/a'\}^3 \cdot \mathcal{V}(v_1 * v_2)(\lambda\beta.\lambda\bar{\bar{\rho}}.\gamma_\epsilon\langle a \leftarrow \beta\rangle(\rho))$$
$$(\rho\{a_1/v_1, a_2/v_2\})(\sigma\{1/a', 1/a_1, 2/a_2\})$$

$$= \ldots$$

$$= \sigma^2 \cdot \sigma\{1/a'\}^3 \cdot \sigma\{1/a', 1/a_1, 2/a_2\}^2 \cdot$$
$$\mathcal{V}(2)(\lambda\beta.\lambda\bar{\bar{\rho}}.\gamma_\epsilon\langle a \leftarrow \beta\rangle(\rho))(\rho\{a_1/v_1, a_2/v_2\})(\sigma\{1/a', 1/a_1, 2/a_2\})$$

$$= \sigma^2 \cdot \sigma\{1/a'\}^3 \cdot \sigma\{1/a', 1/a_1, 2/a_2\}^2 \cdot$$
$$(\gamma_\epsilon\langle a \leftarrow 2\rangle))(\rho)(\sigma\{1/a', 1/a_1, 2/a_2\})$$

$$= \sigma^2 \cdot \sigma\{1/a'\}^3 \cdot \sigma\{1/a', 1/a_1, 2/a_2\}^2 \cdot \sigma\{1/a', 1/a_1, 2/a_2, 2/a\}.$$

We are now ready for the discussion which establishes the usual equivalence result for $\mathcal{O}$ and $\mathcal{D}$. First of all, we introduce the weight function for $\mathcal{L}_{fun}$.

Definition 6.23 $wgt: SRes \cup ERes \cup Stat \cup Exp \to \mathbb{N}$ is given by

(a) $wgt(\text{E}) = 0$
$wgt(s{:}r) = wgt(s) + wgt(r)$
$wgt(\text{if } \alpha \text{ then } r_1 \text{ else } r_2 \text{ fi}) = max\{ wgt(r_1), wgt(r_2) \} + 1$
$wgt(e{:}g) = wgt(e) + wgt(g)$
$wgt(r\langle a \leftarrow \alpha\rangle) = 1 + wgt(r)$
$wgt(\phi{:}r) = 1 + wgt(r)$

(b) $wgt(\lambda\alpha.r) = wgt(r)$

(c) $wgt(v := e) = wgt(e) + 2$
$wgt(s_1;s_2) = wgt(s_1) + wgt(s_2) + 1$

(d) $wgt(\alpha) = 1$
      $wgt(v) = 1$
      $wgt(u(e_1, e_2)) = wgt(e_1) + wgt(e_2) + 2$
      $wgt(f(e_1, e_2)) = 1$
      $wgt(\text{if } e \text{ then } e_1 \text{ else } e_2 \text{ fi}) = wgt(e_1) + 1 + max\{\, wgt(e_1), wgt(e_2)\,\} + 1$
      $wgt(s;e) = wgt(s) + wgt(e) + 1$

Note that, by this definition, $wgt(r[\bar{\alpha}/\alpha]) = wgt(r)$.

The definition of wgt has been designed such that the following lemma holds:

Lemma 6.24   *If* $r_1 \rightarrow_{0,\rho_0} r_2$, *then* $wgt(r_1) > wgt(r_2)$.

Proof   Four subcases.

$[(v := e):r]$ Choose some ρ, and let $a = \rho(v)$. We have

$$
\begin{aligned}
& wgt((v := e):r) \\
=\ & wgt(v := e) + wgt(r) \\
=\ & wgt(e) + 2 + wgt(r) \\
=\ & wgt(e) + 1 + wgt(r\langle a \leftarrow \alpha\rangle) \\
>\ & wgt(e) + wgt(r\langle a \leftarrow \alpha\rangle) \\
=\ & wgt(e{:}\lambda\alpha.r\langle a \leftarrow \alpha\rangle).
\end{aligned}
$$

$[\alpha{:}\lambda\beta.r]$ $wgt(\alpha{:}\lambda\beta.r)$

$$
\begin{aligned}
=\ & 1 + wgt(\lambda\beta.r) \\
=\ & 1 + wgt(r) \\
>\ & wgt(r) \\
=\ & wgt(r[\alpha/\beta]).
\end{aligned}
$$

$[\text{if } e \text{ then } e_1 \text{ else } e_2 \text{ fi}{:}g]$ $wgt(\text{if } e \text{ then } e_1 \text{ else } e_2 \text{ fi}{:}g)$

$$
\begin{aligned}
=\ & wgt(\text{if } e \text{ then } e_1 \text{ else } e_2 \text{ fi}) + wgt(g) \\
=\ & wgt(e) + 1 + max\{\, wgt(e_1), wgt(e_2)\,\} + 1 + wgt(g) \\
>\ & wgt(e) + max\{\, wgt(e_1{:}g), wgt(e_2{:}g)\,\} + 1 \\
=\ & wgt(e{:}\lambda\alpha.(\text{if } \alpha \text{ then } e_1{:}g \text{ else } e_2{:}g \text{ fi})).
\end{aligned}
$$

$[u(e_1, e_2){:}g]$ $wgt(u(e_1, e_2){:}g)$

$$
\begin{aligned}
=\ & wgt(e_1) + wgt(e_2) + 2 + wgt(g) \\
>\ & wgt(e_1) + wgt(e_2) + 1 + wgt(g) \\
=\ & wgt(e_1{:}\lambda\alpha_1.(e_2{:}\lambda\alpha_2.(\hat{u}(\alpha_1, \alpha_2){:}g))),
\end{aligned}
$$

since $\hat{u}(\alpha_1, \alpha_2) \in Val$, hence $wgt(\hat{u}(\alpha_1, \alpha_2)) = 1$. $\square$

Next, we introduce two intermediate semantics which will serve to link $\mathcal{O}$ and $\mathcal{D}$. The mappings $\mathcal{E}$ and $\mathcal{F}$ assign meanings to the two kinds of resumptions:

$$\mathcal{E}: Env \times SRes \rightarrow \mathbb{P}_O$$
$$\mathcal{F}: Env \times ERes \rightarrow Val \rightarrow \mathbb{P}_O$$

They are given—suppressing the ρ_0-argument as usual—by

Definition 6.25

(a)
$$\mathcal{E}(\mathrm{E}) = \gamma_\epsilon$$
$$\mathcal{E}(s{:}r) = \mathcal{D}(s)(\mathcal{E}(r))$$
$$\mathcal{E}(\text{if } \alpha \text{ then } r_1 \text{ else } r_2 \text{ fi})$$
$$\qquad = \text{if } \alpha \text{ then } \mathcal{E}(r_1) \text{ else } \mathcal{E}(r_2) \text{ fi}$$
$$\mathcal{E}(e{:}g) = \mathcal{V}(e)(\mathcal{F}(g))$$
$$\mathcal{E}(r\langle a \leftarrow \alpha \rangle) = \mathcal{E}(r)\langle a \leftarrow \alpha \rangle \qquad (\text{cf. Definition 6.21a})$$
$$\mathcal{E}(\phi{:}r) = \lambda\rho.\lambda\sigma.\mathcal{E}(r)(\rho')(\sigma') \text{ where } (\rho', \sigma') = \phi(\rho, \sigma)$$

(b) $\mathcal{F}(\lambda\alpha.r) = \lambda\alpha.\mathcal{E}(r)$.

In a moment, we shall show that $\mathcal{E}^*$—the usual variation on $\mathcal{E}$—satisfies the defining equation for $\mathcal{O}$. First, we establish the customary

Lemma 6.26

(a) If $[r_1, \rho, \sigma] \rightarrow_{0,\rho_0} [r_2, \rho, \sigma]$ then $\mathcal{E}(r_1)(\rho)(\sigma) = \mathcal{E}(r_2)(\rho)(\sigma)$.

(b) If $[r_1, \rho_1, \sigma_1] \rightarrow_{\rho_0} [r_2, \rho_2, \sigma_2]$ then $\mathcal{E}(r_1)(\rho_1)(\sigma_1) = \sigma_2 \cdot \mathcal{E}(r_2)(\rho_2)(\sigma_2)$.

Proof

(a) Two subcases.

$[(v := e){:}r]$ Choose some ρ, and assume $v \in dom(\rho)$, $a = \rho(v)$. Then
$$\mathcal{E}((v := e){:}r)(\rho)$$
$$= \mathcal{D}(v := e)(\mathcal{E}(r))(\rho)$$
$$= \mathcal{V}(e)(\lambda\alpha.(\mathcal{E}(r)\langle a \leftarrow \alpha \rangle))(\rho)$$
$$= \mathcal{V}(e)(\lambda\alpha.\mathcal{E}(r\langle a \leftarrow \alpha \rangle))(\rho)$$
$$= \mathcal{V}(e)(\mathcal{F}(\lambda\alpha.r\langle a \leftarrow \alpha \rangle))(\rho)$$
$$= \mathcal{E}(e{:}\lambda\alpha.r\langle a \leftarrow \alpha \rangle)(\rho) .$$

$[u(e_1, e_2)]$ We leave as an exercise the proof of $\mathcal{E}(\beta{:}g) = \mathcal{F}(g)(\beta)$. This is used in the following calculation:

$\mathcal{E}(u(e_1, e_2){:}g)$
$= \mathcal{V}(u(e_1, e_2))(\mathcal{F}(g))$
$= \mathcal{V}(e_1)(\lambda\alpha_1.\mathcal{V}(e_2)(\lambda\alpha_2.\mathcal{F}(g)(\hat{u}(\alpha_1, \alpha_2))))$
$= \mathcal{V}(e_1)(\lambda\alpha_1.\mathcal{V}(e_2)(\lambda\alpha_2.\mathcal{E}(\hat{u}(\alpha_1, \alpha_2){:}g)))$
$= \mathcal{V}(e_1)(\lambda\alpha_1.\mathcal{E}(e_2{:}\lambda\alpha_2.\hat{u}(\alpha_1, \alpha_2){:}g))$
$= \mathcal{E}(e_1{:}\lambda\alpha_1.(e_2{:}\lambda\alpha_2.\hat{u}(\alpha_1, \alpha_2){:}g))\,.$

(b) One subcase.

$[f(e_1, e_2){:}\lambda\beta.r]$ Choose some $\rho, \sigma \neq \perp_\Sigma$, let ρ_0 be the initial environment, and let $D(f) = \lambda(v_1, v_2).e$. For simplicity in notation, we restrict the number of parameters of f to one. We have

$\mathcal{E}(f(e_1){:}\lambda\beta.r)(\rho)(\sigma)$
$= \mathcal{V}(f(e_1))(\mathcal{F}(\lambda\beta.r))(\rho)(\sigma)$
$= [a = \rho(v)]$
$\quad \sigma \cdot \mathcal{V}(e_1)(\lambda\alpha_1.\lambda\bar{\rho}.\lambda\bar{\sigma}.\mathcal{V}(e)$
$\qquad (\lambda\beta.\lambda\bar{\bar{\rho}}.\mathcal{F}(\lambda\beta.r)(\beta)(\rho))(\rho_0\{a_1/v_1\})(\bar{\sigma}\{\alpha_1/a_1\}))(\rho)(\sigma)$

We also have

$\mathcal{E}(e_1{:}\lambda\alpha_1.(set(\rho_0\{a_1/v_1\}, \lambda\bar{\sigma}.\bar{\sigma}\{\alpha_1/a_1\}){:}(e{:}\lambda\beta.(set(\rho){:}r))))(\rho)(\sigma)$
$= \mathcal{V}(e_1)(\mathcal{F}(\lambda\alpha_1.(set(\rho_0\{a_1/v_1\}, \lambda\bar{\sigma}.\bar{\sigma}\{\alpha_1/a_1\}){:}$
$\qquad (e{:}\lambda\beta.(set(\rho){:}r)))))(\rho)(\sigma)$
$= \mathcal{V}(e_1)(\lambda\alpha_1.\mathcal{E}(set(\rho_0\{a_1/v_1\}, \lambda\bar{\sigma}.\bar{\sigma}\{\alpha_1/a_1\}){:}$
$\qquad (e{:}\lambda\beta.(set(\rho){:}r))))(\rho)(\sigma)\,.$

In order to prove the claim of (b) for this case, it is therefore sufficient to show the equality of (6.3) and (6.4) for each ρ:

$$\lambda\bar{\rho}.\lambda\bar{\sigma}.\mathcal{V}(e)(\lambda\beta.\lambda\bar{\bar{\rho}}.\mathcal{E}(r)(\rho))(\rho_0\{a_1/v_1\}, \bar{\sigma}\{\alpha_1/a_1\}) \qquad (6.3)$$

$$\lambda\bar{\rho}.\lambda\bar{\sigma}.\mathcal{E}(set(\rho_0\{a_1/v_1\}, \lambda\bar{\bar{\sigma}}.\bar{\sigma}\{\alpha_1/a_1\}){:}(e{:}\lambda\beta.(set(\rho){:}r)))\,. \qquad (6.4)$$

Applying the various definitions, especially of $set(\rho, \psi)$, the desired result now easily follows. $\square$

Finally, let Φ be the higher-order mapping defining $\mathcal{O}$, and let $\mathcal{E}^*(r, \rho, \sigma) \overset{df}{=} \mathcal{E}(r)(\rho)(\sigma)$. We shall prove

Lemma 6.27 $\Phi(\mathcal{E}^*)(r, \rho, \sigma) = \mathcal{E}^*(r, \rho, \sigma)$.

Proof Induction on $wgt(r)$. Choose $\rho, \sigma \neq \perp_\Sigma$ where necessary (and assume all variables declared, $a = \rho(v)$ where relevant). Three subcases.

$[(v := e){:}r]$ $\Phi(\mathcal{E}^*)((v := e){:}r, \rho, \sigma)$

$= \quad$ [def. $\mathcal{T}_{fun}$] $\Phi(\mathcal{E}^*)(e{:}\lambda\alpha.(r\langle a\leftarrow\alpha\rangle),\rho,\sigma)$

$= \quad$ [ind. hyp.] $\mathcal{E}^*(e{:}\lambda\alpha.(r\langle a\leftarrow\alpha\rangle),\rho,\sigma)$

$= \quad$ [Lemma 6.26] $\mathcal{E}^*((v:=e){:}r,\rho,\sigma)$.

$[v{:}g] \qquad \Phi(\mathcal{E}^*)(v{:}g,\rho,\sigma)$

$= \quad$ [def. $\mathcal{T}_{fun}$] $\sigma\cdot\mathcal{E}^*(\sigma(a){:}g,\rho,\sigma)$

$= \quad$ [def. $\mathcal{E}^*$] $\sigma\cdot\mathcal{V}(\sigma(a))(\mathcal{F}(g))(\rho)(\sigma)$

$= \quad$ [def. $\mathcal{V}$] $\sigma\cdot\mathcal{F}(g)(\sigma(a))(\rho)(\sigma)$

$= \quad$ [def. $\mathcal{V}$] $\mathcal{V}(v)(\mathcal{F}(g))(\rho)(\sigma)$

$= \quad$ [def. $\mathcal{E}^*$] $\mathcal{E}^*(v{:}g,\rho,\sigma)$.

$[f(e_1,e_2){:}\lambda\beta.r]$ Let $D(f)=\lambda(v_1,v_2).e$, and let ρ_0 be as usual.

$\quad \Phi(\mathcal{E}^*)(f(e_1,e_2){:}\lambda\beta.r,\rho,\sigma)$

$= \quad$ [def. $\mathcal{T}_{fun}$]

$\quad \sigma\cdot\mathcal{E}^*(e_1{:}\lambda\alpha_1.(e_2{:}\lambda\alpha_2.(set(\rho_0\{\},\lambda\bar\sigma.\bar\sigma\{\}){:}(e{:}\lambda\beta.(set(\rho){:}r)))),\rho,\sigma)$

$= \quad$ [Lemma 6.26] $\mathcal{E}^*(f(e_1,e_2){:}\lambda\beta.r,\rho,\sigma)$. $\hfill \square$

At last, we have arrived at the main result.

Theorem 6.28 $\mathcal{O}[\![\pi]\!] = \mathcal{D}[\![\pi]\!]$, *for* $\pi\in\mathcal{L}_{fun}$.

Proof Using Lemma 6.27, we have, for each $s\in\mathcal{L}_{fun}$

$\mathcal{O}[\![s]\!]$

$= \lambda\rho.\lambda\sigma.\mathcal{O}(\rho|s{:}\mathrm{E},\rho,\sigma)$

$= \lambda\rho.\lambda\sigma.\mathcal{E}^*(\rho|s{:}\mathrm{E},\rho,\sigma)$

$= \lambda\rho.\lambda\sigma.\mathcal{D}(\rho|s)(\gamma_\epsilon)(\rho)(\sigma)$

$= \mathcal{D}[\![s]\!]$. $\hfill \square$

6.3   Exercises

Exercise 6.1   Discuss the modifications necessary in Section 6.1 to replace the explicit step in the (Rec)-rule by a mechanism with guarded procedure bodies and a zero-step rule of the form

$$\ldots x\ldots \rightarrow_{0,\rho_0} \ldots D(x)\ldots.$$

Consider as well the corresponding changes in the definition of $\mathcal{D}$ for $\mathcal{L}_{block}$.

Exercise 6.2 Discuss the modifications in the semantic design for $\mathcal{L}_{block}$ in case procedures may be declared not only in the outermost block, but in each block of the program.

Exercise 6.3 Let $ivar: Stat \to \mathcal{P}(IVar)$ be the following extension of $ivar$ as given in Definition 6.4: $ivar(v := e)$ is as before,

$ivar(\text{begin var } v; s \text{ end}) = ivar(s)\backslash\{v\}$,

and $ivar(s)$ is defined by syntactic induction on s in the remaining cases. Let $ivar(D|s) = ivar(s) \cup \bigcup\{ ivar(D(x)) \mid x \in PVar\}$. The substitution $s[w/v]$ is defined by syntactic induction on s. All clauses are obvious, but for the case when s is a block:

begin var u; s end$[w/v]$ $=$

— begin var u; s end, if $u \equiv v$

— begin var u; $s[w/v]$ end, if $u \not\equiv v$, $w \not\equiv u$

— begin var $\bar{u}$; $s[\bar{u}/u][w/v]$ end, if $u \not\equiv v$, $w \equiv u$,
$\qquad\qquad\qquad$ for some $\bar{u} \notin ivar(s) \cup \{v, w\}$.

(a) Prove $\mathcal{D}(D|\text{begin var } v; s \text{ end}) = \mathcal{D}(D|\text{begin var } w; s[w/v] \text{ end})$, for $w \notin ivar(s)$.

(b) Assume $ivar(D|s)\backslash\{u\} \subseteq dom(\rho)$, $v, w \notin dom(\rho)$. Prove that

$$\mathcal{D}(D|s[v/u])(\rho\{a/v\}) = \mathcal{D}(D|s[w/v])(\rho\{a/w\}).$$

(c) Discuss the relationship between $\mathcal{D}(D|s)(\rho\{a_1/v\})(\sigma\{\alpha/a_1\})$ and $\mathcal{D}(D|s)(\rho\{a_2/v\})(\sigma\{\alpha/a_2\})$.

Exercise 6.4 Generalize the proof of Lemma 6.22c to the case $f(e_1, e_2)$.

Exercise 6.5 (This exercise assumes knowledge of Section 7.2.) Redesign $\mathcal{T}_{fun}$ such that, instead of resumptions r and g as given in Definition 6.17, it is based on transitions of the following types: $[s_1, \sigma_1] \to [s_2, \sigma_2]$, $[e_1, \sigma_1] \to [e_2, \sigma_2]$ and $[e, \sigma] \to \alpha$.

6.4 Bibliographical notes

The use of environments for individual variables as a tool to handle locality is an
essential ingredient of the original Scott-Strachey style of denotational semantics
and has been used in numerous subsequent semantic studies (cf. the textbooks on
(denotational) semantics mentioned elsewhere in the bibliographical notes). Since
locality induces unbounded nondeterminacy, in a cpo setting continuity problems
arise, as investigated, e.g., in [THM83]. The present metric version of $\mathcal{O}$ and $\mathcal{D}$
for $\mathcal{L}_{block}$, and the proof of their equivalence, have been described here for the
first time. Alternative approaches to the semantics of block structures are, e.g.,
[SRP91, BKPR93a, Hor93a].

Function procedures and parameter mechanisms such as call-by-value are as well
objects of study in a wide variety of classical investigations. The specific approach
adopted in Section 6.2 owes much to the earlier studies of the language POOL.
For example, the method of defining $(\mathcal{D}, \mathcal{V})$ as simultaneous fixed point of some
higher-order mapping goes back to [ABKR89], as does the scheme of evaluating
expressions and passing on their results to expression continuations. The idea of
using in $\mathcal{T}_{fun}$ both statement and expression resumptions stems from [AB88]. An
interesting variation on the way to specify the operational semantics of expressions
is Kahn's natural semantics ([Kah87]).

Another area where the use of metric techniques seems promising is that of
languages manipulating (functions on) *streams*, i.e., possibly infinite sequences of
values which may be specified by recursive equations. In [BK85], a beginning is
made with the study of such constructs (cf. also Section 9.2 for another setting
involving infinite sequences of values).

$\mathcal{L}_{fun}$ is just one representative of a large number of notions belonging to the
functional programming paradigm. Since the emphasis in our book is on control flow
in imperative languages—and related phenomena in logic and concurrent object-
oriented programming—we refrain here from providing further references to this
field. (A few texts will be mentioned in Appendix D on further reading.)

7 Nonuniform Parallelism

In Chapter 4, we have studied uniform parallelism: The languages $\mathcal{L}_{par}$ and $\mathcal{L}_{pc}$ were obtained from $\mathcal{L}_{cf}$ by adding two constructs inducing parallel composition (viz. '$\|$' and $\text{new}(\cdot)$), and the interleaving interpretation of '$\|$' was studied in the framework of compact powerdomains. We now follow a similar route in studying parallelism in a *nonuniform* setting. Our starting point is the language $\mathcal{L}_{wh}$. In Section 7.1, we investigate the language $\mathcal{L}_{svp}$ (with "*svp*" standing for "shared variable parallelism") which results from $\mathcal{L}_{wh}$ by adding the operator '$\|$' to it. In Section 7.2, we vary this by focusing instead on the parallel (or *concurrent*) evaluation of *expressions*. Consider, e.g., an expression $u(e_1, e_2)$. In case the evaluation of e_1 or e_2 exhibits side effects (resulting in changes of the state), it is meaningful to study an interleaved way of evaluating e_1 and e_2, consisting in the arbitrary merge of the steps constituting the evaluation of e_1 and e_2, respectively.

Several new problems arise in the semantic modelling of $\mathcal{L}_{svp}$. The main issue has to do with the fact that the natural definition of $\mathcal{O}$ for $\mathcal{L}_{svp}$ results in a *noncompositional* semantic function: We shall show that it is not possible to define, with respect to this $\mathcal{O}$, a semantic '$\|$' such that $\mathcal{O}(s_1\|s_2) = \mathcal{O}(s_1)\|\mathcal{O}(s_2)$. As a consequence, for $\mathcal{L}_{svp}$ we cannot expect that the—so far—usual equivalence $\mathcal{O} = \mathcal{D}$ holds: By definition, $\mathcal{D}$ *has* to be compositional, and from $\mathcal{O} = \mathcal{D}$ compositionality of $\mathcal{O}$ would then follow, contradicting the just stated fact. Therefore, we shall have to aim for another type of result, where the relationship between $\mathcal{O}$ and $\mathcal{D}$ is not a direct equivalence. Rather, we shall introduce an "abstraction mapping," say *abs*, enabling us to obtain the relationship

$$\mathcal{O} = abs \circ \mathcal{D}. \tag{7.1}$$

Briefly, in order for $\mathcal{D}$ to be compositional, we have to equip the denotational domain $\mathbb{P}_D$ with some more elaborate structure than that of the operational domain $\mathbb{P}_O$. The purpose of the abstraction function then is to delete (i.e., abstract away) the additional structure in order to obtain the $\mathcal{O}$-meaning of a program from its $\mathcal{D}$-meaning.

Focusing on the mathematical details involved in this, it will turn out that, at first sight, the structures employed for $\mathcal{D}$ will be based on the closed powerdomain, whereas the structures for $\mathcal{O}$ will—as usual—be couched in terms of the compact powerdomain. This, in turn, leads to some further questions. Firstly, the definition of the semantic operators will be based on a method which is different from the standard one (the Lifting Lemma or Michael's theorem can now not be invoked). The reader who has studied Section 5.3 will recognize the approach adopted instead. Secondly, in defining the mapping *abs*, we shall see that a simple-minded approach going from the world of closed sets to that of compact sets will not work. Only after identifying a certain kind of restriction on the closed sets used for $\mathbb{P}_D$, will it be possible to formulate a satisfactory definition for *abs*. Another type of finiteness condition will be crucial here. Recall that we have built, so far, on the following two correspondences:

- finitely branching—compact,

  and

- image-finite—closed.

We will now use a third correspondence, expressing an intermediate level result. Briefly, we shall introduce a notion of "locally finitely branching" for the transition system involved, corresponding to the property of "finitary nonempty and closed" on the denotational side. (The latter condition is not a general topological notion, but a slightly ad-hoc strengthening of closedness just serving our present purposes.) Thanks to the fact that we can indeed build our denotational model on the domain of finitary nonempty and closed sets, the relevant definitions can all be justified, and the derivation of (7.1) proceeds more or less along standard lines.

Altogether, the material of Section 7.1 is rather more demanding than that of the previous chapters. Once the reader has comprehended this, Section 7.2 will require little extra effort. It consists essentially of a synthesis of some of the techniques of Section 6.2, dealing with the combined definition of $(\mathcal{D}, \mathcal{V})$ for $(Stat, Exp)$, with the machinery as introduced in Section 7.1.

7.1 Parallel composition with shared variables —relating $\mathcal{O}$ and $\mathcal{D}$ through abstraction

Section 7.1 is devoted to a study of $\mathcal{L}_{svp}$, an extension of $\mathcal{L}_{wh}$ with parallel composition. $\mathcal{L}_{svp}$ assumes a *global* state, shared by all parallel components. For example, in a program $(v := 0; \; w := v + 1)\|(v := 2)$, the variables v, w are shared, and the resulting execution—according to the interleaving interpretation—equals that of any of the three merges

$$
\begin{array}{llll}
v := 0; & w := v + 1; & v := 2 \\
v := 0; & v := 2; & w := v + 1 \\
v := 2; & v := 0; & w := v + 1,
\end{array}
$$

resulting in the final values for (v, w) of (2,1), (2,3) or (0,1), respectively.

(In Chapter 13 (Part III), we shall study a variation on this interpretation where all components in a parallel composition have their own "local" state.)

7.1.1 Syntax and operational semantics

We assume the familiar setting for a nonuniform language, say as for $\mathcal{L}_{wh}$. The syntax for $\mathcal{L}_{svp}$ is given in

Definition 7.1

(a) $s\,(\in Stat) ::= \quad v := e \mid \mathsf{skip} \mid (s;s) \mid \mathsf{if}\ e\ \mathsf{then}\ s\ \mathsf{else}\ s\ \mathsf{fi} \mid$
$\qquad\qquad\qquad \mathsf{while}\ e\ \mathsf{do}\ s\ \mathsf{od} \mid (s\|s)$

(b) $(\pi \in)\,\mathcal{L}_{svp} = Stat$.

The class of resumptions we use in $\mathcal{T}_{svp}$ is simple (cf. the discussion of Res for $\mathcal{T}_{par}$):

Definition 7.2

(a) $r\,(\in Res) ::= \mathrm{E} \mid s$

(b) We identify each of $\mathrm{E};s$, $\mathrm{E}\|s$ and $s\|\mathrm{E}$ with s.

We shall use $(\alpha \in)\,Val$, $(\sigma \in)\,\Sigma = IVar \rightarrow Val$, $\sigma\{\alpha/v\}$ and $\mathcal{V}(e)(\sigma)$ as before. The transition system $\mathcal{T}_{svp}$ is given in

Definition 7.3 $\mathcal{T}_{svp} = (Res\times\Sigma, \Sigma, \rightarrow, Spec)$. $Spec$ is given by

- $\qquad [v := e, \sigma] \rightarrow [\mathrm{E}, \sigma\{\alpha/v\}] \qquad\qquad$ where $\alpha = \mathcal{V}(e)(\sigma)$ $\qquad\qquad$ (Ass)

- $\qquad [\mathsf{skip}, \sigma] \rightarrow [\mathrm{E}, \sigma]$ $\qquad\qquad\qquad\qquad\qquad\qquad\qquad\qquad$ (Skip)

- $\qquad \dfrac{[s_1, \sigma] \rightarrow [r_1, \sigma']}{[s_1;s_2, \sigma] \rightarrow [r_1;s_2, \sigma']}$ $\qquad\qquad\qquad\qquad\qquad\qquad\qquad$ (Seq)

- $\qquad [\mathsf{if}\ e\ \mathsf{then}\ s_1\ \mathsf{else}\ s_2\ \mathsf{fi}, \sigma] \rightarrow_0 [s_1, \sigma] \qquad$ if $\mathcal{V}(e)(\sigma) = tt$ $\qquad$ (If 1)

  $\qquad [\mathsf{if}\ e\ \mathsf{then}\ s_1\ \mathsf{else}\ s_2\ \mathsf{fi}, \sigma] \rightarrow_0 [s_2, \sigma] \qquad$ if $\mathcal{V}(e)(\sigma) = ff$ $\qquad$ (If 2)

- $\qquad [\mathsf{while}\ e\ \mathsf{do}\ s\ \mathsf{od}, \sigma] \rightarrow$ $\qquad\qquad\qquad\qquad\qquad\qquad\qquad$ (While)
  $\qquad\qquad [\mathsf{if}\ e\ \mathsf{then}\ (s;\mathsf{while}\ e\ \mathsf{do}\ s\ \mathsf{od})\ \mathsf{else}\ \mathsf{skip}\ \mathsf{fi}, \sigma]$

•
$$\frac{[s_1, \sigma] \to [r_1, \sigma']}{[s_1 \,\|\, s_2, \sigma] \to [r_1 \,\|\, s_2, \sigma']} \tag{Par}$$

$$[s_2 \,\|\, s_1, \sigma] \to [s_2 \,\|\, r_1, \sigma']$$

Remark Contrary to our earlier approach, we now handle the while statement by introducing an explicit step (we use '$\to$' rather than '$\to_0$'). This will turn out to be somewhat more convenient in later calculations.

Due to the presence of the $\|$-operator, $\mathcal{L}_{svp}$ exhibits nondeterministic behaviour: In executing $s_1 \,\|\, s_2$, $\mathcal{T}_{svp}$ has a choice as to performing the first step by s_1 or s_2. Accordingly, the domain of meanings $\mathbb{P}_O$ used for $\mathcal{L}_{svp}$ has the form

$$(p \in) \mathbb{P}_O \;\; = \;\; \Sigma \to \mathcal{P}_{nco}(\Sigma^\infty), \tag{7.2}$$

which should be contrasted with the deterministic domain $\mathbb{P} = \Sigma \to \Sigma^\infty$ as used in Section 1.2.

$\mathcal{T}_{svp}$ has the usual finiteness property.

Lemma 7.4 *For each s and σ,*

(a) $|\mathcal{S}(\mathrm{E}, \sigma)| = 0.$

(b) $1 \le |\mathcal{S}(s, \sigma)| < \infty.$

Proof (a) is clear; for (b), use structural induction on s.   □

We proceed with the definition of the operational semantics $\mathcal{O}$ for $\mathcal{L}_{svp}$.

Definition 7.5

(a) $\mathcal{O}\colon Res \times \Sigma \to \mathcal{P}_{nco}(\Sigma^\infty)$ is the unique function satisfying $\mathcal{O}(\mathrm{E}, \sigma) = \{\epsilon\}$ and

$$\mathcal{O}(s, \sigma) = \bigcup \{\sigma' \cdot \mathcal{O}(r, \sigma') \mid [s, \sigma] \to [r, \sigma']\}.$$

(b) $\mathcal{O}[\![\cdot]\!]\colon \mathcal{L}_{svp} \to \mathbb{P}_O$ is given by $\mathcal{O}[\![s]\!] = \lambda\sigma \cdot \mathcal{O}(s, \sigma).$

Example Let s_{wh} be short for while $v > 0$ do $u := u + 1$ od. Suppose $\sigma(u) = 0$, $\sigma(v) > 0$.

$\mathcal{O}[\![\text{while } v > 0 \text{ do } u := u + 1 \text{ od} \| v := 0]\!](\sigma)$

$= \mathcal{O}(\text{while } v > 0 \text{ do } u := u + 1 \text{ od} \| v := 0, \sigma)$

$= \sigma\{1/u\} \cdot \mathcal{O}(s_{\mathrm{wh}} \| v := 0, \sigma\{1/u\}) \ \cup \ \sigma\{0/v\} \cdot \mathcal{O}(s_{\mathrm{wh}}, \sigma\{0/v\})$

$= \sigma\{1/u\} \cdot (\sigma\{2/u\} \cdot \mathcal{O}(s_{\mathrm{wh}} \| v := 0, \sigma\{2/u\}) \ \cup$
$\qquad \sigma\{1/u, 0/v\} \cdot \mathcal{O}(s_{\mathrm{wh}}, \sigma\{1/u, 0/v\})) \ \cup \ \{\sigma\{0/v\}\sigma\{0/v\}\sigma\{0/v\}\}$

$= \sigma\{1/u\} \cdot \sigma\{2/u\} \cdot (\sigma\{3/u\} \cdot \mathcal{O}(s_{\mathrm{wh}} \| v := 0, \sigma\{3/u\}) \ \cup$
$\qquad \sigma\{2/u, 0/v\} \cdot \mathcal{O}(s_{\mathrm{wh}}, \sigma\{2/u, 0/v\})) \ \cup$
$\qquad\qquad \{\sigma\{1/u\} \cdot \sigma\{1/u, 0/v\}^3\} \ \cup \ \{\sigma\{0/v\}^3\}.$

One obtains, assuming $\sigma(u) = 0$, $\sigma(v) > 0$,

$\mathcal{O}[\![\text{while } v > 0 \text{ do } u := u + 1 \text{ od} \| v := 0]\!](\sigma)$
$\quad = \quad \{\, \sigma\{1/u\}\sigma\{2/u\} \cdots \sigma\{n/u\}\sigma\{n/u, 0/v\}^3 \mid n \geq 0 \,\} \cup$
$\qquad\qquad \{\sigma\{1/u\}\sigma\{2/u\} \cdots\}.$

$\mathcal{O}$ may be seen as a quite natural extension of the earlier definitions proposed so far in our book. It may therefore come somewhat as a surprise that we have the following

Fact $\mathcal{O}$ is not compositional on $\mathcal{L}_{svp}$.

One example suffices to prove this fact: We shall exhibit s, s_1, s_2 such that

$$\mathcal{O}[\![s_1]\!] = \mathcal{O}[\![s_2]\!], \tag{7.3}$$

but

$$\mathcal{O}[\![s_1 \| s]\!] \neq \mathcal{O}[\![s_2 \| s]\!]. \tag{7.4}$$

Note that this is, indeed, sufficient. Whatever semantic operator, say '$\hat{\|}$', is chosen as counterpart to the syntactic '$\|$', if we would have that, for any s', s'', $\mathcal{O}[\![s' \| s'']\!] = \mathcal{O}[\![s']\!] \ \hat{\|} \ \mathcal{O}[\![s'']\!]$, then in particular,

$$\begin{aligned}
\mathcal{O}[\![s_1 \| s]\!] &= \mathcal{O}[\![s_1]\!] \ \hat{\|} \ \mathcal{O}[\![s]\!] \\
\mathcal{O}[\![s_2 \| s]\!] &= \mathcal{O}[\![s_2]\!] \ \hat{\|} \ \mathcal{O}[\![s]\!].
\end{aligned} \tag{7.5}$$

Clearly, formulae (7.3), (7.4) and (7.5) taken together are contradictory. Now, taking $s \equiv v := 2$, $s_1 \equiv (v := 0; v := 1)$ and $s_2 \equiv (v := 0; v := v + 1)$, we have statements satisfying (7.1) and (7.2). For easier notation, we simply write i for $\sigma\{i/v\}$, $i = 0, 1$ or 2. Then

$$\mathcal{O}[\![s_1]\!] = \mathcal{O}[\![s_2]\!] = \lambda\sigma.\{0 \cdot 1\}$$

but

$$\begin{aligned}
\mathcal{O}[\![s_1 \| s]\!] &= \lambda\sigma.\{\, 2 \cdot 0 \cdot 1, 0 \cdot 2 \cdot 1, 0 \cdot 1 \cdot 2 \,\} \\
\mathcal{O}[\![s_2 \| s]\!] &= \lambda\sigma.\{\, 2 \cdot 0 \cdot 1, 0 \cdot 2 \cdot 3, 0 \cdot 1 \cdot 2 \,\}.
\end{aligned}$$

Note how the difference just displayed stems from the different effects of the two interleavings $v := 0; v := 2; v := 1$ and $v := 0; v := 2; v := v + 1$.

The phenomenon that $\mathcal{O}$ is not compositional has important consequences. Contrary to the situation in earlier chapters, we shall have to make special efforts to define a denotational, i.e., by definition, compositional meaning function $\mathcal{D}$. This will be done in the next subsection. By the discussion just presented, we are prepared for the fact that the, up to now standard, equivalence $\mathcal{O} = \mathcal{D}$ will not hold.

7.1.2 Denotational semantics, relating $\mathcal{O}$ and $\mathcal{D}$

We are looking for a compositional meaning function $\mathcal{D}$. This means in particular that we want $\mathcal{D}$ to satisfy

$$\mathcal{D}(s_1 \| s_2) = \mathcal{D}(s_1) \hat{\|} \mathcal{D}(s_2), \tag{7.6}$$

for some suitable definition of $\hat{\|}$. Note that the design of $\mathcal{D}$ (and of $\hat{\|}$) assumes a denotational codomain which is not necessarily the same as the codomain $\mathbb{P}_O$ used in Section 7.1.1.

Another way of phrasing (7.6) is that the meaning of examples such as $s_1 \equiv (v := 0; v := 1)$ or $s_2 \equiv (v := 0; v := v + 1)$ should be designed such that they can "absorb" the effect of arbitrary interleaving actions (i.e., assignments stemming from some parallel component, such as $s \equiv v := 2$ in the earlier example). Once again, a meaning $\lambda\sigma.\{\, \sigma\{0/v\} \cdot \sigma\{1/v\} \,\}$ is, typically, not good enough for this purpose.

One plausible—but not satisfactory—method is to assign functions $\phi \colon \Sigma \to \Sigma$ as meanings to the atomic actions (here assignments $v := e$) of $\mathcal{L}_{svp}$, and next to proceed as for $\mathcal{L}_{par}$ in Chapter 4, i.e., to deliver sets of sequences of such functions. Thus, we would take as codomain for $\mathcal{D}$ the set, say $\hat{\mathbb{P}}$, defined as $\hat{\mathbb{P}} = \mathcal{P}_{nco}((\Sigma \to \Sigma)^\infty)$—to be compared with the uniform codomain $\mathcal{P}_{nco}(Act^\infty)$ used in Chapters 2 and 4. For the example above—with $s \equiv v := 2$—writing $\psi_0 = \lambda\sigma.\sigma\{0/v\}$, $\psi_1 = \lambda\sigma.\sigma\{1/v\}$, $\psi_2 = \lambda\sigma.\sigma\{\sigma(v) + 1/v\}$, $\psi = \lambda\sigma.\sigma\{2/v\}$, we would obtain as outcomes

$$\mathcal{D}(s_1 \| s) = \{ \psi \cdot \psi_0 \cdot \psi_1, \psi_0 \cdot \psi \cdot \psi_1, \psi_0 \cdot \psi_1 \cdot \psi \}$$
$$\mathcal{D}(s_2 \| s) = \{ \psi \cdot \psi_0 \cdot \psi_2, \psi_0 \cdot \psi \cdot \psi_2, \psi_0 \cdot \psi_2 \cdot \psi \}.$$

The problem with this method is that it does not work properly for the conditional and the while statement, since their meaning cannot be expressed in a compositional manner as an element of the above $\hat{\mathbb{P}}$, allowing at the same time the treatment of $s_1 \| s_2$ as just sketched.

Rather than following the approach outlined above, we adopt a closely related method, which is sufficiently different to handle the above mentioned problems. In Definition 7.9, we shall introduce $\mathbb{P}_D$ as the collection of all (nonempty and) *closed* subsets of $(\Sigma \times \Sigma)^\infty$, i.e., of all finite and infinite sequences of *pairs* of states. Note firstly that each function of type $\Sigma \to \Sigma$ may be represented by its graph. i.e., by a subset of $\Sigma \times \Sigma$. Therefore, the domain $\hat{\mathbb{P}}$ may be embedded into $\mathbb{P}_D$. However, $\mathbb{P}_D$ has also elements which are not in $\hat{\mathbb{P}}$, hence the greater flexibility of $\mathbb{P}_D$. Secondly, we draw attention to our using closed rather than compact in the definition of $\mathbb{P}_D$ as powerdomain with respect to $(\Sigma \times \Sigma)^\infty$. As we shall see in a moment, already for the simple case of the skip statement, $\mathcal{D}(\mathsf{skip})$ is a noncompact set. The use of closed rather than compact will have twofold consequences. Firstly, we have to use a different scheme for defining the semantic operators (the technical point being that we can no longer use Michael's theorem in the well-definedness argument). Secondly, when we want to link $\mathcal{O}$ and $\mathcal{D}$—to be discussed later in this subsection—we shall find that we have to impose an extra finiteness condition on the elements in $\mathbb{P}_D$—to be added to their closedness. Otherwise, we are not able to derive the desired relationship. Details of this will follow after we have presented the definition of $\mathcal{D}$.

Preparing the way for this, we first introduce the various semantic operators. Their definition will follow a format which is different from that use on most earlier occasions. (It is, in fact, the same as that used in Section 5.3. Since the reader may have skipped that section, we proceed here without further referring to it.) We shall present the scheme first in a *uniform* setting, viz. for operators defined for $\mathbb{P}_D$ equal to the closed powerdomain variant of the (compact powerdomain) $\mathbb{P}_D$ as in Section 2.2, in order to facilitate comparison with the standard method as first described there.

Let *Act* be a, *not necessarily finite*, set of atomic actions. As usual, we assume the discrete metric on *Act*.

Definition 7.6 Let $(p \in) \mathbb{P}_D = \mathcal{P}_{ncl}(\mathbb{Q})$, with $(q \in) \mathbb{Q} = Act^\infty \backslash \{ \epsilon \}$. Let, for each $a \in Act$, $p_a = \{ q \mid a \cdot q \in p, q \neq \epsilon \}$. (Note that p_a may be empty.) Let

$(\phi \in) \, Op = \mathbb{P}_D \times \mathbb{P}_D \xrightarrow{1} \mathbb{P}_D.$

(a) The operator $\Omega_; : Op \rightarrow Op$ is defined by

$$\Omega_;(\phi)(p,p') \;=\; \bigcup\{\, a \cdot \phi(p_a,p') \mid p_a \neq \emptyset, a \in Act\,\} \cup \bigcup\{\, a \cdot p' \mid a \in p\,\}.$$

(b) The operator $\Omega_\| : Op \rightarrow Op$ is defined by

$$\Omega_\|(\phi)(p,p') \;=\; \Omega_;(\phi)(p,p') \cup \Omega_;(\phi)(p',p)$$

(c) $; = \mathit{fix}(\Omega_;)$, $\| = \mathit{fix}(\Omega_\|)$, $\bigsqcup = \Omega_;(\|)$.

(d) $p_1 + p_2 = p_1 \cup p_2$.

Besides the standard arguments, there is one additional step required to justify the above definition.

Lemma 7.7 *For $p,p' \in \mathbb{P}_D$, $\phi \in Op$, $\Omega_; : Op \rightarrow Op$ as just defined, the set $\Omega_;(\phi)(p,p')$ is nonempty and closed.*

Proof Assume $p,p' \in \mathbb{P}_D$. Clearly, for at least one a, either $p_a \neq \emptyset$ or $a \in p$ (or both). For each a, $a \cdot p'$ is nonempty and closed. By the discreteness of Act and the assumption on ϕ, the set $\bigcup\{\, a \cdot \phi(p_a,p') \mid p_a \neq \emptyset\,\}$ is closed. Altogether, we obtain that $\bigcup\{\, a \cdot \phi(p_a,p') \mid p_a \neq \emptyset\,\} \cup \bigcup\{\, a \cdot p' \mid a \in p\,\}$ is nonempty and closed.   □

We leave it as and exercise (see Exercise 7.4) to show that '$;$' and '$\|$' coincide with the operators '$;$' and '$\|$' as defined earlier on $\mathbb{P}'_D \times \mathbb{P}'_D \rightarrow \mathbb{P}'_D$, where $\mathbb{P}'_D = \mathcal{P}_{nco}(Act^\infty \backslash \{\epsilon\})$.

That the new operators '$;$', '$\|$', '$+$' have the familiar properties is stated in

Lemma 7.8

(a) '$;$', '$\|$', '$+$' are nonexpansive in both arguments.

(b) If $\epsilon \notin p$, then $d(p;p', p;p'') \leq \tfrac{1}{2} d(p',p'')$.

Proof Exercise.   □

It is now only a small step to mimic these definitions in a nonuniform setting:

Definition 7.9 Let $(p \in) \mathbb{P}_D = \mathcal{P}_{ncl}(\mathbb{Q}_D)$, and let $(q \in) \mathbb{Q}_D = (\Sigma \times \Sigma)^\infty \setminus \{\epsilon\}$. Let $p[\sigma, \sigma'] = \{q \mid \langle \sigma, \sigma' \rangle \cdot q \in p, \ q \neq \epsilon\}$. (Again, $p[\sigma, \sigma']$ may be the empty set.) The operators $;, \|, +: \mathbb{P}_D \times \mathbb{P}_D \xrightarrow{1} \mathbb{P}_D$ are given as

(a) ';' is the unique function satisfying

$$p;p' = \bigcup\{\langle \sigma, \sigma' \rangle \cdot (p[\sigma, \sigma'];p') \mid \sigma, \sigma' \in \Sigma, p[\sigma, \sigma'] \neq \emptyset\} \cup$$
$$\bigcup\{\langle \sigma, \sigma' \rangle \cdot p' \mid \langle \sigma, \sigma' \rangle \in p\}.$$

(b) The definitions of '$\|$', '$+$' are obvious from clause (a) and Definition 7.6, and omitted.

Lemma 7.8 applies without change to the newly defined operators.

We are now in a position to define the denotational semantics $\mathcal{D}$ for $\mathcal{L}_{svp}$:

Definition 7.10

(a) Let $(S \in) Sem = \mathcal{L}_{svp} \to \mathbb{P}_D$. The mapping $\Psi: Sem_\mathcal{D} \to Sem_\mathcal{D}$ is given by

$$\Psi(S)(v := e) = \{\langle \sigma, \sigma\{\alpha/v\} \rangle \mid \sigma \in \Sigma\}, \quad \text{where } \alpha = \mathcal{V}(e)(\sigma)$$
$$\Psi(S)(\text{skip}) = \{\langle \sigma, \sigma \rangle \mid \sigma \in \Sigma\}$$
$$\Psi(S)(s_1;s_2) = \Psi(S)(s_1);\Psi(S)(s_2) \text{ and similarly for '}\|\text{'}$$
$$\Psi(S)(\text{if } e \text{ then } s_1 \text{ else } s_2 \text{ fi}) =$$
$$\Psi(S)(s_1) \cap \bigcup\{\langle \sigma, \sigma' \rangle \cdot \mathbb{P}_D \mid \sigma, \sigma' \in \Sigma, \mathcal{V}(e)(\sigma) = tt\} \cup$$
$$\Psi(S)(s_2) \cap \bigcup\{\langle \sigma, \sigma' \rangle \cdot \mathbb{P}_D \mid \sigma, \sigma' \in \Sigma, \mathcal{V}(e)(\sigma) = ff\}$$
$$\Psi(S)(\text{while } e \text{ do } s \text{ od}) =$$
$$\bigcup\{\langle \sigma, \sigma \rangle \cdot S(\text{if } e \text{ then } (s;\text{while } e \text{ do } s \text{ od}) \text{ else skip fi}) \mid \sigma \in \Sigma\}.$$

(b) $\mathcal{D} = fix(\Psi), \mathcal{D}[\![s]\!] = \mathcal{D}(s)$.

Examples

(1) $\mathcal{D}[\![(v := 0; v := 1) \| v := 2]\!]$
$= \mathcal{D}((v := 0; v := 1) \| v := 2)$
$= (\mathcal{D}(v := 0); \mathcal{D}(v := 1)) \| \mathcal{D}(v := 2)$
$= (\{\langle \sigma_0, \sigma_0\{0/v\} \rangle \mid \sigma_0 \in \Sigma\}; \{\langle \sigma_1, \sigma_1\{1/v\} \rangle \mid \sigma_1 \in \Sigma\}) \|$

$$\{\, \langle \sigma_2, \sigma_2\{2/v\}\rangle \mid \sigma_2 \in \Sigma \,\}$$

$$= \{\, \langle \sigma_0, \sigma_0\{0/v\}\rangle \langle \sigma_1, \sigma_1\{1/v\}\rangle \mid \sigma_0, \sigma_1 \in \Sigma \,\} \,\|$$
$$\{\, \langle \sigma_2, \sigma_2\{2/v\}\rangle \mid \sigma_2 \in \Sigma \,\}$$

$$= \{\, \langle \sigma_0, \sigma_0\{0/v\}\rangle \langle \sigma_1, \sigma_1\{1/v\}\rangle \langle \sigma_2, \sigma_2\{2/v\}\rangle,$$
$$\langle \sigma_0, \sigma_0\{0/v\}\rangle \langle \sigma_2, \sigma_2\{2/v\}\rangle \langle \sigma_1, \sigma_1\{1/v\}\rangle,$$
$$\langle \sigma_2, \sigma_2\{2/v\}\rangle \langle \sigma_0, \sigma_0\{0/v\}\rangle \langle \sigma_1, \sigma_1\{1/v\}\rangle \mid \sigma_0, \sigma_1, \sigma_2 \in \Sigma \,\}$$

(2) $\mathcal{D}[\![(v := 0; v := v + 1)\|v := 2]\!]$

$\quad = \mathcal{D}((v := 0; v := v + 1)\|v := 2)$

$\quad = \big(\mathcal{D}(v := 0); \mathcal{D}(v := v + 1)\big)\|\mathcal{D}(v := 2)$

$\quad = \big(\{\, \langle \sigma_0, \sigma_0\{0/v\}\rangle \mid \sigma_0 \in \Sigma \,\};$
$\qquad\quad \{\, \langle \sigma_1, \sigma_1\{\alpha + 1/v\}\rangle \mid \sigma_1 \in \Sigma, \alpha = \sigma_1(v) \,\}\big)\|$
$\qquad\qquad \{\, \langle \sigma_2, \sigma_2\{2/v\}\rangle \mid \sigma_2 \in \Sigma \,\}$

$\quad = \big(\{\, \langle \sigma_0, \sigma_0\{0/v\}\rangle \langle \sigma_1, \sigma_1\{\alpha + 1/v\}\rangle \mid \sigma_0, \sigma_1 \in \Sigma, \alpha = \sigma_1(v) \,\}\big)\|$
$\qquad\quad \{\, \langle \sigma_2, \sigma_2\{2/v\}\rangle \mid \sigma_0 \in \Sigma \,\}$

$\quad = \{\, \langle \sigma_0, \sigma_0\{0/v\}\rangle \langle \sigma_1, \sigma_1\{\alpha + 1/v\}\rangle \langle \sigma_2, \sigma_2\{2/v\}\rangle,$
$\qquad\quad \langle \sigma_0, \sigma_0\{0/v\}\rangle \langle \sigma_2, \sigma_2\{2/v\}\rangle \langle \sigma_1, \sigma_1\{\alpha + 1/v\}\rangle,$
$\qquad\qquad \langle \sigma_2, \sigma_2\{2/v\}\rangle \langle \sigma_0, \sigma_0\{0/v\}\rangle \langle \sigma_1, \sigma_1\{\alpha + 1/v\}\rangle \mid$
$\qquad\qquad\quad \sigma_0, \sigma_1, \sigma_2 \in \Sigma, \alpha = \sigma_1(v) \,\}$

(3) Let $s_{\mathrm{wh}} = $ **while** $v > 0$ **do** $u := u + 1$ **od**.

$\quad \mathcal{D}[\![\textbf{while } v > 0 \textbf{ do } u := u + 1 \textbf{ od}]\!]$

$\quad = \mathcal{D}(\textbf{while } v > 0 \textbf{ do } u := u + 1 \textbf{ od})$

$\quad = \bigcup\{\, \langle \sigma_0, \sigma_0\rangle \cdot \langle \sigma_1, \sigma_1\{\alpha_1 + 1/u\}\rangle \cdot \mathcal{D}(s_{\mathrm{wh}}) \mid$
$\qquad\quad \sigma_0, \sigma_1 \in \Sigma, \alpha_1 = \sigma_1(u), \sigma_1(v) > 0 \,\} \cup$
$\qquad\qquad \{\, \langle \sigma_0, \sigma_0\rangle \langle \sigma_1, \sigma_1\rangle \mid \sigma_0, \sigma_1 \in \Sigma, \sigma_1(v) \leq 0 \,\}$

$\quad = \bigcup\{\, \langle \sigma_0, \sigma_0\rangle \cdot \langle \sigma_1, \sigma_1\{\alpha_1 + 1/u\}\rangle \cdot$
$\qquad\quad \langle \sigma_2, \sigma_2\rangle \cdot \langle \sigma_3, \sigma_3\{\alpha_3 + 1/u\}\rangle \cdot \mathcal{D}(s_{\mathrm{wh}}) \mid$
$\qquad\qquad \sigma_i \in \Sigma, \alpha_i = \sigma_i(u), \sigma_1(v) > 0, \sigma_3(v) > 0 \,\} \cup$
$\quad\;\; \{\, \langle \sigma_0, \sigma_0\rangle \cdot \langle \sigma_1, \sigma_1\{\alpha_1 + 1/u\}\rangle \cdot \langle \sigma_2, \sigma_2\rangle \langle \sigma_3, \sigma_3\rangle \mid$
$\qquad\quad \sigma_i \in \Sigma, \alpha_1 = \sigma_1(u), \sigma_1(v) > 0, \sigma_3(v) \leq 0 \,\} \cup$
$\quad\;\; \{\, \langle \sigma_0, \sigma_0\rangle \langle \sigma_1, \sigma_1\rangle \mid \sigma_0, \sigma_1 \in \Sigma, \sigma_1(v) \leq 0 \,\}.$

So one obtains

$\mathcal{D}(\text{while } v > 0 \text{ do } u := u + 1 \text{ od}) =$
$\{ \langle \sigma_0, \sigma_0 \rangle \langle \sigma_1, \sigma_1 \{ \alpha_1 + 1/u \} \rangle \cdots$
$\qquad \langle \sigma_{2n-2}, \sigma_{2n-2} \rangle \langle \sigma_{2n-1}, \sigma_{2n-1} \{ \alpha_{2n-1} + 1/u \} \rangle \cdot$
$\qquad\qquad \langle \sigma_{2n}, \sigma_{2n} \rangle \langle \sigma_{2n+1}, \sigma_{2n+1} \rangle$
$\qquad | \ \sigma_i \in \Sigma, \alpha_{2i-1} = \sigma_{2i-1}(u),$
$\qquad\qquad \sigma_{2i+1}(v) > 0, 0 \le i < n, \sigma_{2n+1}(v) \le 0 \} \cup$
$\{ \langle \sigma_0, \sigma_0 \rangle \langle \sigma_1, \sigma_1 \{ \alpha_1 + 1/u \} \rangle \cdot$
$\qquad \langle \sigma_2, \sigma_2 \rangle \langle \sigma_3, \sigma_3 \{ \alpha_3 + 1/u \} \rangle \cdots | \ \sigma_i \in \Sigma, \alpha_{2i-1} = \sigma_{2i-1}(u) \}.$

Note that, e.g., $\mathcal{D}(\text{skip})$ is not compact, since Σ is in general infinite and, hence, it is not true that each infinite sequence in $\mathcal{D}(\text{skip})$ has a converging subsequence. (Since we have the discrete metric on (Σ and) $\Sigma \times \Sigma$, the only sequences for which this property holds are the sequences which have a constant subsequence.)

The proof of the well-definedness of $\mathcal{D}$ is an easy variation on earlier ones.

Lemma 7.11

(a) $\Psi(S)(s)$ *is nonempty and closed for each* S, s.

(b) Ψ *is contractive in* S.

Proof

(a) Structural induction on s. One subcase.

[while e do s od] By assumption, $S(\text{if } e \text{ then } (s;\text{while } e \text{ do } s \text{ od}) \text{ else skip fi})$ is closed. By the discreteness of $\Sigma \times \Sigma$, then

$$\bigcup \{ \langle \sigma, \sigma \rangle \cdot S(\text{if } e \text{ then } (s;\text{while } e \text{ do } s \text{ od}) \text{ else skip fi}) \mid \sigma \in \Sigma \}$$

is also closed.

(b) Choose some S_1, S_2. We show by structural induction on s that $d(\Psi(S_1)(s), \Psi(S_2)(s)) \le \frac{1}{2} d(S_1, S_2)$. The only nonstandard subcase is if e then s_1 else s_2 fi. By Exercise 7.2 and the induction hypothesis

$$d(\Psi(S_1)(s_1) \cap \bigcup \{ \langle \sigma, \sigma' \rangle \cdot \mathbb{P}_D \mid \mathcal{V}(e)(\sigma) = tt \},$$
$$\Psi(S_2)(s_1) \cap \bigcup \{ \langle \sigma, \sigma' \rangle \cdot \mathbb{P}_D \mid \mathcal{V}(e)(\sigma) = tt \})$$
$$\le d(\Psi(S_1)(s_1), \Psi(S_2)(s_1))$$
$$\le \frac{1}{2} d(S_1, S_2),$$

and similarly for s_2.   □

We now turn to the discussion as to how $\mathcal{O}$ and $\mathcal{D}$ may be related—knowing already that equivalence of $\mathcal{O}$ and $\mathcal{D}$ is not to be expected. Let us look, once again, at the statement $s_1 \equiv (v := 0; v := 1)$. We have $\mathcal{O}[\![s_1]\!] = \lambda\sigma.\{\sigma\{0/v\} \cdot \sigma\{1/v\}\}$, whereas $\mathcal{D}[\![s_1]\!] = \{\langle \sigma, \sigma\{0/v\}\rangle \cdot \langle \bar{\sigma}, \bar{\sigma}\{1/v\}\rangle \mid \sigma, \bar{\sigma} \in \Sigma\}$. The crucial point here is that $\bar{\sigma}$ may be different from $\sigma\{0/v\}$, thus catering for the possibility that an interleaving action (intervening between the execution of $v := 0$ and $v := 1$) may change $\sigma\{0/v\}$.

As first step in the analysis of the relationship between $\mathcal{O}$ and $\mathcal{D}$, we introduce a modified $\mathcal{O}^*$ which is indeed equal to $\mathcal{D}$. The semantics $\mathcal{O}^*$ has a hybrid character in that is is based on $\mathcal{T}_{svp}$, hence operational in nature, but delivers results in the domain $\mathbb{P}_{O^*}$ which is like $\mathbb{P}_D$ (but for the possible presence of ϵ).

Definition 7.12 Let $\mathbb{P}_{O^*} = \mathbb{P}_{ncl}((\Sigma \times \Sigma)^\infty)$.

(a) $\mathcal{T}'_{svp} = (Res, \Sigma \times \Sigma, \rightarrow, Spec')$. The transitions of $\mathcal{T}'_{svp}$ are of the form $r \xrightarrow{\langle \sigma, \sigma' \rangle} r'$. Using instead the notation $[r, \sigma] \rightarrow [r', \sigma']$ as before, we put $Spec' = Spec$. Note however, that the observables are now *pairs* of states $\langle \sigma, \sigma' \rangle$.

(b) $\mathcal{O}^*: Res \rightarrow \mathbb{P}_{O^*}$ is the unique function satisfying $\mathcal{O}^*(\mathrm{E}) = \{\epsilon\}$ and

$$\mathcal{O}^*(s) = \bigcup\{\langle \sigma, \sigma'\rangle \cdot \mathcal{O}^*(r) \mid [s, \sigma] \rightarrow [r, \sigma']\},$$

where '$\rightarrow$' is now taken with respect to $\mathcal{T}'_{svp}$.

Example $\mathcal{O}^*(v := 0; v := 1)$

$= \bigcup\{\langle \sigma, \sigma\{0/v\}\rangle \cdot \mathcal{O}^*(v := 1) \mid \sigma \in \Sigma\}$

$= \bigcup\{\langle \sigma, \sigma\{0/v\}\rangle \cdot (\bigcup\{\langle \bar{\sigma}, \bar{\sigma}\{1/v\}\rangle \cdot \mathcal{O}^*(\mathrm{E}) \mid \bar{\sigma} \in \Sigma\}) \mid \sigma \in \Sigma\}$

$= \{\langle \sigma, \sigma\{0/v\}\rangle \cdot \langle \bar{\sigma}, \bar{\sigma}\{1/v\}\rangle \mid \sigma, \bar{\sigma} \in \Sigma\}.$

Well-definedness of $\mathcal{O}^*$ follows by the usual higher-order contractiveness argument, once it has been established that $\mathcal{O}^*$ has $\mathbb{P}_{O^*}$ as codomain. This is a consequence of

Lemma 7.13

(a) $\mathcal{T}'_{svp}$ *is "locally finitely branching," i.e., for each* r, σ, *the set*

$$\{ [r', \sigma'] \mid [r, \sigma] \to [r', \sigma'] \}$$

is finite.

(b) $\mathcal{T}'_{svp}$ *is image-finite.*

Proof (a) follows from the definition of $\mathcal{T}'_{svp}$, using structural induction on r. Part (b) is immediate from part (a). $\square$

Remark Note that part (b) of this lemma is sufficient to establish that $\mathcal{O}^*$ yields closed results (cf. Section 5.1). The stronger property of part (a) will be applied subsequently in the argument linking $\mathcal{O}$ and $\mathcal{D}$ for $\mathcal{L}_{svp}$.

We return to the question about the relationship between $\mathcal{O}$ (and $\mathcal{O}^*$) and $\mathcal{D}$. Contrary to what we saw for $\mathcal{O}$, $\mathcal{O}^*$ *is* compositional and, moreover, equal to $\mathcal{D}$ (on $\mathcal{L}_{svp}$). This follows by another application of a standard argument: Let $\mathcal{E}: Res \to \mathbb{P}_{O^*}$ denote the obvious extension of $\mathcal{D}$ (with the clause $\mathcal{E}(\mathrm{E}) = \{\epsilon\}$).

Lemma 7.14 $\mathcal{O}^* = \mathcal{E}$.

Proof Let Φ^* be as implicit in in Definition 7.12. It is, by now, routine how to show, by structural induction on r, that $\Phi^*(\mathcal{E})(r) = \mathcal{E}(r)$. Three subcases.

$[s_1; s_2]$ $\quad \Phi^*(\mathcal{E})(s_1; s_2)$

$\quad = \quad \bigcup \{ \langle \sigma, \sigma' \rangle \cdot \mathcal{E}(r) \mid [s_1; s_2, \sigma] \to [r, \sigma'] \}$

$\quad = \quad \bigcup \{ \langle \sigma, \sigma' \rangle \cdot \mathcal{E}(r_1; s_2) \mid [s_1, \sigma] \to [r_1, \sigma'] \}$

$\quad = \quad \bigcup \{ \langle \sigma, \sigma' \rangle \cdot \mathcal{E}(r_1) \mid [s_1, \sigma] \to [r_1, \sigma'] \}; \mathcal{E}(s_2)$

$\quad = \quad \Phi^*(\mathcal{E})(s_1); \mathcal{E}(s_2)$

$\quad = \quad [\text{ind. hyp.}] \ \mathcal{E}(s_1); \mathcal{E}(s_2)$

$\quad = \quad \mathcal{E}(s_1; s_2)$.

$[\text{if } e \text{ then } s_1 \text{ else } s_2 \text{ fi}]$ $\quad \Phi^*(\mathcal{E})(\text{if } e \text{ then } s_1 \text{ else } s_2 \text{ fi})$

$\quad = \quad \bigcup \{ \langle \sigma, \sigma' \rangle \cdot \mathcal{E}(r) \mid [\text{if } e \text{ then } s_1 \text{ else } s_2 \text{ fi}, \sigma] \to [r, \sigma'] \}$

$\quad = \quad \bigcup \{ \langle \sigma, \sigma' \rangle \cdot \mathcal{E}(r') \mid [s_1, \sigma] \to [r', \sigma'], \mathcal{V}(e)(\sigma) = tt \} \cup$
$\qquad \bigcup \{ \langle \sigma, \sigma' \rangle \cdot \mathcal{E}(r'') \mid [s_2, \sigma] \to [r'', \sigma'], \mathcal{V}(e)(\sigma) = ff \}$

$$
\begin{aligned}
= \quad & (\ \bigcup\{\, \langle\sigma,\sigma'\rangle \cdot \mathcal{E}(r') \mid [s_1,\sigma] \to [r',\sigma']\,\} \cap \\
& \ \bigcup\{\, \langle\sigma,\sigma'\rangle \cdot \mathbb{P}_D \mid \sigma,\sigma' \in \Sigma, \mathcal{V}(e)(\sigma) = tt\,\}) \ \cup \ (\text{symm.}) \\
= \quad & (\Phi^*(\mathcal{E})(s_1) \cap \bigcup\{\, \langle\sigma,\sigma'\rangle \cdot \mathbb{P}_D \mid \sigma,\sigma' \in \Sigma, \mathcal{V}(e)(\sigma) = tt\,\}) \ \cup \ (\text{symm.}) \\
= \quad & [\text{ind. hyp.}] \\
& (\mathcal{E}(s_1) \cap \bigcup\{\, \langle\sigma,\sigma'\rangle \cdot \mathbb{P}_D \mid \sigma,\sigma' \in \Sigma, \mathcal{V}(e)(\sigma) = tt\,\}) \ \cup \ (\text{symm.}) \\
= \quad & \mathcal{E}(\text{if } e \text{ then } s_1 \text{ else } s_2 \text{ fi}).
\end{aligned}
$$

[while e do s od] $\Phi^*(\mathcal{E})(\text{while } e \text{ do } s \text{ od})$

$$
\begin{aligned}
= \quad & \bigcup\{\, \langle\sigma,\sigma\rangle \cdot \mathcal{E}(\text{if } e \text{ then } (s;\text{while } e \text{ do } s \text{ od}) \text{ else skip fi}) \mid \sigma \in \Sigma \,\} \\
= \quad & \mathcal{E}(\text{while } e \text{ do } s \text{ od}). \hspace{6cm} \square
\end{aligned}
$$

Finally, we are left with the question how $\mathcal{O}$ and $\mathcal{O}^*$ are to be related. The solution should not be too difficult to appreciate on the basis of the earlier discussion. The relationship between $\mathcal{O}$ and $\mathcal{D}(= \mathcal{O}^* \text{on } \mathcal{L}_{svp})$ will be expressed in terms of an *abstraction* mapping relating, more in general, $\mathbb{P}_D$ to $\mathbb{P}_O$: we shall define the function

$$
\text{abs}: \mathbb{P}_D \to \mathbb{P}_O
$$

in such a manner that *abs* may be taken as deleting information from an element p in $\mathbb{P}_D$, such that the resulting element $abs(p)$ resides in $\mathbb{P}_O$. (The fact that *abs* deletes information may explain that we call it an *abstraction* function.) Let us recall that $\mathbb{P}_D$ consists of sets of sequences of pairs of states, including possibly nonconsecutive sequences, i.e., sequences with segments

$$
\ldots \langle\sigma_i,\sigma_i'\rangle \cdot \langle\sigma_{i+1},\sigma_{i+1}'\rangle \ldots
$$

with $\sigma_i' \neq \sigma_{i+1}$. Moreover, we note that such sequences are included to achieve compositionality of $\mathcal{D}$ (and $\mathcal{O}^*$). In the operational outcome $\mathcal{O}(s,\sigma)$, no counterpart of such non-consecutive sequences is present. In going from $\mathbb{P}_D$ to $\mathbb{P}_O$, we therefore firstly have to get rid of all nonconsecutive sequences. Next, we discuss what to do with the remaining (consecutive) sequences. Note that these can be seen as the result of "complete" executions without having to cope with possible subsequent interleavings. Now, for each finite or infinite sequence

$$
\langle\sigma,\sigma_1\rangle \cdot \langle\sigma_1,\sigma_2\rangle \ldots \langle\sigma_{n-1},\sigma_n\rangle \in p
$$

or

$$
\langle\sigma,\sigma_1\rangle \cdot \langle\sigma_1,\sigma_2\rangle \ldots \langle\sigma_{n-1},\sigma_n\rangle \cdot \langle\sigma_n,\sigma_{n+1}\rangle \ldots \in p,
$$

we want $abs(p)$ to be defined such that we have, for argument σ, that

$$\sigma_1\sigma_2\ldots\sigma_n \in abs(p)(\sigma)$$

or

$$\sigma_1\sigma_2\ldots\sigma_n\sigma_{n+1}\ldots \in abs(p)(\sigma).$$

For the rigorous definition of abs, various preparations are necessary. Let, as before, $\mathbb{Q}_D = (\Sigma \times \Sigma)^\infty\backslash\{\epsilon\}$. As type of abs we want, more in full,

$$abs\colon \mathcal{P}_{ncl}(\mathbb{Q}_D) \to \Sigma \to \mathcal{P}_{nco}(\Sigma^\infty).$$

In order that $abs(p)(\sigma)$ be well-defined, i.e., nonempty and compact for each σ, we have to impose an additional finiteness condition on the (nonempty and) closed subsets of $\mathbb{Q}_D$ used in the denotational domain $\mathbb{P}_D$. Consider, for example, the closed set $p = \{\langle\sigma_1,\sigma_1\rangle, \langle\sigma_2,\sigma_2\rangle, \ldots\}$, for an arbitrary infinite set $\{\sigma_1,\sigma_2,\ldots\}\subseteq \Sigma$. By the definition of $abs(p)$ as just sketched, we would obtain $abs(p)(\sigma) = \{\sigma_1,\sigma_2,\ldots\}$, which is clearly a noncompact set. (To avoid possible confusion here, let us point out that the p just given is in $\mathbb{P}_D$, but not meaning of any s in $\mathcal{L}_{svp}$.) In order to guarantee that $abs(p)(\sigma)$ is nonempty and compact for each σ, we shall specialize $\mathbb{P}_D = \mathcal{P}_{ncl}(\mathbb{Q}_D)$ to the subset $\mathbb{P}_{Df} = \mathcal{P}_{fncl}(\mathbb{Q}_D)$, where $\mathcal{P}_{fncl}(\cdot)$ denotes the collection of all *finitary nonempty* (to be defined in a moment) and closed subsets of $(\cdot)$. Before embarking upon this definition, let us already point out that we shall have to make sure that, for each s, $\mathcal{D}(s) \in \mathbb{P}_{Df}$. This fact will be shown in Lemma 7.17.

For the formulation of the notion of finitary nonempty we introduce some notation. Let $(q \in)\mathbb{Q}^*$ be short for $(\Sigma \times \Sigma)^*$, the set of all *finite* (possibly empty) sequences of pairs of states.

Definition 7.15

(a) For $q \in \mathbb{Q}^*$, $\sigma \in \Sigma$, $p \in \mathbb{P}_D$ we put

$$[q,\sigma,p] = \{\sigma' \mid \exists q' \in \mathbb{Q}^*\colon q \cdot \langle\sigma,\sigma'\rangle \cdot q' \in p\}.$$

(b) We call $p \in \mathbb{P}_D$ finitary nonempty whenever

    (1) $p \neq \emptyset$

    (2) For all $q \in \mathbb{Q}^*$ we have that (precisely) one of the following two conditions holds

(i) For all σ, $[q, \sigma, p] = \emptyset$

(ii) For all σ, $0 < \|[q, \sigma, p]\| < \infty$.

(c) Let $\mathbb{P}_{Df}$ denote the collection of all finitary nonempty and closed subsets of $\mathbb{Q}_D$.

In words, we have that $p \in \mathbb{P}_D$ is finitary nonempty whenever $p \neq \emptyset$ and, for each finite q, either we have that for *no* σ it is possible to extend q through σ into an element of p, i.e., for no σ' can we find a q' such that

$$q \cdot \langle \sigma, \sigma' \rangle \cdot q' \in p, \tag{7.7}$$

or for *all* σ we may extend q through σ into an element of p. However, this extension is then possible in only *finitely* many ways: For finitely many σ', there exists some q' such that (7.7) holds.

In order that $\mathbb{P}_{Df}$ may serve as a carrier for the general theory developed so far, it certainly has to be complete. This is the content of

Lemma 7.16 *If $(p_i)_i$ is a Cauchy sequence of finitary nonempty and closed sets, then $\lim_i p_i$ is a finitary nonempty and closed set.*

Proof Let $(p_i)_i$ be a Cauchy sequence in $\mathbb{P}_{Df}$. By Hahn's theorem (Theorem 2.10), $p = \lim_i p_i$ is nonempty and closed. We now prove that p is finitary nonempty. The following claim is the crucial step in the proof.

Claim: $\forall q \in \mathbb{Q}^*, \sigma \in \Sigma \exists k \forall n \geq k([q, \sigma, p] = [q, \sigma, p_n])$.

Proof of the claim: Choose some $q \in \mathbb{Q}^*$ and σ. Since $(p_i)_i$ converges to p, we may find some k such that, for all $n \geq k$, $d(p_n, p) < 2^{-(lgt(q)+1)}$. Hence, for each σ', a sequence $q \cdot \langle \sigma, \sigma' \rangle$ may be extended to an element of p_n whenever $q \cdot \langle \sigma, \sigma' \rangle$ may be extended to an element of p, and the desired result follows.

We next show that p is finitary nonempty. Assume that p is *not* finitary nonempty. Then there exist q, σ_1, σ_2 such that $[q, \sigma_1, p] \neq \emptyset$ and ($\|[q, \sigma_2, p]\| = 0$ or $\|[q, \sigma_2, p]\| = \infty$). By the claim, if $\|[q, \sigma_2, p]\| = \infty$ then $\|[q, \sigma_2, p_k]\| = \infty$ for some k, contradicting that p_k is finitary nonempty. There remains the case that $[q, \sigma_1, p] \neq \emptyset$ and $[q, \sigma_2, p] = \emptyset$. By the claim, there exist k_1, k_2 such that $[q, \sigma_1, p_n] = [q, \sigma_1, p]$, for all $n \geq k_1$, and $[q, \sigma_2, p_n] = [q, \sigma_2, p]$, for all $n \geq k_2$. Taking $k = max\{k_1, k_2\}$, we have $[q, \sigma_1, p_k] \neq \emptyset$, and $[q, \sigma_2, p_k] = \emptyset$ and contradicting that p_k is finitary nonempty. □

The main semantic motivation for introducing the notion of "finitary nonempty" stems from the fact that the sets delivered by $\mathcal{O}^*$ (and, hence, also by $\mathcal{D}$) are indeed finitary nonempty:

Lemma 7.17 $\mathcal{O}^*(s)$ *is finitary nonempty and closed, for each* $s \in \mathcal{L}_{svp}$.

Proof Let $\mathbb{P}_{O\cdot f} \stackrel{df}{=} \mathcal{P}_{fncl}((\Sigma \times \Sigma)^\infty)$. Put $(S \in)Sem_{O\cdot} = Res \to \mathbb{P}_{O\cdot f}$, and let $\Phi^*\colon Sem_{O\cdot} \to Sem_{O\cdot}$ be given by $\Phi^*(S)(\mathrm{E}) = \{\,\epsilon\,\}$, and

$$\Phi^*(S)(s) = \bigcup\{\,\langle \sigma, \sigma' \rangle \cdot S(r) \mid [s, \sigma] \to [r, \sigma']\,\}, \quad \text{with `}\to\text{' from } \mathcal{T}'_{svp}.$$

By Lemma 7.16, $\mathbb{P}_{O\cdot f}$ is a complete metric space. By the usual argument (based on the image-finiteness of $\mathcal{T}'_{svp}$), $\Phi^*(S)(s)$ is closed. Since we even know the $\mathcal{T}'_{svp}$ is locally finitely branching (Lemma 7.13), the above definition yields that $\Phi^*(S)(s)$ is finitary nonempty, for each S, s. Putting $\mathcal{O}^* = fix(\Phi^*)$ as usual then gives the desired result. $\qquad\square$

At last, we are ready for the definition of the abstraction function:

Definition 7.18

(a) Let $(\psi \in)\, Op = \mathbb{P}_{Df} \to \mathbb{P}_O$. The mapping $\Omega_{abs}\colon Op \to Op$ is given by

$$\Omega_{abs}(\psi)(p)(\sigma) \;\; = \;\; \bigcup\{\,\sigma' \cdot \psi(p[\sigma, \sigma'])(\sigma') \mid p[\sigma, \sigma'] \neq \emptyset\,\} \cup \\ \{\,\sigma' \mid \langle \sigma, \sigma' \rangle \in p\,\}.$$

(b) $abs = fix(\Omega_{abs})$.

Example

$$abs(\{\, \langle \sigma_0, \sigma_0\{0/v\} \rangle \langle \sigma_1, \sigma_1\{\alpha + 1/v\} \rangle \langle \sigma_2, \sigma_2\{2/v\} \rangle,$$
$$\langle \sigma_0, \sigma_0\{0/v\} \rangle \langle \sigma_2, \sigma_2\{2/v\} \rangle \langle \sigma_1, \sigma_1\{\alpha + 1/v\} \rangle,$$
$$\langle \sigma_2, \sigma_2\{2/v\} \rangle \langle \sigma_0, \sigma_0\{0/v\} \rangle \langle \sigma_1, \sigma_1\{\alpha + 1/v\} \rangle \mid$$
$$\sigma_0, \sigma_1, \sigma_2 \in \Sigma, \alpha = \sigma_1(v)\,\})(\sigma)$$
$$= \;\; \{\, \sigma\{0/v\}\sigma\{1/v\}\sigma\{2/v\},$$
$$\sigma\{0/v\}\sigma\{2/v\}\sigma\{1/v\}, \sigma\{2/v\}\sigma\{0/v\}\sigma\{1/v\}\,\}$$

Justification of Definition 7.18 follows in

Lemma 7.19 Ω_{abs} *is well-defined and contractive in* ψ.

Proof Contractiveness of Ω_{abs} is clear. In order to show that $\Omega_{abs}(\psi)(p)(\sigma)$ is nonempty and compact, we argue as follows. Take $\psi \in Op$, $p \in \mathbb{P}_{Df}$, $\sigma \in \Sigma$. We have that, either

- $\forall \sigma \llbracket \epsilon, \sigma, p \rrbracket = \emptyset$, hence $p = \emptyset$ or $p = \{\epsilon\}$. Since $p \in \mathbb{P}_{Df}$, this case cannot occur.

- $\forall \sigma: 0 < \|\llbracket \epsilon, \sigma, p \rrbracket\| < \infty$. Thus, we have that $p[\sigma, \sigma'] \neq \emptyset$ for a finite nonzero number of σ'. Clearly, $p[\sigma, \sigma']$ is finitary nonempty in case p is finitary nonempty. Thus, the union on the right-hand side of the clause for $\Omega_{abs}(\psi)(p)(\sigma)$ is taken over a finite nonempty index set; moreover, each $\psi(p[\sigma, \sigma'])(\sigma')$ belongs to $\mathcal{P}_{nco}(\Sigma^\infty)$. Since finite nonempty unions preserve nonemptiness and compactness, the desired result follows.   □

The following simple lemma states a property of *abs* we shall apply below.

Lemma 7.20 *For I a finite index set, and $p_i \in \mathbb{P}_{Df}$, $i \in I$, we have*

$$abs(\bigcup_i p_i) = \bigcup_i abs(p_i).$$

Proof Exercise.   □

Finally, we can state and prove the theorem relating $\mathcal{O}$ and $\mathcal{D}$ for $\mathcal{L}_{svp}$. By Lemma 7.14, the only thing left to do is to relate $\mathcal{O}$ and $\mathcal{O}^*$:

Lemma 7.21 $\mathcal{O}\llbracket \cdot \rrbracket = abs \circ \mathcal{O}^*$.

Proof Let $(S' \in)Sem'_O = Res \to \mathbb{P}_O$, and let Φ' be (a variation on the usual Φ) given by $\Phi'(S')(\mathrm{E})(\sigma) = \{\epsilon\}$, $\Phi'(S')(s)(\sigma) = \bigcup\{\sigma' \cdot S'(r)(\sigma') \mid [s, \sigma] \to [r, \sigma']\}$. We leave it to the reader to show that $\mathcal{O}\llbracket \cdot \rrbracket = fix(\Phi')$. We next prove that, for each r, $\Phi'(abs \circ \mathcal{O}^*)(r) = (abs \circ \mathcal{O}^*)(r)$. The case $r \equiv \mathrm{E}$ is clear. For $r \equiv s$ we have, for any σ,

$\Phi'(abs \circ \mathcal{O}^*)(s)(\sigma)$

$= \bigcup\{\sigma' \cdot (abs \circ \mathcal{O}^*)(r)(\sigma') \mid [s, \sigma] \to [r, \sigma'], \sigma' \in \Sigma\}$

$=$ [by the definition of *abs* and Lemma 7.20]

$\quad abs(\bigcup\{\langle \sigma_1, \sigma' \rangle \cdot \mathcal{O}^*(r) \mid [s, \sigma_1] \to [r, \sigma'], \sigma_1, \sigma' \in \Sigma\})(\sigma)$

$= abs(\mathcal{O}^*(s))(\sigma)$

$= (abs \circ \mathcal{O}^*)(s)(\sigma)$.

Hence, $\mathcal{O}\llbracket \cdot \rrbracket = abs \circ \mathcal{O}^*$ follows by Banach's theorem (applied to Φ').   □

This brings us to the final theorem for $\mathcal{L}_{svp}$:

Theorem 7.22 $\mathcal{O}[\![\pi]\!] = (abs \circ \mathcal{D})[\![\pi]\!]$, *for each* $\pi \in \mathcal{L}_{svp}$.

Proof By combining Lemmas 7.14 and 7.21. □

Remark In the above, we have introduced $(\mathbb{P}_D,\ abs$ and$)$ $\mathcal{D}$ such that $\mathcal{O} = abs \circ \mathcal{D}$ holds. In principle, one can imagine several such $(\mathbb{P}_{D'},\ abs'$ and$)$ $\mathcal{D}'$ such that $\mathcal{O} = abs' \circ \mathcal{D}'$. The question then arises which of the $\mathcal{D}$, $\mathcal{D}'$, ... should be seen as the "best" denotational semantics. The technical notion referred to here is that of "full abstractness." Chapter 17 discusses these issues in some detail, and quotes the result that the $\mathcal{D}$ introduced above is indeed best possible.

7.2 Concurrent evaluation of expressions —many sorted transition systems

The concept of parallelism occurs not only in the execution of statements, but as well in that of expressions. In principle, when we want to evaluate the arguments of an expression such as $u(e_1, \ldots, e_\ell)$, there is no reason to restrict ourselves to the case that these arguments are evaluated from left to right (as was the case, e.g., for $\mathcal{L}_{fun}$). We may as well consider the parallel or, as it is often called, *concurrent* evaluation of expressions. Assuming that the evaluation of expressions may have side effects upon the state—otherwise the issue does not arise—one may want to interleave the atomic steps occurring in the evaluation of $e_1, \ldots, e_\ell$, in the same manner as this was done in the previous section for $s_1 \| s_2$. We shall study the ensuing problems in terms of the language $\mathcal{L}_{cee}$, a nonuniform language with expressions—with side effects—where the arguments of constructors are evaluated concurrently. For simplicity, we shall consider only the case that each constructor has precisely two arguments, leaving the general case ($\ell \geq 1$ argument) to the industrious reader. We shall combine the technique developed for $\mathcal{L}_{svp}$ with some of the machinery introduced for $\mathcal{L}_{fun}$. More specifically, from $\mathcal{L}_{svp}$ we take over the use of the state-*pair* sequences, and from $\mathcal{L}_{fun}$ we use the idea of defining the denotational mappings $\langle \mathcal{D}, \mathcal{V} \rangle$ as simultaneous fixed point. As new feature we encounter the use of 'many-sorted' transition systems. This phrase refers to the phenomenon that we shall use transitions both of the form $[s, \sigma] \to [s', \sigma']$ and of the form $[e, \sigma] \to [e', \sigma']$. (To be precise, there is even a third kind of transitions. Details about these will be given in a moment.)

7.2.1 Syntax and operational semantics

Let $(v \in) IVar$, $u \in Constr$ and $(\alpha \in) Val$ be as in Section 1.2, with the extra condition that each u is of arity 2.

Definition 7.23

(a) $s\,(\in Stat) ::= \quad v := e \mid \text{skip} \mid (s;s) \mid \text{if } e \text{ then } s_1 \text{ else } s_2 \text{ fi} \mid$
$\quad\quad\quad\quad\quad\quad\quad \text{while } e \text{ do } s \text{ od}$

(b) $e\,(\in Exp) ::= \alpha \mid v \mid u(e,e) \mid (s;e)$

(c) $(\pi \in)\,\mathcal{L}_{cee} = Stat$.

As before, for $u \in Constr$, $\hat{u}$ stands for the interpretation of u, now a function from Val^2 to Val. The set $(\sigma \in)\,\Sigma$ is the usual one; resumptions are as in Definition 7.2, with the additional clause that E;e and e are identified.

Transitions are a little more complex than those employed so far. They are, in fact, of three kinds

$$[r,\sigma] \to [r',\sigma'] \tag{7.8a}$$

$$[e,\sigma] \to [e',\sigma'] \tag{7.8b}$$

$$[e,\sigma] \to \alpha. \tag{7.8c}$$

Transitions of the first and second kind have the natural interpretation; a transition $[e,\sigma] \to \alpha$ expresses that the evaluation of e in state σ yields, in one step, the result α. As a consequence, no further steps are required in this case. As observables in the transitions (7.8a), (7.8b) and (7.8c) we take σ',σ' and σ, respectively.

Definition 7.24 The transition system $\mathcal{T}_{cee} = ((Res \cup Exp) \times \Sigma \cup Exp, \Sigma, \to, Spec)$, where $Spec$ is given by: (Skip) and (While) as in Definition 7.3, and, in addition,

- $$[\alpha,\sigma] \to \alpha \tag{Val}$$

- $$[v,\sigma] \to [\sigma(v),\sigma] \tag{IVar}$$

- $$\frac{[s,\sigma_1] \to [r,\sigma_2]}{[s;s',\sigma_1] \to [r;s',\sigma_2]} \tag{Seq}$$

  $$[s;e,\sigma_1] \to [r;e,\sigma_2]$$

$$\frac{[e_1, \sigma_1] \to [e_2, \sigma_2]}{}$$

$$[v := e_1, \sigma_1] \to [v := e_2, \sigma_2] \qquad\qquad \text{(Ass 1)}$$

$$[\text{if } e_1 \text{ then } s_1 \text{ else } s_2 \text{ fi}, \sigma_1] \to [\text{if } e_2 \text{ then } s_1 \text{ else } s_2 \text{ fi}, \sigma_2] \qquad \text{(If 1)}$$

$$[u(e_1, e), \sigma_1] \to [u(e_2, e), \sigma_2] \qquad\qquad \text{(Conc 1)}$$

$$[u(e, e_1), \sigma_1] \to [u(e, e_2), \sigma_2] \qquad\qquad \text{(Conc 2)}$$

$$\frac{[e, \sigma] \to \alpha}{}$$

$$[v := e, \sigma] \to [\text{E}, \sigma\{\alpha/v\}] \qquad\qquad \text{(Ass 2)}$$

$$[\text{if } e \text{ then } s_1 \text{ else } s_2 \text{ fi}, \sigma] \to [s_1, \sigma] \qquad \text{if } \alpha = tt \qquad \text{(If 2)}$$

$$[\text{if } e \text{ then } s_1 \text{ else } s_2 \text{ fi}, \sigma] \to [s_2, \sigma] \qquad \text{if } \alpha = f\!f \qquad \text{(If 3)}$$

$$\frac{[e_1, \sigma] \to \alpha_1 \qquad [e_2, \sigma] \to \alpha_2}{[u(e_1, e_2), \sigma] \to \hat{u}(\alpha_1, \alpha_2)} \qquad\qquad \text{(Sync)}$$

The operational semantics of $\mathcal{L}_{cee}$ assigns meanings both to $r \in Res$ and to $e \in Exp$. We introduce two operational codomains $\mathbb{P}_{O,r}$ and $\mathbb{P}_{O,e}$, and two operational semantics $\mathcal{O}_r$ and $\mathcal{O}_e$. $\mathbb{P}_{O,r}$ and $\mathcal{O}_r$ are the usual ones, $\mathbb{P}_{O,e}$ and $\mathcal{O}_e$ cater for the situation that, eventually, a value $\alpha \in Val$ is yielded, in general after the delivery of a number of intermediate states.

Below, we shall use the following

Notation 7.25 Let A be an alphabet, A^∞ as usual, and B an arbitrary set. We put $A^\infty ; B = \{\, u;v \mid u \in A^\infty, v \in B \,\}$, where

$$\begin{aligned}
u;v &= u, \text{ if } u \in A^\omega \\
\epsilon;v &= v \\
(au');v &= a \cdot (u';v), \text{ if } au' \in A^*.
\end{aligned}$$

We now give

Definition 7.26 We assume the discrete metric on Val.

(a) $\mathbb{P}_{O,r} = \Sigma \to \mathcal{P}_{nco}(\Sigma^{\infty})$, $\mathbb{P}_{O,e} = \Sigma \to \mathcal{P}_{nco}(\Sigma^{\infty}; Val)$

(b) The mappings $\mathcal{O}_r$ and $\mathcal{O}_e$ have type $\mathcal{O}_r \colon Res \times \Sigma \to \mathcal{P}_{nco}(\Sigma^{\infty})$ and $\mathcal{O}_e \colon Exp \times \Sigma \to \mathcal{P}_{nco}(\Sigma^{\infty}; Val)$, and are given as the unique functions satisfying $\mathcal{O}_r(\mathrm{E}, \sigma) = \{\epsilon\}$ and

$$
\begin{aligned}
\mathcal{O}_r(s, \sigma) &= \bigcup \{\sigma' \cdot \mathcal{O}_r(r, \sigma') \mid [s, \sigma] \to [r, \sigma']\} \\
\mathcal{O}_e(e, \sigma) &= \bigcup \{\sigma' \cdot \mathcal{O}_e(e', \sigma') \mid [e, \sigma] \to [e', \sigma']\} \cup \{\alpha \mid [e, \sigma] \to \alpha\}.
\end{aligned}
$$

(c) $\mathcal{O}_r[\![\cdot]\!] \colon \mathcal{L}_{cee} \to \mathbb{P}_{O,r}$ and $\mathcal{O}_e[\![\cdot]\!] \colon Exp \to \mathbb{P}_{O,e}$ are given by

$$
\mathcal{O}_r[\![s]\!] = \lambda\sigma.\mathcal{O}_r(s, \sigma) \quad \text{and} \quad \mathcal{O}_e[\![e]\!] = \lambda\sigma.\mathcal{O}_e(e, \sigma).
$$

Examples Let σ_i be short for $\sigma\{i/v\}$, $i = 1, 2$.

(1) $\quad \mathcal{O}_e[\![(v := 1; v) + (v := 2; v)]\!](\sigma)$
$\quad = \mathcal{O}_e((v := 1; v) + (v := 2; v), \sigma)$
$\quad = \{\sigma_1\sigma_1\sigma_2\sigma_2 3, \sigma_1\sigma_2\sigma_2\sigma_2 4, \sigma_2\sigma_1\sigma_1\sigma_1 2, \sigma_2\sigma_2\sigma_1\sigma_1 3\}$

(2) $\quad \mathcal{O}_r v := (v := 1; v) + (v := 2; v)(\sigma)$
$\quad = \mathcal{O}_r([\![v := (v := 1; v) + (v := 2; v)]\!], \sigma)$
$\quad = \{\sigma_1\sigma_1\sigma_2\sigma_2\sigma\{3/v\}, \sigma_1\sigma_2\sigma_2\sigma_2\sigma\{4/v\},$
$\quad\quad\quad \sigma_2\sigma_1\sigma_1\sigma_1\sigma\{2/v\}, \sigma_2\sigma_2\sigma_1\sigma_1\sigma\{3/v\}\}$

7.2.2 Denotational semantics, relating $\mathcal{O}$ and $\mathcal{D}$

The denotational meaning functions $\mathcal{D}$ and $\mathcal{V}$ are obtained as simultaneous fixed point of a (higher-order, contractive) mapping Ψ. For the moment, we restrict ourselves to the introduction of the *closed* variety of the respective power domains. Later in this subsection we shall specify the finitary nonempty version of the domains involved.

Definition 7.27

(a) $(q \in) \mathbb{Q}_D = (\Sigma \times \Sigma)^{\infty} \backslash \{\epsilon\}$, $(p \in) \mathbb{P}_D = \mathcal{P}_{ncl}(\mathbb{Q}_D)$

(b) $(z \in) \mathbb{Z}_D = (\Sigma \times \Sigma)^{\omega} \cup (\Sigma \times \Sigma)^*; Val$, $(w \in) \mathbb{W}_D = \mathcal{P}_{ncl}(\mathbb{Z}_D)$.

Thus, elements $z \in \mathbb{Z}_D$ are either infinite sequences of state pairs $\langle \sigma_1, \sigma_1' \rangle \langle \sigma_2, \sigma_2' \rangle \cdots$, or finite such sequences with some $\alpha \in \text{Val}$ appended at the end. An element $w (\in \mathbb{W}_D)$ is—for the moment—a nonempty closed subset of $\mathbb{Z}_D$. On $\mathbb{P}_D$, the operator ';' is defined as in Section 7.1. For $p \in \mathbb{P}_D$, $w \in \mathbb{W}_D$, $p;w$ is defined as explained above.

Clearly, the main problem in the denotational definition consists in the treatment of the case $\mathcal{V}(u(e_1, e_2))$ in its definition. We shall employ an auxiliary mapping $\mathcal{U}(u): \mathbb{W}_D{}^2 \to \mathbb{W}_D$, the definition of which follows in Definition 7.29.

Definition 7.28

(a) Let $(S \in) SSem_D = Stat \to \mathbb{P}_D$, $(T \in) ESem_D = Exp \to \mathbb{W}_D$. Let $\Psi: SSem_D \times ESem_D \to SSem_D \times ESem_D$ be defined by putting $\Psi(S, T) = (\hat{S}, \hat{T})$, and by specifying $\hat{S}$ and $\hat{T}$ for each argument s and e, respectively. In the clauses to given here, various auxiliary functions are used which will be specified in part (b) of this definition.

$$
\begin{aligned}
\hat{S}(v := e) &= \text{ass}(v, \hat{T}(e)) \\
\hat{S}(\text{skip}) &= \text{skip} \\
\hat{S}(s_1; s_2) &= \hat{S}(s_1); \hat{S}(s_2) \\
\hat{S}(\text{if } e \text{ then } s_1 \text{ else } s_2 \text{ fi}) &= if(\hat{T}(e), \hat{S}(s_1), \hat{S}(s_2)) \\
\hat{S}(\text{while } e \text{ do } s \text{ od}) &= \\
&\quad \bigcup \{ \langle \sigma, \sigma \rangle \cdot if(\hat{T}(e), \hat{S}(s); S(\text{while } e \text{ do } s \text{ od}), skip) \mid \sigma \in \Sigma \}.
\end{aligned}
$$

$$
\begin{aligned}
\hat{T}(\alpha) &= \{ \alpha \} \\
\hat{T}(v) &= \{ \langle \sigma, \sigma \rangle \cdot \sigma(v) \mid \sigma \in \Sigma \} \\
\hat{T}(u(e_1, e_2)) &= \mathcal{U}(u)(\hat{T}(e_1), \hat{T}(e_2)) \\
\hat{T}(s; e) &= \hat{S}(s); \hat{T}(e).
\end{aligned}
$$

(b) Below, we use the notation $w[\sigma, \sigma']$ as an obvious variation on the notation used in Definition 7.9—including $\alpha[\sigma, \sigma'] = \emptyset$ as special case. The functions skip, ass and if are defined by

$$ skip = \{ \langle \sigma, \sigma \rangle \mid \sigma \in \Sigma \}. $$

ass is the unique function satisfying

$$
\begin{aligned}
\text{ass}(v, w) = \ &\bigcup \{ \langle \sigma, \sigma' \rangle \cdot \text{ass}(v, w[\sigma, \sigma']) \mid w[\sigma, \sigma'] \neq \emptyset, \sigma, \sigma' \in \Sigma \} \cup \\
&\{ \langle \sigma, \sigma\{\alpha/v\} \rangle \mid \alpha \in w, \sigma \in \Sigma \}.
\end{aligned}
$$

if is the unique function satisfying

$$if(w, p_1, p_2) \; = \\ \bigcup \{ \langle \sigma, \sigma' \rangle \cdot if(w[\sigma, \sigma'], p_1, p_2) \mid w[\sigma, \sigma'] \neq \emptyset, \sigma, \sigma' \in \Sigma \} \cup \\ \bigcup \{ \text{if } \alpha \text{ then } p_1 \text{ else } p_2 \text{ fi} \mid \alpha \in w \}.$$

(c) $\langle \mathcal{D}, \mathcal{V} \rangle = \mathit{fix}(\Psi)$.

Well-definedness of (*ass*, *if* and) Ψ—apart from the still to be treated case of $\mathcal{U}(u)$—may be shown by the familiar argument. Note in particular our use of $S(\text{while } e \text{ do } s \text{ od})$—rather than of $\hat{S}(\text{while } e \text{ do } s \text{ od})$—on the right-hand side of the clause of $\hat{S}(\text{while } e \text{ do } s \text{ od})$. Contractiveness of Ψ in $\langle S, T \rangle$ is standard by structural induction on s, e.

There remains the task of defining $\mathcal{U}(u)$. We are guided in this definition by the following operational scheme for the concurrent evaluation of $u(e_1, e_2)$ in state σ.

Initialize: the value of $u(e_1, e_2)$ in state σ is determined as follows:

(1) If the evaluations of both e_1 and e_2 terminate directly, yielding results α_1 and α_2, then the desired result is $\hat{u}(\alpha_1, \alpha_2)$, and the evaluation is completed. Otherwise a choice is made between 2 and 3:

(2) If the evaluation of e_1 in state σ requires a step, transforming e_1 to e' and σ to σ', then deliver the pair $\langle \sigma, \sigma' \rangle$, replace e_1 by e' and σ by σ', and go to *Initialize*.

(3) If the evaluation of e_2 in state σ requires a step, transforming e_2 to e'' and σ to σ'', then deliver the pair $\langle \sigma, \sigma'' \rangle$, replace e_2 by e'' and σ by σ'', and go to *Initialize*.

This algorithm for the concurrent evaluation of $u(e_1, e_2)$ is reflected in

Definition 7.29 Let $\mathbb{W}_D{}^+$ denote $\mathbb{W}_D \cup \{\emptyset\}$. The mapping $\mathcal{U}: \mathit{Constr} \to \mathbb{W}_D \times \mathbb{W}_D \to \mathbb{W}_D$ yields, for each $u \in \mathit{Constr}$, the unique function $\mathcal{U}(u)$ (and the unique functions $\mathcal{U}(u)_\ell: \mathbb{W}_D \times \mathbb{W}_D \to \mathbb{W}_D{}^+$ and $\mathcal{U}(u)_c: \mathbb{W}_D \times \mathbb{W}_D \to \mathbb{W}_D{}^+$) satisfying

$$\mathcal{U}(u)(w_1, w_2) \; = \; \mathcal{U}(u)_\ell(w_1, w_2) \cup \mathcal{U}(u)_\ell(w_2, w_1) \cup \mathcal{U}(u)_c(w_1, w_2),$$

where

$$\mathcal{U}(u)_\ell(w_1, w_2) \; = \\ \bigcup \{ \langle \sigma, \sigma' \rangle \cdot \mathcal{U}(u)(w_1[\sigma, \sigma'], w_2) \mid w_1[\sigma, \sigma'] \neq \emptyset, \sigma, \sigma' \in \Sigma \} \\ \mathcal{U}(u)_c(w_1, w_2) \; = \; \{ \hat{u}(\alpha_1, \alpha_2) \mid \alpha_1 \in w_1, \alpha_2 \in w_2 \}.$$

Examples

(1) $\quad \mathcal{V}((v := 1;v) + (v := 2;v))$

$\quad = \mathcal{U}(+)(\mathcal{V}(v := 1;v), \mathcal{V}(v := 2;v))$

$\quad = \mathcal{U}(+)(\mathcal{D}(v := 1);\mathcal{V}(v), \mathcal{D}(v := 2);\mathcal{V}(v))$

$\quad = \mathcal{U}(+)(\mathrm{ass}(v, \{1\});\{\,\langle \sigma, \sigma \rangle \cdot \sigma(v) \mid \sigma \in \Sigma\,\},$

$\quad\quad\quad \mathrm{ass}(v, \{2\});\{\,\langle \sigma, \sigma \rangle \cdot \sigma(v) \mid \sigma \in \Sigma\,\})$

$\quad = \mathcal{U}(+)(\{\,\langle \sigma_1, \sigma_1\{1/v\}\rangle\langle \sigma_1', \sigma_1'\rangle \sigma_1'(v) \mid \sigma_1, \sigma_1' \in \Sigma\,\},$

$\quad\quad\quad \{\,\langle \sigma_2, \sigma_2\{2/v\}\rangle\langle \sigma_2', \sigma_2'\rangle \sigma_2'(v) \mid \sigma_2, \sigma_2' \in \Sigma\,\})$

$\quad = \{\,\langle \sigma_1, \sigma_1\{1/v\}\rangle\langle \sigma_1', \sigma_1'\rangle\langle \sigma_2, \sigma_2\{2/v\}\rangle\langle \sigma_2', \sigma_2'\rangle(\sigma_1'(v) + \sigma_2'(v)),$

$\quad\quad\quad \langle \sigma_1, \sigma_1\{1/v\}\rangle\langle \sigma_2, \sigma_2\{2/v\}\rangle\langle \sigma_1', \sigma_1'\rangle\langle \sigma_2', \sigma_2'\rangle(\sigma_1'(v) + \sigma_2'(v)),$

$\quad\quad\quad\quad \langle \sigma_1, \sigma_1\{1/v\}\rangle\langle \sigma_2, \sigma_2\{2/v\}\rangle\langle \sigma_2', \sigma_2'\rangle\langle \sigma_1', \sigma_1'\rangle(\sigma_1'(v) + \sigma_2'(v)),$

$\quad\quad\quad\quad \ldots \mid \sigma_1, \sigma_1', \sigma_2, \sigma_2' \in \Sigma\,\}$

(2) $\quad \mathcal{D}(v := (v := 1;v) + (v := 2;v))$

$\quad = \{\,\langle \sigma_1, \sigma_1\{1/v\}\rangle\langle \sigma_1', \sigma_1'\rangle \cdot$

$\quad\quad\quad\quad \langle \sigma_2, \sigma_2\{2/v\}\rangle\langle \sigma_2', \sigma_2'\rangle\langle \sigma, \sigma\{(\sigma_1'(v) + \sigma_2'(v))/v\}\rangle,$

$\quad\quad\quad \langle \sigma_1, \sigma_1\{1/v\}\rangle\langle \sigma_2, \sigma_2\{2/v\}\rangle \cdot$

$\quad\quad\quad\quad \langle \sigma_1', \sigma_1'\rangle\langle \sigma_2', \sigma_2'\rangle\langle \sigma, \sigma\{(\sigma_1'(v) + \sigma_2'(v))/v\}\rangle,$

$\quad\quad\quad \langle \sigma_1, \sigma_1\{1/v\}\rangle\langle \sigma_2, \sigma_2\{2/v\}\rangle \cdot$

$\quad\quad\quad\quad \langle \sigma_2', \sigma_2'\rangle\langle \sigma_1', \sigma_1'\rangle\langle \sigma, \sigma\{(\sigma_1'(v) + \sigma_2'(v))/v\}\rangle,$

$\quad\quad\quad\quad \ldots \mid \sigma_1, \sigma_1', \sigma_2, \sigma_2', \sigma \in \Sigma\,\}.$

Definition 7.29 may be justified in the customary way. $\mathcal{U}(u)_\ell$ stands for the left merge of w_1 and w_2; it may be compared with the operator $\parallel$ occurring in $p_1 \parallel p_2$. The entity $\mathcal{U}(u)_c(w_1, w_2)$ yields the *completed* part of the result. This has no counterpart in the semantic operators as studied up till now (but a closely related operator will appear in the form of the synchronization operator $p_1|p_2$ in Chapter 11, incidentally, this also explains the name for the (Sync) rule in $\mathcal{T}_{cee}$). Note that the verification of the property that $\mathcal{U}(u)(w_1, w_2) \neq \emptyset$ requires some care since, contrary to the situation in earlier chapters, intermediate (partial) results which are equal to the empty set may now be yielded. More specifically, both $\mathcal{U}(u)_\ell(w_1, w_2)$ and $\mathcal{U}(u)_c(w_1, w_2)$ may be empty. For example, $\mathcal{U}(u)_\ell(\alpha_1, \alpha_2) = \emptyset$, and $\mathcal{U}(u)_c(w_1, w_2) = \emptyset$ in case $w_1, w_2 \subseteq (\Sigma \times \Sigma)^\omega$. However, one easily checks that such cases cannot occur simultaneously and, putting the various summands for $\mathcal{U}(u)(w_1, w_2)$ together, one may establish that $\mathcal{U}(u)(w_1, w_2) \neq \emptyset$.

Before embarking upon an analysis of the relationship between $\mathcal{O}_r$ and $\mathcal{D}$ (and $\mathcal{O}_e$ and $\mathcal{V}$) we state a useful

Lemma 7.30 *For each e, α*

(a) If $[e, \sigma] \to \alpha$ for some σ, then $[e, \sigma] \to \alpha$ for all σ.

(b) $\alpha \in \mathcal{V}(e)$ iff $[e, \sigma] \to \alpha$ for all σ.

Proof Easy by structural induction on e, using the fact that, for any σ, $[e, \sigma] \to \alpha$ iff e contains no individual variable which is *vital* for e in σ. Here we call an individual variable v vital for e in σ if the evaluation of e requires $\sigma(v)$. $\qquad\square$

Our next step is quite similar to what we did for $\mathcal{L}_{svp}$. We introduce the transition system $\mathcal{T}'_{cee}$ with transitions

$$r \xrightarrow{\langle \sigma, \sigma' \rangle} r', \ e \xrightarrow{\langle \sigma, \sigma' \rangle} e', \text{ and } e \xrightarrow{\sigma} \alpha,$$

and with the observables as suggested by this notation. Writing (as before) $[r, \sigma] \to [r', \sigma']$, $[e, \sigma] \to [e', \sigma']$ and $[e, \sigma] \to \alpha$ for the transitions as just given, we may identify $Spec'$ with $Spec$ for $\mathcal{T}_{cee}$. We next introduce the hybrid meaning functions $\mathcal{O}_r^*$, $\mathcal{O}_e^*$—based on $\mathcal{T}'_{cee}$ but delivering results in the denotational domains—in

Definition 7.31 Let $\mathbb{Q}_{O^*} = (\Sigma \times \Sigma)^\infty$, $\mathbb{Z}_{O^*} = \mathbb{Q}_{O^*}; Val$, $\mathbb{P}_{O^*} = \mathcal{P}_{ncl}(\mathbb{Q}_{O^*})$, $\mathbb{W}_{O^*} = \mathcal{P}_{ncl}(\mathbb{Z}_{O^*})$.

(a) The mapping $\mathcal{O}_r^*: Res \to \mathbb{P}_{O^*}$ is the unique function satisfying

$$\begin{aligned} \mathcal{O}_r^*(\mathrm{E}) &= \quad \{\epsilon\} \\ \mathcal{O}_r^*(s) &= \bigcup\{\, \langle \sigma, \sigma' \rangle \cdot \mathcal{O}_r^*(r) \mid [s, \sigma] \to [r, \sigma']\,\} \end{aligned}$$
$$\text{where ' } \to \text{ ' is with respect to } \mathcal{T}'_{cee}.$$

(b) The mapping $\mathcal{O}_e^*: Exp \to \mathbb{W}_{O^*}$ is the unique function satisfying

$$\mathcal{O}_e^*(e) = \bigcup\{\, \langle \sigma, \sigma' \rangle \cdot \mathcal{O}_e^*(e) \mid [e, \sigma] \to [e', \sigma']\,\} \cup \{\, \alpha \mid [e, \sigma] \to \alpha\,\}$$
$$\text{where ' } \to \text{ ' is with respect to } \mathcal{T}'_{cee}.$$

Note that the second summand for $\mathcal{O}_e^*(e)$ does not depend on σ, by Lemma 7.30. With obvious modifications, the arguments used after Definition 7.12 to show well-definedness of $\mathcal{O}^*$ based on the fact that $\mathcal{T}'_{svp}$ is (locally finitely branching, hence) image-finite may be applied here to infer that $\mathcal{O}_r^*$ and $\mathcal{O}_e^*$ are well-defined based on the same property for $\mathcal{T}'_{cee}$.

The next lemma is the key result on the way to settle the relationship between $\mathcal{O}_r$ and $\mathcal{D}$ (and $\mathcal{O}_e$ and $\mathcal{V}$). Let Φ_r^*, Φ_e^* be the higher-order mappings used (implicitly) in the above definitions. First, we extend $\mathcal{D}$ to $\mathcal{E}$, defined on all of Res by putting $\mathcal{E}(\mathrm{E}) = \{\epsilon\}$, $\mathcal{E}(s) = \mathcal{D}(s)$. We have

Lemma 7.32

(a) For each r, e

$$\begin{aligned}
\Phi_r^*(\mathcal{E})(r) &= \mathcal{E}(r) \\
\Phi_e^*(\mathcal{V})(e) &= \mathcal{V}(e)
\end{aligned}$$

(b) $\mathcal{O}_r^* = \mathcal{E}$, $\mathcal{O}_e^* = \mathcal{V}$.

Proof Simultaneous structural induction on (r, e). Two subcases

$[v := e]$ $\quad \Phi_r^*(\mathcal{E})(v := e)$

$\quad = \quad$ [def. Φ_r^*] $\bigcup\{\langle \sigma, \sigma' \rangle \cdot \mathcal{E}(v := e') \mid [e, \sigma] \to [e', \sigma']\} \cup$
$\quad\quad\quad\quad\quad\quad \{\langle \sigma, \sigma\{\alpha/v\}\rangle \mid [e, \sigma] \to \alpha\}$

$\quad = \quad$ [def. $\mathcal{E}$] $\bigcup\{\langle \sigma, \sigma' \rangle \cdot ass(v, \mathcal{V}(e')) \mid [e, \sigma] \to [e', \sigma']\} \cup$
$\quad\quad\quad\quad\quad\quad \{\langle \sigma, \sigma\{\alpha/v\}\rangle \mid [e, \sigma] \to \alpha\}$

$\quad = \quad$ [def. ass]
$\quad\quad ass(v, \bigcup\{\langle \sigma, \sigma' \rangle \cdot \mathcal{V}(e') \mid [e, \sigma] \to [e', \sigma']\} \cup \{\alpha \mid [e, \sigma] \to \alpha\})$

$\quad = \quad$ [def. Φ_e^*] $ass(v, \Phi_e^*(\mathcal{V})(e))$

$\quad = \quad$ [ind. hyp.] $ass(v, \mathcal{V}(e))$

$\quad = \quad \mathcal{E}(v := e)$.

$[u(e_1, e_2)]$ $\quad \Phi_e^*(\mathcal{V})(u(e_1, e_2))$

$\quad = \quad$ [def. Φ_e^*] $\bigcup\{\langle \sigma, \sigma' \rangle \cdot \mathcal{V}(e) \mid [u(e_1, e_2), \sigma] \to [e, \sigma']\} \cup$
$\quad\quad\quad\quad\quad\quad \{\alpha \mid [u(e_1, e_2), \sigma] \to \alpha\}$

$\quad = \quad$ [def. $\mathcal{T}_{cee}$]
$\quad\quad \bigcup\{\langle \sigma, \sigma' \rangle \cdot \mathcal{V}(u(e', e_2)) \mid [e_1, \sigma] \to [e', \sigma']\} \cup$ (symm.) $\cup$
$\quad\quad\quad \{\hat{u}(\alpha_1, \alpha_2) \mid [e_1, \sigma] \to \alpha_1, [e_2, \sigma] \to \alpha_2\}$

$\quad = \quad$ [def. $\mathcal{V}$, Lemma 7.30]
$\quad\quad \bigcup\{\langle \sigma, \sigma' \rangle \cdot \mathcal{U}(u)(\mathcal{V}(e'), \mathcal{V}(e_2)) \mid [e_1, \sigma] \to [e', \sigma']\} \cup$ (symm.) $\cup$
$\quad\quad\quad \{\hat{u}(\alpha_1, \alpha_2) \mid \alpha_1 \in \mathcal{V}(e_1), \alpha_2 \in \mathcal{V}(e_2)\}$

$\quad = \quad$ [by the definition of $\mathcal{U}(u)_\ell$, the added term $\{\alpha \mid [e_1, \sigma] \to \alpha\}$
$\quad\quad$ contributes $\emptyset$ to the result]
$\quad\quad \mathcal{U}(u)_\ell(\bigcup\{\langle \sigma, \sigma' \rangle \cdot \mathcal{V}(e') \mid [e_1, \sigma] \to [e', \sigma']\} \cup \{\alpha \mid [e_1, \sigma] \to \alpha\}, \mathcal{V}(e_2))$
$\quad\quad \cup$ (symm.) $\cup \mathcal{U}(u)_c(\mathcal{V}(e_1), \mathcal{V}(e_2))$

$$= \text{[ind. hyp.]} \; \mathcal{U}(u)_\ell(\mathcal{V}(e_1), \mathcal{V}(e_2)) \cup (\text{symm.}) \cup \mathcal{U}(u)_c(\mathcal{V}(e_1), \mathcal{V}(e_2))$$
$$= \mathcal{U}(u)(\mathcal{V}(e_1), \mathcal{V}(e_2))$$
$$= \mathcal{V}(u(e_1, e_2)). \qquad\qquad\qquad\qquad\qquad\qquad\qquad \square$$

We conclude this section with the introduction of the abstraction operators

$$\text{abs}_r \colon \mathbb{P}_D \to \Sigma \to \mathcal{P}_{nco}(\Sigma^\infty)$$
$$\text{abs}_e \colon \mathbb{W}_D \to \Sigma \to \mathcal{P}_{nco}(\Sigma^\infty; Val).$$

Just as in Section 7.1, in order that these abstraction operators be well-defined, we require an additional finiteness condition on the denotational domains.

Definition 7.33

(a) $\mathbb{P}_{Df} = \mathcal{P}_{fncl}(\mathbb{Q}_D)$ is as in Section 7.1.

(b) Let, for $q \in \mathbb{Q}^*$, the set $[q, \sigma, w]$ be defined by

$$[q, \sigma, w] = \{\, \sigma' \in \Sigma \mid \exists z \in \mathbb{W}_D \,[\, q \cdot \langle \sigma, \sigma' \rangle \cdot z \in w \,] \,\}.$$

(c) We call $w \in \mathbb{W}_D$ finitary nonempty whenever

   (1) $w \neq \emptyset$

   (2) For each $q \in \mathbb{Q}^*$, (precisely) one of the following conditions holds

     (i) For all σ, $[q, \sigma, w] = \emptyset$

     (ii) For all σ, $0 < |[q, \sigma, w]| < \infty$

   (3) We put $\mathbb{W}_{Df} = \mathcal{P}_{fncl}(\mathbb{Z}_D)$.

By a straightforward extension of the arguments used at the end of Section 7.1, one may show that $\mathbb{W}_{Df}$ is a complete metric space, that $\mathcal{D}(s) \in \mathbb{P}_{Df}$ for each $s \in \mathcal{L}_{cee}$, and $\mathcal{V}(e) \in \mathbb{W}_{Df}$, for each $e \in Exp$. This brings us to

Definition 7.34 The functions abs_r, abs_e are of type as just given, with $\mathbb{P}_{Df}$ and $\mathbb{W}_{Df}$ replacing $\mathbb{P}_D$ and $\mathbb{W}_D$, and are specified as the unique functions satisfying

$$\text{abs}_r(p)(\sigma) =$$
$$\bigcup \{\, \sigma' \cdot \text{abs}_r(p[\sigma, \sigma'])(\sigma') \mid p[\sigma, \sigma'] \neq \emptyset \,\} \cup \{\, \sigma' \mid \langle \sigma, \sigma' \rangle \in p \,\}$$
$$\text{abs}_e(w)(\sigma) =$$
$$\bigcup \{\, \sigma' \cdot \text{abs}_e(w[\sigma, \sigma'])(\sigma') \mid w[\sigma, \sigma'] \neq \emptyset \,\} \cup \{\, \alpha \mid \alpha \in w \,\}.$$

Example (continuation of the example following Definition 7.29)

$$abs(\{\ \langle\sigma_1,\sigma_1\{1/v\}\rangle\langle\sigma_1',\sigma_1'\rangle\langle\sigma_2,\sigma_2\{2/v\}\rangle\langle\sigma_2',\sigma_2'\rangle(\sigma_1'(v)+\sigma_2'(v)),$$
$$\langle\sigma_1,\sigma_1\{1/v\}\rangle\langle\sigma_2,\sigma_2\{2/v\}\rangle\langle\sigma_1',\sigma_1'\rangle\langle\sigma_2',\sigma_2'\rangle(\sigma_1'(v)+\sigma_2'(v)),$$
$$\langle\sigma_1,\sigma_1\{1/v\}\rangle\langle\sigma_2,\sigma_2\{2/v\}\rangle\langle\sigma_2',\sigma_2'\rangle\langle\sigma_1',\sigma_1'\rangle(\sigma_1'(v)+\sigma_2'(v)),$$
$$\dots\mid\sigma_1,\sigma_1',\sigma_2,\sigma_2'\in\Sigma\ \})(\sigma)$$
$$=\ \{\ \sigma\{1/v\}\sigma\{1/v\}\sigma\{2/v\}\sigma\{2/v\}3,\sigma\{1/v\}\sigma\{2/v\}\sigma\{2/v\}\sigma\{2/v\}4,$$
$$\sigma\{1/v\}\sigma\{2/v\}\sigma\{2/v\}\sigma\{2/v\}4,\dots\ \}.$$

Note that the last two displayed elements coincide and, hence, collapse in the
resulting set.

The abstraction functions connect $\mathcal{O}_r$, $\mathcal{O}_e$ with $\mathcal{O}_r^*$, $\mathcal{O}_e^*$ as stated in

Lemma 7.35 $\langle\mathcal{O}_r[\![\cdot]\!],\mathcal{O}_e[\![\cdot]\!]\rangle=\langle abs_r\circ\mathcal{O}_r^*,abs_e\circ\mathcal{O}_e^*\rangle$, on $Res\times Exp$.

Proof Equality in the first component of the pairs is almost as in Section 7.1,
and not further discussed. Now let Φ_e' be derived from Φ_e in a way similar to the
manner Φ' is derived from Φ (cf. the proof of Lemma 7.21). We then have

$$\Phi_e'(abs_e\circ\mathcal{O}_e^*)(e)(\sigma)$$
$$=\ \bigcup\{\sigma'\cdot(abs_e\circ\mathcal{O}_e^*)(e')(\sigma')\mid[e,\sigma]\to[e',\sigma']\}\cup\{\alpha\mid[e,\sigma]\to\alpha\}$$
$$=\ abs_e(\bigcup\{\langle\sigma_1,\sigma'\rangle\cdot\mathcal{O}_e^*(e')\mid[e,\sigma_1]\to[e',\sigma']\}\cup\{\alpha\mid[e,\sigma_1]\to\alpha\})(\sigma)$$
$$=\ abs_e(\mathcal{O}_e^*(e))(\sigma),$$

and $abs_e\circ\mathcal{O}_e^*=\mathcal{O}_e[\![\cdot]\!]\ (=fix(\Phi_e'))$ follows.   □

Finally, by combining Lemma 7.32 and 7.35 we obtain

Theorem 7.36 $\quad\begin{aligned}\mathcal{O}_r[\![\cdot]\!]\ &=\ abs_r\circ\mathcal{D}\ on\ \mathcal{L}_{cee}\\ \mathcal{O}_e[\![\cdot]\!]\ &=\ abs_e\circ\mathcal{V}\ on\ Exp.\end{aligned}$

7.3   Exercises

Exercise 7.1 Let $s_1\equiv v:=0;v:=1$, $s_2\equiv v:=0;v:=v+1$, and $s\equiv v:=2$.

(a) Determine $\mathcal{O}^*(s_1\|s)$ and $\mathcal{O}^*(s_2\|s)$.

(b) Determine $(abs\circ\mathcal{O}^*)(s_1\|s)$ and $(abs\circ\mathcal{O}^*)(s_2\|s)$.

Exercise 7.2 Let $p_1, p_2 \in \mathbb{P}_D$ be such that $p_1 \cup p_2 = \mathbb{P}_D$, $p_1 \cap p_2 = \emptyset$, $d(p_1, p_2) = 1$. Prove that, for arbitrary $\bar{p}_1, \bar{p}_2 \in \mathbb{P}_D$,

$$d(\bar{p}_1, \bar{p}_2) \;=\; max\{\, d(\bar{p}_1 \cap p_1, \bar{p}_2 \cap p_1), d(\bar{p}_1 \cap p_2, \bar{p}_2 \cap p_2) \,\}.$$

Exercise 7.3 Let $\mathbb{P}' \stackrel{df}{=} \mathcal{P}_{nco}((\Sigma \to \Sigma)^\infty)$. Discuss the obstacles in defining $\mathcal{D} \colon \mathcal{L}_{svp} \to \mathbb{P}'$ in a compositional manner.

Exercise 7.4

(a) Let Act be a, not necessarily finite, alphabet, let $\mathbb{P}_{nco} \stackrel{df}{=} \mathcal{P}_{nco}(Act^\infty \backslash \{\epsilon\})$, $Op_{nco} = \mathbb{P}_{nco} \times \mathbb{P}_{nco} \to \mathbb{P}_{nco}$, and similarly for $\mathbb{P}_{ncl}$, Op_{ncl}. Let the operator $;_{nco} \in Op_{nco}$ be equal to ';' from Section 2.2 (Definition 2.35), and let $;_{ncl} \in Op_{ncl}$ be equal to ';' from Definition 7.6. Prove

$$;_{ncl} {\restriction} Op_{nco} \;=\; ;_{nco}$$

(where $f{\restriction}X$ denotes the function f restricted to X).

(b) Similarly for '$\|$'.

Exercise 7.5 Extend $\mathcal{L}_{cee}$ to include expressions $u(e_1, \ldots, e_\ell)$, $\ell \geq 1$. Discuss the induced modifications in the semantics for $\mathcal{L}_{cee}$.

Exercise 7.6 (A variation on $\mathcal{T}_{cee}$ with coarser-grained expression evaluation.) Define the class of simple expressions $(t \in)\, SExp$, by putting

$$t ::= \alpha \mid v \mid u(t_1, t_2).$$

(Thus, $SExp$ equals Exp from Section 1.2.3.) Let $\mathcal{V}(t)(\sigma)$ be as usual. $\mathcal{T}'_{cee}$ is the transition system with r as in Subsection 7.2.1, transitions $[r, \sigma] \to [r', \sigma']$ and $[e, \sigma] \to [e', \sigma']$, the rules (Skip), (Seq), (Ass 1), (If 1), (Conc 1), (Conc 2) and (While) from $\mathcal{T}_{cee}$, and, in addition,

- $$[v := t, \sigma] \to [\mathrm{E}, \sigma\{\alpha/v\}] \qquad \text{where } \alpha = \mathcal{V}(t)(\sigma)$$

- [if t then s_1 else s_2 fi, σ] $\to_0$ [s_1, σ]   if $\mathcal{V}(t)(\sigma) = tt$

  [if t then s_1 else s_2 fi, σ] $\to_0$ [s_2, σ]   if $\mathcal{V}(t)(\sigma) = ff$

Discuss the differences between $\mathcal{O}$ based on $\mathcal{T}_{cee}$ and $\mathcal{O}'$ based on $\mathcal{T}'_{cee}$. Design $\mathcal{D}'$ corresponding to $\mathcal{O}'$.

7.4   Bibliographical notes

Nonuniform forms of parallel composition have their origin in language notions such as Dijkstra's parbegin-parend construct ([Dij68]) or ALGOL 68's "collateral elaboration" ([Wij75]). Hoare's CSP ([Hoa78, Hoa85]) extends nonuniform parallelism by adding the notion of communicating processes (a simple form of which will be treated in Section 12.2).

The observation that the sequence based operational model for shared-variable parallelism is noncompositional has been well-known in concurrency semantics for quite a while ([Mil93] is a recent reference). The problem of designing denotational semantics for $\mathcal{L}_{svp}$ has been discussed, e.g., in [BZ82] (the branching model described there appears in our book only in Part III). In the mean time, we realized that a *linear* model is also feasible—as long as the cluster of problems having to do with synchronous communication and deadlock is not addressed. We took the "sequences of pairs of states" denotational model from a number of studies of parallel logic programming (e.g., [GCLS88, BKPR92]); its earliest appearance may be [Abr79]. The thesis of Horita ([Hor93b]) was as well instrumental for our insights in this question (cf. the discussion in Chapter 17). (An alternative would have been to use the resumption model of Hennessy and Plotkin ([HP79]) based on a domain solving a domain equation involving a tensor product. Since at this stage in our book we have not yet introduced domain equations—and since we have no further occasion to work with tensor products—we have preferred to develop the approach as outlined in Section 7.1.2.) The technical results introducing the operational notion of "locally finitely branching" and the denotational one of "finitary nonempty and closed" powerdomain are described in Section 7.1 for the first time (related results are reported in [Hor93b]), as is Theorem 7.22.

$\mathcal{L}_{cee}$ embodies the salient aspects of ALGOL 68's collateral elaboration. The material described in Section 7.2 has not been published before; an earlier exploratory study which had considerable influence on our treatment is [Roo88].

8 Recursion Revisited

Recursion is a fundamental notion in control flow, if only because it is responsible for the possibility of infinite behaviour of a program. Accordingly, a number of techniques which are pervasive in all investigations so far—the use of *complete* metric spaces, of Banach's theorem, of (closed or) compact powerdomains, etc.—have been developed in earlier chapters for the rigorous treatment of recursion. Still, there is a lot more to be said about this concept, and we devote a separate chapter to the presentation of some of its further properties.

In Chapter 1, we started our work with the study of $\mathcal{L}_{rec}$. So far, all versions of general recursion (rather than of iteration) use a formalism with *declarations*. The first aim of the present chapter is to present a variation on this as alternative syntax, which does away with the need for declarations, and which has become known as "the μ-calculus" ($\mathcal{L}_\mu$ in our terminology). We moreover use $\mathcal{L}_\mu$ to discuss another instance of '$\mathcal{D}$ without higher-order' (recall Section 3.1 on $\mathcal{L}_{gc}$); so-called *procedure environments* are the main tool here. In Section 8.3, we focus on the relationship between $\mathcal{L}_\mu$ and the earlier syntax (in the form of $\mathcal{L}_{cf}$), culminating in two algorithms to translate from $\mathcal{L}_{cf}$ to $\mathcal{L}_\mu$, and vice versa. Finally, in Section 8.4 we mention that, in addition to the higher-order $\mathcal{D}$ and the $\mathcal{D}$ based on procedure environments (of Section 8.2), there is even a third way of defining $\mathcal{D}$ for $\mathcal{L}_\mu$.

8.1 The μ-calculus $\mathcal{L}_\mu$—a declaration free formalism

In this section we introduce a variation on the formalism to handle recursive procedures. We present the so-called μ-calculus—couched in terms of the language $\mathcal{L}_\mu$—which exhibits a form of explicitly binding procedure variables to statements: For procedure variable x and statement s, the binding construct is written as $\mu x[s]$. We shall discuss $\mathcal{L}_\mu$ as an alternative to the language $\mathcal{L}_{cf}$ of Section 2.2, and discuss in Section 8.3 the relationship between the two languages. It should be understood, however, that the μ-formalism for recursion may replace the explicit use of declarations in any of the languages considered so far (or to be considered later).

We begin our explanation of $\mathcal{L}_\mu$ by recalling the syntactic format for recursion used up till now. Firstly, we have an alphabet of procedure variables $(x \in) PVar$. Declarations $D (\in Decl)$ map the elements of $PVar$ to (a guarded version of) the statements in the language at hand, determining for each x its body $D(x)$. "Calls" of a procedure x are handled

• operationally, by using rules of the $x \to_{0,D} D(x)$ kind, possibly embellished by some form of resumption

- denotationally, by using equations of the form $\Psi(S)(D|x) = \Psi(S)(D|D(x))$. Well-definedness is ensured here by the guardedness condition.

In the theory of semantics, a declaration-free formalism has also found widespread use. By way of introduction, we discuss the special case that $PVar = \{x\}$, i.e., there is only one procedure variable. In a program $(D|s)$, s will, in general, contain some occurrences of x, and so will $g = D(x)$. We express this by writing $(D|s)$ as (also using the '$\Leftarrow$' notation)

$$(x \Leftarrow g[x] \mid s[x]). \tag{8.1}$$

Here, by writing $g[x]$ and $s[x]$ rather than just g and s, we emphasize that we are interested in possible occurrences of x in these statements. The key idea is now the following: Firstly, we realize that x occurs "bound" in the construct (8.1), both in the declaration $x \Leftarrow g[x]$ and in the statement $s[x]$. As a consequence, the program

$$(y \Leftarrow g[y] \mid s[y]) \tag{8.2}$$

obtained from (8.1) by systematically replacing all occurrences of x by y, has exactly the same meaning as (8.1). (Of course, in order for (8.2) to be a legal program, we now assume $PVar = \{y\}$.) Secondly, we observe that the declaration information in $x \Leftarrow g[x]$ may as well be expressed, slightly varying the syntactic format, by the construct $\mu x[g[x]]$: This expression contains both the information that x is the bound variable—in the form of the μx-prefix—and that x has $g[x]$ as associated procedure body. The next step is now simple: we drop the declaration D from the program, and replace all occurrences of x in $s[x]$ by $\mu x[g[x]]$, obtaining $s[\mu x[g[x]]]$ as a result. An example will help. Consider the program

$$(x \Leftarrow a;x;b + c \mid (d_1;x) + (x;d_2) + e).$$

Performing the manipulations as just described, we obtain the statement

$$d_1;\mu x[a;x;b + c] + \mu x[a;x;b + c];d_2 + e.$$

Altogether, nothing more has been done than replacing the (globally valid) declaration by a program where the body information for each call of a procedure, say x, is available locally—with the exception of inner recursive calls, which are handled by the μx-binding mechanism. The price to be paid for the abolishment of declarations is the repetition in writing the bodies $g \equiv g[x]$ in all occurrences of $\mu x[g[x]]$. On the other hand, a formalism which avoids carrying along the D-information everywhere has a justifiable claim to increased mathematical conciseness and elegance. The reader who has been somewhat bothered in earlier chapters by all the

$(D|s)$ and $(D|r)$ occurrences with only a neglectable role for the D will no doubt appreciate this.

We conclude this introduction with one very natural question: what happens to the above in a situation where we have more than one procedure declaration? We postpone discussion of this till we have developed our new language for recursion $\mathcal{L}_\mu$ in some detail (see Section 8.3).

8.1.1   Syntax and operational semantics

We present the μ-calculus for a language with the concepts of $\mathcal{L}_{cf}$—elementary actions, sequential composition and nondeterministic choice—but with the new format for recursion. Let $(a \in) Act$ and $(x, y \in) PVar$ be as before. As first approximation, we want to define $(s \in) Stat$ by the syntactic clauses

$$s ::= a \mid x \mid (s;s) \mid (s + s) \mid \mu x[s].$$

It is important to note that this syntax allows nested μ's of the form $\mu x[\ldots \mu y[\ldots] \ldots]$; this possibility is in fact essential for the μ-calculus. Actually, the definition for $Stat$ is a bit more complex, since we also have to cater for the notion of guardedness in the present setting.

Definition 8.1

(a) The languages $(s, t \in) Stat$, $(g \in) GStat$ are defined by

$$s ::= a \mid x \mid (s;s) \mid (s + s) \mid \mu x[g]$$
$$g ::= a \mid (g;s) \mid (g + g) \mid \mu x[g].$$

(b) We put $(\pi \in) \mathcal{L}_\mu = Stat$, $\mathcal{L}_\mu^g = GStat$.

Examples $\mu x[a;x;b + c]$, $\mu x[a;x];\mu y[a;y]$, $\mu x[a;\mu y[b;y;x + d] + e]$, $a;x$, $\mu x[a;x] + y$.

The last two examples illustrate that a program may contain *free* variables, i.e., variables x (or y) which are not in the scope of some prefix $\mu x \ldots$ (or $\mu y \ldots$). We shall return to this phenomenon below. Note also that the above syntax does not allow a construct such as (*) $\mu y[a;\mu x[y;x]]$, since $y;x \notin GStat$. According to the definitions to be developed in a moment, we may use, instead of (*), the statement $\mu y[a;\mu x[a;x;x]]$, which is indeed in $\mathcal{L}_\mu$ and which has the same meaning as the intended one for (*). A similar situation occurs in $\mathcal{L}_{cf}$, where the declaration

$D(x) = y;x$, $D(y) = a;x$ is not allowed, whereas $D(x) = a;x;x$, $D(y) = a;x$ is indeed correct. (Cf. Exercise 8.2 for a somewhat more liberal definition of guardedness.)

The transition system for $\mathcal{L}_\mu$ will use the syntactic notion of *substitution* for procedure variables. Its definition involves in turn that of *free* variables of a statement.

Definition 8.2

(a) The set of free procedure variables of a statement s, denoted by $pvar(s)$, with $pvar: \mathcal{L}_\mu \to \mathcal{P}(PVar)$, is defined as follows

$$pvar(a) = \emptyset, pvar(x) = \{x\}$$
$$pvar(s_1;s_2) = pvar(s_1 + s_2) = pvar(s_1) \cup pvar(s_2)$$
$$pvar(\mu x[g]) = pvar(g) \setminus \{x\}.$$

We say that x *occurs free* in s if $x \in pvar(s)$.

(b) We call $t \in \mathcal{L}_\mu$ *closed* is case $pvar(t) = \emptyset$ (i.e., in case t contains no free procedure variables). The collection of closed statements is denoted by $\mathcal{L}_\mu^c$. The set $\mathcal{L}_\mu^{g,c}$ is defined similarly.

(c) For $s, t \in \mathcal{L}_\mu$ with t closed, we define the syntactic construct $s[t/x]$—the result of substituting t for all free occurrences of x in s—as follows

- $a[t/x] = a$, $y[t/x] = \begin{cases} t & \text{if } x \equiv y \\ y & \text{if } x \not\equiv y \end{cases}$

- $(s_1;s_2)[t/x] = s_1[t/x];s_2[t/x]$, and similarly for '+'

- $\mu y[g][t/x] = \begin{cases} \mu y[g] & \text{if } x \equiv y \\ \mu y[g[t/x]] & \text{if } x \not\equiv y. \end{cases}$

(d) For $s \in \mathcal{L}_\mu$, $t_i \in \mathcal{L}_\mu^c$, $1 \le i \le n$ we define the simultaneous substitution $s[t_i/x_i]_{i=1}^n$ as the natural extension of part (c).

Remark Simultaneous substitution should be distinguished from repeated one. E.g., $x[y/x][z/y] = z$, whereas $x[y/x, z/y] = y$.

Since, in $\mathcal{L}_\mu$, free procedure variables have no meaning associated with them, we shall develop the semantic definitions—both the operational and the denotational ones—only for closed statements.

We are now ready for the definitions leading up to the operational semantics for $\mathcal{L}_\mu$.

Definition 8.3

(a) $(p \in) \mathbb{P}_O = \mathcal{P}_{nco}(Act^\infty)$, and the associated mappings ';' and '+' are as in Chapter 2.

(b) $r (\in Res) ::= E \mid s$, with $s \in \mathcal{L}_\mu^c$. We identify E;s and s.

Note that we return here to the simplest form of resumptions—and that a resumption s is always a closed statement. This will—slightly—facilitate some of the subsequent calculations.

We now present the transition system for the closed language $\mathcal{L}_\mu^c$.

Definition 8.4 $\mathcal{T}_\mu = (Res, Act, \rightarrow, Spec)$, where $Spec$ is defined as

$$a \xrightarrow{a} E \tag{Act}$$

$$\mu x[g] \rightarrow_0 g[\mu x[g]/x] \tag{Rec}$$

$$\frac{s_1 \xrightarrow{a} r_1}{s_1;s_2 \xrightarrow{a} r_1;s_2} \tag{Seq}$$

$$s_1 + s_2 \rightarrow_0 s_1 \tag{Choice}$$
$$s_1 + s_2 \rightarrow_0 s_2$$

As with all languages considered so far, we introduce a weight function in order to justify the way $\mathcal{O}$ is to be based on $\mathcal{T}_\mu$. It is probably not so immediate to see that the next definition is indeed well-defined—the content of Lemma 8.6.

Definition 8.5 wgt: $Res \rightarrow \mathbb{N}$ is given by

$$
\begin{aligned}
wgt(E) &= 0 \\
wgt(a) &= 1 \\
wgt(s_1;s_2) &= wgt(s_1) + 1 \\
wgt(s_1 + s_2) &= max\{\, wgt(s_1), wgt(s_2)\,\} + 1 \\
wgt(\mu x[g]) &= wgt(g[\mu x[g]/x]) + 1.
\end{aligned}
$$

Lemma 8.6 *The function wgt is well-defined.*

Proof The well-definedness of $wgt(s)$ is easily established by induction on the syntactic complexity of s, once the following claim has been established: Let g be a guarded statement (in $\mathcal{L}_\mu^g$) which has free occurrences of the n different statement variables $x_1, \ldots, x_n$, and let $t_1, \ldots, t_n$ be closed statements (in $\mathcal{L}_\mu^c$). Then we claim that $wgt(g[t_i/x_i]_{i=1}^n)$ is well-defined.

The proof of the claim proceeds by induction on the syntactic complexity of g. Let us abbreviate the substitution $[t_i/x_i]_{i=1}^n$ by $[\cdot]$. We have the following subcases.

$[g \equiv a]$ $wgt(a[\cdot]) = wgt(a) = 1$.

$[g \equiv g';s]$ $wgt((g';s)[\cdot]) = wgt(g'[\cdot];s[\cdot]) = wgt(g'[\cdot]) + 1$, which is well-defined by induction.

$[g \equiv g_1 + g_2]$ Easy by induction.

$[g \equiv \mu x[g']]$ We discuss only the subcase that $x \not\equiv x_1, \ldots, x_n$. Then

$$
\begin{aligned}
&wgt(\mu x[g'][\cdot]) \\
&= wgt(\mu x[g'[\cdot]]) \\
&= wgt(g'[\cdot][\mu x[g'[\cdot]]/x]) + 1 \\
&= wgt(g'[\cdot, \mu x[g'[\cdot]]/x]) + 1.
\end{aligned}
$$

The desired result now holds since g' is a (guarded) statement of smaller syntactic complexity than $\mu x[g']$ (and with free occurrences of the n variables $x_1, \ldots, x_n$ and, in general, of x).   □

The complexity function wgt may be applied in the familiar way in showing that $\mathcal{T}_\mu$ is finitely branching, thus justifying the next definition:

Definition 8.7

(a) The operational semantics $\mathcal{O}: Res \to \mathbb{P}_O$ is the unique function satisfying $\mathcal{O}(E) = \{\epsilon\}$ and

$$
\mathcal{O}(s) = \bigcup \{ a \cdot \mathcal{O}(r) \mid s \xrightarrow{a} r \}.
$$

(b) $\mathcal{O}[\![s]\!] = \mathcal{O}(s)$, for $s \in \mathcal{L}_\mu^c$.

8.1.2   Denotational semantics, equivalence of $\mathcal{O}$ and $\mathcal{D}$

In this subsection we give the definition of $\mathcal{D}$ (for closed statements only) in terms of the familiar higher order strategy. In the next section, we shall discuss an alternative definition for $\mathcal{D}$. In Definition 8.8, $\mathbb{P}_D$ and the semantic operators are as in Chapter 2.

Definition 8.8

(a) Let $(S \in) Sem_D = \mathcal{L}_\mu^c \to \mathbb{P}_D$ and let $\Psi : Sem_D \to Sem_D$ be given by

$$
\begin{aligned}
\Psi(S)(a) &= \{a\} \\
\Psi(S)(s_1;s_2) &= \Psi(S)(s_1);S(s_2) \\
\Psi(S)(s_1 + s_2) &= \Psi(S)(s_1) + \Psi(S)(s_2) \\
\Psi(S)(\mu x[g]) &= \Psi(S)(g[\mu x[g]/x]).
\end{aligned}
$$

(b) $\mathcal{D} = fix(\Psi)$.

Well-definedness of $\Psi(S)(s)$ for each s follows by induction on $wgt(s)$. Crucial here is the definition of wgt in such a way that it is ensured that

$$wgt(\mu x[g]) > wgt(g[\mu x[g]/x]).$$

Contractiveness of Ψ in S is as usual. On the way to proving that $\mathcal{O} = \mathcal{D}$ on $\mathcal{L}_\mu^c$, we extend $\mathcal{D}$ to the mapping $\mathcal{E}$ with domain Res by putting $\mathcal{E}(\mathrm{E}) = \{\epsilon\}$, $\mathcal{E}(S) = \mathcal{D}(s)$. The next lemma will not come as a surprise:

Lemma 8.9 $\Phi(\mathcal{E})(r) = \mathcal{E}(r)$, *for* $r \in Res$.

Proof   Clear for $r \equiv \mathrm{E}$. We next use induction on $wgt(s)$ to establish that $\Phi(\mathcal{E})(s) = \mathcal{E}(s)$. We exhibit one subcase.

$$
\begin{aligned}
[\mu x[g]] \quad & \Phi(\mathcal{E})(\mu x[g]) \\
= \quad & [\text{def. } \mathcal{T}_\mu] \; \Phi(\mathcal{E})(g[\mu x[g]/x]) \\
= \quad & [\text{ind. hyp.}] \; \mathcal{E}(g[\mu x[g]/x]) \\
= \quad & [\text{def. } \Psi] \; \mathcal{E}(\mu x[g]). \qquad\qquad\qquad\qquad\qquad \square
\end{aligned}
$$

Lemma 8.9 immediately yields

Corollary 8.10 $\mathcal{O}[\![\pi]\!] = \mathcal{D}[\![\pi]\!]$, *for each* $\pi \in \mathcal{L}_\mu^c$.

8.2   Procedure environments—$\mathcal{D}$ without higher order

We now come to the second main topic of the present chapter—the first one being simply the introduction of the μ-calculus as a variation on the syntactic formalism with declarations. One of the advantages of the study of $\mathcal{L}_\mu$ is that it leads, in a natural way, to the consideration of an alternative *semantic* approach to recursion: We shall develop a method which utilizes so-called *procedure environments* rather than following the route where $\mathcal{D}$ is obtained as fixed point of some higher-order mapping Ψ. As a matter of fact, the method we are about to explain was, historically, the first one proposed. The higher-order technique in defining $\mathcal{D}$ was adopted in our work primarily for reasons of (convenience and) symmetry with the way $\mathcal{O}$ is obtained from Φ. Note, however, that at least one (of the $\mathcal{O}$ or $\mathcal{D}$) should be defined in terms of some higher-order mapping in order that the standard approach of our book in proving $\mathcal{O} = \mathcal{D}$ be applicable. (Recall that $\mathcal{L}_{gc}$ from Section 3.1 already provided an instance of the treatment of (the special case of) iteration in terms of local fixed points, avoiding the global $\mathcal{D} = fix(\Psi)$ style of definition.)

We introduce the set of *procedure environments,* i.e., mappings from $P\mathit{Var}$ to $\mathbb{P}_D$, in

Definition 8.11   The set of procedure environments $(\eta \in) \mathrm{H}$ is given as: $\mathrm{H} = P\mathit{Var} \to \mathbb{P}_D$. The update notation $\eta\{p/x\}$ is defined by putting

$$\eta\{p/x\}(y) \quad = \quad \begin{cases} p & \text{if } x \equiv y \\ \eta(y) & \text{if } x \not\equiv y. \end{cases}$$

Similarly, we may define the simultaneous update $\eta\{\, p_i/x_i \,\}_{i=1}^{n}$.

Note the close similarity between $(\sigma \in) \Sigma$ and $(\eta \in) \mathrm{H}$: just as a state σ is used to store and retrieve the meaning (i.e., some $\alpha \in \mathit{Val}$) of an individual variable v, an environment η will be used to store and retrieve the meaning (some $p \in \mathbb{P}_D$) of a procedure variable x. Also, the update notation $\eta\{\, p/x \,\}$ directly mimics the earlier notation $\sigma\{\alpha/v\}$.

The new denotational semantics, to be denoted by $\mathcal{D}^*$, will be defined as a function which expects, besides an argument s, as well an argument η. It is important to note that $\mathcal{D}^*$ is defined on all of $\mathcal{L}_\mu$, rather than just on $\mathcal{L}_\mu^c$.

Definition 8.12   The meaning function $\mathcal{D}^* \colon \mathcal{L}_\mu \to \mathrm{H} \to \mathbb{P}_D$ is given by

$$\begin{aligned}
\mathcal{D}^*(a)(\eta) &= \{a\} \\
\mathcal{D}^*(x)(\eta) &= \eta(x) \\
\mathcal{D}^*(s_1;s_2)(\eta) &= \mathcal{D}^*(s_1)(\eta);\mathcal{D}^*(s_2)(\eta) \\
\mathcal{D}^*(s_1 + s_2)(\eta) &= \mathcal{D}^*(s_1)(\eta) + \mathcal{D}^*(s_2)(\eta) \\
\mathcal{D}^*(\mu x[g])(\eta) &= \text{fix}(\lambda p.\mathcal{D}^*(g)(\eta\{\,p/x\,\})).
\end{aligned}$$

The clause for $\mathcal{D}^*(\mu x[g])(\eta)$ is especially interesting in that we find here a new use of fixed points to treat recursion: This time, we take the (unique) fixed point of a mapping $\lambda p. \cdots$ from $\mathbb{P}_D \to \mathbb{P}_D$, rather than of a mapping $\Psi\colon Sem_D \to Sem_D$, as was the case in all languages considered earlier (with the exception of $\mathcal{L}_{gc}$).

Examples

(1) $\mathcal{D}^*(a + b)(\eta) = \{a, b\}$.

(2) $\mathcal{D}^*(\mu x[a;x])(\eta) = \text{fix}(\lambda p.\mathcal{D}^*(a;x)(\eta\{p/x\})) = \text{fix}(\lambda p.a \cdot p) = \{a^\omega\}$.

(3) $\mathcal{D}^*(a;x)(\eta) = a \cdot \eta(x)$, with $\eta(x) \in \mathbb{P}_D$ some value for x which is not specified by the—non-closed—program $a;x$.

(4) $\mathcal{D}^*(\mu x[a;x + y])(\eta) = a^* \cdot \eta(y) \cup \{a^\omega\}$.

Normally, we shall encounter $\mathcal{D}^*(s)(\eta)$, for s non-closed, only in a setting where s is a subprogram of some closed s'—as in the clause $\mathcal{D}^*(a;x)(\eta\{p/x\}))$ in the second example. Programs as considered in examples (3) or (4) may be considered as "incorrect."

The justification of Definition 8.12 relies on two facts

(a) $\mathcal{D}^*(s)$ is well-defined since it is expressed in terms of (various operations on) $\mathcal{D}^*(s')$ for s' of smaller syntactic complexity than s. (Accordingly, the machinery in terms of the wgt-function is not needed here.)

(b) The existence of the unique fixed point in the clause for $\mathcal{D}^*(\mu x[g])(\eta)$ is a consequence of the next lemma.

Lemma 8.13 *For each $n \geq 1$, $x_1, \ldots, x_n$, $\eta \in H$,*

(a) for each $s \in \mathcal{L}_\mu$, the function

$$\mathcal{G}(s) = \lambda(p_1, \ldots, p_n).\mathcal{D}^*(s)(\eta\{\,p_i/x_i\,\}_{i=1}^n)$$

is nonexpansive in $(p_1, \ldots, p_n)$

(b) for each $g \in \mathcal{L}^g_\mu$, the function

$$\mathcal{H}(s) = \lambda(p_1, \ldots, p_n).\mathcal{D}^*(g)(\eta\{ p_i/x_i \}_{i=1}^n)$$

is $\frac{1}{2}$-contractive in $(p_1, \ldots, p_n)$.

Proof We prove both assertions simultaneously by introduction on the syntactic complexity of $g + s$. We take $n = 1$ for simplicity in notation.

(a) Two subcases

[x] If $x \not\equiv x_1$, then $\mathcal{G}(x)$ is a constant. If $x \equiv x_1$, then $\mathcal{G}(x) = \lambda p_1.p_1$, which is clearly nonexpansive in p_1.

[$\mu y[g']$] This case follows from the stronger case of part (b).

(b) [$g';s$] $d(\mathcal{G}(g';s)(p_1), \mathcal{G}(g';s)(p_2))$
  $=$ [Def. 8.12] $d(\mathcal{G}(g')(p_1);\mathcal{G}(s)(p_1), \mathcal{G}(g')(p_2);\mathcal{G}(s)(p_2))$
  $\leq$ [by the ind. hyp. for g' and s, and Lemma 2.36c]
        $\frac{1}{2}d(p_1, p_2)$.

[$\mu y[g']$] We only discuss the subcase that $y \not\equiv x$. Let us put

$\hat{p}_j = \mathrm{fix}(\lambda p.\mathcal{D}^*(g')(\eta\{p_j/x\}\{p/y\})), \quad j = 1, 2.$
Then, by Definition 8.12,

$$d(\mathcal{G}(\mu y[g'])(p_1), \mathcal{G}(\mu y[g'])(p_2)) = d(\hat{p}_1, \hat{p}_2).$$
Now let $p_1^0 = p_2^0$ be some arbitrary element of $\mathbb{P}_D$, and let, for $i = 0, 1, \ldots$

$p_j^{i+1} = \mathcal{D}^*(g')(\eta\{p_j/x\}\{p_j^i/y\}), \quad j = 1, 2.$
Since, by Banach's theorem, $\hat{p}_j = lim_i p_j^i, j = 1, 2$, it is sufficient to establish that, for all $i = 0, 1, \ldots$
$$d(p_1^i, p_2^i) \leq \frac{1}{2}d(p_1, p_2). \tag{8.3}$$
We use induction on i. The case $i = 0$ is clear. Now assume (8.3) for some i. Then
  $d(p_1^{i+1}, p_2^{i+1})$
  $=$ $d(\mathcal{D}^*(g')(\eta\{p_1/x\}\{p_1^i/y\}), \mathcal{D}^*(g')(\eta\{p_2/x\}\{p_2^i/y\}))$
  $\leq$ [ind. hyp. for g'] $\frac{1}{2}max\{ d(\langle p_1, p_1^i \rangle, \langle p_2, p_2^i \rangle)$
  $\leq$ [ind. hyp. for i] $\frac{1}{2}d(p_1, p_2)$. $\square$

After having settled that $\mathcal{D}^*$ is well-defined, we address the obvious question as to whether $\mathcal{D}^*$ and $\mathcal{D}$ coincide on $\mathcal{L}_\mu^c$. The following lemma for $\mathcal{D}^*$ is the main step in the proof that this is indeed the case:

Lemma 8.14 *For each $s \in \mathcal{L}_\mu$, $t \in \mathcal{L}_\mu^c$, $x \in PVar$, $\eta \in H$,*

$$\mathcal{D}^*(s[t/x])(\eta) = \mathcal{D}^*(s)(\eta\{\mathcal{D}^*(t)(\eta)/x\}).$$

Proof Structural induction on s. We only present the subcase $s \equiv \mu y[g]$, with $y \not\equiv x$. The proof uses the easily shown lemma that, for any s' such that $y \notin pvar(s')$, and any p, $\mathcal{D}^*(s')(\eta\{p/y\}) = \mathcal{D}^*(s')(\eta)$. We have

$$\mathcal{D}^*(\mu y[g][t/x])(\eta)$$
$$= \mathcal{D}^*(\mu y[g[t/x]])(\eta)$$
$$= \text{fix}(\lambda p.\mathcal{D}^*(g[t/x])(\eta\{p/y\}))$$
$$= [\text{ind. hyp.}] \ \text{fix}(\lambda p.\mathcal{D}^*(g)(\eta\{p/y\}\{\mathcal{D}^*(t)(\eta\{p/y\})/x\}))$$
$$= [\ x \not\equiv y\ ] \ \text{fix}(\lambda p.\mathcal{D}^*(g)(\eta\{\mathcal{D}^*(t)(\eta)/x\}\{p/y\}))$$
$$= \mathcal{D}^*(\mu y[g])(\eta\{\mathcal{D}^*(t)(\eta)/x\}). \qquad \qquad \square$$

The question just raised can now be settled affirmatively:

Theorem 8.15 *For $s \in \mathcal{L}_\mu^c$ and any η,*

$$\mathcal{D}(s) = \mathcal{D}^*(s)(\eta).$$

Proof By Lemma 8.14,

$$\mathcal{D}^*(g[\mu x[g]/x])(\eta) = \mathcal{D}^*(g)(\eta[\mathcal{D}^*(\mu x[g])(\eta)/x]) = \mathcal{D}^*(\mu x[g])(\eta),$$

where the last equality follows from the definition of $\mathcal{D}^*(\mu x[g])(\eta)$ as $\text{fix}(\lambda p.\mathcal{D}^*(g)(\eta\{p/x\})$. Putting, for easier notation, $\mathcal{E}^*(s) = \mathcal{D}^*(s)(\eta)$, we see that

$$\begin{aligned} \mathcal{E}^*(a) &= \{a\} \\ \mathcal{E}^*(s_1;s_2) &= \mathcal{E}^*(s_1);\mathcal{E}^*(s_2), \text{ and similarly for `+'} \\ \mathcal{E}^*(\mu x[g]) &= \mathcal{E}^*(g[\mu x[g]/x]). \end{aligned}$$

Thus, $\mathcal{E}^*$ satisfies $\Psi(\mathcal{E}^*) = \mathcal{E}^*$, with Ψ as in Definition 8.8. By Banach's theorem, $\mathcal{E}^*(s) = \mathcal{D}(s)$, and the desired result $\mathcal{D}^*(s)(\eta) = \mathcal{D}(s)$ follows. $\qquad \square$

8.3 $\mathcal{L}_{cf}$ and $\mathcal{L}_\mu$ compared
—simultaneous versus iterated fixed points

In this subsection we discuss the relationship between the μ-calculus and the more familiar framework with (simultaneous) declarations. We do this for the example languages $\mathcal{L}_\mu$ and $\mathcal{L}_{cf}$, though the results to be presented are in fact independent of the programming constructs—in addition to recursive procedures—present in the language considered. Since declarations play a key role in this subsection, we shall return to the explicit writing of D on all its occurrences.

Firstly, we discuss how a program in $\mathcal{L}_{cf}$ may be expressed in an equivalent manner in $\mathcal{L}_\mu$, provided the set $PVar$ is *finite*. The reader who is still waiting for an answer to the question posed at the end of the introduction to Section 8.1 will find the announced information in the method to be described now. (See also Exercise 8.8 for a case where a program from $\mathcal{L}_{cf}$—with $PVar$ infinite—has no equivalent program in $\mathcal{L}_\mu$.)

Let $\mathcal{D}_{cf}$ and $\mathcal{D}_\mu$ denote the denotational meanings introduced for $\mathcal{L}_{cf}$ (in Chapter 2) and $\mathcal{L}_\mu$ (in Section 8.1) respectively. We shall prove

Theorem 8.16 *Let $PVar$ be a finite alphabet. For each program $(D|s)$ in $\mathcal{L}_{cf}$ we may construct a program s' in $\mathcal{L}_\mu^c$ such that $\mathcal{D}_{cf}(D|s) = \mathcal{D}_\mu(s')$.*

Proof We explain the basic idea of the algorithm which obtains s' from $(D|s)$ by presenting the case that $|PVar| = 2$, say $PVar = \{x_1, x_2\}$, leaving the generalization to arbitrary finite $PVar$ as an exercise. Let $D(x_i) = g_i$, $i = 1, 2$, and let $s \in Stat_{cf}$ be arbitrary. Let s_1, s_2 be the following two statements in $\mathcal{L}_\mu$ (which will serve as equivalent statements for the x_1, x_2—considered as calls—in $\mathcal{L}_{cf}$):

$$\begin{aligned}
s_1 &= \mu x_1[g_1[\mu x_2[g_2]/x_2]] \\
s_2 &= \mu x_2[g_2[\mu x_1[g_1]/x_1]],
\end{aligned} \qquad (8.4)$$

and let $s' = s[s_1/x_1, s_2/x_2]$. Then s' is the desired statement in $\mathcal{L}_\mu$, i.e.,

$$\mathcal{D}_{cf}(x_1 \Leftarrow g_1, x_2 \Leftarrow g_2|s) = \mathcal{D}_\mu(s'). \qquad (8.5)$$

(The reader may want to consult here the example presented after the proof of the theorem.) The proof of (8.4) is conveniently given in terms of the denotational semantics $\mathcal{D}_\mu^*$ as developed in the previous section (Section 8.2), and of $\mathcal{D}_{cf}^*$, which we present now. We first introduce an auxiliary semantic mapping $\mathcal{F}{:}Stat_{cf} \to H \to \mathbb{P}_D$ defined as

$$
\begin{aligned}
\mathcal{F}(a)(\eta) &= \{a\} \\
\mathcal{F}(x)(\eta) &= \eta(x) \\
\mathcal{F}(s_1;s_2)(\eta) &= \mathcal{F}(s_1)(\eta);\mathcal{F}(s_2)(\eta), \quad \text{and similarly for `+.'}
\end{aligned}
$$

Next, we provide a simultaneous variation on the fixed point definition as given for $\mathcal{D}^*_\mu$, by putting

$$
\begin{aligned}
\langle p_1, p_2 \rangle = \qquad\qquad\qquad\qquad\qquad\qquad\qquad\qquad\qquad\qquad (8.6) \\
\text{fix}(\lambda(p', p'').\langle \mathcal{F}(g_1)(\eta\{p'/x_1, p''/x_2\}), \mathcal{F}(g_2)(\eta\{p'/x_1, p''/x_2\})\rangle).
\end{aligned}
$$

Moreover, we put $\mathcal{D}^*_{cf}(D|s)(\eta) = \mathcal{F}(s)(\eta\{p_1/x_1, p_2/x_2\})$. By an easy extension of the argument used in the proof of Theorem 8.15, we obtain that $\mathcal{D}_{cf}(D|s)(\eta) = \mathcal{D}_{cf}(D|s)$, for any η.

Proceeding with the proof of (8.5), we first state a key lemma which expresses a (purely semantic) result relating simultaneous versus iterated (unique) fixed points:

Lemma 8.17 *Let M be a complete metric space and let $f, g: M \times M \to M$ be two contractive mappings. Let the (contractive) mapping $\langle f, g \rangle: M \times M \to M \times M$ be given by $\langle f, g \rangle(x, y) = \langle f(x, y), g(x, y) \rangle$. Let*

$$
\begin{aligned}
\langle x_0, y_0 \rangle &= \text{fix}(\langle f, g \rangle) \\
x_1 &= \text{fix}(\lambda x.f(x, \text{fix}(\lambda y.g(x, y)))) \\
y_1 &= \text{fix}(\lambda y.g(\text{fix}(\lambda x.f(x, y)), y))).
\end{aligned}
$$

Then $x_0 = x_1$, $y_0 = y_1$.

Proof We leave it to the reader to show that the functions involved in the definitions of x_1 and y_1 are contractive. Let us introduce the auxiliary y_2, x_2 by putting $y_2 = \text{fix}(\lambda y.g(x_1, y))$, $x_2 = \text{fix}(\lambda x.f(x, y_1))$. Then, by the definition of x_1 and y_2, we have $x_1 = f(x_1, y_2)$, $y_1 = g(x_1, y_2)$, and we conclude $x_1 = x_0$, $y_2 = y_0$. Symmetrically we obtain $x_2 = x_0$, $y_1 = y_0$. Altogether, we have that, indeed, $x_0 = x_1$ and $y_0 = y_1$. $\qquad\qquad\qquad\qquad\qquad\qquad\qquad\qquad\qquad\qquad\qquad\qquad\square$

Continuing the proof of Theorem 8.16, we apply Lemma 8.17 in the following calculations which will yield $\langle \mathcal{D}^*_\mu(s_1), \mathcal{D}^*_\mu(s_2) \rangle$ as simultaneous fixed point of a suitable pair of mappings. We first rewrite $\mathcal{D}^*_\mu(s_1)(\eta)$—with s_1 as in (8.4)—as follows

$$
\begin{aligned}
&\mathcal{D}^*_\mu(s_1)(\eta) \\
&= \mathcal{D}^*_\mu(\mu x_1[g_1[\mu x_2[g_2]/x_2]])(\eta) \\
&= \text{fix}(\lambda p'.\mathcal{D}^*_\mu(g_1[\mu x[g_2]/x_2])(\eta\{p'/x_1\})
\end{aligned}
$$

$= [\text{Lemma } 8.14] \ \text{fix}(\lambda p'.\mathcal{D}^*_\mu(g_1)(\eta\{p'/x_1\}\{\mathcal{D}^*_\mu(\mu x_2[g_2])(\eta\{p'/x_1\})/x_2\}))$

$= \text{fix}(\lambda p'.\mathcal{D}^*_\mu(g_1)(\eta\{p'/x_1\}[\text{fix}(\lambda p''.\mathcal{D}^*_\mu(g_2)(\eta\{p'/x_1\}\{p''/x_2\}))/x_2])).$

Symmetrically, we obtain a similar formula for $\mathcal{D}^*_\mu(s_2)(\mu)$. Writing $\langle F_1, F_2 \rangle: \mathbb{P}_D \times \mathbb{P}_D \to \mathbb{P}_D \times \mathbb{P}_D$ as short-hand for the mapping

$$\lambda(p', p'').\langle \mathcal{D}^*_\mu(g_1)(\eta\{p'/x_1, p''/x_2\}), \mathcal{D}^*_\mu(g_2)(\eta\{p'/x_1, p''/x_2\})\rangle,$$

we see, using Lemma 8.17, that $\text{fix}(F_1, F_2) = \langle \mathcal{D}^*_\mu(s_1)(\eta), \mathcal{D}^*_\mu(s_2)(\eta)\rangle$.

As final step in the proof we use that, for each $s \in Stat_{cf}$, $\mathcal{F}(s)(\eta) = \mathcal{D}^*_\mu(s)(\eta)$. This follows by the definitions of $\mathcal{F}$ and $\mathcal{D}^*_\mu$, together with the fact that $s \in Stat_{cf}$ contains no μ-terms. Comparing the definitions of p_1, p_2 and of $\langle F_1, F_2 \rangle$ we see that $\langle p_1, p_2 \rangle = \text{fix}(F_1, F_2) = \langle \mathcal{D}^*_\mu(s_1)(\eta), \mathcal{D}^*_\mu(s_2)(\eta)\rangle$. We can now show (8.4) by induction on the complexity of s. The only interesting case is that $s \equiv x_1$ or $s \equiv x_2$. Take $s \equiv x_1$. Then $\mathcal{D}^*_{cf}(D|x_1)(\eta) = p_1 = \mathcal{D}^*_\mu(s_1)(\eta) = \mathcal{D}^*_\mu(x_1[s_1/x_1, s_2/x_2])(\eta)$, as was to be shown. $\qquad\square$

We still owe the reader an example of the construction of s_1 and s_2. Consider the program

$$(x_1 \Leftarrow a_1; x_1; x_2 + b_1, \ x_2 \Leftarrow a_2; x_2 + b_2; x_1 \mid x_1 + x_2).$$

As equivalent program in $\mathcal{L}_\mu$ we have

$$\mu x_1[a_1; x_1; \mu x_2[a_2; x_2 + b_2; x_1] + b_1] + \mu x_2[a_2; x_2 + b_2; \mu x_1[a_1; x_1; x_2 + b_1]].$$

This example concludes our treatment of the algorithm which, for each $(D|s)$ in $\mathcal{L}_{cf}$—with finite $PVar$—yields an equivalent statement in $\mathcal{L}_\mu$. We now turn to the converse question, i.e., how to obtain a program in $\mathcal{L}_{cf}$ for any closed statement in $\mathcal{L}_\mu$. We shall exhibit an algorithm to achieve this in Definition 8.18, and prove its correctness in Lemma 8.19. In the following, we shall consider also *partial* declarations $D: PVar \to \mathcal{L}^g_{cf}$ (with $\mathcal{L}^g_{cf} = GStat$ as in Def. 2.22), i.e., functions which may be undefined for certain x in $PVar$. We shall use $\mathcal{L}^{ext}_{cf}$ for the language which is like $\mathcal{L}_{cf}$, but which allows partially defined declarations. Note that, as a consequence, programs in $\mathcal{L}^{ext}_{cf}$ may have free (occurrences of) procedure variables. We leave to the reader the definition of $pvar(D|s)$ for $(D|s) \in \mathcal{L}^{ext}_{cf}$. With $\delta(D)$ we shall denote the set of procedure variables for which D is defined. Note that $\delta(D) = \emptyset$ is possible. Also, by the construction to be presented, it will follow that there is no need here to consider *infinite* sets $PVar$.

Below, we shall need the notion of an *alphabetic variant* of a program $(D|s)$ with respect to the set $\delta(D)$. This is a program $(D'|s')$ which is obtained form $(D|s)$ by systematically replacing some $x \in \delta(D)$ by a *fresh* x'. By "fresh" we mean here that $x' \notin \delta(D)$, and x' does not occur in s or any of the $D(y)$, for each $y \in \delta(D)$. The operation of systematically replacing x by x' in $(D|s)$, yielding $(D'|s')$, is defined as follows: $D' = D[x'/x]$, $s' = s[x'/x]$, where

$$D[x'/x](y) \quad = \quad D(y)[x'/x], \ \ y \in \delta(D), \ y \not\equiv x$$
$$D[x'/x](x') \quad = \quad D(x)[x'/x]$$
$$D[x'/x](z) \text{ is undefined elsewhere.}$$

Note that this definition implies that $\delta(D') = (\delta(D) \setminus \{x\}) \cup \{x'\}$.

The algorithm transforming an element from $\mathcal{L}_\mu$ to an equivalent element in $\mathcal{L}_{cf}^{ext}$ is expressed in terms of a transition relation " $\rightarrow$," here a subset of $\mathcal{L}_\mu \times \mathcal{L}_{cf}^{ext}$. For $\langle s, (D'|s') \rangle \in \ \rightarrow$, we shall write $s \rightarrow (D'|s')$.

Definition 8.18 $(\mathcal{T}_{\mu \rightarrow cf})$ The relation $\rightarrow \ \subseteq \mathcal{L}_\mu \times \mathcal{L}_{cf}^{ext}$ is the least relation satisfying

- $$a \rightarrow (\emptyset|a) \hspace{7cm} \text{(Act)}$$

- $$x \rightarrow (\emptyset|x) \hspace{7cm} \text{(PVar)}$$

- $$\frac{s_1 \rightarrow (D'|s') \quad s_2 \rightarrow (D''|s'')}{s_1;s_2 \rightarrow (D' \cup D''|s';s'')} \hspace{4cm} \text{(Seq)}$$

provided $\delta(D') \cap \delta(D'') = \emptyset$, $\delta(D') \cap pvar(s'') = \emptyset$, $\delta(D'') \cap pvar(s') = \emptyset$

- similarly for '+' $\hspace{7cm}$ (Choice)

- $$\frac{g \rightarrow (D'|g')}{\mu x[g] \rightarrow (D' \cup (x,g')|x)} \quad \text{ provided } x \notin \delta(D') \hspace{2cm} \text{(Rec)}$$

- $$\frac{s \rightarrow (D'|s')}{s \rightarrow (D''|s'')} \hspace{6cm} \text{(Alph)}$$

where $(D''|s'')$ is an alphabetic variant of $(D'|s')$

In the rules (Seq), (Choice) and (Rec) the notation assumes that the functions D', D'' are given as finite sets of pairs (y, g_y), for $y \in \delta(D')$ or $y \in \delta(D'')$.

Before proving the correctness of the algorithm embodied in $\mathcal{T}_{\mu \to cf}$, we first present an example:

We shall show that

$$\mu x[a;\mu y[b;x;y]] \to (\{(x, a;y), (y, b;x;y)\}|x).$$

We have, by (Act), (PVar) and (Seq),

$$a \to (\emptyset|a) \tag{8.7}$$

$$b;x;y \to (\emptyset|b;x;y). \tag{8.8}$$

By (Rec), from (8.8)

$$\mu y[b;x;y] \to (\{(y, b;x;y)\}|y). \tag{8.9}$$

Applying (Seq) to (8.7) and (8.9), we obtain

$$a;\mu y[b;x;y] \to (\{(y, b;x;y)\}|a;y). \tag{8.10}$$

Another application of (Rec) then yields

$$\mu x[a;\mu y[b;x;y]] \to (\{(x, a;y), (y, b;x;y)\}|x).$$

The next lemma formally states the correctness of the above algorithm.

Lemma 8.19 *For each $s \in \mathcal{L}_\mu$ there exists $(D'|s') \in \mathcal{L}_{cf}^{ext}$ such that $s \to (D'|s')$. If $s \to (D'|s')$ then*

- $pvar(s) = pvar(D'|s')$
- $\mathcal{D}_\mu^*(s)(\eta) = \mathcal{D}_{cf}^*(D'|s')(\eta)$, *for each η.*

Before we can give the proof of this lemma, we need one auxiliary result:

Lemma 8.20 *Assume $x \notin \delta(D)$. Then, for each η,*

$$\mathcal{D}_{cf}^*(D \cup (x, g)|x)(\eta) = \mathcal{D}_{cf}^*(D|g)(\eta\{p/x\}),$$

where $p = fix\,[\,\lambda\bar{p}.\mathcal{D}_{cf}^*(D|g)(\eta\{\bar{p}/x\})\,]$.

Proof See Exercise 8.9.   □

The proof of Lemma 8.19 proceeds by structural induction on s. We only discuss the final assertion. The subcases $[a]$, $[x]$ are immediate, and the subcases $[s_1;s_2]$, $[s_1 + s_2]$ are easy by induction. For example,

$\mathcal{D}_\mu^*(s_1;s_2)(\eta)$

$= \mathcal{D}_\mu^*(s_1)(\eta);\mathcal{D}_\mu^*(s_2)(\eta)$

$= [\text{ind. hyp. }] \; \mathcal{D}_{cf}^*(D'|s')(\eta);\mathcal{D}_{cf}^*(D''|s'')(\eta)$

$= \mathcal{D}_{cf}^*(D' \cup D''|s';s'')(\eta),$

where the last equality holds by the condition on the $\delta(D')$, $\delta(D'')$, pvar(s'), pvar(s''). There remains the most interesting subcase:

$[\mu x[g]]$ Assume that $g \to (D'|g')$, with $x \notin \delta(D)$. By induction we have that, for each η, $\mathcal{D}_\mu^*(g)(\eta) = \mathcal{D}_{cf}^*(D'|g')(\eta)$. Consequently, $\lambda p.\mathcal{D}_\mu^*(g)(\eta\{p/x\}) = \lambda p.\mathcal{D}_{cf}^*(D'|g')(\eta\{p/x\})$. Supplying both functions with the argument

p_0

$= \;\; \text{fix}[\lambda\bar{p}.\mathcal{D}_\mu^*(g)(\eta\{p/x\})]$

$= \;\; \text{fix}[\lambda\bar{p}.\mathcal{D}_{cf}^*(D'|g')(\eta\{\bar{p}/x\})]$

$= \;\; p_1,$

we obtain $\mathcal{D}_\mu^*(g)(\eta\{p_0/x\}) = \mathcal{D}_{cf}^*(D'|g')(\eta\{p_1/x\})$. By the definition of p_0 and Lemma 8.20, we have

$$\mathcal{D}_\mu^*(\mu x[g])(\eta) = \mathcal{D}_{cf}^*(D' \cup (x, g')|x)(\eta).$$

which is the desired result.   □

Remark As an immediate corollary of this lemma we have that, if $s \in \mathcal{L}_\mu^c$ then $(D'|s')$ has no free procedure variables, i.e., $(D'|s')$ is a program in $\mathcal{L}_{cf}$ as originally defined in Chapter 2.

8.4   Three semantics for $\mathcal{L}_{cf}$—fixed points at different levels

We close the chapter on Recursion Revisited with a brief section devoted to a *third* way of designing a denotational semantics for $\mathcal{L}_{cf}$. Recall that we have, so far, introduced two semantics: In Chapter 2, we put $\mathcal{D}_{cf} = \text{fix}(\Psi)$, with

$\Psi \colon (\mathcal{L}_{cf} \to \mathbb{P}_D) \to (\mathcal{L}_{cf} \to \mathbb{P}_D).$

In the previous section, we introduced $\mathcal{D}^*_{cf}(D|s)$ which used (an auxiliary $\mathcal{F}$ and) fixed points of mappings

$$\mathbb{P}^n_D \to \mathbb{P}^n_D,$$

for n the number of procedure variables declared in D (hence, this case assumes a finite domain for D). We now describe a third possibility. Let $(x \in) PVar$, $(s \in) Stat$, $((D|s) \in) \mathcal{L}_{cf}$, $(p \in) \mathbb{P}_D$, $(\eta \in) \mathrm{H} = PVar \to \mathbb{P}_D$, and $\mathcal{F} \colon Stat \to \mathrm{H} \to \mathbb{P}_D$ be as before. Let the mapping

$$\mathcal{X}_D \colon \mathrm{H} \to \mathrm{H}$$

be given by $\mathcal{X}_D(\eta)(x) = \mathcal{F}(D(x))(\eta)$, and let $\eta_D = \mathrm{fix}(\mathcal{X}_D)$. Now let

$$\mathcal{D}^{**}_{cf}(D|s) = \mathcal{F}(s)(\eta_D).$$

We then have

(i) $\mathcal{X}_D$ is contractive (in η).
(ii) $\mathcal{D}^*_{cf}(D|s) = \mathcal{D}^{**}_{cf}(D|s)$.

Proof We leave part (a) as an exercise. Part (b) is shown as follows. By the definition of $\mathcal{D}_{cf}$ and Banach's theorem, it is sufficient to prove that, for each $(D|s)$, $\Psi(\mathcal{D}^{**}_{cf})(D|s) = \mathcal{D}^{**}_{cf}(D|s)$. We use structural induction on s. The three subcases $[a]$, $[s_1;s_2]$, $[s_1 + s_2]$ are immediate. There remains the subcase

$[x]$ We have

$$
\begin{aligned}
&\Psi(\mathcal{D}^{**}_{cf})(D|x) \\
={}& \mathcal{D}^{**}_{cf}(D|D(x)) \\
={}& \mathcal{F}(D(x))(\eta_D) \\
={}& \mathcal{X}_D(\eta_D)(x) \\
={}& \eta_D(x) \\
={}& F(x)(\eta_D) \\
={}& \mathcal{D}^{**}_{cf}(D|s).
\end{aligned}
$$
$\qquad\square$

Summarizing the above discussion, we see that recursion in languages such as $\mathcal{L}_{cf}$ may be handled by taking fixed points at three different levels:

- $(\mathcal{L}_{cf} \to P_D) \to (\mathcal{L}_{cf} \to P_D)$ $\hspace{3cm}$ $(\mathcal{D}_{cf})$
- $(PVar \to P_D) \to (PVar \to P_D)$ $\hspace{2.8cm}$ $(\mathcal{D}^{**}_{cf})$
- $P^n_D \to P^n_D.$ $\hspace{6.2cm}$ $(\mathcal{D}^*_{cf})$

8.5   Exercises

Exercise 8.1

(a) Prove, for $s \in \mathcal{L}_\mu$, $t_1, t_2 \in \mathcal{L}_\mu^c$, $x, y \in PVar$,

$$s[t_1/x][t_2/y] \;=\; \begin{cases} s[t_2/y][t_1/x] & \text{for } x \not\equiv y \\ s[t_1/x] & \text{for } x \equiv y. \end{cases}$$

(b) Discuss the consequences of dropping, in Definition 8.2, the condition that t be a closed statement. (E.g., does part (a) of this exercise remain valid?)

Exercise 8.2   The syntactic class $(s \in)\, Stat_X$, for $X \subseteq PVar$, is given by

$$s ::= a \mid s;s' \mid s + s \mid x \mid \mu x'[s''],$$

where

- $s' \in Stat_\emptyset$
- $x \notin X$
- $s'' \in Stat_{X \cup \{x'\}}$.

Let $Stat^{ext} \stackrel{df}{=} Stat_{PVar}$, and let $Stat$ be as in Definition 8.1. Show that $Stat \subseteq Stat^{ext}$, and that, for $x \not\equiv y$, $\mu x[a;\mu y[x;y]] \in Stat^{ext} \backslash Stat$.

Exercise 8.3   Let $r\,(\in Res) ::= E \mid s$, with $s \in \mathcal{L}_\mu$ (thus, we drop the requirement that r be closed). Consider the system $\mathcal{T}_\mu'$ consisting of (Act), (Seq) and (Choice) as in $\mathcal{T}_\mu$, together with the rule

$$\frac{g \stackrel{a}{\to} r}{\mu x[g] \stackrel{a}{\to} r[\mu x[g]/x]}.$$

Let $\mathcal{O}'$ be derived from $\mathcal{T}_\mu'$ in the usual manner. Show that $\mathcal{O}$ and $\mathcal{O}'$ coincide on $\mathcal{L}_\mu^c$.

Exercise 8.4 Show that, for $t \in \mathit{Stat}_{\{x\}}$ (notation as in Exercise 8.2) and $s_1, s_2 \in \mathcal{L}_\mu^c$,

$$d(\mathcal{O}(t[s_1/x]), \mathcal{O}(t[s_2/x])) \leq \tfrac{1}{2}d(\mathcal{O}(s_1), \mathcal{O}(s_2)).$$

Exercise 8.5 Let $s_1 = s_2$ be short for $\mathcal{D}(s_1) = \mathcal{D}(s_2)$. Show the following (with respect to $\mathcal{L}_\mu$):

(a) $\mu x[s_1[s_2/x]] = s_1[\mu x[s_2[s_1/x]]/x]$

(b) $\mu x[(g;x) + (s_1;s_2)] = \mu x[(g;x) + s_1];s_2$ if $x \notin \mathit{pvar}(s_1;s_2)$

(c) $\mu x[s[x/y]] = \mu x[s[\mu x[s[x/y]]/y]]$.

Exercise 8.6 Assume that it is known that $\mathcal{O}(\mu x[g]) = \mathit{lim}_n \, \mathcal{O}(g^{(n)})$, where $g^{(0)}$ is arbitrary and $g^{(n+1)} = g[g^{(n)}/x]$. (This is easy using Corollary 8.10 and Banach; a direct, and considerably more difficult, proof is possible based on an analysis of the transition sequences for $\mu x[g]$.) Prove—without using Corollary 8.10 or Theorem 8.15—for $s \in \mathcal{L}_\mu$, $x_i \in \mathit{PVar}$, $t_i \in \mathcal{L}_\mu^c$, $i = 1, \ldots, k$, that

$$\mathcal{O}(s[t_i/x_i]_{i=1}^k) \quad = \quad \mathcal{D}^*(s)(\eta\{p_i/x_i\}_{i=1}^k),$$

where

(a) $\mathit{pvar}(s) \subseteq \{\, x_1, \ldots, x_k \,\}$

(b) $\mathcal{O}(t_i) = p_i$, $i = 1, \ldots, k$.

Exercise 8.7 (A fourth way of defining $\mathcal{D}$ for $\mathcal{L}_\mu$.) Let $(\eta \in) \mathrm{H}$ be as in Section 8.2, and let $(S \in) \mathit{Sem}_D = \mathcal{L}_\mu \to \mathrm{H} \to \mathbb{P}_D$. We define $\Psi \colon \mathit{Sem}_D \to \mathit{Sem}_D$ by putting

$$
\begin{aligned}
\Psi(S)(a)(\eta) &= \{a\} \\
\Psi(S)(x)(\eta) &= \eta(x) \\
\Psi(S)(s_1 \,\mathsf{op}\, s_2)(\eta) &= \Psi(S)(s_1)(\eta) \,\mathsf{op}\, \Psi(S)(s_2)(\eta), \quad \mathsf{op} \in \{;, +\} \\
\Psi(S)(\mu x[g])(\eta) &= \Psi(S)(g)(\eta\{S(\mu x[g])(\eta)/x\}).
\end{aligned}
$$

Prove that Ψ is $\tfrac{1}{2}$-contractive in S. Putting $\mathcal{D}^\dagger = \mathit{fix}(\Psi)$, state and prove the relationship between $\mathcal{D}^\dagger$ and the various $\mathcal{D}$-functions discussed in Chapter 8. (This definition combines the global fixed point approach with a definition by syntactic induction on the argument s. Its advantage with respect to Definition 8.8 is that it avoids the use of the "nondenotational" operation of substitution.)

Exercise 8.8 Let $PVar = \{\, x_0, x_1, \ldots \,\}$, and let

$$\pi = (\{\, x_i \Leftarrow a_i; x_{i+1} \,\}_{i=0}^{\infty} | x_0).$$

Show that this program in $\mathcal{L}_{cf}$ has no equivalent program in $\mathcal{L}_{\mu}$.

Exercise 8.9 Prove Lemma 8.20

8.6 Bibliographical notes

Ever since its appearance in higher programming languages (cf. Section 1.4), recursion has played a central role in semantic studies. In a cpo-style semantics, it is characterized in terms of least fixed points. Early references for this are [BS69, Par70, Bek84a]; for a comprehensive discussion of the early literature we refer to [Bak80]. The syntactic formalism of the μ-calculus goes back to [BS69]; [Bak71] is an early monograph on this topic. The metric semantics for $\mathcal{L}_{\mu}$ as developed in Section 8.1 owes much to [Bre94b]; in particular, the crucial definition of wgt for $\mathcal{L}_{\mu}$ (in Definition 8.5) is due to Van Breugel. The way we have imposed the guardedness restriction on $\mathcal{L}_{\mu}$ can be (slightly) weakened; this is described in [KR90] and [Bre94b]. An operational semantics for a language with unguarded recursion has been presented in [BKMOZ85, BMOZ88] and in [BV90]. In [KR90], an alternative transition rule for recursion is given. Both rules induce the same operational semantics, as has been shown in [BD91] (see also Lemma 9.3 of [BM94]).

The use of procedure environments as a tool in the fixed point definition of recursion is the traditional one (see the standard texts on denotational semantics); only later, the global approach as used mostly in our book was proposed ([KR90]).

The comparison of $\mathcal{L}_{cf}$ and $\mathcal{L}_{\mu}$ relies on the crucial Lemma 8.17. This result relating simultaneous to iterated fixed points is another classical result in the theory of recursion. It was obtained—in the slightly more involved case concerning least fixed points rather than unique fixed points—simultaneously (and independently) by Bekić ([Bek84a]), De Bakker and Scott ([BS69]) and Leszczylowski ([Les71]). Once this is available, the translation from $\mathcal{L}_{cf}$ to $\mathcal{L}_{\mu}$ follows naturally; the algorithm translating $\mathcal{L}_{\mu}$ to $\mathcal{L}_{cf}$ may be new.

The third way of defining fixed points to deal with recursive procedures is as well part of the standard toolkit of the denotational semanticist.

9 Nested Resumptions

In Chapter 9, we bring together two language concepts which have in common that in their semantic analysis fruitful use can be made of the notion of *nested* resumptions. Roughly, instead of working with just one resumption (say r), we shall now employ nested constructs, (essentially) consisting of sequences of n ($\geq$ 0) resumptions. In Section 9.1, we shall be concerned with a language $\mathcal{L}_{bt}$ with *backtracking* as its main feature, and we shall use, besides the usual r (of the form E or s), also constructs t given by

$$t ::= \Delta \,|\, (r\!:\!t), \tag{9.1}$$

for Δ some given constant. The rules for accessing/updating the t will have a *stack*-like flavour. In Section 9.2, we study a nonuniform language with a *fork*-construct ($\mathcal{L}_{fork}$). This is maybe less familiar, and we pay some special attention to its informal explanation. In terms of the nested resumption perspective, we shall work with entities as defined by

$$\rho ::= w \,|\, [\rho, r, \sigma]. \tag{9.2}$$

Here the r, σ are (variations on) the standard notions as used for nonuniform languages, and w is a new kind of entity (a sequence of values) which we do not explain further in this introduction. Repeatedly applying rules (9.1) and (9.2), we obtain as instances of t and ρ, respectively, entities such as

$$t = (r_1\!:\!(r_2\!:\ldots(r_n\!:\!\Delta)\ldots))$$

$$\rho = [\ldots[[w, r_1, \sigma_1], r_2, \sigma_2], \ldots, r_n, \sigma_n].$$

For the moment, it is sufficient that the reader observes the similarity in the structure for the t and ρ as displayed. The way they are used in the development of the semantics for $\mathcal{L}_{bt}$ and $\mathcal{L}_{fork}$ will be presented in some detail in Sections 9.1 and 9.2.

9.1 Backtracking—success and failure prolongations

We study the language $\mathcal{L}_{bt}$ which extends the language $\mathcal{L}_{rec}$ with the programming concepts of *failure* and *backtracking*. Failure appears syntactically in the form of the special atomic action fail. Backtracking is expressed by the language construct $s_1 \square s_2$. In a first approximation, its effect may be explained as follows: Execution of $s_1 \Box s_2$ is started with the execution of s_1. If, during this execution the action fail is not encountered, then the execution of $s_1 \Box s_2$ terminates if and when execution of s_1 terminates. Otherwise, i.e., when an action fail is indeed performed, the execution of s_1 is terminated and the execution of $s_1 \Box s_2$ resumes with that of s_2. Actually, this explanation needs some refinement which requires the resumption mechanism for its precise explanation. This we shall introduce in a moment. Let us already remark that we explain backtracking, for simplicity, by extending $\mathcal{L}_{rec}$ with the notions just described. With minor modifications, the same approach may be applied to most of the other languages in Part II. (Cf. Exercise 9.2 for a treatment of backtracking in a simple nonuniform language.)

9.1.1 Syntax and operational semantics

Let $(a \in) Act$ and $(x \in) PVar$ be as usual. Let fail be a new atomic action, i.e., fail $\notin Act$.

Definition 9.1

(a) $s (\in Stat) ::= a \mid \mathsf{fail} \mid x \mid (s;s) \mid (s \Box s)$

(b) $g (\in GStat) ::= a \mid \mathsf{fail} \mid (g;s) \mid (g \Box g)$

(c) $(D \in) Decl = PVar \to GStat$

(d) $(\pi \in) \mathcal{L}_{bt} = Decl \times Stat.$

Remark Note that the $\mathcal{L}_{bt}$-statement fail;x is guarded, whereas fail$\Box x$ is not.

The transition system $\mathcal{L}_{bt}$ employs two kinds of resumptions, viz. $(r \in) SRes$, the set of *success resumptions*, and $(t \in) FRes$, the set of *failure resumptions*. Each statement s is executed in the presence of both a success resumption r and a failure resumption t. Accordingly, we shall specify in $\mathcal{T}_{bt}$ how to execute triples $\langle s, r, t \rangle$. For consistency with our earlier notation, we rather write such a triple as $(s{:}r){:}t$.

We now give the syntax for the two classes of resumptions. Let E be as always, and let Δ be a new symbol—the "atomic" failure resumption.

Definition 9.2

(a) $r (\in SRes) ::= \mathrm{E} \mid (s{:}r)$

(b) $t (\in FRes) ::= \Delta \mid (r{:}t)$

We see that success resumptions are the same as before (for simple sequential languages). A failure resumption t consists of a sequence of $n \geq 0$ success resumptions of the form $r_1:(r_2:\ldots:(r_n:\Delta)\ldots)$. The way in which such a t is accessed—see later—implies that it may be seen, more precisely, as a *stack* of success resumptions, with Δ acting as bottom of the stack. There are no "automatic" identification rules for r or t. In particular, we do not identify E:t with t.

The failure resumptions t are the configurations of the transition system T_{bt}, which is presented in

Definition 9.3 $T_{bt} = (FRes, Act, \rightarrow, Spec)$. *Spec consists of*

- $$(a:r):t \xrightarrow{a} r:t \qquad\qquad\qquad\qquad\qquad\qquad\qquad\qquad \text{(Act)}$$

- $$(\text{fail}:r):t \rightarrow_0 t \qquad\qquad\qquad\qquad\qquad\qquad\qquad\qquad \text{(Fail)}$$

- $$(x:r):t \rightarrow_0 (D(x):r):t \qquad\qquad\qquad\qquad\qquad\qquad \text{(Rec)}$$

- $$((s_1;s_2):r):t \rightarrow_0 (s_1:(s_2:r)):t \qquad\qquad\qquad\qquad \text{(Seq)}$$

- $$((s_1 \,\square\, s_2):r):t \rightarrow_0 (s_1:r):((s_2:r):t) \qquad\qquad \text{(Backtrack)}$$

The (Fail)-rule tells us that a statement which fails should resume with its failure resumption. The (Backtrack)-rule specifies that $((s_1 \,\square\, s_2):r):t$ should be executed by executing s_1 with success resumption r and failure resumption $(s_2:r):t$. Hence, if, during execution of $s_1:r$ somewhere a fail is encountered, execution continues with that of $(s_2:r):t$, i.e., s_2 is performed with r and t as success and failure resumption. In this way, the failure causes execution to *backtrack* to execution of s_2 (with r and t as originally valid for $s_1 \,\square\, s_2$). Note that we have, altogether, introduced a *stack* mechanism for failure resumptions: The effect of the (Fail)-rule is to pop the stack, whereas the (Backtrack)-rule pushes a fresh element onto the stack—which is the first to be retrieved upon subsequent execution of a fail. We can now also explain to what extent the discussion at the introduction of this section (just above 9.1.1) was not yet complete: There, we did not mention that the effect of $s \equiv s_1 \,\square\, s_2$ also influences execution of the r following s, in that encountering some fail while executing r (and not only while executing s_1) will cause backtracking to $(s_2:r):t$—provided that no more recent pushing of the failure resumption stack has taken place.

On the way to the definition of $\mathcal{O}$ in terms of T_{bt} we need two preparations. Firstly, we introduce the customary weight function, and, secondly, we shall need the definition of the notions "t terminates" and "t fails."

The definition of the weight function exhibits the usual pattern in that it is related to, but slightly different from, previous definitions of this function in the context of earlier languages.

Definition 9.4 $wgt: FRes \cup SRes \cup Stat \to \mathbb{N}$ is defined by putting

(a) $wgt(\Delta) = 0$, $wgt(r{:}t) = wgt(r) + wgt(t)$

(b) $wgt(\mathrm{E}) = 0$, $wgt(s{:}r) = wgt(s)$

(c) $wgt(a) = wgt(\mathsf{fail}) = 1$
$wgt(x) = wgt(D(x)) + 1$, $wgt(s_1;s_2) = wgt(s_1) + 1$
$wgt(s_1 \,\square\, s_2) = wgt(s_1) + wgt(s_2) + 1$.

Observe that, in the formula for $wgt(s{:}r)$, r does not contribute to the result. It is not difficult to show

Lemma 9.5 *wgt is well-defined for each s, r and t.*

Proof The cases r are t are immediate by structural induction. The case s follows by the usual arguments, establishing well-definedness first for each g and then for each s. $\qquad\square$

The definition of wgt has been designed such that the following lemma—familiar from earlier chapters—holds:

Lemma 9.6 *If $t \to_0 t'$, then $wgt(t) > wgt(t')$.*

Proof Two subcases

$[((s_1;s_2){:}r){:}t]$ $\quad wgt(((s_1;s_2){:}r){:}t) = wgt(s_1;s_2) + wgt(t) = wgt(s_1) + 1 + wgt(t) > wgt(s_1) + wgt(t) = wgt(s_1{:}((s_2{:}r){:}t))$.

$[((s_1 \,\square\, s_2){:}r){:}t]$ $\quad wgt(((s_1 \,\square\, s_2){:}r){:}t) = wgt(s_1 \,\square\, s_2) + wgt(t) = wgt(s_1) + wgt(s_2) + 1 + wgt(t) > wgt(s_1) + wgt(s_2) + wgt(t) = wgt(s_1{:}r) + wgt((s_2{:}r){:}t) = wgt((s_1{:}r){:}((s_2{:}r){:}t))$. $\qquad\square$

We continue with the definitions of "t terminates" and "t fails."

Definition 9.7

(a) Let $\overset{*}{\to}_0$ denote the reflexive and transitive closure of the $\to_0$ relation.

(b) We say that t *terminates* if $t \overset{*}{\to}_0 \mathrm{E}{:}t'$, for some t'.

(c) We say that t *fails* if $t \overset{*}{\to}_0 \Delta$.

Examples (fail:r):(E:Δ) terminates, and, for $D(x) =$ fail;a, we have that $(x{:}r){:}\Delta$ fails.

These notions play a role in

Lemma 9.8 *For each t we have that precisely one of the following holds*

(1) t terminates;

(2) t fails;

(3) there exist a, t' such that $t \xrightarrow{a} t'$.

Proof Induction on $wgt(t)$. Four subcases.

[Δ]   Then t fails.

[$E{:}t'$] t terminates.

[$(a{:}r){:}t'$]   Now $t \xrightarrow{a} r{:}t'$.

[$((s_1;s_2){:}r){:}t'$]   Putting $t \equiv ((s_1;s_2){:}r){:}t'$, we have that $t \to_0 \bar{t}$, with $\bar{t}$ as prescribed by (Seq). Since, by Lemma 9.6, $wgt(t) > wgt(\bar{t})$, the desired result follows by the induction hypothesis.

The remaining cases are similar. $\square$

We are now sufficiently prepared for the definition of $\mathcal{O}$ for $\mathcal{L}_{bt}$. Since $\mathcal{L}_{bt}$ exhibits no nondeterminism, the codomain for $\mathcal{O}$ only involves sequences of atomic actions in the form as given in

Definition 9.9

(a) Let ∂ be some symbol not in Act, and let $Act_\partial = Act \cup \{\partial\}$.

(b) Let $\mathbb{P}_O = Act_\partial^\infty$, where

$$Act_\partial^\infty = Act^* \cup Act^* \cdot \{\partial\} \cup Act^\omega.$$

We use ∂ here as semantic counterpart of the syntactic fail. (Note that we deviate here from our general convention that we do not distinguish between the use of $a \in Act$ in a syntactic and a semantic context.) The set $\mathbb{P}_O$ consists of all finite and infinite sequences of elements in Act (i.e., Act^∞ as before), together with all finite sequences of elements from Act with ∂ concatenated at the end.

The definition of $\mathcal{O}$ follows in

Definition 9.10

(a) $\mathcal{O}: FRes \to \mathbb{P}_O$ is the unique function satisfying

$$\mathcal{O}(t) \;=\; \begin{cases} \epsilon & \text{if } t \text{ terminates} \\ \partial & \text{if } t \text{ fails} \\ a \cdot \mathcal{O}(t') & \text{if } t \xrightarrow{a} t'. \end{cases}$$

(b) $\mathcal{O}[\![s]\!] = \mathcal{O}((s{:}\text{E}){:}\Delta)$.

Well-definedness of $\mathcal{O}$ may be shown by the standard argument involving a higher order contractive Φ, together with an application of Lemma 9.8.

Examples

(1) $\mathcal{O}[\![a \,\square\, \text{fail}]\!]$
    $= \mathcal{O}((a \,\square\, \text{fail}{:}\text{E}){:}\Delta)$
    $= \mathcal{O}((a{:}\text{E}){:}(\text{fail}{:}\text{E}){:}\Delta)$
    $= a \cdot \mathcal{O}(\text{E}{:}(\text{fail}{:}\text{E}){:}\Delta)$
    $= a$

(2) $\mathcal{O}[\![\text{fail} \,\square\, a]\!]$
    $= \mathcal{O}((\text{fail} \,\square\, a{:}\text{E}){:}\Delta)$
    $= \mathcal{O}((\text{fail}{:}\text{E}){:}((a{:}\text{E}){:}\Delta))$
    $= \mathcal{O}((a{:}\text{E}){:}\Delta)$
    $= a \cdot \mathcal{O}(\text{E}{:}\Delta)$
    $= a$

(3) $\mathcal{O}[\![\text{fail} \,\square\, \text{fail}]\!]$
    $= \mathcal{O}((\text{fail} \,\square\, \text{fail}{:}\text{E}){:}\Delta)$
    $= \mathcal{O}((\text{fail}{:}\text{E}){:}((\text{fail}{:}\text{E}){:}\Delta))$
    $= \mathcal{O}((\text{fail}{:}\text{E}){:}\Delta)$
    $= \mathcal{O}(\Delta)$
    $= \partial$

(4) Let $D(x) = (\text{fail};x) \,\square\, a$.
    $\mathcal{O}[\![x]\!]$
    $= \mathcal{O}((x{:}\text{E}){:}\Delta)$

$$= \mathcal{O}((((\mathsf{fail};x)\Box a){:}E){:}\Delta)$$
$$= \mathcal{O}(((\mathsf{fail};x{:}E){:}((a{:}E){:}\Delta))$$
$$= \mathcal{O}(((\mathsf{fail}{:}x{:}E){:}((a{:}E){:}\Delta))$$
$$= \mathcal{O}((a{:}E){:}\Delta)$$
$$= a.$$

9.1.2   Denotational semantics, equivalence of $\mathcal{O}$ and $\mathcal{D}$

Corresponding to the two kinds of resumptions employed in the operational semantics, we shall introduce two kinds of semantic continuations, viz. *success continuations* and *failure continuations*. These notions are defined in

Definition 9.11

(a) $\mathbb{P}_D = \mathbb{P}_O$

(b) $(\phi \in) SCont = FCont \xrightarrow{1} \mathbb{P}_D, \ \phi_\epsilon = \lambda\gamma.\epsilon$

(c) $(\gamma \in) FCont = \mathbb{P}_D, \ \gamma_\epsilon = \partial.$

The denotational semantics $\mathcal{D}$ is given in the next definition. Its structure closely follows that of $\mathcal{T}_{bt}$, based on the correspondence between r and ϕ, and t and γ, respectively.

Definition 9.12

(a) $(S \in) Sem_D = Stat \to SCont \xrightarrow{1} FCont \xrightarrow{1} \mathbb{P}_D.$ The mapping $\Psi : Sem_D \to Sem_D$ is given by

$$
\begin{aligned}
\Psi(S)(a)(\phi)(\gamma) &= a \cdot \phi(\gamma) \\
\Psi(S)(\mathsf{fail})(\phi)(\gamma) &= \gamma \\
\Psi(S)(x)(\phi)(\gamma) &= \Psi(S)(D(x))(\phi)(\gamma) \\
\Psi(S)(s_1;s_2)(\phi)(\gamma) &= \Psi(S)(s_1)(S(s_2)(\phi))(\gamma) \\
\Psi(S)(s_1\Box s_2)(\phi)(\gamma) &= \Psi(S)(s_1)(\phi)(\Psi(S)(s_2)(\phi)(\gamma))
\end{aligned}
$$

(b) $\mathcal{D} = \mathrm{fix}(\Psi), \ \mathcal{D}[\![s]\!] = \mathcal{D}(s)(\phi_\epsilon)(\gamma_\epsilon).$

Examples

(1) $\mathcal{D}[\![a \square \mathsf{fail}]\!]$

$= \mathcal{D}(a \square \mathsf{fail})(\phi_\epsilon)(\gamma_\epsilon)$

$= \mathcal{D}(a)(\phi_\epsilon)\big(\mathcal{D}(\mathsf{fail})(\phi_\epsilon)(\gamma_\epsilon)\big)$

$= a \cdot \phi_\epsilon(\mathcal{D}(\mathsf{fail})(\phi_\epsilon)(\gamma_\epsilon))$

$= a \cdot \epsilon$

$= a$

(2) Let $D(x) = (\mathsf{fail};x) \square a$.

$\mathcal{D}[\![x]\!]$

$= \mathcal{D}(x)(\phi_\epsilon)(\gamma_\epsilon)$

$= \mathcal{D}((\mathsf{fail};x) \square a)(\phi_\epsilon)(\gamma_\epsilon)$

$= \mathcal{D}(\mathsf{fail};x)(\phi_\epsilon)\big(\mathcal{D}(a)(\phi_\epsilon)(\gamma_\epsilon)\big)$

$= \mathcal{D}(\mathsf{fail})\big(\mathcal{D}(x)(\phi_\epsilon)\big)\big(\mathcal{D}(a)(\phi_\epsilon)(\gamma_\epsilon)\big)$

$= \mathcal{D}(a)(\phi_\epsilon)(\gamma_\epsilon)$

$= a \cdot \phi_\epsilon(\gamma_\epsilon)$

$= a \cdot \epsilon$

$= a.$

The next lemma states a number of results necessary to justify this definition.

Lemma 9.13 *For each S, s, ϕ:*

(a) The mapping $\Psi(S)(s)(\phi)$ is nonexpansive (in γ).

(b) The mapping $\Psi(S)(s)$ is $\frac{1}{2}$-contractive (in ϕ).

(c) The mapping Ψ is $\frac{1}{2}$-contractive (in S).

Proof Structural induction on s.

(a) Two subcases.

[fail] $d(\Psi(S)(\mathsf{fail})(\phi)(\gamma_1), \Psi(S)(\mathsf{fail})(\phi)(\gamma_2)) = d(\gamma_1, \gamma_2).$

$[s_1;s_2]$ $d(\Psi(S)(s_1;s_2)(\phi)(\gamma_1), \Psi(S)(s_1;s_2)(\phi)(\gamma_2))$

$= \quad d(\Psi(S)(s_1)(S(s_2)(\phi))(\gamma_1), \Psi(S)(s_1)(S(s_2)(\phi))(\gamma_2))$

$\leq \quad$ [ind. hyp., which applies since $S(s_2)(\phi) \in SCont$] $d(\gamma_1, \gamma_2).$

(b) Choose some γ. Two subcases.

$$[a] \quad d(\Psi(S)(a)(\phi_1)(\gamma), \Psi(S)(a)(\phi_2)(\gamma))$$
$$= \quad d(a \cdot \phi_1(\gamma), a \cdot \phi_2(\gamma))$$
$$\leq \quad \tfrac{1}{2} d(\phi_1, \phi_2).$$

$$[s_1 \square s_2] \quad d(\Psi(S)(s_1 \square s_2)(\phi_1)(\gamma), \Psi(S)(s_1 \square s_2)(\phi_2)(\gamma))$$
$$= \quad d(\Psi(S)(s_1)(\phi_1)(\Psi(S)(s_2)(\phi_1)(\gamma))$$
$$\quad\quad \Psi(S)(s_1)(\phi_2)(\Psi(S)(s_2)(\phi_2)(\gamma))$$
$$= \quad [d \text{ an ultrametric}]$$
$$\quad max\{d(\Psi(S)(s_1)(\phi_1)(\Psi(S)(s_2)(\phi_1)(\gamma)),$$
$$\quad\quad\quad \Psi(S)(s_1)(\phi_1)(\Psi(S)(s_2)(\phi_2)(\gamma)),$$
$$\quad\quad\quad d(\Psi(S)(s_1)(\phi_1)(\Psi(S)(s_2)(\phi_2)(\gamma)),$$
$$\quad\quad\quad \Psi(S)(s_1)(\phi_2)(\Psi(S)(s_2)(\phi_2)(\gamma)) \}$$
$$\leq \quad [\text{part (a), ind. hyp. for } s_1]$$
$$\quad max\{ d(\Psi(S)(s_2)(\phi_1)(\gamma), \Psi(S)(s_2)(\phi_2)(\gamma)), \tfrac{1}{2} d(\phi_1, \phi_2) \}$$
$$\leq \quad [\text{ind. hyp. for } s_2] \ \tfrac{1}{2} d(\phi_1, \phi_2).$$

(c) Choose some ϕ, γ. One subcase.

$$[s_1; s_2] \quad d(\Psi(S_1)(s_1; s_2)(\phi)(\gamma), \Psi(S_2)(s_1; s_2)(\phi)(\gamma))$$
$$= \quad d(\Psi(S_2)(s_1)(S_1(s_2)(\phi))(\gamma), \Psi(S_2)(s_1)(S_1(s_2)(\phi))(\gamma))$$
$$\leq \quad [d \text{ an ultrametric}]$$
$$\quad max\{d(\Psi(S_1)(s_1)(S_1(s_2)(\phi))(\gamma), \Psi(S_1)(s_1)(S_2(s_2)(\phi))(\gamma)),$$
$$\quad\quad\quad d(\Psi(S_1)(s_1)(S_2(s_2)(\phi))(\gamma), \Psi(S_2)(s_1)(S_2(s_2)(\phi))(\gamma)) \}$$
$$\leq \quad [\text{part (b), ind. hyp. for } s_1]$$
$$\quad max\{ \tfrac{1}{2} d(S_1(s_2)(\phi), S_2(s_2)(\phi)), \tfrac{1}{2} d(S_1, S_2) \}$$
$$\leq \quad \tfrac{1}{2} d(S_1, S_2). \qquad\qquad \square$$

We continue with the argument resulting in the equivalence $\mathcal{O} = \mathcal{D}$. We define the intermediate semantic mappings $\mathcal{E}$ and $\mathcal{F}$, relating (success and failure) resumptions and continuations.

Definition 9.14

(a) $\mathcal{E}: SRes \rightarrow SCont$ is given by

$$\mathcal{E}(\mathrm{E}) \quad = \quad \phi_\epsilon$$
$$\mathcal{E}(s{:}r) \quad = \quad \mathcal{D}(s)(\mathcal{E}(r)).$$

(b) $\mathcal{F}: FRes \rightarrow FCont$ is given by

$$\mathcal{F}(\Delta) \quad = \quad \gamma_\epsilon$$
$$\mathcal{F}(r{:}t) \quad = \quad \mathcal{E}(r)(\mathcal{F}(t)).$$

The next lemma states the characteristic property of $\mathcal{F}$, which will be used subsequently in the proof of Lemma 9.16

Lemma 9.15

(a) If $t_1 \rightarrow_0 t_2$, then $\mathcal{F}(t_1) = \mathcal{F}(t_2)$.

(b) $\mathcal{F}(E{:}t) = \epsilon$,
$\mathcal{F}((a{:}r){:}t) = a \cdot \mathcal{F}(r{:}t)$.

Proof

(a) One subcase.

$$
\begin{aligned}
[((s_1 \,\square\, s_2){:}r){:}t] \quad & \mathcal{F}(((s_1 \,\square\, s_2){:}r){:}t) \\
= \quad & \mathcal{E}((s_1 \,\square\, s_2){:}r)(\mathcal{F}(t)) \\
= \quad & \mathcal{D}(s_1 \,\square\, s_2)(\mathcal{E}(r))(\mathcal{F}(t)) \\
= \quad & \mathcal{D}(s_1)(\mathcal{E}(r))(\mathcal{D}(s_2)(\mathcal{E}(r))(\mathcal{F}(t))) \\
= \quad & \ldots \\
= \quad & \mathcal{F}((s_1{:}r){:}((s_2{:}r){:}t)).
\end{aligned}
$$

(b) Left to the reader.   □

We can now show

Lemma 9.16 $\Phi(\mathcal{F}) = \mathcal{F}$.

Proof We show that, for each t, $\Phi(\mathcal{F})(t) = \mathcal{F}(t)$, using induction on $wgt(t)$. Two subcases.

$[(a{:}r){:}t']$ $\quad \Phi(\mathcal{F})((a{:}r){:}t') = a \cdot \mathcal{F}(r{:}t') = $ (Lemma 9.15b) $\mathcal{F}((a{:}r){:}t')$.

$$
\begin{aligned}
[((s_1;s_2){:}r){:}t'] \quad & \Phi(\mathcal{F})(((s_1;s_2){:}r){:}t') \\
= \quad & [\text{def } \mathcal{T}_{bt}] \ \Phi(\mathcal{F})((s_1{:}(s_2{:}r)){:}t') \\
= \quad & [\text{ind. hyp.}] \ \mathcal{F}((s_1{:}(s_2{:}r)){:}t') \\
= \quad & [\text{Lemma 9.15a}] \ \mathcal{F}(((s_1;s_2){:}r){:}t').
\end{aligned}
$$
                                                                               □

Finally, we have

Theorem 9.17

(a) $\mathcal{O} = \mathcal{F}$.

(b) $\mathcal{O}[\![\pi]\!] = \mathcal{D}[\![\pi]\!]$, for all $\pi \in \mathcal{L}_{bt}$.

Proof

(a) As always.

(b) $\mathcal{O}[\![\pi]\!] = \mathcal{O}((s{:}E){:}\Delta) = \mathcal{F}((s{:}E){:}\Delta) = \mathcal{E}(s{:}E)(\mathcal{F}(\Delta)) = \mathcal{D}(s)(\mathcal{E}(E))(\mathcal{F}(\Delta)) = \mathcal{D}(s)(\phi_\epsilon)(\gamma_\epsilon) = \mathcal{D}[\![\pi]\!]$.   □

9.2   The fork statement—contractiveness through hiatons

Our second example language featuring the use of nested resumptions in its semantics is the language $\mathcal{L}_{fork}$. This is an extension of $\mathcal{L}_{wh}$ which, though syntactically quite modest, adds a new dimension to programming: We shall investigate a cluster of concepts which together result in the possibility to program with a (linear) array of processes which are linked by channels. To $\mathcal{L}_{wh}$ we add three further constructs: read(v), write(e) and fork(v). The syntax for $\mathcal{L}_{fork}$ follows:

$s ::= v := e \mid \text{skip} \mid (s;s) \mid \text{if } e \text{ then } s \text{ else } s \text{ fi} \mid \text{while } e \text{ do } s \text{ od} \mid$
$\qquad \text{read}(v) \mid \text{write}(e) \mid \text{fork}(v).$

In the sequel, a program in execution will be called a *process*. Each process has exactly one input channel and one output channel connected to it. (See Figure 9.1).

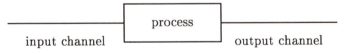

Figure 9.1

Execution of the *write statement* write(e) has the effect that the current value of the expression e is written on the output channel, and the effect of the *read statement* read(v) is that a new value is read from the input channel which is then assigned to the variable v. If there are no more values on the input channel then the process blocks.

A process can be modeled by a function which takes an input stream as an argument and yields an output stream as a result. The input stream is the sequence of all values assumed to be preloaded on the input channel, and the output stream is the sequence of all values successively written by the process on the output channel. Both streams may very well be infinite, implying that we may have to deal with nonterminating computations. We give as first example a "2-filter," described by the program

```
while   true
do      read(v);
        if v mod 2 ≠ 0 then write(v) else skip fi
od
```

In this example, we assume that all values are integers; v mod 2 denotes the remainder of dividing v by 2. The program filters all even number, passing only the odd numbers from its input channel to its output channel.

The other new concept in the language is the *fork statement,* appearing in the form fork(v). When a process executes the statement fork(v), the effect is that an almost identical copy of the process is constructed. We call the original process the *parent* and the new process the *child.* After the fork statement has been executed both processes continue execution with the statement following the fork-statement. There is no sharing of variables, each process has its own set of variables all (but for the variable v, see below) having the value they had in the parent process when the fork statement was executed. There are two differences between the two processes. The first has to do with the fact that executing fork(v) has as a side effect that a value is assigned to v. In the parent process the assignment $v := 1$ is performed, in the child process the value 0 is assigned to v. The other difference has to do with the input and output channels of the original process. On execution of the fork statement a new intermediate channel is constructed. The parent process remains connected to the original input channel, but from now on writes on the new intermediate channel. The child will write on the original output channel, but reads from the intermediate channel. The effect of a fork statement is depicted in Figure 9.2.

The second example is the program

```
read(v);write(v);fork(w);
if      w = 1
then    while   true
        do      read(v);if v mod 2 ≠ 0 then write(v) else skip fi
else    while   true
        do      read(v);if v mod 3 ≠ 0 then write(v) else skip fi
fi.
```

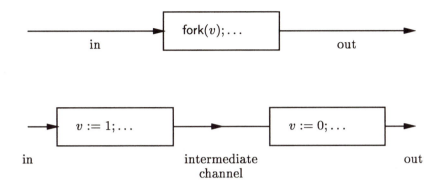

Figure 9.2

The original process passes one value from the input to the output unaltered, and then splits into two filters: the parent filters out all even numbers, passing only the odd numbers to the child. The child filters out all the numbers which are a multiple of 3. The effect is a filter that passes its first input number unaltered, and then passes only those input values that are not multiples of 2 or 3.

Since the fork statement is maybe less familiar to the reader than (most of) the programming notions studied so far, we have spent some extra effort in explaining it. Let us add here one further introductory comment. We recall that in our earlier analyses of nonuniform languages, we took as basic building block for the design of the various transition systems the notion of a change of state, say from σ to some σ' (recorded in transitions of the form $[r, \sigma] \to [r', \sigma']$). For $\mathcal{L}_{fork}$, this is not convenient, since we are primarily interested here in the transformations from input streams to output streams. Therefore, we shall be working with transitions $\rho \xrightarrow{\alpha} \rho'$, for ρ some extension of r to be introduced in a moment[1], and α some value. We shall then obtain the output stream in some way from the successive α's. Now, as we shall see, it is not possible to associate in a natural way a value α from *Val* with each such transition. Rather, certain transitions will involve a "silent" step, denoted by a new symbol τ.[2] Thus, we shall also employ transitions $\rho \xrightarrow{\tau} \rho'$. Another name for such τ is a "hiaton." With this, we have provided an initial explanation of the subtitle of Section 9.2

---

[1]The ρ used here has nothing to do with the ρ from Chapter 6, denoting an environment.

[2]Silent steps τ will reappear on the scene in Chapter 11, where they serve a key role in the handling of synchronous communication.

9.2.1   Syntax and operational semantics

Let $v \in IVar$ and $e \in Exp$ be as usual for a nonuniform language. The syntax for $\mathcal{L}_{fork}$ is given in

Definition 9.18

(a) $s\,(\in Stat) ::= \;\; v := e \mid \text{skip} \mid (s;s) \mid \text{if } e \text{ then } s \text{ else } s \text{ fi} \mid$
$\qquad\qquad\qquad \text{while } e \text{ do } s \text{ od} \mid \text{read}(v) \mid \text{write}(e) \mid \text{fork}(v)$

(b) $(\pi \in)\,\mathcal{L}_{fork} = Stat$.

     As we saw above, programs in $\mathcal{L}_{fork}$ operate on streams of input values, delivering streams of output values. In addition to the set of values Val as used in earlier chapters, we shall also employ the "silent" value τ. Let us use $(\alpha \in)\, Val_\tau = Val \cup \{\tau\}$, and let, in this section, β range over Val only (thus we always have $\beta \neq \tau$). The role of the τ-value (sometimes also called *hiaton*) will be to signal an empty transition, i.e., a transition which does not correspond to outputting a "normal" value. The metric framework needs such silent transitions in order to achieve contractiveness at appropriate places (cf. the definition of $\mathcal{T}_{fork}$ and the notes following it).

     The resumptions which appear in $\mathcal{T}_{fork}$ are of two kinds. The first are the usual r-resumptions; the resumptions in the second category have a nested structure. In fact, the form of the latter is close to the failure resumptions (the t's) of Section 9.1. Since in $\mathcal{L}_{fork}$ there is no phenomenon of (success or) failure, we do not adopt here the earlier terminology.

Definition 9.19

(a) $(w \in)\, Val_\tau^\infty = Val_\tau^* \cup Val_\tau^\omega$. Thus, Val_τ^∞ is the set of finite or infinite sequences of values from Val_τ.

(b) $r\,(\in Res) ::= \mathrm{E} \mid (s{:}r)$.

(c) $\rho\,(\in NRes) ::= w \mid [\rho, r, \sigma]$.

     Whereas a typical failure resumption t (from Section 9.1) has the form $r_1{:}r_2{:}\ldots{:}r_n{:}\Delta$, the general form of a nested resumption ρ is

$$[\ldots[[w, r_1, \sigma_1], r_2, \sigma_2], \ldots, r_n, \sigma_n].$$

     We see three differences: Firstly, for *NRes* we are in a nonuniform setting, with σ's featuring in the ρ's. Secondly, the fixed element Δ is replaced here by the varying input stream w. Thirdly, the order for *NRes* is the reverse one: t's end in Δ, ρ's start with some w.

Nested resumptions ρ correspond to (possibly empty) process arrays described in the introduction in the following way:

(a) $\rho = w$. Here ρ consists of (no more than) the input stream w:

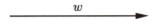

(b) $\rho = [w, r, \sigma]$. Now ρ executes the program as specified by r, for state σ and input w.

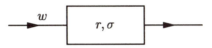

(c) $\rho = [[w, r_1, \sigma_1], r_2, \sigma_2]$. Here ρ consists of two processes: the parent process $[r_1, \sigma_1]$ (with input w), the output of which is to be transmitted to the child process $[r_2, \sigma_2]$.

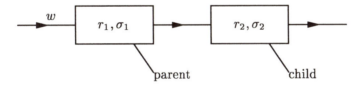

(d) For $n > 2$ we obtain a process array of length n extending the above in the natural way.

We now define $\mathcal{T}_{fork}$. Transitions are of the form $\rho \xrightarrow{\alpha} \rho'$. The notation $\rho \rightarrow_0 \rho'$ has the usual meaning, i.e., $\rho \rightarrow_0 \rho'$ is short for a rule of the form

$$\frac{\rho' \xrightarrow{\alpha} \bar{\rho}}{\rho \xrightarrow{\alpha} \bar{\rho}} \ .$$

Also, $(\sigma \in) \Sigma = IVar \rightarrow Val$ and $\mathcal{V}: Exp \rightarrow \Sigma \rightarrow Val$ are as usual. We emphasize that the codomain of Σ equals *Val* (and not *Val$_\tau$*).

Definition 9.20 $\mathcal{T}_{fork} = (NRes, Val_\tau, \rightarrow, Spec)$. *Spec* is defined as

- $$\alpha \cdot w \xrightarrow{\alpha} w \qquad\qquad\qquad\qquad\qquad\qquad\qquad \text{(Val)}$$

- $$[\rho, (v := e):r, \sigma] \rightarrow_0 [\rho, r, \sigma\{\beta/v\}] \qquad\qquad \text{where } \beta = \mathcal{V}(e)(\sigma) \qquad \text{(Ass)}$$

- $$[\rho, \mathsf{skip}{:}r, \sigma] \rightarrow_0 [\rho, r, \sigma] \tag{Skip}$$

- $$[\rho, (s_1;s_2){:}r, \sigma] \rightarrow_0 [\rho, s_1{:}(s_2{:}r), \sigma] \tag{Seq}$$

- $$[\rho, \mathsf{if}\ e\ \mathsf{then}\ s_1\ \mathsf{else}\ s_2\ \mathsf{fi}{:}r, \sigma] \rightarrow_0 [\rho, s_1{:}r, \sigma] \qquad \text{if } \mathcal{V}(e)(\sigma) = tt \tag{If}$$
  $$[\rho, \mathsf{if}\ e\ \mathsf{then}\ s_1\ \mathsf{else}\ s_2\ \mathsf{fi}{:}r, \sigma] \rightarrow_0 [\rho, s_2{:}r, \sigma] \qquad \text{if } \mathcal{V}(e)(\sigma) = ff$$

- $$[\rho, \mathsf{while}\ e\ \mathsf{do}\ s\ \mathsf{od}{:}r, \sigma] \xrightarrow{\tau} \tag{While}$$
  $$[\rho, \mathsf{if}\ e\ \mathsf{then}\ (s;\mathsf{while}\ e\ \mathsf{do}\ s\ \mathsf{od})\ \mathsf{else}\ \mathsf{skip}\ \mathsf{fi}{:}r, \sigma]$$

- $$\frac{\rho \xrightarrow{\beta} \rho'}{[\rho, \mathsf{read}(v){:}r, \sigma] \xrightarrow{\tau} [\rho', r, \sigma\{\beta/v\}]} \tag{Read 1}$$

- $$\frac{\rho \xrightarrow{\tau} \rho'}{[\rho, \mathsf{read}(v){:}r, \sigma] \xrightarrow{\tau} [\rho', \mathsf{read}(v){:}r, \sigma]} \tag{Read 2}$$

- $$[\rho, \mathsf{write}(e){:}r, \sigma] \xrightarrow{\beta} [\rho, r, \sigma] \qquad \text{where } \beta = \mathcal{V}(e)(\sigma) \tag{Write}$$

- $$[\rho, \mathsf{fork}(v){:}r, \sigma] \rightarrow_0 [[\rho, r, \sigma\{1/v\}], r, \sigma\{0/v\}] \tag{Fork}$$

We add several explanations:

(1) A transition $\rho \xrightarrow{\alpha} \rho'$ expresses that the nested resumption ρ performs a one-step transition to ρ' while producing a value α—which is either a normal value β or a silent value τ. Later, we shall define $\mathcal{O}(\rho)$ in such a way that the α produced in this transition is the first element of the (output) stream which is the result of executing ρ.

(2) We observe that there is no transition defined for $[\rho, \mathrm{E}, \sigma]$. Consequently, neither is there a transition possible for, e.g., $[\rho, (v := e){:}\mathrm{E}, \sigma]$ or $[[\rho, \mathrm{E}, \sigma], \mathsf{read}(v){:}r, \sigma]$, etc. We emphasize that transitions become observable only by delivering output values (including an occasional silent value); note that this is quite different from earlier models where state changes, from σ to some σ', are the observables.

(3) The rules for $v := e$, skip, $s_1;s_2$ and the if statement should be clear. The while statement always induces a silent step. A zero-step transition would not work in this case, since it seems incompatible with the (standard) property that, for some suitable complexity measure wgt (to be defined later), we have, for each ρ, ρ' with $\rho \rightarrow_0 \rho'$, that $wgt(\rho) > wgt(\rho')$.

(4) For a read(v) statement—with respect to current ρ, r and σ—we distinguish three cases. In the normal situation, an input β is available, produced (as output) when ρ turns itself in ρ'. We then assign β to v and continue with r, the updated state $\sigma\{\beta/v\}$, and the new ρ'. Otherwise when ρ produces a silent step τ, we reject this as possible value for v—recall that the codomain of any state equals Val rather than Val_τ—maintain the request for an input read(v), and continue with r, σ and ρ'. Thirdly, if ρ blocks (for no α, ρ', we have that $\rho \xrightarrow{\alpha} \rho'$) then the read($v$)-statement blocks as well.

(5) The fork statement fork(v)—for given ρ, r, σ—creates two processes, the parent process $[r, \sigma\{1/v\}]$ and the child process $[r, \sigma\{0/v\}]$. We observe that

- the fork statement is handled by a zero-step transition;
- both parent and child execute the resumption r; the former with the fork variable v set to 1, the latter with v set to 0;
- since the resulting ρ' has the form $[[\rho, r, \sigma\{1/v\}], r, \sigma\{0/v\}]$, the net effect of this is that the output of $[\rho, r, \sigma\{1/v\}]$ acts as input for $[r, \sigma\{0/v\}]$, cf. also the way the read and write rules are defined.

Example We derive the successive transitions determined by $\mathcal{T}_{fork}$ for

$s \equiv$ fork(v);read(v);write(v),

for $r \equiv$ E, $\rho_0 = w = 8$, and any σ. The initial nested resumption has the form $\rho_1 = [8, (\text{fork}(v);\text{read}(v);\text{write}(v)):\text{E}, \sigma]$ as depicted by

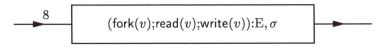

$$\xrightarrow{\quad 8 \quad} \boxed{(\text{fork}(v);\text{read}(v);\text{write}(v)):\text{E}, \sigma} \longrightarrow$$

We give a detailed specification of the transition for this ρ_1. We list the intermediate transitions $1, 2, \ldots$, each of which is justified by an appeal to $\mathcal{T}_{fork}$ and, possibly, by an earlier intermediate transition.

(1) $8 \xrightarrow{8} \epsilon$ (Val)

(2) $[8, \text{read}(v):(\text{write}(v):\text{E}), \sigma\{1/v\}] \xrightarrow{\tau} [\epsilon, \text{write}(v):\text{E}, \sigma\{8/v\}]$ (1,Read 1)

(3) $[8, (\text{read}(v);\text{write}(v)):\text{E}, \sigma\{1/v\}] \xrightarrow{\tau} [\epsilon, \text{write}(v):\text{E}, \sigma\{8/v\}]$ (2,Seq)

(4) $[[8, (\text{read}(v);\text{write}(v)):\text{E}, \sigma\{1/v\}], \text{read}(v):(\text{write}(v):\text{E}), \sigma\{0/v\}] \xrightarrow{\tau}$
$\qquad\qquad [[\epsilon, \text{write}(v):\text{E}, \sigma\{8/v\}], \text{read}(v):(\text{write}(v):\text{E}), \sigma\{0/v\}]$

                                               (3,Read 2)

(5) $[[8, (\text{read}(v);\text{write}(v)):\text{E}, \sigma\{1/v\}], (\text{read}(v);\text{write}(v)):\text{E}, \sigma\{0/v\}] \xrightarrow{\tau}$
$\qquad\qquad [\epsilon, \text{write}(v):\text{E}, \sigma\{8/v\}], \text{read}(v):(\text{write}(v):\text{E}), \sigma\{0/v\}]$

$\qquad\qquad\qquad\qquad\qquad\qquad\qquad\qquad\qquad\qquad\qquad\qquad\qquad\qquad$ (4,Seq)

(6) $[8, \text{fork}(v):(\text{read}(v);\text{write}(v)):\text{E}, \sigma] \xrightarrow{\tau}$
$\qquad [\epsilon, \text{write}(v):\text{E}, \sigma\{8/v\}], \text{read}(v):(\text{write}(v):\text{E}), \sigma\{0/v\}]$

$\qquad\qquad\qquad\qquad\qquad\qquad\qquad\qquad\qquad\qquad\qquad\qquad\qquad\qquad$ (5,Fork)

(7) $[8, (\text{fork}(v);\text{read}(v);\text{write}(v)):\text{E}, \sigma] \xrightarrow{\tau}$
$\qquad [\epsilon, \text{write}(v):\text{E}, \sigma\{8/v\}], \text{read}(v):(\text{write}(v):\text{E}), \sigma\{0/v\}].$

$\qquad\qquad\qquad\qquad\qquad\qquad\qquad\qquad\qquad\qquad\qquad\qquad\qquad\qquad$ (6,Seq)

Putting $\rho_2 = [[\epsilon, \text{write}(v):\text{E}, \sigma\{8/v\}], \text{read}(v):(\text{write}(v):\text{E}), \sigma\{0/v\}]$ we have derived $\rho_1 \xrightarrow{\tau} \rho_2$. We depict ρ_2 with output τ in

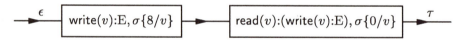

Next we infer that $\rho_2 \xrightarrow{\tau} \rho_3$—details are left to the reader—where ρ_3 and the cumulative output (resulting from the two transitions) are given in the next figure:

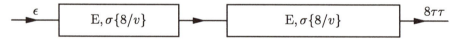

Finally, we have $\rho_3 \xrightarrow{8} \rho_4$, where ρ_4 and the final output stream are described in

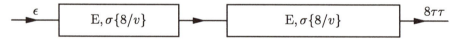

In order to stick to the operational intuition about the graphical representation of processes in execution, the leftmost element of the output is the most recently produced one.

Caution In our subsequent definition of $\mathcal{O}$—Definition 9.24—we shall define $\mathcal{O}(\rho) = w$ such that w contains the successively produced values from left to right. Thus, for the example just treated we shall have that $\mathcal{O}(\rho_1) = \tau\tau 8!$

We add two further comments on the definition of $\mathcal{T}_{fork}$.

(1) We note that, by the way the read (and write) rules are defined, we have that a value is produced by a parent only when it may simultaneously be consumed by the child. Thus, our semantic model avoids the storing of intermediate values

on linking channels, waiting for subsequent consumption by the child process at a later stage. A different model, with nested resumptions explicitly containing both input *and* output values, would be necessary to render such intermediate streams on channels.

(2) Note how the rules (While) and (Read 1,2) prescribe silent steps and, thus, presuppose the presence of the hiaton τ.

As we shall prove in a moment, $\mathcal{T}_{fork}$ specifies *deterministic* behavior. This allows us to define the operational meaning of a program as a transformation from input streams to output streams—rather than to *sets* of output streams, as would be in order when dealing with a nondeterministic mechanism. For the proof of this fact, we introduce once again a complexity measure, this time geared to the proof of Lemma 9.22.

Definition 9.21 The complexity measure $wgt: NRes \rightarrow \mathbb{N}$ is given by

$$wgt(w) = 1$$
$$wgt([\rho, r, \sigma]) = wgt(\rho) + wgt(r)$$

where $wgt: Res \rightarrow \mathbb{N}$ is given by

$$wgt(\mathrm{E}) = 1$$
$$wgt(s{:}r) = wgt(s) \times wgt(r)$$

with $wgt: Stat \rightarrow \mathbb{N}$ given by

$$wgt(\mathsf{write}(e)) = wgt(\mathsf{read}(v)) = 1$$
$$wgt(v := e) = wgt(\mathsf{skip}) = wgt(\mathsf{while}\ e\ \mathsf{do}\ s\ \mathsf{od}) = 2$$
$$wgt(\mathsf{fork}(v)) = 3$$
$$wgt(s_1; s_2) = wgt(s_1) \times wgt(s_2) + 1$$
$$wgt(\mathsf{if}\ e\ \mathsf{then}\ s_1\ \mathsf{else}\ s_2\ \mathsf{fi}) = max\ \{\ wgt(s_1), wgt(s_2)\ \} + 1.$$

This—somewhat ad-hoc—definition of the measure wgt allows a smooth proof of the next lemma.

Lemma 9.22 *For all ρ, ρ', if $\rho \rightarrow_0 \rho'$ then $wgt(\rho) > wgt(\rho')$.*

Proof Three subcases.

$[\bar{\rho}, (v := e){:}r, \sigma]$ $\quad wgt([\bar{\rho}, (v := e){:}r, \sigma]) = 2 * wgt(r) + wgt(\bar{\rho}) > wgt(r) + wgt(\bar{\rho}) = wgt([\bar{\rho}, r, \sigma\{\beta/v\}])$

$$[\bar{\rho}, (s_1;s_2){:}r, \sigma] \qquad wgt([\bar{\rho}, (s_1;s_2){:}r, \sigma])$$
$$= \quad wgt(\bar{\rho}) + wgt((s_1;s_2){:}r)$$
$$= \quad wgt(\bar{\rho}) + wgt(s_1;s_2) \times wgt(r)$$
$$= \quad wgt(\bar{\rho}) + (wgt(s_1) \times wgt(s_2) + 1) \times wgt(r)$$
$$> \quad wgt(\bar{\rho}) + wgt(s_1) \times wgt(s_2) \times wgt(r)$$
$$= \quad wgt([\bar{\rho}, s_1{:}(s_2{:}r), \sigma])$$

$$[\bar{\rho}, \mathsf{fork}(v){:}r, \sigma] \qquad wgt([\bar{\rho}, \mathsf{fork}(v){:}r, \sigma])$$
$$= \quad wgt(\bar{\rho}) + 3 \times wgt(r)$$
$$> \quad wgt(\bar{\rho}) + 2 \times wgt(r)$$
$$= \quad wgt([[\bar{\rho}, r, \sigma\{0/v\}], r, \sigma\{1/v\}]). \qquad\qquad \square$$

From Lemma 9.22, the proof that $\mathcal{T}_{fork}$ is deterministic is straightforward.

Lemma 9.23 $\mathcal{T}_{fork}$ *is deterministic.*

Proof Recall that we use the notation $\mathcal{S}(\rho)$ for the set $\{\, \langle \alpha, \rho' \rangle \mid \rho \xrightarrow{\alpha} \rho' \,\}$. We shall show that $|\mathcal{S}(\rho)| \leq 1$, by induction on $wgt(\rho)$. Two subcases.

$$[\bar{\rho}, (v := e){:}r, \sigma] \qquad |\mathcal{S}([\bar{\rho}, (v := e){:}r, \sigma])|$$
$$= \quad [\text{put } \beta = \mathcal{V}(e)(\sigma)]\ |\mathcal{S}([\bar{\rho}, r, \sigma\{\beta/v\}])|$$
$$\leq \quad [\text{by the induction hypothesis}]\ 1.$$

$$[\bar{\rho}, \mathsf{while}\ e\ \mathsf{do}\ s\ \mathsf{od}{:}r, \sigma] \qquad |\mathcal{S}([\bar{\rho}, \mathsf{while}\ e\ \mathsf{do}\ s\ \mathsf{od}{:}r, \sigma])|$$
$$= \quad |\{\, [\tau, [\bar{\rho}, \mathsf{if}\ e\ \mathsf{then}\ (s;\mathsf{while}\ e\ \mathsf{do}\ s\ \mathsf{od})\ \mathsf{else}\ \mathsf{skip}\ \mathsf{fi}{:}r, \sigma]) \,\}|$$
$$= \quad 1. \qquad\qquad\qquad \square$$

We next describe how to obtain the operational semantics $\mathcal{O}$ for $\mathcal{L}_{fork}$. In the customary manner, we first specify how to obtain $\mathcal{O}{:}\,NRes \to \mathbb{P}'$ from $\mathcal{T}_{fork}$, for suitable $\mathbb{P}'$. Since the outcome of the execution of a nested resumption should consist of a stream, i.e., a (finite or infinite) sequence of values, we put $\mathbb{P}' = Val^{\infty}_{\tau}$. We moreover use the familiar notion of *blocking* for $\mathcal{T}_{fork}$: We say that ρ *blocks* whenever, for no α, ρ', we have $\rho \xrightarrow{\alpha} \rho'$. It is now simple to define $\mathcal{O}$:

Definition 9.24 $\mathcal{O}{:}\,NRes \to Val^{\infty}_{\tau}$ is the unique function satisfying

$$\mathcal{O}(\rho) \quad = \quad \begin{cases} \epsilon & \text{if } \rho \text{ blocks} \\ \alpha \cdot \mathcal{O}(\rho') & \text{if } \rho \xrightarrow{\alpha} \rho'. \end{cases}$$

Example For ρ_1 as defined in the example after Definition 9.20, we obtain $\mathcal{O}(\rho_1)$ $= \tau.\mathcal{O}(\rho_2) = \tau\tau.\mathcal{O}(\rho_3) = \tau\tau8.\mathcal{O}(\rho_4) = \tau\tau8$, since $\mathcal{O}(\rho_4) = \epsilon$.

Well-definedness of $\mathcal{O}$ is completely standard.

Finally, we discuss how to obtain the operational meaning for a statement $s \in$ $\mathcal{L}_{fork}$ from the definition of $\mathcal{O}: NRes \rightarrow Val_\tau^\infty$. In order to execute s, we have to supply it with

- the empty resumption E;
- an input stream w;
- an initial state σ.

We then expect as output a stream w'. This explains the following

Definition 9.25

(a) $\mathbb{P}_O = \Sigma \rightarrow Val_\tau^\infty \rightarrow Val_\tau^\infty$.

(b) $\mathcal{O}[\![\cdot]\!]: \mathcal{L}_{fork} \rightarrow \mathbb{P}_O$ is given by

$$\mathcal{O}[\![s]\!] = \lambda\sigma.\lambda w \cdot \mathcal{O}([w, s{:}\text{E}, \sigma]).$$

Example For $s \equiv$ fork(v);read(v);write(v), we have $\mathcal{O}[\![s]\!](\sigma)(8) = \mathcal{O}([8, s{:}\text{E}, \sigma]) = \tau\tau8$.

9.2.2 Denotational semantics, equivalence of $\mathcal{O}$ and $\mathcal{D}$

The denotational semantics for $\mathcal{L}_{fork}$ uses the set of continuations $(\gamma \in) Cont = \mathbb{P}_D$ (with $\mathbb{P}_D = \mathbb{P}_O$). Let $\gamma_\epsilon = \lambda\sigma.\lambda w.\epsilon$. Continuations correspond to resumptions in the sense that, as we shall see in Definition 9.28a, meanings of Res reside in $Cont$.

We shall use $first(w)$ to denote the first element of the nonempty sequence w, and $rest(w)$ to denote the result of omitting the first element of the nonempty sequence w.

The denotational semantics $\mathcal{D}$ for $\mathcal{L}_{fork}$ is presented in

Definition 9.26

(a) Let $(S \in) Sem_D = \mathcal{L}_{fork} \rightarrow Cont \xrightarrow{1} \mathbb{P}_D$ and let $\Psi: Sem_D \rightarrow Sem_D$ be given by

$$\Psi(S)(v := e)(\gamma)(\sigma)(w) \ = \ \gamma(\sigma\{\,\beta/v\,\})(w), \ \text{where } \beta = \mathcal{V}(e)(\sigma)$$

$$\Psi(S)(\mathsf{skip})(\gamma)(\sigma)(w) \ = \ \gamma(\sigma)(w)$$

$$\Psi(S)(s_1;s_2)(\gamma)(\sigma)(w) \ = \ \Psi(S)(s_1)(\Psi(S)(s_2)(\gamma))(\sigma)(w)$$

$$\Psi(S)(\text{if } e \text{ then } s_1 \text{ else } s_2 \text{ fi})(\gamma)(\sigma)(w) \ = $$

$$\left\{ \begin{array}{ll} \Psi(S)(s_1)(\gamma)(\sigma)(w) & \text{if } \mathcal{V}(e)(\sigma) = tt \\ \Psi(S)(s_2)(\gamma)(\sigma)(w) & \text{if } \mathcal{V}(e)(\sigma) = ff \end{array} \right.$$

$$\Psi(S)(\text{while } e \text{ do } s \text{ od})(\gamma)(\sigma)(w) \ = $$

$$\tau \cdot S(\text{if } e \text{ then } (s;\text{while } e \text{ do } s \text{ od}) \text{ else skip fi})(\gamma)(\sigma)(w)$$

$$\Psi(S)(\mathsf{read}(v))(\gamma)(\sigma)(w) \ = $$

$$\left\{ \begin{array}{ll} \epsilon & \text{if } w = \epsilon \\ \tau \cdot \gamma(\sigma\{\mathit{first}(w)/v\})(\mathit{rest}(w)) & \text{if } w \neq \epsilon, \ \mathit{first}(w) \neq \tau \\ \tau \cdot S(\mathsf{read}(v))(\gamma)(\sigma)(\mathit{rest}(w)) & \text{if } w \neq \epsilon, \ \mathit{first}(w) = \tau \end{array} \right.$$

$$\Psi(S)(\mathsf{write}(e))(\gamma)(\sigma)(w) \ = \ \beta \cdot \gamma(\sigma)(w), \ \text{where } \beta = \mathcal{V}(e)(\sigma)$$

$$\Psi(S)(\mathsf{fork}(v))(\gamma)(\sigma)(w) \ = \ \gamma(\sigma\{0/v\})(\gamma(\sigma\{1/v\})(w)).$$

(b) $\mathcal{D} = \mathit{fix}(\Psi)$, $\mathcal{D}[\![\cdot]\!]\colon \mathcal{L}_{fork} \to \mathbb{P}_D$ is given by $\mathcal{D}[\![s]\!] = \mathcal{D}(s)(\gamma_\epsilon)$.

Much of the structure of the above clauses may be understood by consulting $\mathcal{T}_{fork}$. For example, consider the clause for the fork statement, resulting in

$$\mathcal{D}(\mathsf{fork}(v))(\gamma)(\sigma)(w) = \gamma(\sigma\{0/v\})(\gamma(\sigma\{1/v\})(w)).$$

Using the correspondence between the semantic continuation γ and the syntactic resumptions r, we see that this is an immediate counterpart of the transition from $\mathcal{T}_{fork}$

$$[w, \mathsf{fork}(v){:}r, \sigma] \to_0 [[w, r, \sigma\{1/v\}], r, \sigma\{0/v\}]$$

(where we have instantiated ρ to w). As second example, we discuss the clause for the read statement, in a situation where $w = \tau \cdot \mathit{rest}(w)$. By the rule (Read 2), with $\rho = w$, we infer, also using that $\tau \cdot \mathit{rest}(w) \xrightarrow{\tau} \mathit{rest}(w)$, that

$$[w, \mathsf{read}(v){:}r, \sigma] \xrightarrow{\tau} [\mathit{rest}(w), \mathsf{read}(v){:}r, \sigma]$$

which directly corresponds to the clause

$$\mathcal{D}(\mathsf{read}(v))(\gamma)(\sigma)(w) = \tau \cdot \mathcal{D}(\mathsf{read}(v))(\gamma)(\sigma)(\mathit{rest}(w)).$$

Definition 9.26 is justified in

Lemma 9.27 *For all S, s, γ and σ:*

(a) $\Psi(S)(s)(\gamma)(\sigma)$ *is nonexpansive (in w).*

(b) $\Psi(S)(s)$ *is nonexpansive (in γ).*

(c) Ψ *is contractive (in S).*

Proof We only discuss part (b). We use structural induction on s. Two subcases.

$[\text{read}(v)]$ Choose some σ, w. We distinguish three sub-subcases.

$\quad [w = \epsilon]$ $\quad d(\Psi(S)(\text{read}(v))(\gamma_1)(\sigma)(w), \Psi(S)(\text{read}(v))(\gamma_2)(\sigma)(w))$
$\quad\quad = \quad d(\epsilon, \epsilon)$
$\quad\quad \leq \quad d(\gamma_1, \gamma_2).$

$\quad [w \neq \epsilon, \text{first}(w) \neq \tau]$
$\quad\quad d(\Psi(S)(\text{read}(v))(\gamma_1)(\sigma)(w), \Psi(S)(\text{read}(v))(\gamma_2)(\sigma)(w))$
$\quad\quad = \quad d(\tau \cdot \gamma_1(\sigma\{\text{first}(w)/v\})(\text{rest}(w)), \tau \cdot \gamma_2(\sigma\{\text{first}(w)/v\})(\text{rest}(w)))$
$\quad\quad \leq \quad \frac{1}{2}d(\gamma_1, \gamma_2).$

$\quad [w \neq \epsilon, \text{first}(w) = \tau]$
$\quad\quad d(\Psi(S)(\text{read}(v))(\gamma_1)(\sigma)(w), \Psi(S)(\text{read}(v))(\gamma_2)(\sigma)(w))$
$\quad\quad = \quad d(\tau \cdot S(\text{read}(v))(\gamma_1)(\sigma)(\text{rest}(w)), \tau \cdot S(\text{read}(v))(\gamma_2)(\sigma)(\text{rest}(w)))$
$\quad\quad \leq \quad \frac{1}{2}d(S(\text{read}(v))(\gamma_1), S(\text{read}(v))(\gamma_2))$
$\quad\quad \leq \quad [S(\text{read}(v)) \text{ nonexpansive in } \gamma]\; \frac{1}{2}d(\gamma_1, \gamma_2)$

$[\text{fork}(v)]$ $\quad d(\Psi(S)(\text{fork}(v))(\gamma_1)(\sigma)(w), \Psi(S)(\text{fork}(v))(\gamma_2)(\sigma)(w))$
$\quad = \quad d(\gamma_1(\sigma\{0/v\})(\gamma_1(\sigma\{1/v\})(w)), \gamma_2(\sigma\{0/v\})(\gamma_2(\sigma\{1/v\})(w)))$
$\quad \leq \quad [\text{ultrametricity}]$
$\quad\quad max\{\, d(\gamma_1(\sigma\{0/v\})(\gamma_1(\sigma\{1/v\})(w)), \gamma_1(\sigma\{0/v\})(\gamma_2(\sigma\{1/v\})(w))),$
$\quad\quad\quad\quad d(\gamma_1(\sigma\{0/v\})(\gamma_2(\sigma\{1/v\})(w)), \gamma_2(\sigma\{0/v\})(\gamma_2(\sigma\{1/v\})(w)))\}$
$\quad \leq \quad [\gamma_1(\sigma\{0/v\}) \text{ is nonexpansive in } w]$
$\quad\quad max\{\, d(\gamma_1(\sigma\{1/v\})(w), \gamma_2(\sigma\{1/v\})(w)), d(\gamma_1, \gamma_2)\,\}$
$\quad \leq \quad d(\gamma_1, \gamma_2).$ $\square$

We continue with the preparations for the proof that $\mathcal{O}$ and $\mathcal{D}$ are equivalent on $\mathcal{L}_{fork}$. Closely following the type of argument in Section 9.1, we first introduce two intermediate semantics:

Definition 9.28

(a) The mapping $\mathcal{E}: Res \to Cont$ is defined by

$$\mathcal{E}(\mathrm{E}) \;=\; \gamma_\epsilon$$
$$\mathcal{E}(s{:}r) \;=\; \mathcal{D}(s)(\mathcal{E}(r)).$$

(b) The mapping $\mathcal{F}\colon NRes \to Val_\tau^\infty$ is defined by

$$\mathcal{F}(w) \;=\; w$$
$$\mathcal{F}([\rho,r,\sigma]) \;=\; \mathcal{E}(r)(\sigma)(\mathcal{F}(\rho)).$$

The following familiar properties for $\mathcal{F}$ are satisfied:

Lemma 9.29

(a) If $\rho \to_0 \rho'$, then $\mathcal{F}(\rho) = \mathcal{F}(\rho')$.

(b) If $\rho \xrightarrow{\alpha} \rho'$, then $\mathcal{F}(\rho) = \alpha \cdot \mathcal{F}(\rho')$.

Proof

(a) Induction on $wgt(\rho)$. Two subcases.

$\quad [\bar{\rho}, (v := e){:}r, \sigma]\quad$ Let $\beta = \mathcal{V}(e)(\sigma)$.

$$\begin{aligned}
&\mathcal{F}([\bar{\rho}, (v := e){:}r, \sigma])\\
&=\; \mathcal{E}((v := e){:}r)(\sigma)(\mathcal{F}(\bar{\rho}))\\
&=\; \mathcal{D}(v := e)(\mathcal{E}(r))(\sigma)(\mathcal{F}(\bar{\rho}))\\
&=\; \mathcal{E}(r)(\sigma\{\beta/v\})(\mathcal{F}(\bar{\rho}))\\
&=\; \mathcal{F}([\bar{\rho}, r, \sigma\{\beta/v\}]).
\end{aligned}$$

$\quad [\bar{\rho}, \mathsf{fork}(v){:}r, \sigma]\quad \mathcal{F}([\bar{\rho}, \mathsf{fork}(v){:}r, \sigma])$

$$\begin{aligned}
&=\; \mathcal{E}(\mathsf{fork}(v){:}r)(\sigma)(\mathcal{F}(\bar{\rho}))\\
&=\; \mathcal{D}(\mathsf{fork}(v))(\mathcal{E}(r))(\sigma)(\mathcal{F}(\bar{\rho}))\\
&=\; \mathcal{E}(r)(\sigma\{0/v\})(\mathcal{E}(r)(\sigma\{1/v\})(\mathcal{F}(\bar{\rho}))\\
&=\; \mathcal{E}(r)(\sigma\{0/v\})(\mathcal{F}([\bar{\rho}, r, \sigma\{1/v\}]))\\
&=\; \mathcal{F}([[\bar{\rho}, r, \sigma\{1/v\}], r, \sigma\{0/v\}]).
\end{aligned}$$

(b) Induction on $wgt(\bar{\rho})$. One subcase.

$\quad [\bar{\rho}, \mathsf{read}(v){:}r, \sigma]\quad$ One sub-subcase.

$\qquad [\bar{\rho} \xrightarrow{\beta} \bar{\rho}']\quad$ We have to show:

$$\mathcal{F}([\bar{\rho}, \mathsf{read}(v){:}r, \sigma]) \;=\; \tau \cdot \mathcal{F}([\bar{\rho}', r, \sigma\{\beta/v\}]).$$
By induction, $\mathcal{F}(\bar{\rho}) = \beta \cdot \mathcal{F}(\bar{\rho}')$. Now

$$\mathcal{F}([\bar{\rho}, \text{read}(v){:}r, \sigma])$$
$$= \quad \mathcal{D}(\text{read}(v))(\mathcal{E}(r))(\sigma)(\beta \cdot \mathcal{F}(\bar{\rho}'))$$
$$= \quad \tau \cdot \mathcal{E}(r)(\sigma\{\beta/v\})(\mathcal{F}(\bar{\rho}'))$$
$$= \quad \tau \cdot \mathcal{F}([\bar{\rho}', r, \sigma\{\beta/v\}]). \qquad\qquad\qquad\qquad \square$$

The main step in the equivalence proof now follows. Let Φ be the higher-order operator (implicitly) used in the definition of $\mathcal{O}$.

Lemma 9.30 $\Phi(\mathcal{F}) = \mathcal{F}$.

Proof We show that, for all ρ, $\Phi(\mathcal{F})(\rho) = \mathcal{F}(\rho)$, by induction on $wgt(\rho)$. Two subcases.

$[\rho', (v := e){:}r, \sigma]$ Let $\beta = \mathcal{V}(e)(\sigma)$.

$$\Phi(\mathcal{F})([\rho', (v := e){:}r, \sigma])$$
$$= \quad [\text{by (Ass)}] \ \Phi(\mathcal{F})([\rho', r, \sigma\{\beta/v\}])$$
$$= \quad [\text{by ind. hyp.}] \ \mathcal{F}([\rho', r, \sigma\{\beta/v\}])$$
$$= \quad [\text{Lemma 9.29a}] \ \mathcal{F}([\rho', (v := e){:}r, \sigma]).$$

$[\rho', \text{read}(v){:}r, \sigma]$ Three sub-subcases:

(i) Assume $\rho' \xrightarrow{\beta} \rho''$. Then

$$\Phi(\mathcal{F})([\rho', \text{read}(v){:}r, \sigma])$$
$$= \quad [\text{by (Read 1)}] \ \tau \cdot \mathcal{F}([\rho'', r, \sigma\{\beta/v\}])$$
$$= \quad [\text{Lemma 9.29b}] \ \mathcal{F}([\rho', \text{read}(v){:}r, \sigma]).$$

(ii) Assume $\rho' \xrightarrow{\tau} \rho''$. Then

$$\Phi(\mathcal{F})([\rho', \text{read}(v){:}r, \sigma])$$
$$= \quad [(\text{Read 2})] \ \tau \cdot \mathcal{F}([\rho'', \text{read}(v){:}r, \sigma])$$
$$= \quad [\text{Lemma 9.29b}] \ \mathcal{F}([\rho', \text{read}(v){:}r, \sigma]).$$

(iii) Assuming ρ' blocks we have that $[\rho', \text{read}(v){:}r, \sigma]$ blocks and, hence, $\Phi(\mathcal{F})([\rho', \text{read}(v){:}r, \sigma]) = \epsilon$. Since ρ' blocks, $\Phi(\mathcal{F})(\rho') = \epsilon$. By induction, $\mathcal{F}(\rho') = \epsilon$. Consequently, $\mathcal{F}([\rho', \text{read}(v){:}r, \sigma]) = \epsilon$. $\qquad\qquad \square$

We are ready for the proof of

Theorem 9.31 $\mathcal{O}[\![s]\!] = \mathcal{D}[\![s]\!]$, for each $s \in \mathcal{L}_{fork}$.

Proof By the previous lemma and Banach's theorem $\mathcal{O}$ and $\mathcal{F}$ coincide on *NRes*. Therefore,

$\mathcal{O}[\![s]\!](\sigma)(w)$

$= \mathcal{O}(s{:}\mathrm{E})(\sigma)(w)$

$= \mathcal{F}(s{:}\mathrm{E})(\sigma)(w)$

$= \mathcal{E}(s{:}\mathrm{E})(\sigma)(\mathcal{F}(w))$

$= \mathcal{D}(s)(\mathcal{E}(\mathrm{E}))(\sigma)(w)$

$= \mathcal{D}(s)(\lambda\sigma.\lambda w.\epsilon)(\sigma)(w)$

$= \mathcal{D}[\![s]\!](\sigma)(w).$ □

9.3   Exercises

Exercise 9.1 Prove the following equivalences for $\mathcal{L}_{bt}$-programs:

(a) $\mathcal{O}[\![D|\mathsf{fail}\,\square\,s]\!] = \mathcal{O}[\![D|s\,\square\,\mathsf{fail}]\!]$

(b) $\mathcal{O}[\![D|(s_1\,\square\,s_2)\,\square\,s_3]\!] = \mathcal{O}[\![D|s_1\,\square\,(s_2\,\square\,s_3)]\!].$

Exercise 9.2 (A nonuniform version of $\mathcal{L}_{bt}$.) Let $(s \in)\,\mathcal{L}_{bt,n}$ be given by

$$s \quad ::= \quad v := e \mid \mathsf{skip} \mid \mathsf{fail} \mid (s;s) \mid (s\,\square\,s) \mid$$
$$\text{if } e \text{ then } s \text{ else } s \text{ fi} \mid \text{while } e \text{ do } s \text{ od}.$$

Let $\mathbb{P}_D = \Sigma \to \Sigma^\infty$, and let $(\phi \in)\,SCont = FCont \xrightarrow{1} \mathbb{P}_D$, $(\gamma \in)\,FCont = \mathbb{P}_D$. We define $\mathcal{D}{:}\,\mathcal{L}_{bt,n} \to SCont \xrightarrow{1} FCont \xrightarrow{1} \mathbb{P}_D$ as the unique function satisfying

$$\begin{aligned}
\mathcal{D}(v := e)(\phi)(\gamma) &= \lambda\sigma.\sigma \cdot \phi(\gamma)(\sigma\{\alpha/v\}), \quad \alpha \text{ as usual}\\
\mathcal{D}(\mathsf{fail})(\phi)(\gamma) &= \gamma\\
\mathcal{D}(s_1;s_2)(\phi)(\gamma) &= \mathcal{D}(s_1)\big(\mathcal{D}(s_2)(\phi)\big)(\gamma)\\
\mathcal{D}(s_1\,\square\,s_2)(\phi)(\gamma) &= \mathcal{D}(s_1)(\phi)\big(\mathcal{D}(s_2)(\phi)(\gamma)\big),
\end{aligned}$$

and the usual clauses for the skip, if...fi and while-statements. Define $\mathcal{T}_{bt,n}$, $\mathbb{P}_O$ and $\mathcal{O}{:}\,\mathcal{L}_{bt,n} \to \mathbb{P}_O$, and state and prove the equivalence result concerning $\mathcal{O}$ and $\mathcal{D}$ for $\mathcal{L}_{bt,n}$.

Exercise 9.3 Design $\mathcal{D}$ for $\mathcal{L}_{fork}$ in a properly compositional manner (in the sense as discussed earlier for $\mathcal{L}_{gc}$, Section 3.1, and $\mathcal{L}_\mu$, $\mathcal{L}_{cf}$, Sections 8.2 to 8.4).

Exercise 9.4 Let $s^n_{fork} \stackrel{df}{=} \mathsf{fork}(v); \ldots; \mathsf{fork}(v)$ (n times $\mathsf{fork}(v)$).

(a) What is the maximum length of the process array generated while executing s^n_{fork}?

(b) Let σ and w be arbitrary. Determine $\mathcal{O}[\![s^n_{fork}]\!](\sigma)(w)$.

Exercise 9.5 Consider the following program for the "sieve of Eratosthenes":

```
while  true
do     read(u₁); write(u₁); fork(v);
       if     v = 1
       then   while   true
              do      read(u₂);
                      if u₂ mod u₁ ≠ 0 then write(u₂) else skip fi
              od
       else   skip
       fi
od.
```

Here $u_2 \bmod u_1$ denotes the remainder of dividing u_2 by u_1. Show that, for $w = 2.3.4.5.\ldots$, and ignoring the τ's in the output, this program prints the sequence of primes $2.3.5.7\ldots$.

Exercise 9.6 The execution of a $[\rho, r, \sigma]$-triple is "demand-driven" by the r-component: only if the r requests this, the process ρ performs a step. Discuss an extension of the semantic model for $\mathcal{L}_{fork}$ which allows a form of parallel execution of the ρ and r in $[\rho, r, \sigma]$. (Hint: Extend the formalism for resumptions with a fourth component used to buffer output produced but not yet consumed.)

9.4   Bibliographical notes

A survey of programming constructs involving backtracking is [Coh79]. Languages incorporating forms of backtracking are, e.g., SNOBOL ([GPP71], see also [Ten73]) and PROLOG ([CKRP73, CM94]). The denotational models described in Chapter 9 have been profoundly influenced by [Bru86].

The correspondence between nested resumptions on the operational side, and success and failure continuations on the denotational side has been studied in [Bak91]

for a uniform version of a language with a logic programming flavour; operational
and denotational semantics of PROLOG are developed, e.g., in [Vin89, BV89]. The
paper [Bak91] has been extended considerably in the work of Eliëns ([Eli92]) where
a synthesis of notions from logic and concurrent object-oriented programming (as
in [AR89a]) was aimed for. Both in [BV89] and in [Vin89, Bak91], PROLOG's cut
construct is dealt with as well. (Due to the complexities of its semantic models,
we have not included this material in our book.) A tutorial exposition of much of
Section 9.1 is given in [BV91].

The language $\mathcal{L}_{fork}$ and its denotational model are from [Bru86]. The operational
model and the proof that the operational and denotational semantics coincide are
taken from [BBB93]. A language with a dynamic network of processes which can
be seen as an extension of $\mathcal{L}_{fork}$ is described in [BB85], where also a denotational
model for this language is developed.

III MODELS BASED ON DOMAIN EQUATIONS

Part III starts with a chapter on solving domain equations. After Section 2.1, this is the first occasion where further topological theory is developed. All domains applied in Part III are of the branching type, in that their elements have a tree-like structure, sometimes combined with functional/nonuniform aspects. Once the reader has acquired some familiarity with these domains, he will appreciate that the general semantic methodology as developed in Part I—transition systems, higher-order operators and the like—may be applied in this more abstract setting with only minor adaptations. All concepts investigated in Part III have to do with *parallelism,* including topics such as deadlock and synchronization, communication with value-passing, parallel objects and the rendezvous, and atomization and action refinement.

10 Domain Equations and Bisimulation

In Parts I and II, we have encountered many examples of semantic domains. Recalling some of them, we have worked with

- Act^∞
- $\Sigma \to \Sigma^\infty$
- $\mathcal{P}_{nco}(Act^\infty)$
- $\Sigma \to \mathcal{P}_{nco}(\Sigma^\infty)$
- $\mathcal{P}_{ncl}((\Sigma \times \Sigma)^\infty)$

and several others. The listing brings out in a clear fashion that these domains all deserve to be called *linear,* in that they are all expressed, ultimately, in terms of the operator $(\cdot)^\infty$ of taking finite and infinite *sequences.* For a number of programming constructs this type of domain is not sufficiently expressive. In Part III, we shall be concerned with constructs which require some form of *branching* structure—trees or variations thereof—for their modeling. In Part IV, we shall present an example of a language construct demanding yet another type of domain structure.

Rather than introducing the new domains separately as the need arises, we shall develop a general theory of specifying domains in terms of solving *domain equations.* The reader might compare this, for example, with the way in which in algebra new entities are introduced as solutions of equations: rational numbers (e.g., solving $2x - 1 = 0$), algebraic numbers ($x^2 - 2 = 0$), or complex numbers ($x^2 + 1 = 0$).

All domains considered so far are complete metric spaces, and it is natural to expect that we are looking for means to specify further instances of such spaces. Thus, the question arises as to how one might specify equations over them. Clearly, this presupposes the availability of certain *operators* on (complete) metric spaces. Fortunately, we have already encountered earlier several of the operators we shall need below, viz. disjoint union, product, function space, and the power domains of closed and compact subsets. What is missing so far is a general framework to discuss equations over complete metric spaces in terms of these (and a few other) operators.

A second important point of inspiration for such a general theory is our earlier use, in many forms, of specifying objects in terms of fixed points. We have defined a large variety of operational and denotational semantics, and of semantic operators, by equations such as

$$\mathcal{O} = \Phi(\mathcal{O}) \tag{10.1}$$
$$\mathcal{D} = \Psi(\mathcal{D}) \tag{10.2}$$

$$; \quad = \quad \Omega_;(;) \tag{10.3}$$

$$\| \quad = \quad \Omega_\|(\|) \tag{10.4}$$

etc. Combining the two perspectives just outlined, we want to develop a theory for the solution of domain equations of the form

$$\mathbb{P} \quad = \quad \mathcal{F}(\mathbb{P}) \tag{10.5}$$

where $\mathbb{P}$ is the complete (ultra) metric space we want to determine, and $\mathcal{F}$ is an operator composed from already known operators such as the ones listed above, and, possibly, a few new ones. (For examples of (10.5), the reader may consult the end of Section 10.2.)

In solving equations (10.1) to (10.4), we always followed the same pattern, in that the characteristic mappings $\Phi, \ldots, \Omega_\|$ were defined as ($\frac{1}{2}$-) contractive on an appropriate complete metric space, and then Banach's theorem was invoked.

In Section 10.1, we shall develop a general setting in which equations such as (10.5) may be solved. More specifically, we shall closely follow our earlier treatment of Banach's theorem, and introduce a framework in which it is meaningful to discuss contractive and nonexpansive $\mathcal{F}$. Using CMS to denote the collection of all complete metric spaces, we have that $\mathcal{F} \colon CMS \to CMS$ maps a space (M, d) to some space $(M', d') = \mathcal{F}(M, d)$. Borrowing a term from category theory, we shall call such a mapping $\mathcal{F}$ a *functor*. Note that—in line with the operators on complete metric spaces as discussed in earlier chapters—we have that a functor $\mathcal{F}$ acts both on the set M *and* on the metric d (with (M', d') as result). In order for the metric tools to apply to CMS itself, it is necessary to develop some kind of metric on complete metric spaces. Though not feasible in general, it is possible to do this for a restricted setting which is just sufficient for our purposes. In this way, we shall be able to mimic much of (the proof of) Banach's theorem in showing that (10.5) has a solution for $\mathcal{F}$ contractive.

In Section 10.2, we shall have another look at the various specific instances of functors on CMS as introduced in earlier chapters, and show that they are all nonexpansive. Thanks to the use of an elementary additional operator, we shall also be able to ensure that the operators we work with are contractive, where needed.

In Section 10.3 we present the notions of bisimulation/bisimilarity, first on a transition system and then on domains as introduced in Section 10.2. As main result we shall obtain that bisimilarity on metric domains collapses to identity, thus enabling us to ignore the notion in the subsequent developments.

The theory to be developed in the present chapter is not the most general as known to date. We shall impose two restrictions on the $\mathcal{F}$ occurring in (10.5). The first condition restricts the way in which general function spaces may be formed. Roughly, we shall not allow occurrences of the unknown $\mathbb{P}$ on the left-hand side of the arrow in the function space formation, i.e., we do not allow equations of the form

$$\mathbb{P} \quad = \quad \ldots \mathbb{P} \rightarrow \ldots \tag{10.6}$$

(A more precise formulation will follow.) Two comments are in order concerning this restriction:

(1) The theory supporting the solution of equations (10.5) with $\mathcal{F}$ restricted as indicated can be developed wholly within the metric framework. In fact, we shall see that it is, in essence, a not too drastic extension of our earlier metric machinery, with the theorem of Banach as a key tool.

(2) The applications as discussed in Part III of our book can all be based on the restricted theory.

The second restrictive condition referred to above is more of a technical nature and will be mentioned in due course.

Our reluctance to develop the theory of domain equations in full generality at the present stage stems from the fact that this general theory requires a certain (modest) amount of category theory—which we have not presented at all so far in our work. Rather than disrupting our semantic designs at this point with the presentation of another body of foundational tools, we prefer to postpone an outline of the general category theoretic approach to solving equation (10.5) till Appendix C. (In order to whet the reader's appetite for the general theory, we have included in Part IV an example of a programming notion, viz. second-order assignment, which does need the general theory—in particular an equation of the form (10.6)—in an essential way.)

10.1   Domain equations

Let $\mathcal{F}\colon CMS \rightarrow CMS$ be a functor (in the sense as described in the introduction). In order to be able to apply the general metric tools developed up till now to the solution of equation (10.5), we need the notion of a metric on complete metric spaces. That is, we want to be able to reason about

$$d((M_1, d_1), (M_2, d_2)),$$

for (M_1, d_1) and (M_2, d_2) themselves complete metric spaces. In the general case, it is not clear how one could determine such a d on which to build the theory as developed below. (One has then to resort to category theory, see Appendix C.) However, there is an important subcase where it is indeed feasible to define d, viz. in case (M_1, d_1) is a subspace of (M_2, d_2). This is the case when we have that [1]

$$M_1 \subseteq M_2 \atop d_2 \restriction M_1 = d_1. \tag{10.7}$$

In the sequel, when we are dealing with two spaces satisfying these conditions, we shall express this by writing

$$M_1 \triangleleft M_2. \tag{10.8}$$

Thanks to the assumption that M_1 is complete, we have that M_1 is a *closed* subset of M_2. This allows us to define the sought for d—in case (10.8) is satisfied—simply as

$$d((M_1, d_1), (M_2, d_2)) \quad = \quad (d_2)_H(M_1, M_2),$$

i.e., we take the Hausdorff metric (induced by d_2) to determine the distance between M_1 and M_2. From now on, we shall use the notation

$$\delta(M_1, M_2),$$

as short-hand for $(d_2)_H(M_1, M_2)$—assuming, of course, that (10.8) is satisfied. Recalling our earlier definitions, we have that (assuming (10.8))

$$\delta(M_1, M_2) = sup\{\, inf\{\, d_2(y, x) \mid x \in M_1 \,\} \mid y \in M_2 \,\}.$$

As we shall see, it will be possible to develop a modified form of Banach's theorem solving (10.5) for $\mathcal{F}$ contractive wholly in terms of this δ-metric. Recall, however, that we assumed that $\mathcal{F}$ satisfies two conditions—no $\mathbb{P} \xrightarrow{1} \ldots$ parts, and a not yet stated technical one.

Various preparations are required before we can present the theory in full detail. We start with the introduction of a further fundamental notion for metric spaces in general, viz. that of *isometry*.

---

[1] Recall that $f \restriction X$ denotes the function f restricted to the domain X.

Definition 10.1

(a) Two metric spaces (M_1, d_1) and (M_2, d_2) are called *isometric* in case there exists a bijection $f: M_1 \to M_2$ satisfying, for all $x, y \in M_1$,

$$d_2(f(x), f(y)) \quad = \quad d_1(x, y) . \tag{10.9}$$

(b) In case M_1 and M_2 are isometric, we write $M_1 \simeq M_2$.

Remark It is sufficient to require that the mapping $f: M_1 \to M_2$ is a surjection, since injectivity of f is a consequence of (10.9): If $f(x) = f(y)$, then $0 = d_2(f(x), f(y)) = d_1(x, y)$, whence $x = y$.

Examples

(1) The spaces $([0, 1], d_{\mathbb{R}})$ and $([2, 4], d'_{\mathbb{R}})$, where $d'_{\mathbb{R}}(x, y) = \frac{1}{2}|x - y|$, are isometric (e.g., via the linear function mapping 0 to 2 and 1 to 4).

(2) Any two discrete spaces with the same finite number of elements are isometric. (More generally, any two equipollent discrete spaces are isometric.)

The following simple lemma links isometries and nonexpansive mappings:

Lemma 10.2 *Let* $f: M_1 \xrightarrow{1} M_2$ *and* $g: M_2 \xrightarrow{1} M_1$ *be such that* $f \circ g$ ($= \lambda x \in M_2.f(g(x))$) $= id_{M_2}$, *and* $g \circ f = id_{M_1}$, *where* id_{M_i} *is the identity function on* M_i, $i = 1, 2$. *Then* $M_1 \simeq M_2$.

Proof Exercise. $\qquad\qquad\qquad\qquad\qquad\qquad\qquad\qquad\qquad\qquad\qquad\qquad$ $\square$

The notion of isometry is crucial for the precise formulation of the notion of domain equation over *CMS*. Rather than using (10.5), we shall from now on be concerned with the solution *up to isometry* of the equation, now written as

$$\mathbb{P} \simeq \mathcal{F}(\mathbb{P}) . \tag{10.10}$$

With some abuse of language, we shall refer to (10.10) as a domain *equation* (rather than the more precise domain *isometry*). We shall now present the two conditions which together guarantee that (10.10) is solvable. (Note that no statements on the uniqueness of the solution are made here; we shall return to this issue at a later stage.) The first condition is, simply, a form of the familiar contractiveness notion, here in a somewhat sharpened form, necessary to ensure the existence of the δ-metric for the spaces concerned.

Definition 10.3

(a) A functor $\mathcal{F}\colon CMS \to CMS$ is called *monotonic* if, for each $M_1, M_2 \in CMS$,

$$M_1 \triangleleft M_2 \Rightarrow \mathcal{F}(M_1) \triangleleft \mathcal{F}(M_2)\,.$$

(b) Let α be a real number with $0 \le \alpha \le 1$. A functor $\mathcal{F}\colon CMS \to CMS$ is called α-Lipschitz if it is monotonic and, for all $M_1, M_2 \in CMS$ with $M_1 \triangleleft M_2$, we have

$$\delta(\mathcal{F}(M_1), \mathcal{F}(M_2)) \le \alpha \cdot \delta(M_1, M_2)\,.$$

(c) Let $\mathcal{F}$ be as in (b).

- If $\mathcal{F}$ is 1-Lipschitz, it is called nonexpansive
- If $\mathcal{F}$ is α-Lipschitz $(0 \le \alpha < 1)$, it is called α-contractive
- If $\mathcal{F}$ is α-contractive for some $\alpha(0 \le \alpha < 1)$, it is called contractive.

We now formulate the announced conditions guaranteeing the solvability of (10.10).

(1) $\mathcal{F}$ is contractive.

(2) There exists a space, denoted by $\mathbb{1}$, say, such that $\mathbb{1} \triangleleft \mathcal{F}(\mathbb{1})$.

Condition (1) is, by now, quite familiar. Condition (2) will enable us to mimic an argument in the proof of Banach's theorem, viz. that the fixed point concerned may be obtained as limit of the sequence

$$x_0,\ f(x_0),\ \ldots,\ f^n(x_0), \ldots\,.$$

In the present setting, we want to make sure that there exists an approximating sequence of the form

$$\mathbb{1} \triangleleft \mathcal{F}(\mathbb{1}) \triangleleft \ldots \triangleleft \mathcal{F}^n(\mathbb{1}) \triangleleft \ldots\,.$$

Simply starting in an arbitrary point (here, space) and iterating $\mathcal{F}$ will not work, since the condition as to the well-definedness of the δ-metric is then not necessarily satisfied. On the other hand, condition (2) is, in most of the cases considered in (semantic) practice, easy to satisfy. Various examples will be discussed in Section 10.2.

Altogether, we shall devote the remainder of this section to the proof of the following main theorem.

Theorem 10.4 *Let $\mathcal{F}\colon CMS \to CMS$ be a functor satisfying the two conditions just stated. Then the domain equation*

$$\mathbb{P} \simeq \mathcal{F}(\mathbb{P})$$

has a solution in CMS.

Profiting from our earlier work on metric (hyper) spaces, we have already several ingredients available which play a role in the proof of this important theorem. We begin with the discussion of a result which refines an earlier one (mentioned without proof after Theorem 1.29). First, we give a definition.

Definition 10.5 Let (M, d) be a metric space. A *completion* of (M, d) is a *complete* metric space (N, d') such that

(1) $M \vartriangleleft N$.

(2) For each $x \in N$ we have: $x = lim_n \, x_n$, with $x_n \in M$, $n = 0, 1, \dots$ (and with the limit taken with respect to d').

The next theorem states that each metric space *has* a completion. That is, each (not necessarily complete) metric space M can be enlarged to a complete metric space (N, d')—with M a subspace of N—such that the "extra" points in N are all limits of sequences of points in M. Note how this definition implies a certain minimality condition for N, in that no more points are added to M than those necessary to turn it into a complete space. A trivial example in $(\mathbb{R}, d_{\mathbb{R}})$ may clarify this: The space $([0, 1), d_{\mathbb{R}})$ is incomplete, and the space $([0, 1], d_{\mathbb{R}})$ is a completion of $([0, 1), d_{\mathbb{R}})$. The space $([0, 2], d_{\mathbb{R}})$, though complete, is not a completion of $([0, 1], d_{\mathbb{R}})$.

The announced theorem now follows.

Theorem 10.6 *Each metric space has a completion which is unique up to isometry.*

Proof The proof of the *existence* of a completion is somewhat involved; it is described in some detail in Appendix A. The result on the uniqueness of completions (up to isometry) is easier to obtain: Assume that both (N_1, d_1) and (N_2, d_2) are completions of (M, d). We define a bijection $f\colon N_1 \to N_2$ by putting $f(x) = x$, for $x \in M$, and $f(x) = lim_n^{(2)} \, x_n$, for $x \in N_1 \setminus M$, x of the form $lim_n^{(1)} \, x_n$, where the limits $lim^{(i)}$ are taken with respect to d_i, $i = 1, 2$. Clearly, f is a bijection. Also, we easily see that $d_2(f(x), f(y)) = d_1(x, y)$. Take, e.g., the case that $x, y \in N_1 \setminus M$, $x = lim_n^{(1)} \, x_n$, $y = lim_n^{(1)} \, y_n$. Then

$d_2(f(x), f(y))$

$= d_2(lim_n^{(2)} x_n, lim_n^{(2)} y_n)$

$= [\text{cont. of } d_2]\ lim_n\, d_2(x_n, y_n)$

$= [d_1 = d_2 \text{ on } M]\ lim_n\, d_1(x_n, y_n)$

$= [\text{cont. of } d_1]\ d_1(lim_n^{(1)} x_n, lim_n^{(1)} y_n)$

$= d_1(x, y)\,,$

where lim is taken with respect to the (standard) metric on $[0, 1]$.   □

We now come to the first main step in the proof of Theorem 10.4. In its formulation, we use the notion of a δ-Cauchy sequence, which we define first.

Definition 10.7

(a) A δ-Cauchy sequence is a sequence $(X_n)_n$ with $X_n \in CMS$, $n = 0, 1, \ldots$, such that

  (1) $X_n \triangleleft X_{n+1}$, $n = 0, 1, \ldots$.

  (2) $\forall \varepsilon > 0 \exists i \forall j, k\, [i \leq j \leq k \Rightarrow \delta(X_j, X_k) \leq \varepsilon]$.

(b) A space $X \in CMS$ is a completion of a δ-Cauchy sequence $(X_n)_n$, in case it is a completion of $\bigcup_n X_n$. Here we assume the following metric d on $\bigcup_n X_n$: Let $x, y \in \bigcup_n X_n$, and let m be such that $x, y \in X_m$. Then $d(x, y) = d_m(x, y)$.

Condition (a2) is a one-sided version of the familiar condition on Cauchy sequences; condition (a1) ensures well-formedness of condition (a2).

Remark The space $\bigcup_n X_n$ is, in general, not complete. For example, take $X_n = (\{a, a^2, \ldots, a^n\}, d_B)$ (d_B the Baire metric). Then $\bigcup_n X_n = (a^*, d_B)$, which is a noncomplete space.

We can now state

Theorem 10.8 Let $(X_n)_n$ be a δ-Cauchy sequence in CMS, and let $X \stackrel{df}{=} \bigcup_n X_n$. Then we have, for each $\bar{X} \in CMS$ with $X \triangleleft \bar{X}$,

$\bar{X}$ is a completion of $X \Leftrightarrow \lim_n \delta(X_n, \bar{X}) = 0\,.$

Proof

[⇒]   We show that, for $\bar{X}$ a completion of X, $lim_j\, \delta(X_j, \bar{X}) = 0$. Choose $\varepsilon > 0$. Since (X_n) is δ-Cauchy, we have

$$\forall j, k \,[\, i \le j \le k \Rightarrow \delta(X_j, X_k) \le \varepsilon/4\,] \tag{10.11}$$

Let $\ell \ge i$. In order to prove that $\delta(X_\ell, \bar{X}) \le \varepsilon$, it suffices to show that

$$\forall x \in \bar{X} \exists x_\ell \in X_\ell \,[\, d(x_\ell, x) \le \varepsilon\,] .$$

Let $x \in \bar{X}$. Since $\bar{X}$ is a completion of $X = \bigcup_n X_n$, we have that $x = lim_h\, x_h$, with $x_h \in X$. Consequently, there exists an $x_h \in X_m$ such that $d(x_h, x) \le \varepsilon/2$. We distinguish two cases.

($m \le \ell$) Now $X_m \subseteq X_\ell$, and we may put $x_\ell = x_h \in X_\ell$.

($m > \ell$) By (10.11), we can choose $x_\ell \in X_\ell$ such that $d(x_\ell, x_h) \le d(X_\ell, X_m) + \varepsilon/4 \le \varepsilon/2$, and we have that $d(x_\ell, x) \le d(x_\ell, x_h) + d(x_h, x) \le \varepsilon$.

[⇐]   Choose $x \in \bar{X}$. Choose, for $i \in \mathbb{N}$, an index j such that $\delta(X_j, \bar{X}) < 2^{-(i+1)}$. By the definition of the Hausdorff distance, we may choose some $x_i \in X_j$ such that $d(x_i, x) \le 2 \cdot 2^{-(i+1)} = 2^{-i}$. Thus the sequence $(x_i)_i$ converges to x, and we see that $\bar{X}$ is a completion of X.   □

Theorem 10.8 is used as the main step in the proof of the following

Lemma 10.9 *Let $\mathcal{F}: CMS \to CMS$ be a nonexpansive functor, and let $(X_n)_n$ be a δ-Cauchy sequence in CMS. Then we have*

If $\bar{X}$ is a completion of $(X_n)_n$, then $\mathcal{F}(\bar{X})$ is a completion of $(\mathcal{F}(X_n))_n$.

Proof We first remark that, thanks to the fact that $\mathcal{F}$ is (monotonic and) non-expansive, we have that, for $(X_n)_n$ a δ-Cauchy sequence, also $(\mathcal{F}(X_n))_n$ is a δ-Cauchy sequence. Now let $\bar{X}$ be a completion of $(X_n)_n$. By Theorem 10.8, we have that $lim_n\, \delta(X_n, \bar{X}) = 0$. Since $\mathcal{F}$ is nonexpansive we also have that $lim_n\, \delta(\mathcal{F}(X_n), \mathcal{F}(\bar{X})) = 0$. Another appeal to Theorem 10.8 now yields that $\mathcal{F}(\bar{X})$ is a completion of $(\mathcal{F}(X_n))_n$.   □

We are close to finishing the

Proof of Theorem 10.4 Let $\mathcal{F}\colon CMS \to CMS$ be α-contractive ($0 \leq \alpha < 1$), and assume that $\mathbb{1} \in CMS$ is such that $\mathbb{1} \vartriangleleft \mathcal{F}(\mathbb{1})$. By the monotonicity of $\mathcal{F}$ and this assumption, we easily see that $\mathcal{F}^n(\mathbb{1}) \vartriangleleft \mathcal{F}^{n+1}(\mathbb{1})$, $n = 0, 1, \ldots$. Exactly as in the proof of Banach's theorem (Theorem 1.34), we can now show that $(\mathcal{F}^n(\mathbb{1}))_n$ is a δ-Cauchy sequence. Next, we put $X_n = \mathcal{F}^n(\mathbb{1})$, and let $\bar{X}$ be a completion of $(X_n)_n$. By Lemma 10.9, $\mathcal{F}(\bar{X})$ is a completion of $(\mathcal{F}(X_n))_n$. Now since $\bigcup_n X_n = \bigcup_n X_{n+1} = \bigcup_n \mathcal{F}(X_n)$, and because $\bar{X}$ is a completion of $\bigcup_n X_n$ and $\mathcal{F}(\bar{X})$ is a completion of $\bigcup_n \mathcal{F}(X_n)$, we have, by the uniqueness of completions up to isometry, that

$$\bar{X} \;\simeq\; \mathcal{F}(\bar{X}),$$

as was to be shown. $\square$

Remark It is also known that, under the stated conditions, the space $\bar{X}$ is the *unique* solution—up to isometry—of the equation $\mathbb{P} \simeq \mathcal{F}(\mathbb{P})$. The formalism developed in Appendix C allows a proof of this fact, but we shall have no occasion to appeal to it in our semantic modelling.

Analyzing the proof of Theorem 10.4, we see that we have, indeed, stayed close to the original proof of Banach's theorem. The main technical modifications necessary for the proof as just given were

- the need to restrict the setting to pairs M_1, M_2 with $M_1 \vartriangleleft M_2$, in order to allow the definition of $\delta(M_1, M_2)$

- the use of the existence of a completion for each metric space, and its uniqueness up to isometry

- the interplay between the completion of a δ-Cauchy sequence $(X_n)_n$, and its limit in terms of the δ-metric.

After having analyzed the solvability of (10.10) in terms of conditions on the functor $\mathcal{F}$, we are of course interested in seeing concrete examples of such $\mathcal{F}$, and in particular in the question whether the various operators encountered earlier (and listed in the introduction to Chapter 10) allow us to build contractive $\mathcal{F}$ in a sufficiently general way. The next section is devoted to a treatment of these questions.

10.2 Nonexpansive and contractive functors

In this section we shall review various functors $\mathcal{F}\colon CMS \to CMS$ (or $CMS \times CMS \to CMS$, as the case may be). Most of them were already introduced previously (in Sections 1.1.2 and 2.1); in addition, a few new ones will be presented. The functors $\mathcal{F}$ will be analyzed as to their nonexpansiveness or contractiveness. In the majority of cases, we shall conclude that the $\mathcal{F}$ concerned are nonexpansive. Thanks to one—quite elementary—special case, we shall be able to work with contractive $\mathcal{F}$ as the need arises.

So far, our theory has been rather abstract, and it is perhaps desirable to pay some attention to a concrete case, in view of providing some intuition for what we are doing here. We consider a prime case of a domain with a branching structure, viz. that of (edge-labelled) trees. For our purposes, we are not interested in their most concrete variety, but in a somewhat abstracted version, viz. "trees" which are

- commutative
- absorptive
- closed.

The first condition expresses that, for each node of the tree, the collection of successors of this node is *unordered*. E.g., we identify the two trees of Figures 10.1a and 10.1b.

Figure 10.1a   Figure 10.1b

The second condition states that the successors of each node form a set rather than a multi-set. We identify, e.g., the two trees depicted in Figure 10.2a and 10.2b.

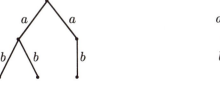

Figure 10.2a   Figure 10.2b

(We postpone for a little while discussion of the condition of closedness of a "tree.")

Consider a typical case: Let $(a \in) A$ be the alphabet of labels. A "tree" t over A has the form of Figure 10.3, where $n \geq 0$ and each t_i, $i = 1, \ldots, n$ is itself a "tree." (The case $n = 0$ specifies the empty "tree.")

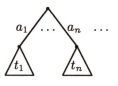

Figure 10.3

Leaving aside the question as to what purpose is served by these entities—a question receiving ample treatment in Chapters 11 to 14—we now discuss how one might specify the collection of such "trees" in terms of a domain equation. We claim that we may take, in first approximation, the domain specified as

$$\mathbb{P} = \mathcal{P}(A \times \mathbb{P}). \tag{10.12}$$

This equation specifies $\mathbb{P}$ such that each element t in $\mathbb{P}$ is a subset of $A \times \mathbb{P}$, i.e., for each $t \in \mathbb{P}$ we have that

$$t = \{\langle a_1, t_1 \rangle, \ldots, \langle a_n, t_n \rangle, \ldots \},$$

which is just the form as suggested by Figure 10.3.

Various refinements are necessary before we can say that (10.12) makes sense mathematically. An important one is the following: A basic fact from set theory is that, for each set X, $\mathcal{P}(X)$ has larger cardinality than X. Using $|X|$ to denote the cardinality of X, we have that, for $A \neq \emptyset$, $|\mathcal{P}(A \times X)| \geq |\mathcal{P}(X)| > |X|$, contradicting (10.12)—since equality should at least imply equal cardinality. (Reading (10.12) as an isometry does not help, since the same cardinality argument applies.) Fortunately, the way out of this impasse is relatively simple: We can replace $\mathcal{P}(\cdot)$ by $\mathcal{P}_{cl}(\cdot)$—with $\mathcal{P}_{cl}(\cdot)$ the powerdomain of closed subsets of—and refine (10.12) to the domain equation (or, rather, isometry) over CMS, now written as

$$\mathbb{P} \simeq \mathcal{P}_{cl}(A \times \mathbb{P}). \tag{10.13}$$

As an equation over complete metric spaces, (10.13) does have a solution (provided the metrics concerned are defined as described below)! This is one of the key results of the metric approach to semantics. Both in the form as given, and in numerous generalized forms, it will play a central role in all semantic modelling to be described in Part III.

Equation (10.13) serves to illustrate the general theory on equations $\mathbb{P} \simeq \mathcal{F}(\mathbb{P})$. Let us pause now to discuss how the $\mathcal{F}$ of (10.13) is built from basic components, and whether this $\mathcal{F}$ satisfies the conditions as referred to in Theorem 10.4.

On closer scrutiny, we observe four constituents in the functor on the right-hand side of (10.13), viz. the (known) space A, equipped with the (tacitly assumed as given) metric d_A, the unknown space $\mathbb{P}$ with the unknown metric $d_{\mathbb{P}}$, and the product and closed powerdomain functors. That is, if we write

- $\times \colon CMS \times CMS \to CMS$ given by

$$\times((M_1, d_1), (M_2, d_2)) = (M_1 \times M_2, d_1 \times d_2), \quad \text{with } d_1 \times d_2 = d_P.$$

- $\mathcal{P}_{cl}(\cdot) \colon CMS \to CMS$ given by

$$\mathcal{P}_{cl}(M, d) = (\mathcal{P}_{cl}(M), d_H)$$

then equation (10.13) can be reformulated as

$$(\mathbb{P}, d_{\mathbb{P}}) \quad \simeq \quad (\mathcal{P}_{cl}(A \times \mathbb{P}), (d_A \times d_{\mathbb{P}})_H),$$

thus bringing out that domain equations are equations both in the carrier part $(\mathbb{P} \simeq \mathcal{P}_{cl}(A \times \mathbb{P})$, and in the metrics part $(d_{\mathbb{P}} = (d_A \times d_{\mathbb{P}})_H)$. (At the end of this subsection, we shall discuss how the $\mathcal{F}$ concerned may be built as *composition* of the respective constituents.)

So far, we have neglected one further—and essential—point: the $\mathcal{F}$ displayed in (10.13) is not contractive, thus preventing the use of the general theory of Section 10.1. However, it is not difficult to remedy this. We introduce a special functor, tailor-made for this purpose, viz. the functor $id_\alpha \colon CMS \to CMS$, with $0 \leq \alpha < 1$ (and id abbreviating "identity"), defined by

$$id_\alpha(M, d) \quad = \quad (M, \alpha \cdot d).$$

Thus, id_α is the functor which leaves the underlying set untouched, and replaces the metric d by $\alpha \cdot d$ (with the obvious definition $(\alpha \cdot d)(x, y) = \alpha \cdot d(x, y)$). With the id_α-functor as a tool, we can, at last, give the equation defining the "tree" in its final form:

$$\mathbb{P} \quad \simeq \quad \mathcal{P}_{cl}(A \times id_{\frac{1}{2}}(\mathbb{P})). \tag{10.14}$$

In its full version, it reads

$$(\mathbb{P}, d_{\mathbb{P}}) \simeq (\mathcal{P}_{cl}(A \times \mathbb{P}), (d_A \times \tfrac{1}{2} \cdot d_{\mathbb{P}})_H),$$

but we shall, from now on, suppress the metrics part in the domain equations (apart from the id_{α}'s).

Equation (10.14) satisfies the conditions of Theorem 10.4. That the $\mathcal{F}$ involved is contractive is a consequence of the $id_{\frac{1}{2}}$-operator. (Soon, we shall present the tools to verify this claim.) For the space $\mathbb{1}$ such that

$$\mathbb{1} \lhd \mathcal{F}(\,\mathbb{1}\,), \tag{10.15}$$

we here simply take the space $(\{\emptyset\}, d)$, that is, the one-point set—with $\emptyset$ as only element—equipped with the discrete metric. Verification of (10.15) for $\mathcal{F}$ as in (10.14) is left as an exercise.

In order to develop some further intuition for a domain $\mathbb{P}$ such as the one specified by (10.14), we look at various examples. From now on, we shall use the term "process" as a generic name for the elements of domains $\mathbb{P}$. Most of the applications of domain equations in our book have to do with branching structures devised to handle notions in concurrency, and it has become customary to refer to the entities considered here as "processes."

We begin with a listing of some finite processes in $\mathbb{P}$, with $\mathbb{P}$ the solution of (10.14).

p_1: $\emptyset$

p_2: $\{\,\langle a, \emptyset \rangle, \langle b, \emptyset \rangle\,\}$

p_3: $\{\,\langle a, \{\,\langle b, \emptyset \rangle\,\} \rangle\,\}$

p_4: $\{\,\langle a, \{\,\langle b, \emptyset \rangle, \langle c, \emptyset \rangle\,\} \rangle\,\}$

p_5: $\{\,\langle a, \{\,\langle b, \emptyset \rangle\,\} \rangle, \langle a, \{\,\langle c, \emptyset \rangle\,\} \rangle\,\}$.

The "tree" structure in these processes may be somewhat obscured by the many parentheses. In a pictorial presentation, this structure is much more transparent. For example, the processes p_4 and p_5 may be represented by the "trees" of Figure 10.4a and 10.4b.

The reader may want to verify that, e.g., the following distances apply to these processes:

$$d_{\mathbb{P}}(p_1, p_2) = 1,\ d_{\mathbb{P}}(p_2, p_3) = 1,\ d_{\mathbb{P}}(p_3, p_4) = \tfrac{1}{2},\ d_{\mathbb{P}}(p_4, p_5) = \tfrac{1}{2}\ .$$

Later—in Chapter 11—we shall see how the two processes p_4 and p_5 serve (with minor modifications) as (denotational) meanings for the two statements $a;(b+c)$ and $(a;b) + (a;c)$, respectively.

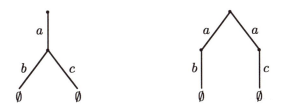

Figure 10.4a: 'tree' for p_4 Figure 10.4b: 'tree' for p_5

The benefit of using *complete* spaces to solve equations such as (10.14) is especially manifest when we want to discuss *infinite* processes. By the completeness of the domain $\mathbb{P}$ solving (10.14), it includes both finite and infinite elements—the latter occurring as limits of (Cauchy) sequences of finite ones. For example, let us consider the elementary infinite binary tree of Figure 10.5

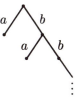

Figure 10.5

This tree can be specified as $p = lim_n p_n$, with $p_0 = \emptyset$, $p_{n+1} = \{\langle a, \emptyset\rangle, \langle b, p_n\rangle\}$. How can we see that this p belongs to $\mathbb{P}$? Let us define $\mathbb{P}_0 = \{\emptyset\}$, $\mathbb{P}_{n+1} = \mathcal{P}_{cl}(A \times id_{\frac{1}{2}}(\mathbb{P}_n))$. Clearly, we have that $p_n \in \mathbb{P}_n$, $n = 0, 1, \ldots$. We leave it as an exercise to verify that $(p_n)_n$ is a Cauchy sequence. By the general theory of Section 10.1, we have that the solution of (10.14) may be obtained as a completion of $\bigcup_n \mathbb{P}_n$, thus proving the claim that $p = lim_n p_n$ is an element of $\mathbb{P}$. Another way of specifying p is require it to satisfy the equation $p = \{\langle a, \emptyset\rangle, \langle b, p\rangle\}$. More precisely, we should employ here the isometry, say f, between $\mathbb{P}$ and $\mathcal{P}_{cl}(A \times id_{\frac{1}{2}}(\mathbb{P}))$, by writing

$p = \{\langle a, \emptyset\rangle, \langle b, f(p)\rangle\}$.

However, here and in all comparable situations below, we shall take the mapping f (or f^{-1}) for granted, and omit writing it explicitly.

A second example of an infinite process is specified as follows: Let $q_0 = \emptyset$, $q_{n+1} = \{\langle a, q_n\rangle\}$, $n = 0, 1, \ldots$, and let

$$\begin{aligned} p_n &= \{ \langle a, q_0 \rangle, \dots, \langle a, q_n \rangle \}, \; n = 0, 1, \dots \\ p &= \lim_n p_n. \end{aligned} \qquad (10.16)$$

We leave it as an exercise to verify that $p \in \mathbb{P}$. There is one important consequence of the general theory we draw attention to. In the world of (ordinary) trees, one should distinguish between the trees of Figure 10.6a and Figure 10.6b.

Figure 10.6a: A (nonclosed) tree   Figure 10.6b: A (closed) tree
which is not a process   which is a process

The first figure (10.6a) depicts the tree consisting of all branches of length $1, 2, \dots, n, \dots$ (with all edges labelled by a), and the second figure (10.6b) is like the first, but with the *infinite* branch of a-labelled edges added. Now it should be carefully noted that the process p as defined in (10.16) corresponds to the tree of Figure 10.6b. The tree t of Figure 10.6a has no counterpart in $\mathbb{P}$: it is a non-closed object, since the Cauchy sequence $(\langle a, q_n \rangle)_n$ residing in t has no limit in t.

With the last example, we have also shed some light on the third property of trees referred to above (where we required the processes concerned to be commutative, absorptive and *closed*). Note how the first two could be stated in an elementary way, but the third one presupposes the metric definitions.

This concludes our discussion of the process domain $\mathbb{P}$ solving (10.14) (and of several processes from this $\mathbb{P}$). Our aim here was to provide some background for the general theory, with the presentation of which we now continue.

We shall list a collection of functors $\mathcal{F}$ mapping (pairs of) complete metric spaces to complete metric spaces, and then present a theorem stating the nonexpansiveness or contractiveness properties of these $\mathcal{F}$.

Definition 10.10

(a) (constant functor) Let $(A, d_A) \in CMS$. The functor $A\colon CMS \to CMS$ is given by

$$A(M, d) = (A, d_A).$$

(b) (α-identity functor, $0 \leq \alpha \leq 1$) The functor $id_\alpha \colon CMS \to CMS$ is given by

$$id_\alpha(M, d) \;\; = \;\; (M, \alpha \cdot d) \,.$$

(c) (disjoint union functor) The functor $+ \colon CMS \times CMS \to CMS$ is given by

$$+((M_1, d_1), (M_2, d_2)) \;\; = \;\; (M_1 + M_2, d_U) \,;$$

where the right-hand side is as in Definition 1.23a.

(d) (product functor) The functor $\times \colon CMS \times CMS \to CMS$ is given by

$$\times((M_1, d_1)\,(M_2, d_2)) \;\; = \;\; (M_1 \times M_2, d_1 \times d_2) \,,$$

where the right-hand side is as in Definition 1.23a (and $d_1 \times d_2$ is another notation for d_P).

(e) (restricted function space functor) Let A be an arbitrary set. The functor $A \to (\cdot) \colon CMS \to CMS$ is given by

$$A \to (M, d) \;\; = \;\; (A \to M, d_F) \,,$$

where the right-hand side is as in Definition 1.23b.

(f) (compact powerdomain functor) The functor $\mathcal{P}_{co}(\cdot) \colon CMS \to CMS$ is given by

$$\mathcal{P}_{co}(M, d) \;\; = \;\; (\mathcal{P}_{co}(M), d_H) \,.$$

(g) (closed powerdomain functor) As part (f), with $\mathcal{P}_{cl}(\cdot)$ replacing $\mathcal{P}_{co}(\cdot)$.

(h) (nonempty compact/closed powerdomain functors) As above, with $\mathcal{P}_{nco}$ or $\mathcal{P}_{ncl}$ replacing $\mathcal{P}_{co}$ or $\mathcal{P}_{cl}$.

We draw special attention to the $A \to (\cdot)$ functor from clause (e). It is important here that the left-hand side of the function space operator is a constant, since this ensures its monotonicity: if $M_1 \lhd M_2$, then $(A \to M_1) \lhd (A \to M_2)$. The general definition of the function space functor, say $\mathcal{F}^* \colon CMS \times CMS \to CMS$, as given by

$$\mathcal{F}^*((M_1, d_1), (M_2, d_2)) \;\; = \;\; (M_1 \xrightarrow{1} M_2, d_F)$$

does not fit into the theory of Section 10.1, since $\mathcal{F}^*$ is not monotonic[2] in its first argument: we do *not* have that, for M_2 arbitrary,

---

[2] In category theory, one would express this by saying that $\mathcal{F}^*$ is not *covariant* in its first argument.

$M_1 \vartriangleleft M_1' \Rightarrow \mathcal{F}^*(M_1, M_2) \vartriangleleft \mathcal{F}^*(M_1', M_2)$.

(See Exercise 10.2 for another example of a monotonic function space operator.)

Apart from the indicated problem with the general function space operator, all other functors as listed in Definition 10.10 behave satisfactorily. We have

Theorem 10.11

(a) *The constant functor A is 0-contractive.*

(b) *The identity functor id_1 is nonexpansive.*

(c) *The α-identity functor $(0 \leq \alpha < 1)$ is α-contractive.*

(d) *The disjoint union and product functors are nonexpansive in both their arguments.*

(e) *The function space functor $A \to (\cdot)$ is nonexpansive.*

(f) *The (nonempty) compact and closed powerdomain functors are nonexpansive.*

Proof Clauses (a) to (d) are clear from the definitions and earlier results. Parts (e) and (f) require somewhat more work.

(e) Choose $M, N \in CMS$ with $M \vartriangleleft N$. Clearly, $(A \to M) \vartriangleleft (A \to N)$. We now verify that $A \to$ is nonexpansive, viz. that

$$\delta(A \to M, A \to N) \leq \delta(M, N). \tag{10.17}$$

By the definition of the Hausdorff metric, it is sufficient to show that

$$\forall \varepsilon > 0 \forall g \in A \to N \exists f \in A \to M \, [d(f, g) \leq \delta(M, N) + \varepsilon].$$

By the definition of $\delta(M, N)$ we have, for given ε, that $\forall a \in A \exists x \in M \, [d(x, g(a)) \leq \delta(M, N) + \varepsilon]$. This determines $f \in A \to M$ such that

$$\forall a \in A \, [d(f(a), g(a)) \leq \delta(M, N) + \varepsilon].$$

By the sup-definition of $d(f, g)$, this yields (10.17), as desired.

(f) We treat only the cases $\mathcal{P}_{co}(\cdot)$ and $\mathcal{P}_{cl}(\cdot)$. We begin with $\mathcal{P}_{co}$. Choose $M, N \in CMS$ with $M \vartriangleleft N$. Clearly, then $\mathcal{P}_{co}(M) \vartriangleleft \mathcal{P}_{co}(N)$. We now prove

$$\delta(\mathcal{P}_{co}(M), \mathcal{P}_{co}(N)) \leq \delta(M, N) .$$

Let $\delta \stackrel{df}{=} \delta(M, N)$. Choose $\varepsilon > 0$ and $Y \subseteq N$, Y compact. We verify the existence of a compact $X \subseteq M$ such that $d(X, Y) \leq \delta + \varepsilon$. Consider the collection of open balls

$$\{ B_{\varepsilon/2}(y) \mid y \in Y \}.$$

Clearly, $Y \subseteq \bigcup_{y \in Y} B_{\varepsilon/2}(y)$. Since Y is compact, there exist $y_1, \ldots, y_n$ such that

$$Y \subseteq \bigcup_{i=1}^{n} B_{\varepsilon/2}(y_i).$$

Since $\delta(M, N) < \delta + \varepsilon/2$, we can choose $x_1, \ldots, x_n$ in M such that

$$d(x_i, y_i) < \delta + \varepsilon/2.$$

Clearly, the subset $X = \{ x_1, \ldots, x_n \}$ of M is compact. Moreover, $d(X, Y) \leq \delta + \varepsilon$. This can be seen as follows: Choose $x = x_i \in X$. Then $d(x, y_i) = d(x_i, y_i) \leq \delta + \varepsilon/2$. Now choose $y \in Y$. Then $y \in B_{\varepsilon/2}(y_j)$, for some j, $1 \leq j \leq n$. Hence $d(y, x_j) \leq d(y, y_j) + d(y_j, x_j) \leq \delta + \varepsilon/2 + \varepsilon/2 = \delta + \varepsilon$. Altogether, we have shown that $\forall x \in X \exists y \in Y \, [d(x, y) \leq \delta + \varepsilon]$ and $\forall y \in Y \exists x \in X \, [d(y, x) \leq \delta + \varepsilon]$, and $d(X, Y) \leq \delta + \varepsilon$ follows.

Finally, we discuss the functor $\mathcal{P}_{ncl}(\cdot)$. Suppose $M \triangleleft N$, and let $\delta = \delta(M, N)$. Clearly, $\mathcal{P}_{ncl}(M) \triangleleft \mathcal{P}_{ncl}(N)$. We now show that

$$\delta(\mathcal{P}_{ncl}(M), \mathcal{P}_{ncl}(N)) \leq \delta.$$

Choose $\varepsilon > 0$ and let $Y \subseteq N$ be nonempty and closed. Let the subset X of M be the closure (Definition 2.1b), in M, of

$$X_0 \stackrel{df}{=} \bigcup \{ B_{\delta+\varepsilon}(y) \cap M \mid y \in Y \}.$$

By the definition of $\delta(M, N)$ we have that $\forall y \in N \exists x \in M \, [d(y, x) \leq \delta + \varepsilon]$. In particular, we have that $\forall y \in Y \exists x \in M \, [d(y, x) \leq \delta + \varepsilon]$. By the definition of X_0 this implies both that $X_0 \neq \emptyset$ and that $\forall y \in Y \exists x \in X_0 \, [d(y, x) \leq \delta + \varepsilon]$. Also, by the definition of X_0 we have that $\forall x \in X_0 \exists y \in Y \, [d(x, y) \leq \delta + \varepsilon]$. Altogether, we have shown that $d(X_0, Y) \leq \delta + \varepsilon$, from which $d(\bar{X}_0, Y) = d(X, Y) \leq \delta + \varepsilon$ follows. $\square$

Now that we have analyzed the various functors encountered so far as to their contractiveness or nonexpansiveness, there is one remaining step to settle: How does the composition of functors affect the contractiveness coefficients involved. For a general statement of the pertinent result, it is convenient to somewhat generalize the theory developed up to now, in that we design a general setting for functors on n-tuples ($n \geq 1$) of complete metric spaces.

Definition 10.12 Let $CMS^k = CMS \times \cdots \times CMS$ (k factors), and let

$$CMS^+ = \bigcup_{k \geq 1} CMS^k .$$

Let $\mathcal{C}_i \in CMS^+$, $i = 0, 1, \ldots$. We define the *tupling* and *projection* functors, and the *composition* of functors as follows:

(a) For $\mathcal{F}_i : \mathcal{C}_0 \to \mathcal{C}_i$, $1 \leq i \leq n$, we define $\langle \mathcal{F}_1, \ldots, \mathcal{F}_n \rangle : \mathcal{C}_0 \to \mathcal{C}_1 \times \cdots \times \mathcal{C}_n$ by putting

$$\langle \mathcal{F}_1, \ldots, \mathcal{F}_n \rangle (M, d) = \langle \mathcal{F}_1(M, d), \ldots, \mathcal{F}_n(M, d) \rangle .$$

(b) The functor $\pi_k : \mathcal{C}_1 \times \cdots \times \mathcal{C}_n \to \mathcal{C}_k$ ($1 \leq k \leq n$) is given by

$$\pi_k \langle (M_1, d_1), \ldots, (M_n, d_n) \rangle = (M_k, d_k) .$$

(c) Let $\mathcal{F}_1 : \mathcal{C}_1 \to \mathcal{C}_2$ and $\mathcal{F}_2 : \mathcal{C}_0 \to \mathcal{C}_1$, then $\mathcal{F}_1 \circ \mathcal{F}_2 : \mathcal{C}_0 \to \mathcal{C}_2$ is given by

$$\mathcal{F}_1 \circ \mathcal{F}_2 (M, d) = \mathcal{F}_1 (\mathcal{F}_2 (M, d)) .$$

It is straightforward to verify that all results of Section 10.1 concerning (contractive) functors $\mathcal{F} : CMS \to CMS$ can be generalized to a setting with (contractive) functors $\mathcal{F} : CMS^+ \to CMS^+$, and we shall not take the trouble to spell out the details. Assuming this to be done, we can now state

Theorem 10.13 *Let $\mathcal{C}_0, \ldots \mathcal{C}_n \in CMS^+$.*

(a) If the functors $\mathcal{F}_i : \mathcal{C}_0 \to \mathcal{C}_i$ are α_i-Lipschitz ($1 \leq i \leq n$, $0 \leq \alpha_i \leq 1$) then $\langle \mathcal{F}_1, \ldots, \mathcal{F}_n \rangle$ is α-Lipschitz, with $\alpha = max\{ \alpha_1, \ldots, \alpha_n \}$.

(b) Each projection functor $\pi_k : \mathcal{C}_1 \times \cdots \mathcal{C}_n \to \mathcal{C}_k$ is nonexpansive, $k = 1, \ldots, n$.

(c) If $\mathcal{F}_1 \colon \mathcal{C}_1 \to \mathcal{C}_2$ is α_1-Lipschitz and $\mathcal{F}_2 \colon \mathcal{C}_0 \to \mathcal{C}_1$ is α_2-Lipschitz, then $\mathcal{F}_1 \circ \mathcal{F}_2$ is $\alpha_1 \cdot \alpha_2$-Lipschitz.

Proof Immediate by the definitions. $\square$

We conclude this section with the discussion of a few examples—all of which will return in Chapters 11 to 14.

Example 1 (Cf. the introduction of this section.) Consider the domain equation

$$\mathbb{P} \simeq \mathcal{P}_{co}(A \times id_{\frac{1}{2}}(\mathbb{P})) \,.$$

Let $\mathcal{F} = \lambda M.\mathcal{P}_{co}(A \times id_{\frac{1}{2}}(M))$ be the functor associated with this equation. We claim that $\mathcal{F}$ is $\frac{1}{2}$-contractive. A direct proof proceeds as follows: Assume $M_1 \triangleleft M_2$. Then

$$\delta(\mathcal{F}(M_1), \mathcal{F}(M_2))$$
$$= \delta(\mathcal{P}_{co}(A \times id_{\frac{1}{2}}(M_1)), \mathcal{P}_{co}(A \times id_{\frac{1}{2}}(M_2)))$$
$$\leq [\text{Theorem 10.11, part (f)}] \; \delta(A \times id_{\frac{1}{2}}(M_1), A \times id_{\frac{1}{2}}(M_2))$$
$$\leq [\delta(A, A) = 0] \; \delta(id_{\frac{1}{2}}(M_1), id_{\frac{1}{2}}(M_2))$$
$$= \tfrac{1}{2}\delta(M_1, M_2) \,.$$

A proof based on Theorem 10.13 runs as follows: We have $\mathcal{F} = \mathcal{P}_{co} \circ \times \circ \langle A, id_{\frac{1}{2}} \rangle$. This functor is α-Lipschitz, with $\alpha = 1 \cdot 1 \cdot max\{0, \frac{1}{2}\} = \frac{1}{2}$. As we saw already, for the space $\mathbb{1}$ such that $\mathbb{1} \triangleleft \mathcal{F}(\mathbb{1})$ we may take $(\{\emptyset\}, d)$, with d the discrete metric.

Example 2 Consider the domain equation

$$\mathbb{P} \simeq A \to \mathcal{P}_{co}(B \times id_{\frac{1}{2}}(\mathbb{P})) \,.$$

(For our present purposes, this is a nonessential variation on the equation used in Chapter 12.) A straightforward application of Theorems 10.11, 10.13 yields that the functor $\mathcal{F} = (A \to (\cdot)) \circ \mathcal{P}_{co} \circ \times \circ \langle B, id_{\frac{1}{2}} \rangle$ is $\frac{1}{2}$-contractive. For the space $\mathbb{1}$ we here may take $(A \to \{\emptyset\}, d_F)$.

Example 3 In Chapter 14, we shall work with the *system* of equations

$$\mathbb{P}_1 \simeq \mathcal{P}_{nco}(\mathbb{P}_2) \tag{10.18}$$
$$\mathbb{P}_2 \simeq A + (A \times id_{\frac{1}{2}}(\mathbb{P}_1)) + (A \times id_{\frac{1}{2}}(\mathbb{P}_2)).$$

Consider the functor $\lambda(M_1, M_2).\langle\mathcal{F}_1(M_1, M_2), \mathcal{F}_2(M_1, M_2)\rangle$ with $\mathcal{F}_1$ and $\mathcal{F}_2$ defined by

$$\mathcal{F}_1 = \lambda(M_1, M_2).\mathcal{P}_{nco}(M_2)$$
$$\mathcal{F}_2 = \lambda(M_1, M_2).A + (A \times id_{\frac{1}{2}}(M_1)) + (A \times id_{\frac{1}{2}}(M_2)),$$

or, alternatively, by

$$\mathcal{F}_1 = \mathcal{P}_{nco} \circ \pi_2$$
$$\mathcal{F}_2 = + \circ \langle A, + \circ \langle \times \circ \langle A, id_{\frac{1}{2}} \circ \pi_1 \rangle, \times \circ \langle A, id_{\frac{1}{2}} \circ \pi_2 \rangle\rangle\rangle.$$

In the form as given, $\langle\mathcal{F}_1, \mathcal{F}_2\rangle$ is not contractive (since it is not contractive in M_2). Putting $\mathcal{F}_3 = \lambda(M_1, M_2).\mathcal{F}_1(M_1, \mathcal{F}_2(M_1, M_2))$, it is not difficult to verify that $\langle\mathcal{F}_3, \mathcal{F}_2\rangle$ *is* $\frac{1}{2}$-contractive. Furthermore, we may take $\mathbb{1} \stackrel{df}{=} \langle\{\emptyset\}, A\rangle$ for the space satisfying $\mathbb{1} \triangleleft \langle\mathcal{F}_3, \mathcal{F}_2\rangle(\mathbb{1})$. By the general theory, $\langle\mathcal{F}_3, \mathcal{F}_2\rangle$ has a fixed point $\langle\mathbb{P}_3, \mathbb{P}_2\rangle$, and it is straightforward to see that this also satisfies (10.18).

10.3 Bisimulation

In this section we discuss the concept of *bisimulation*. This is a certain type of relation which may be introduced in two settings, viz. that of transition systems (cf. Definition 1.2), and that of (branching) domains as specified, e.g., in equation (10.14). Bisimulation is an important notion in the general theory of concurrency, where a variety of graph models for parallel computation is studied. Often, such models are considered modulo the equivalence relation of *bisimilarity* (cf. Definition 10.20). In our framework, bisimulation is in fact less prominent, for the simple reason that, according to Theorem 10.21, bisimilarity coincides with the equality relation. Accordingly, we shall not encounter the notions of bisimulation/bisimilarity at later stages in our work. The primary reason to include the present material here is our wish to establish a bridge with other semantic treatments of concurrency.

   We begin with the definition of bisimulation on a transition system.

Definition 10.14 Let $\mathcal{T} = (Conf, Obs, \rightarrow)$ be a transition system. A *bisimulation* on $\mathcal{T}$ is a relation $R \subseteq Conf \times Conf$ which satisfies the following property: For each $c_1, c_2 \in Conf$, if $c_1 R c_2$ then conditions (a) and (b) hold:

(a) For all a, c', if $c_1 \overset{a}{\to} c'$ then there exists c'' such that $c_2 \overset{a}{\to} c''$ and $c' R c''$.

(b) For all a, c'', if $c_2 \overset{a}{\to} c''$ then there exists c' such that $c_1 \overset{a}{\to} c'$ and $c' R c''$.

Examples Put $Conf = \{ c_0, c_1, c_2, c_3, c_4, c_0', c_1', c_3', c_4' \}$.

(1) If we have

$$\to \; = \{ (c_0, a, c_1), (c_0, a, c_3), (c_1, b, c_2), (c_3, b, c_4) \} \cup \{ (c_0', a, c_1'), (c_1', b, c_2') \},$$

then $R = \{ (c_0, c_0'), (c_1, c_1'), (c_3, c_1'), (c_2, c_2'), (c_4, c_2') \}$ is a bisimulation.

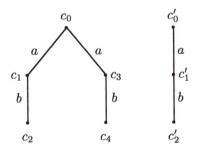

(2) On $\to \; = \{ (c_0, a, c_1), (c_1, b, c_2), (c_1, a, c_3) \} \cup \{ (c_0', a, c_1'), (c_0', a, c_3'), (c_1', b, c_2'), (c_3', a, c_4') \}$ there exists no bisimulation.

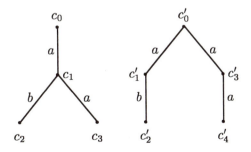

A key property of bisimulation can be expressed by exploiting the framework of domain equations characterizing *branching* domains as discussed in Section 10.2.

We shall in particular be concerned with the domain $\mathbb{P}$ solving (10.14)—which we repeat here for convenience:

$$\mathbb{P} \simeq \mathcal{P}_{cl}(A \times id_{\frac{1}{2}}(\mathbb{P})).$$

Now let $\mathcal{T}$ be an *image-finite* transition system, with $Obs = A$. In Chapter 5, we presented the general (higher-order) definition of the linear operational semantics $\mathcal{O}: Conf \rightarrow \mathcal{P}_{ncl}(A^\infty)$ associated with each such $\mathcal{T}$, viz. as the mapping characterized by the equation

$$\mathcal{O}(c) \;=\; \bigcup\{\,a \cdot \mathcal{O}(c') \mid c \xrightarrow{a} c'\,\} \cup \{\epsilon \mid c \not\rightarrow \}.$$

As important generalization of this equation—embodying a change from linear to branching domains—we now give (for $\mathbb{P}$ as in (10.14)):

Definition 10.15

(a) Let $(S \in)\, Sem = Conf \rightarrow \mathbb{P}$, and let $\Phi^*: Sem \rightarrow Sem$ be given by

$$\Phi^*(S)(c) \;=\; \{\,\langle a, S(c')\rangle \mid c \xrightarrow{a} c'\,\}.$$

(b) $\mathcal{O}^* = fix(\Phi^*)$.

This definition is justified in

Lemma 10.16 $\mathcal{O}^*$ *is well-defined, for $\mathcal{T}$ image-finite. That is*

(a) *For each S, c, the set $\Phi^*(S)(c)$ is closed, and*

(b) Φ^* *is contractive.*

Proof

(a) Let $(\langle a_n, S(c_n)\rangle)_n$ be a converging sequence in $\Phi^*(S)(c)$ with limit $\langle a, p\rangle$. We prove that $\langle a, p\rangle \in \Phi^*(S)(c)$. The sequences $(a_n)_n$ and $(S(c_n))_n$ converge to a and p, respectively. Since A has the discrete metric, almost all a_n equal a. Since $\mathcal{T}$ is image-finite, the set $\{\,c_n \mid c \xrightarrow{a} c_n\,\}$ is finite. Consequently, there exists a c' such that almost all c_n equal c'. Clearly, $p = S(c')$.

(b) Routine. $\square$

The branching semantics $\mathcal{O}^*$ enables us to phrase the announced key property of a bisimulation relation on an image-finite $\mathcal{T}$:

Theorem 10.17 *Let $\mathcal{T}$ be image-finite, and let $\mathcal{O}^*$ be as in Definition 10.15. If R is a bisimulation on $\mathcal{T}$, then we have*

$$c_1 R c_2 \quad \Rightarrow \quad \mathcal{O}^*(c_1) = \mathcal{O}^*(c_2).$$

Proof Another example of the '$\varepsilon \leq \varepsilon/2$' argument. We put

$$\varepsilon \;=\; sup\{\, d(\mathcal{O}^*(c_1), \mathcal{O}^*(c_2)) \mid c_1 R c_2 \,\} \qquad\qquad (10.19)$$

and we shall show that $\varepsilon \leq \varepsilon/2$. Take two elements c_1, c_2 with $c_1 R c_2$. We prove that $d(\mathcal{O}^*(c_1), \mathcal{O}^*(c_2)) \leq \varepsilon/2$. By the definition of the Hausdorff metric d_H, it is sufficient to show that, for each $\langle a, p \rangle \in \mathcal{O}^*(c_1)$, there exists $\langle a, p'' \rangle \in \mathcal{O}^*(c_2)$ such that $d(\langle a, p' \rangle, \langle a, p'' \rangle) \leq \varepsilon/2$, and a symmetric statement. Consider some $\langle a, p' \rangle$. By the definition of $\mathcal{O}^*$, there exists c' such that $p' = \mathcal{O}^*(c')$ and $c_1 \xrightarrow{a} c'$. Since $c_1 R c_2$, we infer that there exists c'' such that $c_2 \xrightarrow{a} c''$ and $c' R c''$. We now take $p'' = \mathcal{O}^*(c'')$. Clearly, $d(\langle a, p' \rangle, \langle a, p'' \rangle) = \frac{1}{2} d(p', p'') = \frac{1}{2} d(\mathcal{O}^*(c'), \mathcal{O}^*(c''))$. Since $c' R c''$ we have that $d(\mathcal{O}^*(c'), \mathcal{O}^*(c'')) \leq \varepsilon$, by (10.19). Altogether, we have shown that $d(\mathcal{O}^*(c_1), \mathcal{O}^*(c_2)) \leq \varepsilon/2$, and $\varepsilon \leq \varepsilon/2$, i.e., $\varepsilon = 0$ follows. $\square$

Remark In Exercise 10.7, a stronger version of Theorem 10.17 is given.

In the above, we have introduced the notion of a bisimulation R as a relationship on a transition system, and shown as main result that, for $\mathcal{T}$ image-finite, if $c_1 R c_2$ then c_1 and c_2 have the same branching (operational) semantics. It is also possible to consider bisimulations purely in a domain-theoretic setting, without referring to some transition system. This view on bisimulation may in fact be developed for any domain solving a domain equation of the kind as studied in Section 10.2. We shall not aim at a fully general treatment here: The notion of bisimulation will not reappear in our later considerations, and a representative example should suffice for our present purposes.

Let $\mathbb{P}$ be the domain solving the equation

$$\mathbb{P} \;\simeq\; A \to \mathcal{P}_{co}(B \times id_{\frac{1}{2}}(\mathbb{P})), \qquad\qquad (10.20)$$

where A, B are given (discrete) complete metric spaces. The definition of a bisimulation $R_{\mathbb{P}}$ on $\mathbb{P}$ will be given in terms of auxiliary relations $R_{\mathbb{P}'}$ on domains $\mathbb{P}'$. Let us put, for easier notation, $\mathbb{Q} = \mathcal{P}_{co}(\mathbb{T})$ and $\mathbb{T} = B \times id_{\frac{1}{2}}(\mathbb{P})$.

Definition 10.18

(a) For $p_1, p_2 \in \mathbb{P}$, we put $p_1 R_{\mathrm{P}} p_2$ if, for all a, $p_1(a) R_{\mathrm{Q}} p_2(a)$.

(b) For $q_1, q_2 \in \mathbb{Q}$, we put $q_1 R_{\mathrm{Q}} q_2$ in case

    (i) $\forall t' \in q_1 \exists t'' \in q_2 \, [\, t' R_{\mathrm{T}} t'' \,]$

    (ii) $\forall t'' \in q_2 \exists t' \in q_1 \, [\, t' R_{\mathrm{T}} t'' \,]$.

(c) For $\langle b_1, p' \rangle, \langle b_2, p'' \rangle \in \mathbb{T}$, we put $\langle b_1, p' \rangle R_{\mathrm{T}} \langle b_2, p'' \rangle$ in case

    (i) $b_1 = b_2$

    (ii) $p' R_{\mathrm{P}} p''$.

Note how the $id_{\frac{1}{2}}$ has no effect on the definition of R_{P}—though it remains essential for the next lemma.

As a modest variation on Theorem 10.17, we may now show

Lemma 10.19 *For $\mathbb{P}$ as in (10.20) and R_{P} as in Definition 10.18, we have*

$$r_1 R_{\mathrm{P}} p_2 \quad \Rightarrow \quad p_1 = p_2.$$

Proof A minor extension of the $\varepsilon \leq \varepsilon/2$-type of argument of Theorem 10.17, and left to the reader. $\qquad\qquad\square$

We are now close to the formulation of the main result of this section. We first introduce the relation of *bisimilarity*, to be denoted by '$\simeq$', on $\mathbb{P}$ (as in (10.20)).

Definition 10.20 $p_1 \simeq p_2$ if, for some bisimulation R_{P}, $p_1 R_{\mathrm{P}} p_2$.

An alternative definition would be to put

$$\simeq \;=\; \bigcup \{\, R_{\mathrm{P}} \mid R_{\mathrm{P}} \text{ is a bisimulation on } \mathbb{P} \,\}.$$

The following results are now immediate from the above:

Theorem 10.21

(a) '$\simeq$' is the largest bisimulation on $\mathbb{P}$.

(b) '$\simeq$' equals the identity relation on $\mathbb{P}$.

Proof

(a) It is sufficient to note that '$\simeq$' is itself a bisimulation.

(b) From Definition 10.18 it is immediate that '=' is a bisimulation, hence $= \subseteq \simeq$. By Lemma 10.19, we have that $R_\mathrm{P} \subseteq =$, for each bisimulation R_P. Hence, $\simeq \subseteq =$, and the result follows. $\square$

   Theorem 10.21 tells us that we may ignore bisimilarity in a setting where the domains are complete metric spaces as discussed in Section 10.2. The identification of bisimilar processes which is often to be made explicitly in other theories of concurrency is here handled as it were automatically.

10.4   Exercises

Exercise 10.1 Let $M_1 \hookrightarrow M_2$ denote that M_1 may be isometrically embedded into M_2. Use the spaces $M_1 = \{\,0\,\} \cup [1, \infty)$, $M_2 = [1, \infty)$—equipped with the usual metric on the reals—to show that we may have $M_1 \hookrightarrow M_2$ (by $\lambda x.x + 1$) and $M_2 \hookrightarrow M_1$ (obvious), but $M_1 \not\simeq M_2$.

Exercise 10.2 Let A, B be (complete) metric spaces, and let $\mathcal{F} \colon CMS \to CMS$ be given by (omitting the d-arguments)

$$\mathcal{F}(M) \;\; = \;\; (M \overset{1}{\to} A) \overset{1}{\to} B.$$

Prove that M is monotonic.

Exercise 10.3 Let A be a given set, let (A^∞, d_B) be as usual (d_B the Baire-metric), and let (M, d) be a given complete metric space. Let $(A \times id_{\frac{1}{2}}(M), \bar{d})$ denote the space

$$\{\,(a, m) \mid a \in A, m \in M\,\},$$

with $\bar{d}$ is defined by

$$\bar{d}((a_1, m_1), (a_2, m_2)) \;\; = \;\; \begin{cases} 1 & \text{if } a_1 \neq a_2 \\ \tfrac{1}{2} d(m_1, m_2) & \text{if } a_1 = a_2. \end{cases}$$

Let $\{\epsilon\}$ be the (discrete) space with the empty word (from A^∞) as only element. Prove the following isometry (in which the metrics are suppressed for easier notation):

$$\{\epsilon\} + (A \times id_{\frac{1}{2}}(A^\infty)) \;\; \simeq \;\; A^\infty.$$

Exercise 10.4 Let $\mathbb{P}$ be the domain from Example 1 (following Theorem 10.13). Let $\mathbb{P}_0 = \emptyset$, $\mathbb{P}_{n+1} = \mathcal{P}_f(A \times \mathbb{P}_n)$, where $\mathcal{P}_f(\cdot)$ denotes the collection of all *finite* subsets of $(\cdot)$. Let $\mathbb{P}_\omega = \bigcup_n \mathbb{P}_n$, and let $\bar{\mathbb{P}}_\omega$ denote the completion of $\mathbb{P}_\omega$. Prove that

$$\bar{\mathbb{P}}_\omega \simeq \mathbb{P}.$$

Exercise 10.5

(a) Let $\mathcal{T} = (\{\, c, c_0, c_1, \dots \,\}, \{a, b\}, \rightarrow)$, where '$\rightarrow$' is given by

$$c \xrightarrow{a} c \quad c_n \xrightarrow{a} c_n \quad \text{for } n = 0, 1, \dots$$
$$c \xrightarrow{b} c \quad c_n \xrightarrow{b} c_n \quad \text{for } n = 0, 1, \dots$$

Prove that $c \simeq c_n$ (c is bisimilar with c_n), for each $n = 0, 1, \dots$.

(b) Let us view Figures 10.6a,b in a natural way as a transition system (uniting the sets of transitions induced by the two trees), and let c_0, c_1 be configurations corresponding to the two roots. Is it true that $c_0 \simeq c_1$?

Exercise 10.6 Supply the details of the proof of Lemma 10.19.

Exercise 10.7 Let, for $\mathcal{T}$ a transition system, '$\simeq$' on $\mathcal{T}$ be defined similar to Definition 10.20. Prove that, for $\mathcal{T}$ image-finite, we have, for all $c_1, c_2 \in Conf$,

$$c_1 \simeq c_2 \quad \Longleftrightarrow \quad \mathcal{O}^*(c_1) = \mathcal{O}^*(c_2).$$

(Hint: '$\Rightarrow$" follows from Theorem 10.17. For '$\Leftarrow$', put $c'Rc''$ iff $\mathcal{O}^*(c') = \mathcal{O}^*(c'')$, and show that R is a bisimulation on $\mathcal{T}$.)

10.5   Bibliographical notes

The development of techniques for solving domain equations has been a central theme in denotational semantics from the beginning. Seminal references are [Sco76] and [Plo76]; since [SP82], the category-theoretic approach has become a standard tool. Our presentation in this chapter generalizes that of [BZ82], in that it provides a systematic account of the techniques solving equation (10.5) for $\mathcal{F}$ monotonic, using solely metric means. (The present form of this account has not been published before.) In Appendix C, the principles will be outlined of the method which combines metric with category-theoretic techniques for solving (10.5) for an (arbitrary, i.e., not necessarily monotonic) contractive functor $\mathcal{F}$. (References will follow there.)

Besides the branching domains as studied in Chapter 10, essentially solving equations of the form

$$\mathbb{P} \simeq \mathcal{P}_{co}(A \times id_{\frac{1}{2}}(\mathbb{P})) \tag{10.21}$$

$$\mathbb{P} \simeq \mathcal{P}_{cl}(A \times id_{\frac{1}{2}}(\mathbb{P})) \tag{10.22}$$

a third kind of branching domains has been studied solving (10.5) for an (arbitrary, i.e., not necessarily in [Bre93, Bre94b], viz. those solving

$$\mathbb{P} \simeq A \xrightarrow{1} \mathcal{P}_{co}(id_{\frac{1}{2}}(P)). \tag{10.23}$$

Under certain conditions (on the cardinality of A), these domains are located properly between those of the first two kinds. In [Bre94b], it is argued that they have advantages in cases where the use of (10.21) is not feasible (for phenomena inducing noncompactness) and that of (10.22) is problematic (in view of the proper definition of the semantic operators). For an example illustrating this (due to Jeroen Warmerdam), cf. Exercise 11.6.

The notion of bisimulation was proposed by Park ([Par81], putting an earlier concept due to Milner ([Mil80]) in a better perspective (cf. [Mil94]). The result that bisimilarity collapses to identity for domains as studied in Chapter 10 is due to [GR89]. Though not so much visible in our framework, bisimulation is a key concept in concurrency semantics. Only a few references must suffice here: It plays a key role in comparative semantics (e.g., [Gla90a, Gla90b] and in foundational studies (e.g., [BK89]) More recently, bisimulation has been studied from domain-theoretic or categorical perspectives in papers such as [AM89, Abr91, Rut92, RT93, RT94].

11 Branching Domains at Work

In semantic applications, a central role is played by domain equations of the form

$$\mathbb{P} \simeq \mathcal{P}_{co}(A \times id_{\frac{1}{2}}(\mathbb{P})), \tag{11.1}$$

or variations thereof. As we saw in Section 10.2, the processes p residing in such a $\mathbb{P}$ have a tree-like structure, and we shall use the generic name "branching domain" for $\mathbb{P}$ solving (11.1) (or some generalization of it). For all language notions studied in Part III, we shall base the denotational semantics on branching domains. For the operational semantics, we will stick to the linear models. Consequently, in all cases we shall have to aim for a relationship between $\mathcal{O}$ and $\mathcal{D}$ which is not a simple equivalence (due to the difference in their codomains). Abstraction mappings reminiscent of the one used in Chapter 7 will have to be employed.

Though the structure of the elements of the branching domains is essentially different from those of the linear ones, the design of the denotational semantics and, in particular, of the semantic operators, will turn out to bear a close resemblance to the linear framework as developed in Part I and applied in Part II. In fact, we are here rewarded for the introduction of the maybe somewhat heavy metric machinery, in that the semantic analysis of more advanced language notions may now be seen, to a large extent, as minor variations on the earlier models.

In Section 11.1 we introduce what is probably the prime language notion responsible for the interest in branching domains, viz. that of *deadlock*. It is first studied—somewhat in isolation—in a simple setting, viz. of the language $\mathcal{L}_\delta$ which is a small extension of $\mathcal{L}_{cf}$. Next, in Section 11.2 we investigate it together with *synchronization* (in the language $\mathcal{L}_{syn}$). By this we refer to a refinement of (uniform) parallelism. The interleaving model as developed in Chapter 4 is extended in that actions are now divided into internal actions and synchronization actions. The latter are a means to establish synchronization between different components in a parallel execution. The operational intuition for this notion is convincingly expressed in a new rule of the transition system $\mathcal{T}_{syn}$. In the denotational model, we will then define the corresponding extension of the semantic parallel composition operator. For both $\mathcal{L}_\delta$ and $\mathcal{L}_{syn}$, we shall link $\mathcal{O}$ and $\mathcal{D}$ through an intermediate $\mathcal{O}^*$, hybrid in the sense that it is based on the transition system concerned ($\mathcal{T}_\delta$ or $\mathcal{T}_{syn}$), but it delivers results in the *denotational codomain*.

11.1 Deadlock—a branching domain for $\mathcal{D}$

The first language notion illustrating the use of domains specified as solutions of domain equations, as described in Chapter 10, is that of *deadlock*. We shall investigate it in the setting of a modest extension of $\mathcal{L}_{cf}$ (as in Section 2.2): We introduce a new elementary action stop (with stop $\notin Act$), and define $\mathcal{L}_\delta$ as a language with the same operators as $\mathcal{L}_{cf}$ (but now over the extended action set). In the next section (Section 11.2) we shall discuss a somewhat more realistic situation, where deadlock may be caused by failing attempts at synchronization.[1] In the *semantics* for $\mathcal{L}_\delta$, we shall use the symbol δ to denote deadlock.[2]

Two properties are characteristic for the concept of deadlock. In stating them, we use formulae of the form $s_1 = s_2$, meaning that s_1 and s_2 are semantically equal, i.e., with respect to the $\mathcal{O}$ and $\mathcal{D}$ still to be defined we have $\mathcal{O}(s_1) = \mathcal{O}(s_2)$, or $\mathcal{D}(s_1) = \mathcal{D}(s_2)$. The properties are

(1) Once a program has arrived in a situation of deadlock, after that nothing further can happen. Accordingly, we expect that, for any s,

stop;s = stop.

(2) In case a program has a choice between deadlock and a "normal" statement s, it will always choose for the alternative s. Thus, we expect that, for each s,

stop $+ s = s$.

Deadlock induces "abnormal" termination, to be distinguished from "normal" termination. For the latter, no explicit construct is included in $\mathcal{L}_\delta$ (or in any of the other languages studied in our book). Note, however, that in all transition systems used so far, we use the *resumption* E to model normal termination. The characteristic feature distinguishing normal termination from deadlock is that, after a normally terminating s, a sequentially succeeding s' (following s in a composition $s;s'$) will be executed normally, whereas after a deadlocking statement, say of the form s;stop, a sequentially succeeding s' (in a composition s;stop;s') will have no effect.

An important consequence of having the notion of deadlock present in a language is that it is no longer natural that the left-distributivity law

$s;(s_1 + s_2) = (s;s_1) + (s;s_2)$

---

[1] An earlier version of deadlock was already encountered in Section 3.1 (on $\mathcal{L}_{gc}$) in a situation where all guards of an if-fi statement have the value *ff*.

[2] Note that this is unusual in that, normally, we do not distinguish between syntactic action symbols and their semantic counterparts. One further exception to this rule was encountered in Chapter 9.1, where we used fail versus ∂.

is valid. Consider, for example, the two statements $s' \equiv a;(b + \mathsf{stop})$ and $s'' \equiv (a;b) + (a;\mathsf{stop})$. The first statement is executed by first performing an a-step and after that choosing between b and stop. By property (2), it will then choose for b, and altogether we obtain ab as (only) possible behavior, i.e. $\mathcal{O}(s') = \{ab\}$. The second statement first chooses between $a;b$ and $a;\mathsf{stop}$. At the moment of choice, it is not yet observable that the second alternative will deadlock, so both behaviors ab (of $a;b$) and $a\delta$ (of $a;\mathsf{stop}$) should be delivered, resulting in $\mathcal{O}(s'') = \{ab, a\delta\}$. We conclude that s' and s'' have different meanings. Our aim in the present section is to make this precise, and to design $\mathcal{O}$ and $\mathcal{D}$ for $\mathcal{L}_\delta$. Note that a linear model for $\mathcal{D}$ will not work, at least not if we assume the familiar semantic operators. The distributive laws for ';' and '+', together with the compositional definition of $\mathcal{D}$, would yield that, contrary to what we just saw,

$\mathcal{D}(s;(s_1 + s_2))$

$= [\mathcal{D} \text{ compositional}] \; \mathcal{D}(s);\mathcal{D}(s_1 + s_2)$

$= [\text{idem}] \; \mathcal{D}(s);(\mathcal{D}(s_1) + \mathcal{D}(s_2))$

$= [\text{distributivity of ';' over '+'}] \; (\mathcal{D}(s);\mathcal{D}(s_1)) + (\mathcal{D}(s);\mathcal{D}(s_2))$

$= \ldots$

$= \mathcal{D}((s;s_1) + (s;s_2)).$

11.1.1 Syntax and operational semantics

Let $(a \in) Act$ and $(x \in) PVar$ be as usual, and let stop be a new symbol. We emphasize that stop is not one of the possible values for the variable a ranging over Act.

Definition 11.1

(a) $s(\in Stat) ::= a \mid \mathsf{stop} \mid x \mid (s;s) \mid (s + s)$

(b) $g(\in GStat) ::= a \mid \mathsf{stop} \mid (g;s) \mid (g + g)$

(c) $(d \in) Decl = PVar \rightarrow GStat$

(d) $(\pi \in) \mathcal{L}_\delta = Decl \times Stat.$

Declarations D will be suppressed in the usual way.

Examples $a;(\mathsf{stop} + b), (a;\mathsf{stop}) + (a;b), (x \Leftarrow (a;x) + \mathsf{stop} \mid x;b).$

The syntax for $\mathcal{L}_\delta$ is as explained above. Note that stop, though not in Act, does guard occurrences of procedure variables. Resumptions are simple (as in Section 2.2.1):

Definition 11.2 $r(\in Res) ::= \mathrm{E} \mid s.$

Transitions are of the form $r \xrightarrow{a} r'$. (Note that there are no transitions $r \xrightarrow{\delta} r'$.) The transition system $\mathcal{T}_\delta$ is given in

Definition 11.3 $\mathcal{T}_\delta = \mathcal{T}_{cf}.$

Thus, $\mathcal{T}_\delta$ simply coincides with $\mathcal{T}_{cf}$ (from Definition 2.23). Implicitly, this means that no transitions are defined for stop or for any stop;s. Also, as a consequence of the (Choice) rule—now referring to $\mathcal{L}_\delta$—we infer that, e.g., the only possible transition for $a + \mathsf{stop}$ is

$$a + \mathsf{stop} \xrightarrow{a} \mathrm{E}.$$

Let δ be a symbol not in the set (of semantic actions) Act. (Note that, by our standard convention, this set coincides with the set of syntactic actions, for which we assumed that stop does not belong to it.) Let

$$\mathbb{Q}_O = Act^* \cup Act^\omega \cup Act^* \cdot \{\delta\}$$
$$\mathbb{P}_O = \mathcal{P}_{nco}(\mathbb{Q}_O).$$

We are almost ready for the definition of $\mathcal{O}$ for $\mathcal{L}_\delta$. One final point: Just as in the case of $\mathcal{L}_{gc}$ (Section 3.1) we now have a transition system which may yield no transitions for some programs. Recalling that the presence of the empty set may result in the absence of contractiveness (cf. the discussion following Theorem 2.3), we have to take the usual measures to ensure that this does not cause problems.

Definition 11.4

(a) We say that s *blocks* if there are no a, r such that $s \xrightarrow{a} r$.

(b) Let $(S \in) Sem_O = Res \to \mathbb{P}_O$, and let $\Phi{:}Sem_O \to Sem_O$ be defined as follows: $\Phi(S)(\mathrm{E}) = \{\epsilon\}$, and

$$\Phi(S)(s) \;=\; \left\{ \begin{array}{ll} \{\delta\} & \text{if } s \text{ blocks} \\ \bigcup\{\, a \cdot S(r) \mid s \xrightarrow{a} r \,\} & \text{otherwise.} \end{array} \right.$$

(c) $\mathcal{O} = \mathrm{fix}(\Phi)$, $\mathcal{O}[\![s]\!] = \mathcal{O}(s)$.

Well-definedness of Φ includes the fact that $\Phi(S)(r) \neq \emptyset$, for each r. This would not be satisfied if the special clause (delivering $\{\delta\}$ in case of blocking) had not been added. The $\frac{1}{2}$-contractiveness of Φ (in S), and the well-definedness of $\mathcal{O}$ are then routine.

Examples

$\mathcal{O}[\![a;(\text{stop} + b)]\!] = \{ab\}$
$\mathcal{O}[\![(a;\text{stop}) + (a;b)]\!] = \{a\delta, ab\}$
$\mathcal{O}[\![x \Leftarrow (a;x) + \text{stop} \mid x;b]\!] = \{a^\omega\}$.

11.1.2 Denotational semantics, relating $\mathcal{O}$ and $\mathcal{D}$

In the denotational semantics for $\mathcal{L}_\delta$, we will employ for the first time a domain as solution of a domain equation.

Definition 11.5 Let $(p \in) \mathbb{P}_D$ be the complete metric space which is the (unique) solution of the equation

$$\mathbb{P}_D \simeq \{p_\epsilon\} + \mathcal{P}_{co}(Act \times id_{\frac{1}{2}}(\mathbb{P}_D)) \tag{11.2}$$

In this equation $\{p_\epsilon\}$ and Act are given (discrete, ultrametric) spaces, and the operators $+$, $\times$, $\mathcal{P}_{co}(\cdot)$ and $id_{\frac{1}{2}}$ are as in the general theory presented in Chapter 10. According to (11.2), a process p in $\mathbb{P}_D$ is either

- the nil-process p_ϵ, or
- a compact (possibly empty) set of pairs $\langle a_1, p_1 \rangle, \ldots, \langle a_i, p_i \rangle, \ldots$, with $a_i \in Act$ and each p_i a process.

Examples

(1) Simple examples of finite processes in $\mathbb{P}_D$ are $\{\langle a, \{\langle a_1, p_\epsilon \rangle, \langle a_2, p_\epsilon \rangle \} \rangle \}$, $\{\langle a, \{\langle a_1, p_\epsilon \rangle \} \rangle, \langle a, \{\langle a_2, p_\epsilon \rangle \} \rangle \}$, $\emptyset$ or $\{\langle a, \{\langle b, p_\epsilon \rangle \} \rangle, \langle a, \emptyset \rangle \}$ which can be represented as

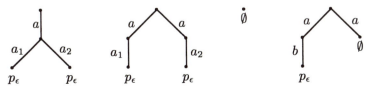

(2) Infinite processes are (small variations on) the examples given in Section 10.2, the process p satisfying $p = \{ \langle a, p \rangle, \langle b, p \rangle \}$, or the process p satisfying

$$p = \{ \langle a, q \rangle \}$$
$$q = \{ \langle a, q \rangle, \langle b, p \rangle \}$$

Note that $\mathbb{P}_D$ does not mention δ. In the denotational model, the process $\emptyset$ models deadlock (or abnormal termination), and p_ϵ expresses normal termination. In a moment we shall define the semantic operators on $\mathbb{P}_D$. It will then become clear that the properties mentioned in the introduction to this section are indeed satisfied using $\emptyset$ to model deadlock. More specifically, it will be the case that $\emptyset; p = \emptyset$, and $\emptyset + p = p$.

The definition of the semantic operators is structured in a way which is quite analogous to the earlier definitions in Part I, II. In fact, this will be a recurring phenomenon in part III. Here we enjoy the benefits of our earlier efforts which may have looked somewhat excessively formal in their systematic use of higher-order definitions.

Definition 11.6 Let $(\phi \in) Op = \mathbb{P}_D \times \mathbb{P}_D \xrightarrow{1} \mathbb{P}_D$.

(a) The operator $\Omega_; : Op \to Op$ is defined by putting

$$\Omega_;(\phi)(p_\epsilon, p) = p$$
$$\Omega_;(\phi)(p_1, p_2) = \{ \langle a, \phi(p', p_2) \rangle \mid \langle a, p' \rangle \in p_1 \}, \quad p_1 \neq p_\epsilon$$

(b) $; = \text{fix}(\Omega_;)$

(c) $p_\epsilon + p = p + p_\epsilon = p$, and, for $p_1, p_2 \neq p_\epsilon$, $p_1 + p_2 = p_1 \cup p_2$, with '$\cup$' the set-theoretic union of (the sets) p_1, p_2.

The pattern in the definition of ';' is the customary one, but for one important difference: it is not necessary here to give a two-layer definition. (Recall that, in Section 2.2, we defined ';' on $\mathbb{P}_D \times \mathbb{P}_D$ in terms of the earlier definition of ';' on $\mathbb{Q}_D \times \mathbb{Q}_D$.) Pictorially, $p_1; p_2$ may be viewed as the result of "grafting" p_2 onto all leaves of (the tree associated with) p_1 which are equal to p_ϵ. Branches in the tree for p_1, which end in $\emptyset$, or infinite branches, do not contribute to the result. These facts are an immediate consequence of the definition of ';', which has as corollary that $p_\epsilon; p = p$ and, for $p_1 \neq p_\epsilon$, $p_1; p_2 = \{ \langle a, p'; p_2 \rangle \mid \langle a, p' \rangle \in p_1 \}$.

Examples

(1) $\{\langle a, \{\langle b, p_\epsilon\rangle, \langle b, \emptyset\rangle\}\rangle\};\{\langle c, p_\epsilon\rangle\} = \{\langle a, \{\langle b, \{\langle c, p_\epsilon\rangle\}\rangle, \langle b, \emptyset\rangle\}\rangle\}$.

(2) Let p be the process satisfying $p = \{\langle a, p\rangle\}$, hence $p = \{\langle a, \{\langle a, \ldots\rangle\}\rangle\}$. Then we have $p;\{\langle b, p_\epsilon\rangle\} = p$.

(3) Let p be given by $p = \{\langle a, p_\epsilon\rangle, \langle b, p\rangle\}$, thus

$$p = \{\langle a, p_\epsilon\rangle, \langle b, \{\langle a, p_\epsilon\rangle, \langle b, \{\ldots\}\rangle\}\rangle\}.$$

Then we have $p;\{\langle c, p_\epsilon\rangle\} = p'$ with p' the unique process satisfying $p' = \{\langle a, \{\langle c, p_\epsilon\rangle, \{\langle b, p'\rangle\}\}\rangle\}$.

Lemma 11.7

(a) The operators ';' and '+' are well-defined. In particular $p_1;p_2$ is a compact set for each p_1, p_2.

(b) ';' and '+' are nonexpansive in both arguments. Also, for $p \neq p_\epsilon$, $d(p;p_1, p;p_2) \leq \frac{1}{2}d(p_1, p_2)$.

Proof

(a) Let $p_1, p_2, \phi, \Omega_;$ be as above. We show that $\Omega_;(\phi)(p_1, p_2)$ is a compact set. Let $\langle a, p'\rangle \in p_1$. Then $\phi(p', p_2) \overset{df}{=} \bar{p}$ is a compact set residing in $\mathbb{P}_D$ (by the continuity of ϕ and Lemma 2.13c), and $\langle a, \bar{p}\rangle \in Act \times \mathbb{P}_D$. Putting $\psi = \lambda\langle a, p\rangle.\langle a, \bar{p}\rangle$, we have that ψ is (nonexpansive, hence) continuous, and $\Omega_;(\phi)(p_1, p_2) = \psi(p_1)$ is a compact (again by Lemma 2.13c).

(b) We sketch the standard argument for ';'. Let, for $\phi \in Op$, $\Gamma(\phi)$ denote the property that ϕ is nonexpansive in both arguments, and that, for $p \neq p_\epsilon$, $d(\phi(p, p_1), \phi(p, p_2)) \leq \frac{1}{2}d(p_1, p_2)$. Let $V = \{\phi \mid \Gamma(\phi)\}$. We may then show

(i) V is nonempty (e.g., $\lambda(p_1, p_2).p_1 \in V$);

(ii) V is closed;

(iii) $\Omega_;(V) \subseteq V$.

From (i) to (iii) it is immediate that $; = lim_n \Omega_;^n(\lambda(p_1, p_2).p_1) \in V$. $\qquad\square$

The denotational semantics $\mathcal{D}$ for $\mathcal{L}_\delta$ is straightforward, now that the necessary semantic operators are available.

Definition 11.8

(a) $\mathcal{D}: \mathcal{L}_\delta \to \mathbb{P}_D$ is the unique function satisfying

$$
\begin{aligned}
\mathcal{D}(a) &= \{\langle a, p_\epsilon \rangle\} \\
\mathcal{D}(\text{stop}) &= \emptyset \\
\mathcal{D}(x) &= \mathcal{D}(D(x)) \\
\mathcal{D}(s_1; s_2) &= \mathcal{D}(s_1); \mathcal{D}(s_2) \\
\mathcal{D}(s_1 + s_2) &= \mathcal{D}(s_1) + \mathcal{D}(s_2),
\end{aligned}
$$

(b) $\mathcal{D}[\![s]\!] = \mathcal{D}(s)$.

Examples

(1) $\mathcal{D}[\![D|a;(\text{stop} + b)]\!] = \{\langle a, \{\langle b, p_\epsilon \rangle\}\rangle\}$
    $\mathcal{D}[\![D|(a;\text{stop}) + (a;b)]\!] = \{\langle a, \emptyset \rangle, \langle a, \{\langle b, p_\epsilon \rangle\}\rangle\}$

(2) $\mathcal{D}[\![x \Leftarrow (a;x) + \text{stop} \mid x;b]\!] = \{\langle a, \{\langle a, \ldots\rangle\}\rangle\}$. This may be seen as follows: Put $p_0 = p_\epsilon$, $p_{i+1} = \{\langle a, p_i \rangle\} + \emptyset$. Then $\mathcal{D}[\![x \Leftarrow (a;x) + \text{stop} \mid x;b]\!] = (lim_i\, p_i); \{\langle b, p_\epsilon \rangle\} = lim_i\, p_i = \{\langle a, \{\langle a, \ldots\rangle\}\rangle\}$.

Well-definedness of $\mathcal{D}$ may be shown in the usual way (cf. Lemma 2.38).

We next address the question as to how $\mathcal{O}$ and $\mathcal{D}$ are related. The codomains for $\mathcal{O}$ and $\mathcal{D}$ being different, we cannot expect that $\mathcal{O}[\![\pi]\!] = \mathcal{D}[\![\pi]\!]$ on $\mathcal{L}_\delta$. $\mathcal{D}[\![\pi]\!]$ exhibits a branching structure; hence, it contains more information than the linear outcome $\mathcal{O}[\![\pi]\!]$. We shall, similarly to what we did in Chapter 7, define an abstraction function $abs: \mathbb{P}_D \to \mathbb{P}_O$, and aim for a result of the form $\mathcal{O}[\![\pi]\!] = (abs \circ \mathcal{D})[\![\pi]\!]$. In proving this, we use an intermediate semantics $\mathcal{O}^*$ which is based on $\mathcal{T}_\delta$ but yields results in the denotational domain $\mathbb{P}_D$.

Definition 11.9 Let $(S \in) Sem_{O^*} = Res \to \mathbb{P}_D$.

(a) The mapping $\Phi^*: Sem_{O^*} \to Sem_{O^*}$ is given by $\Phi^*(S)(\mathrm{E}) = p_\epsilon$, and

$$\Phi^*(S)(s) = \{\, \langle a, S(r)\rangle \mid s \xrightarrow{a} r \,\}.$$

(b) $\mathcal{O}^* = fix(\Phi^*)$.

Examples $\mathcal{O}^*(\text{stop}) = \emptyset$,
$\mathcal{O}^*((a;\text{stop}) + (a;b)) = \{ \langle a, \emptyset \rangle, \langle a, \{\langle b, p_\epsilon \rangle\} \rangle \}$.

Well-definedness of (Φ^* and) $\mathcal{O}^*$ once more relies on the property that $\mathcal{T}_\delta$ is finitely branching, implying that $\Phi^*(S)(r)$ is compact for each $S \in \textit{Sem}_{\mathcal{O}^*}$ and $r \in \textit{Res}$. Contractiveness of Φ^* is a variation on standard results.

We see that $\mathcal{O}^*(r)$ yields a branching process, determined by collecting the successive transitions prescribed by $\mathcal{T}_\delta$ for r. This should be contrasted with the linear result (set of sequences) obtained by applying $\mathcal{O}$ to r. Remarkably, though $\mathcal{O}^*(r)$ is quite different in structure from $\mathcal{O}(r)$, this outcome is achieved by imposing a seemingly small variation in the main clause for Φ^*—compared with that for Φ—and with no changes in $\mathcal{T}_\delta$.

It is not difficult to show that $\mathcal{O}^*$, the branching operational semantics, and $\mathcal{E}$, the (branching) denotational semantics, coincide for each r. First, we define $\mathcal{E}$ in the usual way.

Definition 11.10 $\mathcal{E}\colon \textit{Res} \to \mathbb{P}_D$ is given by

$$
\begin{aligned}
\mathcal{E}(\mathrm{E}) &= p_\epsilon \\
\mathcal{E}(s) &= \mathcal{D}(s).
\end{aligned}
$$

Lemma 11.11 $\mathcal{O}^* = \mathcal{E}$.

Proof We show that $\Phi^*(\mathcal{E})(r) = \mathcal{E}(r)$, by induction on $wgt(r)$ (as in Definition 2.25, with $wgt(\text{stop}) = 1$ added). The proof is a minor variant on earlier arguments, in that it has to be adapted to the branching setting. One subcase.

$$
\begin{aligned}
[s_1;s_2] \quad & \Phi^*(\mathcal{E})(s_1;s_2) \\
={} & \{ \langle a, \mathcal{E}(r) \rangle \mid s_1;s_2 \xrightarrow{a} r \} \\
={} & \{ \langle a, \mathcal{E}(r';s_2) \rangle \mid s_1 \xrightarrow{a} r' \} \\
={} & \{ \langle a, \mathcal{E}(r');\mathcal{E}(s_2) \rangle \mid s_1 \xrightarrow{a} r' \} \\
={} & [\text{def. ';'}] \; \{ \langle a, \mathcal{E}(r') \rangle \mid s_1 \xrightarrow{a} r' \};\mathcal{E}(s_2) \\
={} & \Phi^*(\mathcal{E})(s_1);\mathcal{E}(s_2) \\
={} & [\text{ind. hyp.}] \; \mathcal{E}(s_1);\mathcal{E}(s_2) \\
={} & \mathcal{E}(s_1;s_2). \qquad \qquad \qquad \qquad \qquad \qquad \square
\end{aligned}
$$

We next introduce the announced abstraction mapping. Some comments explaining the definition will follow.

Definition 11.12

(a) Let $(\phi \in) Op = \mathbb{P}_D \xrightarrow{1} \mathbb{P}_O$. We define $\Omega_{abs}:Op \to Op$ by putting

$$\begin{aligned}
\Omega_{abs}(\phi)(p_\epsilon) &= \{\epsilon\} \\
\Omega_{abs}(\phi)(\emptyset) &= \{\delta\},
\end{aligned}$$

and, for $p \neq p_\epsilon, \emptyset$,

$$\Omega_{abs}(\phi)(p) = \bigcup\{ a \cdot \phi(p') \mid \langle a, p' \rangle \in p \}.$$

(b) $abs = fix(\Omega_{abs})$.

Examples $abs(\mathcal{D}[\![a;(\mathsf{stop} + b)]\!]) = abs(\{\langle a, \{\langle b, p_\epsilon \rangle\}\rangle\}) = \{ ab \}$,
$abs(\mathcal{D}[\![(a;\mathsf{stop}) + (a;b)]\!]) = abs(\{\langle a, \emptyset \rangle, \langle a, \{\langle b, p_\epsilon \rangle\}\rangle\}) = \{ a\delta, ab \}$,
$abs(\mathcal{D}[\![x \Leftarrow (a;x) + \mathsf{stop} \mid x;b]\!]) = abs(\{\langle a, \{\langle a, \ldots \rangle\}\rangle\}) = \{a^\omega\}$.

For the proof of the well-definedness of $abs(p)$, the essential step is the fact that $\Omega_{abs}(\phi)(p)$ is compact. Now this is the case since

- p' and, hence, $a \cdot \phi(p')$ are compact by assumption
- the right-hand side of the clause for $\Omega_{abs}(\phi)(p)$ yields the union of a compact collection of compact sets and is hence compact by Michael's theorem (Theorem 2.15).

The operator of abstraction combines two aspects. For its description we introduce the notion of *subprocess* of a process p. A subprocess of p is defined as follows

- p is subprocess of itself
- (for $p \neq p_\epsilon$) for each $\langle a, p' \rangle \in p$, each subprocess of p' is a subprocess of p.

This terminology enables us to say that the operator of abstraction

- collapses the branching structure of p, delivering instead the set of all its paths
- replaces all subprocesses of p which are equal to $\emptyset$ by $\{\delta\}$: the denotational element modeling deadlock is replaced by its operational counterpart.

The key property of abs is stated in

Lemma 11.13 $\mathcal{O} = abs \circ \mathcal{O}^*$.

Proof We show that $\Phi(abs \circ \mathcal{O}^*) = abs \circ \mathcal{O}^*$. The claim is clear in the argument E. Now consider an argument s. We have that s either blocks, in which case

$$\Phi(abs \circ \mathcal{O}^*)(s) = \{\delta\} = abs(\emptyset) = abs(\mathcal{O}^*(s)) = (abs \circ \mathcal{O}^*)(s)$$

or $\mathcal{O}^*(s) = \{\ \langle a, \mathcal{O}^*(r)\rangle \mid s \xrightarrow{a} r\ \}$. In that case,

$(abs \circ \mathcal{O}^*)(s)$

$= abs(\{\ \langle a, \mathcal{O}^*(r)\rangle \mid s \xrightarrow{a} r\ \}$

$= [\text{def. } abs]\ \bigcup\{\ a \cdot (abs \circ \mathcal{O}^*)(r) \mid s \xrightarrow{a} r\ \}$,

i.e., $(abs \circ \mathcal{O}^*)(s) = \Phi(abs \circ \mathcal{O}^*)(s)$. In all cases, we have verified that $abs \circ \mathcal{O}^*$ is a fixed point of Φ, whence the desired result $\mathcal{O} = abs \circ \mathcal{O}^*$. $\qquad\square$

Combining Lemmas 11.11 and 11.13, we finally obtain

Theorem 11.14 $\mathcal{O}[\![\pi]\!] = (abs \circ \mathcal{D})[\![\pi]\!]$, *for all* $\pi \in \mathcal{L}_\delta$.

Proof Clear. $\qquad\square$

Remark By introducing extra (branching) information in the codomain of $\mathcal{D}$, we have been able to give a compositional definition for $\mathcal{D}$, and to obtain the theorem just stated. Still, we cannot be sure that we have derived an optimal result here: we may have put too much information in $\mathbb{P}_D$. One may well imagine some alternative $\mathbb{P}_D^*$—and associated $\mathcal{D}^*$, abs^*—such that we have as well that $\mathcal{O}[\![\pi]\!] = (abs^* \circ \mathcal{D}^*)[\![\pi]\!]$, for $\pi \in \mathcal{L}_\delta$, but with less extra information added (to $\mathbb{P}_O$) in obtaining $\mathbb{P}_D^*$ than was added for $\mathbb{P}_D$. We shall return to these matters in Part IV (Chapter 17) where we shall show that, indeed, a considerably simpler $\mathcal{D}^*$ is possible.

11.2 Synchronization—refining the parallel composition

Synchronization is a programming construct which occurs in the presence of (uniform) parallel composition. It is intended to refine the latter in the following sense: Imagine that we have two parallel components, one which has the program

$s_1 \equiv a_1;a_2;a_3$ to execute, and the other one with program $s_2 \equiv b_1;b_2$. *Arbitrary* parallel execution of $s_1 \| s_2$ would yield 10 possible interleavings, including the instances $a_1a_2a_3b_1b_2$ and $b_1b_2a_1a_2a_3$. Now suppose that we want to restrict the number of possibilities by requiring that first $a_1;a_2$ and b_1 execute in parallel (yielding any of their arbitrary merges), and next the two executions "synchronize." This may be seen as an act of checking that both processes have reached a predetermined point in their execution. (In subsequent refinements of the synchronization concept, this point may be used, for example, to transmit information. See Section 12.2.) After this, execution of $s_1 \| s_2$ will continue with the parallel execution of the remaining actions, here a_3 and b_2. In other words, we want a programming construct to enforce that the synchronized outcome of $s_1 \| s_2$ equals $((a_1;a_2) \| b_1);(a_3 \| b_2)$, possibly with some flag at the second ';' indicating the successful completion of synchronization.

In order to implement the goal just sketched, we introduce a collection of synchronization actions $(c \in)$ *Sync*. These come in pairs: for each $c \in$ *Sync* we assume an associated $\bar{c}$, which in turn has c as its partner. Mathematically, we assume a mapping $\bar{\cdot} :$ *Sync* $\rightarrow$ *Sync*, such that $\bar{\bar{c}} = c$, for all c. We moreover introduce a special action τ—often referred to as the *silent* action—such that the effect of synchronization of a c in one parallel component with a $\bar{c}$ in a second one remains visible as a τ-action in the outcome. Thus, τ serves as the above mentioned flag. In the example discussed earlier, we would intersperse s_1 and s_2 with some c and $\bar{c}$ at the appropriate points, and obtain the equivalence

$$(a_1;a_2;c;a_3) \| (b_1;\bar{c};b_2) = ((a_1;a_2) \| b_1);\tau;(a_3 \| b_2).$$

As further example, consider a program

$$(x \Leftarrow a;c;x, y \Leftarrow b;\bar{c};y \mid x \| y).$$

A typical outcome of this program is any sequence

$$e_1 e_1' \tau e_2 e_2' \tau \cdots$$

where $e_i = a$ and $e_i' = b$, or vice versa, $i = 1, 2, \ldots$.

Of course, an attempt at synchronization may fail: If, in a parallel composition $s_1 \| s_2$, s_1 is ready to execute some c, whereas s_2 is not able to execute the corresponding $\bar{c}$, a failure occurs. A simple example is $(b_1;c) \| b_2$ (no $\bar{c}$ at all; more subtle is the example $(b_1;c_1;\bar{c}_2) \| (b_2;c_2;\bar{c}_1)$. In cases like this, a "deadlock" will result (a failure without alternative), and it was especially to prepare the reader for this phenomenon in the context of parallel languages—the most familiar setting for it—that we have treated it in the previous section.

It will appear that the semantic modeling of $\mathcal{L}_{syn}$—the language with synchronization studied in this section—is not so difficult once the reader has understood firstly our models for $\mathcal{L}_{par}$, and, secondly, the branching model for $\mathcal{L}_\delta$. Only a little extra machinery is required to deal with $\mathcal{L}_{syn}$, consisting firstly in the addition of a new transition rule for synchronization, and secondly in a refined version of the semantic '$\|$'.

11.2.1 Syntax and operational semantics

Let $(b \in) IAct$ be the set of *internal* actions, let $(c \in) Sync$ be the set of *synchronization* actions, and let $(a \in) Act = IAct \cup Sync$. Let τ be some distinguished element of $IAct$, and let $\bar{\cdot} : Sync \to Sync$ be a mapping such that $\bar{\bar{c}} = c$. Let $(x \in) PVar$ be as usual. We emphasize that, in the present section, use of the variable b implies that we refer to an action which is *not* a synchronization action. (This will be essential in the subsequent definition of $\mathcal{O}$.) On the other hand, a variable a refers to either an element of $IAct$ (including the possibility that $a = \tau$), or to an element of $Sync$.

Definition 11.15

(a) $s \,(\in Stat) ::= a \mid x \mid (s;s) \mid (s + s) \mid (s \| s) \mid s \backslash c$

(b) $g \,(\in GStat) ::= a \mid (g;s) \mid (g + g) \mid (g \| g) \mid g \backslash c$

(c) $(D \in) Decl = PVar \to GStat$

(d) $(\pi \in) \mathcal{L}_{syn} = Decl \times Stat.$

Unspecified D's will be dropped as usual. The statement $s \backslash c$—pronounced as "s *restricted by* c"—is executed just as s, with the exception of possible $c, \bar{c}$ steps of s (which are blocked in the execution of $s \backslash c$). E.g., the statements $c \backslash c$ and $(x \Leftarrow c; x \mid x \backslash c)$ both deadlock, and $(b + c) \backslash c$ is semantically equal to b.

Examples $(b_1;c) \| (b_2;\bar{c})$, $(b_1;c) \| b_2$, $(x \Leftarrow (b_1;x) + c, \, y \Leftarrow (b_2;y) + \bar{c} \mid x \| y)$. $((c;a) \| (\bar{c};b)) \backslash c.$

Resumptions are given in

Definition 11.16

(a) $r \,(\in Res) ::= \mathrm{E} \mid s.$

(b) We identify $\mathrm{E};s$, $\mathrm{E} \| s$ and $s \| \mathrm{E}$ with s, and $\mathrm{E} \| \mathrm{E}$ and $\mathrm{E} \backslash c$ with E.

Transitions are of the form $r \xrightarrow{a} r'$. The system $\mathcal{T}_{syn}$ is obtained by extending $\mathcal{T}_{par}$ with two extra rules.

Definition 11.17 $\mathcal{T}_{syn}$ consists of all the rules of $\mathcal{T}_{par}$ (but note that the actions a occurring in these rules are now either internal (b) or synchronization actions (c)), to which the following two rules have been added

$$\bullet \qquad \frac{s_1 \xrightarrow{c} r' \qquad s_2 \xrightarrow{\bar{c}} r''}{s_1 \| s_2 \xrightarrow{\tau} r' \| r''} \qquad\qquad\qquad\qquad\qquad \text{(Sync)}$$

$$\bullet \qquad \frac{s \xrightarrow{a} r}{s \backslash c \xrightarrow{a} r \backslash c} \qquad a \neq c, \bar{c} \qquad\qquad\qquad \text{(Restr)}$$

(Sync) is the rule embodying synchronization: If s_1 can make a c-step resulting in r', and s_2 can make a $\bar{c}$-step to r'', then $s_1 \| s_2$ can make a τ-step resulting in $r' \| r''$. Note firstly that this rule is symmetric in s_1, s_2 (since $\bar{\bar{c}} = c$), and secondly that the construct $s_1 \| s_2$ always has the option to make one-sided steps (only an a-step by s_1, or only an a-step by s_2), on the basis of the rule (Par). Altogether, $s_1 \| s_2$ has the following choice in making transition steps

- to perform a step by s_1 (only)
- to perform a step by s_2 (only)
- (in case the two premises of (Sync) hold) to perform a synchronization step (affecting both operands).

The rule (Restr) has as effect that $s \backslash c$ can make precisely those a-steps which s can make, for $a \neq c, \bar{c}$. In case s can make only $c, \bar{c}$-steps, $s \backslash c$ can make no steps (and deadlock will result).

Examples

(1) $(b_1 + c) \| (b_2 + \bar{c}) \;\overset{b_1}{\to}\; b_2 + \bar{c},$ $(b_1 + c) \| (b_2 + \bar{c}) \;\overset{c}{\to}\; b_2 + \bar{c},$

   $(b_1 + c) \| (b_2 + \bar{c}) \;\overset{b_2}{\to}\; b_1 + c,$ $(b_1 + c) \| (b_2 + \bar{c}) \;\overset{\bar{c}}{\to}\; b_1 + c,$

   $(b_1 + c) \| (b_2 + \bar{c}) \;\overset{\tau}{\to}\; E$

(2) $((c;a) \| (\bar{c};b)) \backslash c \;\overset{\tau}{\to}\; (a \| b) \backslash c \;\overset{a}{\to}\; b \backslash c \;\overset{b}{\to}\; E,$

   $((c;a) \| (\bar{c};b)) \backslash c \;\overset{\tau}{\to}\; (a \| b) \backslash c \;\overset{b}{\to}\; a \backslash c \;\overset{a}{\to}\; E.$

As a consequence of the definition of $\mathcal{O}$ to be given below, one sided c-steps—which may be seen as unsuccessful attempts at synchronization—will leave no trace in the result *unless* the statement making such a one-sided step has no alternative internal step to make. In that case δ, i.e., the symbol representing deadlock, will be the result.

We now give

Definition 11.18

(a) We say that a program $s \in \mathcal{L}_{syn}$ *blocks* whenever it cannot make any b-step. Formally, s blocks if for no b and r, we have $s \overset{b}{\to} r$.

(b) Let $(p \in) \mathbb{P}_O = \mathcal{P}_{nco}(IAct_\delta^\infty)$, where

$$IAct_\delta^\infty = IAct^* \cup IAct^\omega \cup IAct^* \cdot \{\delta\}.$$

(c) Let $(S \in) Sem_O = Decl \times Res \to \mathbb{P}_O$. The mapping $\Phi \colon Sem_O \to Sem_O$ is given by $\Phi(S)(E) = \{\epsilon\}$, and

$$\Phi(S)(s) \;=\; \begin{cases} \{\delta\} & \text{if } s \text{ blocks} \\ \bigcup\{\, b \cdot S(r) \mid s \overset{b}{\to} r \,\} & \text{otherwise.} \end{cases}$$

(d) $\mathcal{O} = fix(\Phi)$, $\mathcal{O}[\![\cdot]\!] \colon \mathcal{L}_{syn} \to \mathbb{P}_O$ is given by $\mathcal{O}[\![s]\!] = \mathcal{O}(s)$.

The essential element in this definition—when compared with that of Section 2.2—is the restriction to $b\,(\in IAct)$ in the main clause. Only internal steps b—and no synchronization steps c—are included in the result.

Examples $\mathcal{O}[\![(b_1;c) \| (b_2;\bar{c})]\!] = \{\, b_1 b_2 \tau,\; b_2 b_1 \tau \,\}$,
$\mathcal{O}[\![(b_1;c) \| b_2]\!] = \{\, b_1 b_2 \delta,\; b_2 b_1 \delta \,\}$,
$\mathcal{O}[\![x \Leftarrow (b_1;x) + c,\; y \Leftarrow (b_2;y) + \bar{c} \mid x \| y]\!] = \{b_1, b_2\}^* \cdot \tau \cup \{b_1, b_2\}^\omega$.

In the third example, $\{b_1, b_2\}^*$ ($\{b_1, b_2\}^\omega$) is the set of all finite (infinite) sequences each element of which is either b_1 or b_2. Note that the outcome includes "unfair" results in which, from a given position in the infinite sequence onwards, *all* elements equal b_1 or *all* elements equal b_2. This kind of behaviour was already present in $\mathcal{L}_{par}$.

11.2.2 Denotational semantics, relating $\mathcal{O}$ and $\mathcal{D}$

The domain $\mathbb{P}_D$ used for $\mathcal{L}_{syn}$'s denotational semantics satisfies the same domain equation as the one used in the preceding section.

Definition 11.19 $\mathbb{P}_D$ is the domain (uniquely) solving the equation

$$\mathbb{P}_D \simeq \{p_\epsilon\} + \mathcal{P}_{co}(Act \times id_{\frac{1}{2}}(\mathbb{P}_D)). \tag{11.3}$$

Note, however, that (11.3) now refers to the set $Act = IAct \cup Sync$.

We begin the design of $\mathcal{D}$ for $\mathcal{L}_{syn}$ with the definition of the operators ';', '$\|$', '+'. The sequential and alternative composition are the same as those given in the preceding section for $\mathcal{L}_\delta$. The definition of $p_1 \| p_2$ combines two ideas.

- Firstly, it follows the same pattern as in Section 4.1 (on $\mathcal{L}_{par}$, Definition 4.7), but now involving the branching version of $\Omega_;$, as defined already in the previous section, yielding the two leftmerges $(p_1 \,\|\!\!\!\lfloor\, p_2)$ and $(p_2 \,\|\!\!\!\lfloor\, p_1)$ as part of the outcome.

- Secondly, it yields a third component which results from synchronization. We shall introduce a further, auxiliary, operator written as '$|$'. The combined effect of these operators should result in the equality

$$p_1 \| p_2 = (p_1 \,\|\!\!\!\lfloor\, p_2) + (p_2 \,\|\!\!\!\lfloor\, p_1) + (p_1 | p_2).$$

The intended meaning of '$|$' is expressed, informally, by the equation $c | \bar{c} = \tau$: synchronization of c with $\bar{c}$ yields the silent step τ. Formally, this should be rewritten as an equation in terms of elements of $\mathbb{P}_D$ as follows

$$\{\langle c, p_\epsilon \rangle\} | \{\langle \bar{c}, p_\epsilon \rangle\} = \{\langle \tau, p_\epsilon \rangle\}.$$

Definition 11.20 Let $(\phi \in) Op = \mathbb{P}_D \times \mathbb{P}_D \xrightarrow{1} \mathbb{P}_D$. Let $\Omega_;$, $\Omega_\|$ and $\Omega_|$: $Op \to Op$ be given by

(a) $\Omega_;(\phi)(p_\epsilon, p) \;=\; p$

$\Omega_;(\phi)(p_1, p_2) \;=\; \{\, \langle a, \phi(p', p_2)\rangle \mid \langle a, p'\rangle \in p_1\,\}, \quad p_1 \neq p_\epsilon$

(b) $\Omega_{\|}(\phi)(p_1, p_2) \;=\; \Omega_;(\phi)(p_1, p_2) + \Omega_;(\phi)(p_2, p_1) + \Omega_{|}(\phi)(p_1, p_2)$

(See part (d) for the definition of '+'.)

(c) $\Omega_{|}(\phi)(p_1, p_2) \;=\;$

$$\begin{cases} \emptyset & \text{if } p_1 = p_\epsilon \text{ or } p_2 = p_\epsilon \\ \{\, \langle \tau, \phi(p', p'')\rangle \mid \langle c, p'\rangle \in p_1, \langle \bar{c}, p''\rangle \in p_2 \,\} & \text{otherwise.} \end{cases}$$

(d) $p + p_\epsilon = p_\epsilon + p = p$. For $p_1, p_2 \neq p_\epsilon$, $p_1 + p_2 = p_1 \cup p_2$ (the set-theoretic union of p_1 and p_2).

(e) $; = \text{fix}(\Omega_;)$, $\| = \text{fix}(\Omega_{\|})$, $\text{\textvisiblespace\textvisiblespace} = \Omega_;(\|)$, $| = \Omega_{|}(\|)$.

Example $\{\langle b_1, \{\langle c, p_\epsilon\rangle\}\rangle\} \| \{\langle b_2, p_\epsilon\rangle\} =$
$\{\langle b_1, \{\langle c, \{\langle b_2, p_\epsilon\rangle\}\rangle\}\rangle, \langle b_2, \{\langle c, p_\epsilon\rangle\}\rangle\rangle, \langle b_2, \{\langle b_1, \{\langle c, p_\epsilon\rangle\}\rangle\}\rangle\rangle\}$.

We next define the semantic restriction operator.

Definition 11.21 $\cdot\backslash c \colon \mathbb{P}_D \xrightarrow{1} \mathbb{P}_D$ is the unique function satisfying $p_\epsilon\backslash c = p_\epsilon$, and, for $p \neq p_\epsilon$,

$$p\backslash c = \{\, \langle a, p'\backslash c\rangle \mid \langle a, p'\rangle \in p,\ a \neq c, \bar{c}\,\}.$$

Examples $\{\langle b_1, \{\langle c, p'\rangle\}\rangle\}\backslash c \;=\; \{\langle b_1, \emptyset\rangle\}, \quad \langle b_1, \{\langle c, p'\rangle, \langle b_2, p''\rangle\}\rangle\backslash c \;=\;$
$\{\langle b_1, \{\langle b_2, p''\backslash c\rangle\}\rangle\}$.

Justification of the Definition 11.21 is left to the reader. It is furthermore not difficult to prove that the familiar properties are satisfied.

Lemma 11.22

(a) The operators ';', '$\|$', '+' are well-defined and nonexpansive in both their arguments. Also, $d(p_1\backslash c, p_2\backslash c) \leq d(p_1, p_2)$.

(b) Assume $p_1, p_1' \neq p_\epsilon$. Then

$$d(p_1;p_2, p_1';p_2') \leq max\{\, d(p_1, p_1'), \tfrac{1}{2}d(p_2, p_2')\,\}$$

(c) $p_1\|p_2 = (p_1 \,\text{\textvisiblespace\textvisiblespace}\, p_2) + (p_2 \,\text{\textvisiblespace\textvisiblespace}\, p_1) + (p_1|p_2)$.

We can now give

Definition 11.23

(a) $\mathcal{D}\colon \mathcal{L}_{syn} \to \mathbb{P}_D$ is the unique function satisfying

$$
\begin{aligned}
\mathcal{D}(a) &= \{\langle a, p_\epsilon \rangle\} \\
\mathcal{D}(x) &= \mathcal{D}(D(x)) \\
\mathcal{D}(s_1 \operatorname{op} s_2) &= \mathcal{D}(s_1) \operatorname{op} \mathcal{D}(s_2), \quad \operatorname{op} \in \{;, \|, +\} \\
\mathcal{D}(s\backslash c) &= \mathcal{D}(s)\backslash c.
\end{aligned}
$$

(b) $\mathcal{D}[\![\pi]\!] = \mathcal{D}(\pi).$

Example

$\mathcal{D}[\![(b_1; c) \| (b_2; \bar{c})]\!]$

$= \{\langle b_1, \{\langle c, p_\epsilon \rangle\}\rangle\} \| \{\langle b_2, \{\langle \bar{c}, p_\epsilon \rangle\}\rangle\}$

$= \{\,\langle b_1, \{\langle c, \{\langle b_2, \{\langle \bar{c}, p_\epsilon \rangle\}\rangle\}\rangle\}\rangle, \langle b_2, \{\langle c, \{\langle \bar{c}, p_\epsilon \rangle\}\rangle\}\rangle, \langle \bar{c}, \{\langle c, p_\epsilon \rangle\}\rangle, \langle \tau, p_\epsilon \rangle\}\rangle,$
$\quad \langle b_2, \{\ldots\}\rangle\,\}.$

In a picture we have

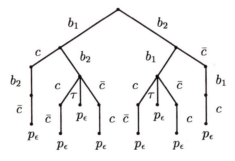

$\mathcal{D}$ has been designed to preserve the full branching structure in the result $\mathcal{D}(s)$. Consequently—just as we saw for $\mathcal{L}_\delta$—$\mathbb{P}_O$ and $\mathbb{P}_D$ are quite different, and no simple result of the form $\mathcal{O} = \mathcal{D}$ (on $\mathcal{L}_{syn}$) is possible. Instead, we again introduce an operator $abs\colon \mathbb{P}_D \to \mathbb{P}_O$. This operator does two things: Firstly, it collapses the branching structure of a process p, delivering the set of all its paths. Secondly, it deletes all $\langle c, \cdot \rangle$ pairs from p and all its subprocesses (defined as in the previous section). In case these deletions result in some subprocess of p being turned into the empty set, this set is then replaced by $\{\delta\}$—the linear element representing deadlock.

The precise definition of abs follows.

Definition 11.24

(a) Let $(\phi \in) Op = \mathbb{P}_D \xrightarrow{1} \mathbb{P}_O$, and let $\Omega_{abs} : Op \to Op$ be given by

$$\Omega_{abs}(\phi)(p_\epsilon) \quad = \quad \{\epsilon\}$$

and, for $p \neq p_\epsilon$,

$$\Omega_{abs}(\phi)(p_\epsilon) \quad = \quad \left\{ \begin{array}{ll} \{\delta\} & \text{if } p \subseteq Sync \times \mathbb{P}_D \\ \bigcup\{b \cdot \phi(p') \mid \langle b, p' \rangle \in p\} & \text{otherwise.} \end{array} \right.$$

(b) $abs = fix(\Omega_{abs})$.

Examples $abs(\mathcal{D}((b_1;c) \| (b_2;\bar{c}))) = \{b_1 b_2 \tau, b_2 b_1 \tau\}$,
$abs(\mathcal{D}((b_1;c) \| b_2)) = \{b_1 b_2 \delta, b_2 b_1 \delta\}$.

Our next task is to show that $\mathcal{O} = abs \circ \mathcal{D}$ on $\mathcal{L}_{syn}$. For this purpose, we introduce an intermediate semantics $\mathcal{O}^* : \mathcal{L}_{syn} \to \mathbb{P}_D$ in

Definition 11.25 $\mathcal{O}^*$ is the unique function satisfying

$$\begin{array}{ll} \mathcal{O}^*(E) & = \quad p_\epsilon \\ \mathcal{O}^*(s) & = \quad \{\langle a, \mathcal{O}^*(r) \rangle \mid s \xrightarrow{a} r\}. \end{array}$$

Example
$\mathcal{O}^*((b_1;c) \| b_2) = \{\langle b_1, \{\langle c, \{\langle b_2, p_\epsilon \rangle\}\rangle, \langle b_2, \{\langle c, p_\epsilon \rangle\}\rangle\}\rangle, \langle b_2, \{\langle b_1, \{\langle c, p_\epsilon \rangle\}\rangle\}\rangle \}$.
The outcome is depicted below:

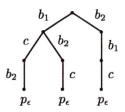

$\mathcal{O}^*$ has two features which distinguish it from $\mathcal{O}$. Firstly, $\mathcal{O}^*(s)$ delivers processes (in $\mathbb{P}_D$) as a result, i.e., elements with full branching structure. In this respect, $\mathcal{O}^*$ extends $\mathcal{O}$ just as this is the case for $\mathcal{L}_\delta$. Secondly, *all* a-steps contribute to the outcome—contrary to what we found in Definition 11.18, where only b-steps are included. Therefore, $\mathcal{O}^*(s)$ delivers the same information as $\mathcal{D}(s)$, and the next lemma, stating that $\mathcal{O}^* = \mathcal{D}$ on $\mathcal{L}_{syn}$, should not come as a surprise.

One small step is still necessary: We extend $\mathcal{D}$ to $\mathcal{E}$ on *Res*, putting $\mathcal{E}(\mathrm{E}) = p_\epsilon$, $\mathcal{E}(s) = \mathcal{D}(s)$. Now let Φ^* be the higher-order mapping with $\mathcal{O}^*$ (Definition 11.25) as its unique fixed point. We have the usual

Lemma 11.26 $\Phi^*(\mathcal{E}) = \mathcal{E}$.

Proof We show by induction on $wgt(r)$ that $\Phi^*(\mathcal{E})(r) = \mathcal{E}(r)$. Two subcases.

$[s_1 \| s_2]$ $\Phi^*(\mathcal{E})(s_1 \| s_2)$

$= \quad \{ \langle a, \mathcal{E}(r) \rangle \mid s_1 \| s_2 \xrightarrow{a} r \}$

$= \quad \{ \langle a, \mathcal{E}(r' \| s_2) \rangle \mid s_1 \xrightarrow{a} r' \} \cup \text{(symm.)} \cup$
$\quad\quad \{ \langle \tau, \mathcal{E}(r' \| r'') \rangle \mid s_1 \xrightarrow{c} r', s_2 \xrightarrow{\bar{c}} r'' \}$

$= \quad [\text{Exercise 11.2}]$
$\quad\quad \{ \langle a, \mathcal{E}(r') \rangle \mid s_1 \xrightarrow{a} r' \} \mathbin{\underline{\|}} \mathcal{E}(s_2) \cup \text{(symm.)} \cup$
$\quad\quad \{ \langle \tau, \mathcal{E}(r') \| \mathcal{E}(r'') \rangle \mid \langle c, \mathcal{E}(r') \rangle \in \Phi^*(\mathcal{E})(s_1) \wedge \langle \bar{c}, \mathcal{E}(r'') \rangle \in \Phi^*(\mathcal{E})(s_2) \}$

$= \quad \Phi^*(\mathcal{E})(s_1) \mathbin{\underline{\|}} \mathcal{E}(s_2) \cup \text{(symm.)} \cup (\Phi^*(\mathcal{E})(s_1) \mid \Phi^*(\mathcal{E})(s_2))$

$= \quad [\text{ind. hyp.}] \ \mathcal{E}(s_1) \mathbin{\underline{\|}} \mathcal{E}(s_2) \cup \text{(symm.)} \cup (\mathcal{E}(s_1) \mid \mathcal{E}(s_2))$

$= \quad \mathcal{E}(s_1) \| \mathcal{E}(s_2)$

$[s\backslash c]\quad \Phi^*(\mathcal{E})(s\backslash c)$

$\quad = \quad \{\,\langle a, \mathcal{E}(r_1)\rangle \mid s\backslash c \overset{a}{\to} r_1\,\}$

$\quad = \quad \{\,\langle a, \mathcal{E}(r\backslash c)\rangle \mid s \overset{a}{\to} r,\, a \neq c, \bar{c}\,\}$

$\quad = \quad \{\,\langle a, \mathcal{E}(r)\backslash c\rangle \mid s \overset{a}{\to} r,\, a \neq c, \bar{c}\,\}$

$\quad = \quad \{\,\langle a, \mathcal{E}(r)\rangle \mid s \overset{a}{\to} r\,\}\backslash c$

$\quad = \quad \Phi^*(\mathcal{E})(s)\backslash c$

$\quad = \quad [\text{ind. hyp.}]\ \ \mathcal{E}(s)\backslash c$

$\quad = \quad \mathcal{E}(s\backslash c).$

From this lemma, we immediately obtain

Lemma 11.27 $\mathcal{O}^* = \mathcal{E}$, *on Res.*

Almost exactly as in Section 11.1, we can now show

Theorem 11.28

(a) $\mathcal{O} = \text{abs} \circ \mathcal{O}^*$, *on Res.*

(b) $\mathcal{O}[\![\pi]\!] = (\text{abs} \circ \mathcal{D})[\![\pi]\!]$, *for* $\pi \in \mathcal{L}_{syn}$.

As in the previous section, we may ask the question whether there exists a simpler $\mathbb{P}_D{}^{**}$, $\mathcal{D}^{**}$ (and accompanying abs**) such that $\mathcal{O} = \text{abs}^{**} \circ \mathcal{D}^{**}$. As we shall see in Chapter 17, the answer to this question is, again, affirmative.

11.3 Exercises

Exercise 11.1 Draw the "trees" corresponding to the processes defined by

- $p = \{ \langle a, p \rangle, \langle b, p \rangle \}$
- $p = \{ \langle a, q \rangle \}$, $q = \{ \langle a, q \rangle, \langle b, p \rangle \}$
- $p_0 = \{ \langle a, p_1 \rangle \}$, $p_n = \{ \langle a, p_{n+1} \rangle, \langle b, p_{n-1} \rangle \}$, $n = 1, 2, \dots$.

Exercise 11.2 Let $\mathbb{P}_O$, $\mathbb{P}_D$ and the semantic operators be as in Section 11.1.

(a) Assume that p satisfies $p = \{ \langle a, p \rangle, \langle b, p \rangle \}$. Prove that $p;p' = p$, for each $p' \in \mathbb{P}_D$.

(b) Verify the right-distributive law

$$(p_1 + p_2);p \;\; = \;\; (p_1;p) + (p_2;p).$$

(c) Show by means of a counterexample that the left-distributive law

$$p;(p_1 + p_2) \;\; = \;\; (p;p_1) + (p;p_2)$$

does not hold, in general, on $\mathbb{P}_D$.

(d) Do the two distributive laws hold on $\mathbb{P}_O$?

(e) Let $p, p_i \in \mathbb{P}_D$, $i = 1, \dots, n$. Prove that

$$\{ \langle a, p_i \| p \rangle \mid 1 \le i \le n \} \;\; = \;\; \{ \langle a, p_i \rangle \mid 1 \le i \le n \} \mathbin{\underline{\|}} p.$$

(f) Prove $(p_1 \mathbin{\underline{\|}} p_2) \mathbin{\underline{\|}} p_3 \;=\; p_1 \mathbin{\underline{\|}} (p_2 \| p_3)$.

Exercise 11.3 Let $\mathcal{L}_{par,\delta}$ be given by the syntax

$$s ::= a \mid \text{stop} \mid x \mid (s;s) \mid (s + s) \mid (s \| s).$$

(a) Design $\mathcal{O}$ and $\mathcal{D}$ for $\mathcal{L}_{par,\delta}$.

(b) Show that

$$\mathcal{O}(x \Leftarrow a;x \mid x \| \text{stop}) \;\; = \;\; \{ a^\omega \}.$$

Exercise 11.4 Let $\mathcal{L}_{syn}$, $\mathcal{O}$ be as in Section 11.2. Elaborate the details of

(a) $\mathcal{O}((b_1;c)\|b_2)$

(b) $\mathcal{O}((b_1;c)\|(b_2;\bar{c}))$

(c) $\mathcal{O}(x \Leftarrow (b_1;x) + c, y \Leftarrow (b_2;y) + \bar{c} \mid x\|y)$.

Exercise 11.5 Let '$\|$', '$\underline{\|}$', '$|$' be as in Definition 11.20, let $p_1,\ldots,p_n \in \mathbb{P}_D$ (as in Equation (11.3)), and let $\underset{i\in I}{\|}\ p_i$ have the obvious meaning. Prove

$$
\underset{1\leq i\leq n}{\|}\ p_i \quad = \quad \bigcup_{1\leq i\leq n} \left(p_i \underline{\|} \left(\underset{1\leq j\leq n,j\neq i}{\|} p_j\right)\right) \cup
$$
$$
\bigcup_{1\leq i,j\leq n,i\neq j} \left((p_i|p_j) \underline{\|} \left(\underset{1\leq k\leq n,k\neq i,j}{\|} p_k\right)\right).
$$

Exercise 11.6 (replacing $\mathcal{P}_{co}(\cdot)$ by $\mathcal{P}_{cl}(\cdot)$ induces problems in the definition of ';')
Let $\mathbb{P}$ be as specified in Equation (11.3), with $\mathcal{P}_{co}(\cdot)$ replaced by $\mathcal{P}_{cl}(\cdot)$. Let us define the following elements of $\mathbb{P}$:

$$
\begin{aligned}
pb_0 &= p_\epsilon \\
pb_{n+1} &= \{\langle b, pb_n\rangle\}, \quad n = 0, 1, \ldots \\
pb_\omega &= \lim_n pb_n,
\end{aligned}
$$

and similarly for pc_ω. Let, for $n = 1, 2, \ldots$,

$$
\begin{aligned}
p_n &= \{\langle b, pb_{n-1}\rangle, \langle a_1, p_\epsilon\rangle, \ldots, \langle a_{n-1}, p_\epsilon\rangle, \langle a_n, pc_\omega\rangle, \langle a_{n+1}, p_\epsilon\rangle, \ldots\} \\
p &= \{\langle a, p_n\rangle \mid n = 1, 2, \ldots\} \\
q &= pc_\omega \\
r &= \{\langle b, pb_\omega\rangle, \langle a_1, pc_\omega\rangle, \ldots, \langle a_{n-1}, pc_\omega\rangle, \langle a_n, pc_\omega\rangle, \langle a_{n+1}, pc_\omega\rangle \ldots\}.
\end{aligned}
$$

(a) Show that $(p_n)_n$ is not a Cauchy sequence.

(b) The "natural" definition of $p;q$ would yield

$$
p;q \quad = \quad \{\langle a, p_n;q\rangle \mid n = 1, 2, \ldots\}.
$$

Show that $p;q$ is not a closed set. (Hint: $p;q$ contains the Cauchy sequence $(\langle a, p_n;q\rangle)_n$ such that its limit $\langle a, r\rangle$ does not belong to $p;q$.)

11.4   Bibliographical notes

The language $\mathcal{L}_\delta$ is a particularly simple vehicle to study deadlock; as such, it is comparable, e.g., to the language BPA$_\delta$ of process algebra ([BW91a]). The linear operational model for $\mathcal{L}_\delta$ is a simple variation on that of $\mathcal{L}_{cf}$; the branching denotational model goes back to [BZ82]. There is, in fact, an extensive hierarchy of models between the linear and branching ones (applicable in cases where the language concerned contains communication and concurrency). In Chapter 17, we shall discuss two of these; much more information can be found, e.g., in [Gla90a, Gla90b].

A first paper relating linear and branching models where metric techniques play a role is [BBKM84]. (Note, however, that the linear model in that paper is based on an order in terms of reverse set inclusion.)

The language $\mathcal{L}_{syn}$ is essentially based on CCS ([Mil80]), though some minor (e.g., renaming) and at least one major topic in CCS is not covered (viz. the material having to do with weak observational equivalence and the τ-laws). Our system $\mathcal{T}_{syn}$ is also close to the transition system used for CCS. Of the differences between our approach and that of [Mil80] we mention

- CCS does not address issues having to do with infinite behaviour, and

- we use linear operational and branching denotational models, whereas Milner employs *synchronization trees* as (another kind of) branching domain.

Two different such trees (or, more in general, process graphs) may be bisimilar, a phenomenon not possible in our setting (since, as we saw in Section 10.3, we have that bisimilarity coincides with equality). Related references are [GR83, Rou85]. Exercise 11.6 is due to Jeroen Warmerdam.

The use of branching domains to handle parallelism has its roots in earlier work in domain theory—where the solutions are cpo- rather than metric based. Since these domains are usually applied to deal with nonuniform parallelism, we postpone the relevant references till the next chapter.

12 Extensions of Nonuniform Parallelism

In this chapter, we use branching domains in the study of nonuniform parallelism. We shall treat two extensions of $\mathcal{L}_{svp}$ (from Chapter 7), each with a different language notion which might induce deadlock. The first kind, also known as *suspension*, occurs in a language ($\mathcal{L}_{aw}$) with the so-called await statement (await e then s end). In case evaluation of e yields tt, s is executed (possibly in an "atomized" way). If e evaluates to ff, execution of the statement is suspended. In case this suspension is not ended (thanks to the effect of some parallel component), a deadlock may result (depending on the availability of an alternative). A branching domain of the nonuniform variety is used for the denotational modeling of this notion.

The second type of deadlock occurs in the language $\mathcal{L}_{com}$, which is the nonuniform counterpart of $\mathcal{L}_{syn}$. Instead of the communication actions $c, \bar{c}$ of $\mathcal{L}_{syn}$ (with the communication as suggested by $c|\bar{c} = \tau$), we now have as communication actions $c?v$, $c!e$, with $c?v|c!e = (v: = e)$ as intended communication. The branching domain used for $\mathcal{L}_{com}$ is a fairly straightforward extension of the domain for $\mathcal{L}_{syn}$. In both $\mathcal{L}_{aw}$ and $\mathcal{L}_{com}$, nonuniformity is modeled by having the elements $p(\in \mathbb{P}_D)$ depend on an argument σ and adapting the semantic operators accordingly.

12.1 Suspension and the await statement
—a nonuniform domain equation

We investigate the notion of *suspension* in the context of a language with parallel composition, shared variables and the *await statement*. We take as starting point $\mathcal{L}_{svp}$, the nonuniform language studied in Chapter 7, and we add to it as a new construct the await statement, expressed syntactically as await e then s end. The resulting language will be called $\mathcal{L}_{aw}$. The construct await e then s end is to be read as: wait for the expression e to be satisfied (i.e., to evaluate to tt), and then execute s. In general, await e then s end occurs in one of a number of parallel components, and, in case e is not true in the current state, the component in which the await statement occurs waits or *suspends*. If, eventually, an interleaving action of some other component results in setting the current value of e to tt, then the execution of the suspended statement is resumed with the execution of s. If this situation does not arise, i.e., e remains false ($= ff$), and there is no alternative available, then the program gets into a deadlock.

We shall follow our earlier treatment of $\mathcal{L}_\delta$ in that we include a special action stop in $\mathcal{L}_{aw}$, and then treat the await statement as nothing but syntactic sugar (i.e., a syntactic variant, possibly more palatable, of an already present programming construct) for if e then s else stop fi. (An alternative interpretation will be mentioned in Exercise 12.1.)

There is one important further characteristic of the await statement not yet mentioned, viz. the property that, in await e then s end, s should be executed in an *atomized* fashion. Whereas execution of s may consist of several steps which may, in general, be interleaved with actions from parallel components, its atomized version does not admit interleavings. Hence, the semantic model should treat it just as, e.g., one single assignment statement, i.e., as a mapping from input states to output states, without recording intermediate states which might be subjected to the effect of interleaving actions.

It is the aim of the present section to provide a mathematical model for the notions just outlined. For this purpose, we shall invoke the branching time machinery already applied in the previous chapter, but now extended to a *nonuniform* version. We shall introduce a codomain $\mathbb{P}_D$ to be used in the design of $\mathcal{D}$ for $\mathcal{L}_{aw}$, which we specify as solution of a domain equation $\mathbb{P}_D \simeq \mathcal{F}(\mathbb{P}_D)$, where $\mathcal{F}$ involves—besides the operations as encountered earlier ('+', '×', $\mathcal{P}_{co}(\cdot)$)—as well the function space operator, here in the simple form $\Sigma \to \mathcal{F}_1(\mathbb{P}_D)$ with Σ, as always, the set of states.

In order not to overload the reader with too much material in one go, we have organized this section into three subsections. The first two describe, in the familiar way, operational and denotational semantics for $\mathcal{L}_{aw}$ and their relationship. However, in $\mathcal{L}_{aw}$ the atomization aspect (of s in await e then s end) is not yet taken into account. In a third subsection we complete the picture by also dealing with the semantic modeling of atomization.

12.1.1 Syntax and operational semantics

Let $v \in IVar$, $e \in Exp$ be as before.

Definition 12.1

(a) $s\,(\in Stat) ::=\;\; v := e \mid \mathsf{skip} \mid \mathsf{stop} \mid (s;s) \mid \mathsf{if}\ e\ \mathsf{then}\ s\ \mathsf{else}\ s\ \mathsf{fi} \mid$
$\qquad\qquad\qquad$ while e do s od $\mid (s\|s)$

(b) await e then s end abbreviates if e then s else stop fi

(c) $(\pi \in)\,\mathcal{L}_{aw} = Stat$.

Resumptions are—as always when '$\|$' is around—particularly simple.

Definition 12.2

(a) $r\ (\in Res) ::= \mathrm{E}\mid s$.

(b) Each of E;s, E$\|s$ or $s\|$E is identified with s.

The sets $(\sigma \in)\, \Sigma$ and $(\alpha \in)\, Val$ are the usual ones. The transition system $\mathcal{T}_{aw}$ is defined in

Definition 12.3 $\mathcal{T}_{aw} = \mathcal{T}'_{svp}$, where $\mathcal{T}'_{svp}$ is as $\mathcal{T}_{svp}$, but with the while rule replaced by

$\bullet$ [while e do s od:r, σ] $\rightarrow_0$ (While$'$)
          [if e then (s;while e do s od) else skip fi, σ]

Remark The replacement of the rule (While) (from $\mathcal{T}_{svp}$) by (While$'$), though not essential for the subsequent arguments, slightly simplifies certain complexity considerations below.

Note that, once again (cf. Section 11.1), there is no rule for stop.

We shall say that $[s, \sigma]$ *suspends* if for no r, σ' we have $[s, \sigma] \rightarrow [r, \sigma']$. $\mathcal{O}$ is based on $\mathcal{T}_{aw}$ in

Definition 12.4

(a) $\Sigma_\delta^\infty = \Sigma^* \cup \Sigma^* \cdot \{\delta\} \cup \Sigma^\omega$.

(b) $\mathbb{P}_O = \Sigma \rightarrow \mathcal{P}_{nco}(\Sigma_\delta^\infty)$.

(c) $\mathcal{O}: \mathcal{L}_{aw} \times \Sigma \rightarrow \mathcal{P}_{nco}(\Sigma_\delta^\infty)$ is the unique function satisfying, $\mathcal{O}(\mathrm{E}, \sigma) = \{\epsilon\}$, and

$$\mathcal{O}(s, \sigma) = \begin{cases} \{\delta\} & \text{if } [s, \sigma] \text{ suspends} \\ \bigcup\{\sigma' \cdot \mathcal{O}(r, \sigma') \mid [s, \sigma] \rightarrow [r, \sigma']\} & \text{otherwise.} \end{cases}$$

(d) $\mathcal{O}[\![\cdot]\!]: \mathcal{L}_{aw} \rightarrow \mathbb{P}_O$ is given by $\mathcal{O}[\![s]\!] = \lambda\sigma.\mathcal{O}(s, \sigma)$.

Example Assume $v, w \in IVar$.

$$\mathcal{O}((v := 0;(\text{await } v = 1 \text{ then } w := 2 \text{ end}))\|(v := 1))(\sigma) \tag{12.1}$$
$$= \{\sigma\{0/v\}\cdot\sigma\{1/v\}\cdot\sigma\{1/v, 2/w\}, \sigma\{1/v\}\cdot\sigma\{0/v\}\cdot\delta\}.$$

This example reflects that the interleaving

$v := 1; v := 0;$ await $v = 1$ then $w := 2$ end

results in deadlock, whereas the interleaving

$v := 0; v := 1;$ await $v = 1$ then $w := 2$ end

yields a final state $\sigma[1/v, 2/w]$. On the other hand, the interleaving

$v := 0;$ await $v = 1$ then $w := 2$ end$; v := 1$

does not contribute to the result since, at the moment the await statement would suspend, the alternative $v := 1$—and only then the await statement—is available. The various choices are probably best expressed in a picture (reflecting the denotational branching model to be developed in the next subsection).

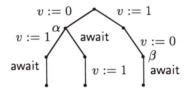

Pruning the suspended branch in node α (but not in node β, where there is no alternative), and simplifying await e then s end to either s or stop, we obtain

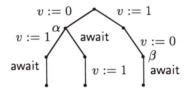

Now the effect of executing this tree in some given σ is, indeed, the set of state sequences as given in (12.1).

12.1.2 Denotational semantics, relating $\mathcal{O}$ and $\mathcal{D}$

The denotational domain $\mathbb{P}_D$ is specified as the solution of a (nonuniform) domain equation, as described in

Definition 12.5 $\mathbb{P}_D$ is the (unique) domain satisfying

$$\mathbb{P}_D \simeq \{p_\epsilon\} + (\Sigma \to \mathcal{P}_{co}(\Sigma \times id_{\frac{1}{2}}(\mathbb{P}_D))). \tag{12.2}$$

We see that, as announced earlier, the defining functor $\mathcal{F}$ for $\mathbb{P}_D$ is built from the operators '+', '×', $\mathcal{P}_{co}(\cdot)$ and in addition, a functional term of the form $\Sigma \to \mathcal{F}_1(\mathbb{P}_D)$—with $\mathcal{F}_1(\mathbb{P}_D) = \mathcal{P}_{co}(\Sigma \times id_{\frac{1}{2}}(\mathbb{P}_D))$. From (12.2) we conclude that a process p in $\mathbb{P}_D$ is either

- the nil process p_ϵ, or
- a function which, given an input σ, yields as result an output which consists of a (compact, possibly empty) set of pairs $\langle \sigma_1, p_1 \rangle, \langle \sigma_2, p_2 \rangle, \ldots$.

The provision for a *set* of outcomes is explained by the nondeterminacy induced by the interleaving model for parallel composition. A pair such as $\langle \sigma_1, p_1 \rangle \in p(\sigma)$ expresses that—for input σ—an output state σ_1 is delivered, together with a continuation process p_1. In a setting where p arises as meaning of a (part of a) program, p_1 is the meaning of the remainder of the program resulting after the execution of the action transforming σ to σ_1. A natural consequence of this view would seem to be that the further computation may be modeled by supplying σ_1 as argument to p_1. However, this is not the case in general: The computation which resulted in σ_1 may be interleaved—immediately after the yielding of p_1—with some action from a parallel component. Only *after* one or more of such interleavings the computation may resume with p_1.

The reader will recognize here a phenomenon which is very similar to that encountered in the semantic model for $\mathcal{L}_{svp}$ (Chapter 7). There, we employed possibly non-consecutive sequences $\langle \sigma_1, \sigma_1' \rangle \langle \sigma_2, \sigma_2' \rangle \ldots$, where, possibly, $\sigma_i' \neq \sigma_{i+1}$, $i = 1, 2, \ldots$. Here as well, the state σ_1 may be changed by an interleaving action to σ_1', and only then—or even later—the execution of the remainder of the program (as modeled by p_1) is resumed. Just as in Chapter 7, the desire to always account for the possibility of interleaving actions from some other parallel component is explained by the requirement that $\mathcal{D}$ be compositional: In order to enable a proper definition of $p_1 \| p_2$ (for, say, $p_1 = \mathcal{D}(s_1)$, $p_2 = \mathcal{D}(s_2)$), at each intermediate step of p_1 an interleaving action of p_2 should be allowed for, and vice versa. The same example as used in Section 7.1 may be used to show that the codomain $\mathbb{P}_O$ as used for $\mathcal{O}$ does not admit a compositional definition.

The essential difference between $\mathbb{P}_D$ as used for $\mathcal{L}_{svp}$ (viz. $\mathbb{P}_D = \mathcal{P}_{fncl}((\Sigma \times \Sigma)^\infty)$) and $\mathbb{P}_D$ from Definition 12.5 is that the latter has a fully branching structure. In the

uniform case, the domain $\mathbb{P}_D$ provides the branching extension of the linear domain
$\mathbb{P} = \mathcal{P}_{nco}(Act^\infty)$. In the nonuniform case, an additional layer in the representation
of an element from the branching domain $\mathbb{P}_D$ (as in (12.2)) stems from the functional
nature of the processes ($\neq p_\epsilon$) in $\mathbb{P}_D$. A typical element $p \in \mathbb{P}_D$ may be pictured
as in Figure 12.1. In this picture, we observe one level of "branching" (indicated
by α) which is due to the functional nature of p (thus, this has nothing to do
with the modeling of nondeterminacy), a second level (indicated by β) which does
indeed stem from the wish to reflect nondeterministic behavior. Note that processes
in $\mathbb{P}_D$ from (12.2) may, just as in the uniform case, exhibit cycles, e.g., as in
$p = \lambda\sigma.\{\langle\sigma, p\rangle\}$. These may, if one desires, be unwound to infinite trees.

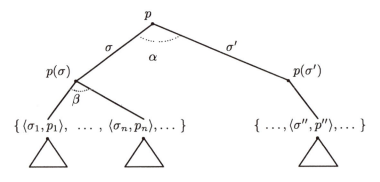

Figure 12.1

We continue with the various definitions leading to the definition of $\mathcal{D}$ for $\mathcal{L}_{aw}$.
We first introduce the semantic operators.

Definition 12.6

(a) The operator $+: \mathbb{P}_D \times \mathbb{P}_D \to \mathbb{P}_D$ is defined by putting $p + p_\epsilon = p_\epsilon + p = p$, and, for
$p_1, p_2 \neq p_\epsilon$,

$$p_1 + p_2 = \lambda\sigma.(p_1(\sigma) \cup p_2(\sigma)).$$

(b) Let $(\phi \in) Op = \mathbb{P}_D \times \mathbb{P}_D \overset{1}{\to} \mathbb{P}_D$, and let the mappings $\Omega_;, \Omega_\| : Op \to Op$ be given
by

$$\Omega_;(\phi)(p_\epsilon, p) = p$$
$$\Omega_;(\phi)(p_1, p_2) = \lambda\sigma.\{\langle\sigma', \phi(p', p_2)\rangle \mid \langle\sigma', p'\rangle \in p_1(\sigma)\}, \quad p_1 \neq p_\epsilon$$
$$\Omega_\|(\phi)(p_1, p_2) = \Omega_;(\phi)(p_1, p_2) + \Omega_;(\phi)(p_2, p_1).$$

(c) $; = fix(\Omega_;)$, $\| = fix(\Omega_\|)$, $\mathbb{L} = \Omega_;(\|)$.

We omit the proof of

Lemma 12.7

(a) '$;$', '$\|$' (and '$\mathbb{L}$', '$+$') are well-defined and nonexpansive in both their arguments.

(b) If $p \neq p_\epsilon$, then $d(p;p_1, p;p_2) \leq \frac{1}{2}d(p_1, p_2)$.

Definition 12.8

(a) Let $(S \in) Sem_D = \mathcal{L}_{aw} \to \mathbb{P}_D$. The mapping $\Psi: Sem_D \to Sem_D$ is defined by

$$\Psi(S)(v := e) = \lambda\sigma.\{\langle\sigma\{\alpha/v\}, p_\epsilon\rangle\}, \quad \alpha = \mathcal{V}(e)(\sigma)$$
$$\Psi(S)(\mathsf{skip}) = \lambda\sigma.\{\langle\sigma, p_\epsilon\rangle\}$$
$$\Psi(S)(\mathsf{stop}) = \lambda\sigma.\emptyset$$
$$\Psi(S)(s_1 \text{ op } s_2) = \Psi(S)(s_1) \text{ op } \Psi(S)(s_2), \quad \text{op} \in \{;, \|, +\}$$
$$\Psi(S)(\mathsf{if}\ e\ \mathsf{then}\ s_1\ \mathsf{else}\ s_2\ \mathsf{fi}) =$$
$$\lambda\sigma.\mathsf{if}\ \mathcal{V}(e)(\sigma)\ \mathsf{then}\ \Psi(S)(s_1)(\sigma)\ \mathsf{else}\ \Psi(S)(s_2)(\sigma)\ \mathsf{fi}$$
$$\Psi(S)(\mathsf{while}\ e\ \mathsf{do}\ s\ \mathsf{od}) =$$
$$\lambda\sigma.\{\langle\sigma, S(\mathsf{if}\ e\ \mathsf{then}\ (s;\mathsf{while}\ e\ \mathsf{do}\ s\ \mathsf{od})\ \mathsf{else}\ \mathsf{skip}\ \mathsf{fi})\rangle\}.$$

(b) $\mathcal{D} = fix(\Psi)$, $\mathcal{D}[\![s]\!] = \mathcal{D}(s)$.

Example

$$\mathcal{D}[\![(v := 0;\mathsf{await}\ v = 1\ \mathsf{then}\ w := 2\ \mathsf{end}) \| v := 1]\!]$$
$$= \big(\mathcal{D}(v := 0);\mathcal{D}(\mathsf{await}\ v = 1\ \mathsf{then}\ w := 2\ \mathsf{end})\big) \| \mathcal{D}(v := 1)$$
$$= \big(\lambda\sigma_0.\{\langle\sigma_0\{0/v\}, p_\epsilon\rangle\};$$
$$\lambda\sigma_1.\mathsf{if}\ \sigma_1(v) = 1\ \mathsf{then}\ \{\langle\sigma_1\{2/w\}, p_\epsilon\rangle\}\ \mathsf{else}\ \emptyset\ \mathsf{fi}) \|$$
$$\lambda\sigma_2.\{\langle\sigma_2\{1/v\}, p_\epsilon\rangle\}$$

$$= (\lambda\sigma_0.\{\langle\sigma_0\{0/v\}, \lambda\sigma_1.\text{if } \sigma_1(v) = 1 \text{ then } \{\langle\sigma_1\{2/w\}, p_\epsilon\rangle\} \text{ else } \emptyset \text{ fi}\rangle\}) \parallel$$
$$\lambda\sigma_2.\{\langle\sigma_2\{1/v\}, p_\epsilon\rangle\}$$
$$= \lambda\sigma.\{\langle\sigma\{0/v\}, \lambda\sigma'.$$
$$\quad\text{if } \sigma'(v) = 1 \text{ then } \langle\sigma'\{2/w\}, \lambda\sigma''.\{\langle\sigma''\{1/v\}, p_\epsilon\rangle\}\rangle\} \text{ else } \emptyset \text{ fi } \cup$$
$$\quad\quad\{\langle\sigma'\{1/v\}, \lambda\sigma''.\text{if } \sigma''(v) = 1 \text{ then } \{\langle\sigma''\{2/w\}, p_\epsilon\rangle\} \text{ else } \emptyset \text{ fi}\rangle,$$
$$\quad\quad\langle\sigma\{1/v\}, \lambda\sigma'.\{\langle\sigma'\{0/v\},$$
$$\quad\quad\quad\lambda\sigma''.\text{if } \sigma''(v) = 1 \text{ then } \{\langle\sigma''\{2/w\}, p_\epsilon\rangle\} \text{ else } \emptyset \text{ fi}\rangle\}\rangle\}$$

We now investigate how $\mathcal{O}$ and $\mathcal{D}$ for $\mathcal{L}_{aw}$ are related. As before, the main step is the introduction of an abstraction function $abs \colon \mathbb{P}_D \to \mathbb{P}_O$. This function combines three features, two of which were already present in the abs-functions from Chapter 11. (It should be noted that points (a) to (c) should be taken simultaneously, rather than as consecutive in time.)

(a) Firstly, it collapses the branching structure of a process $p \in \mathbb{P}_D$, yielding the set of all its paths.

(b) Secondly, it replaces all "instances" of p which are equal to $\emptyset$ to $\{\delta\}$. Here "instance" is defined (as the nonuniform extension of the notion of "subprocess" as introduced in Chapter 11) as follows: For $p \neq p_\epsilon$ an instance of p is either

  • $p(\sigma)$, for some $\sigma \in \Sigma$

  • an instance of any p' such that, for some σ and σ', $\langle\sigma', p'\rangle \in p(\sigma)$.

(c) Thirdly, it "develops" p: The result of $abs(p)$—which should yield an element of $\Sigma \to \mathcal{P}_{nco}(\Sigma_\delta^\infty)$—is defined as the function which, for any σ, yields the union of the sets $\sigma' \cdot abs(p')(\sigma')$, for all $\langle\sigma', p'\rangle \in p(\sigma)$. Note how, in the recursive application of abs to p' and σ', the state σ' will be supplied as argument to p'. This is the place where a pair $\langle\sigma', p'\rangle$—which is still able to accommodate interleaving actions from some parallel $\bar{p}$—loses this ability, in that it is replaced by $p'(\sigma')$, whence σ' as an intermediate state in the execution has disappeared. Note also that we deliver the entities $\sigma' \cdot abs(p')(\sigma')$, ..., rather than just $abs(p')(\sigma')$. The role of the prefix $\sigma' \cdot \ldots$ is (here and elsewhere for nonuniform languages) to build *sequences* of states (here and almost everywhere required by the metric machinery).

It may be instructive to contrast the definition of abs with that of the atomization operator in the next subsection. Though lacking the sequence building feature, it is well-formed since its domain is restricted to the *finite* processes in $\mathbb{P}_D$.

The precise definition of abs follows.

Definition 12.9

(a) Let $(\phi \in) Op = \mathbb{P}_D \xrightarrow{1} \mathbb{P}_O$. The mapping $\Omega_{abs} \colon Op \to Op$ is defined as follows:

$$\Omega_{abs}(\phi)(p_\epsilon) = \lambda\sigma.\{\epsilon\}$$
$$\Omega_{abs}(\phi)(p) = \lambda\sigma.\text{if } p(\sigma) = \emptyset \text{ then } \{\delta\}\text{else}$$
$$\bigcup\{\sigma' \cdot \phi(p')(\sigma') \mid \langle\sigma', p'\rangle \in p(\sigma)\} \text{ fi}, \quad p \neq p_\epsilon$$

(b) $abs = fix(\Omega_{abs})$.

Example

$abs(\lambda\sigma.\{$
$\quad \langle\sigma\{0/v\}, \lambda\sigma'.$
$\qquad \text{if } \sigma'(v) = 1 \text{ then } \{\langle\sigma'\{2/w\}, \lambda\sigma''.\{\langle\sigma''\{1/v\}, p_\epsilon\rangle\}\rangle\} \text{ else } \emptyset \text{ fi} \cup$
$\qquad \{\langle\sigma'\{1/v\}, \lambda\sigma''.\text{if } \sigma''(v) = 1 \text{ then } \{\langle\sigma''\{2/w\}, p_\epsilon\rangle\} \text{ else } \emptyset \text{ fi}\rangle\},$
$\quad \langle\sigma\{1/v\}, \lambda\sigma'.$
$\qquad \{\langle\sigma'\{0/v\}, \lambda\sigma''.\text{if } \sigma''(v) = 1 \text{ then } \{\langle\sigma''\{2/w\}, p_\epsilon\rangle\} \text{ else } \emptyset \text{ fi}\rangle\}$
$\quad \})(\sigma)$
$= \quad \bigcup\{\sigma\{0/v\} \cdot \sigma\{1/v\} \cdot \sigma\{1/v, 2/w\}\{\epsilon\}, \sigma\{1/v\} \cdot \sigma\{0/v\} \cdot \{\delta\}\}$
$= \quad \{\sigma\{0/v\}\sigma\{1/v\}\sigma\{1/v, 2/w\}, \sigma\{1/v\}\sigma\{0/v\}\delta\}$

An alternative way of defining the *abs*-function is described in Exercise 12.3. The usual intermediate semantics $\mathcal{O}^* \colon Res \to \mathbb{P}_D$ is introduced in

Definition 12.10

(a) Let $(S \in) Sem_D = Res \to \mathbb{P}_D$. The mapping $\Phi^* \colon Sem_D \to Sem_D$ is given as, $\Phi^*(S)(E) = p_\epsilon$, and

$$\Phi^*(S)(s) = \lambda\sigma.\{\langle\sigma', S(r)\rangle \mid [s, \sigma] \to [r, \sigma']\}.$$

(b) $\mathcal{O}^* = fix(\Phi^*)$.

Putting $\mathcal{E}(E) = p_\epsilon$, $\mathcal{E}(s) = \mathcal{D}(s)$, we have

Lemma 12.11 $\Phi^*(\mathcal{E}) = \mathcal{E}$.

Proof Choose some σ. One subcase.

$[s_1 \| s_2]$ $\quad \Phi^*(\mathcal{E})(s_1 \| s_2)(\sigma)$

$\quad = \quad \{\, \langle \sigma', \mathcal{E}(r) \rangle \mid [s_1 \| s_2, \sigma] \to [r, \sigma'] \,\}$

$\quad = \quad \{\, \langle \sigma', \mathcal{E}(r' \| s_2) \rangle \mid [s_1, \sigma] \to [r', \sigma'] \,\} \cup \text{(symm.)}$

$\quad = \quad \{\, \langle \sigma', \mathcal{E}(r') \| \mathcal{E}(s_2) \rangle \mid [s_1, \sigma] \to [r', \sigma'] \,\} \cup \text{(symm.)}$

$\quad = \quad \{\, \langle \sigma', \mathcal{E}(r') \rangle \mid [s_1, \sigma] \to [r', \sigma'] \,\} \| \mathcal{E}(s_2) \cup \text{(symm.)}$

$\quad = \quad \Phi^*(\mathcal{E})(s_1)(\sigma) \| \mathcal{E}(s_2) \cup \text{(symm.)}$

$\quad = \quad [\text{ind. hyp.}] \; \mathcal{E}(s_1)(\sigma) \| \mathcal{E}(s_2) \cup \text{(symm.)}$

$\quad = \quad \mathcal{E}(s_1 \| s_2)(\sigma) \,.$ $\hfill \square$

Corollary 12.12 $\mathcal{O}^* = \mathcal{E}$.

Let $\mathcal{O}[\![E]\!] = \lambda\sigma.\{\,\epsilon\,\}$, and let $\mathcal{O}[\![s]\!]$ be as before. We have

Theorem 12.13

(a) *For each $r \in \text{Res}$, $(\text{abs} \circ \mathcal{O}^*)(r) = \mathcal{O}[\![r]\!]$.*

(b) $\mathcal{O}[\![\pi]\!] = (\text{abs} \circ \mathcal{D})[\![\pi]\!]$, *for $\pi \in \mathcal{L}_{aw}$.*

Proof

(a) We show that for each r and each σ, $(\text{abs} \circ \mathcal{O}^*)(r)(\sigma) = \mathcal{O}[\![r]\!](\sigma)$. The case $r \equiv E$ is clear. Otherwise, we have

$\quad \text{abs}(\mathcal{O}^*(s))(\sigma)$

$\quad = \quad \text{abs}(\{\, \langle \sigma', \mathcal{O}^*(r) \rangle \mid [s, \sigma] \to [r, \sigma'] \,\})$

$\quad = \quad \bigcup \{\, \sigma' \cdot (\text{abs} \circ \mathcal{O}^*)(r)(\sigma') \mid [s, \sigma] \to [r, \sigma'] \,\} \,.$

Now let $\Phi' : (\text{Res} \to \mathbb{P}_O) \to (\text{Res} \to \mathbb{P}_O)$ be given by $\Phi'(S)(E) = \lambda\sigma.\{\,\epsilon\,\}$ and

$$\Phi'(S)(s) = \lambda\sigma. \bigcup \{\, \sigma' \cdot S(r)(\sigma') \mid [s, \sigma] \to [r, \sigma'] \,\}.$$

Clearly, we have $\mathcal{O}[\![\cdot]\!] = \text{fix}(\Phi')$. Also, from the above we see that $\Phi'(\text{abs} \circ \mathcal{O}^*) = \text{abs} \circ \mathcal{O}^*$, and we conclude that $\text{abs} \circ \mathcal{O}^* = \mathcal{O}[\![\cdot]\!]$.

(b) Clear. $\hfill \square$

12.1.3 Atomization

In this subsection, we refine the earlier semantic treatment of the await statement, in the sense that we now also take into account the atomization feature of await e then s end: In case the test e succeeds, the statement s is to be executed in an atomized way, i.e., it should not be possible to interrupt the execution of s by some interleaving action of a parallel component. For example, the statement

await true then $(v := 0; v := v + 1)$ end $\|(v := 2)$

has as possible final values for v only $v = 1$ or $v = 2$. Thus, the interleaved execution $v := 0; v := 2; v := v + 1$—with $v = 3$ as final value—is now excluded. The method adopted to achieve atomization is simple: for given input state σ, we determine all final values $\bar{\sigma}$ resulting from the execution of s for input σ, *without* recording the intermediate states σ' (and processes p') as described in the previous subsection. Two points are important here: Firstly, note that the treatment in terms of such intermediate $\langle \sigma', p' \rangle$ was necessitated by the very wish to accommodate interleaving actions, a wish which, by definition, does not apply here. Secondly, the determination of the σ as stated above is easy for programs s without occurrences of a while statement, since the calculation of $\bar{\sigma}$ is then a finite process. In the general case, this is not so simple (and not elaborated here). However, since it is customary to consider only await statements without constituent while statements, this does not bother us too much. Since the semantic modeling to be presented in this subsection is incremental with respect to the earlier design, we shall allow ourselves a somewhat more terse treatment.

We now first give the syntax for the refined $\mathcal{L}_{aw}$, say $\mathcal{L}_{aw,at}$ (await with atomization). The new syntax distinguishes, in addition to the constructs as considered earlier, as well *finite* statements f ($\in$ *FStat*). These are characterized by the omission of the while statement from their definition. In addition, a new operator $[f]$—to be read as "the atomized version of f"—is introduced.

Definition 12.14

(a) s ($\in$ *Stat*) ::= $v := e \mid$ skip $\mid$ stop $\mid [f] \mid (s;s) \mid$ if e then s else s fi $\mid$
         while e do s od $\mid (s\|s)$.

(b) f ($\in$ *FStat*) ::= $v := e \mid$ skip $\mid$ stop $\mid [f] \mid (f;f) \mid$ if e then f else f fi $\mid (f\|f)$.

(c) $(\pi \in)\mathcal{L}_{aw,at} = Stat$.

(d) await e then f end is an abbreviation for if e then $[f]$ else stop fi.

Note that $FStat \subseteq Stat$. Hence, in every phrase below where we use $s \ (\in Stat)$—in a definition, rule, lemma, etc.—as a special case the same phrase applies with f replacing s.

Resumptions for $\mathcal{L}_{aw,at}$ are as for $\mathcal{L}_{aw}$. We now present $\mathcal{T}_{aw,at}$.

Definition 12.15 $\mathcal{T}_{aw,at}$ consists of all rules from $\mathcal{T}_{aw}$ extended with the two rules

$$\bullet \qquad \frac{[f,\sigma] \to [\mathrm{E},\sigma']}{[[f],\sigma] \to [\mathrm{E},\sigma']} \qquad\qquad\qquad\qquad\qquad\qquad \text{(Atom 1)}$$

$$\bullet \qquad \frac{[f,\sigma] \to [f',\sigma'] \qquad [[f'],\sigma'] \to [\mathrm{E},\sigma'']}{[[f],\sigma] \to [\mathrm{E},\sigma'']} \qquad\qquad \text{(Atom 2)}$$

The rules (Atom 1) and (Atom 2) may be understood as follows: (Atom 1) expresses that if f may terminate after one step, then so may $[f]$. If f can make a step to some f' (changing σ to σ'), then, assuming that we already know that $[[f'],\sigma']$ yields—in one step—$[\mathrm{E},\sigma'']$, we can combine the two steps, as indicated by (the conclusion of) (Atom 2). Note that for this to work properly, we rely on the fact that $[f']$ is of smaller syntactic complexity than $[f]$ (cf. the comments below).

Remarks

(1) As in $\mathcal{T}_{aw}$, no rule is given for stop.

(2) The rules from $\mathcal{T}_{aw}$ are stated in terms of $s \in Stat$, and, hence, also apply to the $f \in FStat$.

By induction on the syntactic complexity of f, one easily shows that, for all σ, σ', if $[f,\sigma] \to [f',\sigma']$, then f' has smaller syntactic complexity than f. This property is in fact crucial for the subsequent development—and, of course, only valid by our assumption that f is without while statements. The proof that $\mathcal{T}_{aw,at}$ satisfies, for each s, σ, the (familiar) property that

$$\{ [r,\sigma'] \mid [s,\sigma] \to [r,\sigma'] \}$$

is a finite set, relies in turn on the just stated claim. We omit the (standard) definition of $\mathcal{O}$ for $\mathcal{L}_{aw,at}$ as based on $\mathcal{T}_{aw,at}$.

We next turn to the denotational definitions. As first step, we introduce the finitary variant $\mathbb{P}_D^*$ of the domain $\mathbb{P}_D$ as specified in (12.2). $\mathbb{P}_D^*$ will serve as the codomain for $\mathcal{D}$ on $FStat$.

Definition 12.16 $\mathbb{P}_D^* = \bigcup_n \mathbb{P}_D^{(n)}$, where $\mathbb{P}_D^{(0)} = \{p_\epsilon\}$, and

$$\mathbb{P}_D^{(n+1)} = \{p_\epsilon\} + (\Sigma \to \mathcal{P}_{co}(\Sigma \times id_{\frac{1}{2}}(\mathbb{P}_D^{(n)}))), \quad n = 0, 1, \ldots$$

Thus, $\mathbb{P}_D^*$ contains only finite processes, and it is possible to argue by simple mathematical induction on $\mathbb{P}_D^*$. (Recalling that $\mathcal{P}_f(\cdot)$ stands for all finite subsets of $(\cdot)$, we have that $\mathcal{P}_{co}(\Sigma \times id_{\frac{1}{2}}(\mathbb{P}_D^{(n)}))$ equals $\mathcal{P}_f(\Sigma \times id_{\frac{1}{2}}(\mathbb{P}_D^{(n)}))$, for all $n \geq 0$.)

Remark $\mathbb{P}_D^*$ is an incomplete space, in that is does not include limit processes. By the general theory (Chapter 10) the topological *completion* $\overline{\mathbb{P}_D^*}$ equals (up to isometry) the domain $\mathbb{P}_D$ as specified in (12.2).

Next, we introduce the operation of atomization on $\mathbb{P}_D^*$.

Definition 12.17 For $p \in \mathbb{P}_D^*$, its *atomized* version $[p]$—a process residing in $\mathbb{P}_D^{(1)}$—is defined by putting $[p_\epsilon] = p_\epsilon$, and for $p \neq p_\epsilon$,

$$[p] = \lambda\sigma.(\ \ \{\langle\sigma', p_\epsilon\rangle \mid \langle\sigma', p_\epsilon\rangle \in p(\sigma)\} \cup$$
$$\bigcup\{[p'](\sigma') \mid \langle\sigma', p'\rangle \in p(\sigma),\ p' \neq p_\epsilon\}).$$

Note that, contrary to the situation everywhere else in our book, the definition of $[\cdot]$ lacks contractiveness. However, this does not cause problems since, clearly, well-definedness of $[p]$ is easy by mathematical induction (on the "degree" of p, i.e., the least n such that $p \in \mathbb{P}_D^{(n)}$), using the fact that, if $p \in \mathbb{P}_D^{(n+1)}$, then, for each σ, σ', p', if $\langle\sigma', p'\rangle \in p(\sigma)$ then $p' \in \mathbb{P}_D^{(n)}$. Altogether, for finite p, $[p]$ simply yields the input-output behaviour of p. The form of the definitions is chosen such that it allows a particularly succinct correspondence with the rules (Atom 1), (Atom 2) from $\mathcal{T}_{aw,at}$.

We can now give

Definition 12.18 $\mathcal{D}\colon \mathcal{L}_{aw,at} \to \mathbb{P}_D$ is the unique function satisfying

- all clauses for $\mathcal{D}$ on $\mathcal{L}_{aw}$ as given in Definition 12.8,
- for $f \in FStat$, $\mathcal{D}([f]) = [\mathcal{D}(f)]$.

Justification of this definition requires the easy proof that, for $f \in FStat$, $\mathcal{D}(f) \in \mathbb{P}_D^*$.

As last step, we verify that Theorem 12.13 also holds when $\mathcal{L}_{aw}$ is extended to $\mathcal{L}_{aw,at}$. All steps in the proof remain the same as before, but for one extra subcase in the proof of

Lemma 12.19 $\Phi^*(\mathcal{E}) = \mathcal{E}$.

Proof One (new) subcase.

[[f]]   Choose some σ. We recall that, if $[f,\sigma] \to [f',\sigma']$, then f' has smaller syntactic complexity than f (abbreviated below to $f' < f$). This enables the following argument

$$\Phi^*(\mathcal{E})([f])(\sigma)$$
$$= \ \{\, \langle \sigma', \mathcal{E}(r)\rangle \mid [[f],\sigma] \to [r,\sigma'] \,\}$$
$$= \ \{\, \langle \sigma', p_\epsilon\rangle \mid [f,\sigma] \to [\mathrm{E},\sigma'] \,\} \cup$$
$$\quad \{\, \langle \sigma'', p_\epsilon\rangle \mid [f,\sigma] \to [f',\sigma'], \ [[f'],\sigma'] \to [\mathrm{E},\sigma''] \,\}$$
$$= \ \{\, \langle \sigma', p_\epsilon\rangle \mid \langle \sigma', p_\epsilon\rangle \in \Phi^*(\mathcal{E})(f)(\sigma) \,\} \cup$$
$$\quad \{\, \langle \sigma'', p_\epsilon\rangle \mid \langle \sigma', \mathcal{E}(f')\rangle \in \Phi^*(\mathcal{E})(f)(\sigma), \ \langle \sigma'', p_\epsilon\rangle \in \Phi^*(\mathcal{E})([f'])(\sigma') \,\}$$
$$= \ [\text{ind. hyp., since } f < [f] \text{ and } f' < f, \text{ hence } [f'] < [f]]$$
$$\quad \{\, \langle \sigma', p_\epsilon\rangle \mid \langle \sigma', p_\epsilon\rangle \in \mathcal{E}(f)(\sigma) \,\} \cup$$
$$\quad \{\, \langle \sigma'', p_\epsilon\rangle \mid \langle \sigma', \mathcal{E}(f')\rangle \in \mathcal{E}(f)(\sigma), \ \langle \sigma'', p_\epsilon\rangle \in \mathcal{E}([f'])(\sigma') \,\}$$
$$= \ \{\, \langle \sigma', p_\epsilon\rangle \mid \langle \sigma', p_\epsilon\rangle \in \mathcal{E}(f)(\sigma) \,\} \cup$$
$$\quad \{\, \langle \sigma'', p_\epsilon\rangle \mid \langle \sigma', \mathcal{E}(f')\rangle \in \mathcal{E}(f)(\sigma), \ \langle \sigma'', p_\epsilon\rangle \in [\mathcal{E}(f')](\sigma') \,\}$$
$$= \ \ \{\, \langle \sigma', p_\epsilon\rangle \mid \langle \sigma', p_\epsilon\rangle \in \mathcal{E}(f)(\sigma) \,\} \cup$$
$$\quad \textstyle\bigcup\{\, [\mathcal{E}(f')](\sigma') \mid \langle \sigma', \mathcal{E}(f')\rangle \in \mathcal{E}(f)(\sigma) \,\}$$
$$= \ [\mathcal{E}(f)](\sigma)$$
$$= \ \mathcal{E}([f])(\sigma). \qquad\qquad\qquad\qquad\qquad\qquad\qquad\qquad\qquad\qquad\qquad \square$$

With this proof, we have completed the semantic analysis of $\mathcal{L}_{aw,at}$.

12.2   Communication with value passing
        —a nonuniform version of $\mathcal{L}_{syn}$

Our next language combines features of $\mathcal{L}_{svp}$ and of $\mathcal{L}_{syn}$. Instead of a simple synchronization of some c and $\bar{c}$ occurring in two parallel components—resulting in the silent step τ when the synchronization succeeds—we now consider communication over *channels*. Let *Chan* denote the alphabet of channel names; for simplicity, we use the variable c to range as well over *Chan*. Communication takes place by means of the receive statement $c?v$ and the send statement $c!v$, to be read as

- $(c?v)$ the variable v is ready to receive a value over the channel c,
- $(c!e)$ the current value of e is to be sent over the channel c.

In case the two parallel components in which the statements $c?v$, $c!e$ occur are each ready to execute these respective actions, the communication succeeds, and the current value of e is transmitted over c and received by v. Note that this may also be expressed by saying that at the moment of communication—the moment of the "handshake" as this is often called—the assignment $v := e$ is executed. Altogether, the uniform c, $\bar{c}$ and τ as present in $\mathcal{L}_{syn}$ are replaced here by the nonuniform $c?v$, $c!e$ and $v := e$. The domain necessary to model this type of communication should not be too difficult to understand for the reader who has studied the sections on $\mathcal{L}_{syn}$ and $\mathcal{L}_{aw}$. (For simplicity, we have not included a restriction construct in $\mathcal{L}_{com}$.) One final introductory remark: In the semantics for $\mathcal{L}_{com}$, we stick to a model with one global state (just as the one used for $\mathcal{L}_{svp}$). This might be considered unsatisfactory, since the very purpose of a language such as $\mathcal{L}_{svp}$ is to model the communication between processes which each have their own "local" state. However, we postpone a treatment of this till the next chapter (Section 13.1), in order that we may focus first on the use of branching domains for nonuniform communication.

12.2.1   Syntax and operational semantics

Let $(v \in)$ *IVar* and $(e \in)$ *Exp* be as before. Let $(c \in)$ *Chan* be an alphabet of *channel names*. (We shall have no need for a '$\bar{\cdot}$'-mapping on *Chan*.)

Definition 12.20

(a) $s\, (\in Stat) ::= v := e \mid \mathsf{skip} \mid c?v \mid c!e \mid (s;s) \mid \mathsf{if}\ e\ \mathsf{then}\ s\ \mathsf{else}\ s\ \mathsf{fi} \mid$
$\qquad\qquad\qquad \mathsf{while}\ e\ \mathsf{do}\ s\ \mathsf{od} \mid (s\|s)$

(b) $(\pi \in)\,\mathcal{L}_{com} = Stat$.

The set of resumptions is given in

Definition 12.21

(a) $r\, (\in Res) ::= \mathrm{E} \mid s$.

(b) We identify each of E;s, E$\|s$ and $s\|$E with s, and E$\|$E with E.

Transitions in $\mathcal{T}_{com}$ are of two kinds. Besides the usual $[r, \sigma] \rightarrow [r', \sigma']$, we also use steps generated by (single-sided) communication actions, i.e., of the form $c?v$ or $c!\alpha$. Therefore, we introduce

Definition 12.22 $(\rho \in) \, Step = \Sigma \cup Chan \times (IVar \cup Val)$.

For easier readability, we denote typical elements of $Chan \times IVar$ or $Chan \times Val$ by $c?v$ or $c!\alpha$, respectively.

Definition 12.23 $\mathcal{T}_{com} = (Res \times Step, Step, \rightarrow, Spec)$. Transitions are written as $[r, \rho] \rightarrow [r', \rho']$ or $[r, \rho] \rightarrow_0 [r', \rho']$. $Spec$ contains the rules (Ass), (Skip), (If) and (While') (as in $\mathcal{T}_{aw}$), and, in addition,

- $$[c?v, \sigma] \rightarrow [\text{E}, c?v] \qquad \qquad \qquad \qquad \text{(Receive)}$$

- $$[c!e, \sigma] \rightarrow [\text{E}, c!\alpha] \qquad \text{where } \alpha = \mathcal{V}(e)(\sigma) \qquad \text{(Send)}$$

- $$\frac{[s, \sigma] \rightarrow [r, \rho]}{[s;s', \sigma] \rightarrow [r;s', \rho]} \qquad \qquad \qquad \qquad \text{(Seq)}$$

- $$\frac{[s, \sigma] \rightarrow [r, \rho]}{[s\|s', \sigma] \rightarrow [r\|s', \rho]} \qquad \qquad \qquad \qquad \text{(Par)}$$

  $$[s'\|s, \sigma] \rightarrow [s'\|r, \rho]$$

- $$\frac{[s, \sigma] \rightarrow [r, c?v] \qquad [s', \sigma] \rightarrow [r', c!\alpha]}{[s\|s', \sigma] \rightarrow [r\|r', \sigma\{\alpha/v\}]} \qquad \qquad \text{(Com)}$$

  $$[s'\|s, \sigma] \rightarrow [r'\|r, \sigma\{\alpha/v\}]$$

In the (Com)-rule, if s_1 (s_2) can make a $c?v$ ($c!\alpha$) step (or vice-versa), we are in a position that s_1 is ready to execute $c?v$ and s_2 is ready to execute some $c!\alpha$ (with $\alpha = \mathcal{V}(e)(\sigma)$), or vice-versa. The synchronized communication then succeeds, and the value α is transmitted to v, resulting in a state change from σ to $\sigma\{\alpha/v\}$.

Contrary to the situation for $\mathcal{T}_{aw}$, $\mathcal{T}_{com}$ prescribes transitions for *all* configurations $[s, \sigma]$. Still, there is the following counterpart of the notion of blocking—which is the nonuniform version of a similar version for $\mathcal{L}_{syn}$:

Definition 12.24 $[s, \sigma]$ *blocks* if there are no r and σ' such that $[s, \sigma] \to [r, \sigma']$.

Note that the criterion here is whether there is some (r and) $\sigma' \in \Sigma$ satisfying the condition (rather than just any $\rho' \in Step$).

Examples of blocking configurations are $[c?v;s, \sigma]$ or $[c!\alpha;s', \sigma]$. In both cases, the only transitions possible yield results $[r, \rho]$ with $\rho \in Step \setminus \Sigma$, i.e., ρ is a step in $Chan \times (IVar \cup Val)$. Note how such transitions model failing attempts at communication, analogous to transitions $s \xrightarrow{c} r$ in the context of $\mathcal{L}_{syn}$.

The operational semantics $\mathcal{O}$ uses the same domain $\mathbb{P}_O = \Sigma \to \mathcal{P}_{nco}(\Sigma_\delta^\infty)$ as used in the previous section.

Definition 12.25

(a) $\mathcal{O}: Res \times \Sigma \to \mathcal{P}_{nco}(\Sigma_\delta^\infty)$ is the unique function satisfying $\mathcal{O}(\mathrm{E}, \sigma) = \{\epsilon\}$, and

$$
\mathcal{O}(s, \sigma) \;=\; \begin{cases} \{\delta\} & \text{if } [s, \sigma] \text{ blocks} \\ \bigcup\{ \sigma' \cdot \mathcal{O}(r, \sigma') \mid [s, \sigma] \to [r, \sigma'] \} & \text{otherwise.} \end{cases}
$$

(b) $\mathcal{O}[\![\cdot]\!]: \mathcal{L}_{com} \to \mathbb{P}_O$ is given by $\mathcal{O}[\![s]\!] = \lambda\sigma.\mathcal{O}(s, \sigma)$.

Examples

(1) $\mathcal{O}[\![(v := 1; c!(v + 1)) \| c?w]\!](\sigma) = \{ \sigma\{1/v\}\sigma\{1/v, 2/w\} \}$

(2) $\mathcal{O}[\![(v := 1; v := 2) \| c?v]\!](\sigma) = \{ \sigma\{1/v\}\sigma\{2/v\}\delta \}$.

12.2.2 Denotational semantics, relating $\mathcal{O}$ and $\mathcal{D}$

The denotational domain for $\mathcal{L}_{com}$ combines the nonuniform branching structure as present in the domain for $\mathcal{L}_{aw}$ with the additional structure induced by using the set $Step$ (Definition 12.22) rather than Σ in the product '$\cdot \times \mathbb{P}_D$'. Also, for the definition of '$\|$' on $\mathbb{P}_D$ we shall provide a nonuniform extension of the treatment of synchronization as described for $\mathcal{L}_{syn}$. We first give

Definition 12.26 The domain $\mathbb{P}_D$ for $\mathcal{L}_{com}$ is given as the (unique) solution of the equation

$$
\mathbb{P}_D \simeq \{p_\epsilon\} + (\Sigma \to \mathcal{P}_{co}(Step \times id_{\frac{1}{2}}(\mathbb{P}_D))).
$$

The semantic operators ';', '$\|$' (and '$\lfloor\!\lfloor$', '$\lfloor$'), and '+' on $\mathbb{P}_D$ are described in the next definition.

Definition 12.27 Let $\phi \in Op = \mathbb{P}_D \times \mathbb{P}_D \xrightarrow{1} \mathbb{P}_D$.

(a) The mapping $\Omega_; : Op \to Op$ is given in

$$\begin{aligned}
\Omega_;(\phi)(p_\epsilon, p) &= p \\
\Omega_;(\phi)(p_1, p_2) &= \lambda\sigma.\{\, \langle \rho, \phi(p', p_2)\rangle \mid \langle \rho, p'\rangle \in p_1(\sigma) \,\}, \quad p_1 \neq p_\epsilon \,.
\end{aligned}$$

(b) The mapping $\Omega_\| : Op \to Op$ is given as

$$\Omega_\|(\phi)(p_\epsilon, p) = \Omega_\|(\phi)(p, p_\epsilon) = p$$

and, for $p_1, p_2 \neq p_\epsilon$,

$$\begin{aligned}
\Omega_\|(\phi)(p_1, p_2) &= \\
&\Omega_;(\phi)(p_1, p_2) + \Omega_;(\phi)(p_2, p_1) + \Omega_\lfloor(\phi)(p_1, p_2) + \Omega_\lfloor(\phi)(p_2, p_1)
\end{aligned}$$

with $\Omega_\lfloor$ and '+' as defined in (c) and (d).

(c) The mapping $\Omega_\lfloor : Op \to Op$ is given as

$$\Omega_\lfloor(\phi)(p_\epsilon, p) = \Omega_\lfloor(\phi)(p, p_\epsilon) = \lambda\sigma.\emptyset$$

and, for $p_1, p_2 \neq p_\epsilon$,

$$\begin{aligned}
\Omega_\lfloor(\phi)(p_1, p_2) &= \\
&\lambda\sigma.\{\, \langle \sigma\{\alpha/v\}, \phi(p', p'')\rangle \mid \langle c?v, p'\rangle \in p_1(\sigma), \langle c!\alpha, p''\rangle \in p_2(\sigma) \,\} \,.
\end{aligned}$$

(d) $p + p_\epsilon = p_\epsilon + p = p$, and for $p_1, p_2 \neq p_\epsilon$, $p_1 + p_2 = \lambda\sigma.(p_1(\sigma) \cup p_2(\sigma))$.

(e) $; = \mathit{fix}(\Omega_;)$, $\| = \mathit{fix}(\Omega_\|)$, $\lfloor\!\lfloor = \Omega_;(\|)$, $\lfloor = \Omega_\lfloor(\|)$.

From the definition it is immediate that, for $p_1, p_2 \neq p_\epsilon$,

$$(p_1 \| p_2)(\sigma) = (p_1 \lfloor\!\lfloor p_2)(\sigma) \cup (p_2 \lfloor\!\lfloor p_1)(\sigma) \cup (p_1 \lfloor p_2)(\sigma) \cup (p_2 \lfloor p_1)(\sigma).$$

Thus, the parallel composition $p_1 \| p_2$ of two processes p_1, p_2 yields a process which, for given σ, consists of the union of four components:

- The leftmerge $(p_1 \; \underline{\|} \; p_2)(\sigma)$ is executed by choosing among the possible elements $\langle \rho, p' \rangle$ in $p_1(\sigma)$, and continuing with $\langle \rho, p' \| p_2 \rangle$.
- Symmetrically for the leftmerge $(p_2 \; \underline{\|} \; p_1)(\sigma)$.
- The communication merge $(p_1 \; \underline{\lfloor} \; p_2)(\sigma)$. This collects all result of successful communication (for the given σ) obtained by matching any $\langle c?v, p' \rangle$ in $p_1(\sigma)$ and the corresponding $\langle c!\alpha, p'' \rangle$ in $p_2(\sigma)$, and continuing with $\langle \sigma\{\alpha/v\}, p' \| p'' \rangle$.
- Symmetrically for $(p_2 \; \underline{\lfloor} \; p_1)(\sigma)$.

Clearly, this denotational definition corresponds to the operational intuition: $s_1 \| s_2$, has, for a given state σ, a choice out of four possibilities for its next step:

- $s_1 \| s_2$ executes a first step by s_1, yielding some ρ and r', and continues with the configuration $[\rho, r' \| s_2]$.
- Symmetric, with s_1 and s_2 interchanged.
- In case s_1 is ready to execute $c?v$ (and turn into r') and s_2 is ready to execute $c!\alpha$ (and become r''), the successful communication sets v to α in σ (yielding $\sigma\{\alpha/v\}$), and $r' \| r''$ is the remaining resumption to be executed.
- Symmetric.

We have completed the preparations for

Definition 12.28

(a) $\mathcal{D}: \mathcal{L}_{com} \rightarrow \mathbb{P}_D$ is the unique function satisfying the usual clauses (cf. Definition 12.8) for $v := e$, skip, if e then s_1 else s_2 fi and while e do s od, and moreover

$$
\begin{aligned}
\mathcal{D}(c?v) &= \lambda\sigma.\{\, \langle c?v, p_\epsilon \rangle \,\} \\
\mathcal{D}(c!e) &= \lambda\sigma.\{\, \langle c!\alpha, p_\epsilon \rangle \,\}, \quad \alpha = \mathcal{V}(e)(\sigma) \\
\mathcal{D}(s_1 \; \text{op} \; s_2) &= \mathcal{D}(s_1) \; \text{op} \; \mathcal{D}(s_2), \quad \text{op} \in \{;, \|\} \,.
\end{aligned}
$$

(b) $\mathcal{D}[\![s]\!] = \mathcal{D}(s)$.

Examples

(1) $\quad \mathcal{D}[\![(v := 1; v := 2) \| c?v]\!]$
$\quad = \big(\mathcal{D}(v := 1); \mathcal{D}(v := 2) \big) \| \mathcal{D}(c?v)$
$\quad = \lambda\sigma_0.\{\langle \sigma_0\{1/v\}, \lambda\sigma_1.\{\sigma_1\{2/v\}, p_\epsilon\rangle\}\rangle\} \| \lambda\sigma_2.\{\langle c?v, p_\epsilon \rangle\}$

$$= \lambda\sigma.\{\langle\sigma\{1/v\},\lambda\sigma'.\{\langle\sigma'\{2/v\},\lambda\sigma''.\{\langle c?v,p_\epsilon\rangle\}\rangle,$$
$$\langle c?v,\lambda\sigma''.\{\langle\sigma''\{2/v\},p_\epsilon\rangle\}\rangle\}\rangle,$$
$$\langle c?v,\lambda\sigma'.\{\langle\sigma'\{1/v\},\lambda\sigma''.\{\langle\sigma''\{2/v\},p_\epsilon\rangle\}\rangle\}\rangle\}\}$$

(2) $\quad \mathcal{D}[\![(v := 1;c!(v+1))\|c?w]\!]$

$\quad = \bigl(\mathcal{D}(v := 1);\mathcal{D}(c!(v+1))\bigr)\|\mathcal{D}(c?w)$

$\quad = \bigl(\lambda\sigma_0.\{\langle\sigma_0\{1/v\},p_\epsilon\rangle\};\lambda\sigma_1.\{\langle c!\alpha_1,p_\epsilon\rangle\}\bigr)\|\lambda\sigma_2.\{\langle c?w,p_\epsilon\rangle\}$

$\quad = \lambda\sigma_0.\{\langle\sigma_0\{1/v\},\lambda\sigma_1.\{\langle c!\alpha_1,p_\epsilon\rangle\}\rangle\}\|\lambda\sigma_2.\{\langle c?w,p_\epsilon\rangle\}$

$\quad = \lambda\sigma_0.\{\langle\sigma\{1/v\},\lambda\sigma'.\{\langle c!\alpha',\lambda\sigma''.\{\langle c?w,p_\epsilon\rangle\}\rangle\}\} \cup$
$\qquad \{\langle c?w,\lambda\sigma''.\{\langle c!\alpha'',p_\epsilon\rangle\}\}\}) \cup \emptyset \cup \{\langle\sigma'\{\alpha'/w\},p_\epsilon\rangle\}) \cup$
$\qquad \{\langle c?w,\lambda\sigma'.\{\langle\sigma'\{1/v\},\lambda\sigma''.\{\langle c!\alpha'',p_\epsilon\rangle\}\rangle\}\}\}\}\}$

$\quad = \lambda\sigma.\{\langle\sigma\{1/v\},\lambda\sigma'.\{\langle c!\alpha',\lambda\sigma''.\{\langle c?w,p_\epsilon\rangle\}\rangle\},$
$\qquad \langle c?w,\lambda\sigma''.\{\langle c!\alpha'',p_\epsilon\rangle\}\rangle,\langle\sigma'\{\alpha'/w\},p_\epsilon\rangle\}\rangle,$
$\qquad \langle c?w,\lambda\sigma'.\{\langle\sigma'\{1/v\},\lambda\sigma''.\{\langle c!\alpha'',p_\epsilon\rangle\}\rangle\}\rangle\}\}$

where $\alpha_1 = \sigma_1(v) + 1, \ldots$.

The abstraction mapping abs: $\mathbb{P}_D \to \mathbb{P}_O$ is almost as that defined in the previous section. One extra feature mirrors the definition of abs in the context of $\mathcal{L}_{syn}$. Recall that, there, $abs(p)$ yields $\{\delta\}$ in case $p \subseteq Sync \times \mathbb{P}_D$. In the nonuniform setting, this has as counterpart that, in case $p(\sigma) \subseteq (Step \setminus \Sigma) \times \mathbb{P}_D$, we yield $abs(p)(\sigma) = \{\delta\}$. Note the correspondence between the role of $Sync$ for $\mathcal{L}_{syn}$ with that of $Chan \times (IVar \cup Val)$ ($= Step \setminus \Sigma$) for $\mathcal{L}_{com}$. We furthermore observe that "developing" p (cf. the discussion just before Definition 12.9) only works in arguments $\sigma \in \Sigma$ (and not in arguments $\rho \in Step \setminus \Sigma$).

Definition 12.29

(a) Let $(\phi \in) Op = \mathbb{P}_D \xrightarrow{1} \mathbb{P}_O$. The mapping $\Omega_{abs}: Op \to Op$ is given by

$$\Omega_{abs}(\phi)(p_\epsilon)(\sigma) \;=\; \{\epsilon\}$$

and, for $p \neq p_\epsilon$,

$\Omega_{abs}(\phi)(p)(\sigma)$
$$= \left\{\begin{array}{ll} \{\delta\} & \text{if } p(\sigma) \subseteq (Step \setminus \Sigma) \times \mathbb{P}_D \\ \bigcup\{\sigma' \cdot \phi(p')(\sigma') \mid \langle\sigma',p'\rangle \in p(\sigma)\} & \text{otherwise.} \end{array}\right.$$

(b) $abs = fix(\Omega_{abs})$.

Examples

(1) $abs(\lambda\sigma.\{\langle\sigma\{1/v\}, \lambda\sigma'.\{\langle c!\alpha', \lambda\sigma''.\{\langle c?w, p_\epsilon\rangle\}\rangle, \langle c?w, \lambda\sigma''.\{\langle c!\alpha'', p_\epsilon\rangle\}\rangle,$

       $\langle\sigma'\{\alpha'/w\}, p_\epsilon\rangle\}\rangle, \langle c?w, \lambda\sigma'.\{\langle\sigma'\{1/v\}, \lambda\sigma''.\{\langle c!\alpha'', p_\epsilon\rangle\}\rangle\}\rangle\}\})(\sigma)$

    $= \quad \bigcup\{\,\sigma\{1/v\}\cdot\sigma\{1/v, 2/w\}\cdot\{\epsilon\}\,\}$

    $= \quad \{\,\sigma\{1/v\}\sigma\{1/v, 2/w\}\,\}$

   where $\alpha' = \sigma'(v) + 1$, $\alpha'' = \sigma''(v) + 1$.

(2) $abs(\lambda\sigma.\{\langle\sigma\{1/v\}, \lambda\sigma'.\{\langle\sigma'\{2/v\}, \lambda\sigma''.\{\langle c?v, p_\epsilon\rangle\}\rangle\},$

      $\langle c?v, \lambda\sigma''.\{\langle\sigma''\{2/v\}, p_\epsilon\rangle\}\rangle\}\rangle,$

        $\langle c?v, \lambda\sigma'.\{\langle\sigma'\{1/v\}, \lambda\sigma''.\{\langle\sigma''\{2/v\}, p_\epsilon\rangle\}\rangle\}\rangle\}\})(\sigma)$

    $= \quad \bigcup\{\,\sigma\{1/v\}\cdot\sigma\{2/v\}\{\delta\}\,\}$

    $= \quad \{\,\sigma\{1/v\}\sigma\{2/v\}\delta\,\}.$

The rest of the story is standard; we therefore present it without proofs.

Definition 12.30 $\mathcal{O}^*\colon Res \to \mathbb{P}_D$ is the unique function satisfying $\mathcal{O}^*(\mathrm{E}) = p_\epsilon$, and

$$\mathcal{O}^*(s) \quad = \quad \lambda\sigma.\{\,\langle\rho, \mathcal{O}^*(r)\rangle \mid [s,\sigma] \to [r,\rho]\,\}.$$

Note that in the clause for $\mathcal{O}^*(s)$, all pairs $[r,\rho]$ such that $[s,\sigma] \to [r,\rho]$ contribute to the result—and not only the pairs $[r,\sigma']$ with $[s,\sigma] \to [r,\sigma']$. Cf. a similar comment for $\mathcal{O}^*(s)$ in Definition 11.24.

Let $\mathcal{E}\colon Res \to \mathbb{P}_D$ be the usual extension of $\mathcal{D}$. We have

Theorem 12.31

(a) $\mathcal{O}^* = \mathcal{E}$.

(b) $abs \circ \mathcal{O}^* = \mathcal{O}[\![\cdot]\!]$, on $\mathcal{L}_{com}$.

(c) $\mathcal{O}[\![\pi]\!] = abs(\mathcal{D}[\![\pi]\!])$, for all $\pi \in \mathcal{L}_{com}$.

12.3   Exercises

Exercise 12.1   Let the await statement await e then s end be interpreted as the equivalent of the procedure declared by

$x \Leftarrow$ if e then s else x fi.

(Effectively, this replaces deadlock as interpretation of suspension by divergence.) Investigate the consequences on the definitions of $\mathcal{O}$ and $\mathcal{D}$ for this view of $\mathcal{L}_{aw}$.

Exercise 12.2 (This exercise assumes knowledge of Chapter 15.) The branching denotational semantics for $\mathcal{L}_{aw}$ may be replaced by a linear model, using a (non-essential) variation on the definitions of $\mathbb{P}_D$ and $\mathcal{D}$ for $\mathcal{L}_{hcl}$ (as in Section 15.1). Analyze the consequences of adopting this model for $\mathcal{L}_{aw}$.

Exercise 12.3 Let $\mathbb{P}_O$, $\mathbb{P}_D$ be as in Definition 12.4, 12.26. Let $\mathbb{P}_{O^*} = \mathcal{P}_{nco}(\Sigma_\delta^\infty)$, and let $\mathbb{P}_D^*$ be the domain solving the equation

$$\mathbb{P}_D^* \;\simeq\; \{p_\epsilon\} + \mathcal{P}_{co}(\Sigma \times id_{\frac{1}{2}}(\mathbb{P}_D^*)).$$

Let $\alpha_1 \colon \mathbb{P}_D \overset{1}{\to} (\Sigma \to \mathbb{P}_D^*)$ be the unique mapping satisfying

$$\alpha_1(p)(\sigma) \;=\; \begin{cases} p_\epsilon & \text{if } p = p_\epsilon \\ \{\, \langle \sigma', \alpha_1(p')(\sigma') \rangle \mid \langle \sigma', p' \rangle \in p(\sigma) \,\} & \text{if } p \neq \epsilon. \end{cases}$$

Let $\alpha_2 \colon \mathbb{P}_D^* \overset{1}{\to} \mathbb{P}_{O^*}$ be the unique mapping satisfying

$$\alpha_2(p) \;=\; \begin{cases} \{\epsilon\} & \text{if } p = p_\epsilon \\ \{\delta\} & \text{if } p = \emptyset \\ \bigcup\{\, \sigma' \cdot \alpha_2(p') \mid \langle \sigma', p' \rangle \in p \,\} & \text{otherwise.} \end{cases}$$

Prove that, for $p \in \mathbb{P}_D$, $\sigma \in \Sigma$, we have $abs(p)(\sigma) = \alpha_2(\alpha_1(p(\sigma)))$.

Exercise 12.4 Assume the setting of Section 12.2. Let $\mathbb{P}_D^*$ be the domain solving

$$\mathbb{P}_D^* \;\simeq\; \{p_\epsilon\} + (\Sigma \to \mathcal{P}_{co}(((\Sigma + (Chan \times Val)) \times id_{\frac{1}{2}}(\mathbb{P}_D^*)) + (Chan \times (Val \to id_{\frac{1}{2}}(\mathbb{P}_D^*)))))).$$

Let $\mathcal{D}^* \colon \mathcal{L}_{com} \to \mathbb{P}_D^*$ be the following modification of $\mathcal{D}$ (from Definition 12.28): We put

$$\begin{aligned} \mathcal{D}^*(c?v) &= \lambda\sigma.\{\langle c, \psi_v \rangle\} \\ \mathcal{D}^*(c!v) &= \lambda\sigma.\{\langle c, \alpha, p_\epsilon \rangle\}. \end{aligned}$$

where ψ_v ($\in Val \to \mathbb{P}_D^*$) is given by

$$\psi_v \;=\; \lambda\bar{\alpha}.\lambda\bar{\sigma}.\{\langle \bar{\sigma}\{\bar{\alpha}/v\}, p_\epsilon \rangle\},$$

$\alpha = \mathcal{V}(e)(\sigma)$, and the other clauses are as to be expected. The main change associated with this definition of $\mathcal{D}^*$ concerns the definition of Ω_{L} (cf. Definition 12.26c) which here takes the form

$$\Omega_{\mathsf{L}}^*(\phi)(p_1, p_2) =$$
$$\lambda\sigma.\{\langle\sigma, \phi(p', p'')\rangle \mid \langle c, \alpha, p'\rangle \in p_1(\sigma), \langle c, \psi_v\rangle \in p_2(\sigma), \psi_v(\alpha) = p''\}.$$

Complete the semantic definitions as outlined here, and investigate the relationship between $\mathcal{D}$ and $\mathcal{D}^*$ for $\mathcal{L}_{com}$.

Exercise 12.5 (an example of a definition "by degree," cf. Definition 12.17) Let $\mathbb{P}_D^{(n)}$, $\mathbb{P}_D^*$ be as in Definition 12.17 (and $\mathbb{P}_D$ as in Definition 12.5). For $p \in \mathbb{P}_D^*$, $p' \in \mathbb{P}_D$ we define $p;p'$ as follows: First we introduce the operator '$;_n$' of type $\mathbb{P}_D^{(n)} \times \mathbb{P}_D \to \mathbb{P}_D$ by

- $p;_0 p' = p'$, for $p\,(= p_\epsilon) \in \mathbb{P}_D^{(0)}$
- for $n = 0, 1, \ldots$

$$p;_{n+1}p' = \begin{cases} p' & \text{if } p = p_\epsilon \in \mathbb{P}_D^{(n+1)} \\ \lambda\sigma.\{\langle\tilde{\sigma}, \tilde{p};_n p'\rangle \mid \langle\tilde{\sigma}, \tilde{p}\rangle \in p(\sigma)\} & \text{if } p \neq p_\epsilon \in \mathbb{P}_D^{(n+1)}. \end{cases}$$

Now let $p \in \mathbb{P}_D$, and assume that $p = \lim_n p^{(n)}$ with $p^{(n)} \in \mathbb{P}_D^{(n)}$. We put

$$p;p' \quad = \quad \lim_n(p^{(n)};_n p').$$

Prove that the ';' defined here, and the ';' from Definition 12.6 coincide.

12.4   Bibliographical notes

The first time we saw a domain equation used for modeling nonuniform concurrency was in work by Bekič ([Bek84b]) and Milner ([Mil73]). The seminal paper laying firm (order-theoretic) foundations for this type of equation was [Plo76] (where such domains are called "resumption models"), subsequently applied in, e.g., [Mil79]. In [BZ82], the metric approach to solving equations such as (12.2) was introduced (albeit with $\mathcal{P}_{cl}(\cdot)$ rather than $\mathcal{P}_{co}(\cdot)$ as powerdomain functor).

The await statement was proposed in [OG76], primarily from the perspective of using it in the prooftheoretic analysis of synchronized concurrency (cf. also the textbook [AO91]). The metric models of Section 12.1, especially the treatment of atomization, are new.

The language $\mathcal{L}_{com}$ is a simplified version of CSP ([Hoa78, Hoa85]). Its use of channels c and the constructs $c?v$, $c!e$ is taken from the language occam ([Inm84]). The semantic models as described in Section 12.2 have also been presented in [BM88, KR90] and, in the form as suggested by Exercise 12.4 in [BZ82].

[Plo83] is a detailed study of the operational semantics of CSP. Comparisons between semantic models for CSP include [MZ94] and [Spa93].

13 Concurrent Object-oriented Programming

Concurrent object-oriented programming has two key features. Firstly, a program consists of a—dynamically varying—configuration of processes operating in parallel. Each process has its own "private" variables affecting only the *local* state belonging to that process. Secondly, the parallel processes communicate through the sending and receiving of *messages.* In a simple model, this can be described as a modest variation on the language $\mathcal{L}_{com}$ of Section 12.2. A more complex version uses the *rendezvous* construct, where synchronized communication of two *method* names $(m, \bar{m})$, occurring in two parallel components, results in the execution of the method $s = D(m)$ associated with m in a (new kind of) declaration D.

In Section 13.1, we describe the variations on $\mathcal{L}_{com}$ which are necessary to deal with local states. For simplicity, we restrict ourselves here to a static configuration of $n\,(\geq 1)$ processes. In Section 13.2, we model the rendezvous style of communication, now for configurations which may evolve dynamically thanks to the new-construct. This requires the introduction of yet another version of the parallel composition operator, this time more involved since we have to deal with a situation where the definitions of $\mathcal{D}$ and '‖' are mutually dependent: $\mathcal{D}$ depends on the definition of '‖' (in the usual way), but it is also the case that '‖' depends on the definition of $\mathcal{D}$. To keep matters somewhat tractable, we return in Section 13.2 to the case of one global state.

It should be noted that this chapter deals especially with the concurrency aspects of object-oriented programming. Other important topics such as inheritance or subtyping will not be considered—in accordance with our general strategy to focus on control flow notions.

13.1   Parallel objects—local states and encapsulation

The language studied in this section is quite close to $\mathcal{L}_{com}$, in the sense that it also deals with value-passing between parallel components, but now in a version where each parallel component has a *local* state. Recall that, up to now, in our treatment of nonuniform languages we assumed a *global* state: all variables are global, i.e., each occurrence of some v anywhere in the program refers to the same variable for which values are stored in one shared memory.

We now discuss a language paradigm where variables of different parallel processes—i.e., of different parts of a program executing in parallel—are disjoint. The only means by which any given process may affect variables of another process is by the sending and receiving of values by means of communicating actions. In this way, the variables of one process are "encapsulated," i.e., they are protected against arbitrary access from other processes. Disjointness of variables in parallel processes is not achieved by the use of different variable names. On the contrary, one may well encounter programs such as $(\ldots v := 0 \ldots) \| (\ldots v := 1 \ldots)$. Still, the two v's displayed here have nothing to do with each other.

We shall introduce a simple scheme for distinguishing variables in separate processes. Briefly, each parallel process will be named by some identifier, its so-called "object-name." A parallel process together with its name will be referred to as a "parallel object" (a terminology stemming from the perspective of concurrent object-oriented programming). A further essential part of the naming scheme is that states now also depend on object names: for state σ and object name o, $\sigma(o)$ will denote the local state belonging to the parallel process named by o. Such a local state $\sigma(o)$, when applied to a variable v, will yield its (local) value $\alpha = \sigma(o)(v)$.

13.1.1 Syntax and operational semantics

Let the sets $(v \in) IVar$, $(\alpha \in) Val$, $(u \in) Constr$ be as usual. Let $(o \in) Obj$ be a set of object names, to be used to distinguish between (variables in) different parallel processes. The semantic framework will be designed in such a way that each statement s is executed as part of a process named by some o. Also, communication statements take the form $o?v$ or $o!e$. If $o_1?v$ occurs in a statement named by o_2, and $o_2!e$ occurs in a statement named by o_1, and if the statements are ready to execute the respective communication actions, then the communication succeeds and the current value of e—determined in the local state corresponding to o_1—is transmitted to o_2, and the value of v in the local state for o_2 is updated.

Definition 13.1

(a) $s\,(\in Stat) ::= v := e \mid \mathsf{skip} \mid o?v \mid o!e \mid (s;s) \mid$
$\qquad\qquad\quad \mathsf{if}\ e\ \mathsf{then}\ s\ \mathsf{else}\ s\ \mathsf{fi} \mid \mathsf{while}\ e\ \mathsf{do}\ s\ \mathsf{od}$

(b) $e\,(\in Exp) ::= \alpha \mid v \mid u(\vec{e})$.

In *Stat* we do not yet see a construct for parallel execution. Rather, we shall specify a program as a (fixed) number of (sequential) statements running in parallel, each supplied with a (different) object name for identification purposes. It will be convenient to use the syntactic tool of resumptions for this purpose.

Definition 13.2

(a) $r\,(\in Res) ::= (o, \mathrm{E}) \mid (o, s) \mid (r_1, r_2)$, provided all object names occurring in r_1 are different from all object names in r_2.

(b) We identify $((o, \mathrm{E}), r)$ and $(r, (o, \mathrm{E}))$ with r, and $\mathrm{E};s$ with s.

(c) $(\pi \in)\,\mathcal{L}_{po} = Res$.

Thus, elements π of the language $\mathcal{L}_{po}$ of parallel objects are typically of the form

$$((o_1, s_1), \ldots, (o_n, s_n)),\ n \geq 1,$$

where we have omitted some superfluous parentheses (which may be justified—later—by the associativity of the semantic '$\|$'). A program consists of n sequential statements $s_1, \ldots, s_n$, named by the (different) $o_1, \ldots, o_n$, each with its own state, and communicating through (matching) $o_i?v$, $o_j!e$ statements.

Remark By a combination of the set-up as described here with the new-construct of Chapter 4, one may also handle a system with a dynamically growing number of parallel objects. See also Exercise 13.1.

Before we can define the transition system $\mathcal{T}_{po}$, we need some preparations. Firstly, we introduce the extended set of states, now depending on arguments in Obj as well.

Definition 13.3

(a) $\Sigma = Obj \to IVar \to Val$.

(b) $\sigma\{\alpha/v, o\}$ is short for $\sigma\{\sigma(o)\{\alpha/v\}/o\}$.

Thus, $\sigma\{\alpha/v, o\}$ denotes a state which is like σ, but for its value in o. This equals $\sigma(o)\{\alpha/v\}$, i.e., it equals that function: $IVar \to Val$ which is like $\sigma(o)$, but for its value in v, which equals α. The net effect of this is that $\sigma\{\alpha/v, o\}$ is like σ but for its argument v local to o, which equals α.

We next give the natural definition of the evaluation of expressions, now with respect to some object name (and state).

Definition 13.4 $\mathcal{V} \colon Exp \to Obj \to \Sigma \to Val$ is given by

$$\begin{aligned}
\mathcal{V}(\alpha)(o)(\sigma) &= \alpha \\
\mathcal{V}(v)(o)(\sigma) &= \sigma(o)(v) \\
\mathcal{V}(u(e_1, \ldots, e_\ell))(o)(\sigma) &= \hat{u}(\mathcal{V}(e_1)(o)(\sigma), \ldots, \mathcal{V}(e_\ell)(o)(\sigma)),
\end{aligned}$$

where $\hat{u} \colon Val^{\,\ell} \to Val$ is the usual interpretation of u.

We are almost ready for the definition of $\mathcal{T}_{po}$. We still need the appropriate notion of step. Instead of extending Σ with $Chan \times (IVar \cup Val)$, as we did in Chapter 12, we here use

Definition 13.5 $(\rho \in)\ Step = \Sigma \cup Obj \times Obj \times (IVar \cup Val)$.

This is as expected: instead of communicating over channels, we find here communication by linking two objects. The $c?v$ and $c!\alpha$ of Chapter 12 are to be replaced by $((o_1, o_2), v)$ or $((o_2, o_1), \alpha)$ pairs.

Transitions are of the form $[r, \sigma] \to [r', \rho]$ (or the $\to_0$ -variant), i.e., as in Chapter 12, but, of course, with respect to the newly defined r, σ and ρ.

Definition 13.6 $\mathcal{T}_{po} = (Res \times Step, Step, \to, Spec)$, where $Spec$ is given as

- $[(o, v := e), \sigma] \to [(o, \mathrm{E}), \sigma\{\alpha/v, o\}]$ where $\alpha = \mathcal{V}(e)(o)(\sigma)$ (Ass)

- $[(o, \mathsf{skip}), \sigma] \to [(o, \mathrm{E}), \sigma]$ (Skip)

- $[(o_1, o_2?v), \sigma] \to [(o_1, \mathrm{E}), (o_1, o_2, v)]$ (Receive)

- $[(o_2, o_1!e), \sigma] \to [(o_2, \mathrm{E}), (o_2, o_1, \alpha)]$ where $\alpha = \mathcal{V}(e)(o_2)(\sigma)$ (Send)

- $$\frac{[(o, s), \sigma] \to [(o, r), \rho]}{[(o, s;s'), \sigma] \to [(o, r;s'), \rho]} \qquad \text{(Seq)}$$

- $[(o, \mathsf{if}\ e\ \mathsf{then}\ s_1\ \mathsf{else}\ s_2\ \mathsf{fi}), \sigma] \to_0 [(o, s_1), \sigma]$ if $\mathcal{V}(e)(o)(\sigma) = tt$ (If 1)

  $[(o, \mathsf{if}\ e\ \mathsf{then}\ s_1\ \mathsf{else}\ s_2\ \mathsf{fi}), \sigma] \to_0 [(o, s_2), \sigma]$ if $\mathcal{V}(e)(o)(\sigma) = ff$ (If 2)

- $[(o, \mathsf{while}\ e\ \mathsf{do}\ s\ \mathsf{od}), \sigma] \to$ (While)
  $\qquad [(o, \mathsf{if}\ e\ \mathsf{then}\ (s;\mathsf{while}\ e\ \mathsf{do}\ s\ \mathsf{od})\ \mathsf{else}\ \mathsf{skip}\ \mathsf{fi}), \sigma]$

- $$\frac{[r_1, \sigma] \to [r_2, \rho]}{[(r_1, r), \sigma] \to [(r_2, r), \rho]} \qquad \text{(Par)}$$
  $$[(r, r_1), \sigma] \to [(r, r_2), \rho]$$

- $$\frac{[r_1, \sigma] \to [r', (o_1, o_2, v)] \qquad [r_2, \sigma] \to [r'', (o_2, o_1, \alpha)]}{[(r_1, r_2), \sigma] \to [(r', r''), \sigma\{\alpha/v, o_1\}]} \qquad \text{(Com)}$$
  $$[(r_2, r_1), \sigma] \to [(r'', r'), \sigma\{\alpha/v, o_1\}]$$

The rule (Com) expresses the following: Assume that

- r_1 can make an (o_1, o_2, v)-step, i.e., a step inside object o_1, requesting a value for v from object o_2, and then becomes r',
- r_2 can make an (o_2, o_1, α)-step, i.e., a step inside o_2, ready to send the value α to object o_1, and then becomes r'',

then the communication results in the value α being assigned to v in o_1, and the resumption of the computation equals (r', r'') (for (r_1, r_2)) or (r'', r') (for (r_2, r_1)).

The definition of "blocking" is the standard one.

Definition 13.7 $[r, \sigma]$ *blocks* if there is no $[r', \sigma']$ such that $[r, \sigma] \rightarrow [r', \sigma']$.

Note that σ' is required to be in Σ (rather than in *Step*). $\mathcal{O}$ is obtained from $\mathcal{T}_{po}$ in the usual way.

Definition 13.8

(a) $\mathbb{P}_O = \Sigma \rightarrow \mathcal{P}_{nco}(\Sigma_\delta^\infty)$.

(b) $\mathcal{O}: Res \times \Sigma \rightarrow \mathcal{P}_{nco}(\Sigma_\delta^\infty)$ is the unique function satisfying $\mathcal{O}((o, \mathrm{E}), \sigma) = \{\epsilon\}$, and, for $r \neq (o, \mathrm{E})$,

$$
\mathcal{O}(r, \sigma) = \begin{cases} \{\delta\} & \text{if } [r, \sigma] \text{ blocks} \\ \bigcup \{\sigma' \cdot \mathcal{O}(r', \sigma') \mid [r, \sigma] \rightarrow [r', \sigma']\} & \text{otherwise.} \end{cases}
$$

(c) $\mathcal{O}[\![\cdot]\!]: \mathcal{L}_{po} \rightarrow \mathbb{P}_O$ is given by

$$
\mathcal{O}[\![\pi]\!] = \lambda\sigma.\mathcal{O}(\pi, \sigma).
$$

Examples

(1) $\quad \mathcal{O}[\![((o_1, v := 1; o_2!(v+1)), (o_2, o_1?v))]\!](\sigma)$

$\quad = \mathcal{O}(((o_1, v := 1; o_2!(v+1)), (o_2, o_1?v)), \sigma)$

$\quad = \sigma\{1/v, o_1\} \cdot \mathcal{O}(((o_1, o_2!(v+1)), (o_2, o_1?v)), \sigma\{1/v, o_1\})$

$\quad = [\mathcal{V}(v+1)(o_1)(\sigma\{1/v, o_1\}) = 2]$

$\qquad \sigma\{1/v, o_1\} \cdot \sigma\{1/v, o_1\}\{2/v, o_2\} \cdot$

$\qquad\qquad \mathcal{O}(((o_1, \mathrm{E}), (o_2, \mathrm{E})), \sigma\{1/v, o_1\}\{2/v, o_2\})$

$\quad = \{\sigma\{1/v, o_1\}\sigma\{1/v, o_1\}\{2/v, o_2\}\}$

(2) $\mathcal{O}[\![((o_1, v := 1; v := 2), (o_2, o_1?v))]\!](\sigma)$

$= \mathcal{O}(((o_1, v := 1; v := 2), (o_2, o_1?v)), \sigma)$

$= \sigma\{1/v, o_1\} \cdot \mathcal{O}(((o_1, v := 2), (o_2, o_1?v)), \sigma\{1/v, o_1\})$

$= \sigma\{1/v, o_1\} \cdot \sigma\{2/v, o_1\} \cdot \mathcal{O}(((o_2, o_1?v)), \sigma\{2/v, o_1\})$

$= \sigma\{1/v, o_1\} \cdot \sigma\{2/v, o_1\} \cdot \{\delta\}$

$= \{\sigma\{1/v, o_1\}\sigma\{2/v, o_1\}\delta\}.$

13.1.2 Denotational semantics, relating $\mathcal{O}$ and $\mathcal{D}$

The denotational semantics for $\mathcal{L}_{po}$ is a modest variation on that for $\mathcal{L}_{com}$. The changes consist primarily in the addition, throughout, of arguments o from Obj, and induced changes in the definition of '$\|$'. We begin with

Definition 13.9 $\mathbb{P}_D$ is the domain determined by

$$\mathbb{P}_D \simeq \{p_\epsilon\} \cup (\Sigma \to \mathcal{P}_{co}(Step \times id_{\frac{1}{2}}(\mathbb{P}_D))).$$

We omit the definitions of ';' and '+'. The operator $\| : \mathbb{P}_D \times \mathbb{P}_D \to \mathbb{P}_D$ is specified in

Definition 13.10 '$\|$' is the (unique) function satisfying $p\|p_\epsilon = p_\epsilon\|p = p$, and, for $p_1, p_2 \neq p_\epsilon$,

$$p_1\|p_2 = (p_1 \, \underline{\|} \, p_2) + (p_2 \, \underline{\|} \, p_1) + (p_1 \, \underline{\lfloor} \, p_2) + (p_2 \, \underline{\lfloor} \, p_1)$$

where '$\underline{\|}$' and '$\underline{\lfloor}$' are the unique functions satisfying

$$p_1 \, \underline{\|} \, p_2 = \lambda\sigma.\{ \langle \rho, p'\|p_2 \rangle \mid \langle \rho, p' \rangle \in p_1(\sigma) \}$$

$$p_1 \, \underline{\lfloor} \, p_2 = \lambda\sigma.\{ \langle \sigma\{\alpha/v, o_1\}, p'\|p'' \rangle \mid$$
$$\langle (o_1, o_2, v), p' \rangle \in p_1(\sigma), \langle (o_2, o_1, \alpha), p'' \rangle \in p_2(\sigma) \} .$$

$\mathcal{D}$ is given in

Definition 13.11

(a) $\mathcal{D}\colon Stat \to Obj \to \mathbb{P}_D$ is the (unique) function satisfying

$$
\begin{aligned}
\mathcal{D}(v := e)(o) &= \lambda\sigma.\{\,\langle\sigma\{\alpha/v, o\}, p_\epsilon\rangle\,\}, \quad \alpha = \mathcal{V}(e)(o)(\sigma) \\
\mathcal{D}(\mathsf{skip})(o) &= \lambda\sigma.\{\,\langle\sigma, p_\epsilon\rangle\,\} \\
\mathcal{D}(s_1; s_2)(o) &= \mathcal{D}(s_1)(o); \mathcal{D}(s_2)(o) \\
\mathcal{D}(o_2?v)(o_1) &= \lambda\sigma.\{\,\langle(o_1, o_2, v), p_\epsilon\rangle\,\} \\
\mathcal{D}(o_2!e)(o_1) &= \lambda\sigma.\{\,\langle(o_1, o_2, \alpha), p_\epsilon\rangle\,\}, \quad \alpha = \mathcal{V}(e)(o_1)(\sigma),
\end{aligned}
$$

where we have left the obvious clauses for if e then s_1 else s_2 fi and while e do s od to the reader.

(b) $\mathcal{D}[\![\cdot]\!]\colon \mathcal{L}_{po} \to \mathbb{P}_D$ is given as

$$
\begin{aligned}
\mathcal{D}[\![(o, \mathrm{E})]\!] &= p_\epsilon \\
\mathcal{D}[\![(o, s)]\!] &= \mathcal{D}(s)(o) \\
\mathcal{D}[\![(r_1, r_2)]\!] &= \mathcal{D}[\![r_1]\!] \| \mathcal{D}[\![r_2]\!].
\end{aligned}
$$

Examples

(1) $\quad \mathcal{D}[\![((o_1, v := 1; o_2!(v+1)), (o_2, o_1?v))]\!]$

$= \mathcal{D}[\![(o_1, v := 1; o_2!(v+1))]\!] \| \mathcal{D}[\![(o_2, o_1?v)]\!]$

$= \mathcal{D}(v := 1; o_2!(v+1))(o_1) \| \mathcal{D}(o_1?v)(o_2)$

$= [\alpha_1 = \mathcal{V}(v+1)(o_1)(\sigma_1)]$

$\quad \big(\lambda\sigma_0.\{\langle\sigma_0\{1/v, o_1\}, p_\epsilon\rangle\}; \lambda\sigma_1.\{\langle(o_1, o_2, \alpha_1), p_\epsilon\rangle\}\big) \| \lambda\sigma_2.\{\langle(o_2, o_1, v), p_\epsilon\rangle\}$

$= \big(\lambda\sigma_0.\{\langle\sigma_0\{1/v, o_1\}, \lambda\sigma_1.\{\langle(o_1, o_2, \alpha_1), p_\epsilon\rangle\}\rangle\}\big) \| \lambda\sigma_2.\{\langle(o_2, o_1, v), p_\epsilon\rangle\}$

$= \lambda\sigma.\{\langle\sigma\{1/v, o_1\}, \lambda\sigma'.\{$

$\qquad \langle(o_1, o_2, \alpha_1), \lambda\sigma''.\{\langle(o_2, o_1, v), p_\epsilon\rangle\}\rangle,$

$\qquad \langle(o_2, o_1, v), \lambda\sigma''.\{\langle(o_1, o_2, \alpha_1), p_\epsilon\rangle\}\rangle, \},$

$\qquad \langle(o_2, o_1, v), \lambda\sigma'.\{\langle\sigma'\{1/v, o_1\}, \lambda\sigma''.\{\langle(o_1, o_2, \alpha_1), p_\epsilon\rangle\}\rangle\}\rangle\}$

(2) $\quad \mathcal{D}[\![((o_1, v := 1; v := 2), (o_2, o_1?v))]\!]$

$= \mathcal{D}(v := 1; v := 2)(o_1) \| \mathcal{D}(o_1?v)(o_2)$

$= \lambda\sigma_0.\{\langle\sigma_0\{1/v, o_1\}, \lambda\sigma_1.\{\langle\sigma_1\{2/v, o_1\}, p_\epsilon\rangle\}\rangle\} \| \lambda\sigma_2.\{\langle(o_2, o_1, v), p_\epsilon\rangle\}$

$= \lambda\sigma.\{\langle\sigma\{1/v, o_1\}, \lambda\sigma'.\{$

$\qquad \langle\sigma'\{2/v, o_1\}, \lambda\sigma''.\{\langle(o_2, o_1, v), p_\epsilon\rangle\}\rangle,$

$\qquad \langle(o_2, o_1, v), \lambda\sigma''.\{\langle\sigma''\{2/v, o_1\}, p_\epsilon\rangle\}\rangle\}\rangle,$

$\qquad \langle(o_2, o_1, v), \lambda\sigma'.\{\langle\sigma'\{1/v, o_1\}, \lambda\sigma''.\{\langle\sigma''\{2/v, o_1\}, p_\epsilon\rangle\}\rangle\}\rangle\}\rangle\}.$

We conclude this section with the formulation of the relationship between $\mathcal{O}$ and $\mathcal{D}$. The intermediate semantics $\mathcal{O}^*$ is given in

Definition 13.12 $\mathcal{O}^*: \mathcal{L}_{po} \to \mathbb{P}_D$ is the (unique) function satisfying

$$\mathcal{O}^*(o, \mathrm{E}) \;=\; p_\epsilon \,,$$

and, for $r \neq (o, \mathrm{E})$,

$$\mathcal{O}^*(r) \;=\; \lambda\sigma.\{ \, \langle \rho, \mathcal{O}^*(r') \rangle \mid [r, \sigma] \to [r', \rho] \, \}.$$

In the usual way, one may show

Lemma 13.13 $\mathcal{O}^*(\pi) = \mathcal{D}[\![\pi]\!]$, for each $\pi \in \mathcal{L}_{po}$.

The abstraction function is defined in

Definition 13.14 abs: $\mathbb{P}_D \to \mathbb{P}_O$ is the unique function satisfying $abs(p_\epsilon)(\sigma) = \{\epsilon\}$, and, for $p \neq p_\epsilon$,

$$abs(p)(\sigma) \;=$$
$$\left\{ \begin{array}{ll} \{\delta\} & \text{if } p(\sigma) \subseteq (Step \setminus \Sigma) \times \mathbb{P}_D \\ \bigcup\{ \sigma' \cdot abs(p')(\sigma') \mid \langle \sigma', p' \rangle \in p(\sigma) \} & \text{otherwise.} \end{array} \right.$$

Finally we have

Theorem 13.15

(a) $\mathcal{O}[\![\cdot]\!] = abs \circ \mathcal{O}^*$.

(b) $\mathcal{O}[\![\pi]\!] = (abs \circ \mathcal{D})[\![\pi]\!]$, for each $\pi \in \mathcal{L}_{po}$. $\square$

13.2 The rendezvous
—dependent and independent resumptions

The rendezvous programming concept provides a powerful form of communication between parallel processes; it is a key notion of modern programming languages such as ADA. Communication by rendezvous generalizes the notion of synchronization or communication with value passing as discussed in Chapter 11.2 or 12.2. We recall that, in $\mathcal{L}_{syn}$, successful synchronization involves two components executing in parallel, one of them ready to perform a c-step and the other ready for a $\bar{c}$-step. Synchronized execution then results in a τ-step. In $\mathcal{L}_{com}$, this is very similar: one component is ready to do a $c?v$-step, the other a $c!e$-step, and the handshake execution results in the performance of the (atomic) assignment $v := \alpha$, with α the current value of e. For the rendezvous, we replace the $c, \bar{c}$ or $c?v, c!e$ simply by a pair $m, \bar{m}$ (m for *method*, a terminology borrowed from the field of object-oriented programming). The crucial idea in the generalization is that synchronized execution of m and $\bar{m}$ results in the execution of a, possibly composite, statement $s = D(m)$, associated with m via declaration D. The execution of s may take a number of steps (possibly infinitely many), and the two components in the synchronized execution, i.e., the two components in which the m and $\bar{m}$ occur, both have to wait until completion of s before they may resume. The *other* components, not involved in the rendezvous, may proceed independently, i.e., their actions may interleave with those of s. In order to model this difference between the behavior of the two components involved in the rendezvous, and the remaining components of the program, we shall make use of another variation upon the notion of resumption, viz. that of *dependent* versus *independent* resumptions.

We shall study the rendezvous construct in the setting of the language $\mathcal{L}_{rv}$. This is an extension of $\mathcal{L}_{wh}$ to which parallelism has been added in terms of the process creation construct. For simplicity, we return to a model with *global* states, rather than sticking to a form a distributed states as in the previous section. We leave the straightforward extension of the semantics for $\mathcal{L}_{rv}$ with the notion of object naming to the reader (cf. Exercise 13.3).

13.2.1 Syntax and operational semantics

Let $(m \in) Meth$ be an alphabet of *method names,* and let us assume a mapping $\bar{\cdot}: Meth \to Meth$ with the property that $\bar{\bar{m}} = m$. (The $m, \bar{m}$ will play a role which is very similar to that of the $c, \bar{c}$ in Chapter 11.2.)

Definition 13.16

(a) $s\,(\in Stat) ::= v := e \mid \text{skip} \mid m \mid (s;s) \mid \text{if } e \text{ then } s \text{ else } s \text{ fi} \mid$
$\qquad\qquad\text{while } e \text{ do } s \text{ od} \mid \text{new}(s)$.

(b) $(D \in)\,Decl$ is the set of all functions in $Meth \to Stat$ which satisfy $D(m) = D(\bar{m})$ for all $m \in Meth$.

(c) $(\pi \in)\,\mathcal{L}_{rv} = Decl \times Stat$.

Remark Since the role of the declaration D is somewhat different from that in earlier languages, we return to a treatment where D is explicitly carried along in the notation.

The resumptions for $\mathcal{L}_{rv}$ are the same as those for $\mathcal{L}_{pc}$.

Definition 13.17

(a) $r\,(\in Res) ::= \text{E} \mid (s{:}r) \mid (r,r)$.

(b) (E,r) and (r,E) are identified with r.

The transitions used in the transition system $\mathcal{T}_{rv}$ for $\mathcal{L}_{rv}$ are of the form

$$[r,\rho] \to_D [r',\rho'] \tag{13.1}$$

with $D \in Decl$, and ρ,ρ' ranging over the set of steps defined in

Definition 13.18 $(\rho \in)\,Step_O = \Sigma \cup (Meth \times Res)$.

Steps of the form (m,r) will play a role in the rule for handling methods. The name "$Step_O$" stands for "operational steps," to be contrasted with the denotational steps used in the next subsection. We now define $\mathcal{T}_{rv}$:

Definition 13.19 $\mathcal{T}_{rv} = (Decl \times Res \times Step_O, Step_O, \to, Spec)$. Transitions are written as in (13.1). The set $Spec$ is given by

- (Ass), (Skip), (If), (While$'$) are as usual

- $\qquad (s_1;s_2){:}r \to_{0,D} s_1{:}(s_2{:}r)$ \hfill (Seq)

- $\qquad [m{:}r, \sigma] \to_D [\text{E}, (m,r)]$ \hfill (Meth)

- $\qquad \text{new}(s){:}r \to_{0,D} (s{:}\text{E}, r)$ \hfill (New)

$$\bullet \quad \frac{[r_1, \sigma] \rightarrow_D [r_2, \rho]}{[(r_1, r), \sigma] \rightarrow_D [(r_2, r), \rho]} \quad \text{(Par)}$$

$$[(r, r_1), \sigma] \rightarrow_D [(r, r_2), \rho]$$

$$\bullet \quad \frac{[r_1, \sigma] \rightarrow_D [r_1', (m, r_1'')] \qquad [r_2, \sigma] \rightarrow_D [r_2', (\bar{m}, r_2'')]}{[(r_1, r_2), \sigma] \rightarrow_D [(D(m){:}(r_1'', r_2''), (r_1', r_2')), \sigma]} \quad \text{(Rendezvous)}$$

The rules of $\mathcal{T}_{rv}$ may be explained as follows:

(1) The rules (Ass), (Skip), (If) are the usual ones (of $\mathcal{T}_{wh}$). The rule (While$'$) is as in $\mathcal{T}_{aw}$.

(2) The rules (Seq) and (New) are as in $\mathcal{T}_{pc}$. (Par) is (almost) as in $\mathcal{L}_{svp}$, but for the appearance of ρ rather than σ in the configurations on the right-hand side of the '$\rightarrow$'.

(3) A one-sided (attempt at) rendezvous—in the form $m{:}r$ stores the pair (m, r) for subsequent use, viz. in the (Rendezvous) rule. In the pair (m, r), r is the so-called dependent resumption. As we shall see in a moment, it will be used in such a way that it may resume execution only *after* the execution of $s = D(m)$—associated with m in the declaration D—has been completed.

(4) The rendezvous rule works as follows: Assume that two parallel components are ready to perform a step (*): $[r_1, \sigma] \rightarrow_D [r_1', (m, r_1'')]$ and a step (**): $[r_2, \sigma] \rightarrow_D [r_2', (\bar{m}, r_2'')]$, respectively. Note that such as situation arises from two applications of the (Meth)-rule, each followed by zero or more applications of the (Par)-rule in which the E-component in (Meth) is changed into some r_1' or r_2', respectively. The latter changes reflect activities from other components (not involved in the rendezvous). For this reason, the r_1' and r_2' are called independent resumptions (which don't have to wait for completion of $s = D(m)$).

For example, an application of (Meth) followed by one application of (Par)—also invoking the identification of (E, r) and r—will result in a step $[(m{:}r_1, r_2), \sigma] \rightarrow_D [r_2, (m, r_1)]$. Now the actual rendezvous resulting from the steps (*) and (**) delivers a step $[(r_1, r_2), \sigma] \rightarrow_D [r, \sigma]$, where r—as specified by (Rendezvous)—is given as the parallel composition of three resumptions:

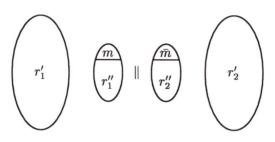

Figure 13.1a: Before the rendezvous

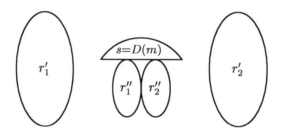

Figure 13.1b: After the rendezvous

- $D(m)$:(r_1'', r_2''). After completion of the execution of $D(m)$, execution resumes with that of r_1'' and r_2'' in parallel. Here r_1'', r_2'' are the dependent resumptions introduced earlier.

- r_1'.

- r_2'.

The latter two are the independent resumptions: By, possibly repeated, application of (Par), on the right-hand side of the steps (*), (**) the resumptions r_1' and r_2' have been accumulated, representing the activities of all components executing in parallel to (i) the component responsible for the m-step and (ii) the component responsible for the $\bar{m}$-step.

Parallel execution of these three resumptions properly represents the total effect of the rendezvous. Figures 13.1a and b illustrate the above description. Note that each of the r_1', r_2', r_1'', r_2'' in Figures 13.1a and b may in turn consist of more than one component executing in parallel.

Example We have

$$[m;v := 1{:}E, \sigma] \to [E, (m, v := 1{:}E)]$$

and

$$[(\bar{m};v := 2{:}E, v := 3{:}E), \sigma] \to [v := 3{:}E, (\bar{m}, v := 2{:}E)],$$

hence

$$[(m;v := 1{:}E, ((\bar{m};v := 2{:}E, v := 3{:}E)), \sigma] \to [(D(m){:}(v := 1{:}E, v := 2{:}E), v := 3{:}E), \sigma].$$

In the definition of $\mathcal{O}$ from $\mathcal{T}_{rv}$, we again use the notion of blocking.

Definition 13.20   A configuration $[r, \sigma]$ *blocks* if, for no r', σ', we have $[r, \sigma] \to_D [r', \sigma']$.

As before, the possibility of a step $\sigma' \in \Sigma$ (rather than any $\rho \in Step$) is the criterion here.

The format for the definition of $\mathcal{O}$ is the familiar one.

Definition 13.21

(a) $(p \in) \, \mathbb{P}_O = \Sigma \to \mathcal{P}_{nco}(\Sigma_\delta^\infty)$.

(b) $\mathcal{O}{:}\ Decl \times Res \times \Sigma \to \mathcal{P}_{nco}(\Sigma_\delta^\infty)$ is the unique function satisfying $\mathcal{O}(D|E, \sigma) = \{\epsilon\}$, and, for $r \not\equiv E$,

$$\mathcal{O}(D|r, \sigma)$$
$$= \begin{cases} \{\delta\} & \text{if } [r, \sigma] \text{ blocks} \\ \bigcup\{\sigma' \cdot \mathcal{O}(D|r', \sigma') \mid [r, \sigma] \to_D [r', \sigma']\} & \text{otherwise.} \end{cases}$$

(c) $\mathcal{O}[\![\cdot]\!]{:}\ \mathcal{L}_{rv} \to \mathbb{P}_O$ is given by $\mathcal{O}[\![D|s]\!] = \lambda\sigma \cdot \mathcal{O}(D|s{:}E, \sigma)$.

Example Let $D(m) = v := 0$. (Below we suppress the declaration D.)

$$\mathcal{O}[\![\mathsf{new}(m;v := 1);\mathsf{new}(\bar{m};v := 2);v := 3]\!](\sigma)$$
$$= \mathcal{O}(\mathsf{new}(m;v := 1);\mathsf{new}(\bar{m};v := 2);v := 3, \sigma)$$
$$= \mathcal{O}((m;v := 1{:}E, \mathsf{new}(\bar{m}, v := 2);v := 3{:}E), \sigma)$$

$$= \mathcal{O}((m;v := 1\text{:E}, (\bar{m}\text{:}v := 2\text{:E}, v := 3\text{:E})), \sigma)$$

$$= \mathcal{O}((v := 0\text{:}(v := 1\text{:E}, v := 2\text{:E}), v := 3\text{:E}), \sigma)$$

$$= \sigma\{0/v\} \cdot \mathcal{O}(((v := 1\text{:E}, v := 2\text{:E}), v := 3\text{E}), \sigma\{0/v\}) \cup$$
$$\quad \sigma\{3/v\} \cdot \mathcal{O}(v := 0\text{:}(v := 1\text{:E}, v := 2\text{:E}), \sigma\{3/v\})$$

$$= \{\, \sigma\{0/v\}\sigma\{1/v\}\sigma\{2/v\}\sigma\{3/v\}, \sigma\{0/v\}\sigma\{1/v\}\sigma\{3/v\}\sigma\{2/v\},$$
$$\quad \sigma\{0/v\}\sigma\{3/v\}\sigma\{1/v\}\sigma\{2/v\}, \ldots,$$
$$\quad \sigma\{3/v\}\sigma\{0/v\}\sigma\{1/v\}\sigma\{2/v\}, \sigma\{3/v\}\sigma\{0/v\}\sigma\{2/v\}\sigma\{1/v\} \,\}.$$

13.2.2   Denotational semantics, relating $\mathcal{O}$ and $\mathcal{D}$

The domain $\mathbb{P}_D$ used in the definition of $\mathcal{D}$ for $\mathcal{L}_{rv}$ is given in

Definition 13.22 $\mathbb{P}_D$ is the unique solution of the equation

$$\mathbb{P}_D \;\simeq\; \{p_\epsilon\} + (\Sigma \to \mathcal{P}_{co}(Step_D \times id_{\frac{1}{2}}(\mathbb{P}_D))), \tag{13.2}$$

where $Step_D$, the collection of "denotational steps" is given as

$$(\theta \in) Step_D \;=\; \Sigma \cup (Meth \times \mathbb{P}_D).$$

The form of (13.2) resembles the equation used in Chapter 12.2 (cf. Definition 12.22). Whereas, for $\mathcal{L}_{com}$, only given (discrete) spaces occur in the definition of $Step$, here the domain to be defined, i.e., $\mathbb{P}_D$, occurs in the definition of $Step_D$. The structure of $Step_D$ may be understood better by comparing it with $Step_O$ (cf. Definition 13.18):

$$Step_O \;=\; \Sigma \cup (Meth \times Res).$$

We observe a correspondence between operational steps which are (specified with respect to some D and) either of the form σ or of the form $\langle m, r \rangle$, and denotational steps which are of the form σ or $\langle m, p \rangle$, with $p \in \mathbb{P}_D$. In this correspondence, p features as the intended meaning of $(D|r)$.

We proceed with the definiton of the semantic operators on $\mathbb{P}_D$. These definitions combine the earlier ones for $\mathcal{L}_{wh}$ and $\mathcal{L}_{pc}$, to which will be added a mechanism to handle the rendezvous construct. We recall that, for languages with some form of (synchronization or) communication the semantic parallel composition operator satisfies an equation of the form

$$p_1 \| p_2 \quad = \quad (p_1 \mathbin{\rlap{\rule[-.2ex]{.6em}{.1ex}}\rule{.1ex}{1.4ex}} p_2) + (p_2 \mathbin{\rlap{\rule[-.2ex]{.6em}{.1ex}}\rule{.1ex}{1.4ex}} p_1) + (p_1 | p_2) \,,$$

where the first two summands specify the left- and rightmerge, respectively, and the third caters for the actual communication. In the third part, the intended effect—in an informal notation—$m|\bar{m} = D(m)$, generalizing the earlier $c|\bar{c} = \tau$ or $c?v \mathbin{\rule{.1ex}{1.2ex}\rule{.5em}{.1ex}} c!\alpha = (v := \alpha)$, will have to be embodied. Since we are now in a purely semantic setting, we shall need the meaning $\mathcal{D}(s)$ of $s = D(m)$ in some way. Summarizing, we see that the definition of '$\|$' involves the meaning function $\mathcal{D}$. On the other hand, $\mathcal{D}$ itself of course employs '$\|$' (at the moment the new construct obtains its meaning). The pattern observed here requires, for a fully rigorous treatment, the introduction of a higher-order operator in two arguments—one argument a meaning function S and the other an operator ϕ—and the definition of $(\mathcal{D}, \|)$ as its simultaneous (and unique) fixed point. Since, on the one hand, we are afraid that the details would somewhat obscure the transparency of the definition, and, on the other hand, we are confident that the reader has by now sufficient maturity in such manipulations to supplement the "definitions" below with a full higher-order treatment, we refrain from presenting the details here. Instead, we simply state the various equations which should be satisfied by $\mathcal{D}$ and '$\|$' (and which uniquely determine them). One detail has been omitted so far: both the denotational semantics $\mathcal{D}$ *and* the operator '$\|$' depend on the argument D. For $\mathcal{D}$, this is as always, for '$\|$' this holds since, as just remarked, the rendezvous part of '$\|$' reflects the intended effect $m \mid \bar{m} = D(m)$. Consequently, we shall work below with '$\|_D$' rather than just with '$\|$'.

Definition 13.23

(a) Let $(\gamma \in)\ Cont = \mathbb{P}_D$, and let γ_ϵ be the nil-continuation.

(b) $\mathcal{D}: \mathcal{L}_{rv} \rightarrow Cont \xrightarrow{1} \mathbb{P}_D$ is the unique function satisfying

$$
\begin{aligned}
\mathcal{D}(D|v := e)(\gamma) &= \lambda\sigma.\{\, \langle \sigma\{\alpha/v\}, \gamma \rangle \,\}, \quad \alpha = \mathcal{V}(e)(\sigma) \\
\mathcal{D}(D|\mathsf{skip})(\gamma) &= \lambda\sigma.\{\, \langle \sigma, \gamma \rangle \,\} \\
\mathcal{D}(D|m)(\gamma) &= \lambda\sigma.\{\, \langle (m, \gamma), \gamma_\epsilon \rangle \,\} \\
\mathcal{D}(D|s_1;s_2)(\gamma) &= \mathcal{D}(D|s_1)(\mathcal{D}(D|s_2)(\gamma)) \\
\mathcal{D}(D|\mathsf{new}(s))(\gamma) &= \mathcal{D}(D|s)(\gamma_\epsilon)\|_D\,\gamma \,.
\end{aligned}
$$

We omit the standard clauses for if e then s_1 else s_2 fi and while e do s od (cf. Definition 12.8).

(c) $\mathcal{D}[\![\pi]\!] = \mathcal{D}(\pi)(\gamma_\epsilon)$.

(d) The operators $+, ;, \|_D, \bigsqcup_D, |_D : \mathbb{P}_D \times \mathbb{P}_D \to \mathbb{P}_D$ satisfy

- $p + p_\epsilon = p_\epsilon + p = p$. For $p_1, p_2 \neq p_\epsilon$, $p_1 + p_2 = \lambda\sigma.(p_1(\sigma) \cup p_2(\sigma))$.

- $p_\epsilon; p = p$. For $p_1 \neq p_\epsilon$,

$$p_1; p_2 \;=\; \lambda\sigma.\{\, \langle \theta, p'; p_2 \rangle \mid \langle \theta, p' \rangle \in p_1(\sigma) \,\}\,.$$

-

$$p_1 \|_D p_2 \;=\; (p_1 \bigsqcup_D p_2) + (p_2 \bigsqcup_D p_1) + (p_1 |_D p_2)$$

- $p_\epsilon \bigsqcup_D p = p$. For $p_1 \neq p_\epsilon$,

$$p_1 \bigsqcup_D p_2 \;=\; \lambda\sigma.\{\, \langle \theta, p' \|_D p_2 \rangle \mid \langle \theta, p' \rangle \in p_1(\sigma) \,\}\,.$$

- $p_\epsilon |_D p = p |_D p_\epsilon = p$. For $p_1, p_2 \neq p_\epsilon$,

$$p_1 |_D p_2 \;=\; \lambda\sigma.\{\, \langle \sigma, \mathcal{D}(D|D(m))(p_1'' \|_D p_2'') \|_D p_1' \|_D p_2' \rangle$$
$$\mid \langle (m, p_1''), p_1' \rangle \in p_1(\sigma), \langle (\bar{m}, p_2''), p_2' \rangle \in p_2(\sigma) \,\}\,.$$

The reader who wants to work out the details should note that the recursive occurrence of $\mathcal{D}$ in the definition of '$|_D$' is guarded by a $\langle \sigma, \ldots \rangle$ step. Moreover, the unguarded appearance of '$\|_D$' in the clause for $\mathcal{D}(D|\mathsf{new}(s))(\gamma)$ is harmless, since one may get rid of it by once unwinding the definition of '$\|_D$'. Note also how, in the definition of $p_1 |_D p_2$, the processes p_1'', p_2'' are the semantic counterparts of the dependent resumptions, whereas p_1', p_2' correspond to independent resumptions.

Example Let $D(m) = v := 0$ (D will be suppressed in the calculation below), $\gamma_i = \lambda\sigma.\{\langle \sigma\{1/v\}, p_\epsilon \rangle\}$, $i = 0, 1, 2, 3$, $\gamma = \lambda\sigma.\{\langle (m, \gamma_1), \gamma_\epsilon \rangle\}$, $\bar{\gamma} = \lambda\sigma.\{\langle (\bar{m}, \gamma_2), \gamma_\epsilon \rangle\}$.

$\mathcal{D}[\![\mathsf{new}(m; v := 1); \mathsf{new}(\bar{m}; v := 2); v := 3]\!]$

$= \mathcal{D}(m)(\gamma_1) \| \mathcal{D}(\bar{m})(\gamma_2) \| \gamma_3$

$= \gamma \| \bar{\gamma} \| \gamma_3$

$= \lambda\sigma.\{\langle (m, \gamma_1), \bar{\gamma} \| \gamma_3 \rangle, \langle (\bar{m}, \gamma_2), \gamma \| \gamma_3 \rangle,$
$\qquad \langle \sigma\{3/v\}, \gamma \| \bar{\gamma} \rangle, \langle \sigma, \mathcal{D}(D(m))(\gamma_1 \| \gamma_2) \| \gamma_3 \rangle\}$

$= \lambda\sigma.\{\langle (m, \gamma_1), \lambda\sigma'.\{\langle (\bar{m}, \gamma_2), \gamma_3 \rangle, \langle \sigma'\{3/v\}, \bar{\gamma} \rangle\}\rangle,$

$$\langle(\bar{m},\gamma_2),\lambda\sigma'.\{\langle(m,\gamma_1),\gamma_3\rangle,\langle\sigma'\{3/v\},\gamma\rangle\}\rangle,$$
$$\langle\sigma\{3/v\},\lambda\sigma'.\{\langle(m,\gamma_1),\bar{\gamma}\rangle,\langle(\bar{m},\gamma_2),\gamma\rangle,\langle\sigma',\mathcal{D}(D(m))(\gamma_1\|\gamma_2)\rangle\}\rangle,$$
$$\langle\sigma,\lambda\sigma'.\{\langle\sigma'\{0/v\},\gamma_1\|\gamma_2\|\gamma_3\rangle,\langle\sigma'\{3/v\},\mathcal{D}(D(m))(\gamma_1\|\gamma_2)\rangle\}\rangle\}$$

$$= \lambda\sigma.\{\langle(m,\gamma_1),\lambda\sigma'.\{\langle(\bar{m},\gamma_2),\gamma_3\rangle,\langle(\sigma'\{3/v\},\bar{\gamma})\rangle\}\rangle,$$
$$\langle(\bar{m},\gamma_2),\lambda\sigma'.\{\langle(m,\gamma_1),\gamma_3\rangle,\langle\sigma'\{3/v\},\gamma\rangle\}\rangle,$$
$$\langle\sigma\{3/v\},\lambda\sigma'.\{\langle(m,\gamma_1),\bar{\gamma}\rangle,$$
$$\langle(\bar{m},\gamma_2),\gamma\rangle,\langle\sigma',\lambda\sigma''.\{\langle\sigma''\{0/v\},\gamma_1\|\gamma_2\rangle\}\rangle\}\rangle,$$
$$\langle\sigma,\lambda\sigma'.\{\langle\sigma'\{0/v\},\gamma_1\|\gamma_2\|\gamma_3\rangle,$$
$$\langle\sigma'\{3/v\},\lambda\sigma''.\{\langle\sigma''\{0/v\},\gamma_1\|\gamma_2\rangle\}\rangle\}\rangle\}.$$

There remains the task of settling the relationship between $\mathcal{O}$ and $\mathcal{D}$. Due to the interplay between (the definition of) $\mathcal{D}$ and '$\|$', this is a bit more complicated than preceding similar analyses. The first step is a familiar one, viz. the introduction of the intermediate $\mathcal{O}^*$, based on $\mathcal{T}_{rv}$ but with the denotational $\mathbb{P}_D$ as its range:

Definition 13.24 $\mathcal{O}^*: Decl \times Res \rightarrow \mathbb{P}_D$ is the unique function satisfying $\mathcal{O}^*(D|\mathrm{E}) = p_\epsilon$, and, for $r \not\equiv \mathrm{E}$,

$$\mathcal{O}^*(D|r) = \lambda\sigma.(\{\,\langle\sigma',\mathcal{O}^*(D|r')\rangle \mid [r,\sigma]\rightarrow[r',\sigma']\,\} \cup$$
$$\{\,\langle(m,\mathcal{O}^*(D|r'')),\mathcal{O}^*(D|r')\rangle \mid [r,\sigma]\rightarrow[r',(m,r'')]\,\}\,).$$

Next, we define the auxiliary $\mathcal{E}$.

Definition 13.25 $\mathcal{E}: Decl \times Res \rightarrow \mathbb{P}_D$ is given by

$$\mathcal{E}(D|\mathrm{E}) = p_\epsilon$$
$$\mathcal{E}(D|s\mathord{:}r) = \mathcal{D}(D|s)(\mathcal{E}(D|r))$$
$$\mathcal{E}(D|(r_1,r_2)) = \mathcal{E}(D|r_1)\|_D\mathcal{E}(D|r_2).$$

The main step in connecting $\mathcal{O}$ and $\mathcal{D}$ is the next lemma. Let Φ^* be the higher-order mapping (implicitly) used in the definition of $\mathcal{O}^*$.

Lemma 13.26 $\Phi^*(\mathcal{E}) = \mathcal{E}.$

For the proof of this lemma, we once more introduce a weight function.

Definition 13.27 $wgt(Res \cup Stat) \to \mathbb{N}$ is defined by

$$
\begin{array}{rcl}
wgt(\mathrm{E}) & = & 0 \\
wgt(s{:}r) & = & wgt(s) + wgt(r) \\
wgt(r_1, r_2) & = & wgt(r_1) + wgt(r_2) \\
wgt(v := e) & = & wgt(\mathsf{skip}) = wgt(m) = 1 \\
wgt(\mathsf{while}\ e\ \mathsf{do}\ s\ \mathsf{od}) & = & 1 \\
wgt(s_1{;}s_2) & = & wgt(s_1) + wgt(s_2) + 1 \\
wgt(\mathsf{if}\ e\ \mathsf{then}\ s_1\ \mathsf{else}\ s_2\ \mathsf{fi}) & = & max\{\, wgt(s_1), wgt(s_2) \,\} + 1 \\
wgt(\mathsf{new}(s)) & = & wgt(s) + 1
\end{array}
$$

Remarks

(1) Note that the definition of wgt does not depend on D.

(2) One easily sees that $wgt(s) > 0$, and $wgt(r) > 0$, for $r \not\equiv \mathrm{E}$.

(3) As always, wgt is designed such that, for $r_1 \to_{0,D} r_2$, $wgt(r_1) > wgt(r_2)$. We omit the easy proof of this fact.

We can now give the

Proof (of Lemma 13.26) We show that $\Phi^*(\mathcal{E})(D|r) = \mathcal{E}(D|r)$, by induction on $wgt(r)$. Two subcases.

$[\mathsf{new}(s){:}r]$ $\Phi^*(\mathcal{E})(D|\mathsf{new}(s){:}r)$

$\quad = \quad$ [def. $\mathcal{T}_{rv}$] $\Phi^*(\mathcal{E})(D|(s{:}\mathrm{E}, r))$

$\quad = \quad$ [ind. hyp.] $\mathcal{E}(D|(s{:}\mathrm{E}, r))$

$\quad = \quad$ [def. $\mathcal{E}, \mathcal{D}$] $\mathcal{E}(D|\mathsf{new}(s){:}r)$.

$[(r_1, r_2)]$ Choose some σ.

$\quad \Phi^*(\mathcal{E})(D|(r_1, r_2)(\sigma)$

$\quad = \quad \{\, \langle \theta', \mathcal{E}(D|(r', r_2)) \rangle \mid [r_1, \sigma] \to_D [r', \theta'] \,\} \cup$ (symm.) $\cup$
$\qquad\quad \{\, \langle \sigma, \mathcal{E}(D|(D(m){:}(r_1'', r_2''), (r_1', r_2''))) \rangle \mid$
$\qquad\qquad [r_1, \sigma] \to_D [r_1', (m, r_1'')], [r_2, \sigma] \to_D [r_2', (\bar{m}, r_2'')] \,\}$

$\quad = \quad$ [def. $\mathcal{E}$, properties of $\|_D$]
$\qquad\quad \{\, \langle \theta', \mathcal{E}(D|r') \rangle \mid [r_1, \sigma] \to_D [r', \theta'] \,\} \|\!\|_D \mathcal{E}(D|r_2) \cup$ (symm.) $\cup$
$\qquad\quad \{\, \langle \sigma, \mathcal{D}(D|D(m))(\mathcal{E}(D|r_1'')\|_D \mathcal{E}(D|r_2''))\|_D \mathcal{E}(D|r_1')\|_D \mathcal{E}(D|r_2') \rangle \mid$
$\qquad\qquad [r_1, \sigma] \to_D [r_1', (m, r_1'')], [r_2, \sigma] \to_D [r_2', (\bar{m}, r_2'')] \,\}$

$\overset{(\dagger)}{=}$ [def. Φ^*, see below for $(\dagger)$]

$(\Phi^*(\mathcal{E})(D|r_1) \mathbin{\|\mkern-6mu\|}_D \mathcal{E}(D|r_2))(\sigma) \cup$ (symm.) $\cup$

$(\Phi^*(\mathcal{E})(D|r_1)|_D \Phi^*(\mathcal{E})(D|r_2))(\sigma)$

$=$ [ind. hyp., def. $\|_D$] $\mathcal{E}(D|(r_1, r_2))$,

where the step marked $(\dagger)$ is justified as follows:

$(\Phi^*(\mathcal{E})(D|r_1)|_D \Phi^*(\mathcal{E})(D|r_2))(\sigma)$

$=$ [def. Φ^*, $\mathcal{E}$]

$\{\, \langle \sigma, \mathcal{D}(D|D(m))(p_1''\|_D p_2'')\|_D p_1'\|_D p_2' \rangle \mid$

$\quad \langle (m, p_1''), p_1' \rangle \in \Phi^*(\mathcal{E})(D|r_1)(\sigma), \langle (\bar{m}, p_2''), p_2' \rangle \in \Phi^*(\mathcal{E})(D|r_2)(\sigma) \,\}$

$=$ [def. Φ^*]

$\{\, \langle \sigma, \mathcal{D}(D|D(m))(p_1''\|_D p_2'')\|_D p_1'\|_D p_2' \rangle \mid$

$\quad \langle (m, p_1''), p_1' \rangle \in \{\, \langle (m, \mathcal{E}(D|r_1'')), \mathcal{E}(D|r_1') \rangle \mid$

$\quad\quad\quad [r_1, \sigma] \to_D [r_1', (m, r_1'')] \,\},$

$\quad \langle (\bar{m}, p_2''), p_2' \rangle \in \{\, \langle (\bar{m}, \mathcal{E}(D|r_2'')), \mathcal{E}(D|r_2') \rangle \mid$

$\quad\quad\quad [r_2, \sigma] \to_D [r_2', (\bar{m}, r_2'')] \,\} \,\}$

$=$ $\{\, \langle \sigma, \mathcal{D}(D|D(m))(\mathcal{E}(D|r_1'')\|_D \mathcal{E}(D|r_2''))\|_D \mathcal{E}(D|r_1')\|_D \mathcal{E}(D|r_2') \rangle \mid$

$\quad [r_1, \sigma] \to_D [r_1', (m, r_1'')], [r_2, \sigma] \to_D [r_2', (\bar{m}, r_2'')] \,\}.$ $\qquad\square$

We conclude the section on the rendezvous by providing (without going into formal details) the definition of the abstraction function $abs\colon \mathbb{P}_D \to \mathbb{P}_O$, and the theorem connecting $\mathcal{O}[\![\pi]\!]$ with $\mathcal{D}[\![\pi]\!]$.

Definition 13.28 $abs\colon \mathbb{P}_D \to \mathbb{P}_O$ is the unique function satisfying $abs(p_\epsilon) = \lambda\sigma.\{\epsilon\}$, and, for $p \neq p_\epsilon$,

$abs(p)(\sigma) =$

$\left\{ \begin{array}{ll} \{\delta\} & \text{if } p(\sigma) \subseteq (Meth \times \mathbb{P}_D) \times \mathbb{P}_D \\ \bigcup\{\, \sigma' \cdot abs(p')(\sigma') \mid \langle \sigma', p' \rangle \in p(\sigma) \,\} & \text{otherwise.} \end{array} \right.$

Putting all the usual ingredients together, we can conclude with

Theorem 13.29 $\mathcal{O}[\![\pi]\!] = (abs \circ \mathcal{D})[\![\pi]\!]$, for each $\pi \in \mathcal{L}_{rv}$.

13.3   Exercises

Exercise 13.1 Design syntax and semantics for a language in which the parallel composition construct of $\mathcal{L}_{po}$ is replaced by a form of process creation (as in Section 4.2).

(Hint: Introduce a new type of assignment $w := \mathsf{new}(s)$, with as effect

- a fresh object name o is created and stored as value for w, and next
- the pair (o, s) is executed in parallel to the processes already in execution.

Communication statements include constructs of the form $w?v$ and $w!e$, where, for o_2 the current value of w, the effect of $(o_1, w?v)$ is as described by the (Receive)-rule of Definition 13.6, and similarly for $w!e$.)

Exercise 13.2 Let the $\mathcal{L}_{rv}$-program π be given as

$$\pi = (D|v := 1;\mathsf{new}(w := 2;m);\bar{m}),$$

where $D(m) = u := v + w$.

(a) Prove that $\mathcal{D}[\![\pi]\!] =$

$$\lambda\sigma_1.\{\langle\sigma_1\{1/v\},$$
$$\lambda\sigma_2.\{\langle\sigma_2\{2/w\}, \lambda\sigma_3.\{\langle\sigma_3, \lambda\sigma_4.\langle\sigma_4\{\sigma_4(v) + \sigma_4(w)/u\}, \gamma_\epsilon\rangle\}\rangle,$$
$$\langle m, \lambda\sigma_4.\{\langle\bar{m}, \gamma_\epsilon, \gamma_\epsilon\rangle\}, \gamma_\epsilon\rangle, \langle\bar{m}, \lambda\sigma_4.\{\langle m, \gamma_\epsilon, \gamma_\epsilon\rangle\}, \gamma_\epsilon\rangle\}\rangle,$$
$$\langle\bar{m}, \lambda\sigma_3.\{\langle\sigma_3\{2/w\}, \lambda\sigma_4.\{\langle m, \gamma_\epsilon, \gamma_\epsilon\rangle\}, \gamma_\epsilon\rangle\}\rangle\}\rangle\}.$$

(b) Determine $\mathcal{O}[\![\pi]\!]$.

Exercise 13.3 Design syntax and semantics for a language combining the constructs of $\mathcal{L}_{po}$ and $\mathcal{L}_{rv}$.

13.4   Bibliographical notes

This chapter is based on our studies of (the semantics of) the parallel object-oriented language POOL, designed by America at Philips Research Laboratories around 1985. Both the design and the semantics of POOL have been described in the joint Ph.D. thesis of America and Rutten ([AR89a]). Since most of its chapters have been published as separate papers, we shall refer below to these papers in view of their easier accessibility.

The languages $\mathcal{L}_{po}$ and $\mathcal{L}_{rv}$ embody two main features of POOL, the former focusing on the machinery to ensure locality of the states in processes executing in parallel, and the latter on the rendezvous construct as a means to achieve communication (a notion inspired by a similar construct in the language ADA ([DoD83])). Both sections rely in essential ways on the operational semantics of POOL (as described in [ABKR86]), and its denotational semantics (given in [ABKR89]). In the paper [Rut90], the precise relationship between the two semantics is investigated. The paper [AR89c] provides a somewhat more tutorial presentation of these results. Our treatment of the rendezvous mechanism is based on a considerably streamlined version of the models from the just quoted papers, reported in [BV93]. A layered development of the semantics of parallel object-oriented languages which distinguishes three levels (statements, objects and the whole program) is given in [AR92].

The overview [Ame91] contains further material on formal studies of parallel object-oriented programming. The reader should be aware of the fact that we have covered only a small part of the full theory of OOP. E.g., we have not addressed any of the mostly type-theoretical issues having to do with the OO notions of subtyping and inheritance. The collection [BRR91] may provide some pointers to a large body of further work.

14 Atomization, Commit, and Action Refinement

In this chapter we study the programming notions of *atomization* and *commit,* and of *action refinement.* The first two have to do with controlling the interleaving possibilities of a construct in a setting with parallelism. A modest version of atomization was already studied in Chapter 12, through the language $\mathcal{L}_{aw,at}$. There, we did not attack the problem in full generality: the atomization operator was applied only to statements the execution of which was guaranteed to be finite (recall that this was enforced by syntactic means). In the present chapter, we address a version of the full problem by studying an extension (to be called $\mathcal{L}_{atc}$) of the uniform parallel language $\mathcal{L}_{par}$. Firstly, we include, for each $s \in \mathcal{L}_{atc}$, its atomized version $[s]$.Secondly, we introduce a variant on the sequential composition operator. We call this variant the "commit" operator, and denote it by ':'.[1] The intended effect of $(s{:}s)$ is close to that of $(s;s)$. However, no interleavings are possible at the position of the ':'.

The next concept we discuss is that of *action refinement.* We extend $\mathcal{L}_{atc}$ to $\mathcal{L}_{ref}$, by adding the construct $s_1\langle a \leadsto s_2 \rangle$, to be read as: In executing s_1, each occurrence of the atomic action a is *refined* to an execution of $[s_2]$. Note the atomization brackets around s_2: Without these, action refinement in a framework with interleaving parallelism would cause the following problem. Consider the two programs $(a \| b)\langle a \leadsto a_1;a_2 \rangle$ and $(a;b + b;a)\langle a \leadsto a_1;a_2 \rangle$. According to the intended meaning of action refinement, the first statement would be equivalent to $(a_1;a_2)\|b$, with semantics $\{\, a_1 a_2 b, a_1 b a_2, b a_1 a_2 \,\}$. On the other hand, the second statement would obtain the same meaning as $a_1;a_2;b + b;a_1;a_2$, that is the set $\{\, a_1 a_2 b, b a_1 a_2 \,\}$. Using '=' as before to denote semantic equivalence, we have obtained that, though $a\|b = a;b + b;a$, it is not true that $(a\|b)\langle a \leadsto a_1;a_2 \rangle = (a;b + b;a)\langle a \leadsto a_1;a_2 \rangle$. In order to avoid the drastic remedy of having to redesign our denotational model (such that it is no longer true that $\mathcal{D}(a\|b) = \mathcal{D}(a;b+b;a)$), we rather choose as way out that the refining statement is postulated to be atomic (through the implicit $[\cdot]$ around the s_2 in $s_1\langle a \leadsto s_2 \rangle$. The reader may easily convince himself that, in the version with atomization, $(a\|b)\langle a \leadsto a_1;a_2 \rangle = (a;b + b;a)\langle a \leadsto a_1;a_2 \rangle$: both have as meaning the set $\{\, a_1 a_2 b, b a_1 a_2 \,\}$.

To simplify the above explanations, they are couched in a linear terminology. However, this is not what we shall use in the treatment below. Rather, we shall employ a branching model. The main motivation for this is didactic: It provides us with the opportunity to illustrate the use of *systems* of domain equations in the

---

[1]The symbol ':' for commit should not be confused with ':' used sometimes in resumptions (though not in the present chapter).

specification of the underlying domain (for both $\mathcal{O}$ and $\mathcal{D}$). Instead of specifying a domain $\mathbb{P}$ through an equation $\mathbb{P} \simeq \mathcal{F}(\mathbb{P})$—as we have done so far in Part III—we shall now introduce the domains $\mathbb{P}, \mathbb{Q}$ as solution of a system

$$\mathbb{P} \simeq \mathcal{F}_1(\mathbb{P}, \mathbb{Q})$$
$$\mathbb{Q} \simeq \mathcal{F}_2(\mathbb{P}, \mathbb{Q}).$$

As a consequence, two further interesting phenomena appear. Firstly, the transition systems $\mathcal{T}_{atc}$ and $\mathcal{T}_{ref}$ will employ *two* kinds of transitions (to be denoted by $\xrightarrow{a}_1$ and $\xrightarrow{a}_2$), induced in a way by the presence of the two domains $\mathbb{P}$ and $\mathbb{Q}$.[2] Secondly, the definition of the various semantic operators (such as ';', '$\|$' or ':') now requires the use of a *system* (again with $n = 2$) of higher-order operators.

Though primarily introduced as a vehicle to illustrate a somewhat more advanced use of domain equations, let us add here the remark that if (synchronization and) deadlock were to be added to the languages $\mathcal{L}_{atc}$ or $\mathcal{L}_{ref}$, the need for a branching domain would arise in just the same way as was discussed in Chapter 11.

14.1   Atomization and commit—systems of equations

The concepts of *atomization* and *commit*—in the syntactic form of $[s]$ and $s{:}s$, respectively—are used to control the interleaving possibilities in a setting of a language with uniform parallelism. For any s, its atomized version $[s]$ acts as an atom, i.e., it is not interruptible by an interleaving action from a parallel statement. Consider, for example, the two statements $s_1 \equiv (a;b)\|c$ and $s_2 \equiv [a;b]\|c$. In a branching model as developed in Chapter 11, s_1 would obtain as meaning the process depicted by Figure 14.1.

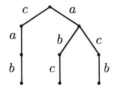

Figure 14.1: Process p_1 for s_1

In this outcome, the branch

---

[2] Recall that the earlier '$\rightarrow_0$' is an abbreviation rather than a separate kind of transition.

results from the interleaving of c *between* the actions a and b. It is precisely this possibility we want to exclude in our treatment of s_2: The to be designed semantic model should assign a meaning to s_2 such that c either precedes all of $a;b$ or follows all of $a;b$. Thus, one might expect the outcome of Figure 14.2.

Figure 14.2: Process p_2 for s_2

However, this is not what we shall do. In fact, process p_2 does not contain the information that between a and b, no interleavings are possible. Thus, a subsequent merge of p_2 with some d would allow d to come between a and b. Instead, we shall design the model such that, rather than p_2, we obtain the process p_3 as depicted in Figure 14.3.

Figure 14.3: Process p_3

We observe a major change in the semantic framework. Instead of using processes which correspond to tree-like objects with edges labeled by actions $a \in Act$, we shall in this chapter study processes which may be seen as tree-like objects where the edges are labeled by (finite or infinite) *words*. Moreover, the semantic atomization operator at will be organized such that, for any p, $at(p)$ results in a tree without inner branching structure (the only possible branching occurring at the root of the tree). Since no interleaving is possible anyway, there is no reason to preserve inner (i.e., different from the root) interleaving points. For example, for p_1 from Figure 14.1, $at(p_1)$ has the form

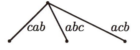

and $at(p_1)\|d$ will result in

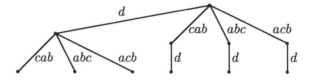

The intended meaning of the commit operator ':'—a "tightly binding" version of the sequential composition—is similar. It may be seen as a more *local* version, in that the use of ':' results in only one point where interleaving is not allowed. Consider $s_1{:}s_2$. We want its meaning to be such that no interleaving is possible at the place of the ':', i.e., between s_1 and s_2. *Within* s_1 and s_2, the possibility of interleaving is controlled by the presence of inner [·] or ':'. If these are absent, then within s_1 and s_2 interleavings are possible at all inner ';' and '$\|$'.

14.1.1 Syntax and operational semantics

We study the notions of atomization and commit by extending the language $\mathcal{L}_{par}$ of Chapter 4 with two new constructs, viz. $[s]$ and $s{:}s$.

Let $(a \in)\, Act$ and $(x \in)\, PVar$ be as usual. The language $\mathcal{L}_{atc}$ is defined in

Definition 14.1

(a) $s\,(\in Stat) ::= a \mid x \mid (s;s) \mid (s{:}s) \mid (s+s) \mid (s\|s) \mid [s]$

(b) $g\,(\in GStat) ::= a \mid (g;s) \mid (g{:}s) \mid (g+g) \mid (g\|g) \mid [g]$

(c) $(D \in)\, Decl = PVar \rightarrow GStat$

(d) $(\pi \in)\, \mathcal{L}_{atc} = Decl \times Stat.$

In the transition system $\mathcal{T}_{atc}$, we need the left merge $s_1 \| s_2$. For this purpose, we define $\mathcal{L}_{atc}^{+}$, the extension of $\mathcal{L}_{atc}$ obtained by adding the clauses

$$s ::= \ldots \mid s_1 \parallel\!\!\!\parallel s_2$$
$$g ::= \ldots \mid g_1 \parallel\!\!\!\parallel g_2$$

to the definition of *Stat* and *GStat*, respectively, and introducing the obvious definitions of $Decl^+$ and $\mathcal{L}_{atc}^+$. We next give

Definition 14.2

(a) $r\,(\in Res) ::= \mathrm{E} \mid s$, with $s \in \mathcal{L}_{atc}^+$.

(b) We identify $\mathrm{E};s$, $\mathrm{E}{:}s$, $\mathrm{E}\|s$ and $\mathrm{E}\parallel\!\!\!\parallel s$ with s, and $[\mathrm{E}]$ with E.

A key element in the design of $\mathcal{T}_{atc}$ is the use of two types of transitions, denoted by $s \xrightarrow{a}_1 r$ and $s \xrightarrow{a}_2 r$. We begin with the latter: A transition $s \xrightarrow{a}_2 r$ specifies that s may perform an a-step to r, *without* allowing an interleaving action (from some parallel statement $\bar{s}$) immediately after completion of this a-step. Rather, even in the presence of this $\bar{s}$, the next step (after the a-step) *has* to be taken by r. On the other hand, $s \xrightarrow{a}_1 r$ does allow an interleaving action just after performing the a-step. Thus, $s \xrightarrow{a}_1 r$ coincides with the $s \xrightarrow{a} r$ transition as studied, e.g., in Chapters 4 and 11.

The difference between the $\xrightarrow{a}_1$ and $\xrightarrow{a}_2$ transitions plays a role in the handling of three language constructs.

(1) $s_1\|s_2$. In order to be able to express the desired effect, we firstly introduce the rules

$$s_1\|s_2 \quad \rightarrow_0 \quad s_1 \parallel\!\!\!\parallel s_2$$
$$s_1\|s_2 \quad \rightarrow_0 \quad s_2 \parallel\!\!\!\parallel s_1$$

with the usual meaning for $\rightarrow_0$. The difference between $\xrightarrow{a}_1$ and $\xrightarrow{a}_2$ is now embodied in (the difference between) the two rules

$$\frac{s \xrightarrow{a}_1 r}{s \parallel\!\!\!\parallel \bar{s} \xrightarrow{a}_1 r\|\bar{s}} \quad \text{and} \quad \frac{s \xrightarrow{a}_2 r}{s \parallel\!\!\!\parallel \bar{s} \xrightarrow{a}_2 r \parallel\!\!\!\parallel \bar{s}} \ .$$

We see that an $\xrightarrow{a}_2$-step preserves the left merge: the next step *has* to come from r. On the other hand, from an $\xrightarrow{a}_1$-step the full merge $r\|\bar{s}$ may be inferred, thus allowing as well that $\bar{s}$ performs the next step—which then would constitute the interleaving action referred to above. One might say that the $\xrightarrow{a}_1$-steps are the "normal" ones, corresponding to the earlier $\xrightarrow{a}$-steps. The $\xrightarrow{a}_2$-steps are special, they are introduced as a result of handling $[s]$ and $s_1{:}s_2$, see (2) and (3) below.

(2) $[s]$. Atomization will be handled, essentially, by the $\xrightarrow{a}_2$-introduction rule

$$\frac{s \xrightarrow{a}_1 s'}{[s] \xrightarrow{a}_2 [s']}.$$

Thus, the possibility of interleaving present in the $\xrightarrow{a}_1$-step in the premise, disappears in the conclusion through the use of the $\xrightarrow{a}_2$-step. Repeated application of this rule will have as effect that no interleavings are possible throughout the execution of $[s]$.

(3) $s_1{:}s_2$. No interleaving is possible at the moment the commit (':') is executed. This is embodied in

$$\frac{s_1 \xrightarrow{a}_1 \mathrm{E}}{s_1{:}s_2 \xrightarrow{a}_2 s_2}.$$

Thus, after completing the execution of s_1, the execution of $s_1{:}s_2$ continues, via an $\xrightarrow{a}_2$-step, with the execution of s_2 *without* allowing an interleaving action (as explained in case (1) above).

Another way of describing the difference between $\xrightarrow{a}_1$ and $\xrightarrow{a}_2$ is to use pictures in the style of the introduction to this section. Let $q \in Act^\infty$, and let qa be the result of postfixing a to q. Consider the transitions $s \xrightarrow{a}_1 s'$ and $s \xrightarrow{a}_2 s'$, and assume that $\mathcal{O}(s)$ has the form as suggested by Figure 14.4a. Then $\mathcal{O}(s')$ will have the form of Figure 14.4b and Figure 14.4c, respectively, depending on whether the $\xrightarrow{a}_1$ – or the $\xrightarrow{a}_2$ – step has been performed.

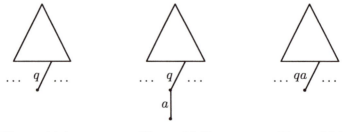

Figure 14.4a   Figure 14.4b   Figure 14.4c

We now give

Definition 14.3 $\mathcal{T}_{atc} = (Decl \times Res, Act \times \{1,2\}, \rightarrow, Spec)$. A transition $((D|r), \langle a, i \rangle, (D|r')) \in \rightarrow$ is written as $r \xrightarrow{a}_i r'$, for $i = 1$ or 2. The notation $r \rightarrow_0 r'$ abbreviates

$$\frac{r' \xrightarrow{a}_i \bar{r}}{r \xrightarrow{a}_i \bar{r}}, \quad i = 1 \text{ or } 2 .$$

Spec is given by

- $$a \xrightarrow{a}_1 E \hspace{8cm} \text{(Act)}$$

- $$x \rightarrow_0 D(x) \hspace{7.5cm} \text{(Rec)}$$

- $$s_1 + s_2 \rightarrow_0 s_1 \hspace{7cm} \text{(Choice)}$$
  $$s_1 + s_2 \rightarrow_0 s_2$$

- $$s_1 \| s_2 \rightarrow_0 s_1 \mathbin{\underline{\|}} s_2 \hspace{6.5cm} (\underline{\|}\text{-intro})$$
  $$s_1 \| s_2 \rightarrow_0 s_2 \mathbin{\underline{\|}} s_1$$

- $$\frac{s_1 \xrightarrow{a}_1 r}{\begin{array}{l} s_1;s \xrightarrow{a}_1 r;s \\ s_1 \mathbin{\underline{\|}} s \xrightarrow{a}_1 r \| s \end{array}} \hspace{5cm} \begin{array}{l} \text{(Seq 1)} \\ \text{(Left merge 1)} \end{array}$$

- $$\frac{s_1 \xrightarrow{a}_2 r}{\begin{array}{l} s_1;s \xrightarrow{a}_2 r;s \\ s_1{:}s \xrightarrow{a}_2 r{:}s \\ s_1 \mathbin{\underline{\|}} s \xrightarrow{a}_2 r \mathbin{\underline{\|}} s \\ [s_1] \xrightarrow{a}_2 [r] \end{array}} \hspace{4.5cm} \begin{array}{l} \text{(Seq 2)} \\ \text{(Commit 1)} \\ \text{(Left merge 2)} \\ \text{(Atom 1)} \end{array}$$

- $$\frac{s_1 \xrightarrow{a}_1 E}{\begin{array}{l} s_1{:}s \xrightarrow{a}_2 s \\ [s_1] \xrightarrow{a}_1 E \end{array}} \hspace{4.5cm} \begin{array}{l} (\rightarrow_2\text{-Intro 1}) \\ \text{(Atom 2)} \end{array}$$

- $$\frac{s_1 \xrightarrow{a}_1 s_2}{\begin{array}{l} s_1{:}s \xrightarrow{a}_1 s_2{:}s \\ [s_1] \xrightarrow{a}_2 [s_2] \end{array}} \hspace{4.5cm} \begin{array}{l} \text{(Commit 2)} \\ (\rightarrow_2\text{-Intro 2}) \end{array}$$

Examples Since

$$[a;b] \mathbin{\|\!\!\underline{}} c \xrightarrow{a}_2 [b] \mathbin{\|\!\!\underline{}} c$$

and

$$c \mathbin{\|\!\!\underline{}} [a;b] \xrightarrow{c}_1 [a;b]$$

we have for $[a;b] \| c$ the two transitions

$$[a;b] \| c \xrightarrow{a}_2 [b] \mathbin{\|\!\!\underline{}} c, \qquad [a;b] \| c \xrightarrow{c}_1 [a;b].$$

We add some explanations.

(1) The rules (Act), (Rec) and (Choice) are standard. The ($\mathbin{\|\!\!\underline{}}$-Intro) rule is necessary to specify the different treatment of $s_1 \mathbin{\|\!\!\underline{}} s_2 \xrightarrow{a}_1$ and $s_1 \mathbin{\|\!\!\underline{}} s_2 \xrightarrow{a}_2$, as described.

(2) By (Left merge 1), from $s_1 \xrightarrow{a}_1 r$ we infer $s_1 \mathbin{\|\!\!\underline{}} s \xrightarrow{a}_1 r \| s$. Thus, in the outcome we find $r \| s$, allowing the next step both from r and from s. In this way, after s_1 has performed an a-step to r, an interleaving step from s is possible. This is different from $s_1 \xrightarrow{a}_2 r$, which, by (Left merge 2), only allows the inference of $s_1 \mathbin{\|\!\!\underline{}} s \xrightarrow{a}_2 r \mathbin{\|\!\!\underline{}} s$. Consequently, the next step has to be taken by r, and an interleaving from s is not possible.

(3) The $\xrightarrow{a}_2$-introduction rules stem either from the handling of ':' or of [·]. In the first case, from $s_1 \xrightarrow{a}_1 \mathrm{E}$ we infer $s_1{:}s \xrightarrow{a}_2 s$, disallowing interrupts upon the completion of s_1. In the second, an $\xrightarrow{a}_1$-step from s_1 to s_2 induces an $\xrightarrow{a}_2$-step from $[s_1]$ to $[s_2]$, with a similar effect.

(4) By inspection of $\mathcal{T}_{atc}$ we see that no transitions of the form $s \xrightarrow{a}_2 \mathrm{E}$ are derivable.

$\mathcal{T}_{atc}$ has the familiar finitely-branching property. We employ a standard complexity measure, and obtain this property in a routine manner.

Definition 14.4 $wgt{:}\, Res \to \mathbb{N}$ is given by

$$
\begin{aligned}
wgt(\mathrm{E}) &= 0 \\
wgt(a) &= 1 \\
wgt(x) &= wgt(D(x)) + 1 \\
wgt(s_1;s_2) &= wgt(s_1) + 1, \text{ and similarly for ':'} \\
wgt(s_1 + s_2) &= wgt(s_1) + wgt(s_2) + 1, \text{ and similarly for '}\|\text{', '}\mathbin{\|\!\!\underline{}}\text{'} \\
wgt([s]) &= wgt(s) + 1 .
\end{aligned}
$$

We have the usual

Lemma 14.5

(a) wgt is well-defined.

(b) $\mathcal{T}_{atc}$ satisfies, for all s,

$$0 < |\{\, \langle a, r \rangle \mid s \xrightarrow{a}_i r, i = 1 \ or \ 2 \,\}| < \infty\,.$$

Proof Exercise.   □

Our next task is to specify $\mathcal{O}$ for $\mathcal{L}_{atc}$. We shall define a branching domain $\mathbb{P}$—to be used as codomain of both $\mathcal{O}$ and $\mathcal{D}$ for $\mathcal{L}_{atc}$—by means of a *system* of domain equations. By way of introduction we recall two domains used in earlier chapters. Firstly, we have made extensive use of the domain $\mathcal{P}_{nco}(Act^\infty \backslash \{\, \epsilon \,\})$. A very similar domain (we leave it to the reader to pinpoint the difference, cf. Exercise 14.1) is the one specified by the system of equations (here and below we write $\ldots /2$ as short-hand for $id_{\frac{1}{2}}(\ldots)$)

$$\mathbb{P} \simeq \mathcal{P}_{nco}(\mathbb{Q})$$
$$\mathbb{Q} \simeq Act + (Act \times \mathbb{Q}/2).$$

We also employed (e.g., in Chapter 11) the branching domain $\mathbb{P} \simeq \{\, p_\epsilon \,\} \cup \mathcal{P}_{co}(A \times \mathbb{P}/2)$. A modest variation on this is the domain $\mathbb{P}$ satisfying the system

$$\mathbb{P} \simeq \mathcal{P}_{co}(\mathbb{Q})$$
$$\mathbb{Q} \simeq Act + (Act \times \mathbb{P}/2).$$

The domain we shall use as semantic universe for $\mathcal{L}_{atc}$ combines the two systems above in the sense given in

Definition 14.6 The domains $\mathbb{P}$, $\mathbb{Q}$—to be used for $\mathcal{L}_{atc}$—are given as (first and second solution of) the system of equations

$$\mathbb{P} \simeq \mathcal{P}_{nco}(\mathbb{Q})$$
$$\mathbb{Q} \simeq Act + (Act \times \mathbb{P}/2) + (Act \times \mathbb{Q}/2)\,.$$

We see that each $p \in \mathbb{P}$ is a nonempty (see below) and compact set, the elements of which are either atomic actions ($a \in Act$), or pairs of the form $\langle a, p \rangle$ or $\langle a, q \rangle$. There is an essential difference between (the way we shall use) $\langle a, p \rangle$ and $\langle a, q \rangle$, in that the former represents a situation where we have the possibility to perform an interleaving action after a, but before continuing with p, whereas for $\langle a, q \rangle$, after having performed a we *have* to continue with q. That is, there is no possibility to perform an interleaving action after a. The two trees depicted earlier (Figures 14.1 and 14.3 from the introduction to Section 14.1) are represented by the following elements in $\mathbb{P}$:

$$p_1 = \{ \langle a, \{ \langle b, \{c\} \rangle, \langle c, \{b\} \rangle \} \rangle, \langle c, \{ \langle a, \{b\} \rangle \} \rangle \}$$
$$p_3 = \{ \langle c, \{ \langle a, b \rangle \} \rangle, \langle a, \langle b, \{c\} \rangle \rangle \} \,.$$

In Section 14.1.2, we shall define the semantic operator $\|: \mathbb{P} \times \mathbb{P} \to \mathbb{P}$ in such a way that the intended interpretation of $\langle a, p \rangle$ versus $\langle a, q \rangle$ is indeed satisfied.

Remark A comment on the necessity of avoiding empty processes (note that we used $\mathcal{P}_{nco}(\cdot)$ rather than $\mathcal{P}_{co}(\cdot)$) follows after the definition of the semantic ':' (Definition 14.8).

We now connect our earlier discussion of the different $\xrightarrow{a}_i$-transitions (for $i = 1$ or $i = 2$) to the design of the domain $\mathbb{P}$. On the basis of the earlier explanations, it is fairly clear how to design $\mathcal{O}(s)$ in terms of the various possibilities for $s \xrightarrow{a}_i r$.

(1) $s \xrightarrow{a}_1 \mathrm{E}$. (Recall that $s \xrightarrow{a}_2 \mathrm{E}$ is not derivable from $\mathcal{T}_{atc}$.) We then, simply, include a in the outcome $\mathcal{O}(s)$.

(2) $s \xrightarrow{a}_1 s'$. This is a step of the interruptible kind, and we include $\langle a, \mathcal{O}(s') \rangle$, i.e., an element of the $\langle a, p \rangle$-kind, in the outcome $\mathcal{O}(s)$.

(3) $s \xrightarrow{a}_2 s'$. Now no interrupts are allowed, and we expect results of the $\langle a, q \rangle$-variety. In fact, we here include all $\langle a, q \rangle$, for $q \in \mathcal{O}(s')$, in the outcome $\mathcal{O}(s)$. Putting the three cases together, we have

Definition 14.7

(a) $\mathcal{O}: \mathcal{L}_{atc} \to \mathbb{P}$ is the unique function satisfying

$$\mathcal{O}(s) = \{ a \mid s \xrightarrow{a}_1 \mathrm{E} \} \cup \{ \langle a, \mathcal{O}(s') \rangle \mid s \xrightarrow{a}_1 s' \} \cup \{ \langle a, q \rangle \mid s \xrightarrow{a}_2 s' \wedge q \in \mathcal{O}(s') \}$$

(b) $\mathcal{O}[\![\pi]\!] = \mathcal{O}(\pi)$.

Well-definedness of $\mathcal{O}$ follows by a standard contractiveness argument.

Examples

(1) $\mathcal{O}[\![a;b]\!]\,\|c]\!]$
$$= \{\langle c, \mathcal{O}([a;b]))\rangle\} \ \cup \ \{\,\langle a, q\rangle \mid q \in \mathcal{O}([b]\ \underline{\|\,}\ c)\,\}$$
$$= \{\langle c, \mathcal{O}([a;b]))\rangle\} \ \cup \ \{\,\langle a, q\rangle \mid q \in \{\langle b, \{c\}\rangle\}\,\}$$
$$= \{\,\langle c, \{\langle a, b\rangle\}, \langle a, \langle b, \{c\}\rangle\rangle\,\}$$

(2) Let $\pi \equiv (D|[x])$, with $D(x) = a;x$. Since $[x] \xrightarrow{a}_2 [x]$ we obtain $\mathcal{O}(D|x) = \{\,\langle a, q\rangle \mid q \in \mathcal{O}(D|[x])\,\}$, from which $\mathcal{O}[\![\pi]\!] = \{\,\langle a, \langle a, \ldots\rangle\rangle\,\}$ follows. This outcome may be represented by the picture

$$a^{\omega}\Bigg|$$

We see that atoms may well be infinite. This should be contrasted with the situation for $\mathcal{L}_{aw,at}$, where finiteness of all atoms was enforced by syntactic means.

14.1.2   Denotational semantics, relating $\mathcal{O}$ and $\mathcal{D}$

The denotational semantics $\mathcal{D}\colon \mathcal{L}_{atc} \to \mathbb{P}$ employs the same codomain $\mathbb{P}$ as that used for the operational semantics. The main issue in the design of $\mathcal{D}$ is the definition of the various semantic operators. Moreover, we shall need several properties of these operators which play a role in establishing that $\mathcal{O} = \mathcal{D}$ on $\mathcal{L}_{atc}$. Corresponding to the use of a *system* of domain equations (with $n = 2$) for the specification of $\mathbb{P}$, in the definition of the operators we shall, throughout, use *systems* of higher-order mappings (again with $n = 2$). Apart from this use of systems, the further machinery used in the various definitions is a straightforward extension of earlier techniques. We begin with the definitions of ';', ':', '$\|$' (and '$\underline{\|}$') and '+', using auxiliary ';', ':' and '$\underline{\|}$'. The semantic atomization operator at will follow in the next definition.

Definition 14.8   Let $(\phi \in)\, Op = \mathbb{P} \times \mathbb{P} \xrightarrow{1} \mathbb{P}$, $(\psi \in)\, Op' = \mathbb{Q} \times \mathbb{P} \xrightarrow{1} \mathbb{Q}$ and $(\chi \in)\, Op'' = \mathbb{Q} \times \mathbb{P} \xrightarrow{1} \mathbb{P}$. The mappings

$$\Omega_; : Op \times Op' \to Op$$
$$\Omega_{;'} : Op \times Op' \to Op'$$

$$\Omega_: : Op \times Op'' \to Op$$
$$\Omega_{:'} : Op \times Op'' \to Op''$$

$$\Omega_\| : Op \times Op' \to Op$$

are given by

(a) $\quad \Omega_;(\phi,\psi)(p_1,p_2) \quad = \quad \{\, \Omega_{;'}(\phi,\psi)(q,p_2) \mid q \in p_1 \,\}$
$\quad\quad \Omega_:(\phi,\chi)(p_1,p_2) \quad = \quad \bigcup \{\, \Omega_{:'}(\phi,\chi)(q,p_2) \mid q \in p_1 \,\}$
$\quad\quad \Omega_\|(\phi,\psi)(p_1,p_2) \quad = \quad \Omega_;(\phi,\psi)(p_1,p_2) \,\cup\, \Omega_;(\phi,\psi)(p_2,p_1) \,.$

(b) $\quad\quad \Omega_{;'}(\phi,\psi)(a,p) \quad = \quad \langle a,p \rangle$
$\quad\quad \Omega_{;'}(\phi,\psi)(\langle a,p' \rangle,p) \quad = \quad \langle a, \phi(p',p) \rangle$
$\quad\quad \Omega_{;'}(\phi,\psi)(\langle a,q \rangle,p) \quad = \quad \langle a, \psi(q,p) \rangle \,.$

(c) $\quad\quad \Omega_{:'}(\phi,\chi)(a,p) \quad = \quad \{\, \langle a,q \rangle \mid q \in p \,\}$
$\quad\quad \Omega_{:'}(\phi,\chi)(\langle a,p' \rangle,p) \quad = \quad \{\, \langle a, \phi(p',p) \rangle \,\}$
$\quad\quad \Omega_{:'}(\phi,\chi)(\langle a,q \rangle,p) \quad = \quad \{\, \langle a,q' \rangle \mid q' \in \chi(q,p) \,\} \,.$

(d) $\quad\quad \langle ;, ;' \rangle \quad = \quad \mathit{fix}(\Omega_;, \Omega_{;'})$
$\quad\quad \langle \|, \|' \rangle \quad = \quad \mathit{fix}(\Omega_\|, \Omega_{;'})$
$\quad\quad \langle :, :' \rangle \quad = \quad \mathit{fix}(\Omega_:, \Omega_{:'})$
$\quad\quad\quad \| \quad = \quad \Omega_;(\|, \|') \,.$

(e) $p_1 + p_2 = p_1 \cup p_2$ (the set-theoretic union of p_1 and p_2).

The justifications for these definitions are collected in

Lemma 14.9

(a) The mappings $\Omega_;$, $\Omega_\|$, $\Omega_:$, $\Omega_{;'}$, $\Omega_{:'}$ are well-defined.

(b) $\langle \Omega_;, \Omega_{;'} \rangle$ and $\langle \Omega_\|, \Omega_{;'} \rangle$ are contractive in the argument $\langle \phi, \psi \rangle$. $\langle \Omega_:, \Omega_{:'} \rangle$ is contractive in the argument $\langle \phi, \chi \rangle$.

Proof

(a) Clearly, we have that $\Omega_{;'}(\phi,\psi)(q,p) \in \mathbb{Q}$, for each ϕ, ψ, q, p. Next, let $F \colon \mathbb{Q} \to \mathbb{Q}$ be short-hand for the mapping $\lambda q . \Omega_{;'}(\phi,\psi)(q,p_2)$. Since F is nonexpansive (in q), it is continuous. Therefore the image $\hat{F}(p_1) \overset{df}{=} \{\, F(q) \mid q \in p_1 \,\}$ $(= \{\, \Omega_{;'}(\phi,\psi)(q,p_2) \mid$

$q \in p_1$ }) of the compact set p_1 is itself a compact set (by Theorem 2.13c). The proof that $\langle \Omega_{\parallel}, \Omega_{;'} \rangle$ is well-defined is obvious from this. We now discuss the pair $\langle \Omega_{:}, \Omega_{:'} \rangle$. Take some ϕ, χ, p_1, p_2 and q as specified. By the assumptions on ϕ, χ we have that the set $\Omega_{:'}(\phi, \chi)(q, p_2)$ is compact for each of the three subcases $q = a$, $q = \langle a, p' \rangle$ or $q = \langle a, q' \rangle$. Moreover, the set $\{ \Omega_{:'}(\phi, \chi)(q, p_2) \mid q \in p_1 \}$ is a compact set (of compact sets) by the same argument as just used for $\Omega_{:}$. By Michael's theorem (Theorem 2.15) we then have that

$$\Omega_{:}(\phi, \psi)(p_1, p_2) \;=\; \bigcup \{ \Omega_{:'}(\phi, \psi)(q, p_2) \mid q \in p_1 \}$$

is also a compact set.

(b) Routine. □

By a straightforward extension (to the case of systems) of earlier proof techniques, one obtains

Lemma 14.10

(a) ';' and ':' are nonexpansive in their first argument and contractive in their second argument.

(b) '$\parallel$' and '$\underline{\parallel}$' are nonexpansive in both arguments.

Remark Part (a) requires the assumption that all $p \in \mathbb{P}$ are nonempty. Applying the definitions without this assumption would yield $\{a\}{:}\emptyset = \emptyset$, violating the desired property that $d(\{a\}{:}p_1, \{a\}{:}p_2) \leq \frac{1}{2} d(p_1, p_2)$, for all p_1, p_2.

We now state some simple properties of ';', '$\underline{\parallel}$' and ':' for later use.

Lemma 14.11

(a) $\{\langle a, p_1 \rangle\}{;}p_2 = \{\langle a, p_1{;}p_2 \rangle\}$, and similarly for '$\underline{\parallel}$', ':'.

(b) $\{\langle a, q \rangle \mid q \in p_1 \}{;}p_2 = \{\langle a, q \rangle \mid q \in p_1{;}p_2 \}$, and similarly for '$\underline{\parallel}$', ':'.

Proof We only discuss claim (b) for ':'. We have

$$\{\langle a, q \rangle \mid q \in p_1 \}{:}p_2$$
$$= \bigcup \{ \langle a, q \rangle :' p_2 \mid q \in p_1 \}$$
$$= \bigcup \{ \{ \langle a, \bar{q} \rangle \mid \bar{q} \in q :' p_2 \} \mid q \in p_1 \}$$

$$= \bigcup \{ \langle a, \bar{q} \rangle \mid q \in p_1, \bar{q} \in q :' p_2 \}$$
$$= \{ \langle a, \bar{q} \rangle \mid \bar{q} \in p_1 : p_2 \} \,. \qquad\qquad\qquad\qquad\qquad\qquad\qquad \square$$

We next introduce the semantic operator *at* (for atomization) corresponding to the syntactic atomization [·]. We need a domain $\mathbb{R}$ which is essentially simpler than $\mathbb{P}$ in that it lacks the branching structure of $\mathbb{P}$.

Definition 14.12 The domain $\mathbb{R}$ is the first component of the solution of the system of equations

$$\begin{aligned} \mathbb{R} &\simeq \mathcal{P}_{nco}(\mathbb{T}) \\ \mathbb{T} &\simeq Act + Act \times \mathbb{T}/2. \end{aligned}$$

Note that $\mathbb{R}$ is (almost) the domain $\mathcal{P}_{nco}(Act^{\infty}\backslash\{\,\epsilon\,\})$. It is presented here as given in order to organize the definitions of *at* (and *at'*) as mappings which collapse the branching structure from some p (or q) yielding $at(p)$ (or $at'(q)$) as elements of the linear domain $\mathbb{R}$.

Remark One might argue that it is not necessary to collapse the branching structure of a process p in order to obtain its atomized version $at(p)$. In fact, one could imagine a framework where $at(p)$ is derived from p by surrounding it in some way by begin and end markers, but preserving its branching structure. This assumes that the $\|$-operator is defined in such a way that interleaving actions may occur only completely before or after $at(p)$. For example, for p as specified in Figure 14.1 above, $at(p)\|d$ would result in the process depicted by

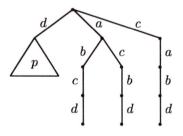

Though valid in principle, this view of atomization—leaving aside the elaboration of the details in the definitions—results in an unnecessarily complicated semantic model: The branching points interior to p do not allow interleaving anyway, so there seems to be little point in preserving them as such.

We proceed with the precise definitions of at.

Definition 14.13 Let $(\phi \in)\, Op = \mathbb{P} \overset{1}{\to} \mathbb{R}$, $(\psi \in)\, Op' = \mathbb{Q} \overset{1}{\to} \mathbb{R}$.

(a) The mappings $\Omega_{at} \colon Op \times Op' \to Op$ and $\Omega_{at'} \colon Op \times Op' \to Op'$ are defined by putting

$$
\begin{aligned}
\Omega_{at}(\phi, \psi)(p) &= \bigcup \{\, \Omega_{at'}(\phi, \psi)(q) \mid q \in p \,\} \\
\Omega_{at'}(\phi, \psi)(a) &= \{a\} \\
\Omega_{at'}(\phi, \psi)(\langle a, p \rangle) &= \{\, \langle a, t \rangle \mid t \in \phi(p) \,\} \\
\Omega_{at'}(\phi, \psi)(\langle a, q \rangle) &= \{\, \langle a, t \rangle \mid t \in \psi(q) \,\}\,.
\end{aligned}
$$

(b) $(at, at') = \mathrm{fix}(\Omega_{at}, \Omega_{at'})$.

We leave to the reader the proof of the next lemma which states various properties of at, at' which are direct variations on earlier properties of ';', ';'' or ':', ':''.

Lemma 14.14

(a) $\Omega_{at}(\phi, \psi) \in Op$, $\Omega_{at'}(\phi, \psi) \in Op'$.

(b) $(\Omega_{at}, \Omega_{at'})$ is contractive in (ϕ, ψ).

(c) at is nonexpansive in p.

(d) $at(\{\, \langle a, q \rangle \mid q \in p \,\}) = \{\, \langle a, t \rangle \mid t \in at(p) \,\}$.

Proof Exercise.   □

We are ready for the definition of $\mathcal{D} \colon \mathcal{L}_{atc} \to \mathbb{P}$. The format of the definition is the usual one.

Definition 14.15

(a) Let $(S \in)\, Sem = \mathcal{L}_{atc} \to \mathbb{P}$, and let $\Psi \colon Sem \to Sem$ be given by

$$
\begin{aligned}
\Psi(S)(a) &= \{a\} \\
\Psi(S)(x) &= \Psi(S)(D(x)) \\
\Psi(S)(s_1 \text{ op } s_2) &= \Psi(S)(s_1) \text{ op } S(s_2), \quad \text{op} \in \{;, :\} \\
\Psi(S)(s_1 \text{ op } s_2) &= \Psi(S)(s_1) \text{ op } \Psi(S)(s_2), \quad \text{op} \in \{+, \|\} \\
\Psi(S)([s]) &= at(\Psi(S)(s))\,.
\end{aligned}
$$

(b) $\mathcal{D} = \mathrm{fix}(\Psi)$, $\mathcal{D}[\![\pi]\!] = \mathcal{D}(\pi)$.

Example

$$\mathcal{D}([a;b]\,\|\,c)$$
$$=\ \mathsf{at}(\mathcal{D}(a;b))\,\|\,\mathcal{D}(c)$$
$$=\ \mathsf{at}(\{\langle a,\{b\}\rangle)\})\,\|\,\{c\}$$
$$=\ \{\langle a,b\rangle\}\,\|\,\{c\}$$
$$=\ \{\,\langle a,\langle b,\{c\}\rangle\rangle,\langle c,\{\langle a,b\rangle\}\,\}.$$

For the purpose of comparing $\mathcal{O}$ and $\mathcal{D}$ on $\mathcal{L}_{atc}$, it is necessary to extend $\mathcal{D}$ to $\mathcal{L}_{atc}^{+} \to \mathbb{P}$. This is easily achieved by replacing $\mathcal{L}_{atc}$ by $\mathcal{L}_{atc}^{+}$ in the above definition, and extending the clause indexed by $\mathsf{op} \in \{+, \|\}$ to one indexed by $\mathsf{op} \in \{+, \|, \|\!\_\}$.

One simple lemma is necessary before we can prove that $\mathcal{O} = \mathcal{D}$ on $\mathcal{L}_{atc}$.

Lemma 14.16 *Let* $t \in \mathbb{T}$, *and let* $p_i \in \mathbb{P}$, $i \in I$ *be such that* $\bigcup_{i \in I} p_i \in \mathbb{P}$. *Then*

$$t :' \bigcup_{i \in I} p_i = \bigcup_{i \in I} (t :' p_i)\,.$$

Proof Let X be defined as

$$X = \{\,(\phi, \psi) \in Op \times Op' \mid \ \phi(r, \textstyle\bigcup_i p_i) = \bigcup_i \phi(r, p_i), \ \text{for all } r \in \mathbb{R}$$
$$\psi(t, \textstyle\bigcup_i p_i) = \bigcup_i \psi(t, p_i), \ \text{for all } t \in \mathbb{T}\,\}\,.$$

We have that X is a nonempty and closed subset of $Op \times Op'$. To establish nonemptiness, take $(\phi, \psi) = (\lambda r.\lambda p.r, \lambda t.\lambda p.t)$. Closedness of X is left as an exercise (cf. Exercise 14.2). We clearly have that $(\Omega_:, \Omega_{:'})(X) \subseteq X$. By completeness of X (as subspace of $Op \times Op'$), we obtain that $\langle :, :'\rangle = \mathit{fix}(\Omega_:, \Omega_{:'}) \in X$, thus proving the desired result. $\qquad\square$

Remark Note that the above lemma does not hold when we replace $t \in \mathbb{T}$ by arbitrary $q \in \mathbb{Q}$.

We are ready for the proof of

Lemma 14.17 *Let Φ be the higher-order mapping used (implicitly) in the definition of $\mathcal{O}$. Then*

$$\Phi(\mathcal{D}) = \mathcal{D} .$$

Proof We prove that $\Phi(\mathcal{D})(s) = \mathcal{D}(s)$, for each $s \in \mathcal{L}_{atc}^{+}$, by induction on $wgt(s)$. Three subcases.

$[s_1;s_2]$ $\Phi(\mathcal{D})(s_1;s_2)$

$\quad = \quad \{\, a \mid s_1;s_2 \xrightarrow{a}_1 \mathrm{E} \,\} \cup \{\, \langle a, \mathcal{D}(\bar{s}) \rangle \mid s_1;s_2 \xrightarrow{a}_1 \bar{s} \,\} \cup$
$\qquad \{\, \langle a, q \rangle \mid s_1;s_2 \xrightarrow{a}_2 \bar{s}, q \in \mathcal{D}(\bar{s}) \,\}$

$\quad = \quad \emptyset \cup \{\, \langle a, \mathcal{D}(s_2) \rangle \mid s_1 \xrightarrow{a}_1 \mathrm{E} \,\} \cup \{\, \langle a, \mathcal{D}(s';s_2) \rangle \mid s_1 \xrightarrow{a}_1 s' \,\} \cup$
$\qquad \{\, \langle a, q \rangle \mid s_1 \xrightarrow{a}_2 s', q \in \mathcal{D}(s';s_2) \,\}$

$\quad = \quad \{\, \langle a, \mathcal{D}(s_2) \rangle \mid s_1 \xrightarrow{a}_1 \mathrm{E} \,\} \cup \{\, \langle a, \mathcal{D}(s');\mathcal{D}(s_2) \rangle \mid s_1 \xrightarrow{a}_1 s' \,\} \cup$
$\qquad \{\, \langle a, q \rangle \mid s_1 \xrightarrow{a}_2 s', q \in \mathcal{D}(s');\mathcal{D}(s_2) \,\}$

$\quad = \quad$ [Lemma 14.11]
$\qquad \{\, a \mid s_1 \xrightarrow{a}_1 \mathrm{E} \,\};\mathcal{D}(s_2) \cup \{\, \langle a, \mathcal{D}(s') \rangle \mid s_1 \xrightarrow{a}_1 s' \,\};\mathcal{D}(s_2) \cup$
$\qquad \{\, \langle a, q \rangle \mid s_1 \xrightarrow{a}_2 s', q \in \mathcal{D}(s') \,\};\mathcal{D}(s_2)$

$\quad = \quad \Phi(\mathcal{D})(s_1);\mathcal{D}(s_2)$

$\quad = \quad$ [ind. hyp.] $\mathcal{D}(s_1);\mathcal{D}(s_2)$

$\quad = \quad \mathcal{D}(s_1;s_2) .$

$[s_1{:}s_2]$ $\Phi(\mathcal{D})(s_1{:}s_2)$

$\quad = \quad \{\, a \mid s_1{:}s_2 \xrightarrow{a}_1 \mathrm{E} \,\} \cup \{\, \langle a, \mathcal{D}(s) \rangle \mid s_1{:}s_2 \xrightarrow{a}_1 s \,\} \cup$
$\qquad \{\, \langle a, q \rangle \mid s_1{:}s_2 \xrightarrow{a}_2 s, q \in \mathcal{D}(s) \,\}$

$\quad = \quad \emptyset \cup \{\, \langle a, \mathcal{D}(s'{:}s_2) \rangle \mid s_1 \xrightarrow{a}_1 s' \,\} \cup \{\, \langle a, q \rangle \mid s_1 \xrightarrow{a}_1 \mathrm{E}, q \in \mathcal{D}(s_2) \,\} \cup$
$\qquad \{\, \langle a, q \rangle \mid s_1 \xrightarrow{a}_2 s', q \in \mathcal{D}(s'{:}s_2) \,\}$

$\quad = \quad \{\, \langle a, \mathcal{D}(s'){:}\mathcal{D}(s_2) \rangle \mid s_1 \xrightarrow{a}_1 s' \,\} \cup \{\, \langle a, q \rangle \mid s_1 \xrightarrow{a}_1 \mathrm{E}, q \in \mathcal{D}(s_2) \,\} \cup$
$\qquad \{\, \langle a, q \rangle \mid s_1 \xrightarrow{a}_2 s', q \in \mathcal{D}(s'){:}\mathcal{D}(s_2) \,\}$

$\quad = \quad$ [Def. $a{:}p$, Lemma 14.11]
$\qquad \{\, a \mid s_1 \xrightarrow{a}_1 \mathrm{E} \,\}{:}\mathcal{D}(s_2) \cup \{\, \langle a, \mathcal{D}(s') \rangle \mid s_1 \xrightarrow{a}_1 s' \,\}{:}\mathcal{D}(s_2) \cup$
$\qquad \{\, \langle a, q \rangle \mid s_1 \xrightarrow{a}_2 s', q \in \mathcal{D}(s') \,\}{:}\mathcal{D}(s_2)$

$\quad = \quad \Phi(\mathcal{D})(s_1){:}\mathcal{D}(s_2)$

$\quad = \quad$ [ind. hyp.] $\mathcal{D}(s_1) : \mathcal{D}(s_2)$

$\quad = \quad \mathcal{D}(s_1{:}s_2) .$

$[[s]]$ $\Phi(\mathcal{D})([s])$

$= \{ a \mid [s] \xrightarrow{a}_1 \mathrm{E} \} \cup \{ \langle a, \mathcal{D}(\bar{s}) \rangle \mid [s] \xrightarrow{a}_1 \bar{s} \} \cup \{ \langle a, q \rangle \mid [s] \xrightarrow{a}_2 \bar{s}, q \in \mathcal{D}(\bar{s}) \}$

$= \quad [\text{by (Atom) and } (\to_1\text{-Intro 2})]$
$\quad \{ a \mid s \xrightarrow{a}_1 \mathrm{E} \} \cup \emptyset \cup \{ \langle a, q \rangle \mid s \xrightarrow{a}_1 s', q \in \mathcal{D}([s']) \} \cup$
$\quad \{ \langle a, q \rangle \mid s \xrightarrow{a}_2 s'', q \in \mathcal{D}([s'']) \}$

$= \quad [\text{def. } \mathcal{D}([s'])]$
$\quad \{ a \mid s \xrightarrow{a}_1 \mathrm{E} \} \cup \{ \langle a, q \rangle \mid s \xrightarrow{a}_1 s', q \in at(\mathcal{D}(s')) \} \cup$
$\quad \{ \langle a, q \rangle \mid s \xrightarrow{a}_2 s'', q \in at(\mathcal{D}(s'')) \}$

$=$
$\quad at\big(\{ a \mid s \xrightarrow{a}_1 \mathrm{E} \} \cup \{ \langle a, \mathcal{D}(s') \rangle \mid s \xrightarrow{a}_1 s' \} \cup \{ \langle a, q \rangle \mid s \xrightarrow{a}_2 s'', q \in \mathcal{D}(s'') \} \big)$

$= \quad at\big(\Phi(\mathcal{D})(s) \big)$

$= \quad [\text{ind. hyp.}] \ at(\mathcal{D}(s))$

$= \quad \mathcal{D}([s]) .$ $\square$

From Lemma 14.17 we obtain in the usual way

Theorem 14.18 $\mathcal{O}[\![\pi]\!] = \mathcal{D}[\![\pi]\!]$, *for all* $\pi \in \mathcal{L}_{atc}$.

14.2   Action refinement—proving $\mathcal{O} = \mathcal{D}$ may be difficult

The language $\mathcal{L}_{ref}$ is obtained from $\mathcal{L}_{atc}$ by adding the construct $s_1\langle a \rightsquigarrow s_2 \rangle$. This requires an interesting extension of $\mathcal{T}_{atc}$ with rules to handle action refinement. Moreover, a semantic counterpart of the refinement construct is defined and studied. For r the meaning of an atomized s (and p as usual), we introduce the semantic operator $p\langle a \rightsquigarrow r \rangle$. The main achievement of the present section is the proof that $\mathcal{O} = \mathcal{D}$ for $\mathcal{L}_{ref}$. Though conceptually fitting in the line of earlier proofs, the technicalities involved lead to a proof which is an order of magnitude more complex than the equivalence proofs encountered up till now.

14.2.1   Syntax and operational semantics

The language $\mathcal{L}_{ref}$ is obtained from $\mathcal{L}_{atc}$ by the addition of the language construct of refinement, expressed by $s\langle a \rightsquigarrow s' \rangle$. We emphasize that, in this notation, s' is always assumed to be atomized. Thus, a more precise notation would be $s\langle a \rightsquigarrow [s'] \rangle$.

Definition 14.19

(a) $s \, (\in Stat) ::= \ldots \mid s\langle a \rightsquigarrow s' \rangle$ (with $\ldots$ as in Definition 14.1a).

(b) $g\,(\in \mathit{GStat}) ::= \dots \mid g\langle a \rightsquigarrow g'\rangle.$

(c) $D \in \mathit{Decl}$ and $\pi \in \mathcal{L}_{ref}$ are as expected.

We extend $\mathcal{L}_{ref}$ to $\mathcal{L}_{ref}^{+}$ by the inclusion of $s_1 \parallel s_2$ (in the same way as in Section 14.1). The complexity $wgt\colon \mathcal{L}_{ref}^{+} \to \mathbb{N}$ is obtained from $wgt\colon \mathcal{L}_{atc}^{+} \to \mathbb{N}$ by adding the clause $wgt(s\langle a \rightsquigarrow s'\rangle) = wgt(s) + wgt(s') + 1.$

Resumptions for $\mathcal{L}_{ref}^{+}$ are as usual, with the additional convention that we identify $s;\mathrm{E}$ with s and $\mathrm{E}\langle a \rightsquigarrow s\rangle$ with E. The transition system $\mathcal{T}_{ref}$ consists of the following extension of $\mathcal{L}_{atc}$:

Definition 14.20 $\mathcal{T}_{ref}$ consists of all the rules of $\mathcal{T}_{atc}$ (where all s now refer to $\mathcal{L}_{ref}^{+}$) to which are added

$$\bullet \quad \frac{s_1 \xrightarrow{b}_i r}{s_1\langle a \rightsquigarrow s\rangle \xrightarrow{b}_i r\langle a \rightsquigarrow s\rangle} \quad (a \neq b,\ i = 1 \text{ or } 2) \qquad (\text{Ref 1})$$

$$\bullet \quad \frac{s_1 \xrightarrow{a}_i r \qquad [s] \xrightarrow{b}_1 \mathrm{E}}{s_1\langle a \rightsquigarrow s\rangle \xrightarrow{b}_i r\langle a \rightsquigarrow s\rangle} \quad (i = 1 \text{ or } 2) \qquad (\text{Ref 2})$$

$$\bullet \quad \frac{s_1 \xrightarrow{a}_1 r \qquad [s] \xrightarrow{b}_2 s'}{s_1\langle a \rightsquigarrow s\rangle \xrightarrow{b}_2 s';r\langle a \rightsquigarrow s\rangle} \qquad\qquad (\text{Ref 3})$$

$$\bullet \quad \frac{s_1 \xrightarrow{a}_2 r \qquad [s] \xrightarrow{b}_2 s'}{s_1\langle a \rightsquigarrow s\rangle \xrightarrow{b}_2 s':r\langle a \rightsquigarrow s\rangle} \qquad\qquad (\text{Ref 4})$$

Examples

(1) From $\bar{a}\|c \xrightarrow{\bar{a}}_1 c$ and $[a;b] \xrightarrow{a}_2 [b]$ it follows that $(\bar{a}\|c)\langle \bar{a} \rightsquigarrow a;b\rangle \xrightarrow{a}_2 [b];c\langle \bar{a} \rightsquigarrow a;b\rangle$ by (Ref 3).

(2) From $[a;b]\|c \xrightarrow{a}_2 [b] \parallel c$ and $[a_1;a_2] \xrightarrow{a_1}_2 [a_2]$ it follows that $([a;b]\|c)\langle a \rightsquigarrow a_1;a_2\rangle \xrightarrow{a_1}_2 [a_2]:([b] \parallel c)\langle a \rightsquigarrow a_1;a_2\rangle$ by (Ref 4).

An explanation of the refinement rules follows:

(1) If $s_1 \xrightarrow{b}_i r$ for some $b \neq a$, the possible effects of a-refinement are simply transmitted to r.

(2) If $s_1 \xrightarrow{a}_i r$ then the effect of refining a has to be taken into account, and we see which step can be taken by $[s]$, viz. a $\xrightarrow{b}_1$-step to E, or a $\xrightarrow{b}_2$-step to some s'. In the former case, the effect of refining a by the atomized $[s]$ results in a b-step, after which we continue with $r\langle a \rightsquigarrow s \rangle$. In the latter case,

(3) We distinguish between the subcases $s_1 \xrightarrow{a}_1 r$ and $s_1 \xrightarrow{a}_2 r$. In the former, we replace the $\xrightarrow{a}_1 r$ step from s_1 by the $\xrightarrow{b}_2 s'$ step from $[s]$, and continue with s', sequentially composed with the remaining $r\langle a \rightsquigarrow s \rangle$. In the latter

(4) We replace the $\xrightarrow{a}_2$-step from s_1 by the $\xrightarrow{b}_2 s'$ step taken by $[s]$, and we continue with $s' {:} r \langle a \rightsquigarrow s \rangle$.

(5) Thus, the distinction between the $\rightarrow_1$ and $\rightarrow_2$-steps taken by s_1 is inherited by the distinction between the $s'; \ldots$ and $s'{:}\ldots$ constructs in the conclusion of the rules (Ref 3) and (Ref 4).

(6) By the way $\mathcal{T}_{ref}$ (and $\mathcal{T}_{atc}$) is designed, we firstly have that it will not be possible to derive a transition $[s] \xrightarrow{b}_1 s'$. This explains why there are no variants of (Ref 3) or (Ref 4) with such transitions in the premise. Moreover, we note that the s' delivered by $[s] \xrightarrow{b}_2 s'$ is itself of the form $[s'']$, a fact we shall use below (in the proof of Lemma 14.24).

The operational semantics $\mathcal{O} {:} \mathcal{L}_{ref} \rightarrow \mathbb{P}$ uses $\mathbb{P}$ as introduced in Section 14.1 (Definition 14.6). Also, the way we obtain $\mathcal{O}$ from $\mathcal{T}_{ref}$ is exactly as before.

Definition 14.21 $\mathcal{O} {:} \mathcal{L}_{ref} \rightarrow \mathbb{P}$ is the unique function satisfying

$$\mathcal{O}(s) = \{ a \mid s \xrightarrow{a}_1 E \} \cup \{ \langle a, \mathcal{O}(s') \rangle \mid s \xrightarrow{a}_1 s' \} \cup$$
$$\{ \langle a, q \rangle \mid s \xrightarrow{a}_2 s', q \in \mathcal{O}(s') \}.$$

Examples

(1) $\mathcal{O}((\bar{a} \| c)\langle \bar{a} \rightsquigarrow a; b\rangle) = \{ \langle a, \langle b, \{c\}\rangle \rangle, \langle c, \{\langle a, b\rangle\}\rangle \}$

(2) $\mathcal{O}(([a;b] \| c)\langle a \rightsquigarrow a_1; a_2\rangle) = \{ \langle a_1, \langle a_2, \langle b, \{c\}\rangle\rangle\rangle, \langle c, \{\langle a_1, \langle a_2, b\rangle\rangle\}\rangle \}$.

14.2.2 Denotational semantics, relating $\mathcal{O}$ and $\mathcal{D}$

The only semantic operator left to define is that of "semantic refinement," which is to correspond to the syntactic refinement construct $s \equiv s_1\langle a \rightsquigarrow s_2\rangle$. For p the meaning of s_1 and r the meaning of $[s_2]$ (recall that, by convention, we suppressed the atomization brackets in the notation for s), we are thus faced with the task of defining the semantic refinement $p\langle a \rightsquigarrow r\rangle$—using a notation which suggests the intended correspondence.

Definition 14.22 The mappings $\cdot\langle a \rightsquigarrow \cdot\rangle\colon \mathbb{P} \times \mathbb{R} \to \mathbb{P}$ and $\cdot\langle a \rightsquigarrow'\cdot\rangle\colon \mathbb{Q} \times \mathbb{R} \to \mathbb{P}$ are the unique functions satisfying

$$
\begin{aligned}
p\langle a \rightsquigarrow r\rangle &= \bigcup\{\, q\langle a \rightsquigarrow'r\rangle \mid q \in p \,\} \\
b\langle a \rightsquigarrow'r\rangle &= \quad r, \quad \text{if } a = b \\
&\qquad \{b\}, \quad \text{if } a \neq b. \\
\langle b, p\rangle\langle a \rightsquigarrow'r\rangle &= \quad r;p\langle a \rightsquigarrow r\rangle, \quad \text{if } a = b \\
&\qquad \{b\};p\langle a \to r\rangle, \quad \text{if } a \neq b \\
\langle b, q\rangle\langle a \rightsquigarrow'r\rangle &= \quad r;q\langle a \rightsquigarrow'r\rangle, \quad \text{if } a = b \\
&\qquad \{b\};q\langle a \rightsquigarrow'r\rangle, \quad \text{if } a \neq b.
\end{aligned}
$$

We next define $\mathcal{D}$ for $\mathcal{L}_{ref}$.

Definition 14.23 Let $(S \in)\, Sem = \mathcal{L}_{ref} \to \mathbb{P}$.

(a) The mapping $\Psi\colon Sem \to Sem$ is defined by extending the clauses as specified in Definition 14.15 with the clause

$$
\Psi(S)(s\langle a \rightsquigarrow s'\rangle) = \Psi(S)(s)\langle a \rightsquigarrow (\Psi(S)([s']))\rangle .
$$

(b) $\mathcal{D} = fix(\Psi)$, $\mathcal{D}[\![\pi]\!] = \mathcal{D}(\pi)$, for $\pi \in \mathcal{L}_{ref}$.

In the obvious way we can now also define $\mathcal{D}(s_1 \,\|\!\|\, s_2)$.

Examples

(1) $\quad \mathcal{D}((\bar{a}\|c)\langle \bar{a} \rightsquigarrow a;b\rangle)$

$= (\mathcal{D}(\bar{a}\|c))\langle \bar{a} \rightsquigarrow \mathcal{D}([a;b])\rangle$

$= \{\, \langle \bar{a}, \{c\}\rangle, \langle c, \{\bar{a}\}\rangle \,\}\langle \bar{a} \rightsquigarrow \{\langle a, b\rangle\}\rangle)$

$= \bigcup\{\, \langle \bar{a}, \{c\}\rangle\langle \bar{a} \rightsquigarrow \{\langle a, b\rangle\}\rangle), \langle c, \{\bar{a}\}\rangle\langle \bar{a} \rightsquigarrow \{\langle a, b\rangle\}\rangle) \,\}$

$$= \bigcup\{\,\{\langle a,b\rangle\};\{c\},\{c\};\bar{a}\langle\bar{a}\leadsto\{\langle a,b\rangle\}\rangle\,\}$$
$$= \{\,\langle a,\langle b,\{c\}\rangle\rangle,\langle c,\{\langle a,b\rangle\}\rangle\,\}$$

(2) $\mathcal{D}(([a;b]\,\|\,c)\langle a\leadsto a_1;a_2\rangle)$
$$= \{\,\langle a,\langle b,\{c\}\rangle\rangle,\langle c,\{\langle a,b\rangle\}\rangle\,\}\langle a\leadsto\{\langle a_1,a_2\rangle\}\rangle$$
$$= \bigcup\{\,\{\langle a_1,a_2\rangle\};(\langle b,\{c\}\rangle\langle a\leadsto\{\langle a_1,a_2\rangle\}\rangle),\{c\};(\{\langle a,b\rangle\}\langle a\leadsto\{\langle a_1,a_2\rangle\}\rangle)\,\}$$
$$= \ldots$$
$$= \{\,\langle a_1,\langle a_2,\langle b,\{c\}\rangle\rangle\rangle,\langle c,\{\langle a_1,\langle a_2,b\rangle\rangle\}\rangle\,\}.$$

Due to the several case distinctions in the refinement rules, the difference between the ';' and ':' composition, and the not so easy interplay between the $\to_1$ and $\to_2$-rules, the proof that $\mathcal{O}=\mathcal{D}$ for $\mathcal{L}_{ref}$—obtained from the usual $\Phi(\mathcal{D})=\mathcal{D}$ method—is more difficult than we have encountered so far. We show

Lemma 14.24 $\Phi(\mathcal{D})(\bar{s})=\mathcal{D}(\bar{s})$, for all $\bar{s}\in\mathcal{L}_{ref}^{+}$.

Proof We only consider the case $\bar{s}\equiv s_1\langle a\leadsto s\rangle$. We shall use r as shorthand for $\mathcal{D}([s])$. Firstly we have, by the definition of Φ, that

$$\Phi(\mathcal{D})(s_1\langle a\leadsto s\rangle)=(1)\cup(2)\ldots(9)$$

where

$$
\begin{aligned}
(1) \;&=\; \{b|s_1\xrightarrow{b}_1 E,\, a\neq b\}\\
(2) \;&=\; \{b|s_1\xrightarrow{a}_1 E,\,[s]\xrightarrow{b}_1 E\}\\
(3) \;&=\; \{\langle b,q\rangle|s_1\xrightarrow{b}_2 s',\, a\neq b,\, q\in\mathcal{D}(s'\langle a\leadsto s\rangle)\}\\
(4) \;&=\; \{\langle b,q\rangle|s_1\xrightarrow{a}_2 \bar{s},\,[s]\xrightarrow{b}_1 E,\, q\in\mathcal{D}(\bar{s}\langle a\leadsto s\rangle)\}\\
(5) \;&=\; \{\langle b,q\rangle|s_1\xrightarrow{a}_1 E,\,[s]\xrightarrow{b}_2 s',\, q\in\mathcal{D}(s')\}\\
(6) \;&=\; \{\langle b,q\rangle|s_1\xrightarrow{a}_2 \bar{s},\,[s]\xrightarrow{b}_2 s',\, q\in\mathcal{D}(s':\bar{s}\langle a\leadsto s\rangle)\}\\
(7) \;&=\; \{\langle b,q\rangle|s_1\xrightarrow{a}_1 \bar{s},\,[s]\xrightarrow{b}_2 s',\, q\in\mathcal{D}(s';\bar{s}\langle a\leadsto s\rangle)\}\\
(8) \;&=\; \{\langle b,\mathcal{D}(\bar{s}\langle a\leadsto s\rangle)\rangle|s_1\xrightarrow{b}_1 \bar{s},\, a\neq b\}\\
(9) \;&=\; \{\langle b,\mathcal{D}(\bar{s}\langle a\leadsto s\rangle)\rangle|s_1\xrightarrow{a}_1 \bar{s},\,[s]\xrightarrow{b}_1 E\}.
\end{aligned}
$$

Here, (1), (3) and (8) are obtained by (Ref 1), (2), (4) and (9) by (Ref 2), (5) and (7) by (Ref 3), and (6) by (Ref 4). Moreover, we have that

$$\mathcal{D}(s_1\langle a\leadsto s\rangle)$$
$$=\mathcal{D}(s_1)\langle a\leadsto r\rangle$$

= [induction hypothesis for s_1]

$$(\{\, b \mid s_1 \xrightarrow{b}_1 E \,\} \cup \{\, \langle b, q \rangle \mid s_1 \xrightarrow{\iota}_2 \bar{s},\, q \in \mathcal{D}(\bar{s}) \,\}$$
$$\cup \{\, \langle b, \mathcal{D}(\bar{s}) \rangle \mid s_1 \xrightarrow{b}_1 \bar{s} \,\}) \langle a \rightsquigarrow r \rangle$$

$$= (1') \cup (2') \cup \cdots \cup (6')$$

where

$$\begin{aligned}
(1') &= \bigcup \{ r \mid s_1 \xrightarrow{a}_1 E \} \\
(2') &= \{ b \mid s_1 \xrightarrow{b}_1 E,\, a \neq b \} \\
(3') &= \bigcup \{ r{:}q \langle a \rightsquigarrow' r \rangle \mid s_1 \xrightarrow{a}_2 \bar{s},\, q \in \mathcal{D}(\bar{s}) \} \\
(4') &= \{ \langle b, q' \rangle \mid s_1 \xrightarrow{b}_2 \bar{s},\, q \in \mathcal{D}(\bar{s}),\, q' \in q \langle a \rightsquigarrow' r \rangle,\, a \neq b \} \\
(5') &= \bigcup \{ r{;}\mathcal{D}(\bar{s}) \langle a \rightsquigarrow r \rangle \mid s_1 \xrightarrow{a}_1 \bar{s} \} \\
(6') &= \{ \langle b, \mathcal{D}(\bar{s}) \langle a \rightsquigarrow r \rangle \rangle \mid s_1 \xrightarrow{b}_1 \bar{s},\, a \neq b \}.
\end{aligned}$$

We have $(2') = (1)$, $(4') = (3)$, $(6') = (8)$ and by the induction hypothesis (replacing $r = \mathcal{D}([s])$ by $\Phi(\mathcal{D})([s])$),

$(1')$

$$= \{ b \mid [s] \xrightarrow{b}_1 E,\, s_1 \xrightarrow{a}_1 E \} \cup$$
$$\{ \langle b, q' \rangle \mid [s] \xrightarrow{b}_2 s',\, q' \in \mathcal{D}(s'),\, s_1 \xrightarrow{a}_1 E \}$$

$$= (2) \cup (5).$$

Next we show $(3') = (4) \cup (6)$. First suppose $[s] \xrightarrow{b}_2 s'$. By inspection of the transition system it follows that $s' = [s'']$ for some suitable s''. Therefore it then holds that $\mathcal{D}(s') \in \mathbb{R}$ and

$$\mathcal{D}(s' : \bar{s} \langle a \rightsquigarrow s \rangle)$$

$$= [\text{definition of } \mathcal{D}] \; \mathcal{D}(s') : \mathcal{D}(\bar{s}) \langle a \rightsquigarrow r \rangle$$

$$= [\text{definition } :,\, \mathcal{D}(s') \in R] \; \bigcup \{ t' :' \mathcal{D}(\bar{s}) \langle a \rightsquigarrow r \rangle \mid t' \in \mathcal{D}(s') \}$$

$$= [\text{definition } \langle a \rightsquigarrow r \rangle] \; \bigcup \{ t' :' (\bigcup \{ \bar{q} \langle a \rightsquigarrow' r \rangle \mid \bar{q} \in \mathcal{D}(\bar{s}) \}) \mid t' \in \mathcal{D}(s') \}$$

$$= [\text{Lemma 14.16}] \; \bigcup \{ q' :' \bar{q} \langle a \rightsquigarrow' r \rangle \mid \bar{q} \in \mathcal{D}(\bar{s}),\, q' \in \mathcal{D}(s') \}.$$

Now we reason as follows

$(3')$

$$= [\text{induction hypothesis (for } r), \text{ definition } \Phi]$$
$$\bigcup \{ (\{ b \mid [s] \xrightarrow{b}_1 E \} \cup \{ \langle b, q' \rangle \mid [s] \xrightarrow{b}_2 s',\, q' \in \mathcal{D}(s') \}) : \bar{q} \langle a \rightsquigarrow' r \rangle \mid s_1 \xrightarrow{a}_2 \bar{s},\, \bar{q} \in \mathcal{D}(\bar{s}) \}$$

= [definition :]

$\{\langle b,\bar{q}\rangle \mid \bar{q} \in \bar{q}\langle a\rightsquigarrow'r\rangle,\ [s] \xrightarrow{b}_1 \text{E},\ s_1 \xrightarrow{a}_2 \bar{s},\ \bar{q} \in \mathcal{D}(\bar{s})\} \cup$

$\{\langle b,\bar{q}\rangle \mid \bar{q} \in q': \bar{q}\langle a\rightsquigarrow'r\rangle,\ q' \in \mathcal{D}(s'),\ [s] \xrightarrow{b}_2 s',\ s_1 \xrightarrow{a}_2 \bar{s},\ \bar{q} \in \mathcal{D}(\bar{s})\}$

= [by the above] (4) $\cup$ (6).

Similarly, we have by the definitions of $\mathcal{D}$ and ';'

$$\mathcal{D}(s';\bar{s}\langle a\rightsquigarrow s\rangle) = \{q';\mathcal{D}(\bar{s}\langle a\rightsquigarrow s\rangle) \mid q' \in \mathcal{D}(s')\}$$

and therefore

$(5')$

= [induction hypothesis]

$\bigcup\{ (\{b \mid [s] \xrightarrow{b}_1 \text{E}\} \cup$

$\quad \{\langle b,q'\rangle \mid [s] \xrightarrow{b}_2 s',\ q' \in \mathcal{D}(s')\});\mathcal{D}(\bar{s}\langle a\rightsquigarrow r\rangle) \mid s_1 \xrightarrow{a}_1 \bar{s}\}$

= [Lemma 14.11a]

$\{\langle b,\mathcal{D}(\bar{s}\langle a\rightsquigarrow r\rangle)\rangle \mid [s] \xrightarrow{b}_1 \text{E},\ s_1 \xrightarrow{a}_1 \bar{s}\} \cup$

$\{\langle b,q';\mathcal{D}(s\langle a\rightsquigarrow r\rangle)\rangle \mid [s] \xrightarrow{b}_2 s',\ q' \in \mathcal{D}(s'),\ s_1 \xrightarrow{a}_1 \bar{s}\}$

= (9) $\cup$ (7).

Altogether, we have proven that $\Phi(\mathcal{D})(s_1\langle a\rightsquigarrow s\rangle) = \mathcal{D}(s_1\langle a\rightsquigarrow s\rangle)$ as desired.   □

Finally, we have

Theorem 14.25 $\mathcal{O}[\![\pi]\!] = \mathcal{D}[\![\pi]\!]$, *for all π in $\mathcal{L}_{ref}$.*

Proof By Lemma 14.24.   □

14.3   Exercises

Exercise 14.1 Let $\mathbb{P}_1 = \mathcal{P}_{nco}(\mathbb{Q}_1)$, $\mathbb{Q}_1 = Act^\infty \backslash \{\epsilon\}$, and let $\mathbb{P}_2$, $\mathbb{Q}_2$ be equal to the $\mathbb{P}$, $\mathbb{Q}$ as specified immediately after Lemma 14.5. Let the metric d_1 on $\mathbb{P}_1$ be the usual metric on a hyperspace of words (as in Chapter 2), and let d_2 be the metric on $\mathbb{P}_2$ as explained in Section 10.2. Show that, for $a, b \in Act$,

$$d_1(a, ab) = \tfrac{1}{2}, \quad d_2(a, \langle a, b\rangle) = 1$$

(thus showing that $\mathbb{P}_1$ and $\mathbb{P}_2$ are not isometric).

Exercise 14.2 Supply (the details of) the proofs of Lemma 14.14, 14.16.

Exercise 14.3 Introduce the notions of bisimulation/bisimilarity on the domain(s) of Definition 14.6, and formulate and prove a theorem analogous to Theorem 10.21.

Exercise 14.4 (changing the step-size in transitions) Let $\mathcal{L}_{ct}$ be as $\mathcal{L}_{atc}$, but with the atomization operator omitted (for simplicity). Assume that $u, v \in Act^+ \cup Act^\omega$, and that we replace transitions $s \xrightarrow{a}_i r$ by $s \xrightarrow{u}_i r$. Let $\mathcal{T}_{ct}$ be as $\mathcal{T}_{atc}$, but with the rules dealing with $[\cdot]$ omitted, and with u replacing a throughout (except in the (Act) axiom). Let $\mathcal{T}_{ct}$ contain in addition the rule

$$\frac{s_1 \xrightarrow{u}_1 \mathrm{E} \qquad s_2 \xrightarrow{v}_i r}{s_1 : s_2 \xrightarrow{uv}_i r}.$$

Let us put

$$\mathcal{O}^*(s) \;=\; cl(\{\, v \mid s \xrightarrow{v}_1 \mathrm{E} \,\} \cup \bigcup \{\, v \cdot \mathcal{O}^*(s') \mid s \xrightarrow{v}_1 s' \,\} \cup \\ \{\, \langle v, \mathcal{O}^*(s') \rangle \mid s \xrightarrow{v}_2 s' \,\}),$$

where $cl(\cdot)$ denotes the closure of $(\cdot)$. Determine the appropriate codomain for $\mathcal{O}^*$, and, putting

$$\begin{aligned}
\tilde{\mathcal{O}} &= \mathcal{O} \!\restriction\! \mathcal{L}_{ct} \quad (\mathcal{O} \text{ as in Definition 14.7}) \\
\tilde{\mathcal{D}} &= \mathcal{D} \!\restriction\! \mathcal{L}_{ct} \quad (\mathcal{D} \text{ as in Definition 14.15}),
\end{aligned}$$

determine the relationship between $\mathcal{O}^*$ and $\tilde{\mathcal{O}}, \tilde{\mathcal{D}}$.

Exercise 14.5 (refinement as syntactic substitution) Let $\mathcal{T}_{ref}$ consist of the rules of $\mathcal{T}_{atc}$, together with the rules ('$\to_0$' as in Definition 14.3)

$$\begin{aligned}
a\langle a \rightsquigarrow s' \rangle &\to_0 [s'] \\
b\langle a \rightsquigarrow s' \rangle &\to_0 b \quad \text{if } a \neq b \\
(s_1 \text{ op } s_2)\langle a \rightsquigarrow s' \rangle &\to_0 (s_1 \langle a \rightsquigarrow s' \rangle) \text{ op } (s_2 \langle a \rightsquigarrow s' \rangle) \\
x\langle a \rightsquigarrow s' \rangle &\to_0 D(x)\langle a \rightsquigarrow s' \rangle \\
[s]\langle a \rightsquigarrow s' \rangle &\to_0 [s\langle a \rightsquigarrow s' \rangle].
\end{aligned}$$

(a) Complete this list with a rule for the handling of $(s_0 \langle b \leadsto s'' \rangle)\langle a \leadsto s' \rangle$.
    (Hint: this necessitates the introduction of a simultaneous refinement notation $s \langle a_i \leadsto s_i \rangle_{i=1}^n$, and of a rule to deal with $s \langle a_i \leadsto s_i \rangle_{i=1}^n \langle b_j \leadsto s'_j \rangle_{j=1}^m$.)

(b) Investigate whether the rules stated above may replace the transition rules (Ref 1) to (Ref 4), and how the equality of $\mathcal{O}$ and $\mathcal{D}$ would have to be handled in this setting.

14.4 Bibliographical notes

This chapter is based on [BV94]. Linear models for a uniform language with atomization close to $\mathcal{L}_{atc}$ are studied in [KK91, KK93]. Our transition system for action refinement owes much to the work of Degano and Gorrieri ([DG91, Gor91]). The problem signaled in the introduction of the chapter was noted in [CMP87, Pra86]. The commit operator appears in 'committed choice' parallel logic programming languages (cf. [Sha89]). Atomization and, especially, action refinement have been studied in numerous papers in the concurrency literature. Overviews in the setting of process algebra are [Gla90a, Ace90, Ren93], and in that of Petri nets [BGV91].

IV PERSPECTIVES

The main purpose of Part IV is to outline the connections with a number of further areas of semantic interest. In contrast to Parts I to III, we do not always aim here at a self-contained treatment with full coverage of all mathematical details. We have chosen four themes:

- The language paradigm of Logic Programming. Only control flow aspects are considered here, leaving the modeling of those notions which are primarily of a logical nature to the well-established theory of *declarative* semantics (not to be treated in our book).

- The "true concurrency" style of modeling parallelism, as alternative to the interleaving model used (almost) everywhere in earlier chapters.

- The difficult topic of full abstractness, giving a precise meaning to the notion of "optimality"—for any given language—of a denotational semantics with respect to an operational one. This issue often requires mathematically difficult combinatorial arguments, and only a first orientation in the problem area will be provided.

- Second-order assignment, exemplifying the class of higher-order control flow notions in imperative programming. Though higher-order notions abound in functional languages, this is not so much the case for languages within the scope of our work. In concurrency, higher-order processes have recently entered the scene, and the approach described in Chapter 18 provides a first step on the way to the use of metric techniques in the modeling of such processes.

15 The Control Flow Kernel of Logic Programming

Logic programming (LP) is a computational paradigm rooted in (first-order) predicate logic, more specifically in the version of so called "resolution logic." Accordingly, the framework of LP is traditionally described in logical terms, at considerable distance from the methodology set forth in our book. It is the aim of the present chapter to argue that a substantial part of LP, viz. what we would like to call its control flow kernel, is amenable to a treatment in terms of operational and denotational semantic models of the same kind as those studied for earlier languages.

In this chapter, we assume that the reader has at least some basic knowledge of the conceptual principles of LP, sufficient to understand, for example, the following simple program, written in a self-explanatory syntax:

$$
\begin{aligned}
(\text{ancestor}(u_1, u_2) \quad &\Leftarrow \quad \text{father } (u_1, u_2) \\
\text{ancestor } (u_1, u_2) \quad &\Leftarrow \quad \text{ancestor } (u_1, v), \text{father } (v, u_2) \\
\text{father } (a, b) \quad &\Leftarrow \quad \text{E} \\
\text{father } (b, c) \quad &\Leftarrow \quad \text{E} \\
&\mid \quad \text{ancestor } (u, c) \;)
\end{aligned} \quad (15.1)
$$

In this program, we distinguish a declaration part—the four clauses involving '$\Leftarrow$'—and a statement part, viz. the "goal" $\text{ancestor}(u, c)$. The left-hand sides of the declaration clauses each consist of an *atom*—$\text{ancestor}(u_1, u_2)$, $\text{ancestor}(u_1, u_2)$, $\text{father}(a, b)$ and $\text{father}(b, c)$, respectively – and the right-hand sides of each clause consist of a sequence of zero or more atoms separated by ',' (LP's symbol '$\square$' for the empty sequence is here, for consistency with our earlier notation, denoted by E). The computational process of LP compares the goal with the left-hand sides of the declaration clauses (in some arbitrary order), tries to *unify* them (determining their *most general unifier*) and, in case the unification succeeds, applies the resulting substitution to the corresponding right-hand side of the clause and evaluates all the resulting atoms *in parallel*.

In the example at hand, the evaluation of $\text{ancestor}(u, c)$ will terminate successfully with as "computed answer substitution" either $[b/u]$ or $[a/u]$. Since it is the very purpose of this chapter to abstract from the details of the definitions of substitution, unification or most general unifier, we shall not go into this here. Rather, we shall design the control flow kernel referred to above by abstracting from the logic layer, preserving only the basic "skeleton" of the program. In this abstraction, we apply the following key ideas:

- Firstly, all atoms of the program are simply represented by procedure variables from some (fresh) alphabet, say $(x, y, \ldots, \xi, \ldots \in) PVar$

- Secondly, the choice inherent in the appearance of different right-hand sides for the same left-hand side is expressed through the (usual) +-operator
- Thirdly, we model the parallel execution of the sequence of atoms on a right-hand side by the (usual) ‖-operator.

Applying the above to our example program, we obtain the skeleton

$$(\ x \ \Leftarrow \ y + (y_1 \| y_2)$$
$$z_1 \ \Leftarrow \ \mathrm{E} \qquad\qquad\qquad\qquad (15.2)$$
$$z_2 \ \Leftarrow \ \mathrm{E} \ | \ z \ )$$

This construct should give the reader already some intimation of what we are aiming at, since it exhibits strong resemblance to a program in, say, $\mathcal{L}_{par}$. There is, however, one element not yet addressed, viz. the place where the unification actions are invoked—whatever their precise meaning may be. We shall design the semantics for a program like (15.2) by implicitly viewing it as having the (even more abstract) form of the next program, which consists of

- an (infinite) *set* of declarations, consisting of a declaration for each element in $PVar$ (i.e., for each atom)
- one procedure call as main statement.

Also incorporating the various unification actions, we obtain as resulting program

$$(\{\xi \ \Leftarrow \ \mathsf{unify}(\xi, x); (y + (y_1 \| y_2)) +$$
$$\mathsf{unify}(\xi, z_1) + \mathsf{unify}(\xi, z_2)\}_{\xi \in PVar} \ | \ z \ ) \qquad (15.3)$$

The elaboration of the procedure call z – on the basis of the declaration $z \Leftarrow \mathsf{unify}(z, x); (\cdots) + \mathsf{unify}(z, z_1) + \mathsf{unify}(z, z_2)$ – leads to a choice between three terms. Choosing the first prescribes the evaluation of $\mathsf{unify}(z, x)$. Assuming it succeeds—with an associated (but not specified here) resulting substitution—the statement $y + (y_1 \| y_2)$ is executed. Choosing the second alternative, this amounts to the parallel execution of the procedure calls y_1 and y_2, and for each of these the mechanism just described applies (now with z replaced by y_1 or y_2).

Assuming that the $\mathsf{unify}(-, -)$ constructs are interpreted according to their usual LP meaning, we have as main result that the semantics of (15.3) coincides with the usual (say, the "declarative") meaning of (15.1). More precisely, we have the following: On the one hand, we determine the customary "computed answer substitutions" as prescribed by the LP definitions.

(For a brief summary of these, we refer to Section 15.3, starting just before Definition 15.31). On the other hand, we follow the semantic approach as defined for $\mathcal{L}_{svp}$, modified in that the states $(\sigma\epsilon)\Sigma$ are now replaced by substitutions (and the basic transformations determined by assignment statements are replaced by operations in terms of most general unifiers). Applying this approach to (15.3), we obtain that the final elements of the finite sequences of σ's delivered by its operational semantics (defined as an appropriate modification of that of Section 7.1) yields precisely the computed answer substitutions just mentioned.[1]

Summarizing, we shall design a language $\mathcal{L}_{hcl}$ – named after *Horn clause logic*, a subset of predicate logic – and its associated semantics such that it enables us to construct the control flow kernel of each LP program as a program from $\mathcal{L}_{hcl}$. The latter program has the property that its semantics delivers a set of sequences of substitutions such that, if we provide the abstract unify-operator in the $\mathcal{L}_{hcl}$ setting with the usual LP-interpretation, then the collection of final elements of the finite sequences in this set coincides with the declarative semantics (in terms of the computed answer substitutions) of the original program.

The language $\mathcal{L}_{hcl}$ will actually be supplied with operational and denotational semantics in two ways (to be described in Section 15.1 and 15.2, respectively). The first one closely follows our earlier definitions for $\mathcal{L}_{svp}$: $\mathcal{L}_{hcl}$ is treated as a nonuniform language, involving transformations of states (here substitutions) and delivering sequences of states as a result. More specifically, the operational semantics will be expressed in terms of transitions $[s, \sigma] \to [s', \sigma']$, just as in Chapter 7, and the familiar treatment of '$\|$' in terms of arbitrary interleaving will be adopted again. The second way of viewing $\mathcal{L}_{hcl}$ is uniform: We shall employ transitions (in the uniform style, i.e.) $s \xrightarrow{\sigma} s'$. This approach is made feasible by the introduction of a special operation on substitutions, viz. *parallel composition*, written as $\sigma_1 \| \sigma_2$. This operation – which has no counterpart in a setting such as $\mathcal{L}_{svp}$ – allows us to employ the following rule to handle the parallel composition of statements:

$$\frac{s_1 \xrightarrow{\sigma_1} s', \; s_2 \xrightarrow{\sigma_2} s''}{s_1 \| s_2 \xrightarrow{\sigma_1 \| \sigma_2} s' \| s''}$$

(ignoring one refinement to be discussed later). Repeated application of this rule to a construct $s_1 \| s_2 \| \ldots \| s_n$ results in the *simultaneous* evaluation of $\sigma_1 \| \ldots \| \sigma_n$. We draw special attention to this so-called *maximal parallelism* model. Elsewhere,

---

[1]The announced result only concerns the finite successful computations. The complementary case of infinite or "failing" computations will not be addressed in this chapter.

this form of parallelism is also called the *synchronous* one: All components in the parallel construct proceed simultaneously, without any role for a form of arbitrary interleaving (as used throughout in our earlier models for parallelism).

In Section 15.3, we shall address the relationship between the various models. We shall formulate (and outline the proof of) a precise theorem relating the nonuniform/interleaving and uniform/maximal parallelism models for $\mathcal{L}_{hcl}$. Moreover, we shall sketch a proposition relating $\mathcal{L}_{hcl}$ to traditional LP. In this proposition, we do not aim at full rigour. Not having introduced the details of the substitution or unification notions—let alone the tedious precautions to avoid clashes of variables by means of LP's "standardizing apart"—we are not prepared for complete statements (let alone proofs). Instead, our main aim with this chapter is to provide a view on LP which brings out its imperative aspects. As a bonus of this view, we obtain a transparent perspective on a generalization of LP in terms of the so-called *concurrent constraint* programming model (couched in terms of the language $\mathcal{L}_{cc}$). LP's use of substitutions and unification is replaced in $\mathcal{L}_{cc}$ by the manipulation of constraints ("partial descriptions of the current state of affairs") by means of $\mathsf{ask}(\sigma)$ and $\mathsf{tell}(\sigma)$ actions. The former asks whether a given constraint σ is implied ("entailed") by the current constraint (say σ'). If yes, the effect of $\mathsf{ask}(\sigma)$ is to leave σ' unchanged; if no, failure arises. The latter results in an extension of the current σ' to the enlarged constraint $\sigma \sqcup \sigma'$ (assuming that no consistency problems arise in joining σ with σ'). Very few modifications are necessary to adapt the (nonuniform) model for $\mathcal{L}_{hcl}$ to one for $\mathcal{L}_{cc}$.

We close this introduction with the remark that the approach advocated in this chapter has as distinct advantage that the many specializations of LP in concrete programming languages (such as PROLOG or "committed choice" parallel LP languages) can be accommodated through this perspective by varying the control flow primitives employed. At the end of Section 15.3 we shall say a bit more about this.

15.1 Horn clause logic viewed as a nonuniform parallel language

In this section, we introduce $\mathcal{L}_{hcl}$ and design its semantics as a variation on that of $\mathcal{L}_{svp}$. The two main ingredients in this variation are

- the replacement of $(\sigma \in) \Sigma$ as a set of states by a set of substitutions (not specified in detail but only in terms of certain associated operations)

- the introduction of unification ($\mathsf{unify}(x, y)$)—and associated semantic function $mgu(x, y)$—as basic action transforming the new states.

For completeness sake, we begin by recalling the basic features of the nonuniform parallel language $\mathcal{L}_{svp}$.

(1) Firstly, we have a set of *states* Σ (given as $\Sigma = IVar \rightarrow Val$), together with *assignments* as elementary actions, interpreted as functions transforming states to states.

(2) Secondly, $\mathcal{L}_{svp}$ includes various rules to build composite programs from basic ones, including the

- sequential composition
- conditional
- while statement
- parallel composition.

(3) Thirdly, programs are assigned as meanings functions from states to sets of sequences of

- states (for $\mathcal{O}$)
- pairs of states (for $\mathcal{D}$).

We now introduce the language $\mathcal{L}_{hcl}$ as a fairly modest variation on $\mathcal{L}_{svp}$. For the moment, we treat $\mathcal{L}_{hcl}$ on a high level of abstraction, ignoring most of the more specific logical features of Horn clause logic. In Section 15.3 we shall provide some (but not too many) more details.

The difference between $\mathcal{L}_{svp}$ and $\mathcal{L}_{hcl}$ is firstly located in the underlying domain of discourse—the entities manipulated by the program—and the associated basic actions which transform these entities. Whereas for $\mathcal{L}_{svp}$ we have Σ as the set of states as just mentioned, for $\mathcal{L}_{hcl}$ we take Σ as the set of *substitutions*. For the moment we do not have to go into much detail about the nature of these substitutions. It suffices to assume the following:

(1) There is a (for the moment abstract) set $(\sigma, \tau, \rho, \theta \in) \Sigma$ of substitutions.

(2) From Σ, the domains $\Sigma_\delta^\infty = \Sigma^* \cup \Sigma^\omega \cup \Sigma^* \cdot \{\delta\}$ and $\mathcal{P}_{nco}(\Sigma_\delta^\infty)$ are built in the usual way. (As always, $\delta\,(\notin \Sigma)$ will be used to model deadlock.)

(3) On Σ, an operation of *composition* $\circ: \Sigma \times \Sigma \rightarrow \Sigma$ is given. We shall always suppress the '$\circ$', and write $\sigma\sigma'$ rather than $\sigma \circ \sigma'$. Moreover, we assume the so-called *empty* substitution λ, such that $\lambda\sigma = \sigma\lambda = \sigma$. The operation of composition is assumed to be associative.

Caution The reader should distinguish between the empty sequence of substitutions (as always denoted by ϵ) and the empty substitution λ. Also, the concatenation of two substitutions (written as $\sigma_1 \cdot \sigma_2$) is a two-element sequence which should be distinguished from the (single) substitution $\sigma\sigma'$ resulting from composing σ and σ'. (In the next section, we shall introduce, as further binary operation on Σ the operator '$\|$' of *parallel* composition.)

(4) Next, $\mathcal{L}_{hcl}$ has recursion rather than $\mathcal{L}_{svp}$'s iteration (in the form of the while statement). Thus, in $\mathcal{L}_{hcl}$ we have procedure variables $x, y, \ldots \in PVar$ in the usual way. Though seemingly a small variation, we shall encounter these $x, y, \ldots$ in the next point which constitutes a key feature of $\mathcal{L}_{hcl}$.

(5) The atomic actions of $\mathcal{L}_{hcl}$—to be introduced in a moment—will obtain their meaning in terms of a *partial* function $mgu: PVar \times PVar \to \Sigma$. In case $mgu(x, y)$ is defined, say $mgu(x, y) = \sigma$, we say that σ is the *most general unifier* of x and y. The phrase "$mgu(x, y)$ is defined and equal to σ" will be written as $mgu(x, y){\downarrow}\sigma$. In case $mgu(x, y)$ is undefined, we write $mgu(x, y){\uparrow}$.

(6) With each $\sigma \in \Sigma$ we associate a function $PVar \to PVar$. This function will be denoted as well by σ; its result, given the argument x, is denoted by $x\sigma$—rather than by the more customary $\sigma(x)$.

After these introductory remarks, we are ready for the first definition. Let $(x, y \in) PVar$ be as always, and similarly for E. The elementary actions of $\mathcal{L}_{hcl}$ are of the form $\mathsf{unify}(x, y)$. According to the subsequent definitions, an action $\mathsf{unify}(x, y)$ will obtain as meaning a function which transforms a given input substitution σ either to output σ', or to δ. Instead of the more customary sequential composition, $\mathcal{L}_{hcl}$ has only "action prefixing" (in the form of $\mathsf{unify}(x, y);s$). This is sufficient for our present purposes and somewhat more convenient later (in the setting of Section 15.2).

Definition 15.1

(a) $s\, (\in Stat) ::= \mathsf{unify}(x, y) \mid \mathsf{unify}(x, y);s \mid x \mid (s + s) \mid (s \| s)$

(b) $g\, (\in GStat) ::= r \mid (g + g)$ (see clause (d) for r)

(c) $(\pi \in)\, \mathcal{L}_{hcl} = Decl \times Stat$ (where, as usual, $Decl = PVar \to GStat$)

(d) $r\, (\in Res) ::= \mathrm{E} \mid s$.

Remark The form of g is chosen to accommodate empty right-hand sides (g has no connotation of "guarding" here).

The customary identifications involving r are again assumed. Here they are of the form E;$s = s$;E $=$ E$\|s = s\|$E $= s$, E$\|$E $=$ E.

The syntax of $\mathcal{L}_{hcl}$ is more or less as expected (after our introductory remarks about $\mathcal{L}_{svp}$).

We proceed with the design of the transition system $\mathcal{T}_{hcl}$. In order to distinguish the present (nonuniform) interleaving approach from the (uniform) noninterleaving one of the next section, we shall throughout use sub- and superscripts I for our main semantic notions in the present section. Accordingly, from now on we use $\mathcal{T}_{hcl}^{I}$, etc. As announced, the underlying semantic domain for $\mathcal{T}_{hcl}^{I}$ is based on substitutions. The details are repeated in the next definition (and one technical condition is added):

Definition 15.2

(a) $(\sigma, \tau, \rho, \theta \in)\,\Sigma$ is a set of substitutions. On Σ, an associative binary operation '$\circ$' is given which is always suppressed in the notation. The *empty* substitution λ satisfies $\lambda\sigma = \sigma\lambda = \sigma$.

(b) Let $\delta \notin \Sigma$. The domains Σ_{δ}^{∞} and $\mathcal{P}_{nco}(\Sigma_{\delta}^{\infty})$ are defined in the usual manner. We put

$$\mathbb{P}_{O}^{I} \;=\; \Sigma \to \mathcal{P}_{nco}(\Sigma_{\delta}^{\infty}).$$

(c) $mgu\colon PVar \times PVar \to \Sigma$ is given as *partial* function. Each $\sigma \in \Sigma$ induces a function (also denoted by σ): $PVar \to PVar$ mapping x to $x\sigma$.

(d) For each $x, mgu(x, y)$ is defined only for finitely many y.[2]

Definition 15.3 $\mathcal{T}_{hcl}^{I} = (Decl \times Res \times \Sigma, \Sigma, \to, Spec)$. Transitions are written as $[r, \sigma] \to_{I,D} [r', \sigma']$; zero-step relations are denoted by $[r, \sigma] \to_{0,I,D} [r', \sigma']$. In order not to burden the notation too much, we shall usually suppress writing the D as index. $Spec$ is given by

•	$[\mathsf{unify}(x, y), \sigma] \to_{I} [\mathrm{E}, \sigma\rho]$	if $mgu(x\sigma, y)\!\downarrow\!\rho$	(Unify 1)
•	$[\mathsf{unify}(x, y);s, \sigma] \to_{I} [s, \sigma\rho]$	if $mgu(x\sigma, y)\!\downarrow\!\rho$	(Unify 2)
•	$[x, \sigma] \to_{0,I} [\mathsf{unify}(x, y);D(y), \sigma]$	for each $y \in PVar$	(PVar)

---

[2] A comment explaining this finiteness condition follows after Definition 15.33.

- $$[s_1 + s_2, \sigma] \to_{0,I} [s_1, \sigma] \qquad\qquad\qquad\text{(Choice)}$$

$$[s_1 + s_2, \sigma] \to_{0,I} [s_2, \sigma]$$

- $$\frac{[s, \sigma] \to_I [r, \sigma']}{[s \,\|\, \bar{s}, \sigma] \to_I [r \,\|\, \bar{s}, \sigma']} \qquad\qquad\qquad\text{(Par)}$$

$$[\bar{s} \,\|\, s, \sigma] \to_I [\bar{s} \,\|\, r, \sigma']$$

The rules (Choice) and (Par) are standard and need no explanation. The rule (Unify 1) expresses that, for given x, y and σ, if $mgu(x\sigma, y)$ is (defined and) equal to ρ, then $\mathsf{unify}(x, y)$ transforms σ to $\sigma\rho$. (Unify 2) is similar. The rule (PVar) is somewhat more involved than encountered so far. Instead of searching for x in the declaration and continuing with $D(x)$, we here prescribe a zero-step transition to $\mathsf{unify}(x, y); D(y)$. This implies that execution of x proceeds in two stages. The second is familiar in that it consists in the execution of the appropriate g-statement retrieved from D. The first, which invokes a call of $\mathsf{unify}(x, y)$, is typical for logic programming, in that this is the very place where an atomic action of $\mathcal{L}_{hcl}$ appears on the scene. Note that the seemingly infinite choice induced here is reduced to a finite one since $mgu(x\sigma, y)\uparrow$ for almost all $y \in PVar$. No transition is specified for $[\mathsf{unify}(x, y), \sigma]$ in a situation where $mgu(x\sigma, y)\uparrow$. This explains the need for the usual notion of *blocking*.

Definition 15.4 A configuration $[s, \sigma]$ *blocks* (with respect to $\mathcal{T}^I_{hcl}$) if there exists no $[r, \sigma']$ such that $[s, \sigma] \to_I [r, \sigma']$. The notation $[s, \sigma] \not\to_I$ will be used to the same effect.

The (interleaving) operational semantics $\mathcal{O}_I$ for $\mathcal{L}_{hcl}$ can now be defined.

Definition 15.5

(a) $\mathcal{O}_I \colon Decl \times Res \times \Sigma \to \mathcal{P}_{nco}(\Sigma_\delta^\infty)$ is given by $\mathcal{O}_I(D|\mathrm{E}, \sigma) = \{\epsilon\}$ and

$$\mathcal{O}_I(D|s, \sigma) \;=\; \bigcup\{\, \sigma' \cdot \mathcal{O}_I(D|r, \sigma') \mid [s, \sigma] \to_I [r, \sigma'] \,\} \cup \{\, \delta \mid [s, \sigma] \not\to_I \,\}.$$

(b) $\mathcal{O}_I[\![\cdot]\!] \colon \mathcal{L}_{hcl} \to \mathbb{P}^I_O$, is given by $\mathcal{O}_I[\![D|s]\!] = \lambda\sigma.\mathcal{O}_I(D \mid s, \sigma)$.

Well-definedness of $\mathcal{O}_I$ is established in the customary way from the fact that $\mathcal{T}_{hcl}$ is locally finitely branching. The latter property is, in turn, based on the finiteness condition on $mgu(x, y)$ (clause (d) of Definition 15.2).

We now turn to the discussion of the denotational semantics $\mathcal{D}$ for $\mathcal{L}_{hcl}$. As we just saw, $\mathcal{L}_{hcl}$ exhibits possible deadlock behaviour. From the study of $\mathcal{L}_\delta$ in Chapter 11, the reader might expect that we shall develop a branching model for $\mathcal{L}_{hcl}$ as well. However, this will not be necessary: it will turn out that a linear domain—with some extra care exercised in defining the semantic operators—suffices for $\mathcal{L}_{hcl}$. (In fact, the same holds for $\mathcal{L}_\delta$, as we shall see in Chapter 17 on Full Abstractness.) What we *do* need in the (co)domain for $\mathcal{D}$ is

- Firstly, a framework which is close to that developed for the denotational semantics for $\mathcal{L}_{svp}$, in particular the use of sets of sequences of *pairs* of states (here substitutions), with the associated refinement of the use of *finitary nonempty* (and closed) such sets.

- Secondly, defining the semantic operators in such a way that the deadlock behaviour embodied in the definition of $\mathcal{T}_{hcl}^I$ is reflected in the definitions.

The definition of $\mathbb{P}_{Df}^I$ for $\mathcal{L}_{hcl}$ follows. The symbol $\delta (\notin \Sigma)$ is as before.

Definition 15.6 Let Σ be as in Definition 15.2.

$$\mathbb{P}_{Df}^I = \mathcal{P}_{fncl}((\Sigma \times \Sigma)^+ \cup (\Sigma \times \Sigma)^\omega \cup (\Sigma \times \Sigma)^* \cdot (\Sigma \times \{\delta\})).$$

Here $\mathcal{P}_{fncl}(\cdot)$ stands, as usual, for the collection of all finitary nonempty and closed subsets of $(\cdot)$, the sets $(\Sigma \times \Sigma)^+$ and $(\Sigma \times \Sigma)^\omega$ are as before, and $(\Sigma \times \Sigma)^* \cdot (\Sigma \times \{\delta\})$ denotes the set of all finite (possibly empty) sequences of pairs of substitutions postfixed with a pair $\langle \sigma, \delta \rangle$. (The definition of $[q, \sigma, p]$ being independent of the presence of δ, the definition of "finitary nonempty" is exactly as in Chapter 7, Definition 7.15.)

The presence of the pair $\langle \sigma, \delta \rangle$ indicates a nonuniform—parameterized by σ—deadlock possibility. In order to understand the definitions of the semantic operators '+' and '$\|$', the reader should keep in mind that from $\mathcal{T}_{hcl}^I$ it follows that $s_1 + s_2$ blocks in σ only if *both* s_1 and s_2 block in σ, and similarly for $s_1 \| s_2$. This observation should explain the next definition. (For the notation $p[\sigma, \sigma']$ see Definition 7.9.)

Definition 15.7 The operators $;, +, \| \colon \mathbb{P}_{Df}^I \times \mathbb{P}_{Df}^I \to \mathbb{P}_{Df}^I$ are the unique functions satisfying

(a) $\quad p_1;p_2 \;=\; \bigcup\{\, \langle \sigma, \sigma' \rangle \cdot (p_1[\sigma, \sigma'];p_2) \mid p_1[\sigma, \sigma'] \neq \emptyset \,\} \cup$
$\qquad\qquad \bigcup\{\, \langle \sigma, \sigma' \rangle \cdot p_2 \mid \langle \sigma, \sigma' \rangle \in p_1 \,\} \cup \{\, \langle \sigma, \delta \rangle \mid \langle \sigma, \delta \rangle \in p_1 \,\}.$

(b) $\quad p_1 + p_2 \;=\; \bigcup\{\, \langle \sigma, \sigma' \rangle \cdot p_1[\sigma, \sigma'] \mid p_1[\sigma, \sigma'] \neq \emptyset \,\} \cup$
$\qquad\qquad \bigcup\{\, \langle \sigma, \sigma' \rangle \cdot p_2[\sigma, \sigma'] \mid p_2[\sigma, \sigma'] \neq \emptyset \,\} \cup$
$\qquad\qquad \{\, \langle \sigma, \delta \rangle \mid \langle \sigma, \delta \rangle \in p_1 \cap p_2 \,\}.$

(c) $\quad p_1 \| p_2 \;=\; (p_1 \mathbin{\mathbb{L}} p_2) \cup (p_2 \mathbin{\mathbb{L}} p_1) \cup (p_1 | p_2), \quad\text{where}$
$\qquad p_1 \mathbin{\mathbb{L}} p_2 \;=\; \bigcup\{\, \langle \sigma, \sigma' \rangle \cdot (p_1[\sigma, \sigma'] \| p_2) \mid p_1[\sigma, \sigma'] \neq \emptyset \,\} \cup$
$\qquad\qquad \bigcup\{\, \langle \sigma, \sigma' \rangle \cdot p_2 \mid \langle \sigma, \sigma' \rangle \in p_1 \,\}$
$\qquad p_1 | p_2 \;=\; \{\, \langle \sigma, \delta \rangle \mid \langle \sigma, \delta \rangle \in p_1 \cap p_2 \,\}.$

Remarks

(1) Though $\mathcal{L}_{hcl}$ has sequential composition only in the form of prefixing, we have given the definition of $p_1;p_2$ for the general case, since we shall need the general definition for a subsequent application (in Section 15.4, on a concurrent constraint language).

(2) For later use (in the proof of lemma 15.10) we observe that $\{\langle \sigma, \delta \rangle\} \mathbin{\mathbb{L}} p = \emptyset$. Elements $\langle \sigma, \delta \rangle$ in $p_1 \| p_2$ are delivered only (via $p_1 | p_2$) in case $\langle \sigma, \delta \rangle$ is element of both p_1 and p_2.

Next, we define $\mathcal{D}_I$ on $\mathcal{L}_{hcl}$.

Definition 15.8

(a) $\mathcal{D}_I \colon \mathcal{L}_{hcl} \to \mathbb{P}_{Df}^I$ is the unique function satisfying

$$\mathcal{D}_I(D|\mathsf{unify}(x, y)) =$$
$$\{\, \langle \sigma, \sigma\rho \rangle \mid mgu(x\sigma, y)\!\downarrow\!\rho \,\} \cup \{\, \langle \sigma, \delta \rangle \mid mgu(x\sigma, y)\!\uparrow \,\}$$
$$\mathcal{D}_I(D|x) = \bigcup\{\, \mathcal{D}_I(D|\mathsf{unify}(x, y); D(y)) \mid y \in PVar \,\}$$
$$\mathcal{D}_I(D|s_1 \text{ op } s_2) = \mathcal{D}_I(D|s_1) \text{ op } \mathcal{D}_I(D|s_2), \quad \text{op} \in \{;, +, \| \}.$$

(b) $\mathcal{D}_I[\![\pi]\!] = \mathcal{D}_I(\pi)$, for each $\pi \in \mathcal{L}_{hcl}$.

Well-definedness of $\mathcal{D}_I$ follows by the usual argument.

On the way to link $\mathcal{O}_I$ and $\mathcal{D}_I$ for $\mathcal{L}_{hcl}$, we introduce the customary intermediate semantics $\mathcal{O}_I^*$ in

Definition 15.9 Let $\mathbb{P}^I_{O\cdot f} = \mathbb{P}^I_{Df} \cup \{\{\epsilon\}\}$. The function $\mathcal{O}^*_I: Decl \times Res \to \mathbb{P}^I_{O\cdot f}$ is the unique function satisfying $\mathcal{O}^*_I(D|E) = \{\epsilon\}$, and

$$\mathcal{O}^*_I(D|s) = \bigcup \{ \langle \sigma, \sigma' \rangle \cdot \mathcal{O}^*_I(D|r) \mid [s,\sigma] \to_I [r,\sigma'] \} \cup \\ \{ \langle \sigma, \delta \rangle \mid [s,\sigma] \not\to_I \} .$$

Putting $\mathcal{E}_I(D|E) = \{\epsilon\}$, $\mathcal{E}_I(D|s) = \mathcal{D}_I(D|s)$, we have that $\mathcal{O}^*_I = \mathcal{E}_I$ on $Decl \times Res$. This is an immediate corollary of

Lemma 15.10 Let Φ^*_I be the operator defining $\mathcal{O}^*_I$. Then

$$\Phi^*_I(\mathcal{E}_I) = \mathcal{E}_I .$$

Proof We show that $\Phi^*_I(\mathcal{E}_I)(D|r) = \mathcal{E}_I(D|r)$, by induction on $wgt(D|r)$ (defined in the usual way). Two subcases (suppressing the subscript I and most occurrences of the D).

$[x]$ $\Phi^*(\mathcal{E})(x)$

$= \bigcup \{ \Phi^*(\mathcal{E})(\mathrm{unify}(x,y);D(y)) \mid y \in PVar \}$

$= [\text{ind. hyp.}] \bigcup \{ \mathcal{E}(\mathrm{unify}(x,y);D(y) \mid y \in PVar \}$

$= \mathcal{E}(x) .$

$[s_1 \| s_2]$ $\Phi^*(\mathcal{E})(s_1 \| s_2)$

$= \bigcup \{ \langle \sigma, \bar{\sigma} \rangle \cdot \mathcal{E}(\bar{s}) \mid [s_1 \| s_2, \sigma] \to [\bar{s}, \bar{\sigma}] \} \cup \{ \langle \sigma, \delta \rangle \mid [s_1 \| s_2, \sigma] \not\to \}$

$= \bigcup \{ \langle \sigma, \sigma' \rangle \cdot \mathcal{E}(s' \| s_2) \mid [s_1, \sigma] \to [s', \sigma'] \} \cup$
    $\bigcup \{ \langle \sigma, \sigma'' \rangle \cdot \mathcal{E}(s_1 \| s'') \mid [s_2, \sigma] \to [s'', \sigma''] \} \cup$
    $\{ \langle \sigma, \delta \rangle \mid [s_1, \sigma] \not\to , [s_2, \sigma] \not\to \}$

$= (\bigcup \{ \langle \sigma, \sigma' \rangle \cdot \mathcal{E}(s') \mid [s_1, \sigma] \to [s', \sigma'] \} \cup \{ \langle \sigma, \delta \rangle \mid [s_1, \sigma] \not\to \}) \, \| \, \mathcal{E}(s_2)$
    $\cup \text{ (symm.)} \cup (\Phi^*(\mathcal{E})(s_1) | \Phi^*(\mathcal{E})(s_2))$

$= (\Phi^*(\mathcal{E})(s_1) \, \| \, \mathcal{E}(s_2)) \cup \text{ (symm.)} \cup (\Phi^*(\mathcal{E})(s_1) | \Phi^*(\mathcal{E})(s_2))$

$= [\text{ind. hyp.}] \, \mathcal{E}(s_1) \| \mathcal{E}(s_2)$

$= \mathcal{E}(s_1 \| s_2),$

where we have used the two properties

(i) $\{ \langle \sigma, \delta \rangle \} \, \| \, p = \emptyset .$

(ii) $\langle \sigma, \delta \rangle \in \Phi^*(\mathcal{E})(s)$ iff $[s,\sigma] \not\to .$ $\square$

We continue with the definition of the abstraction function abs connecting $\mathbb{P}^I_{Df}$ to $\mathbb{P}^I_O$. Next, abs will be used to relate $\mathcal{D}_I$ and $\mathcal{O}_I$ for $\mathcal{L}_{hcl}$ in the familiar manner.

Definition 15.11 $abs: \mathbb{P}^I_{Df} \to \mathbb{P}^I_O$ is the unique function satisfying

$$abs(p)(\sigma) = \bigcup\{\,\sigma' \cdot abs(p[\sigma, \sigma'])(\sigma') \mid p[\sigma, \sigma'] \neq \emptyset\,\} \cup$$
$$\{\,\sigma' \mid \langle\sigma, \sigma'\rangle \in p\,\} \cup \{\,\delta \mid \langle\sigma, \delta\rangle \in p\,\}.$$

As in Chapter 7, we have the

Theorem 15.12

(a) $\mathcal{O}_I = abs \circ \mathcal{O}_I^*$, on $Decl \times Res$.

(b) $\mathcal{O}_I[\![\pi]\!] = abs(\mathcal{D}_I[\![\pi]\!])$, for $\pi \in \mathcal{L}_{hcl}$.

Proof Standard.   □

15.2   Horn clause logic viewed as a uniform parallel language

The view of $\mathcal{L}_{hcl}$ developed in the previous section is based on the interleaving approach to parallel execution, where the execution of $s_1 \| s_2$ consists in choosing either of the two components, performing a step from that component, e.g., from s_1 to s', and continuing with $s' \| s_2$ (or the symmetric case). We now discuss an alternative interpretation of parallel execution where, in the elaboration of $s_1 \| s_2$, we simultaneously perform steps by s_1 and s_2, combine the result in the some way, and continue with $s' \| s''$. Note that, when handling a composed parallel term, e.g., of the form $(s_1 \| s_2) \| s_3$, we simultaneously perform steps from s_1, and s_2 and combine these to some resulting step which we in turn combine with a step as prescribed by s_3. In the general case, *all* components of a parallel statement in whatever nested form will perform a step when possible, explaining the term "maximal parallelism" (abbreviated as MP) for this model. (The noninterleaving view of concurrency will be studied also in Chapter 16 on True Concurrency.)

The combination of steps referred to above is done with the following operator:

Definition 15.13 The operator '$\|$' of *parallel composition* of substitutions is given as a *partial* function: $\Sigma \times \Sigma \to \Sigma$. We shall write $(\sigma_1 \| \sigma_2)\downarrow\sigma$ in case $\sigma_1 \| \sigma_2$ is defined and equal to σ, and $(\sigma_1 \| \sigma_2)\uparrow$ otherwise. Moreover, we require

(a) $\sigma_1 \| \sigma_2 = \sigma_2 \| \sigma_1$, or, more precisely, for all $\sigma_1, \sigma_2, \sigma$, $(\sigma_1 \| \sigma_2) \downarrow \sigma$ iff $(\sigma_2 \| \sigma_1) \downarrow \sigma$.

(b) $(\sigma_1 \| \sigma_2) \| \sigma_3 = \sigma_1 \| (\sigma_2 \| \sigma_3)$, or, more precisely, for all $\sigma_1, \sigma_2, \sigma_3, \rho$, the following two conditions are equivalent:

  (1) There exists σ' such that $(\sigma_1 \| \sigma_2) \downarrow \sigma'$, $(\sigma' \| \sigma_3) \downarrow \rho$.

  (2) There exists σ'' such that $(\sigma_2 \| \sigma_3) \downarrow \sigma''$, $(\sigma_1 \| \sigma'') \downarrow \rho$.

(c) $(\sigma \| \lambda) \downarrow \sigma$, $(\lambda \| \sigma) \downarrow \sigma$.

In the maximal parallelism model we shall have no need for the sequential composition $(\sigma \circ \sigma')$ of substitutions. In Section 15.3, when discussing the correspondence between the interleaving and the maximal parallelism view on $\mathcal{L}_{hcl}$, we shall appeal to a property linking the two outcomes $\sigma \circ \sigma'$, and $\sigma \| \sigma'$.

We now develop $\mathcal{T}_{hcl}^{MP}$ for $\mathcal{L}_{hcl}$. Instead of transitions $[s, \sigma] \to_{I,D} [r, \sigma']$ as used in $\mathcal{T}_{hcl}^{I}$, we simply use labeled transitions $s \overset{\sigma}{\to}_{MP,D} r$.

Definition 15.14 $\mathcal{T}_{hcl}^{MP} = (Decl \times Res, \Sigma, \to, Spec)$. The notation $\to_{0,MP,D}$ is the usual one. The index D will, from now on, be suppressed. *Spec* is given by

- $\quad$ $\mathsf{unify}(x, y) \overset{\sigma}{\to}_{MP} \mathrm{E}$ $\qquad$ if $mgu(x, y) \downarrow \sigma$ $\qquad\qquad$ (Unify 1)

- $\quad$ $\mathsf{unify}(x, y); s \overset{\sigma}{\to}_{MP} s$ $\qquad$ if $mgu(x, y) \downarrow \sigma$ $\qquad\qquad$ (Unify 2)

- $\quad$ $x \to_{0,MP} \mathsf{unify}(x, y); D(y)$ $\qquad$ for each $y \in PVar$ $\qquad\qquad$ (PVar)

- $\quad$ $s_1 + s_2 \to_{0,MP} s_1$ $\qquad\qquad\qquad\qquad\qquad\qquad\qquad$ (Choice)

  $\quad$ $s_1 + s_2 \to_{0,MP} s_2$

- $\quad$ $\dfrac{s_1 \overset{\sigma_1}{\to} r_1 \quad s_2 \overset{\sigma_2}{\to} r_2}{s_1 \| s_2 \overset{\sigma}{\to} r_1 \| r_2}$ $\qquad$ if $(\sigma_1 \| \sigma_2) \downarrow \sigma$ $\qquad\qquad$ (Par)

A statement s *blocks* (with respect to $\mathcal{T}_{hcl}^{MP}$) if, for no σ, r, we have that $s \overset{\sigma}{\to}_{MP} r$. Note that, contrary to the situation for $\mathcal{T}_{hcl}^{I}$, we here have that $s_1 \| s_2$ blocks if

(1) s_1 blocks or s_2 blocks, or

(2) both s_1 and s_2 do not block (i.e., for some $\sigma_1, r_1, \sigma_2, r_2$, $s_1 \overset{\sigma_1}{\to}_{MP} r_1$, $s_2 \overset{\sigma_2}{\to}_{MP} r_2$), but $(\sigma_1 \| \sigma_2) \uparrow$.

The (Unify) rules are close to those of T^I_{hcl}, but they do not depend on a current state. The rules (PVar) and (Choice) are the natural uniform counterparts of the rules of T^I_{hcl}.

Let $\mathbb{P}^{MP}_O = \mathcal{P}_{nco}(\Sigma^\infty_\delta)$. We first introduce an auxiliary operator defined for each $p \in \mathcal{P}_{nco}(\Sigma^\infty_\delta)$. This operator—written as p_δ—deletes δ from p in case p does not consist solely of δ—and leaves p untouched if $p = \{\delta\}$.

Definition 15.15 $p_\delta \;=\; \begin{cases} p & \text{if } p = \{\delta\} \\ p \backslash \{\delta\} & \text{otherwise.} \end{cases}$

For the definition of $\mathcal{O}_{MP}\colon \mathcal{L}_{hcl} \to \mathbb{P}^{MP}_O$ we need a further operator which extends the parallel composition $\|\colon \Sigma \times \Sigma \to_{part} \Sigma$ defined on substitutions to $\|\colon \Sigma \times \mathbb{P}^{MP}_O \to \mathbb{P}^{MP}_O$.

Definition 15.16 The operators $\|\colon \Sigma \times \mathbb{P}^{MP}_O \to \mathbb{P}^{MP}_O$ and $\|'\colon \Sigma \times \Sigma^\infty_\delta \to \mathbb{P}^{MP}_O$ are the unique functions satisfying

$$\sigma \| p \;=\; \{\sigma \|' q \mid q \in p\}_\delta$$
$$\sigma \|' \epsilon \;=\; \sigma$$
$$\sigma \|' \delta \;=\; \delta$$
$$\sigma \|'(\tau \cdot q) \;=\; \begin{cases} \rho \cdot (\sigma \|' q) & \text{if } (\sigma \| \tau) \downarrow \rho \\ \delta & \text{otherwise.} \end{cases}$$

Note how $\sigma \| q$ composes σ successively with all elements of the sequence q. We next give

Definition 15.17

(a) $\mathcal{O}_{MP}\colon Decl \times Res \to \mathbb{P}^{MP}_O$ is the unique function satisfying

$$\mathcal{O}_{MP}(D|\mathrm{E}) \;=\; \{\epsilon\}$$
$$\mathcal{O}_{MP}(D|s) \;=\; \bigcup\{\sigma \cdot (\sigma \| \mathcal{O}_{MP}(D|r)) \mid s \xrightarrow{\sigma}_{MP} r\} \cup \{\delta \mid s \not\to_{MP}\}$$

(b) $\mathcal{O}_{MP}[\![\pi]\!] = \mathcal{O}_{MP}(\pi)$, for $\pi \in \mathcal{L}_{hcl}$.

The denotational semantics $\mathcal{D}_{MP}$ for $\mathcal{L}_{hcl}$ is easier than $\mathcal{D}_I$, since the complications due to the nonuniform framework—especially the use of sequences of *pairs*— are absent here. $\mathcal{D}_{MP}$ uses the domain $\mathbb{P}^{MP}_D = \mathcal{P}_{nco}(\Sigma^\infty_\delta \backslash \{\epsilon\})$. In the next definition, we first introduce the semantic operators, and next give the definition of $\mathcal{D}_{MP}$ in the usual style. We draw attention to the definition of '$\|$' on $\mathbb{P}^{MP}_D$, especially its lack of any interleaving features.

Definition 15.18

(a) The mappings $+, \|: \mathbb{P}_D^{MP} \times \mathbb{P}_D^{MP} \to \mathbb{P}_D^{MP}$ are the unique functions satisfying

$$
\begin{aligned}
p_1 + p_2 &= \{\, \sigma \cdot q \mid \sigma \cdot q \in p_1 \cup p_2 \,\} \cup \{\, \delta \mid \delta \in p_1 \cap p_2 \,\} \\
p_1 \| p_2 &= \{\, q_1 \| q_2 \mid q_1 \in p_1, q_2 \in p_2 \,\}_\delta \\
\epsilon \| q &= q \| \epsilon = q \\
\delta \| q &= q \| \delta = \delta \\
(\sigma_1 \cdot q_1) \| (\sigma_2 \cdot q_2) &= \begin{cases} \rho \cdot (q_1 \| q_2) & \text{if } (\sigma_1 \| \sigma_2){\downarrow}\rho \\ \delta & \text{otherwise.} \end{cases}
\end{aligned}
$$

(b)
$$
\begin{aligned}
\mathcal{D}_{MP}(D|\mathsf{unify}(x,y)) &= \begin{cases} \{\sigma\} & \text{if } mgu(x,y){\downarrow}\sigma \\ \{\delta\} & \text{otherwise} \end{cases} \\
\mathcal{D}_{MP}(D|\mathsf{unify}(x,y);s) &= \begin{cases} \sigma \cdot (\sigma \| \mathcal{D}_{MP}(D|s)) & \text{if } mgu(x,y){\downarrow}\sigma \\ \{\delta\} & \text{otherwise} \end{cases} \\
\mathcal{D}_{MP}(D|x) &= \bigcup\{\, \mathcal{D}_{MP}(D|\mathsf{unify}(x,y);D(y)) \mid y \in PVar \,\} \\
\mathcal{D}_{MP}(D|s_1 \text{ op } s_2) &= \mathcal{D}_{MP}(D|s_1) \text{ op } \mathcal{D}_{MP}(D|s_2), \quad \text{op} \in \{+, \|\}.
\end{aligned}
$$

(c) $\mathcal{D}_{MP}[\![\pi]\!] = \mathcal{D}_{MP}(\pi)$, for $\pi \in \mathcal{L}_{hcl}$.

For $\mathcal{E}_{MP}$ the usual extension of $\mathcal{D}_{MP}$, we next prove

Lemma 15.19 *For Φ_{MP} the operator defining $\mathcal{O}_{MP}$, we have*

$$
\Phi_{MP}(\mathcal{E}_{MP}) = \mathcal{E}_{MP}.
$$

Proof We follow the customary argument (and suppress the MP-subscript and most occurrences of D). Two subcases.

$[\mathsf{unify}(x,y);s]$ $\quad \Phi(\mathcal{E})(\mathsf{unify}(x,y);s)$
$$
\begin{aligned}
&= \bigcup\{\, \sigma \cdot (\sigma \| \mathcal{E}(s)) \mid \mathsf{unify}(x,y) \xrightarrow{\sigma} \mathrm{E} \,\} \cup \{\, \delta \mid \mathsf{unify}(x,y) \not\rightarrow \,\} \\
&= \text{if } mgu(x,y){\downarrow}\sigma \text{ then } \sigma \cdot (\sigma \| \mathcal{E}(s)) \text{ else } \{\delta\} \text{ fi} \\
&= \mathcal{E}(\mathsf{unify}(x,y);s)
\end{aligned}
$$

$[s_1 \| s_2]$ $\quad \Phi(\mathcal{E})(s_1 \| s_2)$
$$
\begin{aligned}
&= \bigcup\{\, \sigma \cdot (\sigma \| \mathcal{E}(r)) \mid s_1 \| s_2 \xrightarrow{\sigma} r \,\} \cup \{\, \delta \mid s_1 \| s_2 \not\rightarrow \,\} \\
&= \bigcup\{\, \sigma \cdot (\sigma \| \mathcal{E}(r_1 \| r_2)) \mid s_1 \xrightarrow{\sigma_1} r_1, s_2 \xrightarrow{\sigma_2} r_2, (\sigma_1 \| \sigma_2){\downarrow}\sigma \,\} \cup \\
&\quad\;\; \{\, \delta \mid (s_1 \not\rightarrow) \vee (s_2 \not\rightarrow) \vee ((s_1 \xrightarrow{\sigma_1} r_1) \wedge (s_2 \xrightarrow{\sigma_2} r_2) \wedge (\sigma_1 \| \sigma_2){\uparrow}) \,\}
\end{aligned}
$$

$$
\begin{aligned}
&= \bigcup \{\, (\sigma_1 \| \sigma_2) \cdot (\sigma_1 \| \sigma_2) \| (\mathcal{E}(r_1) \| \mathcal{E}(r_2)) \mid s_1 \overset{\sigma_1}{\to} r_1, s_2 \overset{\sigma_2}{\to} r_2, (\sigma_1 \| \sigma_2){\downarrow}\sigma \,\} \cup \\
&\qquad \{\, \delta \mid s_1 \not\to \,\} \cup \{\, \delta \mid s_2 \not\to \,\} \cup \{\, \delta \mid s_1 \overset{\sigma_1}{\to} r_1, s_2 \overset{\sigma_2}{\to} r_2, (\sigma_1 \| \sigma_2){\uparrow} \,\} \\
&= (\bigcup \{\, \sigma_1 \cdot (\sigma_1 \| \mathcal{E}(r_1)) \mid s_1 \overset{\sigma_1}{\to} r_1 \,\} \cup \{\, \delta \mid s_1 \not\to \,\}) \| \\
&\qquad (\bigcup \{\, \sigma_2 \cdot (\sigma_2 \| \mathcal{E}(r_2)) \mid s_2 \overset{\sigma_2}{\to} r_2 \,\} \cup \{\, \delta \mid s_2 \not\to \,\}) \\
&= \Phi(\mathcal{E})(s_1) \| \Phi(\mathcal{E})(s_2) \\
&= [\text{ind. hyp.}] \ \mathcal{E}(s_1) \| \mathcal{E}(s_2) \\
&= \mathcal{E}(s_1 \| s_2),
\end{aligned}
$$

where we have used that $(\sigma_1 \| \sigma_2) \| (p_1 \| p_2) = (\sigma_1 \| p_1) \| (\sigma_2 \| p_2)$. $\square$

Finally, we have

Theorem 15.20 $\mathcal{O}_{MP}[\![\pi]\!] = \mathcal{D}_{MP}[\![\pi]\!]$, for $\pi \in \mathcal{L}_{hcl}$.

Proof By Lemma 15.19. $\square$

15.3   Relating the various views

This section is devoted firstly to a discussion of the relationship between the two kinds of semantics for $\mathcal{L}_{hcl}$ developed in the two preceding sections, and secondly to the connection between (the semantics for) Horn clause logic and $\mathcal{L}_{hcl}$. The material is, altogether, somewhat peripheral to the major themes of our work. Accordingly, we adopt a somewhat more terse style in its presentation.

We begin with a discussion of $\mathcal{O}_I$ versus $\mathcal{O}_{MP}$ for $\mathcal{L}_{hcl}$. It is not difficult to see that $\mathcal{O}_I$ and $\mathcal{O}_{MP}$ do not coincide. Consider a statement $s \equiv s_1 \| s_2$, where s_1 allows an infinite computation and s_2 (only) deadlocks. Then $\mathcal{O}_I(s)(\lambda)$ includes an infinite sequence, whereas $\mathcal{O}_{MP}(s) = \{\delta\}$. More precisely, this situation arises, e.g., when $PVar = \{x, y\}$, $D(x) = x$, $D(y)$ is undefined, $mgu(x, x){\downarrow}\lambda$, $mgu(y, y){\downarrow}\lambda$, $mgu(x, y){\uparrow}$, $mgu(y, x){\uparrow}$. By the various definitions, then $\lambda \cdot \lambda \cdots \in \mathcal{O}_I(D|x\|y)(\lambda)$, and $\mathcal{O}_{MP}(D|x\|y) = \{\delta\}$.

This example shows that we shall have to be satisfied with a more restricted relationship between $\mathcal{O}_I$ and $\mathcal{O}_{MP}$. In its formulation, we use the notion of set of *last* elements of a set of sequences.

Definition 15.21 Let $p \in \mathcal{P}_{nco}(\Sigma_\delta^\infty)$. Define $last: \mathcal{P}_{nco}(\Sigma_\delta^\infty) \to \mathcal{P}(\Sigma)$ by

$$
last(p) = \{\, \sigma \mid \sigma_1 \cdot \ldots \cdot \sigma_n \in p, \sigma = \sigma_n \,\}.
$$

Thus, $last(p)$ collects all the final elements of the finite sequences in p which do not end in δ.

We can now state the theorem relating $\mathcal{O}_I$ and $\mathcal{O}_{MP}$.

Theorem 15.22 *Let $\pi \in \mathcal{L}_{hcl}$, and assume that all $\rightarrow_I$-computations and all $\rightarrow_{MP}$-computations of π terminate successfully (i.e. without blocking). Then*

$$last(\mathcal{O}_I[\![\pi]\!](\lambda)) \quad = \quad last(\mathcal{O}_{MP}[\![\pi]\!]).$$

We shall develop a sequence of lemmas leading up to the proof of this theorem. The first step is stated here as a proposition without proof. The reason for this is that the result depends on detailed properties of substitutions and of the *mgu*-function. Since we do not develop this machinery in our book, we are not able to present the proof here (see Section 15.5 for references to standard texts on Logic Programming).

The proposition we need is

Proposition 15.23 *Let $x, y \in PVar$, $\sigma \in \Sigma$ be such that $y\sigma = y$. Then, for all ρ_1, ρ_2, θ the following two conditions are equivalent*

(1) $mgu(x, y)\downarrow\rho_1$, $(\sigma\|\rho_1)\downarrow\theta$,

(2) $mgu(x\sigma, y)\downarrow\rho_2$, $\theta = \sigma\rho_2$.

In other words, the proposition expresses that, in case $y\sigma = y$, we have that $\sigma \| mgu(x, y) = \sigma mgu(x\sigma, y)$.

Next, we introduce two relations ($\twoheadrightarrow_I$ and $\twoheadrightarrow_{MP}$), built from $\rightarrow_I$ and $\rightarrow_{MP}$, respectively. In both cases, the intended meaning is to serve as a finite (nonempty) iteration of the original relation. The actual definition of $\twoheadrightarrow_{MP}$ is a little more involved.

Definition 15.24

(a) $\twoheadrightarrow_I$ is the transitive closure of $\rightarrow_I$. That is, we have that $[s, \sigma] \twoheadrightarrow_I [r, \tau]$ if either $[s, \sigma] \rightarrow_I [r, \tau]$, or, for some s', σ', we have that $[s, \sigma] \rightarrow_I [s', \sigma']$, and $[s', \sigma'] \twoheadrightarrow_I [r, \tau]$.

(b) $s \xrightarrow{\theta}_{MP} r$ holds if either $s \xrightarrow{\theta}_{MP} r$, or, for some s', θ', θ'' we have $s \xrightarrow{\theta'}_{MP} s'$, $s' \xrightarrow{\theta''}_{MP} r$, and $(\theta'\|\theta'')\downarrow\theta$.

Note that $\twoheadrightarrow_I$ is, indeed, the transitive closure of $\to_I$, but $\twoheadrightarrow_{MP}$ is built firstly by iterating $\to_{MP}$ one or more times and, secondly, taking the iterated $\|$-composition of the substitutions labeling the constituent $\to_{MP}$-transitions.

The definitions of $\twoheadrightarrow_I$ and $\twoheadrightarrow_{MP}$ have been designed such that the following holds.

Lemma 15.25

(a) $last(\mathcal{O}_I[\![s]\!](\sigma)) = \{\, \sigma' \mid [s,\sigma] \twoheadrightarrow_I [\mathrm{E},\sigma'] \,\}$

(b) $last(\mathcal{O}_{MP}[\![s]\!]) = \{\, \sigma \mid s \stackrel{\sigma}{\twoheadrightarrow}_{MP} \mathrm{E} \,\}$.

Proof Clear from the definitions. $\qquad\square$

We next present a lemma which analyzes in which situation execution of a statement terminates after one step.

Lemma 15.26 *Let $\twoheadrightarrow_{0,I}$ denote the reflexive and transitive closure of $\to_{0,I}$, and similarly for $\twoheadrightarrow_{0,MP}$.*

(a) $[s,\sigma] \to_I [\mathrm{E},\tau]$ *if there exist x,y such that*

    (1) $[s,\sigma] \twoheadrightarrow_{0,I} [\mathsf{unify}(x,y),\sigma]$,

    (2) $mgu(x\sigma,y)\!\downarrow\!\rho$, $\tau = \sigma\rho$.

(b) $s \stackrel{\theta}{\to}_{MP} \mathrm{E}$ *if there exist x,y such that*

    (1) $s \twoheadrightarrow_{0,MP} \mathsf{unify}(x,y)$,

    (2) $mgu(x,y)\!\downarrow\!\theta$.

Proof Clear by an analysis of the cases in which either $\mathcal{T}_{hcl}^I$ or $\mathcal{T}_{hcl}^{MP}$ determines a single-step transition. $\qquad\square$

By combining this lemma with the proposition stated at the beginning of this section, it is not difficult to prove

Lemma 15.27 *The following two conditions are equivalent*

(1) $[s,\sigma] \to_I [\mathrm{E},\tau]$,

(2) $(s \stackrel{\theta}{\to}_{MP} \mathrm{E})$ *and* $(\sigma\|\theta)\!\downarrow\!\tau$.

Proof By Proposition 15.23 and Lemma 15.26. $\qquad\square$

We are almost ready for the main lemma on which we base the proof of Theorem 15.22. One important preparatory step is still to be made:

Lemma 15.28 *Assume* $[s_1 \| s_2, \sigma] \rightarrow_I [s_2, \tau] \rightarrow_I [\mathrm{E}, \rho]$. *Then, for some* θ, *we have*

$[s_1 \| s_2, \sigma] \rightarrow_I [s_1, \theta] \rightarrow_I [\mathrm{E}, \rho]$.

Proof Since $[s_1 \| s_2, \sigma] \rightarrow_I [s_2, \tau]$, we have that $[s_1, \sigma] \rightarrow_I [\mathrm{E}, \tau]$. By Lemma 15.27, for some θ_1, we have $s \xrightarrow{\theta_1}_{MP} \mathrm{E}$, $(\sigma \| \theta_1) \downarrow \tau$. Since $[s_2, \tau] \rightarrow_I [\mathrm{E}, \rho]$, we also have, for some θ_2, $s_2 \xrightarrow{\theta_2}_{MP} \mathrm{E}$, $(\tau \| \theta_2) \downarrow \rho$. Hence, $(\sigma \| \theta_1) \| \theta_2 \downarrow (\tau \| \theta_2) \downarrow \rho$. By associativity and commutativity of $\|$, we also have $(\sigma \| \theta_2) \| \theta_1 \downarrow \rho$ and we may take $\theta = \sigma \| \theta_2$ obtaining $[s_1 \| s_2, \sigma] \rightarrow_I [s_1, \theta] \rightarrow_I [\mathrm{E}, \rho]$, as desired.   □

By repeated application of this lemma, one obtains the following consequence:

Lemma 15.29 *The following two conditions are equivalent.*

(1) $[s_1 \| s_2, \sigma] \twoheadrightarrow_I [\mathrm{E}, \tau]$.

(2) *For some* ρ, $[s_1, \sigma] \twoheadrightarrow_I [\mathrm{E}, \rho]$ *and* $[s_2, \rho] \twoheadrightarrow_I [\mathrm{E}, \tau]$.

Proof (Sketch, refer to Figure 15.1) That $(2 \Rightarrow 1)$ is immediate from the definition of $\mathcal{T}_{hcl}^I$. That $(1 \Rightarrow 2)$ can be obtained by repeated application of Lemma 15.28 (stating that the transitions 3 and then 4 may equivalently be replaced by 1 and then 2). From this we infer that each path from top (T) to bottom (B) in Figure 15.1 may equivalently be replaced by a path from T to A, and then from A to B, reorganizing an arbitrary transition sequence from $s_1 \| s_2$ to E in a sequence which first rewrites s_1 to E, and then s_2 to E.   □

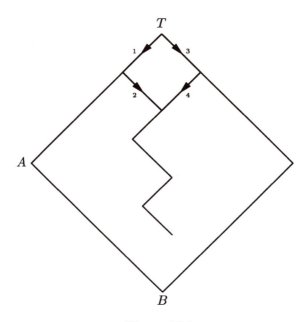

Figure 15.1

The next lemma states the n-step equivalent of the 1-step Lemma 15.27.

Lemma 15.30 *For each s and each σ, τ, θ such that $(\sigma \| \theta) {\downarrow} \tau$, there exists a computation (1) iff there exists a computation (2), where*

(1) $[s, \sigma] \twoheadrightarrow_I [E, \tau]$.

(2) $s \stackrel{\theta}{\twoheadrightarrow}_{MP} E$.

Proof Let ν_1 denote the number of $\rightarrow_I$-steps in (1), and similarly for ν_2. Let $wgt(s)$ be as usual. The proof uses induction on the entity $(\nu_1 + \nu_2, wgt(s))$, ordered lexicographically (i.e., $(\nu', w') < (\nu'', w'')$ iff $\nu' < \nu''$ or $\nu' = \nu''$ and $w' < w''$). Three subcases.

[unify(x, y)] We have that $[\text{unify}(x, y), \sigma] \rightarrow_I [E, \tau]$ iff
$[\text{unify}(x, y), \sigma] \rightarrow_I [E, \tau]$, and a similar claim holds for $\twoheadrightarrow_{MP}$. Now apply Lemma 15.27.

[x] By the definition of $\mathcal{T}_{hcl}^I$ we have that $[x, \sigma] \twoheadrightarrow_I [E, \tau]$ iff

$[\mathsf{unify}(x,y);D(y),\sigma] \twoheadrightarrow_I [\mathrm{E},\tau]$, for some $y \in PVar$, and similarly for the MP-case. By the induction hypothesis we have, for each $y \in PVar$, that, for $(\sigma\|\theta)\!\downarrow\!\theta$, $[\mathsf{unify}(x,y);D(y),\sigma] \twoheadrightarrow_I [\mathrm{E},\tau]$ iff $\mathsf{unify}(x,y);D(y) \overset{\theta}{\twoheadrightarrow}_{MP} \mathrm{E}$, and the desired result follows.

$[s_1\|s_2]$ We have, by Lemma 15.29, that $[s_1\|s_2,\sigma] \twoheadrightarrow_I [\mathrm{E},\tau]$ iff, for some ρ,

$$[s_1,\sigma] \twoheadrightarrow_I [\mathrm{E},\rho] \tag{15.4}$$

$$[s_2,\rho] \twoheadrightarrow_I [\mathrm{E},\tau] . \tag{15.5}$$

By the induction hypothesis we have that (15.4) and (15.5) are equivalent with, respectively

$$s_1 \overset{\theta_1}{\twoheadrightarrow}_{MP} \mathrm{E}, (\sigma\|\theta_1)\!\downarrow\!\rho \tag{15.6}$$

$$s_2 \overset{\theta_2}{\twoheadrightarrow}_{MP} \mathrm{E}, (\rho\|\theta_2)\!\downarrow\!\tau . \tag{15.7}$$

Thus, $(\sigma\|\theta_1)\|\theta_2\!\downarrow\!(\rho\|\theta_2)\!\downarrow\!\tau$, from which we infer that $(\theta_1\|\theta_2)\!\downarrow\!\theta$, for some θ. By (Par) from $\mathcal{T}_{hcl}^{MP}$, from (15.6) and (15.7) one obtains $s_1\|s_2 \overset{\theta}{\twoheadrightarrow}_{MP} \mathrm{E}$, with $(\sigma\|\theta)\!\downarrow\!\tau$, as desired.   □

The proof of Theorem 15.22 is now easy:

Proof (of Theorem 15.22) Assume that all $\rightarrow_I$—and $\rightarrow_{MP}$—computations for s terminate successfully. We have

$\sigma \in last(\mathcal{O}_I(D|s)(\lambda))$

$\Longleftrightarrow$ [Lemma 15.25] $[s,\lambda] \twoheadrightarrow_I [\mathrm{E},\sigma]$

$\Longleftrightarrow$ [Lemma 15.30] $s \overset{\theta}{\twoheadrightarrow}_{MP} \mathrm{E}, (\lambda\|\theta)\!\downarrow\!\sigma$

$\Longleftrightarrow$ [Definition 15.13] $s \overset{\theta}{\twoheadrightarrow}_{MP} \mathrm{E}, \theta = \sigma$

$\Longleftrightarrow$ [Lemma 15.25] $\sigma \in last(\mathcal{O}_{MP}(D|s)) .$ □

Combining Theorem 15.22 with Theorem 15.12 and 15.20, one obtains as a corollary a relationship between $\mathcal{D}_I$ and $\mathcal{D}_{MP}$ for $\mathcal{L}_{hcl}$. Since this does not contain new information, we do not bother to state it. What we do discuss briefly is the possibility of introducing variations in the operational behaviour of $\mathcal{L}_{hcl}$.

The arbitrary interleaving mechanism prescribed by (Par) from $\mathcal{T}_{hcl}^I$ might be replaced by a more rigid rule, e.g., one embodying the breadth-first strategy. This is achieved by replacing the rule (Par) by (Par') in

•
$$\frac{[x,\sigma] \to [r,\sigma']}{[x \,\|\, s, \sigma] \to [s \,\|\, r, \sigma']} \cdot \qquad\qquad (\text{Par}')$$

Combining this with a further new rule, viz. $(s_1 \,\|\, s_2) \,\|\, s_3 \to_0 s_1 \,\|\, (s_2 \,\|\, s_3)$, one obtains the desired effect. Consider, for example, the statement $x \,\|\, (y \,\|\, z)$, and assume that the revised T_{hcl} prescribes transitions $x \to s_x$, and similarly for y, z (for brevity, we drop all states in this example). We then obtain

$$x \,\|\, (y \,\|\, z) \to (y \,\|\, z) \,\|\, s_x \to_0 y \,\|\, (z \,\|\, s_x) \to$$
$$(z \,\|\, s_x) \,\|\, s_y \to_0 z \,\|\, (s_x \,\|\, s_y) \to (s_x \,\|\, s_y) \,\|\, s_z,$$

etc. Various further variations on the rewriting strategy for $\mathcal{L}_{hcl}$, and the associated $\mathcal{O}$ and $\mathcal{D}$, have been studied in the logic programming literature.

After having settled the relationship between $\mathcal{O}_I$ and $\mathcal{O}_{MP}$ for $\mathcal{L}_{hcl}$, we now turn to a discussion of the connection between $\mathcal{L}_{hcl}$ and standard Horn clause logic—abbreviated from now on as HCL. HCL is a world of its own, with a rich semantic theory. For our purposes, it is sufficient to provide a quick introduction to the basic syntax and operational semantics of HCL, which we shall then use to state a somewhat—but not fully—rigorous proposition relating (the respective operational semantics of) $\mathcal{L}_{hcl}$ and HCL.

As always, we begin with the syntax. The key idea bridging the two languages consists in identifying the procedure variables ($x \in PVar$) of $\mathcal{L}_{hcl}$ with HCL's set of *atoms*—a standard ingredient of each logical first order language.

Definition 15.31

(a) Let $(c \in)\, Const$ be the set of constants and let $(v, w \in)\, IVar$ be the (infinite) set of individual variables, $(f \in)\, FSym$ the set of function symbols, and $(X \in)\, PSym$ the set of predicate symbols.

(b) $e\,(\in Exp) ::= c \mid v \mid f(e_1, \ldots, e_k)$, where $k = ar(f) \geq 1$,
   $x\,(\in Atom) ::= X(e_1, \ldots, e_\ell)$, $\ell = ar(X)$.

(c) $G\,(\in Goal) ::= x_1, \ldots, x_n$ $(n \geq 0)$. The empty sequence of atoms is denoted by $\square$.

(d) A *clause* in HCL is a pair (x, G)—always written $x \leftarrow G$.

(e) A program in HCL is pair (S, G), consisting of

   • a finite set of clauses $S = \{\, x_i \leftarrow G_i \,\}_{i=1}^p$,

   • a goal G.

The intended correspondence between $\mathcal{L}_{hcl}$ and HCL may already be transparent from this syntax. The basic building blocks of both languages are the $x, y, \ldots$, in $\mathcal{L}_{hcl}$ taken from an arbitrary alphabet $PVar$, in HCL instantiated to (i.e., taken as elements of) the syntactic set $Atom$. In brief, we take $PVar = Atom$, when connecting $\mathcal{L}_{hcl}$ and HCL. Next, a construct $G = x_1, \ldots, x_n$ of HCL corresponds with a statement $s = x_1 \| \ldots \| x_n$ of $\mathcal{L}_{hcl}$ (where E corresponds to $\square$). A subset of clauses $x \leftarrow G_1, \ldots, x \leftarrow G_n$ of S—collecting all pairs with x as left-hand side—returns as a declaration $D(x) = g_1 + \ldots + g_n$ (g_i corresponds to G_i, g_i may equal E) of $\mathcal{L}_{hcl}$. Note that HCL has no explicit atomic actions unify(x, y), nor (syntactically visible) forms of ';' or '+'. However, as we shall see soon, these composition mechanisms do play a role in the operational semantics for HCL.

We proceed with some semantic preparations.

Definition 15.32

(a) $\Sigma = IVar \rightarrow Exp$ is the set of *substitutions*. We write $v\sigma$ to denote the result of applying σ to v. For $\sigma, \sigma' \in \Sigma$ we shall employ the (total) operation of sequential composition (written as $\sigma \circ \sigma'$ or $\sigma\sigma'$) and the partial operation of parallel composition ($\sigma \| \sigma'$). These operations satisfy the properties as specified in Definitions 15.2, 15.13. (We omit precise definitions of '$\circ$' and '$\|$'.)

(b) Each $\sigma \in \Sigma$ is extended in a natural way to act on $e \in Exp$, $x \in Atom$ and $G \in Goal$, the results being written as $e\sigma$, $x\sigma$ and $G\sigma$.

(c) We postulate a partial function $mgu: Atom \times Atom \rightarrow \Sigma$, satisfying (at least) the property stated in Proposition 15.23.

We now come to the main step in the definition of the operational semantics for HCL. The key notion is that of *resolvent* of a set of clauses S and a goal G.

Definition 15.33

(a) We say that G' is a resolvent of (S, G)—with associated substitution θ—in case $G = x_1, \ldots, x_n$ ($n \geq 1$), and we can find some i, $1 \leq i \leq n$ and a clause $y \leftarrow y_1, \ldots, y_m$ ($m \geq 0$) in S, such that

(1) $mgu(x_i, y) \downarrow \theta$.

(2) $G' = (x_1, \ldots, x_{i-1}, y_1, \ldots, y_m, x_{i+1}, \ldots, x_n)\theta$.

(b) We write $G \xrightarrow{\theta}_S G'$—in words, S determines a θ-transition step from G to G'—if G' is a resolvent of (S, G) with associated substitution θ.

(c) We say that θ is a *computed answer substitution* (*cas*) of (S, G) in case there exists a sequence of transition steps

$$G = G_0 \overset{\theta_1}{\to}_S G_1 \to \cdots \overset{\theta_n}{\to}_S G_n = \Box, \text{ such that } \theta = \theta_1 \theta_2 \cdots \theta_n.$$

(d) We use $cas(S, G)$ to denote the collection of all computed answer substitutions of (S, G).

Remark In determining G', we search for a clause $y \Leftarrow y_1, \ldots, y_m$ in S such that $mgu(x_i, y) \downarrow \theta$. Since S is finite, there are only finitely many possibilities for such a variable y, explaining the finiteness condition in Definition 15.2, clause d. Note that it would not be feasible to express this phenomenon by postulating a finite domain for each $D \in Decl$: This does not allow us to cope with the alphabetic variant machinery (see below), effectively resulting in the fact that, each time we have $D(y) = y_1, \ldots, y_m$, we simultaneously have that $D(y') = y'_1, \ldots, y'_m$, where the primed variables are arbitrary alphabetic variants of the unprimed ones.

There is, in fact, one important further ingredient to the notion of sequence of transition steps which we have ignored in the above definition, viz., the obligation to take fresh *alphabetic variants*—systematically replacing individual variables by others not used so far in the derivation—of the clause as selected from S in determining the successive resolvents. (LP calls this "standardizing apart.") We shall not go into the—crucial but tedious—details of this, since they are somewhat orthogonal to our main concern here. Let it suffice to say that it is not difficult to mimic the precise definition of this for HCL by a similar one in the framework of the semantic definitions for $\mathcal{L}_{hcl}$.

We now make some comments on Definition 15.33. Firstly, we see that the invocation of $mgu(x, y)$ takes place at the moment one searches for an applicable clause $y \leftarrow G$ when evaluating some x_i, and this is the same scheme used in $\mathcal{L}_{hcl}$. The selection of the index i for the x_i to be processed corresponds to the execution of the associated $x_1 \| \ldots \| x_n$ (parenthesized in an arbitrary way) by selecting the first interleaving step (by (Par)) to be one of x_i. The choice explicit in $\mathcal{L}_{hcl}$'s $s_1 + s_2$ construct is here implicit in the selection of some $y \leftarrow G$. More precisely, if $y \leftarrow G_1, \ldots, y \leftarrow G_n$ are all clauses from S with left-hand side y, then—as we indicated above—the D associated with S will contain the information $D(y) = g_1 + \cdots + g_n$. Furthermore, step 1 and 2 of clause (a) prescribe that the execution of some x_i

proceeds by firstly performing a unify(x_i, y)-step, and, next, executing one of the choices in $D(y)$. Again, these steps return in the $\mathcal{T}_{hcl}^{I}$ specification. One final point: in the (nonuniform) treatment of $\mathcal{L}_{hcl}$, transitions for some $[s, \sigma]$ are always with respect to a current substitution σ. For HCL, the current substitution, when a step affecting G_i is made, consists in the accumulated history $\theta_1 \cdots \theta_{i-1}$ (which has already been applied in the formation of G_i). By resolving G_i with S, the next substitution is determined taking the $\theta_1 \cdots \theta_{i-1}$ into account, just as, in $\mathcal{T}_{hcl}^{I}$ the next substitution, yielded by the next unification step, is derived in terms of the current σ.

There is one further obvious difference between the HCL operational semantics in terms of computed answer substitutions, and $\mathcal{O}_I$ or $\mathcal{O}_{MP}$. Whereas in the former we only deliver the *final* substitution $\theta = \theta_1 \cdots \theta_n$, in $\mathcal{O}_I$ or $\mathcal{O}_{MP}$ we deliver *sequences* of intermediate (and the final) substitutions. As everywhere in our framework, these sequences are necessary to make the metric machinery work; they are in particular essential to ensure appropriate limit behaviour for infinite computations. When we restrict attention to finite computations, we are often interested only in the final elements of computation sequences. For HCL, these are collected in $cas(S, G)$, and for $\mathcal{L}_{hcl}$ in $last(\mathcal{O}_I(D|s)(\lambda))$ ($= last(\mathcal{O}_{MP}(D|s))$). After all these preliminaries, we are rewarded by the

Proposition 15.34 *For each $(S, G) \in HCL$ we can find a $(D|s)$ in $\mathcal{L}_{hcl}$ such that*

$$\theta \in cas(S, G) \text{ iff } \theta \in last(\mathcal{O}_I(D|s)(\lambda)).$$

Since $\mathcal{L}_{hcl}$ has a somewhat more liberal syntax than HCL, a converse claim would require a restriction to an appropriate subset of $\mathcal{L}_{hcl}$. We shall not take the trouble to enter into the details of this. In fact, we shall make no attempt at proving the proposition. A proof would necessitate rather more detail in the definition of HCL. Also, the already mentioned renaming mechanism would burden the proof.

Though we have left some loose ends in our analysis here, we hope to have collected enough evidence to convince the reader that a control flow study of HCL in our framework is indeed fruitful. This will pay off, for example, when looking at variants of HCL where control structures have been modified to enhance effectiveness. Two examples must suffice here. The language PROLOG replaces the quite liberal selection mechanism of HCL—choose any x_i in a goal G, and any $y \leftarrow G'$ in S—by a more structured one: select the x_i from left to right, and impose a backtracking mechanism in selecting the $y \leftarrow G'$ from S. Now one easily sees that our general semantic framework can cope with PROLOG's variations on HCL without undue effort. The left-right selection in a goal simply amounts to replacing $x_1 \| \cdots \| x_n$ by $x_1; \ldots; x_n$. Also, the backtracking mechanism in selecting the clauses from S may directly be handled by the $s_1 \square s_2$-construct as studied in Section 9.1. The second example concerns the family of committed choice parallel LP languages. In the design of their semantics, one should aim for a synthesis between the ideas of the present chapter and the analysis of atomization and commit from Section 14.1.

15.4   A concurrent constraint language

Horn clause logic has been generalized in various ways partly by extending it with more refined (and, hopefully efficient) control structures—more about this in the bibliographic section—and partly by abstracting from the underlying logical framework—but not as drastically as we did in Sections 15.1, 15.2. We shall present the control flow kernel of one version of the species of concurrent constraint languages, by varying the model as developed in Section 15.1.

The first step is to replace the underlying domain of substitutions (remember that this, in turn, replaced the earlier domain of states) by that of *constraints*. So we now take $(\sigma, \sigma' \in) \Sigma$ as an (abstract) set of constraints. Intuitively, we may take a constraint as a "partial description of the current state of affairs." We postulate two binary operations on this set.

Definition 15.35 For $\sigma, \sigma' \in \Sigma$, we use

- the operator $\vdash : \Sigma \times \Sigma \to \{tt, ff\}$ of *entailment* (We shall write $\sigma \vdash \sigma'$ and $\sigma \nvdash \sigma'$ in case $\vdash (\sigma, \sigma') = tt$ and $\vdash (\sigma, \sigma') = ff$, respectively.)

- the operator $\sqcup : \Sigma \times \Sigma \to \Sigma$ of *extension*, written as $\sigma \sqcup \sigma'$.

The first operator may, intuitively, be read as: constraint σ implies constraint σ', and the second as: the constraints σ and σ' are united yielding the constraint $\sigma \sqcup \sigma'$ as outcome. For our present purposes, it is not necessary to articulate these notions (for more information consult the references mentioned in the bibliographical notes).

Instead, in the spirit of our treatment of $\mathcal{L}_{hcl}$, we shall now introduce a language $\mathcal{L}_{cc}$, together with an operational and denotational semantics for it, based on the one hand on the introduction of two new types of elementary actions (replacing the $\mathsf{unify}(x, y)$ of the earlier sections), and on the other hand on a semantic treatment of the composition operators of the language which quite closely follows our earlier treatment (in Section 15.1).

We begin by introducing the two new elementary actions,

- For each σ, $\mathsf{ask}(\sigma)$ is an elementary action.

- For each σ, $\mathsf{tell}(\sigma)$ is an elementary action.

As we shall see below, $\mathsf{ask}(\sigma)$ will be interpreted in terms of the '$\vdash$'-operator, and $\mathsf{tell}(\sigma)$ in terms of the '$\sqcup$'-operator.

Definition 15.36

(a) $s\,(\in Stat) ::= \mathsf{ask}(\sigma) \mid \mathsf{tell}(\sigma) \mid x \mid (s;s) \mid (s+s) \mid (s\|s)$.

(b) $(D \in)\,Decl = PVar \to Stat$.

(c) $(\pi \in)\,\mathcal{L}_{cc} = Decl \times Stat$.

Resumptions are as usual for a parallel language (cf. Definition 4.2). Note that $\mathcal{L}_{cc}$ includes full sequential composition ($s;s$) rather than $\mathcal{L}_{hcl}$'s action prefixing. Also, we have no need for a notion of guarded statement (since we shall prescribe an explicit transition step when dealing with a procedure variable).

The transition system $\mathcal{T}_{cc}$ is a modest variation on earlier nonuniform systems. Transitions are of the form $[s,\sigma] \to [r,\sigma']$ (suppressing the D).

Definition 15.37 $\mathcal{T}_{cc} = (Decl \times Res \times \Sigma, \Sigma, \to, Spec)$. *Spec* is given by

- $\quad [\mathsf{ask}(\sigma'),\sigma] \to [\mathrm{E},\sigma] \qquad$ if $\sigma \vdash \sigma'$ $\hfill$ (Ask)

- $\quad [\mathsf{tell}(\sigma'),\sigma] \to [\mathrm{E},\sigma \sqcup \sigma']$ $\hfill$ (Tell)

- $\quad [x,\sigma] \to [D(x),\sigma]$ $\hfill$ (PVar)

- $$\frac{[s,\sigma] \to [r,\sigma']}{[s;\bar{s},\sigma] \to [r;\bar{s},\sigma']}$$ (Seq)

- $$\frac{[s,\sigma] \to [r,\sigma']}{[s+\bar{s},\sigma] \to [r,\sigma']}$$ (Choice)

  $$[\bar{s}+s,\sigma] \to [r,\sigma']$$

$$\bullet \quad \frac{[s,\sigma] \to [r,\sigma']}{[s \,\|\, \bar{s},\sigma] \to [r \,\|\, \bar{s},\sigma']} \tag{Par}$$

$$[\bar{s} \,\|\, s,\sigma] \to [\bar{s} \,\|\, r,\sigma']$$

A remark on the feasibility of forming $\sigma \sqcup \sigma'$ follows at the end of this section.

As a consequence of the condition in the (Ask)-rule requiring that the current constraint σ implies the asked-for constraint σ', we have that $[s,\sigma] \to \ldots$ may be undefined for certain $[s,\sigma]$. This induces, once more, the need for a notion of blocking, together with the by now familiar consequences of the possible presence of deadlock. The operational semantics $\mathcal{O}$ for $\mathcal{L}_{cc}$ employs the usual (for a nonuniform language) domain $\mathbb{P}_O = \Sigma \to \mathcal{P}_{nco}(\Sigma_\delta^\infty)$. $\mathcal{O}$ is specified in

Definition 15.38 $\mathcal{O}: Decl \times Res \times \Sigma \to \mathcal{P}_{nco}(\Sigma_\delta^\infty)$ is the unique function satisfying $\mathcal{O}(\mathrm{E},\sigma) = \{\epsilon\}$ and

$$\mathcal{O}(s,\sigma) \;=\; \bigcup \{\, \sigma' \cdot \mathcal{O}(r,\sigma') \mid [s,\sigma] \to [r,\sigma'] \,\} \cup \{\, \delta \mid [s,\sigma] \not\to \,\}.$$

The mapping $\mathcal{O}[\![\cdot]\!]:\mathcal{L}_{cc} \to \mathbb{P}_O$ is given by $\mathcal{O}[\![s]\!] = \lambda\sigma.\mathcal{O}(s,\sigma)$.

The denotational semantics for $\mathcal{L}_{cc}$ is obtained as a mild variation on that for $\mathcal{L}_{hcl}$ (in the view of Section 15.1). The domain $\mathbb{P}_{Df}$ and the operators '$;$', '$+$', '$\|$' are exactly as in Section 15.1 (i.e., $\mathbb{P}_{Df}$ equals $\mathbb{P}_{Df}^I$ as given there). What needs to be supplied in addition are the definitions of the meanings of $\mathsf{ask}(\sigma)$ and $\mathsf{tell}(\sigma)$. This is done (suppressing D once again) in

Definition 15.39 $\mathcal{D}: \mathcal{L}_{cc} \to \mathbb{P}_{Df}$ is the unique function satisfying

$$\begin{aligned}
\mathcal{D}(\mathsf{ask}(\sigma')) &= \{\, \langle \sigma,\sigma \rangle \mid \sigma \vdash \sigma' \,\} \cup \{\, \langle \sigma,\delta \rangle \mid \sigma \not\vdash \sigma' \,\} \\
\mathcal{D}(\mathsf{tell}(\sigma')) &= \{\, \langle \sigma, \sigma \sqcup \sigma' \rangle \mid \sigma \in \Sigma \,\} \\
\mathcal{D}(x) &= \bigcup \{\, \langle \sigma,\sigma' \rangle \cdot \mathcal{D}(D(x)) \mid \sigma \in \Sigma \,\} \\
\mathcal{D}(s_1 \ \mathsf{op}\ s_2) &= \mathcal{D}(s_1) \ \mathsf{op}\ \mathcal{D}(s_2), \quad \mathsf{op} \in \{;,+,\|\}.
\end{aligned}$$

Also, $\mathcal{D}[\![\pi]\!] = \mathcal{D}(\pi)$, for $\pi \in \mathcal{L}_{cc}$.

We see that the definitions of $\mathcal{D}$ for $\mathsf{ask}(\sigma')$ and $\mathsf{tell}(\sigma')$ are quite natural counterparts of the operational rules. Moreover, the way $\mathcal{D}$ is given for the composite statements is completely standard. As a bonus from our rather abstract perspective on the languages $\mathcal{L}_{hcl}$ and $\mathcal{L}_{cc}$, only minor variations are incurred in going from one to the other. Also, we can now simply take over *abs* as given in Definition 15.11, and use it in the statement of the final theorem of this chapter:

Theorem 15.40 $\mathcal{O}[\![\pi]\!] = abs(\mathcal{D}[\![\pi]\!])$, *for each* $\pi \in \mathcal{L}_{cc}$. $\square$

We conclude with a

Remark A more refined analysis of the notions underlying the concurrent constraint model would have to address the operation of $\sigma \sqcup \sigma'$ in more detail. A natural requirement would be to require that $\sigma \sqcup \sigma'$ is defined only for certain combinations of σ, σ' —say the so-called *consistent* ones—and to introduce another type of deadlock caused by an attempt to evaluate $\sigma \sqcup \sigma'$ for inconsistent σ, σ' . Moreover, it would be natural to consider this type of deadlock as more "serious." In this analysis, δ would express *temporary* deadlock (or suspension), and a new symbol, say Δ , would stand for definitive deadlock (also called error or abort). (The induced modifications in $\mathcal{T}_{cc}$, $\mathcal{O}$ and $\mathcal{D}$ for $\mathcal{L}_{cc}$ are described in [BKPR92], cf. Section 15.5.)

15.5 Bibliographical notes [3]

A general source for the idea that it may be advantageous to separate logic and control is [Kow79]. The paper [Bak91] is the first reference describing the perspective on logic programming as outlined in this chapter. Concurrently, the specialization of this view to Prolog was developed in [Vin89, BV89, Vin90]. The "translation" of logic programming (in the Horn clause form) to $\mathcal{L}_{hcl}$ was first described in [BK88, BK90].

Standard texts on logic programming are [Apt90] and [Llo87]. [She94] provides further details on the "standardizing apart" problem. A thorough study of denotational (and operational) semantics for Horn clause logic comparing models in the line of our book to the traditional ("declarative" and "fixed point") semantics is [BKPR92]. Much of the material in Section 15.1 and 15.2 is based on this paper (which also contains several further results not reported here). New elements in our treatment are the use of the $\mathcal{P}_{fncl}(\cdot)$ domain, and the definition of the semantic operators with a full coverage of deadlock (with definitions in turn based on [BKPR93b]).

The construct $\sigma_1 \| \sigma_2$, for σ_1, σ_2 substitutions, is Jacquet's "reconciliation" ([Jac91]). This operation has also been investigated in [Pal90] and in [Vin90]. The

---

[3] Since Chapter 15 is not fully self-contained, we have not included a section with exercises in it.

argument used in the proof of Lemma 15.29 is a version of the "diamond lemma" of logic programming.

The notion of constraint logic programming is due to Jaffar and Lassez ([JL87]). Concurrent constraint languages have been investigated, e.g., in [SR90, SRP91]. Our treatment in Section 15.4 is based on [BKPR93b].

Examples of parallel logic programming languages include PARLOG ([Gre87]), GHC ([Ued88]) and Concurrent PROLOG ([Sha88]). In addition to the references given earlier, we cite here a few further semantic studies: [Kok88, GMS89, JM90, BKPR91b].

16 True Concurrency

So far, all our models for parallel execution were based on the *interleaving* interpretation: typically, the meaning of the statement $s \equiv a \| b$ is given as $\{ ab, ba \}$ in a linear model, or as shown below in a branching model.

In recent years, increased attention has been paid to models of the so-called *true concurrency* (or noninterleaving) kind. A variety of domains has been developed where concurrency is modelled without imposing a form of temporal (or "causal") order: in executing $a \| b$, no assumptions are made on the relative order in which a and b are performed. In this chapter, we shall treat a particularly simple example of this, viz. the *pomset* model. We shall show that it is amenable to a metric treatment in a way which closely follows the general methodology advocated so far in our book. Some work needs to be done to construct the precise mathematical groundwork on which to build the metrics. Once this is available, the semantic design may proceed in a way which stays close to our earlier approach. As example language, we have chosen to consider once more $\mathcal{L}_{par}$ (which was modelled according to the interleaving interpretation in Chapter 4). We shall present operational and denotational pomset semantics (yielding *sets* of pomsets as meanings for programs in $\mathcal{L}_{par}$), and establish their equivalence. The denotational semantics is a rather convincing variation on earlier models, but the operational model exhibits certain deficiencies.

In this chapter we do not aim at providing full mathematical details, especially not in the material which lays the foundations for the metric treatment of pomsets. The true concurrency model being somewhat peripheral to the main stream of our work, we have preferred to quote various results without proof (though full details are available in the literature referred to in Section 16.5). We also want to emphasize that the pomset domain is just one out of a spectrum of true concurrency models. Of fundamental importance, both for theoretical investigations and for practical applications, is the notion of *Petri net*. Closer to the pomset model is the so-called *event structure* model, which has been studied in considerable depth. Some more information on the latter will be given at the end of Section 16.3; pointers to the literature follow in Section 16.5.

16.1   Pomsets

In this section we shall introduce the mathematical notion of pomset (which is short
for "partially ordered multiset"), define a *metric* on pomsets and then introduce
the pomset version of the main control flow operators studied so far (';', '+', '∥').
We begin with defining the notion of partially ordered set.

Definition 16.1 A *partially ordered set* (poset) is a pair $(X, \leq)$, where X is a
set and '$\leq$' is a subset of $X \times X$ (we shall write $x \leq y$ instead of $(x, y) \in \leq$) that
satisfies the following conditions

(i) $\forall x\colon x \leq x$

(ii) $\forall x, y\colon x \leq y$ and $y \leq x \Rightarrow x = y$

(iii) $\forall x, y, z\colon x \leq y$ and $y \leq z \Rightarrow x \leq z$.

The notation $x < y$ is short for $(x \leq y$ and $x \neq y)$.

Definition 16.2 Let $(X, \leq)$ be a poset.

(a) For $x \in X$, we define $lev(x) \in \mathbb{N} \cup \{\infty\}$ by

$$lev(x) = sup\{\, n \mid \exists x_1, \ldots, x_n \in X\colon x_1 < x_2 < \ldots < x_n = x \,\}.$$

(b) $lgt(X, \leq) = sup\{\, lev(x) \mid x \in X \,\}$ (with the convention that $sup(\emptyset) = 0$).

(c) For $A \subseteq X$, we call A *downward closed* if $\forall a \in A \forall x \in X\colon x \leq a \Rightarrow x \in A$.

Remark Note that $lgt(X, \leq) \in \mathbb{N} \cup \{\infty\}$.

We shall now introduce the notion of pomset and state some of their technical
properties. Next, we shall turn the set of pomsets into a complete metric space—
using a metric which is strongly reminiscent of the Baire metric of Chapter 1—and
then define the familiar operators on (sets of) pomsets. Let A be a fixed (finite or
infinite) set of actions and let $\mathcal{X}$ be a fixed (infinite) set of nodes, also called *events*.

Definition 16.3 A labeled poset or *causality structure* σ is a three-tuple $(X_\sigma, \leq_\sigma, \lambda_\sigma)$, where $X_\sigma \subseteq \mathcal{X}$ and where $(X_\sigma, \leq_\sigma)$ is a poset satisfying

(i) $\forall n \colon |\{\, x \in X_\sigma \mid lev(x) \leq n \,\}| < \infty$

(ii) $\forall x \in X_\sigma \colon lev(x) < \infty$.

Moreover, $\lambda_\sigma \colon X_\sigma \to A$ is given as the so-called *labeling function*. We shall use $act(\sigma) \stackrel{df}{=} \{\, \lambda_\sigma(x) \mid x \in X_\sigma \,\}$.

The intended meaning of a causality structure (or, briefly, structure) is the following: X_σ is the set of names of events, and, for $x_1 \neq x_2$, $x_1 < x_2$ means that event x_1 has to precede x_2. The meaning of λ_σ is that $\lambda_\sigma(x)$ is the action of event x, or, stated otherwise, x is an occurrence of $\lambda_\sigma(x)$. The two restrictions on the partial ordering are essential for the proof that the distance function introduced below (Definition 16.7) is indeed a metric. Furthermore, they imply that every event has only a finite number of predecessors. Note that different events may be labeled by the same action.

We now introduce the notion of pomset as a causality structure modulo renaming of nodes (i.e., we abstract from the *identity* of the events) as introduced in

Definition 16.4

(a) Two structures σ and ρ are called isomorphic if there exists a bijection $\phi \colon X_\sigma \to X_\rho$ such that $\phi(x) \leq_\rho \phi(y) \Leftrightarrow x \leq_\sigma y$, and $\lambda_\rho \circ \phi = \lambda_\sigma$.

(b) A pomset is an isomorphism class of causality structures. Let $(p, q \in) POM[A]$ denote the collection of pomsets with respect to some action set A. In case A is understood, we shall use POM rather than $POM[A]$. The notation $[\sigma]$ denotes a pomset with representative σ. Also, $act([\sigma])$ is defined by $act(\sigma)$ (which is independent of the representative). The empty pomset $[(\emptyset, \emptyset, \emptyset)]$ is denoted by $[\,]$.

We shall draw pomsets by using the Hasse diagram of the partial order belonging to some representative causality structure, with the labels at the place of the nodes, as in

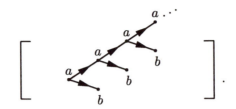

By the length of a structure, we mean the length of the order belonging to that structure. We also extend the notion of length to pomsets by taking the length of some representative. We now introduce the key notion of *truncation* on *POM*:

Definition 16.5

(a) For a causality structure σ and a downward closed subset X of X_σ we define $\sigma{\upharpoonright}X = (X, \leq_\sigma \cap(X \times X), \lambda_\sigma{\upharpoonright}X)$. $\sigma{\upharpoonright}X$ is a causality structure, and $lev(x)$ with respect to $\sigma{\upharpoonright}X$ equals $lev(x)$ with respect to σ.

(b) For σ a causality structure and $n \in \mathbb{N}$, we define $\sigma[n] = \sigma{\upharpoonright}\{\, x \in X_\sigma \mid lev(x) \leq n \,\}$.

(c) For $p \in POM$, $p[n] = \{\, \sigma[n] \mid \sigma \in p \,\}$.

(For clause (c), cf. Exercise 16.2.)

Example Let p be the following pomset

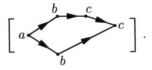

Then $lgt(p) = 4$, $act(p) = \{a, b, c\}$, and p has, e.g., one c at level 3 and one c at level 4. (To be more precise, every representative of p has two nodes labeled with c, one at level 3 and one at level 4.) The truncations $p[0], p[1], \ldots, p[4], p[5]$ are, respectively,

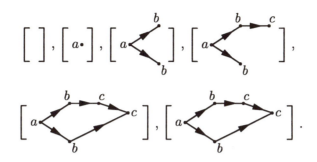

Note how the empty pomset $[\,]$ corresponds to the empty word ϵ in the setting of Chapter 1. On the way to defining a metric structure on POM, we require some properties which we state here without proof.

Lemma 16.6

(a) $\sigma[n][m] = \sigma[min\{n,m\}]$

(b) $p[n][m] = p[min\{n,m\}]$

(c) $(\forall n\colon p[n] = q[n]) \Rightarrow p = q$.

Especially clause (c) requires various technicalities for its proof (based on the finiteness conditions of Definition 16.3). We refer to the literature mentioned in Section 16.5 for full details.

We can now introduce a metric on POM which follows quite closely our earlier definition (cf. Definition 1.20):

Definition 16.7 The distance $d\colon POM \times POM \to [0,1]$ is defined by

$$d(p,q) \;=\; \begin{cases} 0 & \text{if } p = q \\ 2^{-n} & \text{where } n = max\{\, k \mid p[k] = q[k] \,\}, \text{ if } p \neq q. \end{cases}$$

According to the next lemma, d is indeed an (ultra)metric, and (POM, d) is complete. In the familiar way, we can also define the *hyperspace* of nonempty closed subsets of POM (with respect to the Hausdorff metric d_H based on d):

Lemma 16.8

(a) (POM, d) *is a complete ultrametric space.*

(b) $(\mathcal{P}_{ncl}(POM), d_H)$ *is a complete ultrametric space.*

We omit the proof of this lemma: for part (a) see the literature mentioned in Section 16.5; part (b) is standard from part (a) (by Hahn's theorem).

From now on, it will be convenient to use $(P, Q \in) POM^*$ as short-hand for the hyperspace $(\mathcal{P}_{ncl}(POM), d_H)$.

Having completed the introduction of (the metric on) pomsets, we now discuss the motivation for their use in the present context: We want to be able to model the basic operators of parallel languages such as $\mathcal{L}_{par}$ in a way which avoids the interleaving approach as applied everywhere up till now. Rather, we aim at defining a version of parallel composition which deserves to be called "truly concurrent," in that the execution of, e.g., $a \| b$ is modeled by a structure where (the events labeled by) a and b can be seen as *simultaneous*—without committing to an execution which either chooses for first a and then b, or first b and then a. A few pictures— for which the pomset formalism is eminently suitable—should clarify this: Consider the following statements from $\mathcal{L}_{par}$:

- $s_1 \equiv (a;b)$, $s_2 \equiv (c;d)$
- $s_3 \equiv (a;b) \| (c;d)$
- $s_4 \equiv (a;b) + (c \| d)$.

The operators ';' and '$\|$' can simply be explained on the level of pomsets. The pomsets corresponding to s_1, s_2 and s_3 are

$$\left[a \bullet\!\!\longrightarrow\!\!\bullet b \right] \;,\; \left[c \bullet\!\!\longrightarrow\!\!\bullet d \right] \;,\; \left[\begin{array}{c} a \bullet\!\!\longrightarrow\!\!\bullet b \\ c \bullet\!\!\longrightarrow\!\!\bullet d \end{array} \right] \;,$$

respectively. Thus, sequential precedence (a comes before b, c before d) is reflected by the partial order in the (representative of the) pomset, and parallel composition is no more than juxtaposition (note how both operations assume disjoint sets of events). Nondeterministic choice is modeled at the level of *sets* of pomsets in that s_4 has a meaning the structure

$$\left\{ \left[a \bullet\!\!\longrightarrow\!\!\bullet b \right] \;,\; \left[\begin{array}{c} d \bullet \\ c \bullet \end{array} \right] \right\} .$$

We emphasize the essential difference of the latter two cases: the parallel composition $p_1 \| p_2$ of two pomsets will yield a third pomset, whereas nondeterministic choice ('+') will only be defined on two *sets* of pomsets P_1, P_2, yielding their union $P_1 + P_2$ ($= P_1 \cup P_2$) as outcome. (To be fully rigorous, the meaning of, e.g., $a;b$ is also a (singleton) *set* of pomsets, and we should use $\{\, [\, a\bullet\!\!\rightarrow\!\!\bullet b\,]\, \}$ rather than just $[\, a\bullet\!\!\rightarrow\!\!\bullet b\,]$ for the meaning of s_1.)

We now describe the various definitions in a rigorous way, and state the familiar properties of these operators (necessary to make the semantic definitions of the next sections work):

Definition 16.9

(a) (';', '$\|$' for causality structures) Let σ, ρ be such that $X_\sigma \cap X_\rho = \emptyset$.

$$
\begin{aligned}
\sigma;\rho &= \sigma, \text{ if } lgt(\sigma) = \infty \\
&= (X_\sigma \cup X_\rho, \leq_\sigma \cup \leq_\rho \cup (X_\sigma \times X_\rho), \lambda_\sigma \cup \lambda_\rho), \text{ otherwise} \\
\sigma\|\rho &= (X_\sigma \cup X_\rho, \leq_\sigma \cup \leq_\rho, \lambda_\sigma \cup \lambda_\rho).
\end{aligned}
$$

(b) (';', '$\|$' for pomsets) Let $p = [\sigma], q = [\rho]$, with $X_\sigma \cap X_\rho = \emptyset$. Then $p;q = [\sigma;\rho]$, $p\|q = [\sigma\|\rho]$.

(c) (';', '$\|$' for sets of pomsets)

$$
\begin{aligned}
P;Q &= \{\, p;q \mid p \in P, q \in Q \,\} \\
P\|Q &= \{\, p\|q \mid p \in P, q \in Q \,\} \\
P+Q &= P \cup Q.
\end{aligned}
$$

Examples

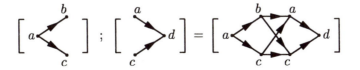

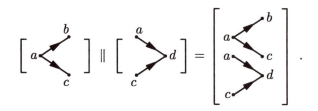

Remark A clear advantage of these definitions is their simplicity: no higher order techniques are needed here to deal with possibly infinite operands. Only the closedness of the outcomes $P;Q$ and $P\|Q$ requires separate proof.

The next lemma expresses that the above operators are well-defined and satisfy the customary properties (necessary to invoke the familiar arguments in the semantic modeling in the next sections):

Lemma 16.10

(a) *For $P, Q \in POM^*$, $P;Q$, $P\|Q$ and $P + Q$ are closed sets.*

(b) *If $p, p' \neq [\,]$ then $d(p;q, p';q') \leq max\{\, d(p, p'), \frac{1}{2}d(q, q')\,\}$.*

(c) *If $[\,] \notin P, P'$ then $d(P;Q, P';Q') \leq max\{\, d(P, P'), \frac{1}{2}d(Q, Q')\,\}$.*

(d) *$\|: POM \times POM \to POM$ is nonexpansive (in both arguments).*

(e) *$\|, +: POM^* \times POM^* \to POM^*$ are nonexpansive (in both arguments).*

Proof See references in Section 16.5.   □

We have now collected enough properties of pomsets to enable us to proceed with their applications in semantic definitions.

16.2   An operational pomset semantics[1] for $\mathcal{L}_{par}$

Let $\mathcal{L}_{par}$ be as in Chapter 4. We shall use POM^* and the operators defined on it in the design of a truly concurrent semantics for $\mathcal{L}_{par}$. The central issue is the treatment of (the meaning of) $s_1\|s_2$, and, as we saw above, the pomset model allows a smooth definition of this which deserves the qualification of "truly concurrent."

---

[1] The semantic models of this and the next section are expressed in terms of closed (rather than the more usual compact) sets. For a—preliminary—explanation of this cf. Exercise 16.3.

As a consequence, it is especially suitable for the denotational modeling (to be described in Section 16.3). However, it is less convenient for a transition system based operational semantics. Recall that—for all uniform languages treated so far—we employed transitions of the form $s \xrightarrow{a} s'$. In a pomset based semantics we run into trouble if we want to follow the same approach, in particular in assembling information from successive steps. Consider the situation that $s_1 \xrightarrow{a_1} s_1'$ and $s_2 \xrightarrow{a_2} s_2'$. If we use this to derive something like

$$s_1 \| s_2 \xrightarrow{\left[\begin{smallmatrix} a_1 \\ a_2 \end{smallmatrix}\right]} s_1' \| s_2',$$

then the information is lost that a_1 stems from s_1 and a_2 stems form a_2. This information is essential, for if $s_1' \xrightarrow{b} s_1''$, we want to combine, in the operational semantics, the b only with the a_1 and not with (all of) $\left[\begin{smallmatrix} a_1 \\ a_2 \end{smallmatrix}\right]$. We know of no convincing way out of this problem [2]. What we shall describe below circumvents the issue of how the successive pomsets in transitions $s_1 \xrightarrow{p_1} s_2$, $s_2 \xrightarrow{p_2} s_3$, ... are to be connected such that the operational intuition is captured. The somewhat crude means to do this is by restricting *all* transitions to be of the form

$$s \xrightarrow{p} E \tag{16.1}$$

(thus avoiding the question just formulated). This has as a consequence that the operational semantics loses its "successive steps" flavour. Still, there remains an interesting issue which the transition system $\mathcal{T}_{par}^{pom}$ *does* settle, viz. how to handle recursion—in particular the task of building infinite p in (16.1)—by suitably extending the so far standard treatment.

Let *Act* be the usual set of actions used in the syntax for $\mathcal{L}_{par}$, and let e be a new symbol not in *Act*. We shall write Act_e for $Act \cup \{e\}$, and we shall work below with the (sets of) pomsets $POM[Act]$ or $POM[Act_e]$ and $POM^*[Act]$ or $POM^*[Act_e]$. We now first present the pomset-based transition system for $\mathcal{L}_{par}$; various comments to explain it will follow. The set *Res* is as in Definition 4.2.

Definition 16.11 $\mathcal{T}_{par}^{pom} = (Res, POM[Act_e], \rightarrow, Spec)$, where *Spec* consists of

$$a \xrightarrow{[a]} E \tag{Act}$$

$$\frac{D(x) \xrightarrow{p} E}{x \xrightarrow{p} E} \tag{Rec}$$

---

[2] Unless one is willing to pay the price of considerably complicating the semantic machinery.

$$\bullet \quad \frac{s_1 \xrightarrow{p_1} \mathrm{E} \qquad s_2 \xrightarrow{p_2} \mathrm{E}}{s_1;s_2 \xrightarrow{p_1;p_2} \mathrm{E}} \qquad\qquad (\text{Seq})$$

$$\bullet \quad \frac{s_1 \xrightarrow{p_1} \mathrm{E} \qquad s_2 \xrightarrow{p_2} \mathrm{E}}{s_1\|s_2 \xrightarrow{p_1\|p_2} \mathrm{E}} \qquad\qquad (\text{Par})$$

$$\bullet \quad \frac{s_1 \xrightarrow{p} \mathrm{E}}{\begin{array}{c} s_1 + s_2 \xrightarrow{p} \mathrm{E} \\[4pt] s_2 + s_1 \xrightarrow{p} \mathrm{E} \end{array}} \qquad\qquad (\text{Choice})$$

$$\bullet \quad x \xrightarrow{[e]} \mathrm{E} \qquad\qquad (\text{Init})$$

$$\bullet \quad \frac{s \xrightarrow{p_i} \mathrm{E},\ i = 1, 2, \ldots \qquad lim_i\, p_i = p}{s \xrightarrow{p} \mathrm{E}} \qquad\qquad (\text{Lim})$$

The following definition tells us how to base the operational semantics $\mathcal{O}$ for $\mathcal{L}_{par}$ on $\mathcal{T}_{par}^{pom}$:

Definition 16.12

(a) $\mathcal{I}\colon \mathcal{L}_{par} \to POM^*[Act_e]$ is given by

$$\mathcal{I}(s) \quad = \quad \{\, p \mid s \xrightarrow{p} \mathrm{E} \,\}.$$

(b) $\mathcal{O}\colon \mathcal{L}_{par} \to POM^*[Act]$ is given by

$$\mathcal{O}(s) \quad = \quad \mathcal{I}(s) \cap POM[Act].$$

Let us first discuss $\mathcal{T}_{par}^{pom}$. The rules (Act), (Rec) are (almost) standard, and the rules (Seq), (Par) and (Choice) clearly capture the intended meanings of the operator (though, for ';', in an arguably too denotational manner). The rules (Init) and (Lim) are included to enable us to handle possibly infinite computations of recursive procedures. Since we only work with transitions $s \to \mathrm{E}$, we have no means to build up an infinite computation without additional measures.

Rule (Init) provides an arbitrary starting point (always fixed at $[e]$) for the execution of a recursive procedure. Rule (Lim) allows us to infer a possibly infinite p in one step (albeit from an infinity of premises). This set-up would allow e to remain in the final outcome of a computation. Therefore, we obtain the desired operational semantics $\mathcal{O}(s)$ by restricting the intermediate semantics $\mathcal{I}(s)$ to those outcomes which contain only pomsets involving actions from Act (thus excluding occurrences of e). The following example should be helpful to understand the handling of recursion here.

Example Let $D(x) \equiv a;(x\|b);c$, and let $s \equiv x$. By applying the rules (Init), (Act), (Seq), (Par) and (Rec), we may derive $s \xrightarrow{p_i} \text{E}$, for p_1, p_2, p_3, p_4, ... equal to

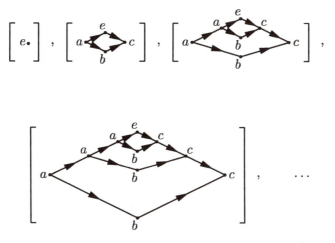

Applying rule (Lim) gives $s \xrightarrow{p} \text{E}$, $p = lim_i\, p_i =$

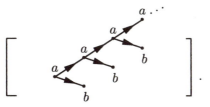

So $\mathcal{I}(s)$ is the set of all pomsets $p_1, p_2, \ldots$ and p listed above, and $\mathcal{O}(s)$ is the singleton set with p as (only) member.

The definitions of $\mathcal{I}$ and $\mathcal{O}$ are formally justified in

Lemma 16.13

(a) $\mathcal{I}(s)$ *is nonempty and closed, for each* $s \in \mathcal{L}_{par}$.

(b) $\mathcal{O}(s)$ *is nonempty and closed, for each* $s \in \mathcal{L}_{par}$.

Proof

(a) By induction on the syntactic complexity of s, one may show that $\mathcal{I}(s) \neq \emptyset$ (use (Init) for $s \equiv x$). By (Lim), $\mathcal{I}(s)$ is closed.

(b) $\mathcal{O}(s)$ is closed since $\mathcal{I}(s)$ is closed. Proving $\mathcal{O}(s) \neq \emptyset$ is more involved. We construct a sequence $(p_i)_i$ with $p_i \in \mathcal{I}(s)$, such that $e \notin act(p_i[i])$ and $p_{i+1}[i] = p_i[i]$. From this it follows that $(p_i)_i$ is a Cauchy sequence, say with limit p, $p \in \mathcal{I}(s)$ and $\forall i: e \notin act(p[i])$, so $e \notin act(p)$. We conclude that $p \in \mathcal{O}(s)$. The sequence is constructed in the following way: $\mathcal{I}(s) \neq \emptyset$, so take some $p_0 \in \mathcal{I}(s)$. Note that $e \notin p_0[0] = [\,]$. If $p_k \in \mathcal{I}(s)$ with $e \notin act(p_k[k])$ then we can find a $p_{k+1} \in \mathcal{I}(s)$ with $p_{k+1}[k] = p_k[k]$ and $e \notin act(p_{k+1}[k+1])$. This is guaranteed by the next lemma. $\square$

Lemma 16.14 *If* $s \xrightarrow{p} E$ *and* $e \notin act(p[n])$ *then* $\exists p': s \xrightarrow{p'} E$, $p'[n] = p[n]$, *and* $e \notin act(p'[n+1])$.

Proof (sketch) First we remark that, for each $g \in GStat$, $\exists p': g \xrightarrow{p'} E$ and $e \notin act(p'[1])$, which can easily be proven by induction on the syntactic complexity of g.

The lemma is proven by transfinite induction on the depth of the proof tree for $s \xrightarrow{p} E$, defined in the usual way.

- If $a \xrightarrow{[a]} E$ by (Act), then we take $p' = [a]$.

- If $x \xrightarrow{p} E$ by (Rec), then $g \xrightarrow{p} E$, with $g = D(x)$. By induction, $\exists p': g \xrightarrow{p'} E$ with $p'[n] = p[n]$ and $e \notin act(p'[n+1])$. Now also $x \xrightarrow{p'} E$.

- If $s_1; s_2 \xrightarrow{p_1; p_2} E$ by (Seq), then $s_1 \xrightarrow{p_1} E$, $s_2 \xrightarrow{p_2} E$. By induction, $\exists p'_1, p'_2: s_1 \xrightarrow{p'_1} E$ and $s_2 \xrightarrow{p'_2} E$, with $e \notin act(p'_1[n+1])$ and $e \notin act(p'_2[n+1])$, $p'_1[n] = p_1[n]$, $p'_2[n] = p_2[n]$. Now $s_1; s_2 \xrightarrow{p'_1; p'_2} E$, $e \notin act((p'_1; p'_2)[n+1])$ and $(p'_1; p'_2)[n] = (p_1; p_2)[n]$.

- The case of (Par) can be treated similarly.
- The case of (Choice) is immediate by induction.
- Assume $x \xrightarrow{[e]} E$ by (Init). By the remark just made we know, putting $g = D(x)$, that $g \xrightarrow{p} E$ for some p with $e \notin act(p[1])$. The transition $x \xrightarrow{p} E$ then satisfies the conditions of the lemma.
- If $s \xrightarrow{p} E$ by (Lim), then $s \xrightarrow{p_i} E$ $(i = 1, 2 \ldots)$ and $lim_i\, p_i = p$. Now $\exists i \colon p_i[n] = p[n]$. By induction $\exists p' \colon s \xrightarrow{p'} E$ and $e \notin act(p'[n+1])$ and $p'[n] = p_i[n] = p[n]$. $\square$

With this lemma, we have concluded our justification of the operational semantics for $\mathcal{L}_{par}$.

16.3   Denotational semantics, equivalence of $\mathcal{O}$ and $\mathcal{D}$

The design of the denotational pomset semantics for $\mathcal{L}_{par}$ is particularly straight-forward, thanks to the preparations in Section 16.1 (especially Lemma 16.10). We adopt the usual definition scheme in

Definition 16.15

(a) Let $(S \in)\, Sem = \mathcal{L}_{par} \to POM^*[Act]$. The mapping $\Psi \colon Sem \to Sem$ is given by

$$
\begin{aligned}
\Psi(S)(a) &= \{[a]\} \\
\Psi(S)(x) &= \Psi(S)(D(x)) \\
\Psi(S)(s_1;s_2) &= \Psi(S)(s_1);S(s_2) \\
\Psi(S)(s_1\ \mathsf{op}\ s_2) &= \Psi(S)(s_1)\ \mathsf{op}\ \Psi(S)(s_2), \quad \mathsf{op} \in \{\|, +\}.
\end{aligned}
$$

(b) $\mathcal{D} = \text{fix}(\Psi)$.

The format of this definition being exactly as in Definition 4.12, it is immediate (by Lemma 16.10) that Ψ has the usual properties (including the fact that $[]\ \notin \Psi(D)(s)$), and that $\mathcal{D}$ is well-defined. There remains the proof that the operational and denotational semantics coincide. We shall not be able to follow the usual route in showing that $\Psi(\mathcal{D}) = \mathcal{D}$, since no higher-order mapping Φ was involved in the definition of $\mathcal{O}$. Rather, we shall prove that $\Psi(\mathcal{O}) = \mathcal{O}$. This will be the contents of Lemma 16.17. Preparatory to this, we first show

Lemma 16.16

(a) $\{[a]\} = \mathcal{I}(a)$

(b) $\mathcal{I}(g) \cup \{[e]\} = \mathcal{I}(x)$, *for* $g = D(x)$

(c) $\mathcal{I}(s_1);\mathcal{I}(s_2) = \mathcal{I}(s_1;s_2)$

(d) $\mathcal{I}(s_1)\|\mathcal{I}(s_2) = \mathcal{I}(s_1\|s_2)$

(e) $\mathcal{I}(s_1) + \mathcal{I}(s_2) = \mathcal{I}(s_1 + s_2)$.

Proof First we show that (a) to (e) hold with '$\subseteq$' replacing '$=$'. Only case (c) is proven since (a) is immediate from (Act), and (b) from (Rec) and (Init). Case (d) is like (c), and case (e) is immediate by (Choice). Let $p \in \mathcal{I}(s_1);\mathcal{I}(s_2)$. Then $p = p_1;p_2$ with $p_1 \in \mathcal{I}(s_1)$ and $p_2 \in \mathcal{I}(s_2)$. So $s_1 \xrightarrow{p_1} \mathrm{E}$ and $s_2 \xrightarrow{p_2} \mathrm{E}$, from which $s_1;s_2 \xrightarrow{p_1;p_2} \mathrm{E}$ is direct by (Seq).

To prove '$=$', define $\mathcal{I}'(s)$ as follows: $\mathcal{I}'(a) = \{[a]\}$, $\mathcal{I}'(x) = \mathcal{I}(g) \cup \{[e]\}$, for $g = D(x)$, $\mathcal{I}'(s_1;s_2) = \mathcal{I}(s_1);\mathcal{I}(s_2)$, $\mathcal{I}'(s_1\|s_2) = \mathcal{I}(s_1)\|\mathcal{I}(s_2)$, and $\mathcal{I}'(s_1 + s_2) = \mathcal{I}(s_1)+\mathcal{I}(s_2)$. It follows immediately that $\forall s\colon \mathcal{I}'(s) \subseteq \mathcal{I}(s)$, and that $\mathcal{I}'(s)$ is closed. Now define the relation $\to'$ by putting $s \xrightarrow{p}{}' \mathrm{E}$ iff $p \in \mathcal{I}'(s)$. We next show that $\to'$ satisfies the rules from *Spec* for T_{par}^{pom}:

(Act) Trivial.

(Rec) Let $D(x) = g$. If $g \xrightarrow{p}{}' \mathrm{E}$ then $p \in \mathcal{I}'(g) \subseteq \mathcal{I}(g) \subseteq \mathcal{I}'(x)$.

(Seq), (Par) If $s_1 \xrightarrow{p_1}{}' \mathrm{E}$, $s_2 \xrightarrow{p_2}{}' \mathrm{E}$, then $p_1 \in \mathcal{I}'(s_1) \subseteq \mathcal{I}(s_1)$ and $p_2 \in \mathcal{I}'(s_2) \subseteq \mathcal{I}(s_2)$,
   so $p_1;p_2 \in \mathcal{I}(s_1);\mathcal{I}(s_2) = \mathcal{I}'(s_1;s_2)$ and $p_1\|p_2 \in \mathcal{I}'(s_1\|s_2)$.

(Choice) If $s_1 \xrightarrow{p}{}' \mathrm{E}$, then $p \in \mathcal{I}'(s_1) \subseteq \mathcal{I}(s_1) \subseteq \mathcal{I}'(s_1 + s_2)$, so $s_1 + s_2 \xrightarrow{p}{}' \mathrm{E}$, and
   similarly $s_2 + s_1 \xrightarrow{p}{}' \mathrm{E}$.

(Init) $[e] \in \mathcal{I}'(x)$, so $x \xrightarrow{[e]}{}' \mathrm{E}$.

(Lim) If $s \xrightarrow{p_i}{}' \mathrm{E}$, $i = 1, 2, \ldots$, and $lim_i\, p_i = p$, then, since $\mathcal{I}'(s)$ is closed, $p \in \mathcal{I}'(s)$,
   hence $s \xrightarrow{p}{}' \mathrm{E}$.

Now, since '$\to$' is the smallest relation satisfying the rules (Act) to (Lim), we have $\to\ \subseteq\ \to'$ or, equivalently, $\mathcal{I}(s) \subseteq \mathcal{I}'(s)$. Altogether, we have shown that $\mathcal{I}(s) = \mathcal{I}'(s)$.   □

Finally, we prove the compositionality of $\mathcal{O}$.

Lemma 16.17

(a) $\mathcal{O}(a) = \{[a]\}$

(b) $\mathcal{O}(x) = \mathcal{O}(g)$, *for* $g = D(x)$

(c) $\mathcal{O}(s_1;s_2) = \mathcal{O}(s_1);\mathcal{O}(s_2)$

(d) $\mathcal{O}(s_1\|s_2) = \mathcal{O}(s_1)\|\mathcal{O}(s_2)$

(e) $\mathcal{O}(s_1 + s_2) = \mathcal{O}(s_1) + \mathcal{O}(s_2)$.

Proof Let $\mathcal{A}$ abbreviate $POM[Act]$.

(a) $\mathcal{O}(a) = \mathcal{I}(a) \cap \mathcal{A} = \{[a]\} \cap \mathcal{A} = \{[a]\}$.

(b) $\mathcal{O}(x) = \mathcal{I}(x) \cap \mathcal{A} = \mathcal{I}(g) \cap \mathcal{A} = \mathcal{O}(g)$

(c) $\mathcal{O}(s_1;s_2) = \mathcal{I}(s_1;s_2) \cap \mathcal{A} = (\mathcal{I}(s_1);\mathcal{I}(s_2)) \cap \mathcal{A} \overset{(1)}{=} (\mathcal{I}(s_1) \cap \mathcal{A});(\mathcal{I}(s_2) \cap \mathcal{A}) = \mathcal{O}(s_1);\mathcal{O}(s_2)$, where the equality (1) is justified as follows:

[$\supseteq$]   Trivial since $\mathcal{A}$ is closed under ';'.

[$\subseteq$] $(\mathcal{I}(s_1);\mathcal{I}(s_2)) \cap \mathcal{A} = \{ p_1;p_2 \in \mathcal{A} \mid p_1 \in \mathcal{I}(s_1), p_2 \in \mathcal{I}(s_2) \} \overset{df}{=} P$. Let $p_1;p_2 \in P$. We have $e \notin act(p_1)$. If $lgt(p_1) = \infty$, take some $p_2' \in \mathcal{O}(s_2) = \mathcal{I}(s_2) \cap \mathcal{A}$ (note that $\mathcal{O}(s_2) \neq \emptyset$). So $p_1;p_2 = p_1 = p_1;p_2' \in (\mathcal{I}(s_1) \cap \mathcal{A});(\mathcal{I}(s_2) \cap \mathcal{A})$. If $lgt(p_1) < \infty$, then also $e \notin act(p_2)$, so $p_1;p_2 \in (\mathcal{I}(s_1) \cap \mathcal{A});(\mathcal{I}(s_2) \cap \mathcal{A})$.

(d) Like (c), but now the equation corresponding to the one marked with (1) above is direct.

(e) Like (d). $\square$

We have reached the

Theorem 16.18 *Let* $\mathcal{O}, \mathcal{D}\colon \mathcal{L}_{par} \to POM^*[Act]$ *be as in Definition 16.12 and 16.15. Then* $\mathcal{O} = \mathcal{D}$.

Proof By Lemma 16.17, $\Psi(\mathcal{O}) = \mathcal{O}$, and $\mathcal{O} = \mathcal{D}$ follows. $\square$

We conclude this section with several remarks which may shed some further light on the usefulness of the pomset model.

(1) The pomset model is (noninterleaving and) *linear*, in the sense that the semantic equivalence

$$s;(s_1 + s_2) \quad = \quad (s;s_1) + (s;s_2) \tag{16.2}$$

holds, for $s, s_1, s_2 \in \mathcal{L}_{par}$ (or similar languages). The reader may recall here the discussion in the introduction of Section 11.1. Formula (16.2) is a consequence of the equality on (sets of) pomsets

$$P;(Q_1 + Q_2) \;=\; (P;Q_1) + (P;Q_2),$$

an identity which is, in turn, immediate by Definition 16.9. Thus, the domain of (sets of) pomsets is not suitable to model branching behaviour (as in Section 11.1 or later in part III). A refinement of the pomset model is then in order; for this, the so-called *event structures* have turned out to be particularly successful (cf. the references in Section 16.5).

(2) A natural question is whether the pomset domain can be obtained by means of the general domain equation approach as described in Chapter 10. Maybe somewhat surprisingly, this turns out not to be the case. Consider the so-called N-pomset, say p_N (depicted in Figure 16.1):

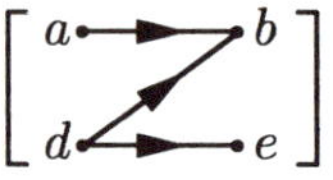

Figure 16.1

No domain which is built from given sets (without any structure) and the usual functors (listed in Chapter 10) exists which has this structure as one of its elements. Of course, the question then arises whether a pomset such as p_N does occur as meaning of some statement. Indeed, one may imagine some s—though in $\mathcal{L}_{syn}$ rather than in $\mathcal{L}_{par}$—for which it is natural to expect that p_N represents (part of) its meaning, viz. $s \equiv (a;c)\|(d;(\bar{c}\|e))$. In fact, replacing b by τ in Figure 16.1 yields a plausible candidate for (an element of) $\mathcal{O}(s)$ (or $\mathcal{D}(s)$).

(3) The tentativeness in what we just wrote stems from the fact that a satisfactory treatment of synchronization in the (metric) pomset setting is not known. Various definitions which have been considered so far lack the essential contractiveness/nonexpansiveness properties, thus leaving open how one might develop a metric treatment in the style as adopted all through our work. (Incidentally, a transparent definition of synchronization in the setting of event structures is as well a challenge which has led to a considerable amount of research.)

16.4   Exercises

Exercise 16.1   Let, for a poset $(X, \leq)$, $x \preceq y$ denote that $(x \leq y) \wedge (\nexists z \,[\, (x \leq z \leq y) \wedge (z \neq x, y) \,]\,)$. Show that the first condition of Definition 16.3 is equivalent with the conjunction of the two conditions

- $\forall x \,[\, |\{ x \mid x \preceq y \}| < \infty \,]$
- $\forall x \,[\, |\{ y \mid \nexists x \colon x < y \}| < \infty \,]$.

Exercise 16.2   Let '$\sim$' denote isomorphism between causality structures. Verify that, if $\sigma \sim \rho$ then $\sigma[n] \sim \rho[n]$. (Note that this implies that $[\sigma][n] = [\sigma[n]]$, thus justifying Definition 16.5c.)

Exercise 16.3   Explain why the standard proof (using induction based on $wgt(s)$) that $\mathcal{T}_{par}^{pom}$ is finitely branching does not work. (Hint: invoking the usual definition $wgt(g;s) = wgt(g) + 1$ is not compatible with the form of the (Seq)-rule.)

Remark   We conjecture that the pomset semantics for $\mathcal{L}_{par}$ may be based on compact sets (rather than on closed sets), but we have no proof for this.

Exercise 16.4   (On the problem of treating $\mathcal{L}_{syn}$ with pomsets.) Assume a semantic model in which we have $\mathcal{D}$ satisfying

$$\mathcal{D}(c \| \bar{c}) \;=\; \left\{ \left[\begin{smallmatrix} c\bullet \\ \bar{c}\bullet \end{smallmatrix} \right], \left[\; \tau\bullet \; \right] \right\}.$$

Take $p = [\, a\bullet\!\!\rightarrow\!\!\bullet c \,]$, $p' = [\, a\bullet\!\!\rightarrow\!\!\bullet d \,]$, $q = q' = [\, \bar{c}\bullet \,]$, and assume we put

$$p \| q \;=\; \left\{ \left[\begin{smallmatrix} a\bullet\!\longrightarrow\!\bullet c \\ \bar{c}\bullet \end{smallmatrix} \right], [\, a\bullet\!\!\rightarrow\!\!\bullet\tau \,] \right\}$$

$$p' \| q' \;=\; \left\{ \left[\begin{smallmatrix} a\bullet\!\longrightarrow\!\bullet d \\ \bar{c}\bullet \end{smallmatrix} \right] \right\}.$$

Show that $d(p \| q, p' \| q') = 1$, whereas $d(p, p') = \frac{1}{2}$, $d(q, q') = 0$, thus establishing that '$\|$' is not nonexpansive.

16.5   Bibliographical notes

The pomset model is due to Grabowski ([Gra81]) and Pratt ([Pra86]). Our metric treatment of pomsets, and their use in the semantics of $\mathcal{L}_{par}$, was first presented in [BW90]. (Most of the mathematical details omitted in Chapter 16 can be found in this reference.) An order-theoretic approach to the use of pomsets to model recursion with merge is [MV89a].

Pomsets provide a noninterleaving *linear* model for concurrency; the so-called event structures can be used as a basis for its noninterleaving *branching* interpretation. Event structures were first described in [NPW81]; from the numerous further studies on this topic we mention [Win89] and [NSW94]. In [LG91], a metric is proposed for event structures which is very similar to the one treated in this chapter; in the paper [BM94], some further properties of (the metric approach to) event structures in concurrency semantics are obtained. Basic references for Petri nets are [Rei85, BRR86]. A recent survey of models for concurrency is [WN95].

An attempt at developing a purely domain-theoretic treatment of noninterleaving concurrency is described in [BW91b].

It is a topic of current research how synchronization could be embedded in the pomset (or event structure) model for concurrency. A few references relating to event structures are [DMN88, Vaa89, BC89, Lan92]. An obstacle in the metric treatment is that simple definitions of synchronization induce operators lacking the necessary nonexpansiveness property ([BW90], cf. Exercise 16.4). (In the order-theoretic approach, monotonicity is problematic, cf. [MV89a].)

The metric treatment of fairness as developed in [DNPY92] (cf. Section 5.5) has been extended to the pomset model for $\mathcal{L}_{par}$ in the thesis of Nolte ([Nol94]).

17 Full Abstractness

17.1 Introduction

On several occasions in earlier chapters, after having derived a relationship of the form

$$\mathcal{O} = abs \circ \mathcal{D}, \tag{17.1}$$

we have raised the question whether such a relationship might qualify as an *optimal* one. We shall devote the present chapter to a more detailed treatment of this issue. In summary, we shall present two instances where the $\mathcal{D}$ (and abs) concerned requires modification to achieve optimality—one simple (for $\mathcal{L}_\delta$) and one rather involved (for $\mathcal{L}_{syn}$). For two further languages ($\mathcal{L}_{aw}$, $\mathcal{L}_{svp}$) we shall quote some results from the literature. As overall picture we have that such optimality results are difficult to obtain, and several open problems remain.

The technical term, for the property to be investigated is that of "full abstractness." More specifically, this notion arises when, for a given language $\mathcal{L}$, we encounter an operational semantics which is not compositional. Since, by definition, any $\mathcal{D}$ for $\mathcal{L}$ has to be compositional, we cannot have that $\mathcal{O} = \mathcal{D}$, and we must look for a more involved relationship. Let us recall a few cases where the $\mathcal{O}$ concerned is not compositional.

Examples

(1) ($\mathcal{L}_{svp}$) We consider the two statements $s_1 \equiv v := 0; v := 1$ and $s_2 \equiv v := 0; v := v + 1$. The $\mathcal{O}$ as defined in Chapter 7 yields that $\mathcal{O}(s_1) = \mathcal{O}(s_2)$, but, taking $s \equiv v := 2$, we found that $\mathcal{O}(s_1 \| s) \neq \mathcal{O}(s_2 \| s)$, thus establishing that $\mathcal{O}$ is not compositional.

(2) ($\mathcal{L}_{syn}$) Let $s_1 \equiv c_1$, $s_2 \equiv c_2$. Then $\mathcal{O}$ (from Chapter 11) yields that $\mathcal{O}(s_1) = \mathcal{O}(s_2) = \{\delta\}$. However, putting $s \equiv \bar{c}_1$, we have that $\mathcal{O}(s_1 \| s) \neq \mathcal{O}(s_2 \| s)$, and the same conclusion holds.

A general pattern can be inferred from these two cases. For both of them, the $\mathcal{O}$ concerned *identifies* too many statements: We provided instances of s_1, s_2 such that $\mathcal{O}(s_1) = \mathcal{O}(s_2)$, but we also supplied a larger program—a *context* $C(\cdot)$—such that putting s_1 and s_2 in this context results in two different $\mathcal{O}$-meanings (i.e., $\mathcal{O}(C(s_1)) \neq \mathcal{O}(C(s_2))$). Note that, in both cases, the context happens to be of the form $\cdot \| s$. In the design of the denotational models for $\mathcal{L}_{svp}$ and $\mathcal{L}_{syn}$, we made sure that $\mathcal{D}$ makes fewer identifications—or, equivalently, makes more distinctions—than $\mathcal{O}$, and we saw that this was sufficient to obtain compositionality for $\mathcal{D}$. At this point, the need arises for a criterion that settles how far one should go in making $\mathcal{D}$ more distinctive. In an extreme case, one could semantically distinguish between all syntactically different s, and this would lead to a particularly un-informative (albeit compositional) semantics. The natural criterion now is that one wants to introduce no more differences between (the meanings of) statements than can be observed operationally in any context. Expressed formally, we require that the pair $(\mathcal{O}, \mathcal{D})$ satisfies

$$\forall s_1, s_2 \in \mathcal{L}\, [\mathcal{D}(s_1) \neq \mathcal{D}(s_2) \Rightarrow \exists C(\cdot)\, [\mathcal{O}(C(s_1)) \neq \mathcal{O}(C(s_2))]\,]. \tag{17.2}$$

In case (17.2) holds for some $\mathcal{D}$—with respect to a given ($\mathcal{L}$ and) $\mathcal{O}$—we call $\mathcal{D}$ *complete* with respect to $\mathcal{O}$. Usually, we assume some fixed $\mathcal{O}$ in the discussion below, and then simply call $\mathcal{D}$ complete. In case $\mathcal{D}$ is also *correct*—a notion to be introduced in a moment—we shall call $\mathcal{D}$ *fully abstract*.

Later in this chapter, we shall quote the result that (17.2) indeed holds for our first example language $\mathcal{L}_{svp}$. It may come as a surprise that this does not hold for $\mathcal{L}_{syn}$, and we shall devote Section 17.3 to a detailed discussion of how this may be remedied by the design of a different (less distinctive) $\mathcal{D}$.

We now fill in some details which have been left open above. We begin by the definition of a *context*. This notion can be defined for any language which is specified syntactically in the style as adopted in our book. We shall not bother to describe the formalities for the general case, but restrict ourselves to two simple examples, viz. contexts for $\mathcal{L}_{par}$ and $\mathcal{L}_{svp}$. For simplicity, we replace the earlier $C(\cdot)$ by C.

Definition 17.1

(a) (contexts for $\mathcal{L}_{par}$)

$C ::= (\cdot) \mid a \mid x \mid (C;C) \mid (C + C) \mid (C \| C).$

(b) (contexts for $\mathcal{L}_{svp}$)

$C ::= (\cdot) \mid v := e \mid \mathsf{skip} \mid (C;C) \mid \mathsf{if}\ e\ \mathsf{then}\ C\ \mathsf{else}\ C\ \mathsf{fi} \mid \mathsf{while}\ e\ \mathsf{do}\ C\ \mathsf{od}.$

For $\mathcal{L}_{par}$, we assume that the sets of guarded statements and of declarations remain unchanged (with respect to the definitions of Section 4.1). In other words, we shall have no occasion to work with contexts involving procedure bodies. (Following the usual conventions, we shall mostly suppress D below.) The above should make it clear how a context can be defined for any $\mathcal{L}$. For a given C, we obtain $C(s)$ as the result of "plugging in" s for all occurrences of the "hole" $(\cdot)$ in C. More formally, we may view $(\cdot)$ as a kind of statement variable, and obtain $C(s)$ as the result of substituting s for all occurrences of $(\cdot)$ in C (i.e., as $C[s/(\cdot)]$).

Besides the property (17.2), it is natural to consider its contrapositive counterpart: We shall call $\mathcal{D}$ *correct* with respect to $\mathcal{O}$ in case

$$\forall s_1, s_2 \in \mathcal{L} \, [\mathcal{D}(s_1) = \mathcal{D}(s_2) \Rightarrow \forall C \, [\mathcal{O}(C(s_1)) = \mathcal{O}(C(s_2))] \,]. \tag{17.3}$$

Whereas completeness is often difficult to establish—and the topic of most of the remainder of this chapter—correctness is usually an easier property. More specifically, we have

Lemma 17.2 *Let $\mathcal{L}$ be any language, and let $\mathcal{O}: \mathcal{L} \to \mathbb{P}_O$, $\mathcal{D}: \mathcal{L} \to \mathbb{P}_D$ and abs$: \mathbb{P}_D \to \mathbb{P}_O$ be such that*

$$\mathcal{O} \;=\; abs \circ \mathcal{D}.$$

Then $\mathcal{D}$ is correct with respect to $\mathcal{O}$.

Proof Let s_1, s_2 be such that $\mathcal{D}(s_1) = \mathcal{D}(s_2)$. By the compositionality of $\mathcal{D}$, it follows that, for any C, $\mathcal{D}(C(s_1)) = \mathcal{D}(C(s_2))$. Therefore, $(abs \circ \mathcal{D})(C(s_1)) = (abs \circ \mathcal{D})(C(s_2))$, and $\mathcal{O}(C(s_1)) = \mathcal{O}(C(s_2))$ follows. $\qquad\square$

Putting the earlier definitions together, we arrive at

Definition 17.3 Let $\mathcal{L}$ be a language, let $\mathcal{O}: \mathcal{L} \to \mathbb{P}_O$ be an operational semantics for $\mathcal{L}$, and $\mathcal{D}: \mathcal{L} \to \mathbb{P}_D$ a denotational one. We call $\mathcal{D}$ *fully abstract* with respect to $\mathcal{O}$ if the following holds:

$$\forall s_1, s_2 \in \mathcal{L} \, [\mathcal{D}(s_1) = \mathcal{D}(s_2) \Leftrightarrow \forall C \, [\mathcal{O}(C(s_1)) = \mathcal{O}(C(s_2))] \,].$$

Remarks

(1) Usually, we assume ($\mathcal{L}$ and) $\mathcal{O}$ given, and simply talk about the full abstractness of $\mathcal{D}$.

(2) Trivially, each $\mathcal{D}$ such that $\mathcal{O} = \mathcal{D}$ is fully abstract.

(3) An alternative characterization of full abstractness may be given in terms of what are called "congruence relations," cf. Exercise 17.2.

We shall devote Sections 17.2, 17.3 and 17.4 to a discussion of the full abstractness problem for the languages $\mathcal{L}_\delta$, $\mathcal{L}_{syn}$ and $\mathcal{L}_{svp}$, $\mathcal{L}_{aw}$, respectively.

17.2   A fully abstract $\mathcal{D}$ for $\mathcal{L}_\delta$

The case of $\mathcal{L}_\delta$ is particularly simple. Though the $\mathcal{D}$ as presented in Section 11.1 is not fully abstract (with respect to the $\mathcal{O}$ given there), it is not difficult to design a $\mathcal{D}'$ for $\mathcal{L}_\delta$ which satisfies $\mathcal{O} = \mathcal{D}'$, and is thus trivially fully abstract. Note that this implies that the branching $\mathcal{D}$ as given in Section 11.1 makes too many distinctions. E.g., there is no $\mathcal{L}_\delta$-context which motivates that $\mathcal{D}(a_1;(a_2 + a_3)) \neq \mathcal{D}((a_1;a_2) + (a_1;a_3))$.

Let $\mathcal{O}$ and $\mathbb{P}_O$ be as in Section 11.1. The new $\mathcal{D}'$ will employ a domain $\mathbb{P}_{D'}$ which equals $\mathbb{P}_O$, but for the customary deletion of ϵ from it. The precise definition follows:

Definition 17.4

(a) $(q \in) \mathbb{Q}_{D'} = Act^+ \cup Act^\omega \cup Act^* \cdot \{\delta\}$.

(b) $(p \in) \mathbb{P}_{D'} = \mathcal{P}_{nco}(\mathbb{Q}_{D'})$.

As we saw in Section 11.1, defining the semantic operators (';', '+') in the usual way—in particular satisfying the left-distributivity law $p;(p_1 + p_2) = (p;p_1) + (p;p_2)$—does not work. Instead of adapting the denotational domain—as we did in Section 11.1—we now follow another route, in that we adapt the semantic operators. The new definitions are uniform simplifications of those of Section 15.1.

Definition 17.5

(a) $;: \mathbb{Q}_{D'} \times \mathbb{Q}_{D'} \xrightarrow{1} \mathbb{Q}_{D'}$ is the unique function satisfying

$$\begin{aligned} a;q &= a \cdot q \\ \delta;q &= \delta \\ (a \cdot q');q &= a \cdot (q';q). \end{aligned}$$

The function $;: \mathbb{P}_{D'} \times \mathbb{P}_{D'} \to \mathbb{P}_{D'}$ is defined from this using the Lifting Lemma.

(b) $p_1 + p_2 = \{\, q \mid q \in p_1 \cup p_2, q \neq \delta \,\} \cup \{\, \delta \mid \delta \in p_1 \cap p_2 \,\}$.

The definition of $\mathcal{D}'$ for $\mathcal{L}_\delta$ is now simple:

Definition 17.6 $\mathcal{D}': \mathcal{L}_\delta \to \mathbb{P}_{D'}$ is the unique function satisfying $\mathcal{D}'(a) = \{a\}$, $\mathcal{D}'(\mathrm{stop}) = \{\delta\}$, $\mathcal{D}'(x) = \mathcal{D}'(D(x))$, and

$$\mathcal{D}'(s_1 \ \mathrm{op}\ s_2) \ = \ \mathcal{D}'(s_1) \ \mathrm{op}\ \mathcal{D}'(s_2), \ \ \mathrm{op} \in \{;, +\}.$$

There remains the proof that $\mathcal{O} = \mathcal{D}'$ on $\mathcal{L}_\delta$. It is convenient to work with $\mathcal{O}$ defined in terms of simple resumptions ($r ::= \mathrm{E} \mid s$) and to base $\mathcal{T}_\delta$ on this. That is, we take $\mathcal{T}_\delta = \mathcal{T}_{cf}$, with $\mathcal{T}_{cf}$ as in Section 2.2.1. Let Φ be the usual operator defining $\mathcal{O}$ (as in Definition 11.4). We prove

Lemma 17.7 $\Phi(\mathcal{D}') = \mathcal{D}'$.

Proof We show that, for all r, $\Phi(\mathcal{D}')(r) = \mathcal{D}'(r)$. Two subcases.

$[s_1;s_2]$

$$\begin{aligned} &\Phi(\mathcal{D}')(s_1;s_2) \\ =\ &\bigcup \{\, a \cdot \mathcal{D}'(r) \mid s_1;s_2 \xrightarrow{a} r \,\} \cup \{\, \delta \mid s_1;s_2 \not\rightarrow \,\} \\ =\ &[s_1;s_2 \not\rightarrow \text{ iff } s_1 \not\rightarrow] \\ &\bigcup \{\, a \cdot \mathcal{D}'(s';s_2) \mid s_1 \xrightarrow{a} s' \,\} \cup \bigcup \{\, a \cdot \mathcal{D}'(s_2) \mid s_1 \xrightarrow{a} \mathrm{E} \,\} \cup \{\, \delta \mid s_1 \not\rightarrow \,\} \\ =\ &[\{\delta\};p = \{\delta\}] \\ &(\bigcup \{\, a \cdot \mathcal{D}'(s') \mid s_1 \xrightarrow{a} s' \,\} \cup \{\, a \mid s_1 \xrightarrow{a} \mathrm{E} \,\} \cup \{\, \delta \mid s_1 \not\rightarrow \,\});\mathcal{D}'(s_2) \\ =\ &\Phi(\mathcal{D}')(s_1);\mathcal{D}'(s_2) \\ =\ &[\text{ind. hyp.}]\ \mathcal{D}'(s_1);\mathcal{D}'(s_2) \\ =\ &\mathcal{D}'(s_1;s_2). \end{aligned}$$

$[s_1 + s_2]$

$$\begin{aligned} &\Phi(\mathcal{D}')(s_1 + s_2) \\ =\ &\bigcup \{\, a \cdot \mathcal{D}'(r) \mid s_1 + s_2 \xrightarrow{a} r \,\} \cup \{\, \delta \mid s_1 + s_2 \not\rightarrow \,\} \\ =\ & \\ &\bigcup \{\, a \cdot \mathcal{D}'(r_1) \mid s_1 \xrightarrow{a} r_1 \,\} \cup \bigcup \{\, a \cdot \mathcal{D}'(r_2) \mid s_2 \xrightarrow{a} r_2 \,\} \cup \{\, \delta \mid s_1 \not\rightarrow \wedge s_2 \not\rightarrow \,\} \end{aligned}$$

$$
\begin{aligned}
&= \quad [\delta \in p_1 + p_2 \text{ iff } (\delta \in p_1) \wedge (\delta \in p_2),\, p + \{\delta\} = p] \\
&\quad\; (\bigcup\{ a \cdot \mathcal{D}'(r_1) \mid s_1 \xrightarrow{a} r_1 \} \cup \{ \delta \mid s_1 \not\rightarrow \}) + \\
&\quad\; (\bigcup\{ a \cdot \mathcal{D}'(r_2) \mid s_2 \xrightarrow{a} r_2 \} \cup \{ \delta \mid s_2 \not\rightarrow \}) \\
&= \quad \Phi(\mathcal{D}')(s_1) + \Phi(\mathcal{D}')(s_2) \\
&= \quad [\text{ind. hyp.}]\ \mathcal{D}'(s_1) + \mathcal{D}'(s_2) \\
&= \quad \mathcal{D}'(s_1 + s_2). \qquad\qquad\qquad\qquad\qquad\qquad\qquad\quad \square
\end{aligned}
$$

$\mathcal{O} = \mathcal{D}'$ now follows in the usual way, and we have shown full abstractness of $\mathcal{D}'$. The $\mathcal{D}$ for $\mathcal{L}_\delta$ from Section 11.1 makes too many distinctions. Our reason for its introduction there was that is provides a particularly simple setting for a branching domain at work, thus preparing the way for the subsequent chapters in Part III. In the next section, we shall show that, for $\mathcal{L}_{syn}$ as well, the full branching domain determines a too refined structure. However, the situation is more challenging than that for $\mathcal{L}_\delta$, in that we cannot simply devise some $\mathcal{D}'$ such that $\mathcal{O} = \mathcal{D}'$. Instead, we shall develop the first non-trivial fully abstract model discussed in our book.

17.3 A fully abstract $\mathcal{D}$ for $\mathcal{L}_{syn}$

17.3.1 Syntax and operational semantics

We first recall the syntax for $\mathcal{L}_{syn}$. We distinguish in the set $(a \in)\, Act$ two disjoint parts:

> $(b \in)\, IAct$ the *internal* actions
> $(c \in)\, SAct$ the *synchronization* actions.

In $IAct$, we also include the silent action τ. For brevity, from now on we abbreviate $SAct$ to S. Moreover, we shall postulate that

S is a *finite* set.

(This postulate results in a simplification of several mathematical arguments below.) We also recall the mapping $\bar{\cdot}\colon S \to S$, satisfying $\bar{\bar{c}} = c$. On the basis of Act, $Stat$ for $\mathcal{L}_{syn}$ has the usual syntax $s ::= a \mid x \mid (s;s) \mid (s + s) \mid (s \| s)$. $GStat$ and $Decl$ are as before.

In Section 11.2 we introduced a linear operational semantics $\mathcal{O}\colon \mathcal{L}_{syn} \to \mathbb{P}_O$ and a branching denotational semantics $\mathcal{D}\colon \mathcal{L}_{syn} \to \mathbb{P}_D$. We moreover employed as auxiliary operational semantics the (branching) $\mathcal{O}^*\colon \mathcal{L}_{syn} \to \mathbb{P}_D$, for which we showed that $\mathcal{O}^* = \mathcal{D}$. In the present subsection, we shall introduce two new *intermediate* (operational and denotational) semantics in terms of what are to be called the *ready domain* and the *failure domain*. In order to distinguish the various types of domains and semantics, we shall from now on use subscripts or superscripts L, R, F and B to distinguish them. The earlier $\mathbb{P}_O$, $\mathcal{O}$, $\mathbb{P}_D$, $\mathcal{D}$ and $\mathcal{O}^*$ will be denoted by $\mathbb{P}_O^L$, $\mathcal{O}_L$, $\mathbb{P}_D^B$, $\mathcal{D}_B$ and $\mathcal{O}_B$ (recall that $\mathcal{O}^*$ is a branching semantics).

We shall now introduce the new domains $\mathbb{P}_O^R$, $\mathbb{P}_O^F$ and the operational semantics $\mathcal{O}_R \colon \mathcal{L}_{syn} \to \mathbb{P}_O^R$ and $\mathcal{O}_F \colon \mathcal{L}_{syn} \to \mathbb{P}_O^F$. The corresponding denotational models will follow in Section 17.3.2. The ready domain and -semantics are introduced not so much for their own sake, but as a step on the way to the understanding of the failure domain and -semantics. The central result of Section 17.3 will be that the denotational failure semantics $\mathcal{D}_F$ is fully abstract with respect to the (linear) operational semantics $\mathcal{O}_L$ (thus implying, among other facts, that the denotational semantics $\mathcal{D}_B$ of Section 11.2 is *not* fully abstract). We first introduce two new notations.

Notation 17.8 Let $(D|s) \in \mathcal{L}_{syn}$.

(a) $init(D|s) = \{\, a \mid \exists r [s \xrightarrow{a}_D r] \,\}$.

(b) $act(D|s)$ equals the set of all actions occurring in s or any of the $D(x)$, for $x \in$ *P Var*.

In the sequel, we shall once more omit the D's. We have that $init(s)$ is the set of all *initial* steps which can be made by s. We shall in particular be interested in the situation that $init(s) \subseteq S$, i.e., that s can perform as first step only synchronization actions. (The set $act(s)$ will play a role in Section 17.3.3.)

We now describe the domain of *readies*. We shall explain it in terms of the associated semantics $\mathcal{O}_R$ which is intermediate between $\mathcal{O}_L$ and $\mathcal{O}_B$ in the sense that it makes more distinctions than $\mathcal{O}_L$ and fewer than $\mathcal{O}_B$. Unlike $\mathcal{O}_L$, $\mathcal{O}_R$ does not yield only sequences of actions, but contains already some branching information (but less than is present in $\mathcal{O}_B$): Instead of using a single symbol (δ) to denote deadlock, in $\mathcal{O}_R$ this information is refined by yielding, in case of deadlock, the set of all $c \in S$ that could be taken next—by the s at hand—if only a matching $\bar{c}$ were to be offered in parallel. We now introduce the domain $\mathbb{P}_O^R$:

Definition 17.9 Let $(w \in) Act^\infty$ be as usual, and let

$$(q \in) Act_R \;=\; Act^\infty \cup Act^* \cdot \mathcal{P}(S).$$

Let X range over $\mathcal{P}(S)$. For easier readability, we shall use the pair (w, X)—rather than $w \cdot X$—to range over $Act^* \cdot \mathcal{P}(S)$. Such a pair will be called a *ready pair*. The set Act_R is supplied with the usual Baire metric. In the definition of this, the set of $\mathcal{P}(S)$ is regarded simply as an alphabet. Thus, for $X_1 \neq X_2$, $d(X_1, X_2) = 1$ and $d((a, X_1), (a, X_2)) = \frac{1}{2}$. Note also that, in the current setting, we do not have that $w \cdot X$ (or, equivalently, (w, X)) equals $\{ w \cdot x \mid x \in X \}$. We next put

$$(p \in) \mathbb{P}_O^R \;=\; \mathcal{P}_{nco}(Act_R).$$

The elements of $\mathbb{P}_O^R$ will be called ready sets or readies. Prefixing on Act_R is defined by taking $a \cdot q$ as usual for $q \in Act^\infty$, and $a \cdot (w, X) = (aw, X)$.

We next define $\mathcal{O}_R[\![\cdot]\!] : \mathcal{L}_{syn} \to \mathbb{P}_O^R$.

Definition 17.10 Let $(r \in) Res$ be as usual. $\mathcal{O}_R : Res \to \mathbb{P}_O^R$ is the unique function satisfying $\mathcal{O}_R(\mathrm{E}) = \{\epsilon\}$ and

$$
\begin{aligned}
\mathcal{O}_R(s) \;=\; & \bigcup \{ a \cdot \mathcal{O}_R(r) \mid s \xrightarrow{a} r \} \cup \\
& \{ (\epsilon, init(s)) \mid init(s) \subseteq S \}.
\end{aligned}
$$

$\mathcal{O}_R[\![\cdot]\!]$ is standard from $\mathcal{O}_R$. Note that, contrary to what we have for $\mathcal{O}_L$, $\mathcal{O}_R[\![s]\!]$ contains sequences which are words on Act rather than on $IAct$ only. Thus, single sided synchronization actions c are visible. Further deadlock information in $\mathcal{O}_R[\![s]\!]$ is represented by a pair (w, X), to be interpreted as follows: After performing the actions in w, the computation has reached a point from which it can only perform synchronization actions; these are collected in the set X.

We proceed with the definition of the failure domain. We use it to define the failure semantics $\mathcal{O}_F$ which is, like $\mathcal{O}_R$, more distinctive than $\mathcal{O}_L$. However, it is less distinctive than $\mathcal{O}_R$. Instead of ready pairs, the function $\mathcal{O}_F$ yields *failure pairs* (w, X) which are again elements in $Act^* \cdot \mathcal{P}(S)$, but now have a different interpretation. The set X is called a refusal set, and contains those synchronization actions (but not necessarily all) that are to be refused, even if a matching action would be offered in parallel. The complete definition is given in

Definition 17.11 Let $Act_F = Act_R$. We call a subset V of Act_F *downward closed* in case, for all $(w, X) \in V$ and $Y \subseteq X$, also $(w, Y) \in V$. We now put

$$\mathbb{P}_O^F \;=\; \{ V \subseteq Act_F \mid V \text{ is nonempty, compact and downward closed} \}.$$

We leave to the reader the easy proof that the additional property of downward closedness preserves completeness of $\mathbb{P}_O^F$. We next define $\mathcal{O}_F$ for $\mathcal{L}_{syn}$:

Definition 17.12 $\mathcal{O}_F\colon Res \to \mathbb{P}_O^F$ is the unique function satisfying $\mathcal{O}_F(\mathrm{E}) = \{\epsilon\}$ and

$$\mathcal{O}_F(s) = \bigcup\{\, a \cdot \mathcal{O}_F(r) \mid s \xrightarrow{a} r \,\} \cup \\ \{\, (\epsilon, X) \mid init(s) \subseteq S, X \subseteq S \setminus init(s) \,\}.$$

$\mathcal{O}_F[\![\cdot]\!]$ is as usual from this. (The reader who checks the details here will note that the compactness of $\mathcal{O}_F[\![s]\!]$ depends upon the finiteness of S.) The fact that $\mathcal{O}_F$ is less distinctive than $\mathcal{O}_R$ is caused by taking the downward closure of $S \setminus init(s)$ in the definition of $\mathcal{O}_F$.

We next present some examples illustrating the difference between $\mathcal{O}_F$ and $\mathcal{O}_R$ (and $\mathcal{O}_L$, $\mathcal{O}_B$). We put

$$
\begin{aligned}
s_1 &= b_1;b_2;(c_1 + c_2) \\
s_2 &= (b_1;b_2;c_1) + (b_1;b_2;(c_1 + c_2)) + (b_1;b_2;c_2) \\
s_3 &= (b_1;b_2;c_1) + (b_1;b_2;c_2) \\
s_4 &= b_1;(b_2;c_1 + b_2;c_2)
\end{aligned}
$$

We now list the $\mathcal{O}_L$, $\mathcal{O}_F$ and $\mathcal{O}_R$ meaning of these statements (leaving the $\mathcal{O}_B$-case to the reader).

$[s_1]$

$$
\begin{aligned}
\mathcal{O}_L[\![s_1]\!] &= \{\, b_1 b_2 \delta \,\} \\
\mathcal{O}_F[\![s_1]\!] &= \{\, b_1 b_2 c_1, b_1 b_2 c_2, \,\} \cup \{\, (b_1 b_2, X) \mid X \subseteq S \setminus \{c_1, c_2\} \,\} \\
\mathcal{O}_R[\![s_1]\!] &= \{\, b_1 b_2 c_1, b_1 b_2 c_2, (b_1 b_2, \{c_1, c_2\}) \,\}.
\end{aligned}
$$

$[s_2]$

$$
\begin{aligned}
\mathcal{O}_L[\![s_2]\!] &= \mathcal{O}_L[\![s_1]\!] \\
\mathcal{O}_F[\![s_2]\!] &= \{\, b_1 b_2 c_1, b_1 b_2 c_2 \,\} \cup \{\, (b_1 b_2, X) \mid X \subseteq S \setminus \{c_1\} \,\} \cup \\
&\quad \{\, (b_1 b_2, X) \mid X \subseteq S \setminus \{c_2\} \,\} \\
\mathcal{O}_R[\![s_2]\!] &= \{\, b_1 b_2 c_1, b_1 b_2 c_2, (b_1 b_2, \{c_1\}), (b_1 b_2, \{c_2\}), (b_1 b_2, \{c_1, c_2\}) \,\}.
\end{aligned}
$$

$[s_3]$

$$
\begin{aligned}
\mathcal{O}_L[\![s_3]\!] &= \mathcal{O}_L[\![s_2]\!] = \mathcal{O}_L[\![s_1]\!] \\
\mathcal{O}_F[\![s_3]\!] &= \mathcal{O}_F[\![s_2]\!] \\
\mathcal{O}_R[\![s_3]\!] &= \{\, b_1 b_2 c_1, b_1 b_2 c_2, (b_1 b_2, \{c_1\}), (b_1 b_2, \{c_2\}) \,\}.
\end{aligned}
$$

$[s_4]$

$$\begin{aligned}
\mathcal{O}_L[\![s_4]\!] &= \mathcal{O}_L[\![s_3]\!] = \mathcal{O}_L[\![s_2]\!] = \mathcal{O}_L[\![s_1]\!] \\
\mathcal{O}_F[\![s_4]\!] &= \mathcal{O}_F[\![s_3]\!] = \mathcal{O}_F[\![s_2]\!] \\
\mathcal{O}_R[\![s_4]\!] &= \mathcal{O}_R[\![s_3]\!].
\end{aligned}$$

Noting that $\mathcal{O}_B[\![s_4]\!] \neq \mathcal{O}_B[\![s_3]\!]$, we conclude that from $\mathcal{O}_L$ to $\mathcal{O}_B$, the semantics are more distinctive.

Since $\mathcal{O}_R$ only serves, for our present purposes, to pave the way for $\mathcal{O}_F$, we shall from now on no longer be concerned with ready sets or ready semantics, and consider solely the failure models (in addition to the linear ones).

17.3.2 Denotational semantics, relating $\mathcal{O}$ and $\mathcal{D}$

As always, the core of the denotational semantics consists in the definitions of the semantic operators. In this—and the next—subsection, we shall not aim at supplying all mathematical details. Rather, we shall be satisfied with outlining the main semantic ideas, and leave some detailed mathematical verifications to the industrious reader. Firstly, we shall work with a denotational domain which is obtained from the operational one by imposing some extra conditions.

Definition 17.13 $(p \in) \, \mathbb{P}_D^F$ consists of all elements of $\mathbb{P}_O^F$ which satisfy the conditions

$$(w, X) \in p \;\; \Rightarrow \;\; \exists c \in S \setminus X, q \in Act_F[wcq \in p] \tag{17.4a}$$
$$wcq \in p \;\; \Rightarrow \;\; \exists b, q'[wbq' \in p] \lor \exists X \subseteq S[(w, X) \in p]. \tag{17.4b}$$

Properties (17.4a,b) are in fact satisfied by all elements of $\mathbb{P}_O^F$ which are obtained as $\mathcal{O}_F$-meaning of some $s \in \mathcal{L}_{syn}$. E.g., if wcq results as meaning of some statement—thus signaling a potential deadlock—then it can either make as well some internal step (some wbq')—thus avoiding the deadlock possibility—or it can make only synchronization steps, thus resulting in a (w, X) term in the outcome.

Well-definedness of $\mathcal{O}_F$ does not depend upon conditions (17.4a,b), but the well-definedness of the semantic operators and of the—still to be defined—abstraction mapping $abs_F : \mathbb{P}_D^F \to \mathbb{P}_O^F$ does rely on it. We omit verification of the fact that conditions (17.4a,b) are preserved under taking limits.

We proceed with the definition of the semantic operators (';', '$\|$', '+') on $\mathbb{P}_D^F$. We follow the approach as used earlier in, e.g., Definition 7.6. In particular, we again use the notation $p_a = \{ q \mid a \cdot q \in p, q \neq \epsilon \}$. Also recall that we have that $(w, X) = w \cdot (\epsilon, X)$.

Definition 17.14 Let, for $X \subseteq S$, $\bar{X} = \{\bar{c} \mid c \in X\}$.

(a) The operators $;, \| : \mathbb{P}_D^F \times \mathbb{P}_D^F \xrightarrow{1} \mathbb{P}_D^F$ are the unique functions satisfying

$$
\begin{aligned}
p_1;p_2 &= \bigcup\{a \cdot ((p_1)_a;p_2) \mid (p_1)_a \neq \emptyset\} \cup \bigcup\{a \cdot p_2 \mid a \in p_1\} \cup \\
&\quad \{(\epsilon, X) \mid (\epsilon, X) \in p_1\} \\
p_1 \| p_2 &= (p_1 \mathbin{\underline{\|}} p_2) \cup (p_2 \mathbin{\underline{\|}} p_1) \cup (p_1 \mathbin{\nparallel} p_2) \cup (p_1 | p_2) \\
p_1 \mathbin{\underline{\|}} p_2 &= \bigcup\{a \cdot ((p_1)_a \| p_2) \mid (p_1)_a \neq \emptyset\} \cup \bigcup\{a \cdot p_2 \mid a \in p_1\} \\
p_1 \mathbin{\nparallel} p_2 &= \{(\epsilon, X) \mid (\epsilon, Z_1) \in p_1, (\epsilon, Z_2) \in p_2, \\
&\qquad\qquad (S \setminus Z_1) \cap (\overline{S \setminus Z_2}) = \emptyset, X \subseteq Z_1 \cap Z_2\} \\
p_1 | p_2 &= \bigcup\{\tau \cdot ((p_1)_c \| (p_2)_{\bar{c}}) \mid (p_1)_c \neq \emptyset, (p_2)_{\bar{c}} \neq \emptyset\} \cup \\
&\quad \bigcup\{\tau \cdot (p_2)_{\bar{c}} \mid c \in p_1, (p_2)_{\bar{c}} \neq \emptyset\} \cup \\
&\quad \bigcup\{\tau \cdot (p_1)_c \mid (p_1)_c \neq \emptyset, \bar{c} \in p_2\} \cup \{\tau \mid c \in p_1, \bar{c} \in p_2\}.
\end{aligned}
$$

(b) The operator $+: \mathbb{P}_D^F \times \mathbb{P}_D^F \xrightarrow{1} \mathbb{P}_D^F$ is defined by

$$
\begin{aligned}
p_1 + p_2 &= \{q \mid q \in (p_1 \cup p_2) \cap (Act^+ \cup Act^\omega \cup Act^+ \cdot \mathcal{P}(S))\} \cup \\
&\quad \{(\epsilon, X) \mid (\epsilon, X) \in p_1 \cap p_2\}.
\end{aligned}
$$

We add some brief explanation on these operators. The definition of ';' implies that $\{(w, X)\};p = \{(w, X)\}$, and, for $w' \in Act^+$, $\{w'\};\{(w, X)\} = \{(w';w, X)\}$ (with the right-hand ';' as in Chapter 1). Note how the expression for $p_1 + p_2$ in its first summand involves only those q which are not of the form (ϵ, X). The element $p_1 + p_2$ can deadlock in its first step only if both p_1 and p_2 contain some failure pair (ϵ, X): the synchronization actions that $p_1 + p_2$ can refuse are those that can be refused both by p_1 and p_2. Downward closedness of $p_1 + p_2$ follows from the downward closedness of p_1 and p_2. The definition of $p_1 \| p_2$ has the following components: $p_1 \mathbin{\underline{\|}} p_2$ and $p_2 \mathbin{\underline{\|}} p_1$ represent the familiar interleaving parts and $p_1 | p_2$ the synchronization case. The term $p_1 \mathbin{\nparallel} p_2$ describes the immediate deadlock behaviour of $p_1 \| p_2$: If p_1 contains some (ϵ, Z_1)—p_1 can refuse all actions in Z_1—and similarly for p_2, then $p_1 \| p_2$ can refuse the elements of each $X \subseteq Z_1 \cap Z_2$, *provided* $(S \setminus Z_1) \cap (\overline{S \setminus Z_2}) = \emptyset$, i.e., no synchronization between p_1 and p_2 is possible.

We omit the proof that these operators are well-defined and that they satisfy the usual nonexpansiveness/contractiveness properties. We immediately proceed with the definition of $\mathcal{D}_F: \mathcal{L}_{syn} \to \mathbb{P}_D^F$.

Definition 17.15 We put

$$\mathcal{D}_F(b) = \{b\}$$
$$\mathcal{D}_F(c) = \{c\} \cup \{(\epsilon, X) \mid X \subseteq S \setminus \{c\}\},$$

and the remaining clauses are as to be expected (as is $\mathcal{D}[\![\cdot]\!]$).

In Definitions 17.13, 17.14 and 17.15 we have prepared the result:

Theorem 17.16 $\mathcal{O}_F[\![\cdot]\!] = \mathcal{D}_F[\![\cdot]\!]$, *on* $\mathcal{L}_{syn}$.

Proof In outline, another application of the $\Phi(\mathcal{D}) = \mathcal{D}$ argument. Some details have to be checked, due to the new operators involved here. We refer to the literature (cf. Section 17.6) for a precise treatment. $\square$

17.3.3   Full abstractness

$\mathcal{D}_F$ is a (or, rather, *the*) fully abstract denotational semantics for $\mathcal{L}_{syn}$ (with respect to $\mathcal{O}_L$). The present section contains an outline of the proof of this fact. We begin with the easy part, establishing correctness.

Lemma 17.17 $\mathcal{D}_F$ *is correct for* $\mathcal{L}_{syn}$ *with respect to* $\mathcal{O}_L$.

Proof By Lemma 17.2 (and Theorem 17.16), it is sufficient to provide an abstraction mapping $abs_F \colon \mathbb{P}_D^F \to \mathbb{P}_O^L$ such that

$$\mathcal{O}_L = abs_F \circ \mathcal{O}_F. \tag{17.5}$$

We take for abs_F the function defined by

$$abs_F(p) = \{w \mid w \in p \cap IAct^\infty\} \cup \{w\delta \mid (w, X) \in p\}.$$

We omit the proof that abs_F is well-defined and satisfies (17.5). $\square$

We next establish completeness of $\mathcal{D}_F$. The proof relies on two technical definitions which form the key element in the construction of distinguishing $\mathcal{O}_L$-contexts (for statements s_1, s_2 with $\mathcal{D}_F(s_1) \neq \mathcal{D}_F(s_2)$). In this construction we shall employ—with respect to some statement s—an auxiliary internal action b such that $b \notin act(s)$ (cf. Notation 17.8b).

Definition 17.18

(a) The mapping $\tilde{\cdot}^b : Act^* \to IAct^*$ is given by

$$\tilde{\epsilon}^b \;=\; b$$
$$(aw)^{\tilde{\cdot}b} \;=\; \begin{cases} a\tilde{w}^b & \text{if } a \in IAct \\ b\tau b\tilde{w}^b & \text{if } a \in S. \end{cases}$$

(b) The mapping $\hat{\cdot}^b : Act^* \to Stat$ is given by

$$\hat{\epsilon}^b \;=\; b$$
$$(aw)^{\hat{\cdot}b} \;=\; \begin{cases} \hat{w}^b & \text{if } a \in IAct \\ b;\bar{a};b;\hat{w}^b & \text{if } a \in S. \end{cases}$$

The mappings $\tilde{\cdot}^b$ and $\hat{\cdot}^b$ have been designed such that the following two lemmas hold:

Lemma 17.19 *For all $s \in \mathcal{L}_{syn}$, $w \in Act^*$ and $b \in IAct \setminus act(s)$, we have*

$$\exists u \in IAct^\infty \cup IAct^* \cdot \{\delta\}[\tilde{w}^b u \in \mathcal{O}_L(s\|\hat{w}^b)] \;\; \textit{iff} \;\; \exists q \in Act_F[wq \in \mathcal{O}_F(s)].$$

Proof Induction on the length of w. $\square$

Lemma 17.20 *For all $s \in \mathcal{L}_{syn}$, $w \in Act^*$, $X \in \mathcal{P}(S)$ such that $X = \{c_1, \ldots, c_n\}$ $(n \geq 0)$ and $b \in IAct \setminus act(s)$, we have*

$$\tilde{w}^b \delta \in \mathcal{O}_L(s\|\hat{w}^b;(\bar{c}_1 + \cdots + \bar{c}_n)) \;\; \textit{iff} \;\; (w, X) \in \mathcal{O}_F(s).$$

Proof Induction of the length of w. $\square$

We are now ready for the proof of the main lemma, on which the proof of the full abstractness of $\mathcal{D}_F$ is based. In this proof, we assume that $IAct$ is an infinite set and that $PVar$ is a finite set. (Some comments on this follow below.)

Lemma 17.21 *Assume that IAct is infinite and PVar is finite. Let s_1, s_2 be such that $\mathcal{O}_F(s_1) \neq \mathcal{O}_F(s_2)$. Then there exists a context C such that $\mathcal{O}_L(C(s_1)) \neq \mathcal{O}_L(C(s_2))$.*

Proof Let $s_1, s_2 \in \mathcal{L}_{syn}$, and let $b \in IAct \setminus (act(s_1) \cup act(s_2))$. (Since we assume IAct to be infinite and PVar finite, the number of internal actions in $(D|s_1)$ and $(D|s_2)$ is finite, and it is always possible to find such a b.) Assume that $\mathcal{O}_F(s_1) \neq \mathcal{O}_F(s_2)$. Without loss of generality, we assume that there exists some $q \in \mathcal{O}_F(s_1) \setminus \mathcal{O}_F(s_2)$. We distinguish the following three cases:

(1) $q = w \in Act^*$. In this case we take $C(\cdot) = \cdot \| \hat{w}^b$. From Lemma 17.19 we deduce that $\tilde{w}^b \in \mathcal{O}_L(C(s_1))$ but $\tilde{w}^b \notin \mathcal{O}_L(C(s_2))$.

(2) $q = w \in Act^\omega$. Since $\mathcal{O}_F(s_1)$ and $\mathcal{O}_F(s_2)$ are closed sets, there exists a prefix v of w which is not a prefix of any element of $\mathcal{O}_F(s_2)$. In this case we take $C(\cdot) = \cdot \| \hat{v}^b$. From Lemma 17.19 we can deduce that $\exists u \in IAct^\infty \cup IAct^* \cdot \{\delta\}$ such that $\tilde{v}^b u \in \mathcal{O}_L(C(s_1))$ but $\tilde{v}^b u \notin \mathcal{O}_L(C(s_2))$.

(3) $q = (w, X)$. Assume $X \cap (act(s_1) \cup act(s_2)) = \{c_1, \ldots, c_n\}$. We take $C(\cdot) = \cdot \| (\hat{w}^b; (\bar{c}_1 + \cdots + \bar{c}_n))$. From Lemma 17.20 we can deduce that $\tilde{w}^b \delta \in \mathcal{O}_L(C(s_1))$ but $\tilde{w}^b \delta \notin \mathcal{O}_L(C(s_2))$. □

Remark Note how the condition that IAct be infinite is essential in the proof, in that it allows the finding of a fresh b. We believe—but have no proof—that $\mathcal{D}_F$ is not fully abstract in a setting where IAct is finite.

We can now state our main result:

Theorem 17.22 *$\mathcal{D}_F$ is fully abstract for $\mathcal{L}_{syn}$ with respect to $\mathcal{O}_L$.*

Proof Combine Theorem 17.16, Lemma 17.17 and Lemma 17.21. □

Besides its technical role in this theorem, the failure semantics is also important since it illustrates the essential role for domains which are situated in between the linear models of Part II and the branching models of Part III. In fact, a whole range of further domains has been developed in (especially) the theory of concurrency, of which the failure model is just one—albeit central—example. (Some references will be given in Section 17.6; cf. also Section 11.4.)

17.4   A fully abstract $\mathcal{D}$ for $\mathcal{L}_{aw}$

In this section, we shall be quite brief. The denotational semantic definitions for $\mathcal{L}_{aw}$ (of the semantic operators and of $\mathcal{D}$) are assembled from earlier material in our book. The proof of the full abstractness of $\mathcal{D}$ is just quoted from the literature, since it is too lengthy and complex to be reproduced here.

We first repeat the syntax for $\mathcal{L}_{aw}$.

Definition 17.23

$$s\,(\in \mathcal{L}_{aw}) \quad ::= \quad v := e \mid \mathsf{skip} \mid \mathsf{stop} \mid (s;s) \mid \mathsf{if}\ e\ \mathsf{then}\ s\ \mathsf{else}\ s\ \mathsf{fi} \mid$$
$$\mathsf{while}\ e\ \mathsf{do}\ s\ \mathsf{od} \mid (s\|s).$$

The definitions of $\mathbb{P}_O$, $\mathcal{T}_{aw}$ and $\mathcal{O}[\![\cdot]\!]\colon \mathcal{L}_{aw} \to \mathbb{P}_O$ are just as in Section 12.1.1. The denotational semantics for $\mathcal{L}_{aw}$ to be used here is essentially different from that of Section 12.1.2, in that we now use a *linear* domain (instead of the branching $\mathbb{P}_D$ used there). Fortunately, we happen to have the right domain already available: We simply used the domain $\mathbb{P}_{Df}^I$ as specified in Definition 15.6—but now with $\Sigma = IVar \to Val$ the usual set of states (and not the set of abstract substitutions used in Chapter 15). For simplicity, we use the notation $\mathbb{P}_{D'}$ instead of $\mathbb{P}_{Df}^I$ in the definitions to follow. We furthermore take over the definitions of the operators ';' and '$\|$' from Definition 15.7. Putting this together with the earlier design for $\mathcal{L}_{svp}$, we altogether have as definition for $\mathcal{D}'$:

Definition 17.24 $\mathcal{D}'\colon \mathcal{L}_{aw} \to \mathbb{P}_{D'}$ is given by

$$
\begin{aligned}
\mathcal{D}'(v := e) &= \{\, \langle \sigma, \sigma\{\alpha/v\}\rangle \mid \sigma \in \Sigma, \alpha = \mathcal{V}(e)(\sigma)\,\} \\
\mathcal{D}'(\mathsf{skip}) &= \{\, \langle \sigma, \sigma\rangle \mid \sigma \in \Sigma\,\} \\
\mathcal{D}'(\mathsf{stop}) &= \{\, \langle \sigma, \delta\rangle \mid \sigma \in \Sigma\,\} \\
\mathcal{D}'(s_1\ \mathsf{op}\ s_2) &= \mathcal{D}'(s_1)\ \mathsf{op}\ \mathcal{D}'(s_2),\ \ \mathsf{op} \in \{;, \|\} \\
&\qquad \text{(with the semantic ';', '$\|$' as in Definition 15.7)}
\end{aligned}
$$
$$\mathcal{D}'(\mathsf{if}\cdots\mathsf{fi}), \mathcal{D}'(\mathsf{while}\cdots\mathsf{od})\colon \text{ as in Definition 7.10.}$$

Let $abs'\colon \mathbb{P}_{D'} \to \mathbb{P}_O$ be as in Definition 15.11. As in Theorem 15.12, we can prove

Theorem 17.25 $\mathcal{O} = abs' \circ \mathcal{D}'$, on $\mathcal{L}_{aw}$.

Proof Standard $\square$

Finally, we have as important result the

Proposition 17.26 $\mathcal{D}'$ *is fully abstract with respect to* $\mathcal{O}$.

We omit the complicated proof of this fact (cf. Section 17.6). For $\mathcal{L}_{svp}$—i.e., $\mathcal{L}_{aw}$ without the stop-statement—almost the same proof applies, and we have the following

Corollary 17.27 *Let* $\mathcal{L}_{svp}$ *and the associated semantic definitions be as in Chapter 7. The denotational semantics for* $\mathcal{L}_{svp}$ *is fully abstract with respect to its operational semantics.*

Nonuniform languages where parallelism is combined with communication require a mixture of the techniques from Section 17.3 and the just quoted results. Both the definitions and the proofs of the relevant theorems are difficult, and we refrain from an attempt to summarize this material here. For many other languages ($\mathcal{L}_{rv}$ is just one example), the full abstractness problem has hardly been explored. In general, the constructions necessary to establish completeness of some $\mathcal{D}$ are quite intricate, and many open problems remain in this area.

17.5   Exercises

Exercise 17.1   Determine $\mathcal{O}_B[\![s_i]\!]$ with s_i as given after Definition 17.12, $i = 1, \ldots, 4$.

Exercise 17.2

(a) Let '$\sim$' be an equivalence relation on $\mathcal{L}$. We call '$\sim$' a *congruence* relation in case, for all contexts $C[\cdot]$,

$$s_1 \sim s_2 \quad \Rightarrow \quad C[s_1] \sim C[s_2].$$

Let $s_1 \sim^c s_2$ be defined by

$$s_1 \sim^c s_2 \quad \Leftrightarrow \quad \forall C[\cdot]\,[\,C[s_1] \sim C[s_2]\,].$$

Prove

(i) $\sim^c$ is a congruence relation

(ii) $\sim^c \subseteq \sim$

(iii) For any congruence relation '$\sim'$' on $\mathcal{L}$, we have $\sim' \subseteq \sim^c$.

(b) For any semantic mapping $\mathcal{M}: \mathcal{L} \to \mathbb{P}$, put

$$s_1 \sim_\mathcal{M} s_2 \quad \Leftrightarrow \quad \mathcal{M}[\![s_1]\!] = \mathcal{M}[\![s_2]\!].$$

Prove: $\mathcal{D}$ is fully abstract with respect to $\mathcal{O}$ iff $\sim_\mathcal{D} = \sim^c_\mathcal{O}$. Infer that $\mathcal{D}$ is fully abstract with respect to $\mathcal{O}$ iff $\sim_\mathcal{D}$ is the largest congruence relation contained in $\sim_\mathcal{O}$.

Exercise 17.3 Complete the proofs of Lemmas 17.19 and 17.20.

17.6 Bibliographical notes

The full abstractness problem for programming languages was first raised by Milner ([Mil73]). The definition of $\mathcal{D}$ for $\mathcal{L}_\delta$ is a greatly simplified version of a definition such as in [BKPR93b] (cf. also [BKPR91a]). The failure set model for $\mathcal{L}_{syn}$ is from [BHR84] (see also [BR84]). The ready set model occurs, e.g., in [OH86] ([BMOZ88] describes an application of it). The first proof of the full abstractness of the failure set model—for a (recursionless) language from the process algebra family—was given in [BKO88]. Our proof is a considerably simplified (unpublished) version, due to Van Breugel, of the metric based proof in [Rut89] (in turn based on [BKO88]). Several results only sketched in Chapter 17—such as the proof of Theorem 17.16—can be found in [Rut89].

The full abstractness results for $\mathcal{L}_{aw}$ (and $\mathcal{L}_{svp}$) are from [HBR94]. Closely related results—for a language which also includes a coroutine construct—have been described in [HP79]. In [Hor93b], several detailed studies are reported about full abstractness for languages with concurrency, including some languages combining features of $\mathcal{L}_{syn}$ and $\mathcal{L}_{aw}$. Further references—often presenting quite complex constructions establishing completeness—include [Hor92, Hor93a].

In the context of logic programming, some references on full abstraction are [GCLS88, BP91, BKPR91a]; references in the area of functional programming are [Mil77, BCL85, KCF93, AMJ94].

18 Second-order Assignment

So far, we have always based the semantics of nonuniform languages (ultimately) upon simple values from *Val*—appearing through the states (from $\Sigma = IVar \rightarrow Val$) in the various domains used up to now. In this chapter, we shall study a generalization of this, in that the objects manipulated are not just simple values, but as well *functions* (from states to (sequences of) states). Such an extension of individual to functional values is usually called a higher-order phenomenon. Here, we shall restrict the attention to a particularly simple setting, where the higher-order—more precisely, second-order—notion takes the form of *second-order assignment*, couched in a language which we baptize $\mathcal{L}_{as,2}$. Our primary motivation for studying this language is that it requires the use of a domain the specification of which necessitates an essential generalization of our earlier techniques. Recall that in Part III we have worked with domains solving a domain equation

$$\mathbb{P} \cong \mathcal{F}(\mathbb{P}) \tag{18.1}$$

with $\mathcal{F}$ *monotonic*. The domain on which we want to base the (denotational) semantics for $\mathcal{L}_{as,2}$ will involve a *nonmonotonic* $\mathcal{F}$. More specifically, we shall employ an $\mathcal{F}$ involving the function space constructor $\cdot \xrightarrow{1} \cdot$, with the unknown $\mathbb{P}$ appearing on the left-hand side. In general (see Exercise 10.2 for a counterexample), such $\mathcal{F}$ are not monotonic, and the method of Chapter 10 does not apply. In Appendix C, we shall describe a generalization of the purely topological approach of Chapter 10 to a setting where we work in a *category* of complete ultrametric spaces. This allows a generalization of the notion of *contractive*, as well as another version of Banach's theorem, resulting in the proposition that (18.1) has a solution for all contractive $\mathcal{F}$ (whether monotonic or not). Once such a solution is available, the semantic definitions proper can be given wholly within the metric framework, without appealing anew to categorical tools. Accordingly, apart from the matter of the solvability of (18.1), we can proceed as usual, applying the, by now standard, techniques. In addition, a few new aspects are treated. E.g., we shall now work with syntactic versus semantic states, where in the former we store statements as values for procedure values, and in the latter *meanings* of statements. This induces the need for a more complex relationship between $\mathcal{O}$ and $\mathcal{D}$ for $\mathcal{L}_{as,2}$, involving a mapping between syntactic and semantic states as an essential ingredient.

18.1 A language with second-order assignment

The language $\mathcal{L}_{as,2}$ is a simple nonuniform language in the style of $\mathcal{L}_{wh}$. As important new feature it includes *second-order assignment*, syntactically expressed by the construct

$$x := s \tag{18.2}$$

for x a procedure variable and s a statement (itself from $\mathcal{L}_{as,2}$). This should be contrasted with the assignment statement $v := e$, with v an *individual* variable (and e some expression). To bring out the difference with (18.2), we might call $v := e$ a *first-order* assignment.

The language $\mathcal{L}_{as,2}$ furthermore includes the notion—just as in $\mathcal{L}_{rec}$, say—of *calling* a procedure variable x by simply writing x as a statement. For example, the combined effect of the statement

$$x := (v := 1); x \tag{18.3}$$

is that to x is assigned the statement $v := 1$, and, next, the 'call' of x results in the execution of $v := 1$. In case (18.3) is followed by a second assignment to x, this overwrites the first one. Consider the program

$$x := (v := 1); x; x := (v := v + 2); x.$$

Here, the second call of x has the effect of executing $v := v + 2$, thus setting v to 3. Briefly, the *static* binding resulting—in various earlier languages—from a declaration D is now replaced by a dynamically changing association of statements with procedure variables. Note also that the assignment $x := s$ allows the same kind of recursion as was possible through declarations. Consider, for example, the assignment $x :=$ if $v = 0$ then $w := 1$ else $v := v - 1; x; v := v + 1$ fi.

We next provide some—as yet informal—intuition for the execution of $x := s$. Let us recall how we assigned a meaning to $v := e$. For any state σ, the value, say α, of the expression e is determined, and the state is updated to $\sigma_1 = \sigma\{\alpha/v\}$. After this, in the operational approach the relevant resumption is executed (acting on σ_1), and in the denotational setting the continuation at hand is applied to σ_1. Note how there is little difference in the actual handling of the assignment, in that both $\mathcal{O}$ and $\mathcal{D}$ determine, for the given σ, $\alpha = \mathcal{V}(e)(\sigma)$, and then continue with $\sigma\{\alpha/v\}$. In the treatment of $x := s$, there is more difference between the operational and the denotational case.

In the operational approach we store the statement s—a *syntactic* entity—as value for x in the state σ. A subsequent call of x will retrieve the current value of x (here s) from σ. In the denotational setting, we instead use what may be called *semantic* states—for which we shall use the variable ρ—and store and retrieve *meanings* $p = \mathcal{D}(s)$ through such a semantic ρ. In outline, we shall have as effect of

$(x := s;x)$ that first the current ρ is updated to $\rho\{p/x\}$, with $p = \mathcal{D}(s)$, and next, the call of x results in retrieving p from ρ, and doing whatever p prescribes. Again, we will have to make sure that the relevant definitions can handle recursion.

18.2   Syntax and operational semantics

In the syntax for $\mathcal{L}_{as,2}$, the syntactic classes $(v \in)IVar$, $(x \in)PVar$ and $(e \in)Exp$ are as usual. Since second order assignment allows expression of (general) recursion, there is no need to include the while statement (let alone skip) in the syntax.

Definition 18.1

(a) $s\,(\in Stat) ::= v := e \mid x := s \mid x \mid (s;s) \mid$ if e then s else s fi.

(b) $(\pi \in)\mathcal{L}_{as,2} = Stat$.

Resumptions have the standard form for a sequential language.

Definition 18.2 $r\,(\in Res) ::= \mathrm{E} \mid (s{:}r)$.

In the semantics for $\mathcal{L}_{as,2}$, we shall work with two kinds of states. The *syntactic* states from $(\sigma \in)\Sigma$ will play a role in the operational definitions, whereas the *semantic* ones from $(\rho \in)\mathrm{R}$ will figure in the denotational ones.

The syntactic states are still quite simple, and involve no more than a natural extension of the states as used on many occasions before (starting with Definition 1.52). The new feature is that the state should now be able to accommodate information both about the individual variables and about the procedure variables. This is taken care of in

Definition 18.3

(a) $\Sigma = (IVar \to Val) \times (PVar \to Stat)$.

(b) For $\sigma = (\sigma_1, \sigma_2)$, we write $\sigma\{\alpha/v\}$ as short-hand for $(\sigma_1\{\alpha/v\}, \sigma_2)$, and $\sigma\{s/x\}$ as short-hand for $(\sigma_1, \sigma_2\{s/x\})$. Also, we shall often use $\sigma(v)$ and $\sigma(x)$ instead of the more precise $\sigma_1(v)$ and $\sigma_2(x)$.

It should be obvious how the definition of $\mathcal{V}(e)(\sigma)$—cf. Definition 1.71—has to be modified to cater for the new type of states.

Once (Res and) Σ is understood, the rules for $\mathcal{T}_{as,2}$ will be clear as straightforward variations on our earlier specifications.

Definition 18.4 $\mathcal{T}_{as,2} = (Res \times \Sigma, \Sigma, \rightarrow, Spec)$, where $Spec$ consists of the following axioms and rules

- $$[(v := e){:}r, \sigma] \rightarrow [r, \sigma\{\alpha/v\}] \qquad \text{where } \alpha = \mathcal{V}(e)(\sigma) \qquad \text{(Ass,1)}$$

- $$[(x := s){:}r, \sigma] \rightarrow [r, \sigma\{s/x\}] \qquad\qquad\qquad\qquad\qquad \text{(Ass,2)}$$

- $$[x{:}r, \sigma] \rightarrow [\sigma(x){:}r, \sigma] \qquad\qquad\qquad\qquad\qquad\quad \text{(PVar)}$$

- $$[(s_1;s_2){:}r, \sigma] \rightarrow_0 [s_1{:}(s_2{:}r), \sigma] \qquad\qquad\qquad\qquad \text{(Seq)}$$

- $$[\text{if } e \text{ then } s_1 \text{ else } s_2 \text{ fi}{:}r, \sigma] \rightarrow_0 [s_1{:}r, \sigma] \qquad \text{if } \mathcal{V}(e)(\sigma) = tt \qquad \text{(If 1)}$$

  $$[\text{if } e \text{ then } s_1 \text{ else } s_2 \text{ fi}{:}r, \sigma] \rightarrow_0 [s_2{:}r, \sigma] \qquad \text{if } \mathcal{V}(e)(\sigma) = ff \qquad \text{(If 2)}$$

The new rules are (Ass,2) and (PVar). By (Ass,2), the statement which is the right-hand side of the assignment is stored in the current state. The rule (PVar) specifies that execution of x in the current state σ amounts to execution of $\sigma(x)$, i.e., of the statement stored in σ as value for x.

The definition of $\mathcal{O}$ for $\mathcal{L}_{as,2}$ based on $\mathcal{T}_{as,2}$ is completely standard. No element of nondeterminism is involved, so we may take $\mathbb{P}_O$ simply as in Definition 1.57. $\mathcal{O}[\![\cdot]\!]{:}\mathcal{L}_{as,2} \rightarrow \mathbb{P}_O$ is given in

Definition 18.5

(a) $\mathbb{P}_O = \Sigma \rightarrow \Sigma^\infty$.

(b) $\mathcal{O}{:}Res \times \Sigma \rightarrow \Sigma^\infty$ is the unique function satisfying $\mathcal{O}(\mathrm{E}, \sigma) = \epsilon$ and

$$\mathcal{O}(s{:}r, \sigma) \;=\; \sigma' \cdot \mathcal{O}(r', \sigma'), \quad \text{where } [s{:}r, \sigma] \rightarrow [r', \sigma'].$$

(c) $\mathcal{O}[\![s]\!] = \lambda\sigma.\mathcal{O}(s{:}\mathrm{E}, \sigma)$.

So far, the treatment of $\mathcal{L}_{as,2}$ has brought hardly anything new. The novelties will appear in the next section.

18.3 Denotational semantics, relating $\mathcal{O}$ and $\mathcal{D}$

Since denotational semantics is concerned with meanings, we want to manipulate meanings of statements when handling second-order assignment. That is, we want that the effect of $x := s$ upon the semantic state ρ is given by the updated state $\rho\{p/x\}$, for $p = \mathcal{D}(s)$. Upon closer scrutiny, this may be problematic: The effect of $x := s$ is described as a function from states to (sequences of) states, where the values stored in the states are (either simple values from *Val* or) themselves state transformations. It is not obvious that we are working here in a well-defined mathematical setting, so let us be somewhat more precise about the various domains involved. First, once R is known, the denotational domain $\mathbb{P}_D$ is, simply, the counterpart of $\mathbb{P}_O$: Instead of $\Sigma \to \Sigma^\infty$, we now want

$$\mathbb{P}_D = \mathrm{R} \xrightarrow{1} \mathrm{R}^\infty, \tag{18.4}$$

where R^∞ is, of course, the set of all finite or infinite sequences over R (and '$\xrightarrow{1}$' replaces '$\to$': all our semantic functions have to be (at least) nonexpansive). We next look at the definition of R. We want, again, the denotational counterpart of the operational definition. Rather than Σ as in Definition 18.3a, we now want to have

$$\mathrm{R} = (IVar \to Val) \times (PVar \to \mathbb{P}_D). \tag{18.5}$$

Note how $\mathbb{P}_D$ replaces *Stat*: instead of $\sigma(x) = s$ as above, we now expect formulae such as $\rho(x) = p$, where p is the denotational meaning of some s. Actually, we even want a mild extension of (18.5), in that, following the general continuation-style format, the meaning of a statement is an element, say ϕ, of $Cont \xrightarrow{1} \mathbb{P}_D$ rather than of $\mathbb{P}_D$. We now put all our wishes together in a *system* of domain equations, for the moment forgetting about the contractiveness factors as prescribed by the general theory:

$$
\begin{aligned}
(p \in) \mathbb{P}_D & \simeq \mathrm{R} \xrightarrow{1} \mathbb{Q} & (18.6a) \\
(q \in) \mathbb{Q} & \simeq \{\epsilon\} + (\mathrm{R} \times \mathbb{Q}) & (18.6b) \\
(\rho \in) \mathrm{R} & \simeq (IVar \to Val) \times (PVar \to (Cont \xrightarrow{1} \mathbb{P}_D)) & (18.6c) \\
(\gamma \in) Cont & \simeq \mathbb{P}_D. & (18.6d)
\end{aligned}
$$

Summarizing the above in words, the definition for *Cont* is obvious, and that for $\mathbb{Q}$ is a standard way of specifying R^∞. The equation for $\mathbb{P}_D$ follows (18.4), and the equation for R—the key part of the whole system—enables us to see a semantic state ρ as a mapping (from *IVar* to *Val* and) from *PVar* to (*Cont* to) $\mathbb{P}_D$, where the elements of the latter are functions transforming ρ's to sequences of ρ's. The expressive power of the ρ's defined in this way will in particular become manifest when we define $\mathcal{D}(x)$ below.

One last foundational point: In order for (18.6) to be solvable, we need to distribute some $id_{\frac{1}{2}}$'s over the equations. A closer analysis tells us that $\mathbb{Q}$ and R depend recursively upon themselves, whereas $\mathbb{P}_D$ and *Cont* are expressed non-recursively in $\mathbb{Q}$ and R. Thus, it suffices to rewrite (18.6b) and (18.6c) in such a way that the associated function $\mathcal{F} = (\mathcal{F}_1, \mathcal{F}_2)$—or, more precisely $\mathcal{F} \circ \mathcal{F}$—is $\frac{1}{2}$-contractive in $(\mathbb{Q}, R)$. This is achieved, e.g., by writing

$$\mathbb{Q} \simeq \{\epsilon\} + (R \times id_{\frac{1}{2}}(\mathbb{Q})) \qquad\qquad (18.7a)$$

$$R \simeq (IVar \rightarrow Val) \times (PVar \rightarrow id_{\frac{1}{2}}((R \xrightarrow{1} \mathbb{Q}) \xrightarrow{1} (R \xrightarrow{1} \mathbb{Q}))). \qquad (18.7b)$$

Once (18.7a) and (18.7b) have been solved in terms of complete ultrametric spaces—which is possible thanks to the general theory as described in Appendix C, we can then, simply, put

$$\mathbb{P}_D = R \xrightarrow{1} \mathbb{Q}$$
$$Cont = \mathbb{P}_D,$$

as indicated already.

Note also that (18.7a) justifies our (informal) notation R^∞ for $\mathbb{Q}$. In fact, for each A we may specify A^∞ as solution of the equation

$$\mathbb{P} \simeq \{\epsilon\} + (A \times id_{\frac{1}{2}}(\mathbb{P}))$$

(see e.g., the discussion after Lemma 14.5).

Having R and $\mathbb{P}_D$ available, the definition of $\mathcal{D}$ is not too hard. It is contained in

Definition 18.6

(a) $\mathcal{D}:\mathcal{L}_{as,2} \rightarrow Cont \xrightarrow{1} \mathbb{P}_D$ is given by

$$\mathcal{D}(v := e)(\gamma)(\rho) = \rho\{\alpha/v\} \cdot \gamma(\rho\{\alpha/v\}), \text{ where } \alpha = \mathcal{V}(e)(\rho)$$
$$\mathcal{D}(x := s)(\gamma)(\rho) = \rho\{\phi/x\} \cdot \gamma(\rho\{\phi/x\}), \text{ where } \phi = \mathcal{D}(s)$$
$$\mathcal{D}(x)(\gamma)(\rho) = \rho \cdot \rho(x)(\gamma)(\rho)$$
$$\mathcal{D}(s_1;s_2)(\gamma)(\rho) = \mathcal{D}(s_1)(\mathcal{D}(s_2)(\gamma))(\rho)$$
$$\mathcal{D}(\text{if } e \text{ then } s_1 \text{ else } s_2 \text{ fi})(\gamma)(\rho)$$
$$\qquad\qquad = \text{ if } \mathcal{V}(e)(\rho) \text{ then } \mathcal{D}(s_1)(\gamma)(\rho) \text{ else } \mathcal{D}(s_2)(\gamma)(\rho) \text{ fi.}$$

(b) $\mathcal{D}[\![s]\!] = \mathcal{D}(s)(\gamma_\epsilon)$, with $\gamma_\epsilon = \lambda\rho.\epsilon$.

In the above, we have tacitly assumed that the reader understands $\mathcal{V}(e)(\rho)$.

In order to appreciate the clauses for $\mathcal{D}$, it is helpful to compare them with the transition rules from $\mathcal{T}_{as,2}$. Let us assume as already given correspondences between σ and ρ, and between r and γ (and their indexed variants). Details of these correspondences will evolve when we relate $\mathcal{O}$ to $\mathcal{D}$. As relationship between the rules from $\mathcal{T}_{as,2}$ and the clauses for $\mathcal{D}$ we shall have the general scheme that, whenever $[s_1:r_1, \sigma_1] \to [s_2:r_2, \sigma_2]$, then

$$\mathcal{D}(s_1)(\gamma_1)(\rho_1) = \rho_2 \cdot \mathcal{D}(s_2)(\gamma_2)(\rho_2),$$

and, whenever $[s_1:r_1, \sigma_1] \to_0 [s_2:r_2, \sigma_2]$, then

$$\mathcal{D}(s_1)(\gamma_1)(\rho_1) = \mathcal{D}(s_2)(\gamma_2)(\rho_2).$$

Focusing on the most demanding denotational rule, i.e., the rule for $\mathcal{D}(x)(\gamma)(\rho)$, we see that its right-hand side may indeed be inferred directly from the operational (PVar)-rule:

$$[x:r, \sigma] \to [\sigma(x):r, \sigma].$$

Assuming the indicated correspondence between ρ and σ, and r and γ, we infer $\mathcal{D}(x)(\gamma)(\rho) = \rho \cdot \mathcal{D}(\sigma(x))(\gamma)(\rho)$. Also using that the indicated correspondence between σ and ρ (to be elaborated below) implies that $\mathcal{D}(\sigma(x)) = \rho(x)$, we obtain $\mathcal{D}(x)(\gamma)(\rho) = \rho \cdot \rho(x)(\gamma)(\rho)$, which is exactly as in Definition 18.6.

This explanation should shed some light on the remarkable rule for $\mathcal{D}(x)$. Note that a key feature of ρ is that it may be applied to (a number of arguments including) itself. It is for this very purpose that the rather heavy machinery for the solution of general domain equations had to be invoked.

As a further comment on the definition of $\mathcal{D}$, we draw attention to the fact that there is no need to involve any higher-order Ψ—not even implicitly—in the definition of $\mathcal{D}$. Though the domains are non-trivial, the definition of $\mathcal{D}$ itself proceeds by a simple structural induction (on the complexity of the argument s).

There is one aspect of the definition of $\mathcal{D}$ which we have not yet addressed, viz. its well-definedness with respect to the various nonexpansiveness conditions. We discuss here only the hardest of the verifications involved: We shall show that, for each $x, \gamma, \rho_1, \rho_2$,

$$d(\mathcal{D}(x)(\gamma)(\rho_1), \mathcal{D}(x)(\gamma)(\rho_2)) \leq d(\rho_1, \rho_2).$$

By Definition 18.6, this can be rewritten as

$$d(\rho_1 \cdot \rho_1(x)(\gamma)(\rho_1), \rho_2 \cdot \rho_2(x)(\gamma)(\rho_2)) \leq d(\rho_1, \rho_2).$$

By (18.7a), we have that it is sufficient to prove that

$$\tfrac{1}{2} d(\rho_1(x)(\gamma)(\rho_1), \rho_2(x)(\gamma)(\rho_2)) \leq d(\rho_1, \rho_2).$$

Since d is an ultrametric, the left-hand side can be bounded as follows:

$\frac{1}{2}d(\rho_1(x)(\gamma)(\rho_1), \rho_2(x)(\gamma)(\rho_2))$

$\leq \frac{1}{2}max\{\, d(\rho_1(x)(\gamma)(\rho_1), \rho_1(x)(\gamma)(\rho_2)), d(\rho_1(x)(\gamma)(\rho_2), \rho_2(x)(\gamma)(\rho_2))\,\}$

$\leq [\rho_1(x)(\gamma)$ is nonexpansive, def. $d(\rho_1, \rho_2)$ and (18.7b)]
$\qquad \frac{1}{2}max\{\, d(\rho_1, \rho_2, 2 \cdot d(\rho_1, \rho_2)\,\}$

$\leq d(\rho_1, \rho_2).$

As always, there remains the task of comparing $\mathcal{O}$ with $\mathcal{D}$. Due to the essential difference between the two kinds of states, we cannot expect a simple result of the form $\mathcal{O} = \mathcal{D}$ or $\mathcal{O} = abs \circ \mathcal{D}$. Rather, we shall aim for a relationship involving as key constituent a mapping, say sem, between syntactic and semantic states. Once sem is available, the relation between $\mathcal{O}$ and $\mathcal{D}$ will turn out to be fairly transparent. Let us first give the definition of sem.

Definition 18.7

(a) The mapping $sem : \Sigma \rightarrow R$ is given by

$$sem(\sigma) = (\sigma_1, \lambda x.\mathcal{D}(\sigma_2(x))) . \tag{18.8}$$

(b) Let τ range over Σ^∞. We extend $sem : \Sigma \rightarrow R$ to a mapping $sem : \Sigma^\infty \rightarrow R^\infty$ by defining it as the unique function satisfying

$$sem(\epsilon) = \epsilon \text{ and } sem(\sigma \cdot \tau) = sem(\sigma) \cdot sem(\tau) .$$

Formula (18.8) is to be understood as follows: For each syntactic state $\sigma = (\sigma_1, \sigma_2)$, we determine the outcome $sem(\sigma) = (\rho_1, \rho_2)$ by putting $\rho_1 = \sigma_1$, and defining ρ_2 such that, for each procedure variable x, its meaning $\rho_2(x)$ equals $\mathcal{D}(\sigma_2(x))$, i.e., in case $\sigma_2(x) = s$, we have $\rho_2(x) = \phi = \mathcal{D}(s)$. Thus, in going from syntactic to corresponding semantic states, a value s for a procedure variable x is replaced by a value $\phi = \mathcal{D}(s)$. As immediate corollary of the definition we have

Lemma 18.8

(a) $sem(\sigma\{s/x\}) = sem(\sigma)\{\mathcal{D}(s)/x\}$.

(b) $sem(\sigma)(x) = \mathcal{D}(\sigma_2(x))$.

Using the mapping *sem*, we can now state our main result on $\mathcal{O}$ versus $\mathcal{D}$ on $\mathcal{L}_{as,2}$.

Theorem 18.9 *For each s, σ*

$$sem(\mathcal{O}[\![s]\!](\sigma)) = \mathcal{D}[\![s]\!](sem(\sigma))\,.$$

Proof Let, as usual, $\mathcal{E}:Res \to \mathbb{P}_D$ be given by $\mathcal{E}(\mathrm{E}) = \lambda\rho.\epsilon$, $\mathcal{E}(s{:}r) = \mathcal{D}(s)(\mathcal{E}(r))$. The desired result is immediate once we have shown that for all r, σ,

$$sem(\mathcal{O}(r,\sigma)) = \mathcal{E}(r)(sem(\sigma))\,.$$

We use the $\varepsilon \leq \frac{1}{2}\varepsilon$ argument. Let

$$\varepsilon = sup\{\, d(sem(\mathcal{O}(r,\sigma)), \mathcal{E}(r)(sem(\sigma))) \mid r \in Res, \sigma \in \Sigma \,\}\,.$$

We use induction on $wgt(r)$, where wgt is as in Definition 1.60 (with $wgt(x := s) = 1$ added). The case $r \equiv \mathrm{E}$ is clear. Now let $r \equiv (s{:}r')$. We discuss two subcases for s.

$[x := s_1]$ Let $\phi = \mathcal{D}(s_1)$.

$$d(sem(\mathcal{O}((x := s_1){:}r',\sigma)), \mathcal{D}(x := s_1)(\mathcal{E}(r'))(sem(\sigma)))$$
$$= \quad d(sem(\sigma\{s_1/x\} \cdot \mathcal{O}(r',\sigma\{s_1/x\})), sem(\sigma\{\phi/x\} \cdot \mathcal{E}(r')(sem(\sigma\{\phi/x\}))))$$
$$\leq \quad [\text{Lemma} \qquad\qquad 18.8a, \qquad\qquad \text{def.} \qquad\qquad sem]$$
$$\qquad \tfrac{1}{2}d(sem(\mathcal{O}(r',\sigma\{\,s_1/x\,\})), \mathcal{E}(r')(sem(\sigma\{\,s_1/x\,\})))$$
$$\leq \quad \tfrac{1}{2}\varepsilon.$$

$[x]$ $\quad d(sem(\mathcal{O}(x{:}r',\sigma)), \mathcal{D}(x)(\mathcal{E}(r'))(sem(\sigma)))$
$$= \quad d(sem(\sigma \cdot \mathcal{O}(\sigma_2(x){:}r',\sigma)), sem(\sigma) \cdot sem(\sigma)(x)(\mathcal{E}(r'))(sem(\sigma)))$$
$$\leq \quad [\text{Lemma} \qquad\qquad 18.8b, \qquad\qquad \text{def.} \qquad\qquad sem]$$
$$\qquad \tfrac{1}{2}d(sem(\mathcal{O}(\sigma_2(x){:}r',\sigma)), \mathcal{D}(\sigma_2(x))(\mathcal{E}(r'))(sem(\sigma)))$$
$$= \quad \tfrac{1}{2}d(sem(\mathcal{O}(\sigma_2(x){:}r',\sigma)), \mathcal{E}(\sigma_2(x){:}r')(sem(\sigma)))$$
$$\leq \quad \tfrac{1}{2}\varepsilon\,. \qquad\qquad\qquad\qquad\qquad\qquad\qquad\qquad \square$$

18.4   Exercises

Exercise 18.1 Let

$$s = (x := \text{if } v = 0 \text{ then } w := 1 \text{ else } v := v - 1; x; v := v + 1 \text{ fi}; x).$$

Determine $\mathcal{O}[\![s]\!]$ and $\mathcal{D}[\![s]\!]$.

Exercise 18.2 Complete the well-definedness analysis of $\mathcal{D}$ as outlined after Definition 18.6.

18.5 Bibliographical notes

This chapter is based on [BB94]. References pertaining to the necessary extensions of the domain theory as developed earlier in Chapter 10 are given in Appendix C.

A variation on $\mathcal{L}_{as,2}$ dealing with second order communication (say $\mathcal{L}_{com,2}$) is also described in [BB94]. The semantic modeling is then more involved since the techniques of Chapter 18 have to be combined with those used for the branching domains as described, e.g., for $\mathcal{L}_{com}$ in Section 12.2. In addition, in establishing the relationship between $\mathcal{O}$ and $\mathcal{D}$ for $\mathcal{L}_{com,2}$, a transition system satisfying an essentially generalized finiteness condition ([Bre94a, Bre94b]) is employed. Full details are provided in [Bre94b].

Our investigation of the language $\mathcal{L}_{as,2}$ is no more than a simple example of a large body of studies of higher-order constructs. In concurrency theory, one encounters systems such as Thomsen's CHOCS ([Tho89, Tho90b], Boudol's γ-calculus ([Bou89]) and Sangiorgi's higher-order π-calculus ([San92, San93]). Furthermore, there is a wealth of higher-order phenomena in the area of functional programming, see, e.g., [Bar92].

A. Proofs of Topological Theorems

In this section we collect the remaining proofs of several topological theorems exploited in the main text. First we prove Hahn's and Kuratowski's theorem, stating the completeness of the hyperspaces of (nonempty and) closed or compact sets, respectively. Then we show the equivalence of the formulations of compactness in terms of sequences as in Definition 2.11 on the one hand, and in terms of open covers as in Definition 2.18 on the other. We close this appendix with the remaining proof of Theorem 10.6, i.e., the existence of a completion of an arbitrary metric space.

We first prove Hahn's theorem presented above as Theorem 2.10.

Theorem A.1 *(Hahn) Let (M, d) be a complete metric space.*

(a) If $(X_n)_n$ is a Cauchy sequence in $(\mathcal{P}_{ncl}(M), d_H)$, then

$$\lim_n X_n = \{ \lim_n x_n \mid \forall n \colon x_n \in X_n,\ (x_n)_n \text{ Cauchy} \}.$$

(b) If $(X_n)_n$ is a Cauchy sequence in $(\mathcal{P}_{cl}(M), d_H)$ then either, for almost all n, $X_n = \emptyset$, and $\lim_n X_n = \emptyset$, or for almost all n, $X_n \neq \emptyset$ (say for $n \geq N$), and

$$\lim_n X_n = \{ \lim_{n \geq N} x_n \mid \forall n \geq N \colon x_n \in X_n,\ (x_n)_{n=N}^\infty \text{ Cauchy} \}.$$

(c) $(\mathcal{P}_{cl}(M), d_H)$ and $(\mathcal{P}_{ncl}(M), d_H)$ are complete.

Proof

(a) Suppose $(X_n)_n$ is a Cauchy sequence in $\mathcal{P}_{ncl}(M)$. Put

$$X \ = \ \{ \lim_n x_n \mid \forall n \colon x_n \in X_n,\ (x_n)_n \text{ Cauchy} \}.$$

First we check that X is nonempty. Let $(i_n)_n$ be a strictly increasing sequence such that $d(X_i, X_j) < 2^{-n}$ for $i, j \geq i_n$. Define a sequence $(x_i)_i$ as follows

$$
\begin{aligned}
&x_i \in X_i \text{ arbitrary, for } i \leq i_0 \\
&x_i \in X_i \text{ such that } d(x_{i_n}, x_i) < 2^{-n}, \text{ for } i_n < i \leq i_{n+1}
\end{aligned}
\tag{A.1}
$$

where the latter construction can be made by the choice of i_n. We claim that $(x_i)_i$ is Cauchy: For $\varepsilon > 0$ we pick n such that $2^{-n} < \varepsilon/4$. For $i, j \geq i_n$, with $i_m \leq i < i_{m+1}$, $i_\ell \leq j < i_{\ell+1}$ we have

$$d(x_i, x_j)$$
$$\leq d(x_i, x_{i_m}) + \sum_{k=m}^{\ell-1} d(x_{i_k}, x_{i_{k+1}}) + d(x_{i_\ell}, x_j)$$
$$\leq 2^{-m} + \sum_{k=m}^{\ell-1} 2^{-k} + 2^{-\ell}$$
$$< \sum_{k=m-1}^{\ell} 2^{-k} < 4 \cdot 2^{-m} \leq 4 \cdot 2^{-n} < \varepsilon.$$

So $(x_i)_i$ is a Cauchy sequence through $(X_i)_i$. By completeness of M, $x = lim_i x_i$ exists and $x \in X$. Hence X is nonempty.

Next, we check that X is closed. Let $(x_i)_i$ be a convergent sequence in X, say $x = lim_i x_i$. We have to check that $x \in X$. Pick Cauchy sequences $(x_{ij})_j$ such that for all j: $x_{ij} \in X_j$ and $x_i = lim_j x_{ij}$, for all i. Let $(i_n)_n$ be a strictly increasing sequence such that $d(x_i, x) < 2^{-n}$ for $i \geq i_n$. Let furthermore $(j_n)_n$ be a strictly increasing sequence such that $\forall i \leq i_n\, [\, d(x_{ij}, x_i) < 2^{-n}$ for $j \geq j_n\,]$.

Now define the sequence $(z_j)_j$ as follows:

$z_j \in X_j$ arbitrary, for $j < j_0$
$z_j = x_{i_k j} \in X_j$ with k such that $j_k \leq j < j_{k+1}$.

Then it holds that $(z_j)_j$ is a sequence through $(X_j)_j$. Moreover, for arbitrary $\varepsilon > 0$,

$$d(z_j, x) \leq d(x_{i_k j}, x_{i_k}) + d(x_{i_k}, x) < 2 \cdot 2^{-k} \leq 2 \cdot 2^{-n} < \varepsilon$$

for k such that $j_k \leq j < j_{k+1}$, $j \geq j_n$ (hence $k \geq n$) and n such that $2^{-n} < \varepsilon/2$. So $(z_j)_j$ converges to x. Hence $x \in X$.

Now we have settled $X \in \mathcal{P}_{ncl}(M)$ we have left to show that $X = lim_i X_i$. Let, again, $(i_n)_n$ be strictly increasing such that $d(X_i, X_j) < 2^{-n}$ for $i, j \geq i_n$. Pick $\varepsilon > 0$ and n such that $2^{-n} < \varepsilon/5$ and $i \geq i_n$. We check $d(X, X_i) < \varepsilon$.

Suppose, on the one hand, $x_i \in X_i$. We construct a sequence $(z_i)_i$ through $(X_i)_i$ as follows

$z_i \in X_i$ arbitrary, for $i < i_n$
$z_{i_n} \in X_{i_n}$ such that $d(z_{i_n}, x_i) < 2^{-n}$
$z_i \in X_i$ such that $d(z_i, z_{i_m}) < 2^{-m}$, for $i_n \leq i_m < i \leq i_{m+1}$.

As for the sequence $(x_i)_i$ constructed in (A.1) above, one can show $d(z_i, z_j) \leq 4 \cdot 2^{-n}$ for $i, j \geq i_n$ implying that $(z_i)_i$ is Cauchy. Now, for $z = lim_i z_i$ we have $z \in X$ by closedness of X and

$$d(z, x_i) \leq d(z, z_{i_n}) + d(z_{i_n}, x_i) \leq 4 \cdot 2^{-n} + 2^{-n} < \varepsilon.$$

Suppose, on the other hand, $x \in X$, say $x = lim_i \, x_i$ for a Cauchy sequence $(x_i)_i$ through $(X_i)_i$. Pick $k \geq i_n$ such that $d(x, x_k) < 2^{-n}$. Since $d(X_k, X_i) < 2^{-n}$ we can choose for $x_k \in X_k$, $x_i \in X_i$ such that $d(x_k, x_i) < 2^{-n}$. Then we have

$$d(x, x_i) \leq d(x, x_k) + d(x_k, x_i) < 2 \cdot 2^{-n} < \varepsilon .$$

This shows $d(X, X_i) < \varepsilon$. Conclusion: $X = lim_i \, X_i \in \mathcal{P}_{ncl}(M)$.

(b) From the observation $d(\emptyset, X) < 1 \Rightarrow X = \emptyset$, for $X \in \mathcal{P}_{cl}(M)$, it follows that a Cauchy sequence in $\mathcal{P}_{cl}(M)$ has either all its elements eventually equal to $\emptyset$, or all its elements eventually different from $\emptyset$. Thus the limit is either $\emptyset$, or the limit of the Cauchy sequence of nonempty elements in $\mathcal{P}_{ncl}(M)$, which exists by part (a).

(c) Completeness of $(\mathcal{P}_{ncl}(M), d_H)$ and $(\mathcal{P}_{ncl}(M), d_H)$ is now immediate from part (a) and (b), respectively.   □

Next we give the proof of Kuratowski's theorem, Theorem 2.14.

Theorem A.2 *(Kuratowski) Let (M, d) be a complete metric space.*

(a) If $(X_n)_n$ is a Cauchy sequence in $(\mathcal{P}_{nco}(M), d_H)$, then

$$lim_n X_n = \{\, lim_n x_n \mid \forall n \colon x_n \in X_n, \; (x_n)_n \; Cauchy \,\}.$$

(b) If $(X_n)_n$ is a Cauchy sequence in $(\mathcal{P}_{co}(M), d_H)$ then either, for almost all n, $X_n = \emptyset$, and $lim_n X_n = \emptyset$, or for almost all n, $X_n \neq \emptyset$ (say for $n \geq N$), and

$$lim_n X_n = \{\, lim_{n \geq N} x_n \mid \forall n \geq N \colon x_n \in X_n, \; (x_n)_{n=N}^{\infty} \; Cauchy \,\}. \tag{A.2}$$

(c) $(\mathcal{P}_{co}(M), d_H)$ and $(\mathcal{P}_{nco}(M), d_H)$ are complete.

Proof We only prove part (a), case $\mathcal{P}_{nco}(\cdot)$, the remainder being similar to the corresponding statements in the proof of A.1. So, let $(X_i)_i$ be a Cauchy sequence in $\mathcal{P}_{nco}(M)$ and put

$$X \quad = \quad \{\, lim_n x_n \mid \forall n \colon x_n \in X_n, \; (x_n)_n \; \text{Cauchy} \,\}.$$

Since compactness implies closedness we have, by Hahn's theorem, that X is nonempty and closed, and $X = lim_i \, X_i$ in $\mathcal{P}_{ncl}(M)$. It remains to show that X is compact.

Let $(j_n)_n$ be a strictly increasing sequence such that $d(X_j, X) < 2^{-n}$ for $j \geq j_n$. Let $(x_i)_i$ be an arbitrary sequence in X. Choose, for each i and j, $x_{ij} \in X_j$ such that $d(x_i, x_{ij}) < 2^{-n}$ if $j_n \leq j < j_{n+1}$.

Put $I_{-1} = \mathbb{N}$ and construct sequences $(I_n)_n$, $(i_n)_n$ such that

I_n is infinite

$I_n \supseteq I_{n+1}$

$(x_{ij_n})_{i \in I_n}$ is converging

$(i_n)_n$ is strictly increasing

$i_n \in I_n$ and $d(x_{ij_n}, x_{hj_n}) < 2^{-n}$ for $i, h \in I_n$, $i, h \geq i_n$,

for all $n \in \mathbb{N}$. This is possible since $(x_{ij_n})_{i \in I_{n-1}}$ is an infinite sequence in the compact set X_{j_n}, and thus has a converging subsequence $(x_{ij_n})_{i \in I_n}$. We check that the sequence $(x_{i_n})_n$ is Cauchy:

$$d(x_{i_n}, x_{i_m}) \leq d(x_{i_n}, x_{i_n j_n}) + d(x_{i_n j_n}, x_{i_m j_n}) + d(x_{i_m j_n}, x_{i_m}) \leq 3 \cdot 2^{-n}$$

for $i_n \leq i_m$. By completeness of M, $x = lim_n x_{i_n}$ exists and $x \in X$ by closedness of X. So $(x_{i_n})_n$ is a convergent subsequence of $(x_i)_i$ with limit in X.   □

Now we turn to the equivalence of sequential and topological compactness (Theorem 2.19) as introduced in Definitions 2.11 and 2.18, respectively, which we repeat first.

Definition A.3 Let (M, d) be a metric space.

(a) A subset $X \subseteq M$ is called (sequentially) compact whenever each infinite sequence $(x_n)_n$ in X has a convergent subsequence with limit in X.

(b) A subset $X \subseteq M$ is called topologically compact whenever each open cover of X has a finite subcover, i.e., if $\{O_\alpha \mid \alpha \in I\}$ is a collection of open sets in M such that $X \subseteq \bigcup\{O_\alpha \mid \alpha \in I\}$, then there exists a finite subset $J \subseteq I$ such that $\{O_\alpha \mid \alpha \in J\}$.

The proof of Theorem 2.19 now follows.

Theorem A.4 *Let (M, d) be a metric space. A subset X of M is (sequentially) compact iff it is topologically compact.*

Proof Suppose $X \subseteq M$ is compact in the sense of Definition 2.11. In order to show topological compactness of X, we have to check that any open cover $\{O_\alpha \mid \alpha \in I\}$ of X has a finite subcover. First we claim: *If $\{O_\alpha \mid \alpha \in I\}$ is an open cover*

of X, then for some real number $\lambda > 0$ it holds that $\forall x \in X \exists \alpha \in I: B_\lambda(x) \subseteq O_\alpha$.
(The number λ is usually called the Lebesgue number of the cover.) Proof of the claim: Suppose such λ does not exist. Then, for all i, there exists $x_i \in X$ such that $B_{2^{-i}}(x_i) \not\subseteq O_\alpha$ for any $\alpha \in I$. Let, by compactness of X, $(x_{i_n})_n$ be a convergent subsequence of $(x_i)_i$ with limit $x \in X$. Say $x \in O_{\alpha_0}$ for some $\alpha_0 \in I$. Since O_{α_0} is open, we can pick $\varepsilon > 0$ satisfying $B_\varepsilon(x) \subseteq O_{\alpha_0}$. But then, for n such that $2^{-n} < \varepsilon/2$ and k such that $i_k > n$, $d(x, x_{i_k}) < 2^{-k}$ and $2^{-k} < \varepsilon/2$, we have

$$B_{2^{-k}}(x_{i_k}) \subseteq B_{2^{-n}+2^{-k}}(x) \subseteq B_\varepsilon(x) \subseteq O_{\alpha_0}.$$

Contradiction. This proves the claim.

Now let $\{ O_\alpha \mid \alpha \in I \}$ be any open cover of X. Let λ be its Lebesgue number which exists by the above claim. Suppose that $\{ O_\alpha \mid \alpha \in i \}$ has no finite subcover. Now, put $U_{-1} = \emptyset$ and define, inductively, x_n, α_n, U_n, for $n \geq 0$, such that

$$x_n \notin U_{n-1}, \quad B_\lambda(x) \subseteq O_{\alpha_n}, \quad U_n = U_{n-1} \cup O_{\alpha_n}.$$

Then $\forall i, j, i \neq j: d(x_i, x_j) \geq \lambda$. So $(x_i)_i$ has no convergent subsequence, contradicting the compactness of X. Conclusion: $\{ O_\alpha \mid \alpha \in I \}$ has a finite subcover, and X is topologically compact.

Now suppose X is topologically compact. To show compactness of X in the sense of Definition 2.11, we have to verify that each sequence $(x_i)_i$ in X has a convergent subsequence $(x_{i_n})_n$ with limit in X. We first claim: X *is complete,* i.e., each Cauchy sequence $(x_i)_i$ in X has a limit in X. Proof of the claim: Let $(x_i)_i$ be a Cauchy sequence and suppose for no $x \in X$, $x = lim_i x_i$. Then we have that each set $\{ x_n, x_{n+1}, \dots \}$ is closed and $\{ O_n \mid n \in \mathbb{N} \}$ where $O_n = M \setminus \{ x_n, x_{n+1}, \dots \}$ is an open cover of X without finite subcover, contradicting the topological compactness of X. This proves the claim.

Now, let $(x_i)_i$ be an arbitrary sequence in X. We will determine a convergent subsequence $(x_{i_n})_n$ with limit x in X. First note that, by topological compactness, each open cover $\{ B_{2^{-n}}(x) \mid x \in X \}$ has a finite subcover. So for each sequence $(y_i)_i$ and $n \in \mathbb{N}$ there exists $y \in X$ such that $y_i \in B_{2^{-n}}(y)$ for infinitely many indices i.

We now define a sequence of infinite index sets $(I_n)_n$ and derive from this a convergent subsequence of $(x_i)_i$. Put $I_{-1} = \mathbb{N}$ and construct I_n, for $n \in \mathbb{N}$, as follows:

I_n is infinite
$I_n \supseteq I_{n+1}$
$x_i \in B_{2^{-n}}(x)$ for some $x \in X$ and all $i \in I_n$.

Let $(i_n)_n$ be a strictly increasing sequence such that $i_n \in I_n$. Then $(x_{i_n})_n$ is Cauchy: $d(x_{i_n}, x_{i_m}) < 2 \cdot 2^{-n}$ for $n \leq m$. By completeness of X, as shown above, $(x_{i_n})_n$ has a limit in X. Conclusion: $(x_{i_n})_n$ is a convergent subsequence of $(x_i)_i$ with limit in X, and X is compact.   □

The last theorem of which the full proof remains, is Theorem 10.6 stating that each metric space can be completed (obtaining an essentially unique complete metric space). First we present an auxiliary lemma.

Lemma A.5 *Let (M, d) be a (1-bounded) metric space. Put $F(M) = M \to [0, 1]$ with the metric d_F induced by the standard metric on $[0, 1]$. Define $\phi \colon M \to F(M)$ by $\phi(x) = f_x$ where*

$$f_x(y) \quad = \quad d(x, y)$$

for all $y \in M$. Then ϕ is an isometry.

Proof Pick $x, x' \in M$. Since, for any $y \in M$, by the triangle inequality $d(x, y) \leq d(x, x') + d(x', y)$ and $d(x', y) \leq d(x', x) + d(x, y)$, we have $|d(x, y) - d(x', y)| \leq d(x, x')$. Therefore

$$d(f_x, f_{x'}) = sup\{|d(x, y) - d(x', y)| \mid y \in M\} \leq d(x, x').$$

On the other hand, by definition of $d(f_x, f_{x'})$,

$$d(x, x') = d(x, x') - d(x', x') = d(f_x(x'), f_{x'}(x')) \leq d(f_x, f_{x'}).$$

Conclusion $d(x, x') = d(f_x, f_{x'}) = d(\phi(x), \phi(x'))$ and ϕ is an isometry.   □

We next repeat the definition of a completion of a metric space as given in Definition 10.5.

Definition A.6 Let (M, d) be a metric space. A *completion* of (M, d) is a *complete* metric space (N, d') such that

(1) $M \vartriangleleft N$.

(2) For each $x \in N$ we have: $x = lim_n x_n$, with $x_n \in M$, $n = 0, 1, \ldots$ (and with the limit taken with respect to d').

Finally, we provide the remaining proof of Theorem 10.6.

Theorem A.7 *Each metric space has a completion which is unique up to isometry.*

Proof Let (M, d) be a metric space. We show the existence of a completion (N, d') for (M, d). (Its uniqueness up to isometry was shown in the main text.) Let $(F(M), d_F)$ and ϕ be as in Lemma A.5. Note that $F(M)$ is complete. Now $\phi(M) \subseteq F(M)$ and we define

$$cl(M) \quad = \quad \{ \, lim_i \, f_i \in F(M) \mid (f_i)_i \text{ convergent } \wedge \forall i \, [\, f_i \in \phi(M) \,] \, \}.$$

If we let $cl(M)$ inherit its metric d_F from $F(M)$, we then clearly have $cl(M) \triangleleft f(M)$. $cl(M)$ is closed in $F(M)$, hence also complete.

Put $bnd(M) = cl(M) \setminus \phi(M)$ and define (N, d') as follows: $N = M \cup bnd(M)$ and the distance d' is given by

$$
\begin{aligned}
d'(x, x') &= d_F(f_x, f_{x'}) && \text{if } x, x' \in M \\
d'(f, f') &= d_F(f, f') && \text{if } f, f' \in bnd(M) \\
d'(x, f) &= d_F(f_x, f) && \text{if } x \in M, \ f \in bnd(M) \\
d'(f, x) &= d_F(f, f_x) && \text{if } f \in bnd(M), \ x \in M.
\end{aligned}
$$

There remains to verify that (N, d') is a completion of (M, d). We have $(M, d) \triangleleft (N, d')$, by isometry of ϕ (Lemma A.5). Now pick $z \in N$ arbitrary. If $z \in M$ then clearly $z = lim_i \, x_i$ with $x_i \in M$: Pick $x_i = z$ for all i. If $z \in bnd(M)$, we have $z = lim_i \, f_{x_i}$ in $F(M)$ with $f_{x_i} \in \phi(M)$, $i \in \mathbb{N}$. Since $d'(z, x_i) = d(z, f_{x_i})$ we then have $z = lim_i \, x_i$ in N. Hence, (N, d') is a completion of (M, d). □

Bibliographical notes

The historical background of the theorems of this appendix is discussed already in Section 2.4. The proofs of the theorems of Hahn and Kuratowski are elementary and formulated anew for this appendix. The same applies to Theorem A.4 stating the equivalence of sequential and topological compactness. In showing topological from sequential compactness the use of the Lebesgue number of an open cover is probably folklore. The proof of the existence of a completion of a metric space follows the presentation given in [Eng89].

B Direct Operational Semantics

In this appendix we provide full proofs of Propositions 2.30 and 5.3. The former states that the direct operational semantics generated by a finitely branching transition system always delivers compact sets of sequences of observables, whereas the latter claims that the direct operational semantics induced by an image-finite transition system generally yields closed subsets of $\mathcal{P}(Obs^\infty)$. First we repeat the definitions of direct operational semantics and of a transition system being finitely branching and image-finite.

Definition B.1 Let $\mathcal{T} = (Conf, Obs, \rightarrow)$ be a transition system.

(a) The direct operational semantics $\mathcal{O}_d: Conf \rightarrow \mathcal{P}(Obs^\infty)$ generated by $\mathcal{T}$ is given as follows:

$$\mathcal{O}_d(c) = \{\, a_1 \cdots a_n \in Obs^* \mid c = c_0 \xrightarrow{a_1} \cdots \xrightarrow{a_n} c_n \not\rightarrow \,\} \cup$$
$$\{\, a_1 a_2 \cdots \in Obs^\omega \mid c = c_0 \xrightarrow{a_1} c_1 \xrightarrow{a_2} \cdots \,\}.$$

(b) A transition system $\mathcal{T}$ is called finitely branching if the set $\{\, \langle a, c' \rangle \mid c \xrightarrow{a} c' \,\}$ is finite, for each $c \in Conf$. $\mathcal{T}$ is called image-finite if the set $\{\, c' \mid c \xrightarrow{a} c' \,\}$ is finite, for each $c \in Conf$, $a \in Obs$.

We first treat the case of finitely branching transition systems, in the main text presented as Proposition 2.30.

Theorem B.2 *Let $(Conf, Obs, \rightarrow)$ be a finitely branching transition system. Then for all $c \in Conf$, it holds that $\mathcal{O}_d(c)$ is a compact subset of Obs^∞.*

Proof Pick $c \in Conf$ and let $(w_i)_i$ be a sequence in $\mathcal{O}_d(c)$. We have to determine a convergent subsequence $(w_{i_n})_n$ of $(w_i)_i$ with limit w in $\mathcal{O}_d(c)$. We distinguish two cases.

First suppose, for some $n \in \mathbb{N}$: $lgt(w_i) = n$ for infinitely many i: Choose n such that $I_0 \overset{df}{=} \{\, i \mid lgt(w_i) = n \,\}$ is infinite. Pick, for $i \in I_0$, $c_{i,0}, c_{i,1}, \ldots, c_{i,n}$ and $a_{i,1}, \ldots, a_{i,n}$ such that

$$c = c_{i,0} \xrightarrow{a_{i,1}} c_{i,1} \cdots \xrightarrow{a_{i,n}} c_{i,n} \not\rightarrow \ \wedge\ w_i = a_{i,1} \cdots a_{i,n}.$$

Put $c_0 = c$. We construct, inductively, $I_1, \ldots, I_n \subseteq \mathbb{N}$, $c_1, \ldots, c_n \in Conf$, $a_1, \ldots, a_n \in Obs$ such that, for all k, $0 < k \leq n$,

I_k is infinite
$I_{k-1} \supseteq I_k$
$c_k = c_{i,k} \wedge a_k = a_{i,k}$ for all $i \in I_k$.

Suppose I_k and c_k are given and $k < n$. Since the set $\{ \langle a, c' \rangle \mid c_k \xrightarrow{a} c' \}$ is finite, whereas the set $\{ i \in I_k \mid c_k \xrightarrow{a_{k+1}} c_{i,k+1} \}$ is infinite, we can choose a_{k+1}, c_{k+1} such that $a_{i,k+1} = a_{k+1} \wedge c_{i,k+1} = c_{k+1}$, for infinitely many $i \in I_k$. Then, put

$$I_{k+1} \quad = \quad \{ i \in I_k \mid a_{i,k+1} = a_{k+1}, c_{i,k+1} = c_{k+1} \}.$$

Once the above sequences have been constructed, consider the transition sequence $c = c_0 \xrightarrow{a_1} c_1 \cdots \xrightarrow{a_n} c_n \nrightarrow$ and put $w \stackrel{df}{=} a_1 \cdots a_n \in Obs^n$. Note $w \in \mathcal{O}_d(c)$, since $c = c_0$ by definition and $c_n \nrightarrow$. For all $i \in I_n$ we have

$$w_i = a_{i,1} \cdots a_{i,n} = a_1 \cdots a_n = w$$

since $I_0 \supseteq I_1 \cdots \supseteq I_n$. So, if $\{ i_k \mid k \in \mathbb{N} \}$ is an enumeration of I_n, we have then that $(w_{i_k})_k$ is a convergent subsequence of $(w_i)_i$ with limit $w \in \mathcal{O}_d(c)$.

Now suppose, for all $n \in \mathbb{N}$: $lgt(w_i) = n$ for finitely many i. Assume, without loss of generality, $lgt(w_n) \geq n$ for all $n \in \mathbb{N}$. Pick $c_{n,0}, c_{n,1}, \ldots, c_{n,n}, a_{n,1}, \ldots, a_{n,n}$ such that

$$c = c_{n,0} \xrightarrow{a_{n,1}} c_{n,1} \cdots \xrightarrow{a_{n,i}} c_{n,i} \wedge a_{n,1} \cdots a_{n,n} \text{ is a prefix of } w_n.$$

We construct, inductively, sequences of configurations $(c_i)_i$, of labels $(a_i)_i$ and of index sets $(I_i)_i$ such that

I_k is infinite
$I_{k-1} \supseteq I_k$
$c_k = c_{i,k} \wedge a_k = a_{i,k}$ for all $i \in I_k$

for all k, $k > 0$. Put $c_0 = c$ and $I_0 = \mathbb{N}$. Suppose I_k and c_k have been chosen. Since the set $\{ \langle a, c' \rangle \mid c_k \xrightarrow{a} c' \}$ is finite, whereas the set $\{ i \in I_k \mid c_k \xrightarrow{a_{i,k+1}} c_{i,k+1} \}$ is infinite, we can pick a_{k+1}, c_{k+1} such that $a_{i,k+1} = a_{k+1} \wedge c_{i,k+1} = c_{k+1}$ for infinitely many $i \in I_k$. Put

$$I_{k+1} \quad = \quad \{ i \in I_k \mid a_{i,k+1} = a_{k+1}, c_{i,k+1} = c_{k+1} \}.$$

Note that $c_k \xrightarrow{a_k} c_{k+1}$ since $c_{i,k} \xrightarrow{a_{i,k+1}} c_{i,k+1}$ for $i \in I_{k+1}$. Once the above sequences have been constructed, let $(i_n)_n$ be a strictly increasing sequence such that $i_n \in I_n$. We have that $a_{i_n,1} a_{i_n,2} \cdots a_{i_n,n} = a_1 a_2 \cdots a_n$ is a prefix of w_{i_n}. So $(w_{i_n})_n$ is a converging subsequence of $(w_i)_i$. Moreover for w given by $w \stackrel{df}{=} a_1 a_2 \cdots \in Obs^\omega$ we have

$$w = \lim_n w_{i_n} \wedge c = c_0 \xrightarrow{a_1} c_1 \xrightarrow{a_2} c_2 \cdots .$$

So $w \in \mathcal{O}_d(c)$. $\square$

As closedness is a weaker notion than compactness, the case of image-finite transition systems, firstly formulated in Section 5.1, is slightly easier to prove.

Theorem B.3 *Let $(Conf, Obs, \rightarrow)$ be an image-finite transition system. Then for all $c \in Conf$, it holds that $\mathcal{O}_d(c)$ is a closed subset of Obs^∞.*

Proof Let $c \in Conf$. Pick any $w \in Obs^\infty$ and suppose there exists a sequence $(w_i)_i$ in $\mathcal{O}_d(c)$ converging to w. We have to show $w \in \mathcal{O}_d(c)$.

First suppose $w \in Obs^*$, say $lgt(w) = n$. Pick i such that $d(w, w_i) < 2^{-n}$. We then have $w = w_i$, so $w \in \mathcal{O}_d(c)$.

Next assume $w \in Obs^\omega$, say $w = a_1 a_2 \cdots$. If $w = w_i$, for some i, we are done. Otherwise we can choose, for each i, n such that $d(w, w_i) = 2^{-n}$ and $c_{i,0}, c_{i,1}, \ldots, c_{i,n}$ such that

$$c_{i,0} \xrightarrow{a_1} c_{i,1} \cdots \xrightarrow{a_n} c_{i,n}.$$

Since $w = \lim_i w_i$ we have, for all n, that $c_{i,n}$ is defined for all but finitely many i. Also note that $c_{i,0}$ always exists and $c = c_{i,0}$. We inductively construct a sequence $(c_i)_i$ such that, for all n,

I_n is infinite
$I_n \supseteq I_{n+1}$
$\forall i \in I_n \, [\, c_{i,n} \text{ is defined and } c_n = c_{i,n} \,]$
$c_n \xrightarrow{a_{n+1}} c_{n+1}.$

Put $I_0 = \mathbb{N}$, $c_0 = c$. Suppose I_n, c_n are given. By image-finiteness of '$\rightarrow$' the set $\{\, c' \mid c_n \xrightarrow{a_{n+1}} c' \,\}$ is finite. By construction the set $\{\, i \in I_n \mid c_{i,n} \xrightarrow{a_{n+1}} c_{i,n+1} \,\}$ is infinite. So, we can choose c_{n+1} such that for infinitely many $i \in I_n$, $c_{i,n+1}$ is defined, $c_{n+1} = c_{i,n+1}$ and $c_{i,n} \xrightarrow{a_{n+1}} c_{i,n+1}$. Let I_{n+1} be the set of indices satisfying these three conditions. We then have, by the choice of c_{n+1} and definition of I_{n+1},

I_{n+1} is infinite
$I_n \supseteq I_{n+1}$
$c_n \xrightarrow{a_{n+1}} c_{n+1}.$

The last property follows from the observation $c_{i,n} \xrightarrow{a_{n+1}} c_{i,n+1}$, $c_{i,n} = c_n$ and $c_{i,n+1} = c_{n+1}$, for any $i \in I_{n+1}$.

Now from the construction above we obtain

$$c = c_0 \xrightarrow{a_1} c_1 \xrightarrow{a_2} c_2 \cdots.$$

Therefore we conclude $w = a_1 a_2 \cdots \in \mathcal{O}_d(c)$. $\qquad\square$

Bibliographical notes

Theorems B.2 and B.3 and variations thereof are frequently cited in the literature (see, e.g., the references mentioned in Section 2.4 and 5.5). Detailled proofs, however, seem not available, apart from [Bre94b]. There the presentation is tuned to a generalization coping with so-called image-compact transition systems. For our situation with finitely branching and image-finite transition systems the slightly simpler proof above suffices.

C Domain Equations *by J.J.M.M. Rutten*

In Section 10.3, domain equations are solved by constructing fixed points for associated functors, satisfying certain restrictions. Notably, functors $\mathcal{F}\colon CMS \to CMS$ are required to be monotone: for any two complete metric spaces M_1 and M_2, if $M_1 \subseteq M_2$ then $\mathcal{F}(M_1) \subseteq \mathcal{F}(M_2)$. There are functors, however, that do *not* have this property: see the discussion in Section 10.2. The aim of this section will therefore be to generalize the constructions of Section 10.3 in order to deal with these examples as well. Attention will be focussed at complete *ultrametric* spaces (all of the constructions can be straightforwardly generalized to complete metric spaces).

C.1 Comparing two metric spaces

We have seen in Section 10.3 that for two spaces (M_1, d_1) and (M_2, d_2) with $M_1 \subseteq M_2$, a "kind of metric" $\delta(M_1, M_2)$ can be defined by putting:

$$\delta(M_1, M_2) = (d_2)_H(M_1, M_2),$$

where $(d_2)_H$ is the Hausdorff metric associated with d_2. Based on this definition, the construction of a fixed point of a monotone and *contractive functor* is very similar to the construction of a fixed point of a *contractive mapping* on a complete metric space (Banach's theorem). All of this can be generalized by means of the following definition. Let (M_1, d_1) and (M_2, d_2) be two complete metric spaces. An *embedding-projection* pair from M_1 to M_2 (e-p pair for short), denoted by $\langle e, p \rangle \colon M_1 \to M_2$, is a pair of nonexpansive mappings $e\colon M_1 \to M_2$ and $p\colon M_2 \to M_1$ (called *embedding* and *projection,* respectively), such that $p \circ e = 1_{M_1}$, the identity mapping on M_1. Because e and p are nonexpansive, it follows that e is an isometric embedding: for all x and y in M_1: $d_2(e(x), e(y)) = d_1(x, y)$. An e-p pair $\langle e, p \rangle \colon M_1 \to M_2$ can be thought of as a *comparison* of M_1 and M_2 by means of e and p. The following number gives a measure for the quality of this comparison:

$$\delta\langle e, p \rangle = sup\{d_2(e \circ p(x), x) \mid x \in M_2\} \ (= d_{M_2 \to M_2}(e \circ p, 1_{M_2})).$$

The smaller this number, the more M_1 and M_2 are alike; in the extreme case that $\delta\langle e, p \rangle = 0$, it follows that e is an isomorphism with p as inverse, meaning that, metrically speaking, M_1 and M_2 are indistinguishable.

The following property holds.

Lemma C.1 *Let M_1 and M_2 be two ultrametric spaces and consider two e-p pairs $\langle e, p \rangle \colon M_1 \to M_2$ and $\langle r, s \rangle \colon M_2 \to M_3$. The composition of $\langle e, p \rangle$ and $\langle r, s \rangle$ is defined by*

$$\langle r, s \rangle \circ \langle e, p \rangle = \langle r \circ e, p \circ s \rangle,$$

and yields again an e-p pair; and $\delta(\langle r, s \rangle \circ \langle e, p \rangle) \leq max\{\delta\langle e, p \rangle, \delta\langle r, s \rangle\}$.

There will in what follows next be two major differences with the approach of Section 10.3. Firstly, the family $CUMS$ of complete ultrametric spaces will be considered as a *category* $CUMS^e$, consisting of *objects* and *arrows*:

- the objects of $CUMS^e$ are complete ultrametric spaces;
- the arrows of $CUMS^e$ are embedding-projection pairs $\langle e, p \rangle \colon M_1 \to M_2$.

Secondly, the functors of Section 10.3, in spite of what the categorical term suggests, do not act on arrows. Instead, we shall here deal with functors in the standard sense of the word: they map not only a complete ultrametric space to a complete ultrametric space, but in addition assign to any arrow $\langle e, p \rangle \colon M_1 \to M_2$ an arrow $F(\langle e, p \rangle) \colon F(M_1) \to F(M_2)$ (in such a manner that composition of arrows is preserved).

The "double arrows" of the category $CUMS^e$ make it possible to compare two metric spaces numerically, as described above. In addition, they allow the definition of functors stemming from contravariant constructions such as the function space (see below).

Although it will not be further explored here, the above can be used to turn the category $CUMS$ (and $CUMS^e$) itself into a "kind of ultrametric space": a "distance" between two spaces M_1 and M_2 is given by

$$D(M_1, M_2) = inf\{\delta\langle e, p \rangle \mid \langle e, p \rangle \colon M_1 \to M_2 \text{ is an e-p pair }\}.$$

It satisfies, for all spaces M_1, M_2, and M_3 in $CUMS$,

1. $D(M_1, M_1) = 0$
2. $D(M_1, M_3) \leq max\{D(M_1, M_2), D(M_2, M_3)\}$.

Thus $(CUMS, D)$ is a (large) so-called pseudo-quasi ultrametric space: it differs from an ordinary ultrametric space in that two different elements can have distance 0 (e.g., two isomorphic spaces) and moreover $D(M_1, M_2)$ is in general different from $D(M_2, M_1)$. Variations on the above are possible—using arbitrary pairs of nonexpansive mappings rather than embedding-projection pairs—in order to turn $CUMS$ into something still closer to an ordinary complete ultrametric space. Cf. the notes at the end of this appendix.

C.2 Fixed points of functors

A functor $\mathcal{F}: CUMS^e \to CUMS^e$ maps a complete ultrametric space to a complete ultrametric space, and an arrow $\langle e, p \rangle$ to an arrow $\mathcal{F}(\langle e, p \rangle)$, which is again an e-p pair. Typically, the action of $\mathcal{F}$ on arrows will be componentwise: $\mathcal{F}(\langle e, p \rangle) = \langle \mathcal{F}(e), \mathcal{F}(p) \rangle$, and only functors with this property will be considered. Let α be a real number with $0 \le \alpha \le 1$. A functor $\mathcal{F}$ is called α-*Lipschitz* if for every e-p pair $\langle e, p \rangle: M_1 \to M_2$,

$$\delta(\mathcal{F}(\langle e, p \rangle)) \le \alpha \cdot \delta \langle e, p \rangle.$$

(Note that this definition differs from Definition 10.3.) A functor $\mathcal{F}$ is called *contractive* if it is α-Lipschitz for some α with $0 \le \alpha < 1$. The following generalizes Theorem 10.4.

Theorem C.2 *A contractive functor $\mathcal{F}: CUMS^e \to CUMS^e$ has a fixed point: there exists a complete ultrametric space M such that $M \cong \mathcal{F}(M)$.*

Proof The proof essentially mimics that of Banach's fixed-point theorem. Let 1 be an arbitrary set containing one element supplied with the trivial ultrametric. Let $M_0 = 1$ and given M_n let $M_{n+1} = \mathcal{F}(M_n)$. The metric on M_n will be denoted by d_n. Let $\langle e_0, p_0 \rangle: M_0 \to M_1$ be an arbitrary e-p pair and given $\langle e_n, p_n \rangle: M_n \to M_{n+1}$, let $\langle e_{n+1}, p_{n+1} \rangle = \mathcal{F}(\langle e_n, p_n \rangle)$. This inductively defines a sequence of e-p pairs

$$\Delta = M_0 \xrightarrow{\langle e_0, p_0 \rangle} M_1 \xrightarrow{\langle e_1, p_1 \rangle} M_2 \xrightarrow{\langle e_2, p_2 \rangle} \cdots .$$

It is an immediate consequence of the contractiveness of $\mathcal{F}$ that it is *Cauchy* in the following sense:

$$\forall \epsilon > 0 \; \exists N \; \forall m > n \ge N, \quad \delta(\langle e_{m-1}, p_{m-1} \rangle \circ \cdots \circ \langle e_n, p_n \rangle) \le \epsilon.$$

The following complete ultrametric space will be shown to be a fixed point of $\mathcal{F}$ (it will be a kind of limit of the Cauchy sequence Δ): let

$$M = \{(x_n)_n \mid \forall n \ge 0, \; x_n \in M_n \text{ and } p_n(x_{n+1}) = x_n\},$$

with metric, for $(x_n)_n$ and $(y_n)_n$ in M,

$$d((x_n)_n, (y_n)_n) = sup\{d_n(x_n, y_n)\}.$$

(It is a little exercise to prove that this defines a complete ultrametric space.) The space M can be related to the sequence Δ by means of the following e-p pairs: for every $n \ge 0$, $x \in M_n$, and $(x_0, x_1, \ldots)$ in M, an e-p pair $\langle f_n, g_n \rangle: M_n \to M$ is defined by

$$f_n(x) = (p_0 \circ \cdots \circ p_{n-1}(x), \ \ldots, p_{n-1}(x), \ x, \ e_n(x), \ e_{n+1} \circ e_n(x), \ \ldots),$$

$$g_n((x_0, x_1, \ldots)) = x_n.$$

Because Δ is Cauchy, it follows that $lim \, \delta \langle f_n, g_n \rangle = 0$, which is equivalent to $lim \, f_n \circ g_n = 1_M$. This means that for increasing n, the spaces M and M_n are more and more alike.

The last step in the proof of the theorem, namely that M is a fixed point of $\mathcal{F}$, consists of a typically categorical argument: by definition, $(\langle f_n, g_n \rangle : M_n \to M)_n$ is a *cone* from Δ to M; that is, for all $n \geq 0$,

$$\langle f_n, g_n \rangle = \langle f_{n+1}, g_{n+1} \rangle \circ \langle e_n, p_n \rangle.$$

(The space M is called the vertex of this cone.) It is not difficult to prove that $lim \, f_n \circ g_n = 1_M$ implies that this cone is moreover *colimiting*: that is, for any other cone $(\langle \bar{f}_n, \bar{g}_n \rangle : M_n \to \bar{M})_n$, from Δ to $\bar{M}$, there is a *unique* e-p pair $\langle r, s \rangle : M \to \bar{M}$ such that, for all $n \geq 0$, $\langle r, s \rangle \circ \langle f_n, g_n \rangle = \langle \bar{f}_n, \bar{g}_n \rangle$. (Cf. the "initiality lemma" of [AR89b].) The uniqueness requirement ensures that if two cones both are colimiting, then their vertices must be isomorphic. Now we have just seen that M is (the vertex of) a colimiting cone for Δ. Applying the functor $\mathcal{F}$ gives a new cone

$$(\langle \mathcal{F}(f_n), \mathcal{F}(g_n) \rangle : M_{n+1} \to \mathcal{F}(M))_n$$

from

$$\mathcal{F}(\Delta) = M_1 \xrightarrow{\langle e_1, p_1 \rangle} M_2 \xrightarrow{\langle e_2, p_2 \rangle} \cdots$$

to $\mathcal{F}(M)$. It follows from the contractiveness of $\mathcal{F}$ that $lim \, \delta \langle \mathcal{F}(f_n), \mathcal{F}(g_n) \rangle = 0$, which is equivalent to $lim \, \mathcal{F}(f_n) \circ \mathcal{F}(g_n) = 1_{\mathcal{F}(M)}$. Therefore this new cone is again colimiting. Because the sequence $\mathcal{F}(\Delta)$ is obtained from Δ by omitting its first element, there is also a cone from $\mathcal{F}(\Delta)$ to M:

$$(\langle f_{n+1}, g_{n+1} \rangle : M_n \to M)_n,$$

and it is still colimiting. Both M and $\mathcal{F}(M)$ are (the vertex of) colimiting cones from $\mathcal{F}(\Delta)$, hence they are isomorphic. $\square$

The above can be easily generalized to functors on $CUMS^e \times CUMS^e$: Let α be a real number with $0 \leq \alpha \leq 1$. A functor

$$\mathcal{F} : (CUMS^e \times CUMS^e) \to (CUMS^e \times CUMS^e)$$

is called α-*Lipschitz* if for every arrow $(\langle e, p \rangle, \langle r, s \rangle)$ in $CUMS^e \times CUMS^e$,

$$\delta(\mathcal{F}(\langle e, p \rangle, \langle r, s \rangle)) \leq \alpha \cdot \delta(\langle e, p \rangle, \langle r, s \rangle),$$

where $\delta(\langle e, p \rangle, \langle r, s \rangle) = max\{\delta\langle e, p \rangle, \delta\langle r, s \rangle\}$. (Similarly for functors from $CUMS^e$ to $CUMS^e \times CUMS^e$ and functors from $CUMS^e \times CUMS^e$ to $CUMS^e$.) Again we have that if $\mathcal{F}$ is contractive then it has a fixed point.

C.3   Contractive functors

For functors built (by composition and pairing) from a number of basic functors, it is fairly easy to determine whether they are contractive. First it can be observed that all functors of Definition 10.10 give rise to corresponding functors on $CUMS^e$ (or $CUMS^e \times CUMS^e$), acting the same on objects and on arrows as one would expect. For instance, the product functor maps any arrow $(\langle e, p \rangle, \langle r, s \rangle) \colon (M, N) \to (M', N')$ to

$$\langle e \times r, p \times s \rangle \colon (M \times N) \to (M' \times N'),$$

where $(e \times r)(m, n) = (e(m), r(n))$, for $(m, n) \in M \times N$. Similarly for the other examples. There is notably one functor that we could not deal with before: The function space functor $\xrightarrow{1} \colon (CUMS^e \times CUMS^e) \to CUMS^e$ is defined, on objects (M, N), by

$$M \xrightarrow{1} N = \{f \colon M \to N \mid f \text{ is nonexpansive}\},$$

and on arrows $(\langle e, p \rangle, \langle r, s \rangle) \colon (M, N) \to (M', N')$ by

$$\langle p \to r, e \to s \rangle \colon (M \xrightarrow{1} N) \to (M' \xrightarrow{1} N'),$$

where $p \to r$ maps f in $M \xrightarrow{1} N$ to $r \circ f \circ p$ in $M' \xrightarrow{1} N'$, and $e \to s$ is defined similarly.

The Lipschitz factor of a compound functor can be calculated from those of its components with the help of a few simple rules:

1. The basic functors are Lipschitz as in Theorem 10.11. E.g., any constant functor is 0-Lipschitz; the α-identity functor $(0 \leq \alpha \leq 1)$ is α-Lipschitz; the powerdomain functors are 1-Lipschitz; and $\times$ and $+$ are 1-Lipschitz.

2. If $\mathcal{F} \colon CUMS^e \to CUMS^e$ is α_1-Lipschitz and $\mathcal{G} \colon CUMS^e \to CUMS^e$ is α_2-Lipschitz $(0 \leq \alpha_1, \alpha_2 \leq 1)$, then

(a) $\mathcal{F} \circ \mathcal{G}$ is α-Lipschitz with $\alpha = \alpha_1 \cdot \alpha_2$;

(b) $\langle \mathcal{F}, \mathcal{G} \rangle \colon CUMS^e \to (CUMS^e \times CUMS^e)$ is α-Lipschitz with $\alpha = max\{\alpha_1, \alpha_2\}$;

(c) $\xrightarrow{1} \circ \langle \mathcal{F}, \mathcal{G} \rangle \colon CUMS^e \to CUMS^e$ is α-Lipschitz with
$\alpha = max\{\alpha_1, \alpha_2\}$.

As an example consider the following variant of the system of equations in Section 18.3. Let A be an arbitrary complete ultrametric space and suppose we are looking for complete ultrametric spaces Q and R such that

$$
\begin{aligned}
Q &\cong R + (R \times Q), \\
R &\cong A \times ((R \xrightarrow{1} Q) \xrightarrow{1} (R \xrightarrow{1} Q)).
\end{aligned}
$$

This leads to the definition of a contractive functor by adding appropriate α-identity functors: let $\mathcal{F}, \mathcal{G} \colon (CUMS^e \times CUMS^e) \to CUMS^e$ be defined, for complete ultrametric spaces M and N, by

$$
\mathcal{F}(M, N) = id_{\frac{1}{2}}(N + (N \times M)),
$$

$$
\mathcal{G}(M, N) = A \times id_{\frac{1}{2}}((N \xrightarrow{1} M) \xrightarrow{1} (N \xrightarrow{1} M)).
$$

It follows from the rules above that both $\mathcal{F}$ and $\mathcal{G}$, and consequently also $\langle \mathcal{F}, \mathcal{G} \rangle$ all are $\frac{1}{2}$-Lipschitz. Thus the latter is a contractive functor on $CUMS^e \times CUMS^e$ and therefore has a fixed point $\langle Q, R \rangle$, satisfying the two equations above. The following variation on the definition of $\mathcal{F}$,

$$
\mathcal{F}(M, N) = N + (N \times id_{\frac{1}{2}}(M)),
$$

leads to a metric on Q that might be considered more natural. In fact, in the definitions (18.7a, 18.7b), the latter $\mathcal{F}$ is used. (Note that though $\mathcal{F}$ is now no longer contractive, the composition $\langle \mathcal{F}, \mathcal{G} \rangle \circ \langle \mathcal{F}, \mathcal{G} \rangle$ still is.)

C.4   Bibliographical notes

The above construction is taken from [AR89b], and generalizes the way of solving recursive domain equations with metric spaces introduced by De Bakker and Zucker in [BZ82]. It is a metric variant of the order-theoretic solution of recursive domain equations by Smyth and Plotkin ([SP82]). A similar metric variation is given in [MZ91]. The results of [AR89b] have been further generalized in [RT93] by dealing with local properties of functors. Similar results have been obtained for compact metric spaces in [BW94]. The idea mentioned above of viewing the family of complete metric spaces itself as a kind of large metric space has recently been carried out somewhat further. In [ABBR95], it is shown that this family can be supplied with a pseudo-metric with respect to which it is complete. The restriction of this large pseudo-metric space to the family of all compact metric spaces satisfies the additional property that two spaces have distance 0 if and only if they are isometric. As a consequence domain equations can be solved by an application of Banach's fixed-point theorem (rather than some categorical variant of it). The latter approach has been motivated by Lawvere's $\mathcal{V}$-categorical view on metric spaces ([Law73]). One of his contributions is the observation that both preordered sets and metric spaces are examples of $\mathcal{V}$-categories and hence have many structural similarities. As a consequence, pseudo-quasi (also called generalized) metric spaces can be supplied with both a preorder and an (ordinary) metric. Some of Lawvere's ideas have been worked out in a number of papers: In [Ken87], some domain equations are solved in a category of generalized (i.e., pseudo-quasi) metric spaces. In [Wag94], domain equations are solved in categories of "abstract preorders," generalizing both preorders and metric spaces. A similar aim underlies [FK94], where a more topological approach is followed. In [Rut95], the category of generalized ultrametric spaces is studied by exploiting the work of Lawvere and Smyth' work on quasi-metric spaces ([Smy91]); as in [Wag94], domain equations are solved—using metric adjoint pairs rather than embedding-projection pairs—for partial orders and metric spaces at the same time. Moreover the subcategory "SFU" of (colimits of) sequences of finite (generalized) ultrametric spaces is identified, having both the category SFP of bifinite partial orders and the category of compact ultrametric spaces as full subcategories.

D Further Reading

Textbooks on semantics

[Sto77] J.E. Stoy, *Denotational Semantics: The Scott-Strachey Approach to Programming Language Theory,* The MIT Press, 1977. The first—and by now classical—text on denotational semantics.

Further textbooks on semantics include

[Gor79] M.J.C. Gordon, *The Denotational Description of Programming Languages,* Springer, 1979.

[Ten81] R.D. Tennent, *Principles of Programming Languages,* Prentice-Hall International, 1981.

[All86] L. Allison, *A Practical Introduction to Denotational Semantics,* Cambridge University Press, 1986.

[Sch86] D.A. Schmidt, *Denotational Semantics: A Methodology for Language Development,* Allyn and Bacon, 1986.

[Hen90] M. Hennessy, *The Semantics of Programming Languages: An Elementary Introduction Using Structural Operational Semantics,* Wiley, 1990.

[Ten91] R.D. Tennent, *Semantics of Programming Languages,* Prentice-Hall International, 1991.

[Wat91] D.A. Watt, *Programming Language Syntax and Semantics,* Prentice-Hall International, 1991.

More recent texts are the following

[Gun92] C.A. Gunter, *Semantics of Programming Languages: Structures and Techniques,* The MIT Press, 1992. An advanced text with thorough coverage of domain theory and type systems

[Mos92] P. Mosses, *Action Semantics,* Cambridge University Press, 1992. Presents a wide range of language features with semantic models expressed in terms of the formal notion of "action." No operational semantics.

[NN92] H.R. Nielson and F. Nielson, *Semantics with Applications: A Formal Introduction,* Wiley, 1992. An introductory text on operational, denotational and "axiomatic" semantics for languages in the style of our $\mathcal{L}_{wh}$. Treats in addition topics on implementation and static analysis techniques.

[Win93] G. Winskel, *The Formal Semantics of Programming Languages,* The MIT
Press, 1993. An intermediate text treating both operational, denotational
and axiomatic semantics. Based on cpo's as mathematical structures, the
book includes material on higher and recursive types, but is less comprehensive in its treatment of control flow.

[Sch94] D.A. Schmidt, *The Structure of Typed Programming Languages,* The MIT
Press, 1994. Starting from lambda calculus and type theory, this text
discusses Algol-like languages such as Pascal and higher-order functional
languages such ML.

Textbooks on programming logics

[Bak80, LS87, Gum89, AO91, Fra92]. Several texts on semantics also deal with
programming logics (or "axiomatic semantics"), e.g., [Ten91, NN92, Win93].

Textbooks on (the foundations of) functional programming

(a small selection) [Bar84, HS86, BW88, HMT90, Mit90].

Advanced topics in (metric) semantics.

In the papers [Bre94a, Bre94b] so-called "metric transition systems" are investigated, where both the set of configurations of the transition system, and its set of
observations are equipped with a metric. This leads in a natural way to the introduction of two generalized finiteness conditions, viz. those of *compactly branching*
and of *image-compact* transition systems. General properties of these systems are
explored, e.g., generalizing Theorem 2.30 and Theorem 5.3. Also, some applications
of such systems are discussed, e.g., dealing with the notion of "compact choice" in
a setting with real-time notions.

Our semantics for nonuniform languages are always "state-based," with state
transformations as a basic ingredient of the various models. It is also possible to
base the semantics on predicates (sets of states determined by logical properties)
and predicate transformations. There is an extensive literature on this topic, with
the (Stone) duality between state transformers and predicate transformers as an

interesting subtheme. We mention only the references [Plo79, Smy83, Hes89, BK94, BVK94, Bon96].

The reader who has worked through the numerous $\mathcal{O} = \mathcal{D}$ proofs may wonder whether it might be possible to "automate" such arguments, essentially by establishing a method to infer $\mathcal{D}$ (and not only $\mathcal{O}$) from the information in the transition system at hand. There are a number of important studies of this question, mostly establishing compositionality of the $\mathcal{O}$ associated with some $\mathcal{T}$—thus verifying a necessary condition for $\mathcal{O}$ to qualify as well as a denotational semantics. References for this include [GV92, Rut92, Ver94, Fok94, OV94]. Though quite promising (from the perspective of making the $\mathcal{O} = \mathcal{D}$ proofs superfluous), for the moment considerable work remains to be done to widen the applicability of these results. E.g., as yet it is not clear how to deal with (most of) our resumption-based specifications. Also, the methods available to date only deal with the case that both $\mathcal{O}$ and $\mathcal{D}$ are branching models. In [RT94, Tur95], these questions are studied with category-theoretic tools, aiming at a better understanding of the underlying structure of the approach.

Besides the metric spaces used to solve domain equations (Chapter 10, Appendix C) and the "classical" cpo's, a third kind of mathematical structure is receiving increased attention, viz. that of Aczel's non-well-founded sets ([Acz88]) or Forti and Honsell's hyperstructures ([FH83, FHL94]). (In [RT93] it is argued that each of the three types of domains is an instance of the categorical notion of *final coalgebra*.)

Bibliography

[AA88]   Y.J. Aalbersberg and P.H.M. America. Personal communication, 1988.

[AB88]   P.H.M. America and J.W. de Bakker. Designing equivalent semantic models for process creation. *Theoretical Computer Science*, 60:109–176, 1988.

[ABBR95]   F. Alessi, P. Baldan, G. Bellè, and J.J.M.M. Rutten. Solutions of functorial and non-functorial metric domain equations. In S. Brookes et al., editor, *Proc. 11th MFPS*, pages 427–438. Electronic Notes in Theoretical Computer Science, 1995.

[ABKR86]   P. America, J.W. de Bakker, J.N. Kok, and J.J.M.M. Rutten. Operational semantics of a parallel object-oriented language. In *Proc. of the 13th Annual ACM Symposium on Principles of Programming Languages*, pages 194–208. ACM, 1986.

[ABKR89]   P. America, J.W. de Bakker, J.N. Kok, and J.J.M.M. Rutten. Denotational semantics of a parallel object-oriented language. *Information and Computation*, 83:152–205, 1989. Reprinted in [BR92].

[Abr79]   K. Abrahamson. Modal logic of concurrent nondeterministic programs. In G. Kahn, editor, *Proc. Semantics of Concurrent Computation*, pages 21–33. LNCS 70, Springer, 1979.

[Abr91]   S. Abramsky. A domain equation for bisimulation. *Information and Computation*, 92:161–218, 1991.

[Ace90]   L. Aceto. *Action Refinement in Process Algebras*. PhD thesis, University of Sussex, 1990.

[Acz88]   P. Aczel. *Non-well-founded Sets*. Lecture Notes 14, CSLI, 1988.

[Ale27]   P. Alexandroff. Über stetige Abbildungen kompakter Räume. *Mathematische Annalen*, 96:555–571, 1927.

[All86]   L. Allison. *A Practical Introduction to Denotational Semantics*. Cambridge Computer Science Texts 23, 1986.

[AM89]   P. Aczel and N. Mendler. A final coalgebra theorem. In D.H. Pitt et al., editors, *Proc. Category Theory and Computer Science*, pages 357–365. LNCS 389, Springer, 1989.

[Ame91]   P.H.M. America. Formal techniques for parallel object-oriented languages. In J.C.M. Baeten and J.F. Groote, editors, *Proc. CONCUR'91*, pages 1–17. LNCS 527, Springer, 1991.

[AMJ94]   S. Abramsky, P. Malacaria, and R. Jagadeesan. Full abstraction for PCF. In M. Hagiya and J.C. Mitchell, editors, *Proc. Theoretical Aspects of Computer Software*, pages 1–15. LNCS 789, Springer, 1994.

[AN80a]   A. Arnold and M. Nivat. Metric interpretations of infinite trees and semantics of nondeterministic recursive programs. *Theoretical Computer Science*, 11:181–205, 1980.

[AN80b]   A. Arnold and M. Nivat. The metric space of infinite trees, algebraic and topological properties. *Fundamenta Informaticae*, 4:445–476, 1980.

[ANN85]   A. Arnold, P. Naudin, and M. Nivat. On semantics of nondeterministic recursive program schemes. In M. Nivat and J.C. Reynolds, editors, *Algebraic Methods in Semantics*, pages 1–33. Cambridge University Press, 1985.

[AO91]   K.R. Apt and E.-R. Olderog. *Verification of Sequential and Concurrent Programs*. Springerg, 1991.

[AP86]   K.R. Apt and G.D. Plotkin. Countable nondeterminism and random assignment. *Journal of the ACM*, 33:724–767, 1986.

[Apt83]   K.R. Apt. Recursive assertions and parallel programs. *Acta Informatica*, 15:219–232, 1983.

[Apt90]   K.R. Apt. Logic programming. In J. van Leeuwen, editor, *Handbook of Theoretical Computer Science*, volume B, pages 493–574. Elsevier, 1990.

[AR89a]   P. America and J.J.M.M. Rutten. *A Parallel Object-Oriented Language: design and semantic foundations*. PhD theses, Vrije Universiteit Amsterdam, 1989. Also published as CWI Tracts, Vol. 81, CWI, Amsterdam, 1991.

[AR89b]   P. America and J.J.M.M. Rutten. Solving reflexive domain equations in a category of complete metric spaces. *Journal of Computer and System Sciences*, 39:343–375, 1989. Reprinted in [BR92].

[AR89c]   P.H.M. America and J.J.M.M. Rutten. A parallel object-oriented language: design and semantic foundations. In J.W. de Bakker, editor, *Languages for Parallel Architectures*, pages 1–49. Wiley Series in Parallel Computing, 1989.

[AR92]   P.H.M. America and J.J.M.M. Rutten. A layered semantics for parallel object-oriented languages. *Formal Aspects of Computing*, 4:376–408, 1992.

[Arn83]   A. Arnold. Topological characterizations of infinite behaviours of transition systems. In J. Diaz, editor, *Proc. of 10th International Colloquium on Automata, Languages and Programming*, pages 28–38. LNCS 154, Springer, 1983.

[Bac83]   R.J. Back. A continuous semantics for unbounded nondeterminism. *Theoretical Computer Science*, 23:187–210, 1983.

[Bai09]   R. Baire. Sur la représentation des fonctions discontinues. *Acta Mathematica*, 32:97–176, 1909.

[Bak71]   J.W. de Bakker. *Recursive Procedures*. Mathematical Centre Tracts 24, Mathematisch Centrum, Amsterdam, 1971.

[Bak76]   J.W. de Bakker. Semantics and termination of nondeterministic recursive programs. In S. Michaelson and R. Milner, editors, *Proc. 3rd International Colloquium on Automata, Languages and Programming*. Edinburg University Press, 1976.

[Bak80]   J.W. de Bakker. *Mathematical Theory of Program Correctness*. Prentice-Hall, 1980.

[Bak89]   J.W. de Bakker. Designing concurrency semantics. In G.X. Ritter, editor, *Proc. 11th IFIP World Computer Congress*, pages 591–598. North-Holland, 1989.

[Bak91]   J.W. de Bakker. Comparative semantics for flow of control in logic programming without logic. *Information and Computation*, 94:123–179, 1991. Reprinted in [BR92].

[Ban22]   S. Banach. Sur les opérations dans les ensembles abstraits et leurs applications aux equations intégrales. *Fundamenta Mathematicae*, 3:133–181, 1922.

[Bar84]   H.P. Barendregt. *The Lambda Calculus, its Syntax and Semantics*. North-Holland, 1984.

[Bar92]   H.P. Barendregt. Lambda calculus with types. In S. Abramsky, D. Gabbay, and T.S.E. Maibaum, editors, *Handbook of Logic in Computer Science*, volume 2, pages 117–309. Oxford University Press, 1992.

[BB85]   A. de Bruin and W. Böhm. The denotational semantics of dynamic networks of processes. *ACM Transactions on Programming Languages and Systems*, 7:656–679, 1985.

[BB94]   J.W. de Bakker and F. van Breugel. Topological models for higher order control flow. In S. Brookes, M. Main, A. Melton, M. Mislove, and D. Schmidt, editors, *Proc. of the 9th International Conference on Mathematical Foundations of Programming Semantics*, pages 122–142. LNCS 802, Springer, 1994.

[BBB93]   J.W. de Bakker, F.C. van Breugel, and A. de Bruin. Comparative semantics for linear arrays of communicating processes. In A. Borzyszkowski and S. Sokolowski, editors, *Proc. 18th Symposium on Mathematical Foundations of Computer Science*, pages 252–261. LNCS 771, Springer, 1993.

[BBKM84]   J.W. de Bakker, J.A. Bergstra, J.W. Klop, and J.-J.Ch. Meyer. Linear time and branching time semantics for recursion with merge. *Theoretical Computer Science*, 34:135–156, 1984. Reprinted in [BR92].

[BC89]   G. Boudol and I. Castellani. Permutations of transitions: an event structure semantics for CCS and SCCS. In [BRR89], pages 411–427, 1989.

[BCL85]   G. Berry, P.L. Curien, and J. Levy. Full abstraction for sequential languages: the state of the art. In M. Nivat and J.C. Reynolds, editors, *Algebraic Methods in Semantics*, pages 90–132. Cambridge University Press, 1985.

[BD91]   E. Badouel and P. Darondeau. On guarded recursion. *Theoretical Computer Science*, 82:403–408, 1991.

[Bek84a]   H. Bekic. Definiable operations in general algebras and the theory of automata and flow charts. In *H. Bekic, Programming Languages and their Definition*, pages 30–55. LNCS 177, Springer, 1984. Reprinted.

[Bek84b]   H. Bekic. Towards a mathematical theory of processes. In *H. Bekic, Programming Languages and their Definition*, pages 168–214. LNCS 177, Springer, 1984. Reprinted.

[Bes93]   E. Best, editor. *Proc. 4th International Conference on Concurrency Theory*. LNCS 715, Springer, 1993.

[BGV91]   W. Brauer, R. Gold, and W. Vogler. A survey of behaviour and equivalence preserving refinements of Petri nets. In G. Rozenberg, editor, *Advances in Petri Nets*, pages 1–46. LNCS 483, Springer, 1991.

[BHR84]   S.D. Brookes, C.A.R. Hoare, and A.W. Roscoe. A theory of communicating sequential processes. *Journal of the ACM*, 31:560–599, July 1984.

[BK85]   J.W. de Bakker and J.N. Kok. Towards a uniform topological treatment of streams and functions on streams. In W. Brauer, editor, *Proc. of the 12th International Colloquium on Automata, Languages and Programming*, pages 140–148. LNCS 194, Springer, 1985.

[BK88]   J.W. de Bakker and J.N. Kok. Uniform abstraction, atomicity and contractions in the comparative semantics of Concurrent Prolog. In *Proc. International Conference on Fifth Generation Computer Systems (FGCS'88)*, pages 347–355, Tokyo, 1988.

[BK89]   J.A. Bergstra and J.W. Klop. Process theory based on bisimulation semantics. In [BRR89], pages 50–122, 1989.

[BK90]   J.W. de Bakker and J.N. Kok. Comparative metric semantics for Concurrent Prolog. *Theoretical Computer Science*, 75:15–43, 1990.

[BK94]   M. Bonsangue and J.N. Kok. The weakest precondition calculus: recursion and duality. *Formal Aspects of Computing*, 6A:788–800, 1994.

[BKMOZ85]   J.W. de Bakker, J.N. Kok, J.-J.Ch. Meyer, E.-R. Olderog, and J.I. Zucker. Contrasting themes in the semantics of imperative concurrency. In [BRR85], pages 51–121, 1985.

[BKO88]   J.A. Bergstra, J.W. Klop, and E.-R. Olderog. Readies and failures in the algebra of communicating processes. *SIAM Journal on Computing*, 17:1134–1177, 1988.

[BKPR91a]   F.S. de Boer, J.N. Kok, C. Palamidessi, and J.J.M.M. Rutten. The failure of failures in a paradigm for asynchronous communication. In J.C.M. Baeten and J.F. Groote, editors, *Proc. CONCUR'91*, pages 111–126. LNCS 527, Springer, 1991.

[BKPR91b]   F.S. de Boer, J.N. Kok, C. Palamidessi, and J.J.M.M. Rutten. Semantic models for concurrent logic languages. *Theoretical Computer Science*, 86:3–34, 1991.

[BKPR92]   F.S. de Boer, J.N. Kok, C. Palamidessi, and J.J.M.M. Rutten. From failure to success: comparing a denotational and a declarative semantics for Horn clause logic. *Theoretical Computer Science*, 101:239–263, 1992. Reprinted in [BR92].

[BKPR93a]   F.S. de Boer, J.N. Kok, C. Palamidessi, and J.J.M.M. Rutten. On blocks: locality and asynchronous communication. In [BRR93], pages 73–90, 1993.

[BKPR93b]   F.S. de Boer, J.N. Kok, C. Palamidessi, and J.J.M.M. Rutten. A paradigm for asynchronous communication and its application to concurrent constraint programming. In K.R. Apt, J.W. de Bakker, and J.J.M.M. Rutten, editors, *Logic Programming Languages — Constraints, Functions and Objects*, pages 82–114. The MIT Press, 1993.

[BM87]   J.W. de Bakker and J.-J.Ch. Meyer. Order and metric in the stream semantics of elemental concurrency. *Acta Informatica*, 24:491–511, 1987. Reprinted in [BR92].

[BM88]   J.W. de Bakker and J.-J.Ch. Meyer. Metric semantics for concurrency. *BIT*, 28:504–529, 1988. Reprinted in [BR92].

[BM94]   Ch. Baier and M.E. Majster-Cederbaum. The connection between an event structure semantics and an operational semantics for TCSP. *Acta Informatica*, 31:81–104, 1994.

[BMOZ88]   J.W. de Bakker, J.-J.Ch. Meyer, E.-R. Olderog, and J.I. Zucker. Transition systems, metric spaces and ready sets in the semantics of uniform concurrency. *Journal of Computer and System Sciences*, 36:158–224, 1988.

[Bon96]   M. Bonsangue. *Topological Dualities in Semantics*. Forthcoming Ph.D thesis, Vrije Universiteit Amsterdam, 1996.

[Bou89]   G. Boudol. Towards a lambda-calculus for concurrent and communicating systems. In J. Diaz and F. Orejas, editors, *Proc. of the International Joint Conference on Theory and Practice of Software Development*, pages 149–162. LNCS 351, Springer, 1989.

[BP91]   F.S. de Boer and C. Palamidessi. A fully abstract model for concurrent constraint programming. In S. Abramsky and T.S.E. Maibaum, editors, *Proc. TAPSOFT/CAAP'91*, pages 296–319. LNCS 493, Springer, 1991.

[BR84]   S.D. Brookes and A.W. Roscoe. An improved failures model for communicating processes. In *Proc. Seminar on Concurrency*, pages 281–305. LNCS 197, Springer, 1984.

[BR92]   J.W. de Bakker and J.J.M.M. Rutten, editors. *Ten Years of Concurrency Semantics, selected papers of the Amsterdam Concurrency Group*. World Scientific, 1992.

[Bre93]   F. van Breugel. Three metric domains of processes for bisimulation. In S. Brookes, M. Main, A. Melton, M. Mislove, and D. Schmidt, editors, *Proc. of the 9th International Conference on Mathematical Foundations of Programming Semantics*, pages 103–121. LNCS 802, Springer, 1993.

[Bre94a]   F. van Breugel. Generalizing finiteness conditions of labelled transition systems. In S. Abiteboul and E. Shamir, editors, *Proc. of the 21th International Colloquium on Automata, Languages, and Programming*, pages 376–387. LNCS 820, Springer, 1994.

[Bre94b]   F.C. van Breugel. *Topological Models in Comparative Semantics*. PhD thesis, Vrije Universiteit Amsterdam, 1994.

[BRR85]   J.W. de Bakker, W.P. de Roever, and G. Rozenberg, editors. *Current Trends in Concurrency: Overviews and Tutorials*. Proc. ESPRIT/LPC Summerschool, LNCS 224, Springer, 1985.

[BRR89]   J.W. de Bakker, W.P. de Roever, and G. Rozenberg, editors. *Linear Time, Branching Time and Partial Order in Logics and Models for Concurrency*. REX School/Workshop, LNCS 354, Springer, 1989.

[BRR91]   J.W. de Bakker, W.P. de Roever, and G. Rozenberg, editors. *Foundations of Object-Oriented Languages*. REX School/Workshop, LNCS 489, Springer, 1991.

[BRR93]   J.W. de Bakker, W.P. de Roever, and G. Rozenberg, editors. *Semantics: Foundations and Applications*. REX School/Workshop, LNCS 666, Springer, 1993.

[BRR94]   J.W. de Bakker, W.P. de Roever, and G. Rozenberg, editors. *A Decade of Concurrency, Reflections and Perspectives*. REX School/Symposium, LNCS 803, Springer, 1994.

[BRR86]   W. Brauer, W. Reisig, and G. Rozenberg, editors. *Petri Nets: Central Models and Their Properties, Advances in Petri Nets 1986 Part I*. LNCS 254, Springer, 1986.

[Bru84]   A. de Bruin. On the existence of Cook semantics. *SIAM Journal on Computing*, 13:59–71, 1984.

[Bru86]   A. de Bruin. *Experiments with Continuation Semantics: Jumps, Backtracking, Dynamic Networks*. PhD thesis, Vrije Universiteit Amsterdam, 1986.

[BS69]   J.W. de Bakker and D.S Scott. A theory of programs. Notes, IBM Seminar, Vienna, 1969. Appeared in *J.W. de Bakker, 25 jaar semantiek*, pages 1–30, CWI, Amsterdam 1989.

[BV89]   A. de Bruin and E.P. de Vink. Continuation semantics for Prolog with cut. In J. Diaz and F. Orejas, editors, *Proc. TAPSOFT'89*, pages 178–192. LNCS 351, Springer, 1989.

[BV90]   A. de Bruin and E.P. de Vink. Denotational semantics for unguarded recursion: the demonic case. In A.J. van de Goor, editor, *Proc. of Computing Science in the Netherlands*, volume 1, pages 51–64. Stichting Mathematisch Centrum, 1990.

[BV91]   J.W. de Bakker and E.P. de Vink. CCS for OO and LP. In S. Abramsky and T.S.E. Maibaum, editors, *Proc. TAPSOFT'91*, pages 1–28. LNCS 494, Springer, 1991.

[BV92]   J.C.M. Baeten and F.W. Vaandrager. An algebra for process creation. *Acta Informatica*, 29:303–334, 1992.

[BV93]   J.W. de Bakker and E.P. de Vink. Rendez-vous with metric semantics. *New Generation Computing*, 12:53–90, 1993.

[BV94]   J.W. de Bakker and E.P. de Vink. Bisimulation semantics for concurrency with atomicity and action refinement. *Fundamenta Informaticae*, 20:3–34, 1994.

[BVK94]   M. Bonsangue, E.P. de Vink, and J.N. Kok. Metric predicate transformers: Towards a notion of refinement for concurrency. In I. Lee and S.A. Smolka, editors, *Proc. CONCUR'95*, pages 363–377, LNCS 962, Springer, 1995.

[BW88]   R.S. Bird and R. Wadler. *Introduction to Functional Programming*. Prentice-Hall International, 1988.

[BW90]   J.W. de Bakker and J.H.A. Warmerdam. Metric pomset semantics for a concurrent language with recursion. In I. Guessarian, editor, *Proc. of the LITP Spring School on Theoretical Computer Science*, pages 21–49. LNCS 469, Springer, 1990.

[BW91a]   J.C.M. Baeten and P. Weyland. *Process Algebra*. Cambridge Tracts in Theoretical
             Computer Science 18, 1991.

[BW91b]   J.W. de Bakker and J.H.A. Warmerdam. Four domains for concurrency. *Theoret-
             ical Computer Science*, 90:127–149, 1991.

[BW94]   F. van Breugel and J.H.A. Warmerdam. Solving domain equations in a category
             of compact metric spaces. Report CS-R9424, CWI, Amsterdam, 1994.

[BZ82]   J.W. de Bakker and J.I. Zucker. Processes and the denotational semantics of
             concurrency. *Information and Control*, 54:70–120, 1982. Reprinted in [BR92].

[BZ83a]   J.W. de Bakker and J.I. Zucker. Compactness in semantics for merge and fair
             merge. In E. Clarke and D. Kozen, editors, *Proc. of 4th Workshop on Logics of
             Programs*, pages 18–33. LNCS 164, Springer, 1983.

[BZ83b]   J.W. de Bakker and J.I. Zucker. Processes and a fair semantics for the ada rendez-
             vous. In J. Diaz, editor, *Proc. of 10th International Colloquium on Automata,
             Languages and Programming*, pages 52–66. LNCS 154, Springer, 1983.

[CKRP73]   A. Colmerauer, H. Kanoui, P. Roussel, and R. Pasero. Un système de commu-
             nication homme-machine en français. Technical report, Groupe de Recherche en
             Intelligence Artificielle, Université d'Aix-Marseille, 1973.

[CM94]   W.F. Clocksin and C.S. Mellish. *Programming in PROLOG, 4th ed.* Springer,
             1994.

[CMP87]   L. Castellano, G. de Michelis, and L. Pomello. Concurrency vs. interleaving: an
             instructive example. *Bulletin of the EATCS*, 31:12–15, 1987.

[Coh79]   J. Cohen. Nondeterministic algorithms. *Computing Surveys*, 11:79–94, 1979.

[Cos85]   G. Costa. A metric charaterization of fair computations in CCS. In H. Ehrig et al.,
             editors, *Proc. Colloquium on Software Engineering*, pages 239–251. LNCS 186,
             Springer, 1985.

[DG91]   P. Degano and R. Gorrieri. Atomic refinement in process description languages. In
             A. Tarlecki, editor, *Proc. MFCS*, pages 121–130. LNCS 520, Springer, 1991.

[Dij68]   E.W. Dijkstra. Cooperating sequential processes. In F. Genuys, editor, *Program-
             ming Languages*, pages 43–112. Academic Press, 1968.

[Dij75]   E.W. Dijkstra. Guarded commands, nondeterminacy and formal derivation of pro-
             grams. *Communications of the ACM*, 18:453–457, 1975.

[DM84]   P. Degano and U. Montanari. Liveness properties as convergence in metric spaces.
             In *Proc. 16th ACM STOC*, pages 31–38, 1984.

[DMN88]   P. Degano, U. Montanari, and R. de Nicola. On the consistency of 'truly concurrent'
             operational and denotational semantics. In *Proc. 3rd Annual Symposium on Logics
             in Computer Science 88*, pages 133–141, 1988.

[DNPY92]   P. Darondeau, D. Nolte, L. Priese, and S. Yoccoz. Fairness, distances and degrees.
             Theoretical Computer Science, 97:131–142, 1992.

[DoD83]   US Department of Defense. *Reference Manual for the ADA Programming Lan-
             guage*, 1983. ANSI/MIL-STD-1815A.

[Eli92]   A. Eliëns. *DLP: A Language for Distributed Logic Programming: Design, Seman-
             tics and Implementation*. Wiley Series in Parallel Computing, 1992.

[Eng89]   R. Engelking. *General Topology*. Sigma Series in Pure Mathematics 6, Heldermann
             Verlag, revised and completed edition, 1989.

[FH83]   M. Forti and F. Honsell. Set theory with free construction principles. *Annali
             Scuola Normale Superiore, Pisa*, X:493–522, 1983.

[FHL94]   M. Forti, F. Honsell, and M. Lenisa. Processes and hyperuniverses. In I. Pri-
            vara et al., editors, *Proc. Symposium on Mathematical Foundations of Computer
            Science 1994*, pages 352–361. LNCS 841, Springer, 1994.

[FK94]   B. Flagg and R. Kopperman. Continuity spaces: reconciling domains and metric
            spaces - part I. Draft, 1994.

[Fok94]   W.J. Fokkink. The tyft/tyxt format reduces to tree rules. In M. Hagiya and J.C.
            Mitchell, editors, *Proc. 2nd International Symposium on Theoretical Aspects of
            Computer Software*, pages 440–453. LNCS 789, Springer, 1994.

[Fra86]   N. Francez. *Fairness*. Springer, 1986.

[Fra92]   N. Francez. *Program Verification*. Addison-Wesley, 1992.

[GCLS88]   R. Gerth, M. Codish, Y. Lichtenstein, and E. Shapiro. Fully abstract denotational
            semantics for Concurrent Prolog. In *Proc. 3rd LICS*, pages 320–335, Edinburgh,
            1988.

[Gla90a]   R.J. van Glabbeek. *Comparative Concurrency Semantics and Refinement of Ac-
            tions*. PhD thesis, Vrije Universiteit Amsterdam, 1990.

[Gla90b]   R.J. van Glabbeek. The linear time - branching time spectrum. In J.C.M. Baeten
            and J.W. Klop, editors, *Proc. of CONCUR'90*, pages 278–297. LNCS 458, Springer,
            1990.

[GMS89]   H. Gaifman, M.J. Maher, and E. Shapiro. Reactive behaviour semantics for concur-
            rent constraint logic programs. In E. Lusk and R. Overbeek, editors, *Proc. North
            American Conference on Logic Programming 1989*, pages 553–572. The MIT Press,
            1989.

[Gor79]   M.J.C. Gordon. *The Denotational Description of Programming Languages*.
            Springer, 1979.

[Gor91]   R. Gorrieri. *Refinement, Atomicity and Transactions for Process Description Lan-
            guages*. PhD thesis, University of Pisa, 1991.

[GPP71]   R.E. Griswold, J.F. Poage, and I.P. Polonsky. *The SNOBOL 4 Programming Lan-
            guage, 2nd ed.* Prentice-Hall, 1971.

[GR83]   W.G. Golson and W.C. Rounds. Connections between two theories of concurrency:
            Metric spaces and synchronization trees. *Information and Control*, 57:102–124,
            May/June 1983.

[GR89]   R.J. van Glabbeek and J.J.M.M. Rutten. The processes of De Bakker and Zucker
            represent bisimulation equivalence classes. In *J.W. de Bakker 25 Jaar Semantiek,
            Liber Amicorum*, pages 243–246. CWI, Amsterdam, 1989.

[Gra81]   J. Grabowski. On partial languages. *Fundamenta Informaticae*, 4:427–498, 1981.

[Gre87]   S. Gregory. *Parallel Logic Programming in PARLOG*. Addison Wesley, 1987.

[Gro14]   W. Gross. Zur Theorie der Mengen in denen ein Distanzbegriff definiert ist.
            Sitzungsberichte der Akademie der Wissenschaften Wien, 123:801–819, 1914.

[Gum89]   R.D. Gumb. *Programming Logics: An Introduction to Verification and Semantics*.
            Wiley, 1989.

[Gun92]   C.A. Gunter. *Semantics of Programming Languages: Structures and Techniques*.
            The MIT Press, 1992.

[GV92]   J.F. Groote and F.W. Vaandrager. Structured operational semantics and bisimu-
            lation as a congruence. *Information and Computation*, 100:202–260, 1992.

[Hah32]   H. Hahn. *Reelle Funktionen I*. Akademische Verlagsgesellschaft, Leizig, 1932.

[Hau14]   F. Hausdorff. *Grundzüge der Mengenlehre*. Leipzig, 1914.

[HBR94]   E. Horita, J.W. de Bakker, and J.J.M.M. Rutten. Fully abstract denotational mod-
            els for nonuniform concurrent languages. *Information and Computation*, 115:125–
            178, 1994.

[Hen88]   M. Hennessy. *Algebraic Theory of Processes*. The MIT Press, 1988.

[Hen90]   M. Hennessy. *The Semantics of Programming Languages: An Elementary Intro-
            duction Using Structural Operational Semantics*. Wiley, 1990.

[Hes89]   W.H. Hesselink. Predicate transformer semantics of general recursion. *Acta Infor-
            matica*, 26:309–332, 1989.

[Hes92]   W.H. Hesselink. *Programs, Recursion and Unbounded Choice*. Cambridge Univer-
            sity Press Tracts in Theoretical Computer Science 27, 1992.

[HMT90]   R. Harper, R. Milner, and M. Tofte. *Definition of Standard ML*. The MIT Press,
            1990.

[Hoa78]   C.A.R. Hoare. Communicating sequential processes. *Communications of the ACM*,
            21:666–677, 1978.

[Hoa85]   C.A.R. Hoare. *Communicating Sequential Processes*. Prentice Hall International,
            1985.

[Hor92]   E. Horita. Fully abstract models for communicating processes with respect to
            weak linear semantics with divergence. *IEICE Transactions on Information and
            Systems*, E75-D:64–77, 1992.

[Hor93a]   E. Horita. A fully abstract model for a nonuniform concurrent language with
            parametrization and locality. In [BRR93], pages 288–317, 1993.

[Hor93b]   E. Horita. *Fully Abstract Models for Concurrent Languages*. PhD thesis, Vrije
            Universiteit Amsterdam, 1993.

[HP79]   M. Hennessy and G.D. Plotkin. Full abstraction for a simple parallel program-
            ming language. In J. Bečvář, editor, *Proc. of 8th Symposium on Mathematical
            Foundations of Computer Science*, pages 108–120. LNCS 74, Springer, 1979.

[HR85]   H.J. Hoogeboom and G. Rozenberg. Infinitary languages: basic theory and appli-
            cations to concurrent systems. In [BRR85], pages 266–342, 1985.

[HS86]   J.R. Hindley and J.P. Seldin. *Introduction to Combinators and λ-Calculus*. Cam-
            bridge University Press, 1986.

[HU79]   J.E. Hopcroft and J.D. Ullman. *Introduction to Automata Theory, Languages, and
            Computation*. Addison-Wesley, 1979.

[Inm84]   INMOS Ltd. *Occam Programming Manual*, 1984. Prentice-Hall.

[Jac91]   J.M. Jacquet. *Conclog — a Methodological Approach to Concurrent Logic Pro-
            gramming*. LNCS 556, Springer, 1991.

[JL87]   J. Jaffar and J.L. Lassez. Constraint logic programming. In *Proc. 14th ACM
            Symposium on POPL*, pages 111–119. ACM, 1987.

[JM90]   J.M. Jacquet and L. Monteiro. Comparative semantics for a parallel contextual
            logic programming language. In S. Debray and M. Hermenegildo, editors, *Proc.
            North American Conference on Logic Programming*, pages 195–214. The MIT
            Press, 1990.

[JP94]   B. Jonsson and J. Parrow, editors. *Proc. 5th International Conference on Concur-
            rency Theory*. LNCS 836, Springer, 1994.

[Kah87]   G. Kahn. Natural semantics. In F.J. Brandenburg et al., editors, *Proc. Symposium
            STACS*, pages 22–39. LNCS 247, Springer, 1987.

[KCF93]   R. Kanneganti, R. Cartwright, and M. Felleisen. SPCF, its model, calculus and computational power. In [BRR93], pages 318–347, 1993.

[Kel76]   R.M. Keller. Formal verification of parallel programs. *Communications of the ACM*, 19:371–384, 1976.

[Ken87]   R.E. Kent. The metric closure powerspace construction. In M. Main, A. Melton, M. Mislove, and D. Schmidt, editors, *Proc. of the 3rd Workshop on Mathematical Foundations of Programming Language Semantics*, volume 298, pages 173–199. LNCS 298, Springer, 1987.

[KK91]   P. Knijnenburg and J.N. Kok. On the semantics of atomized statements: the parallel choice option. In L. Budach, editor, *Proc. Fundamentals of Computation Theory*, pages 297–307. LNCS 529, Springer, 1991.

[KK93]   P. Knijnenburg and J.N. Kok. Divergent models for atomized statements and parallel choice. In *Proc. 2nd Israel Symposium on Theory of Computing and Systems*, pages 231–240. IEEE Computer Society Press, 1993.

[Kle52]   S.C. Kleene. *Introduction to Metamathematics*. D. van Nostrand, 1952.

[Kna28]   B. Knaster. Un théorème sur les fonctions d'ensembles. *Annales Societatis Mathematicae Polonae*, 6:133–134, 1928.

[Kok88]   J.N. Kok. A compositional semantics for Concurrent Prolog. In R. Cori and M. Wirsing, editors, *Proc. STACS 1988*, pages 373–388. LNCS 294, Springer, 1988.

[Kok89]   J.N. Kok. *Semantic Models for Parallel Computation in Data Flow, Logic- and Object-Oriented Programming*. PhD thesis, Vrije Universiteit Amsterdam, 1989.

[Kön26]   D. König. Sur les correspondances multivoques des ensembles. *Fundamenta Mathematicae*, 8:114–134, 1926.

[Kow79]   R. Kowalski. Algorithm = logic + control. *Communications of the ACM*, 22:424–435, 1979.

[KR90]   J.N. Kok and J.J.M.M. Rutten. Contractions in comparing concurrency semantics. *Theoretical Computer Science*, 76:179–222, 1990.

[Kui81]   R. Kuiper. An operational semantics for bounded nondeterminism equivalent to a denotational one. In J.W. de Bakker and J.C. van Vliet, editors, *Proc. of the International Symposium on Algorithmic Languages*, pages 373–398. North-Holland, 1981.

[Kur56]   K. Kuratowski. Sur une méthode de métrisation complète des certains espaces d'ensembles compacts. *Fundamenta Mathematicae*, 43:114–138, 1956.

[Lan64]   P.J. Landin. The mechanical evaluation of expressions. *The Computer Journal*, 6:308–320, 1964.

[Lan69]   L.H. Landweber. Decision problems for ω-automata. *Mathematical Systems Theory*, 3:376–384, 1969.

[Lan92]   R. Langerak. *Transformations and Semantics for LOTOS*. PhD thesis, Universiteit Twente, Enschede, 1992.

[Law73]   F.W. Lawvere. Metric spaces, generalized logic, and closed categories. *Rendiconti del Seminario Matematico e Fisico di Milano*, 43:135–166, 1973.

[Les71]   J. Leszczylowski. A theorem on resolving equations in the space of languages. *Bull. Acad. Pol. Sci., Ser. Sci. Math. Astr. Phys.*, 19:967–970, 1971.

[LG91]   R. Loogen and U. Goltz. Modelling nondeterministic concurrent processes with event structures. *Fundamenta Informaticae*, 14:39–73, 1991.

[Llo87]   J. Lloyd. *Foundations of Logic Programming, 2nd ed.* Springer, 1987.

[LS87]   J. Loeckx and K. Sieber. *The Foundations of Program Verification*. Wiley, 1987.

[LW71]   P. Lucas and K. Walk. On the formal description of PL/1. *Ann. Rev. in Automatic Programming 6*, pages 105–182, 1971.

[Maz71]   A. Mazurkiewicz. Proving algorithms by tail functions. *Information and Control*, 18:220–226, 1971.

[McC62]   J. McCarthy et al. *LISP 1.5 Programmer's Manual*. The MIT Press, 1962.

[Mic51]   E. Michael. Topologies on spaces of subsets. *Transactions of the American Mathematical Society*, 71:152–182, 1951.

[Mil73]   R. Milner. Processes: a mathematical model of computing agents. In Rose and Shepherdson, editors, *Proc. Logic Coll. 73*, pages 157–173. North-Holland, 1973.

[Mil77]   R. Milner. Fully abstract models of typed λ-calculi. *Theoretical Computer Science*, 4:1–22, 1977.

[Mil79]   R. Milner. Flow graphs and flow algebras. *Journal of the ACM*, 26:794–818, 1979.

[Mil80]   R. Milner. *A Calculus of Communicating Systems*. LNCS 92, Springer, 1980.

[Mil89]   R. Milner. *Communication and Concurrency*. Prentice Hall International, 1989.

[Mil93]   R. Milner. Elements of interaction. *Communications of the ACM*, 36:78–89, 1993.

[Mil94]   R. Milner. David Michael Ritchie Park (1935–1990) in memoriam. *Theoretical Computer Science*, 133:187–200, 1994.

[Mit90]   J.C. Mitchell. Type systems for programming languages. In J. van Leeuwen, editor, *Handbook of Theoretical Computer Science*, volume B, pages 367–458. Elsevier, 1990.

[Mos92]   P. Mosses. *Action Semantics*. Cambridge University Press Tracts in Theoretical Computer Science 26, 1992.

[MS76]   R. Milne and C. Strachey. *A Theory of Programming Language Semantics*. Chapman and Hall, 1976. 2 volumes.

[MV88]   J.-J.Ch. Meyer and E.P. de Vink. Applications of compactness in the Smyth powerdomain of streams. *Theoretical Computer Science*, 57:251–282, 1988.

[MV89a]   J.-J. Meyer and E.P. de Vink. Pomset semantics for true concurrency with synchronization and recursion. In A. Kreczmar and G. Mirkowska, editors, *Proc. MFCS'89*, pages 360–369. LNCS 379, Springer, 1989.

[MV89b]   J.-J. Meyer and E.P. de Vink. Step semantics for 'true' concurrency with recursion. *Distributed Computing*, 3:130–145, 1989.

[MZ91]   M.E. Majster-Cederbaum and F. Zetzsche. Towards a foundation for semantics in complete metric spaces. *Information and Computation*, 90:217–243, 1991.

[MZ94]   M.E. Majster-Cederbaum and F. Zetzsche. The comparison of a CPO-based semantics with a CMS-based semantics for CSP. *Theoretical Computer Science*, 124:1–40, 1994.

[Nau63]   P. Naur (editor) et al. Revised report on the algorithmic language Algol 60. *Communications of the ACM*, 6:1–17, 1963.

[Niv77]   M. Nivat. Mots infinis engendrés par une grammaire algébrique. *RAIRO Informatique Théorique*, 11:311–327, 1977.

[Niv78]   M. Nivat. Sur les ensembles des mots infinis engendrés par une grammaire algébrique. *RAIRO Informatique Théorique*, 12:259–278, 1978.

[Niv79]   M. Nivat. Infinite words, infinite trees, infinite computations. In J.W. de Bakker and J. van Leeuwen, editors, *Foundations of Computer Science III*, part 2: Languages, Logic, Semantics, pages 3–52. Mathematical Centre Tracts 109, Mathematical Centre, Amsterdam, 1979.

[NN92]   H.R. Nielson and F. Nielson. *Semantics with Applications: A Formal Introduction.* Wiley, 1992.

[Nol94]   D. Nolte. *Faire Semantiken.* PhD thesis, Univerität Koblenz, 1994.

[NPW81]   M. Nielsen, G. Plotkin, and G. Winskel. Petri nets, event structures and domains, part 1. *Theoretical Computer Science*, 13:85–108, 1981.

[NSW94]   M. Nielsen, V. Sassone, and G. Winskel. Relationships between models of concurrency. In [BRR94], pages 425–476, 1994.

[OG76]   S. Owicki and D. Gries. An axiomatic proof technique for parallel programs. *Acta Informatica*, 6:319–340, 1976.

[OH86]   E.-R. Olderog and C.A.R. Hoare. Specification-oriented semantics for communicating processes. *Acta Informatica*, 23:9–66, 1986.

[Old91]   E.-R. Olderog. *Nets, Terms and Formulas.* Cambridge University Press Tracts in Theoretical Computer Science 23, 1991.

[OV94]   V. van Oostrom and E.P. de Vink. Transition system specifications in stalk format with bisimulation as a congruence. In P. Enjalbert, E.W. Mayer, and K.W. Wagner, editors, *Proc. STACS'94*, pages 569–580. LNCS 775, Springer, 1994.

[Pal90]   C. Palamidessi. Algebraic properties of idempotent substitutions. In M. Paterson, editor, *Proc. 17th ICALP*, pages 386–399. LNCS 443, Springer, 1990.

[Par70]   D.M.R. Park. Fixpoint induction and proofs of program semantics. In B. Meltzer and D. Michie, editors, *Machine Intelligence, Vol. 5*, pages 59–78. Edinburgh University Press, 1970.

[Par81]   D.M.R. Park. Concurrency and automata on infinite sequences. In P. Deussen, editor, *Proc. 5th GI Conference on Theoretical Computer Science*, pages 167–183. LNCS 104, Springer, 1981.

[Plo76]   G. Plotkin. A powerdomain construction. *SIAM Journal on Computing*, 5:522–587, 1976.

[Plo77]   G.D. Plotkin. LCF considered as a programming language. *Theoretical Computer Science*, 5:223–255, 1977.

[Plo79]   G.D. Plotkin. Dijkstra's predicate transformers and Smyth's powerdomains. In D. Bjørner, editor, *Proc. Winter School on Abstract Software Specification*, pages 527–553. LNCS 86, Springer, 1979.

[Plo81]   G.D. Plotkin. A structural approach to operational semantics. Report DAIMI FN-19, Aarhus University, 1981.

[Plo82]   G.D. Plotkin. A powerdomain for countable non-determinism. In M. Nielsen and E.M. Schmidt, editors, *Proc. of the 9th International Colloquium on Automata, Languages and Programming*, pages 418–428. LNCS 140, Springer, 1982.

[Plo83]   G.D. Plotkin. An operational semantics for CSP. In D. Bjørner, editor, *Proc. IFIP Working Conference on Formal Description of Programming Concepts II*, pages 199–223. North-Holland, 1983.

[PN92]   L. Priese and D. Nolte. Strong fairness and ultra metrics. *Theoretical Computer Science*, 99:121–140, 1992.

[Pra86]   V.R. Pratt. Modelling concurrency with partial orders. *International Journal of Parallel Programming*, 15:33–71, 1986.

[Ree89]   G.M. Reed. A hierarchy of domains for real-time distributed computing. In
            M. Main, A. Melton, M. Mislove, and D. Schmidt, editors, *Proc. 5th International
            Conference on Mathematical Foundations of Programming Semantics*, pages 80–
            128. LNCS 442, Springer, 1989.

[Rei85]   W. Reisig. *Petri Nets, an Introduction*, volume 4 of *EATCS Monographs on The-
            oretical Computer Science*. Springerg, 1985.

[Ren93]   A. Rensink. *Models and Methods for Action Refinement*. PhD thesis, Universiteit
            Twente, 1993.

[Rey93]   J.C. Reynolds. *The discovery of continuations*. LISP and Symbolic Computation.
            Kluwer, 1993.

[Roo88]   M. de Rooy. Concurrent evaluation of side-effects. Note CS-N8801, CWI, Amster-
            dam, 1988.

[Rou85]   W.C. Rounds. On the relationship between Scott domains, synchronization trees,
            and metric spaces. *Information and Computation*, 66:6–28, 1985.

[RR88]   G.M. Reed and A.W. Roscoe. A timed model for communicating sequential pro-
            cesses. *Theoretical Computer Science*, 58:249–261, 1988.

[RT93]   J.J.M.M. Rutten and D. Turi. On the foundations of final semantics: non-standard
            sets, metric spaces, partial orders. In [BRR93], pages 477–530, 1993.

[RT94]   J.J.M.M. Rutten and D. Turi. Initial algebra and final coalgebra semantics for
            concurrency. In [BRR94], pages 530–582, 1994.

[Rut89]   J.J.M.M. Rutten. Correctness and full abstraction of metric semantics for concur-
            rency. In [BRR89], pages 628–659, 1989. Reprinted in [BR92].

[Rut90]   J.J.M.M. Rutten. Semantic correctness for a parallel object-oriented language.
            SIAM Journal on Computing, 19:341–383, 1990. Reprinted in [BR92].

[Rut92]   J.J.M.M. Rutten. Processes as terms: Non-well-founded models for bisimulation.
            Mathematical Structures in Computer Science, 2:257–275, 1992.

[Rut95]   J.J.M.M. Rutten. Elements of generalized ultrametric domain theory. Technical
            Report CS–R9507, CWI, Amsterdam, 1995.

[RZ92]   J.J.M.M. Rutten and J.I. Zucker. A semantic approach to fairness. *Fundamenta
            Informaticae*, 16:1–38, 1992.

[San92]   D. Sangiorgi. *Expressing Mobility in Process Algebras: first-order and higher-order
            paradigms*. PhD thesis, University of Edinburgh, 1992.

[San93]   D. Sangiorgi. From π-calculus to higher-order π-calculus - and back. In M.-C.
            Gaudel and J.-P. Jouannaud, editors, *Proc. of the 5th International Conference on
            Theory and Practice of Software Development*, pages 151–166. LNCS 668, Springer,
            1993.

[Sch63]   M.P. Schutzenberger. Push-down automata and context free languages. *Informa-
            tion and Control*, 6:246–264, 1963.

[Sch86]   D.A. Schmidt. *Denotational Semantics: A Methodology for Language Develop-
            ment*. Allyn and Bacon, 1986.

[Sch94]   D.A. Schmidt. *The Structure of Typed Programming Languages*. The MIT Press,
            1994.

[Sco70]   D.S. Scott. Outline of a mathematical theory of computation. In *Proc. 4th Annual
            Princeton Conference on Inf. Sciences and Systems*, pages 169–176, Princeton,
            1970.

[Sco76]   D.S. Scott. Data types as lattices. *SIAM Journal on Computing*, 5:522–587, 1976.

[Sha88]   E.Y. Shapiro. *Concurrent Prolog: Collected Papers*. The MIT Press, 1988. 2 volumes.

[Sha89]   E.Y. Shapiro. The family of concurrent logic programming languages. *ACM Computer Surveys*, 21:412–510, 1989.

[She94]   J.C. Shepherdson. The role of standardising apart in logic programming. *Theoretical Computer Science*, 129:143–166, 1994.

[Smy83]   M.B. Smyth. Power domains and predicate transformers — a topological view. In J. Diaz, editor, *Proc. 10th ICALP*, pages 662–675. LNCS 154, Springer, 1983.

[Smy91]   M.B. Smyth. Totally bounded spaces and compact ordered spaces as domains of computation. In G.M. Reed, A.W. Roscoe, and R.F. Wachter, editors, *Topology and Category Theory in Computer Science*, pages 207–229. Oxford University Press, 1991.

[Smy92]   M.B. Smyth. Topology. In S. Abramsky, D.M. Gabbay, and T.S.E Maibaum, editors, *Handbook of Logic in Computer Science*, volume 1, Background: Mathematical Structures, pages 641–761. Clarendon Press, 1992.

[SP82]   M.B. Smyth and G.D. Plotkin. The category-theoretic solution of recursive domain equations. *SIAM Journal on Computing*, 11:761–783, 1982.

[Spa93]   M. Spanier. *Vergleich zweier Theorien nebenläufigen Prozesse*. PhD thesis, Univ. Mannheim, 1993.

[SR90]   V.A. Saraswat and M. Rinard. Concurrent constraint programming. In *Proc. 17th Ann. Symp. on POPL*, pages 232–245. ACM, 1990.

[SRP91]   V.A. Saraswat, M. Rinard, and P. Panangaden. Semantic foundations of concurrent constraint programming. In *Proc. 18th Annual Symp. on POPL*, pages 333–352. ACM, 1991.

[SS71]   D.S. Scott and C. Strachey. Towards a mathematical semantics for computer languages. In J. Fox, editor, *Proc. of the Symposium on Computers and Automata*, volume 21 of *Microwave Research Institute Symposia Series*, pages 19–46, New York, 1971. Polytechnic Press.

[Sto77]   J.E. Stoy. *Denotational Semantics: The Scott-Strachey Approach to Programming Language Theory*. The MIT Press Series in Computer Science 1, 1977.

[SW74]   C. Strachey and C. Wadsworth. Continuations: a mathematical semantics for handling full jumps. Tech. Monograph PRG–11, Oxford University, 1974.

[Tar55]   A. Tarski. A lattice-theoretical fixpoint theorem and its applications. *Pacific Journal of Mathematics*, 5:285–309, 1955.

[Ten73]   R.D. Tennent. Mathematical semantics of SNOBOL4. In *ACM SIGPLAN/SIGACT Symposium on POPL*, pages 95–107. ACM, 1973.

[Ten81]   R.D. Tennent. *Principles of Programming Languages*. Prentice-Hall International, 1981.

[Ten91]   R.D. Tennent. *Semantics of Programming Languages*. Prentice-Hall International, 1991.

[THM83]   B.A. Trakhtenbrot, J.Y. Halpern, and A.R. Meyer. From denotational to operational and axiomatic semantics for ALGOL-like languages: an overview. In E. Clarke and D. Kozen, editors, *Proc. Logics of Programs*, pages 474–500. LNCS 164, Springer, 1983.

[Tho89]   B. Thomsen. A calculus of higher order communicating systems. In *Proc. of the 16th Annual ACM Symposium on Principles of Programming Languages*, pages 143–154. ACM, 1989.

[Tho90a]   W. Thomas. Automata on infinite objects. In J. van Leeuwen, editor, *Handbook of Theoretical Computer Science, vol. B*, pages 133–191. Elsevier, 1990.

[Tho90b]   B. Thomsen. *Calculi for Higher Order Communicating systems*. PhD thesis, Imperial College, 1990.

[Tur95]   D. Turi. *Functorial Operational Semantics and its Denotational Dual*. Forthcoming Ph.D thesis, Vrije Universiteit Amsterdam, 1995.

[Ued88]   K. Ueda. Guarded Horn clauses: a parallel logic programming language with the concept of a guard. In M. Nivat and K. Fuchi, editors, *Proc. Programming of Future Generation Computers*, pages 441–456. North-Holland, 1988.

[Vaa89]   F. Vaandrager. A simple definition of parallel composition of prime event structures. Report CS–R8903, CWI, Amsterdam, 1989.

[Ver94]   C. Verhoef. A congruence theorem for structured operational semantics with predicates and negative premises. In B. Jonsson and J. Parrow, editors, *Proc. 5th Conference on Concurrency Theory*, pages 433–448. LNCS 836, Springer, 1994.

[Vin89]   E.P. de Vink. Comparative semantics for Prolog with cut. *Science of Computer Programming*, 13:237–264, 1989.

[Vin90]   E.P. de Vink. *Designing Stream Based Semantics for Uniform Concurrency and Logic Programming*. PhD thesis, Vrije Universiteit Amsterdam, 1990.

[Wag94]   K.R. Wagner. *Solving Recursive Domain Equations with Enriched Categories*. PhD thesis, Carnegie Mellon University, Pittsburgh, 1994. Technical Report CMU-CS-94-159.

[Wat91]   D.A. Watt. *Programming Language Syntax and Semantics*. Prentice-Hall International, 1991.

[Wij66]   A. van Wijngaarden. Recursive definition of syntax and semantics. In T.B. Steel, editor, *Formal Language Description Languages for Comp. Prog.*, pages 13–24. North-Holland, 1966.

[Wij75]   A. van Wijngaarden et al. (eds). Revised report on the algorithmic language ALGOL68. *Acta Informatica*, 5:1–236, 1975.

[Win89]   G. Winskel. An introduction to event structures. In [BRR89], pages 364–397, 1989.

[Win93]   G. Winskel. *The Formal Semantics of Programming Languages*. The MIT Press, 1993.

[WN95]   G. Winskel and M. Nielsen. Models for concurrency. In S. Abramsky, D. Gabbay, and T.S.E. Maibaum, editors, *Handbook of Logic in Computer Science*, volume 4, pages 1–148. Oxford University Press, 1995.

Author Index

Subject Index